D1232080

BLACK ROBES AND INDIANS ON THE LAST FRONTIER

Black Robes and Indians on the Last Frontier

A STORY OF HEROISM

SISTER MARIA ILMA RAUFER, O.P.

THE BRUCE PUBLISHING COMPANY
MILWAUKEE

NIHIL OBSTAT:

    JOHN J. COLEMAN
    Censor librorum

IMPRIMATUR:

    ✠ BERNADUS J. TOPEL, D.D., PH.D.
    Episcopus Spokanensis
    July 10, 1963

Library of Congress Catalog Card Number: 65–29168
© 1966 SISTER MARIA ILMA RAUFER, O.P.
MADE IN THE UNITED STATES OF AMERICA

TO MARY,
THE MOTHER OF GOD,
QUEEN OF HEAVEN AND EARTH

Preface

WHEN the Rev. William L. Davis, S.J., then chairman of the History Department at Gonzaga University, Spokane, Washington, assigned to the author as subject of a master's thesis *The History of St. Mary's Mission, Omak, Washington,* she was at a loss. Four years as a teacher at this institution had then passed without her knowing a thing about its long and colorful history. Occasionally fragments of information were rumored, but were they correct? She found discrepancies in dates referring to the same events. With the exception of the old baptismal records and a few old photographs, there was nothing whatsoever available at the Mission. Either the fires of 1919 and 1938 had destroyed very important historical data, or the want of a sense of historical values had kept it from being collected.

For the same reasons, the Oregon Province Archives of the Jesuit Fathers at Crosby Library, Gonzaga University, Spokane, contain only fragmentary material on the subject. But it was here that the author had the opportunity to study the original manuscripts of early missionaries, which furnished a rich background for the examination of the history of the regions of the Upper and Central Columbia and Okanogan Valleys. Acknowledgments are due to the archivist, the Rev. Winfred P. Schoenberg, S.J., for making these manuscripts and rare books available.

Only after the study of early mission activities had been nearly completed did the author have the good fortune of locating prime material on St. Mary's Mission and also gradually of becoming acquainted with former students of the Mission. It meant a new beginning and hard work that proved eventually successful. Heartfelt thanks are expressed to Rev. Mother General Mary Anselm for use of documents from the Archives of the Blessed Sacrament Sisters, Cornwells Heights, Pa. Father de Rougé's correspondence with Rev. Mother Mary Katherine Drexel and with other members of this community are a vital part of this history. Also special appreciation is due to the Most Rev. Bishop Bernard Joseph Topel, D.D., Ph.D., of Spokane, for generous permission to study such files of the Diocesan Archives as pertain to this early history. These documents also were invaluable for the supplying of missing data. The author expresses thanks to the Very Rev. Cornelius M. Power, Chancellor of the Archdiocese of Seattle, for the invitation to do research work at the Chancery. She acknowledges also the friendly help received at the Washington State Historical Society reference room in Tacoma from Mr. Bruce Le Roy and his staff.

Sincere gratitude is also due to Father de Rougé's former students and friends, especially to Dr. Paschal Sherman, Washington, D. C., for the photocopies of historical documents and photographs from the National Archives, for the hand-drawn maps of St. Mary's Mission, and for the detailed answers of the author's questionnaire. Mr. John Cleveland, Monse; Mr. Narcisse Nicholson, Ellisforde; Judge W. C. Brown, Okanogan; Mrs. Nellie Picken, Spokane; Mr. Robert Picken, Tonasket; Mr. Harry Van Coelen, Portland, Oregon; Mr. William Hill, Tonasket; Mr. Francis Favel, Monse; Mrs. Helen Toulou, Kewa; Mrs. Pauline Zacherle, Disautel; Mr. A. F. De Vos, Gresham, Oregon; Mrs. Alyce Hallenius, Omak; Mrs. Anna Bass, Omak; and Mrs. Katie Lacey, Osoyoos, B. C., deserve special thanks for having given so generously of their time for interviews and many other services.

As in a mosaic, this history was constructed of multiple pieces. It would be impossible to name all the good people who have contributed these fragments of information. The footnotes and the bibliography will name many of them and show their contributions. The author wishes to express gratitude to all who have in any way helped her to make this history more complete. We regret that some of our informants have died in the meantime.

The author wishes further to acknowledge the splendid library services of the Washington State Research Library in Olympia; of the Bookmobile that serves St. Mary's Mission, Omak; of the northwest section of the library at the University of Washington in Seattle; of the northwest reference room of the Main Public Library in Spokane, where Mrs. George W. Gilbert and Miss Mary Johnson gave her such friendly service; and of the Crosby Library, Gonzaga University, Spokane, where Father C. Carroll, S.J., and his staff were often called upon for assistance. Her appreciation to Mr. Michael Moyer and his helpers for supplying some of the photographic material; also to Mr. Van Peterson, S.J., of the St. Louis Province for many kindnesses. Her profound thanks are due to those who have contributed to the printing costs, especially Mr. and Mrs. Edward Figlenski and their many friends.

Finally, the author wishes to express gratitude to her Superiors, who gave the means and the opportunity for such extensive research work at a time when there was a shortage of teachers.

Introduction

THE development of Christian civilization in the Oganogan and the Central and Upper Columbia Valleys took root in 1811, when Fort Okanogan was built.

These years, from 1811 to the present, may be divided into two historical eras. The first one saw the establishment of Fort Okanogan and Colville; the planting and the spreading of the Christian faith; the calls for priests; the building of the early missions, St. Paul's at the Kettle Falls of the Columbia River and St. Francis Regis in the Colville Valley; it saw also the open encroachments on the Indians' lands, the uncertain United States Indian policies in action, and the Indian wars and their repercussions in eastern Washington. We see in this era the gradual development of a white pioneer society and the growing of the settlements into towns and cities resulting from the steady influx of prospective miners, farmers, and businessmen. This era also witnessed the creation of the Colville Indian Reservation.

The second era, from 1885 to the present, saw the development of St. Mary's Mission at Omak, Washington, into the largest mission and parish center then in the state of Washington. Its territory extended hundreds of miles in all directions. The early fame of St. Mary's Mission as the only Christian cultural center then in existence in this part of the country, the Okanogan and Central Columbia Valleys, rested to a great extent on its schools. In them, Indian boys, together with their white brothers, received the first adequate education offered to them in a radius of hundreds of miles. The second era, therefore, saw the culture of the white man being assimilated gradually by the various Indian tribes. The founder of St. Mary's Mission, the Reverend Father Etienne de Rougé, S.J., a member of the French nobility, through his educational and pastoral work, must be regarded as contributing greatly to this progress of Christian civilization.

The building of St. Mary's Mission in the Okanogan Valley would have been impossible without the zealous, self-sacrificing Jesuit pioneer priests of earlier times. These missionaries indirectly prepared for the founding of this great institution by their missionary journeys from the first mission centers into the Okanogan and Central and Upper Columbia Valleys. Without an account of the activities of these early missionaries at St. Paul's and St. Francis Regis, the history of St. Mary's Mission, Omak, and of a great part of eastern Washington, would lack a foundation. Therefore this history will take into account early beginnings at other localities that gradually, in 1885, led to the birth of St. Mary's Mission, the great educational center.

A picture of the spreading of the Christian cultural heritage to the Indian tribes and to the incoming white population will show the significance of this institution in the Okanogan Valley as the center of inspiration for Indians and whites, for Catholics and non-Catholics alike, as it gradually grew to fill the needs of the time. At a time when the rough life of the whites on the frontier and their lust for land terrified the Indians, who loved their age-old inheritance, St. Mary's Mission served as a civilizing agent and as a spiritual refuge.

Mission centers were Indian centers. This study will also be the first comprehensive history of the tribes that inhabited this vast area.

List of Abbreviations

TO SAVE lengthy repetitions the following abbreviations were used in the book and in the bibliography:

AAS Archives Archdiocese of Seattle, Wash.

AAQ Archives Archdiocese of Quebec, Canada

ABSS Archives Blessed Sacrament Sisters, Cornwells Heights, Pa.

ADS Archives Diocese Spokane, Wash.

ADSK Archives Dominican Sisters, Kettle Falls, Wash.

AWHS Archives Washington Historical Society, Tacoma, Wash.

BCHS British Columbia Historical Society

BRSTM *Baptismal Records of St. Mary's Mission,* Omak, Wash.

CR, *De Smet* Hiram Chittendon and Alfred Talbot Richardson, *Life, Letters, and Travels of Father Pierre De Smet, S.J., 1801–1873.*

Griva, *History* Rev. Edward M. Griva, S.J., *Fifty Years of My Missionary Life Among Indians and Whites From July 1894 Till the End of September 1944,* Ms. OPA.

HBRS Hudson's Bay Record Society

IECM *The Inland Empire Catholic Messenger*

MDPT *Missione Della Provincia Torinese Della Compagnia De Gesu Nelle Montagne Rocciose Della America Settentrionala,* Torino: Tipografia Giulio Speirani E. Figli, 1887.

LPT *Lettere Della Provincia Torinese.* Torino: Tipografia, Ditto G. Derossi, 1902, 1904.

NA National Archives, Washington, D. C.

OHQ *Oregon Historical Quarterly*

OPA Oregon Province Archives, S.J., Gonzaga University, Crosby Library, Spokane, Wash.

PNQ *Pacific Northwest Quarterly*

RBIA *Records of the Bureau of Indian Affairs*

SM St. Mary's Mission, Omak, Wash.

WL *Woodstock Letters: a Record of Current Events and Historical Notes Connected with the Colleges and Missions of the Society of Jesus.* Woodstock Press, Woodstock, Md., 1887–

WHQ *Washington Historical Quarterly*

Contents

BLACK ROBES AND INDIANS ON THE LAST FRONTIER

CHAPTER I

The Dawn of the White Man's Culture

THE settlement of the Pacific Northwest was greatly determined by its geographical features. No specific name had been designated to this territory when the first white man made his appearance. Various European powers had competed for the possession of the Pacific Northwest. As early as 1542–1543, Juan Rodrigues Cabrillo and Bartolome Ferrelo, two Spaniards, had started an exploratory trip along the coast. For decades Spain had been merely interested in California; later, however, she moved farther north. The Russians under Vitus Bering in 1728 discovered the Bering Strait; in 1741 they reached the Alaskan mainland. It was during the Revolutionary War that the English sent James Cook who sailed in 1778 along the Northwest Coast. Other Englishmen followed and claimed the sole right of trade between the Northwest Coast of America and China.

The Americans were no less enterprising. In 1789 Robert Gray and John Kendrick were exploring the coast. The Spaniards, then at Nootka Sound, seized English ships, but were friendly to the two Americans. The Nootka Sound Controversy ended with the Spaniards surrendering their claims of discovery and exploration.

In 1811, when our story begins, the term "Oregon Country" was still obscure. The second designation, "Washington Territory," was not used until 1853. Today this part of the country is known as eastern Washington.

From time immemorial the great river system of the Columbia with its many tributaries had been the only "highway" available. The tribes that peopled the river valleys often designated their official names according to the names of the rivers that flowed through their valleys. Canoes made of hollowed-out trunks or of bark were the only significant means of transportation.

Historians have demonstrated that probably around 1750 the horse made its appearance in the immense territory of the West. By the time of Lewis and Clark's exploration most of the tribes possessed herds of horses. The southern tribes had stolen or bought horses from the Spaniards. The tribes of eastern Washington knew that the fierce Blackfeet Indians were in possession of fine horses. Okanogan Indians would band together for the express purpose of stealing these animals. Great daring and courage were required to meet the ever alert Blackfeet. Out of one group of fifty Okanogans who had gone to the Blackfeet country only eight returned after two years; each however, riding a horse and leading one.[1]

The Okanogan and Upper Columbia Indians needed horses to overcome the rough terrain of their big territory. Here we find valleys divided by mountain ranges, with summits varying in height from 4000 to 8000 feet. In northeastern Washington the Okanogan Highlands occupy a large part of the country. Here are also the rugged Nespelem Range and the Sanpoil Range. Moses Mountain and Omak Mountain, not too far from St. Mary's Mission, have their local significance. Vast areas of basalt and granite and other igneous rocks point to much primeval volcanic activity. Dense forests cover the slopes of the various mountain ranges. Much of this area was inaccessible during the winter months. During the spring melting of the snow the rivers were not safe even for the best canoe men. But let summer come and the age-worn Indian trails and sparkling rivers became the bustling highways in the quest for food and trade; they also became the means of spreading faith, goodness, culture — in other words, the Christian civilization.

We can justly assume that many of the Indian tribes that play a part in our story had heard of the "Palefaces" before 1811. Intermarriage between tribes was common. The Indians annually roamed far to the east for the buffalo hunt, where they came into contact with other tribes who might have told them about early French traders and their posts along the Great Lakes, Lake Winnepeg, the Canadian prairie, and even in the vicinity of the Rockies. La Verendrye was one of the early traders who made expeditions to the Rockies looking for the "River of the West" whose name was supposed to be "Ouragon" of which Jonathan Carver had told in his travel stories and which name had been made known to him by Major Robert Rogers of Mackinac, Michigan, in about 1766–1767. Rogers was then the English commander of the fort.[2]

---

[1] Cull White, in an interview in Spokane, Wash., January 7, 1961.

[2] Grace Flandrau, ed., "Verendrye Expeditions in Quest of the Pacific," *Oregon Historical Quarterly* (henceforth cited as *OHQ*) (26:2, June, 1925), 65 ff. Also: Lawrence Burpee, *The Search for the Western Sea*, Vol. 1, 294, 298. Consult also: T. C. Elliott, "The Origin of the Name Oregon," *OHQ* (22:2, June, 1921), 91–115.

As the tribes of eastern Washington and British Columbia had no written language, they had some intelligent member memorize important tribal events. He then had the duty to transmit this history to future generations. Chief Pelka-mulox, the then head of the Okanogans and the Colvilles, had his son, Chief Nicola, memorize the speech he gave to the first white men he had seen. Maria Brent, the great-granddaughter of Chief Nicola, in turn was chosen to memorize this speech of her great-great-grandfather. She recited this last in 1955. She tells how her great-great-grandfather did an unusual amount of traveling for his time, visiting the different bands of the Okanogans and of the neighboring tribes. He was acquainted with the Flatheads, the Coeur d'Alenes, the Blackfeet, and the Shoshoni. During his last buffalo hunt he traveled as far as the site of Helena, Montana, where he met some white men, the first he had ever seen. "He thought they were beautiful — not human beings, but good spirits that had come from somewhere to do good for his people and take care of them." Chief Pelka-mulox guided these white men west over the mountains to the Colville country. For some reason he was not able to take care of them and had the Colville subchief promise him that the white men would not be harmed. Before leaving them, Chief Pelka-mulox adressed the white men as follows:

> You are my white children, and I do not want to lose you. I want you to live in my territory. I have a big country, big enough for all of us and for our children and our children's children.
>
> Our mountains are green and full of fruits. We have many roots. We will show you which ones to eat and which ones not to eat so that you will not be poisoned. We have grouse and many other birds for the hunt. We have plenty of deer for the meat and hides. We have all kinds of fur, large and small for our use, and salmon to eat.
>
> As long as the waters run and until yonder hill is no more, you and I stay here, your children and my children. From my waters I drink, you drink. From my fruits I eat, you eat. From my game I eat, you eat. You are my white children. Stay with me.[3]

It is not related if the white men later went along with Chief Pelka-mulox to the Okanogan Valley or if they understood the Okanogan Salish dialect of the chief's speech. However, it shows us the friendly and hospitable attitude of the old Okanogans toward the white men and that this event was important enough to be transmitted to posterity.

The Okanogan Indians were known to have covered the distance to the West Coast in about fifteen days when old Whowhylaugh, or Red

---

[3] Maria Brent, *A Chief's Address to the First White Man.* Courtesy of Mrs. Katie Lacey, member of the Okanogan Historical Society, Osoyoos, B. C.

Fox, was their chief. The Pacific Ocean was called the "Great Salt Lake" which they reached by a trail across the mountains "in about the forty-ninth degree of north latitude."[4] Alexander Ross tells us that:

> Red Fox . . . was the head chief of the Oakinacken nation and had formerly been in the habit of going to the Pacific on trading excursions, carrying with him a kind of wild hemp which the Indians along the Pacific make fishing nets of; and in exchange, the Oakinacken bringing back any marine shells and other trinkets, articles of value among Indians.[5]

This trade with the coastal people and the exchange of news might well have made the inland Indians acquainted with the ships of the white men, who had explored the West Coast since the middle of the sixteenth century. It was on May 11, 1792, that Captain Gray entered the "River of the West" with his ship the *Columbia Rediviva*. He named the river *Columbia* and gave to the young United States a claim to that river based on his discovery eleven years prior to the Louisiana Purchase[6] and prior to any British claim.

In 1805–1806 the Lewis and Clark expedition met many tribes. The big news had traveled to other tribesmen, and when David Thompson, the famous British surveyor, erected the first trading post near East Hope on the Lake Pend Oreille, Kullyspell House, in September of 1809, and Saleesh House near Thompson Falls on the Clark River in November of the same year; and when Jacques Finlay and Finnan McDonald of the Canadian North West Company came to build Spokane House in 1810, "moccasin telegraphy" traveled faster than we might guess. Thompson himself arrived at Spokane House on June 14, 1811. Three days later he followed an old Indian trail along the Colville River that connected the two fishing centers, Spokane Falls and Kettle Falls. At Kettle Falls he stopped two weeks looking for the right cedars with which to build a big canoe. He visited the village of the "Ilthkoyape" or Kettle Falls Indians. He was well received by the Sanpoil Indians, July 3, 1811. He met the Okanogans, July 5, 1811, but seems not to have noticed the mouth of the Okanogan River. The Methow Indians came dancing and singing to meet him on July 6, 1811. All these tribes did not show any great surprise at the sight of white men. When Thompson stopped to visit the Wenatchee Indians, however, he noted

[4] Alexander Ross, *Adventures of the First Settlers on the Oregon or Columbia River,* 1849 ed., Vol. I, 313. Milo Milton Quaife, ed.

[5] Alexander Ross, *The Fur Hunters of the Far West,* 1855 ed., 31.

[6] F. G. Young, ed., "John Boit's Log of the Columbia," *OHQ* (22:4, December, 1921), 258 ff.

their surprise and shyness, and that only gradually did they become friendly.[7]

David Thompson was on his way to the mouth of the Columbia to forestall any attempt by the Americans to establish themselves first. To his consternation he found a trading post, Fort Astoria, in the making. John Jacob Astor had, on June 23, 1810, formed the Pacific Fur Company, an American concern. He had failed to persuade the North West Company to join him in forming a larger establishment, but he succeeded in persuading many of their best and experienced men to forsake their old company and join Astor's. The Astor men, under the leadership of David Stuart, had prepared to make an inland exploration but this, owing to the coming of Thompson, was delayed until Thompson himself would accompany the American men up the Columbia River, which he did a few days later. They finally parted, Thompson stopping again at Kettle Falls to build another boat, and meeting a number of "Okanogan Indians";[8] and David Stuart and his party stopping at the Okanogan peninsula where the Okanogan River flows into the Columbia.

A great crowd of Indians had followed the Astor party and camped with them. They kept on begging the whites to settle among them. After some hesitation and examination of the near surroundings, David Stuart agreed. The Indians showed their pleasure:

> ... the chiefs immediately held a council and then pledged themselves to be always our friends, to kill us plenty of beaver, to furnish us at all times with provisions, and to ensure protection and safety.[9]

The Okanogan peninsula had always been a great meeting place for several tribes for fishing, gambling, and trading. Here on the first of September, 1811, David Stuart selected the historic site of the first American fur trading post in the Inland Empire about half a mile from the mouth and on the east side of the Okanogan River. The nearby driftwood came in handy and was used to begin the construction of the first Fort Okanogan, a house sixteen by twenty feet. Washington Irving tells us that four men were sent back to Astoria because David Stuart was afraid there might not be enough food for them during the winter.[10] Alexander Ross was left alone to complete the structure, while David Stuart, Montigny, and two others went on an exploring trip up the Okanogan River into what was later called "New Caledonia."

---

[7] J. B. Tyrrell, ed., *David Thompson's Narrative of His Explorations in Western America, 1784–1812*, 465–481.

[8] *Ibid.*, 532.

[9] Alexander Ross, *Adventures*, 153.

[10] Washington Irving, "Astoria," in *Works of Washington Irving*, Vol. VII, 175.

Alexander Ross was alone all during the winter in a strange land with strange people; yet these strangers proved to be very peaceful and honorable. They were camped around their only white man. That the Okanogan and related tribes meant what they had promised is revealed by Ross who writes that during Stuart's absence of 188 days he had procured 1550 beavers, and other peltries valued at £ 2,250.[11]

The Astor Fur Company was short-lived. John Clark from the Pacific Fur Company had in the meantime established Fort Spokane near the Spokane House of the North West Company. Constant rivalry between the two companies was the order of the day. Imprudent management, quarrels between the Astor party and the captain of the *Tonquin* (the ship that brought Astor's oversea party around Cape Horn); the blowing up of this ship; the failure of the supply ship of 1813 to arrive; loss of the second ship, the *Beaver,* on the high seas; the disaster of the third ship, the *Lark,* totally wrecked near the Sandwich Islands; and the War of 1812 were some of the factors that finally ended the competition of the British with the Americans by the sale of Astor's property to the North West Company. Fort Okanogan now had a new owner. It was fortunate for the Okanogan tribes that the former partners and Canadian employees went over to the North West Company from which they had been seduced earlier by Astor. The Americans went home.[12]

Not for too long did Alexander Ross feel lonely. He married one of the beautiful girls of the Okanogan tribe and stayed at Fort Okanogan. His little fort became an important inland stopping center for the Northwest brigades on their way either to New Caledonia or to Spokane House. Fort Okanogan lost its prime importance only after Fort Colville was established in 1825.

In the spring of 1816 Alexander Ross was succeeded by Ross Cox, who set about enlarging Fort Okanogan. With the help of a large crew he had by September erected a substantial fort:

> . . . a new dwelling house for the person in charge, containing four excellent rooms and a large dining hall, two good houses for the men, and a spacious store for the furs and merchandise, to which was attached a shop for trading with the natives. The whole was surrounded by strong palisades fifteen feet high and flanked by two bastions. Each bastion had, in its lower story, a light brass four pounder; and in the upper, loop holes were left for the use of musketry.[13]

---

[11] Ross, *op. cit.,* 163.

[12] See: George W. Fuller, *A History of the Pacific North-West,* 104–109, for more detail.

[13] Ross Cox, *The Columbia River,* 320.

During the following years diplomacy was at work to establish more definite possessory rights in the Northwest. By treaty of 1819, the Spanish boundary line was fixed to below 42 degrees of north latitude. In accordance with the Treaty of Ghent, the British in 1818 gave back to the Americans Fort George, the former Fort Astoria. As no Americans were then present, the British fur companies kept on using it. In the same year a British-American Joint Occupation Agreement was reached and was renewed in 1827. Accordingly the British and the Americans had the joint right of trade and settlement in the Oregon Country. The Russians dropped out of the competition for the Northwest Coast in 1824, when by treaty their boundary line was fixed at 54 degrees latitude.

The Hudson's Bay Company had its own boundary policy. When in 1821 the North West Company and the Hudson's Bay Company were amalgamated under the latter's name, they disregarded the American right of joint occupation and became the sole rulers of the West in every sense of the word.[14] Governor Simpson of the Hudson's Bay Company stayed the winter of 1824–1825 at Fort George while the new fort was built on the north side of the Columbia River. On March 19, 1825, he named it Fort Vancouver. He expressed the Hudson's Bay Company's policy concerning the boundaries. "The object of naming it after that distinguished navigator is to identify our claim to the Soil and Trade with his discovery of the River and Coast on behalf of Gt. Britain."[15]

The Indian tribes were told that all the Okanogan country and all the lands north of the Columbia River were "King George's Land." This term was soon understood by the Indians living in that area. But when in 1846, the 49th parallel became the boundary line between Great Britain and the United States, the Indians became confused.[16] It must have been puzzling for them when later suddenly, instead of a King George, a "Great White Father in Washington, D. C." wanted to buy their lands.

The Hudson's Bay Company later moved Fort Okanogan to the side of the Columbia River to assure easier access. There is still speculation as to when the fort was moved. It is assumed that the move had been accomplished before the inspection trip of Governor Simpson in 1824–

---

[14] See Frederick Merk, *Fur Trade and Empire,* 257–259. Governor Pelly of the Hudson's Bay Company asked the Hon. George Canning, British foreign secretary, to propose a boundary line that would follow the Columbia, Snake, Salmon, and Lemhi Rivers. It would reach the summit of the Rocky Mountains at Lemhi Pass in Idaho.

[15] Governor Simpson quoted by Douglas MacKay, *The Honourable Company,* 193.

[16] Mrs. Helen Toulou, in an interview at St. Mary's Mission, Omak, Washington, concerning tribal history, November 3, 1959.

1825. It was then, in 1825, that Fort Vancouver was built on a site chosen by Simpson and that Fort Spokane was abandoned and a new fort built near Kettle Falls of the Columbia River. About the visit of Simpson in 1824 we read:

> Monday, Nov. 1st . . . got to Okanogan at 10 A.M. Mr. Birnie, Clerk in charge with two men. . .
>
> This post is agreeably situated in a fine plain near the forks of the Okanogan and main River; the soil is much the same as at Spokane and produces the finest potatoes I have ever seen in the country. Grain in any quantity might be raised here, but cultivation to any extent has never been attempted. . . .[17]
>
> The Post of Okanogan I think ought to be maintained. It requires an Establishment only of a Clerk and two men and produces about 600 Beavers.[18]

John Work remarked in his *Journal,* "Sunday 24" [July, 1825]: "Continued our route at 4 o'clock and arrived on the opposite side of the River at Okanogan. . . ." A footnote on the same page explains: "Fort Okanogan was then on the Columbia river side of the plateau at the mouth of Okanogan river."[19]

John McLaughlin wrote to Francis Ermatinger, clerk in charge of Kamloops, from Vancouver on January 2, 1829, that he was happy to find a good Boat Shed at Okanogan, something that had been badly needed.[20] Would this remark give us another indication that the fort then was at the side of the Columbia River? A boat shed was not mentioned at the Okanogan site but old records from 1847, which served to confirm the results of excavations made in 1952, give the measurements of the separate buildings and mention a boat shed.[21]

Simpson was again at Fort Oganogon on April 6, 1829. The profits then were insignificant.[22] The fort must by that time have been at the

---

[17] Simpson quoted by Mark, *op. cit.,* 50.

[18] *Ibid.,* 51–52. See also: R. Harvey Fleming, ed., *Minutes of Council Northern Department of Rupert Land,* 1821–1831, xxxiii. The publications of the Hudson's Bay Record Society (henceforth: HBRS), III. The author had been asked many questions on Fort Okanogan and therefore attempted to do more research on this subject than had been originally planned.

[19] T. C. Elliot, ed., "Journal of John Work," *Washington Historical Quarterly* (henceforth cited as *WHQ*) (5:2, April, 1914), 100.

[20] John McLaughlin, quoted by Louis R. Caywood, "Extracts from Hudson's Bay Company Records," Appendix B, 37 (H.B.C. Arch. B.223/4, fo.32d. *Excavations at the Two Fort Okanogan Sites.*

[21] Caywood, *op. cit.,* 9. "One boat shed, 62 x 18 feet."

[22] Simpson quoted by E. E. Rich, ed., *Part of Dispatch From George Simpson Esq, Governor of Ruperts Land to the Governor & Committee of the Hudson's Bay Company, London, 1829* (HBRS, X), 50. "The next Post in the Columbia, below Colvile house is Okanogan, but the few skins it yields are not worth

site of the Columbia. It is reasonable to think that no new establishment was built after the fur trade had declined in this region. On May 31, 1836, Samuel Parker paid a visit to the fort. He definitely stated that it was on the north side of the Columbia River, about at the "confluence with the Okanogan River."[23] When the Wilkes Expedition came to Fort Okanogan, June 8, 1841, they found that the fort showed signs of decay.[24]

Governor Stevens of Washington Territory had sent Captain McClellan to explore the Yakima and Okanogan part of the country for a good route for railroads. He arrived at Okanogan, September 20, 1853, and mentioned the "old and ruinous establishment of the Hudson's Bay Company." Mr. Lafleur was then in charge and told McClellan of the

---

mentioning. The place is maintained almost entirely for the accommodation of New Caledonia and Thompson River, being the point at which the route from those places strikes upon the Main River, and where it is necessary to keep three men throughout the year for the purpose of Watching Boats, Horses, Provisions & c. The Expenses of this Post, are for the sake of regularity charged to Thompson River, which receives credit for the few skins it collects, and it is therefore considered as forming a part of, belonging to, Thompson River."

[23] Samuel Parker, *Journal of an Explorating Tour Beyond the Rocky Mountains, Under the Director of the A.B.D.T.M., Performed in the Years 1835, '36, and '37,* 295–296.

[24] Charles Wilkes, *Narrative of the United States Exploring Expedition During the Years 1838, 1839, 1840, 1841, 1842.* Vol. IV., 433–434. "The post was in charge of a Canadian by the name of Le Pratt; but the whole is going into rapid decay, as it is only retained as an entrepot for the deposit of supplies, & c., in connection with the post in New Caledonia, as the northern part of this country is called by the Hudson's Bay Company. Okanogan lies directly on the route thither, and here they change from land to water transportation. Were it not for the convenience it affords, in this respect, it would not be retained.

"It is inhabited by two Canadian white men and numerous half-breed women and children, the men having gone down the river with Mr. Ogden. It has, as usual at the posts, an Indian encampment on the outside, but there is no Indian settlement within eight miles, where there is a salmon fishery. Few skins are obtained here, and the extreme scarcity of game and fur animals is remarkable throughout all this part of Middle Oregon.

"Okanogan is situated on a poor, flat sandy neck, above two miles from the junction of the river of that name with the Columbia. It is a square picketed in the same manner as those already described, but destitute of bastions, and, removed 60 yards from the Columbia. Within the pickets there is a large house for the reception of the Company's officers, consisting of several apartments, and from each end of it two rows of low mud huts run towards the entrance; these serve as offices and dwellings for the trappers and their families. In the center there is an open space.

"French is the language spoken here, as it is at all the other posts of the Company."

"At this post they have some goats, and thirty-five head of very fine cattle which produce abundant milk and butter."

foot trail from the headwaters of the Methow River to the Puget Sound.[25]
It was this trail that had been used for the early trading expeditions
of the Okanogan tribes with the tribes on the West Coast. Stanley, the
artist, was a member of the Stevens party who made the only sketch
available of Fort Okanogan. The fort was built on a higher elevation;
some of the buildings can be seen outside the stockade. Next to the
river can be seen the dwellings of the Indians.[26]

A special trail connected the transport route between Fort Okanogan
and Fort Alexandria. The fur brigade had camping grounds about thirty-
five miles distant, or a day's travel. One of the camping grounds was
near Lake Osoyoos. As the Hudson's Bay Company pushed farther north
with her trading posts, greater traffic took place through the Okanogan
Valley. The Indian tribes would follow the brigades and congregate at
Fort Okanogan. Here they came in contact not only with the white
man's wares but also with his ideas and his religion. Soon the brigade
trail was used by the Catholic missionaries in quest of souls, and Fort
Okanogan, the only white settlement for many miles, became a hospitable
and convenient stopping place for them.

The second fort that will play a very significant part in our story is
Fort Colville. While George Simpson was on his inspection trip during
November, 1824, he appraised the country and the existing forts in regard to accessibility, security, and profitableness for the fur trade and
for agricultural independence. This he did on the way down to Fort
George. His plans had time to ripen during the winter. On April 8,
1825, he had a "Consultation with Messrs. Kennedy, McMillan, McDonald,
& Ross on the subject of removing the Establishment of Spokane House
to the Kettle Falls."[27] He then traveled to Kettle Falls and had his bag-
gage conveyed around the falls for the boat trip up the Columbia. His
mind was made up; this was the ideal place for a central fur-trading post.
He tells about it in his *Journal:*

> While the people were carrying I went to the Chief's lodge about a
> Mile above the Carrying place; had an interview with him and some
> of his principal followers and intimated my wish to form an Establish-
> ment on his lands provided he undertook to protect it and assured us
> of his Friendly disposition. He received the proposal with much satis-

---

[25] Isaac I. Stevens, "Reports of Explorations and Surveys to Ascertain the
Most Practicable and Economical Route for a Railroad From the Mississippi River
to the Pacific Ocean," *Thirty-Sixth Congress, First Session, House of Representatives,
Executive Doc. No. 56,* Volume XII (Book I), 142.

[26] *Ibid.*

[27] Simpson quoted by Merk, *op. cit.,* 134.

faction and offered me the choice of his Lands in regard to situation eligible in every point of view. An excellent farm can be made at this place where as much grain and potatoes may be raised as would feed all the Natives of the Columbia and a sufficient number of Cattle and Hogs to supply his Majestys Navy with Beef and Pork. . . . I have taken the liberty of naming it Fort Colvile.[28]

Simpson even marked out the garden and fields. Then he went into the boat that brought him to "Columbia Lake." Here he addressed a letter to John Work on April 16, 1825, "which was handed to Work on his arrival at Spokane House on July 20, 1825":[29]

I have lined out the site of a new establishment at the Kettle Falls and wish you to commence building and transporting our property from Spokane as early as possible. Mr. Birnie has been directed to plant about 5 kegs of potatoes. You will . . . take great care of them, the produce to be reserved for seed . . . as next spring I expect that from 30–40 bushels will be planted. Pray let every possible exertion be used to buy up an abundant stock of fish and country produce, as no other provisions in future [will] be forwarded from the East.[30]

George Fuller tells us that McLaughlin hesitated to build Fort Colville because the place chosen was on the south of the Columbia.[31] The place was on a beautiful plain overlooking the Columbia River and about half a mile from the Kettle Falls. The *Journal* of John Work tells about the slow progress made in building the new fort. The potatoes had grown, were harvested, and it was time for the new spring planting before the last occupants of Spokane House could move to the new Fort Colville. John Work's *Journal* entry of April 11, 1826, gives the following information: "The Express arrived in the evening, Messrs. McLeod, Ermatinger & Douglas. They brought 3 pigs & 3 young cows for Fort Colville."[32] This means that the three gentlemen were among the men of the express, the Hudson's Bay Company's special boat. Some authors maintain that David Douglas brought along the animals that started the livestock industry in the Inland Empire. According to Work's and Douglas' *Journals* this is historically incorrect. Under "Thursday 13" (April, 1826), we read:

---

[28] Simpson, *op. cit.*, 13.

[29] J. Orin Oliphant, "Old Fort Colville," *WHQ* (16:1, January, 1925), 30. Also: "Journal of John Work," *ibid.* (5:2, April, 1914), 98.

[30] Simpson quoted by T. C. Elliott, ed., "Journal of John Work," *WHQ* (5:2, April, 1914), 98.

[31] George W. Fuller, *op. cit.*, 121.

[32] John Work, quoted by T. C. Elliott, "Journal of John Work," *WHQ* (5:3, July, 1914), 284 ff.

F. Rivit, Old Philip & Old Paget & Pierre with a number of women and children & all the horses & the young cows, were sent off to Kettle Falls. They have a quantity of seed potatoes with them & tools to commence farming immediately.[33]

The same *Journal* tells us that the man in charge, then a clerk, Archibald McDonald, arrived at Kettle Falls from Okanogan by land on the day before, "Wednesday 12."

David Douglas, the famous botanist who gave the name to the Douglas firs, writes on April 21, 1826:

Arrived at the [Kettle] Falls at six in the evening thoroughly drenched to the skin, and gladly walked over the portage three-quarters of a mile to small circular plain surrounded by high hills on all sides, where the new establishment is to be.[34]

Although the transfer of goods and of the people to Fort Colville took place in the spring of 1826, complete construction of the new fort was slow in progress. In 1827 new boundary negotiations took place. Simpson found it necessary to write to J. W. Dease, the chief trader in charge, July, 1827:

We regret you have not gone on with the Building and improvement at Fort Colvile, and beg that they may be continued as if no such nation as America existed — there is no probability of a boundary line being determined for many years. . . .[35]

Fort Colville, named after the director of the Hudson's Bay Company in London, Andrew Colvile grew in importance and became the main depot in the West after Fort Vancouver was replaced by Fort Victoria, B. C. This was the biggest social as well as religious center of the Northwest for many years. Here would be the residence of the paymaster. Extensive farms and gardens were thriving and supplying all the other posts with the produce.[36] The name of the fort was later misspelled with a double *l*.

---

[33] John Work, *op. cit.*

[34] *Journal Kept by David Douglas During His Travels in North America, 1823—27* (1914 edition), 165.

[35] Simpson, quoted by E. E. Rich, ed., *The Letters of John McLaughlin From Fort Vancouver to the Governor and Committee* (First Series, 1825–1838), HBRS, IV, lvi.

[36] Oliphant in "Old Fort Colville," *WHQ* (16:1, January, 1925), 40–41, quotes Archibald McDonald, January 25, 1837. ". . . the farm at present is on an extensive scale . . . upward of 5000 bushels of grain, 3000 of wheat, 1000 of corn and more than 1200 of other grain . . . your three calves are up to 55 & your Grunters would have swarmed the country if we did not make it a point to keep them down to 150."

Trade was the first object of the Hudson's Bay Company. As the sole rulers of this vast fur empire, the Company had to see that the essentials of morality and honesty were observed by the natives. However, the white traders were often less conscientious than the Indians and reaped large profits. HUM-ISHU-MA relates that when the Hudson's Bay Company's Fort Okanogan, and we may add Colville, was at its height, the Indians would come with priceless furs to be placed in piles equal to the height of the objects they wanted. This was called an "even swap":

> Thus for a cheap, smooth-bored flintlock gun of the musket type — oft times six or seven feet in length — the Company received a pack of the finest variety of skins stacked solidly the standing height of the worthless firearm.[37]

Fort Colville's profits increased from £ 3,200 in 1825 to £ 4,000 in 1827.[38]

Governor Simpson visited the forts in 1841–42. From his writings we can imagine how the two forts of the Hudson's Bay Company looked in 1841:

> Colville is a wooden fort of large size, enclosed with pickets and bastions. The houses are of cedar, neatly built and well finished and the whole place bears a cleaner and more comfortable aspect than any establishment between itself and the Red River. It stands about a mile from the nearest point of the Columbia River, and about two miles from the Chaudiere Falls, where Salmon are so abundant that as many as a thousand, some of them weighing upwards of forty pounds, have been caught in one day in a single basket.[39]

> At eleven in the forenoon, we called at the company's post, Okanogan, situated at the mouth of the stream of the same name, and maintained merely as an entrepot for the district of the Thompson River. We found the post garrisoned by half a dozen women and children, the person in charge being absent at the farm, which, on account of the sterility of the immediate neighborhood, proved to be a few miles distant. . . .[40]

These forts did not need their fortifications. A peaceful people eager to learn from the white inhabited the immense territory. Fort Colville became a small city in itself. At the time of the boundary treaty be-

---

[37] HUM-ISHU-MA, "Mourning Dove," CO-GE-WE-A: The Half-blood, 295.

[38] Fleming, ed., op. cit., LXVIII.

[39] Sir George Simpson, An Overland Journey Around the World During the Years 1841 and 1842, 94.

[40] Ibid., 97.

tween the United States and Great Britain it showed an extensive inventory.[41]

"1 Range of Stores	60 x 25 feet	Solid Logs	81 x 60 feet
1 Range of Stores	50 x 21 feet	Barn Yard	84 x 33 feet
1 Store unfinished	40 x 22 feet	Cattle Yard	
1 Dwelling house	50 x 24 feet	1 Bastion	12 x 12 feet
1 Range of Officers houses	60 x 18 feet	Stockades 208 feet square 14' high	
1 Range of Men's houses	50 x 18 feet	18 M. Fence Poles	
1 House Indian Hall	16 x 16 feet	340 acres cultivated land	
1 Kitchen	27 x 16 feet	One flour Mill complete with	
1 Blacksmithshop	30 x 17 feet	one pair of Stones and bolt-	
1 Meat & Ice Cellar	20 x 16 feet	ing Machine	30 x 20 feet
1 Bake house and ovens	15 x 15 feet	Farm of the White Mud:	
1 Poultry House	20 x 13	1 Dwelling House	16 x 16 feet
1 Pigeon House	9 x 9 feet	1 Barn	30 x 20 feet
1 Root House	40 x 20 feet	1 Stable	20 x 15 feet
Pigs Houses	60 x 15 feet	1 Pig house	8 x 8 feet
1 Stable	17 x 13 feet	$2\frac{1}{2}$ M. fence poles	
1 Barn	50 x 25 feet	30 acres of cultivated land."	
2 Byres, each	65 x 20 feet		
Horse yard, 6' high	127 x 87 feet		

Forts Colville and Okanogan became the vital centers from which Christianity spread into the Upper and Central Columbia and Okanogan Valleys. Here it was that the Christian civilization and culture first asserted themselves. All important men visiting the West stopped at these two forts, among them the Catholic missionaries. The hospitality and helpfulness of the officers of the Hudson's Bay Company in general and of Chief Factor Dr. McLaughlin toward the missionaries and their problems deserves the highest praise.

[41] Oliphant, "Old Fort Colville," *WHQ* (16:1), 43–44, enumerates the Hudson's Bay Company's establishment at Kettle Falls.

CHAPTER II

Okanogan, Middle and Upper Columbia Tribes

WHEN in 1811, David Thompson visited the tribes at Spokane House, he heard that they were preparing a war against the Teekanoggin Indians. Thompson broke up the war party by giving the Indians presents and by talking to them.[1] The Teekanoggin were the Okanogan. Thompson's account provides the first mention of this great tribe that consisted originally of twelve subtribes or bands. Every valley and every watershed had its own tribe and its own chief. For defense purposes they would band together; otherwise each tribe was independent from the other. Alexander Ross gives the following original names:

Skamoynumachs	Kewaughtchenunaughs
Pisscows	Incomecanetook
Tsilane	Intietook
Buttlemuleemauck or	Meawho
Inspellum	Sinpohellechah
Sinwhoyelppetook	Samilkameigh

Oakinacken, which is nearly in the center[2]

Some difficulties have been encountered in identifying these original names. The Skamoynumachs are mentioned by Hodge but cannot be identified. He says that the Ke-waugt-chen-unaughs are the Ke-waught-token-emachs who lived thirty miles above Priest Rapids on the Columbia River.[3] The Sinwhoyelppetook are mentioned in Governor Simpson's

---

[1] J. B. Tyrrell, *David Thompson's Narrative of His Explorations, 1784–1812*, 465.

[2] Alexander Ross, *Adventures of the First Settlers on the Oregon or Columbia River*, 311.

[3] Frederick Webb Hodge, ed., *Handbook of American Indians, Bureau of American Ethnology, Bulletin 30*, Pt. I, 676–677.

Journal, as we shall see. The other modern tribal names are as follows: the Pisscow or Wenatchee, the Tsilane or Chelan, the Methow or Meawho, the Incomecanetook or the Inkameep, the Intietook or the Entiat, the Sinpohelechah or Sanpoil, the Samilkameigh or Similkameen. These tribes were then living on a strip of country about one hundred miles in breadth and about five hundred miles in length along the upper Columbia River and all along the Okanogan Valley into British Columbia. Here, above Lake Okanogan, the last band of Okanogans would be neighbors to their age-old enemies, the Shuswaps, who lived on the other side of the Shuswaps River. Ross simply placed the homes of these aboriginal tribes between the Priest Rapids of the Columbia River in the south to the "She Whaps" in the north; no definite boundary lines were then established for more than three decades.

Governor Simpson in his *Journal* on the occasion of his 1824–1825 inspection trip gives a more detailed account of where these tribes and subtribes then lived:

Iscamoomacks	Priest Rapids
Incomicanatook	above Priest Rapids
Piscowes	River same name
Intietook	" " "
Tsillani	" " "
Meatuho	" " "
Okinagon	North side of River same name
Samilkumeighs	" " " " " "
Nispellum	" " " " " "
Simposllechah	" " " " " "
Isnihoyelps	South side below Kettle River
Sinwhoyelpetook	North side of the same River
Callespellum	South side of the same River
Sinachicks	Lakes of main river.[4]

Simpson mentioned the names of the early Kettle Falls and Lake tribes. who later also were taken care of at St. Mary's Mission in the lower Okanogan Valley.

Isaac I. Stevens in 1854, as Superintendent of Indian Affairs for Washington Territory, named only six Okanogan tribes:

> The Okinakanes comprise the bands lying on the river of that name, as far north as the foot of a great lake. They are six in number viz: The Tekunr-a-tum, at the mouth; the Konekonep, on the Creek of that name; Kluck-hait-kwee, at the falls; Kinakanes, near the forks; and

---

[4] George Simpson quoted by Frederick Merk, *Fur Trade and Empire,* 168–169.

Mil-aket-kun, on the west fork. With them may also be classed the N'pockle or San Puelles, on the Columbia River.[5]

Gibbs, a member of the Stevens party gives about the same account.[6] Teit names the Nicola Okanogan according to the name of their Chief Nicola, who had their headquarters at Douglas Lake, and the Lower Okanogans or River Okanogan as "the real Okanogans." He says that the population of these tribes had originally been at least four times greater.

Lake Tribe	2000 or more
Colville	2500
Okanogan	2500–3000
Sanpoil	1500

Smallpox epidemics in 1800, 1832, 1857, and 1862 had decimated the various tribes.[7] Captain McClellan visited the Okanogan Indians near the mouth of the Okanogan River in 1854, when smallpox was prevailing. Near Fort Okanogan he saw the dead wrapped in blankets and bound upright high in the trees.[8] James A. Teit classifies all the Okanogan and Upper Columbia tribes as "The Okanogan"[9] while Curtis even names several individually distinct bands of Wenatchee Indians.[10]

Walter Cline and others in an ethnographical study made during July and August, 1930, divide the Okanogan tribes into the Northern and the Southern Okanogans. The Okanogan tribes of the South are called here by the name they used, "Sin Equai'tku." In an angelicized version the authors refer to them as the Sinkaietk or Southern Okanogan, the first mention of this name.[11] Early historians did not divide the Upper and the Lower Okanogans. The old Indians who lived in the Okanogan Valley did not know international boundaries. This concept was only gradually developed as the United States and British Canadian Indian policies were shaped and these were slow procedures. The history of St. Mary's Mission is a proof that this was so. Father de Rougé's

---

[5] Isaac I. Stevens to Commissioner of Indian Affairs, September 16, 1854, in *Report of the Secretary of the Interior, Thirty-Third Congress, 2nd Session,* 445.

[6] George Gibbs quoted in Frederick Webb Hodge, *op. cit.* II, 115 (1959 ed.).

[7] James A. Teit, "The Okanogan," in Franz Boas, ed., *Forty-Fifth Annual Report of the Bureau of American Ethnology to the Secretary of the Smithsonian Institution,* 198 ff. (1927–1928).

[8] Steven to Commissioner of Indian Affairs, September 16, 1854, *op. cit.,* 446.

[9] Teit, "The Okanogan," *op. cit.,* 198–294.

[10] Edward S. Curtis, *The North American Indians* (Frederick Webb Hodge, ed.), Vol. 7, 68.

[11] Walter Cline and others, *The Sinkaietk or Southern Okanogan* (Leslie Spier, ed.), 3.

Okanogan Indians came from all directions. They all belonged to the same great people who spoke the same interior Salish language with local variations.[12] The meeting place in front of the church was the scene for joyful greetings and reunions of the various Okanogan bands with their Canadian tribal relatives. The Indians themselves had nothing to do with boundary politics.

The Wenatchees or Pisscows, the Chelans, the Entiats, and the Methows living in their river valleys had certain closer relationships with each other expressed in their Salish dialect; some Shahaptian words were intermingled with Salish due to the nearness of the Yakima tribes. All these tribes came later under the influence of St. Mary's Mission. The Wenatchee had become friendly to the white man very early. Their chief, Sopa, sent his braves to hunt deer for the fur traders. He was concerned about the security of the white man. Having learned that Alexander Ross and his party were on the way to the Yakima nation to buy horses, he sent two of his men to warn the whites to stay away from that fierce warrior tribe.[13]

The principal tribe of the Okanogans were the Konkonelps who had their winter village in what is today Conconully. Smaller bands lived in the side valleys under subchiefs, for instance, the Katar people and the Omak Lake people. The Tukoratum lived at the mouth of the Okanogan River. From 1858 on, we hear of Chief Tonasket's band of Okanogans whose ancestral homes were located from Oliver, British Columbia, down to Tonasket. The Similkameen and the Inkameep tribes came to the Osoyoos gambling and horse racing grounds and, as mentioned before, to Father de Rougé's church gatherings.

The tribes who are distinct but often grouped together, the Nespelems and the Sanpoels, lived about 30 miles apart, separated by the Sanpoil Mountains. Their territory extended from the mouth of the Spokane River down to Grand Coulee on the south side of the Columbia and from the opposite side of the mouth of the Spokane River down to the mouth of the Okanogan on the north side of the Columbia, including also the valleys of the Sanpoil and Nespelem Creeks. According to David Thompson they were different tribes. He had visited the Sanpoil before he met the Nespelem Indians:

----

[12] L. V. McWhorter, in *Hear Me My Chiefs* (Ruth Bordin, ed.), footnote, 10, quotes Duncan McDonald, son of Angus McDonald, last Hudson's Bay Company Factor at Fort Okanogan: "They speak of the native name of the Flatheads as Salish, but I say it is Selish." McDonald's mother spoke Nez Perce and Selish; she was a Nez Perce Indian.

[13] Alexander Ross, *The Fur Hunters of the Far West*, 6.

. . . They are a finer people, several of the Men were six feet in height, the face rather oval, the eyes black, the nose straight and prominent, the cheek-bones moderate, teeth and mouth good, the chin round, on the whole their appearance is manly, mild, open, and friendly. The men were ornamented with a few shells, the women more profusely. . . .[14]

At the greatest fishing center of the Upper Columbia River, the Kettle Falls, we find the Shuelpis or Skoyelpi, named by the fur traders the Chaudieres. The falls were named the Chaudieres meaning "kettle" and "trap" or net. The Indians would catch the salmon in big wicker basket traps. The water fell into gigantic rock cauldrons formed by erosion. These Chaudiere Indians were later called simply the Colville Indians because of the proximity of Fort Colville. These people had their homes along the Colville River and along the Columbia River from Kettle Falls down to the mouth of the Spokane River.

The Snaicksti or Sinajextee were named after a fish which was caught in their region. Later they were known as the Lake Indians. Their homes were on the Upper Columbia River from Kettle Falls north and along the Arrow Lakes.

All of these tribes belonged to the Interior Salish language group among whom a variety of dialects was spoken. Certain words were differently pronounced especialy farther down the Columbia where the Salish language had acquired in the course of time some words from the Shahaptian language, as we have said. David Thompson tells about the Wenatchee:

> They had about one hundred and twenty families, and from the women and children must be about eight hundred souls. The language is still a dialect of the Saleesh, but my Simpoil Interpreters find several words they do not understand.[15]

It is known that all these tribes used a sign language also. The Interior Salish language is slowly dying out. It is to be seriously regretted that the young generation seems not to have much interest in learning it. The elderly Indians still speak it among themselves. Here are historical linguistic values that never can be replaced.

Each tribe that lived in the Okanogan and Columbia Valleys was known under several names given it by the fur traders, ethnologists, and other white men who came in contact with them. A footnote in *The British Columbia Historical Quarterly,* Volume LX, 1945, page 282, states that there were about forty-five different spellings of the word Okanogan. Right

---

[14] David Thompson, quoted by Tyrrell, *op. cit.,* 479.
[15] *Ibid.,* 482.

Reverend Francis Norbert Blanchet was justly incensed about the changing of old Indian names.[16]

As in other tribes, the position of head chief in the Okanogan and related tribes was usually passed on from father to son. The war chief had great influence. Tribal government was very effective on account of the high respect paid the authority of the chief. Alexander Ross tells us that "Their general maxim is that Indians were born free."[17] Hence, the chief would never interfere in private or family matters but only in affairs that concerned the tribe as a whole. Only if a man were rich in horses and wives would he have a right to the obedience of another. Often chieftainship was acquired by a man who possessed high moral leadership. Governor Stevens wrote in his *Report* that:

> During Captain McClellan's examination of the Methow river, six of the bands, belonging in part to each tribe agreed upon Ke-kete-tum-nouse, or Pierre, an Indian from Kla-hum, the site of Astor's old fort, at the mouth of the Okin-a-kane, as their chief.[18]

All important decisions of peace or war required the assistance of a council. Prerequisites for council membership were again many horses, many wives, or the accomplishment of some heroic deed. The use of the ceremonial pipe in council meetings was sacred ancient symbolism. The council would assemble in a ring; the chief would start the meeting by the ceremony of smoking, which was a peace offering for the Great Spirit. The pipe when lighted was held first to the east or rising sun, then to the heavens above, and last to the earth below. Each time three whiffs were drawn. This ceremony was observed only by the chief. After it he would give the pipe to the next man who would smoke without ceremony and give it to the next until all had smoked. Deep silence was observed.

It was mainly by way of speech-making that the chiefs ruled their subjects and asserted their great influence even among neighboring tribes. In 1841 the Shushwaps chief, Tranquille, died. The Indians blamed the whites

---

[16] Rt. Rev. F. N. Blanchet, *Historical Notes and Reminiscences of Early Time in Oregon*, 11. "Okanogan is an Indian name, which has always been so spelled and so written by all from early times, as well as that of Spokane. Now that Indian name has been subjected more than any other to a variety of reforms at the hands of disagreeing reformers of late years, who, despising the long and honored tradition of that Indian name, have changed and varied its spelling into curious and extraordinary variety: some one, in 1846 spelling it Okinakana; other parties have spelled the word . . . Okanagan, Aokinagan, Okanagon, etc. Hence the confusion and a conflict in the camp of the reformers; each one founding the right of spelling that Indian name on his own private judgment which is known to be prolific of sects."

[17] Ross, *Adventures*, 310.

[18] Stevens to Commissioner of Indian Affairs, September 16, 1854, *op. cit.*, 445.

for having given him "bad medicine." A nephew of the dead chief waited for an opportunity and then killed Chief Trader Black. The country of the Okanogans and Upper Columbians was aroused. All trade was stopped. Dr. John McLaughlin was at this time chief factor of the Hudson's Bay Company center at Fort Vancouver, and his letters show that serious consequences were expected. Old John Tod from Alexandria, McKinley and Ermatinger from Fort Okanogan, McLean from Colville were ordered to Kamloops. Tod told the Shushwaps that the murderer had to be delivered up. It was then that Chief Nicola of the Okanogans showed his great eloquence effectively:

> The winter is cold. On all the hills around the deer are plenty; and yet I hear your children crying for food. Why is this? You ask for powder and ball, they refuse you with a scowl. Why do the white man let your children starve? Look here! Beneath you [sic] mound of earth lies him who was your friend, your father. The powder and ball he gave you that you might get food for your famishing wives and children, you turned against him. Great Heavens! And are the Shushwaps such cowards dastardly to shoot their benefactor in the back while his face was turned? Yes, alas, you have killed your father! A mountain has fallen! The earth is shaken! The sun is darkened; My heart is sad. I cannot look at myself in the glass, I cannot look at you, neighbors and friends. He is dead, and we poor Indians shall never see his like again. He was just and generous. His heart was larger than yonder mountain, and clearer than the waters of the lake. Warriors, do not weep, but sore is my breast, and our wives shall wail for him. Wherefore did you kill him? But you did not. You loved him and now you must not rest until you have brought to justice his murderer.[19]

The office of war chief was abandoned during the nineteenth century. The Okanogan, the Colville, and the Lake tribes were peaceful and friendly to their neighboring tribes and to the white man. Enemies or outlaws would often lurk about at night in earlier times. Ross tells about the whoops and yells that alerted him while he was alone in the wilderness. He said that the Nez Perce were the enemies of the Okanogans. James Teit confirms this. Previous to the coming of the fur traders a large war party of the Nez Perce attacked the main camp of the Sanpoil Indians while the able-bodied men were on a hunting trip in the mountains. Nearly 200 women, children, and old people were killed. Then the Sanpoils asked the Okanogans and the Colvilles to help revenge the massacre, and they were prepared therefore when a war party of the Nez Perce and Yakima showed up. The united tribes, whose strength had been concealed,

---

[19] Chief Nicola, quoted by George Bryce, *The Remarkable History of the Hudson's Bay Company*, 403–404.

attacked. Their enemies were completely defeated; after this there was peace. Mrs. Mary Ann Sampson-Timentwa of Omak reported how her grandfather and one of his wives were killed by the enemies, the Nez Perce Indians. Both were pierced by arrows, the shafts of which were so thick they could have supported the bodies. This will explain later difficulties when Chief Joseph of the Nez Perce tribe as a prisoner of war was placed with a group of his people on the Colville Reservation as we will see.

It took many decades to educate the Indians to a more Christian way of thinking about enemies. With the Indians an enemy always remained an enemy. Every tribe had friends and foes; and the attitudes toward them were kept alive from one generation to the next. David Douglas, the famous botanist, while traveling through the Okanogan and Upper Columbia Valleys during 1826, experienced this sudden fighting impulse in one of his guides at the mere sight of members of a supposed enemy tribe:

> The little Wolf, chief of a tribe near Okanogan Lake, a useful fine fellow, was selected to go with me by land the 200 miles. A party of Cootanie Indians arrived, with whom and the Little Wolf's people an old grievance existed . . . war was instantly declared by the Wolf.[20]

After the hostile factions had finally settled their grievances with presents, a big feast had to be celebrated. On a later occasion the "Wolf" repeated his behavior against a party of the same tribe.

Marie Houghton Brent tells the story of how her great-grandfather made Tonasket a subchief. The Shuswaps, the enemies of the Okanogans, had come down to the land of the Okanogans and had ordered her great-grandfather, Chief Nicola, and his people away from their land. Chief Nicola refused to vacate his territory. Thereupon the Shuswaps, outnumbering the Okanogans, gave them time until sunrise. While the Shuswaps moved back a little way and made camp, Chief Nicola held a conference with his people giving them a pep talk, telling them that if they resolved to stand up to the last man and planned their battle carefully they might have a chance. The Okanogans waited until the enemy made the first move and then mowed the first line down and kept on fighting. The dead were piled up on both sides, but finally the Shuswaps were on the run and the Okanogans in pursuit of them. The Shuswaps attempted to make another stand amid some rock and brush, but they were falling right and left and were soon on the run again. Soon they were nearly

---

[20] *Journal Kept by David Douglas During His Travels in North America,* 1823–1827 (1914 ed.), 65–66.

halfway back to their country. After trying another big stand, in which they fought toe to toe, they gave up and were chased back across the Shuswaps River and into their own country. They were told never to put foot on the Okanogan soil again and never to intermarry with Okanogans. The Okanogans then named the various places of the battle.

When the Okanogans came back from the Shuswaps River Chief Nicola gathered all his people and told them that they still were in danger of losing their land to other tribes. He told them that he must go to the head of the Okanogan Lake for the security of that land. This brought about the need for another chief in the lower Okanogan Valley:

> He said he would leave young Tonasket here to help the rest of them. He knew the young man well, being with him a long time and growing up with him. He knew that Tonasket was honest, kind and with good judgment, and he would trust him. Chief Nicola said that he would make Chief Tonasket a sub-chief to take care of the Indians here and that he would marry his daughter to Tonasket. Then Chief Nicola would not be alone and would have help when it was needed. This daughter of Chief Nicola who married Joseph Tonasket was my Mother's aunt and Millie Tonasket's aunt. This was Batiste Tonasket's mother.[21]

Great sorrow was experienced when this mighty tribe was divided by the United States and Canadian boundaries. Chief Nicola regretted very much the separation of his people. It was only then that the people accepted Tonasket as their real chief. After Chief Tonasket's wife (Batiste's mother) died very young, Tonasket after a long time married Antonia Somday, a widow with two children.

All the tribes of the Okanogan and Upper Columbia Rivers had a food-gathering economy. Their summer habitat was chosen on the basis of its ability to provide them with food for the winter. During the fishing season they camped along the famous fishing centers: Kettle Falls, Spokane Falls, mouth of the Okanogan into the Columbia Rivers, and along the other rivers of their big territory. Mr. Richard Hirst, who came in 1901 with covered wagons to St. Mary's Mission, Omak, remembers how the rivers were then filled with fish. He saw the Indians on horseback, the horses standing in the river near the bank, and the Indians spearing the big salmon as they went up the river to spawn. One of the big fish was hung from a horse's saddle and the tail reached the dust.[22] The men brought in the fish, the women prepared them for winter storage. Big

---

[21] Maria Houghton Brent, *Chief Nicola Makes Tonasket A Sub-Chief.* Courtesy of Mrs. Katie Lacey, Ms.

[22] Mr. Richard Hirst, in an interview at St. Mary's Mission, Omak, January 27, 1961.

drying racks and smoking stacks could be seen all along the rivers. At the camping sites the Indians were able to recognize the tribal identity of their neighbors by observing the different customs of slicing and preparing the fish for winter storage. Without a calendar, these children of nature knew exactly the time of the salmon run and the different cycles of the diverse kinds of fish. During the fishing season the Indians built fish traps into the streams that flowed into the Columbia River between Brewster and Kettle Falls. Fish were for some tribes the main winter food. At the Kettle Falls big basket traps were used. Besides the salmon, sturgeon were caught here. David Douglas has left a vivid description of the famous fishing place.[23]

The Indians knew the best time for hunting the various wild animals then roaming the extensive forests. Alexander Ross reports that once an Indian chief came to him and warned him that a strange pack of big wolves was coming. Three days later the wolves did come and on the very first night killed five of the horses of the fur company. Ross set a dozen steel traps in a circle around the carcass of one of the dead horses. Next morning he found that he had trapped four animals. One of the animals caught was a large white wolf still alive. These white wolves must have been caught periodically, for the emblem of the chiefs of the Okanogan tribes was the skin of a white wolf, which hung at the entrance to their lodges. It symbolized strength. The Okanogan chief would say: "While I have this, we have nothing to fear, strange wolves will kill no more horses, and I shall always love the whites."[24]

On hunting excursions the Okanogans would conceal themselves sometimes in a wolf's skin and act like wolves, or they would dress up as deer and walk on all fours right into the herd of deer.[25] The country especially around the Okanogan and upper Columbia Valleys abounded with game, such as bears, coyotes, foxes, wild ducks, blue grouse, prairie chickens, pheasants, prairie dogs, and rabbits. The hunting camp was made in the woods. The braves and their sons hunted the animals; their wives and

---

[23] *Journal Kept by David Douglas*, 166: "The Falls is a perpendicular pitch of 24 feet across the whole northern arm of the river, through which the principal part of the water runs: the south branch is dashed over shattered rocks, making a semicircular curve similar to that on the other channel. They meet a few feet below the Falls, where the whole body of the water is again dashed over a small cascade of 8 feet height. The river is only 43 yards wide, where it leaves the cascades in snowy flakes exceedingly picturesque, and in many places the scene is grand with every variety of appearance that can be called beautiful. The channels are divided by a small oval rocky island with a few stunted trees on it."

[24] Alexander Ross, *The Fur Hunters of the Far West* (1855 edition), Vol. I, 49–50.

[25] Alexander Ross, *Adventures*, 321.

daughters cut, cured, dried, or smoked the meat. Some was used for pemican, a highly concentrated food made of a mixture of dried pounded meat, fats, and berries. Kept in skin pouches, pemican could be preserved for years. During the berry-picking seasons and root diggings the family skin lodge or mat tepee was erected in a convenient place. Often this was not even necessary. The Great Spirit had given these lands to the Indians and they could stretch out anywhere on Mother Earth to enjoy a peaceful sleep.

The four main kinds of roots gathered by the old Indians were the wild carrot, wild onion, bitterroot, and camas root. The camas roots were especially important items in their diet. To cook them the Indian wives used earth ovens. A pit was dug and covered with firewood upon which rocks were piled. Fire was put to the wood, and the heated rocks fell into the pit as the wood burned away. The rocks were then leveled and covered with green grass. The sacks of camas were then placed in the pit and covered with green grass, followed by a layer of earth and then a layer of sod. More firewood was piled on top and covered with wet or green branches and leaves to assure a slow and steady heat. This fire was watched and nourished for nearly forty-eight hours, after which the camas roots were taken out of the pit. The Indian wives made flour out of the camas roots. Certain kinds of roots required skill in cooking; otherwise they would taste bitter. A skillful cook, relative of Chief Smitkin, was called "Sumetalx" which means "sweet-smelling cooking." Various kinds of berries were picked and dried. Stems of the sunflower and other plants were eaten. Nuts, seeds, even the mosslike lichens that grew on the trunks of pine trees served as food.

In spite of all their efforts to store up food, sometimes Okanogan families would starve to death toward spring when the winter supply had run out. Charles Wilkes wrote about this in his reports:

> . . . They are not provident enough to lay up a sufficient supply for their winter's stock and are obliged for the remainder of the year to make use of roots, and a bread which is made from the Moss that grows on trees.[26]

Father Joseph Joset, S.J., who came in contact with the Okanogan Indians near Fort Colville, made the same observation:

> The Okinagans follow about the same kind of life as the Sgoyelpi with the difference that they are most improvident; hence death of hunger is not very rare among them; once, the news being brought that

---

[26] Charles Wilkes, *Narrative of the United States Exploring Expedition During the Years 1838, 1839, 1840, 1841, 1842*, IV, 434.

one family of them had been found all dead of hunger, the missionary made the remark to the Colville chief: "It must be laziness: for moss is found everywhere," meaning the parasite plant hanging from the limbs of pines. The chief answered: "Yes, moss is found everywhere, but after one has lived on it one or two weeks, it becomes impossible to swallow it."[27]

The Okanogan tribes generally had to work hard to provide for the winter. All members of the family had to help; they depended on each other. This explains the closely knit family ties that existed among the Okanogans. Father Joset described a certain interrelationship between the mode of food gathering, the character of the men and women, and consequently the marriage ties. He described the early Skoyelpi or Colvilles as mainly salmon eaters. During the salmon run the basket traps would fill and all the men had to do was to empty the baskets periodically. In a few weeks they had all their supply for the winter. All the other work was done by the women, who had to preserve the fish and keep the provisions. The women considered all the provisions as belonging to them alone. The men depended on the women completely. The men had little to do. They were "lazy, haughty, independent." When the missionary was seen working, the men asked him: "Are you a woman?"[28]

During the berry-picking season and root gatherings all again became the property of the women:

> . . . Communion of goods was very rare; often the writer heard a man say: I have stolen my wife's provisions. That way a man was prevented from gambling away his wife's property; but on the other side how difficult to establish Christian subordination. How often a passionate woman would fill a camp or the whole tribe with disorders: when angry she always could drive the man away, for she could always tell him I don't need thee.[29]

The Lake Indians, or, as Father Joset called them, the "Snaicksti," had to exert themselves by trapping and hunting animals or by spearing fish. The wife needed the husband and the husband needed the wife in the more difficult ways they had to make a living. They even had to travel during the winter over mountains in search of small game with their small children on their backs. The missionary said they were "more noble-minded. So the domestic relations were more the Christian way."[30]

When the fall winds blew over the country these tribes knew that it

[27] Rev. Joseph Joset, S.J., "Colville Mission," *The Joset Papers,* Mss., OPA.
[28] *Ibid.*
[29] *Ibid.*
[30] *Ibid.*

was time to prepare or rebuild the winter home. During the food-providing season the tribes had been scattered in smaller groups. As winter approached they would assemble again in a village. These winter villages were for the most part permanent. Some of the older people would stay here during the summer months and provide the winter wood and help store the food.

The winter shelters were for the most part mat houses or skin houses. The inside was dug out about a foot or two below the surface of the ground. The floor was covered with rye grass. Poles stuck into the ground held the mats or skins; planks, brush, and earth helped to keep them in place. Some families would live together in a "longhouse" where each family had a fire in the center and had to provide the wood for it. The property and privacy of these families were provided for. Later, buffalo-skin lodges were used. The Nepelems formerly had winter pit houses, semisubterranean dwellings; the roofs were either flat or conical in form. A ladder was needed to enter through the same opening that served as an exit for the smoke, or there were doors at the sides in bigger rectangular houses.

David Thompson describes the villages of the "Ilthkoyapes," as he called the Indians he found at Kettle Falls, as made up

> . . . of log sheds of about twenty feet in breath by from thirty to sixty feet in length. They were built of boards which somehow they [the Indians] had contrived to split from large cedars drifted down the River, partly covered with the same and with mats so as to withstand the rain; each shed had many cross poles for smoke drying the Salmon. . . .[31]

The sheds were clean. Thompson said the Indians would have looked clean but they had no soap. He makes this remark in regard to the other tribes also.

As the years passed, the Indians started slowly to imitate the fur traders and the missionaries and build log dwellings. These were for many years without a floor; later hewn log floors were used. Many more years were to pass before sawmills made smooth wooden floors possible. Governor George Simpson wrote on October 22, 1824:

> Passed a lodge of Indians, part of the Kettle Falls Tribe. They appeared more wretched than any I had seen on the East side of the Mountains not having a single article of British Manufacture in their possession but a Gun & Beaver Trap; they were not sufficiently numerous to enable us to form any correct opinion of their disposition or habits.[32]

---

[31] *Journal Kept by David Thompson,* 467.
[32] Frederick Merk, *op. cit.,* 40.

Before the contact with the white man all the tribes of the Okanogan and Upper Columbia Valleys still lived in the Stone Age. Rock formations which split off in layers were used to fashion knives, scrapers, hammers, arrowpoints, and spearheads. The elbow pipes of the Sanpoils, Nespelems, and Okanogans were of steatite and soapstone. Quartzite scrapers with wooden handles are still used by some for hide fleshers or scrapers. Numerous rock tools were found when excavating for the Coulee Dam project when old Indian graves were removed. Jasper, chert, flint, even the bones of animals were used for practical purposes. The Indian wives sewed with bone needles.[33] They knew how to make beads and earrings from river clams.

Besides rocks, wood was used for dishes and spoons. Often spoons were formed out of horns and shells. Furniture was not needed. Mother Earth provided sitting and sleeping space and served as a table also.

Mats of bulrushes, birchbark baskets, skin baskets were made. Others were manufactured by twining, coiling, matting, and weaving. Great artistic talent and practical sense were exhibited in using fibers and animals' hair and skins. Braided buckskin strips became strong cords. The Lake Indians are known to have made soft and warm garments from the fleecy hair of the wild mountain goats and the hair of rabbits and dogs by twisting the hair first into heavy strings and then weaving them. The Okanogans were famous for the art of tanning. Their buckskin garments were beautifully decorated; the men showed off their porcupine quills and teeth of various animals while the higuas and pearls were chiefly used for the dresses of the girls and women. The Okanogan and Upper Columbia beauties wore conical caps into which pretty designs were woven. No European clothing can compare favorably to native dress when worn by Indians on festive occasions. It is to be regretted that in modern times these relics of a former aboriginal culture are disappearing more and more. Because of the great work entailed in making a new Indian outfit, the Indians could not and did not change their clothing until it was often in rags. More and more they came to prefer European clothing. David Douglas, when wandering through the Okanogan and Upper Columbia Valleys in April of 1826, found the natives using a lichen which afforded a "very durable beautiful yellow colour and is used by the natives in Dyeing."[34] Many of these secrets of nature which the Indians possessed in primitive times were lost by using the white man's wares.

The Indians were eager for the exchange of goods by the traders

---

[33] Donald Collier, Alfred E. Hudson, and Arlo Ford, *Archaeology of the Upper Columbia Region,* 63 ff.
[34] *Journal Kept by David Douglas* (1914 edition), 161.

as David Thompson reported when he visited the Sanpoil Indians, July 3, 1811:

> The chief made a long speech in a loud singing voice, and each sentence was responded to by the others by Oy Oy: The speech being ended and interpreted to us, was thanks for our arrival, and hope we would bring them Guns, Ammunition, Axes, Knives, Awls, and not to forget Steels and Flints with many other articles; they were able and willing to hunt, and would be able to pay for everything they wanted, but at present they had only their hands to procure food and clothing.[35]

Alexander Ross and Ross Cox had not much good to say about the Sanpoils. They were the poorest of the Okanogan and Upper Columbia tribes. For the sake of historical accuracy, we will have to make a distinction here. We have seen that David Thompson was well received. This tribe consisted of several bands; it would be bad logic to generalize the fur traders' judgments referring to the whole tribe. The country where the bands of the Sanpoils lived was very poor in game. The natives did not know how to use the net and other easier methods for catching fish. Having no guns and nothing to exchange; being poorly clothed and almost starving, they were forced to keep alive by depredations. These bands were in the most primitive state when the fur traders arrived. Yet there are many fine and noble people among the Sanpoils today. Their early hostile attitude toward the whites was developed by faulty leaders and the bad behavior of the whites.

We can imagine how the Indians by their gatherings conversed and relayed important tribal matters. Mrs. Mary Ann Sampson-Timentwa tells how the old and blind Mary Ann Yatkanolz, who was the historian of the tribal band, used a ball of string like a calendar. Simple knots in the string represented the historical events as they were handed down through three generations.

The greatest sources of evil the Catholic missionaries had to fight before the Indians could become good Christians were gambling, polygamy, and their belief in all kinds of superstitions, magic, and powers. Like all other people the Indians loved games, races, and competitions; for these activities invitations were sent to other friendly tribes. At old Fort Okanogan, at Monse, and at Lake Osoyoos there were race tracks where the Indians vied with each other in horse races. When Chief Tonasket later moved his people into the region of Curlew he had to construct a mile-long race track for the young chiefs. Certain bone games and stick games often occupied days of the Indians' time. They would become so heated by

---

[35] Tyrrell, *op. cit.*, 475.

their gambling passion that nothing could stop them until they had gambled away all their possessions. Special gambling lodges existed.

Polygamy was a sign of honor and distinction. The more wives a man had the richer he was because the wives worked for him. Generally all the chiefs had more than one wife. They were very conscious of rank and would marry only Indian princesses from friendly tribes. The wives had to be bought, the price depending on what the girl was worth in the eyes of her parents. It was seen as degrading to expect a future wife for nothing. Alexander Ross tells of one marriage custom in which

> . . . the husband of the eldest daughter of the family is entitled by their laws to take to wife all her sisters as they grow up, if able to maintain them.[36]

Mrs. Helen Toulou, who was educated at "Ward Mission" and is one of the former members of the Tribal Council, tells of the same custom in her manuscript book:

> There is no record kept of early leaders by Indians, only legendary. However, Kee-Kee-tum-nouse was head chief when the Canadian Fur Comp. first came into the Wild Northwest Territory, about 1810. They found a rather young and active chief, who notwithstanding his tribal leadership, turned out to be an excellent trapper and became the key man for the Trading Co. The factor of the fur Co. encouraged Indian trappers to move their families near the Post and was most insistent that the chief be located near by.
>
> Chief Kee-Kee-tum-nouse had the largest wigwam and well he might, since he had five wives and children by all. As it was the tribal custom those days when a man married, if the wife had sisters he would marry them as soon as they became of marriageable age and live together in one big happy home.
>
> Kee-Kee-tum-nouse was head chief as well as the direct sire of the Lake Tribe.[37]

The earliest knowledge we have about the religious ideas of the Okanogan and Upper Columbia tribes comes from David Thompson, who is speaking of the Sanpoil Indians:

> They seemed to acknowledge a Great Spirit who dwelled in the clouds to be the master of everything, and when they died their souls went to him; the Sun, Moon and Stars were all divinities, but the sun above all; and that he made the Lightning, Thunder and Rain. Their worship was

---

[36] Alexander Ross, *Adventures*, 318.

[37] Mrs. Helen Toulou, Kewa, Washington, *Manuscript Book on Indian Affairs.* We will hear more about this line of chiefs when it fits into our story.

in dancing, and the last dance they gave me was for a safe voyage and return to them.[38]

The Nespelems too danced and prayed for Thompson. The chief lifted his hands to heaven during prayer. The Methow told David Thompson of one of their taboos: all the salmon they caught from the time of the salmon run until the chief would assemble all for the feast and religious ceremonies had to be roasted. Only after those ceremonies could they boil or do as they pleased with the fish. The Wenatchees prayed again for the safety of the white men and for their return.

The Okanogans believed that the world was once just a floating island.[39] The concept of a God was very vague. Superstition and power worship regulated their daily life. Nearly every phase of human living, even death itself, had its rules of superstition which were deeply implanted in their primitive beliefs. Nevertheless, according to Alexander Ross, they had certain fundamental concepts. They believed in a good spirit and in an evil spirit. All good deeds would be rewarded and all evil actions punished in a future state. All important actions, business, hunting, and fishing, were started by a short prayer to the good spirit to ask his help. Smoking belonged to the ritual as we have seen. The Okanogan believed that the lakes and rivers would one day make the earth again a floating island as in the days of their ancestors and then all would be destroyed. They kept on asking the fur traders when this would happen. The Okanogans had

---

[38] Tyrrell, *op. cit.*, quoting Thompson, 477.

[39] Ross, *Adventures*, 287–289: "Long ago, so long ago that the sun was quite young and very small and no bigger than a star, there was an island far out at sea, called Samahtumiwhoolah, or the White Man's Island. It was inhabited by a white race of gigantic stature, and governed by a tall fair woman called Scomalt; and she was a great and strong medicine: the Scomalt. At last the peace of the island was destroyed by war, and the noise of battle was heard, the white man fighting the one with the other; and Scomalt was exceedingly wroth. She rose up and said: 'Lo, now I will drive these wicked far from me; my soul shall be no longer vexed concerning them, neither shall they trouble the faithful of my people with their strivings any more.' And she drove the rebellious together to the uttermost end of the island, and broke off the piece of land on which they were huddled, and pushed it out to sea to drift whither it would. This floating island was tossed to and fro many days, and buffeted by the winds exceedingly, so that all the people thereon died, save one man and one woman, who, seeing their island was ready to sink, made themselves a canoe and got themselves away towards the west. After paddling day and night for many suns, they came to certain islands, whence stearing through them, they came at last to where the mainland was, being the territory that the Okanogan now inhabit; it was, however, much smaller those days, having grown much since. This man and woman were so sorely weather-beaten when they landed that they found their original whiteness quite gone, and a dusky reddish color in its place. All the people of the continent are descended from this pair and the dingy skin of their storm-tossed ancestors has become the characteristic of the race."

clear concepts of honesty; stealing was considered a disgrace. Generally the women were faithful to their husbands. Inconstancy would be punished with death at the hand of any member of her family. But this seems not to have been an offense for the men.

When the girls and boys were nearing their age of puberty they would prepare themselves by a sweat bath for the "Quest." The parents would send them out alone into the wilderness to look for their powers, or, as some authors call it, their guardian spirits. Often the children were several days and nights outside alone looking for their power. Moses Mountain, Omak Mountain, or other isolated places were chosen. Some would dive into Omak Lake to look for their power. The parents often made sure their children had been at the place by assigning them a certain work to do there, for instance piling up a certain heap of rocks. Often the child had to attempt the quest for a power several times. Parents or other relatives sometimes would camp alone at a distance from the place. Being alone at night at the mercy of the elements or near wild animals and fasting often had their psychological effects on the power seekers. They concentrated on and imagined that they had received a certain power from a friendly animal or any other creature. Often they would dance, exhaust themselves, and produce a certain nervous state for the reception of an imagined power. The children thought they had seen visions or had heard their power song. Then they were allowed to go home and rest a while; some even died of fright.

At the time of the next Chinook Dance or winter dance, the youth would show his power and sing his power song and dance himself into a state of frenzy. The audience would help him sing his power song and would reward him with presents. But if he invited the guests he himself would have to give the presents.

The power might be a coyote or any animal, a bird, or an object. This magic power would save him in dangerous situations. The mythology of the Okanogans was centered around the coyote. His name occurred frequently in various legends; he was said to have all kinds of superhuman powers. In general, all objects, either animate or inanimate, were believed to possess supernatural powers.

The one who kept all these superstitions alive among the tribal members was the medicine man or shaman. He knew the medicinal value of herbs. Father De Smet describes the work of the medicine men as follows:

> Conjurers are found here as well as in some parts of Europe. They are a kind of physician. Whatever may be the complaint of the patient these gentlemen have him stretched out on his back, and his friends and relatives are ordered to stand around him, each one armed with two

sticks of unequal length. The doctor or conjurer neither feels his pulse nor looks at the tongue, but with a solemn countenance commences to sing some mournful strain, whilst those present accompany him with their voices and beat time with their sticks. During the singing the doctor operates on the patient, he kneels before him, and placing his closed fists on the stomach, leans on him with all his might. Excessive pain makes the patient roar, but these roarings are lost in the noise, for the doctor and the bystanders raise their voices higher in proportion as the sick man gives utterance to his sufferings. At the end of each stanza the doctor joins his hands, applies them to the patient's lips, and blows with all his strength. The operation is repeated till at last the doctor takes from the patient's mouth, either a little white stone or a claw of some bird or animal which he exhibits to the bystanders, protesting that he has removed the cause of the disease, and that the patient will soon recover.[40]

The influence of the medicine man was often greater than that of the chief. Often he was feared; nobody dared oppose him; he could send "bad medicine" into people. If someone was sick in the family the Indians would ask the medicine man to come. Before seeing the patient, the pay for his services was fixed in horses, blankets, hides, etc. Then he would come and make use of charms and incantations that were supposed to possess a healing power. He might give the patient some of his herbs or do some of the things Father Joset observed:

> The action of the medicine man or as he is called in the Indian language, the Tlekwilish, on the sick consisted in blowing, touching the sick part, in sucking the skin to extract coagulated blood. . . .[41]

Father Joset could not believe that coagulated blood could be sucked through the pores. He was told that a baptized man had done it for his only daughter. He happened to meet this man and wanted an experiment on himself:

> . . . he presented his naked forearm saying: "Suck me." The man smiled, saying: "You are not sick." "I need not be sick: There is blood, and my skin is surely not thicker than an Indian's. Suck me, I am in earnest." "I can't." "And why can't you?" "To do any such thing I must be angry (furious) when calm I can do nothing." The priest had never witnessed any such thing: he questioned other Indians who confirmed the story. "When the medicine man wants to do anything, to blow, to

---

[40] Rev. P. J. De Smet, S. J., to Very Rev. John Roothaan, S. J., St. Mary's (Montana), December 30, 1841, quoted in Hiram Martin Chittendon and Alfred Talbot Richardson, *Life, Letters and Travels of Father Pierre Jean De Smet, S.J., 1801–1873* (henceforth: CR, *De Smet*), III, 1013.

[41] *The Joset Papers*, Mss., OPA.

suck, he begins his song or rather humming (for they never sing words), he orders others to accompany him to sing with him, until he becomes furious, and then they attack the disease."[42]

But woe to the medicine man if his patient dies. Then the relatives would say that he had used "bad medicine" or witchcraft and the suspicious Indians would ambush the medicine man and kill him. Sometimes, however, he was permitted to buy off the relatives with most of his possessions.

Besides employing the medicine man, the tribes used the sweat lodge to cure all kinds of sickness, often expecting superhuman help from it in important undertakings. They would even address special prayers to the sweat lodge. Guy Waring, who came to the Okanogan country in the same year as Father de Rougé, in 1885, when this missionary started his priestly work there, once visited Chief Sarsapkin in Loomis to attend Holy Mass which Father was supposed to say in the chief's house. Sarsapkin was then in his sweat house; he stepped out naked to greet Waring and then went back to finish the bathing job. Waring was interested enough to write a description of this sweat house. It was oval in shape and was made of saplings stuck in the ground. It was about six by eight feet in its two diameters and about four feet high. The frame was covered tightly with coarse buckskin. Inside was a hole for the stones which were heated outside the lodge and then rolled in. When it was warm enough inside, the bather would enter, close the cover, and pour water on the hot stones. It was believed that the steam made the Indians sweat out all sickness and that they would now be cleansed and purified. When the body was bathed in sweat the Indians would run out and plunge themselves in the nearby river.

Not all treatment of sickness was left to the medicine man, as Ross Cox experienced. One of the proprietors had married a beautiful girl and taken her to Fort George. There she became ill. As a last resort her husband had her transported to Fort Okanogan hoping the change of air might improve her condition. Her legs and feet were swollen and hard and were without sensation and she looked like a skeleton. They were waiting for death to come when an old Indian who had observed her offered to try to cure her. Without telling him his method he wanted Cox to agree because he feared he might not be allowed to try it. As there was no hope and not much to lose, Cox consented. The young woman agreed. The old man then killed a dog, cut open his belly and placed the legs and feet of the patient inside and had them warmed by the intestines. When these got cold, he bandaged the legs and feet with warm flannel.

---

[42] The Joset Papers.

Beside the dog treatment the patient had to drink daily a glass of wine in which a certain bark had been soaked. Every day another dog had to die so that the woman could be treated. Slowly the swelling disappeared, the eyes of the patient became more lively. It took thirty-two dogs to bring about a complete recovery.[43]

Each tribe had its common preserves: the hunting regions, fishing places, berry and root grounds. Often other friendly tribes used these preserves with the permission of the chief.

Teit maintains that the Okanogan tribes formerly had slaves, mostly women. Some were bought from the Walla Wallas. They were treated well and their children belonged to the tribe. Cline and others in *The Sinkaietk or Southern Okanogan* refer to their informants, saying that the Okanogans never had slaves.

The foregoing are some of the aspects of the primitive aboriginal culture found by the missionaries, who followed upon the heels of the fur traders. To stoop down to this aboriginal culture of the Indians in order to raise them up into the sphere of Christian civilization required from the missionaries a dauntless and heroic spirit and utter self-sacrifice. Yet they were ready to follow the call.

---

[43] Ross Cox, *The Columbia River*, 235–236.

CHAPTER III

Centers From Which the Faith Spread

THE Catholic faith had been brought to the Pacific Northwest many years before any minister or priest of any denomination had ever set foot on the land. A number of Catholic Canadian voyageurs had been employed in the expeditions of Lewis and Clark in 1805. Samuel Parker at Colville on May 28, 1836, found an old man of this expedition who had stayed in the West and was now employed as an interpreter to the neighboring tribes.[1] When John Jacob Astor formed his Pacific Fur Company he engaged many men of faith. Archbishop Blanchet tells us that "in Astor's expedition there were thirteen Canadians nearly all of whom were Catholics."[2] Hunt's overland expedition had Canadian members who deserted on account of the great hardships of the journey and settled among the Indians. Writing about Fort Astoria and Fort Okanogan, Washington Irving tells about a Canadian Indian who acted differently from the members of the Western tribes:

> Ignace Shonowane, the Iroquois hunter, was a specimen of a different class. He was one of those aboriginals of Canada who had partially conformed to the habits of civilization and the doctrines of Christianity, under the influence of the French colonists and the Catholic priests; who seem generally to have been more successful in conciliating, taming, and converting the savages, than their English and Protestant rivals.[3]

Canadian voyageurs and Iroquois Indians had been employed west of the Rockies during the last decades of the eighteenth century. The French

---

[1] Samuel Parker, *op. cit.*, 292.
[2] Francis Norbert Blanchet, *Historical Sketches of the Catholic Church in Oregon*, 7.
[3] Washington Irving, *op. cit.*, VII, 175.

Canadians were Catholics and many Iroquois had been converted during the seventeenth and eighteenth cnturies by the Jesuit Fathers. Father Isaac Jogues, S.J., who died a most cruel death at the hands of these Indians,[4] and others did not shed their blood in vain. The Iroquois clung to their faith in spite of their "sullen, indolent, fickle, cowardly, and treacherous nature,"[5] a generalization which did not do justice to the Iroquois. There were many faithful servants living their faith and ready to lay down their lives for their fur masters. These Iroquois became living examples of their religion to other tribes.

David Thompson was happy when he found a party of these Canadian Indians who had come over the mountains to hunt. He engaged three of them while he was on the way to Spokane. He found another one at an Indian camp and hired him as a steersman for the great voyage down the Columbia.[6] This is another example of how the Catholic Iroquois then were welcome in the different Indian camps of the Inland Empire. The voyageurs would sing certain boatmen songs that made it easier to paddle by following the rhythm of the song. The Iroquois were in the habit of singing Catholic hymns to the beat of the paddle and most certainly were asked about the content of these songs.

As the North West Company and the Hudson's Bay Company moved farther toward the West Coast, the religious influence of their employees was felt among the tribes. As members of the fur brigades the voyageurs came in contact with many tribes at the various forts where they taught their hymns and prayers to others. Alexander Ross mentions why Canadians were employed:

> Canadians, it is admitted, are the best calculated for the endurance of hardships and expedition in the business of light canoe-men. It is seldom that other men are employed in such arduous labor. Indeed, the Canadians, considered as voyagers, merit the highest praise.[7]

The many Iroquois together with the Canadian employees who were Catholics probably outnumbered the adherents of other denominations:

> Among the people employed are a set of civilized Indians from the neighborhood of Montreal, chiefly of the Iroquois nation. At this period they form nearly a third of the number of men employed by the Company at the Columbia. They are expert voyagers, and especially so in

---

[4] See: John J. Wayne, S.J., *The Jesuit Martyrs of North America;* also: Blanchet, *op. cit.,* 7.

[5] Ross, *The Fur Hunters of the Far West,* I, 286.

[6] George W. Fuller, *The Inland Empire of the Pacific Northwest,* I, 152–154.

[7] Ross, *Fur Hunters,* 282.

the rapids and dangerous runs in the inland waters, which they either stem or shoot with the utmost skill.[8]

The Okanogan Indians probably heard about the faith for the first time from one of the Iroquois Indians at Fort Okanogan.[9]

As no white women were available the officers of the fur companies and the Canadian voyageurs married Indian women and taught their growing families the faith. And the Iroquois Indians married members of other tribes. As early as 1821 these Catholic families voiced the wish to have a Catholic priest. However, the priest shortage was acute, and the Very Reverend Father Rosati, then vicar-general of Upper Louisiana, was unable to answer this wish.[10] This was fourteen years before the first Protestant missionary, the Reverend Samuel Parker, made his trip to the Northwest looking for mission sites. Many of the half-breed families were then living near the forts; some in the lower Columbia Basin.

By license of Parliament in September, 1821, when the North West Company and the Hudson's Bay Company were combined, the Hudson's Bay Company was obliged to take care of the Christianization of the Indians. The committee of this company on February 27, 1822, gave the following directions to Governor Simpson:

> . . . numerous Halfbreed children . . . ought to be removed to Red River where the Catholics will naturally fall under the Roman Catholic Mission which is established there, and the Protestants and such Orphan Children as fail to be maintained and clothed by the Company, may be placed under the Protestant Establishment and Schools under the Revd. Mr. West.[11]

The same policy was to be maintained for women and children at the different trading posts. Director Andrew Colvile urged further fostering of religion in a letter to Governor Simpson "London, 11 March 1824":

> It is incumbent on the Company if there was no settlement to have a chaplain in their country and at least to allow missions to be established at proper places for the conversion of the Indians. . . .[12]

Far-reaching orders were given to the chief factors, chief traders, and clerks in charge of districts and posts at the Council of the Northern

---

[8] Ross, *op. cit.*, 286.

[9] *Ibid.*, 149–150.

[10] Gilbert J. Garraghan, S.J., *The Jesuits of the Middle United States*, II, 236, quoting *Annales de la Propagation de la Foi* (1:2), 52.

[11] Fleming, ed., *op. cit.*, 33.

[12] Merk, ed., *op. cit.*, 205.

Department, July 5, 1823 — which were repeated at the Council that met July 1, 1823 — to assist in and to carry out regulations concerning religion, morality, and education. Among others the following regulations are most significant:

124. That for the moral and Religious improvement of the Servant and more effectual civilization and instruction of the families attached to the different establishments and the Indians, that every Sunday divine services be publicly read with becoming solemnity either once or twice a day to be regulated by the number of people, at which every man [,] woman and child resident will be required to attend together with any of the Indians who may be at hand and whom it will be proper to invite.

125. That for this purpose, the requisite supply of Religious Books will be furnished from time to time by and at the Expense of the Company.

126. That in the course of the week all irregularity, vicious, immoral or indolent habits particularly among women and children be check'd and discountenanced and their opposites encouraged and rewarded.

129. That the parent be encouraged to devote part of his leisure moments to teach his children their A.B.C. Catechism, together with some short appropriate Prayer, to be punctually repeated on going to bed, by which means the instruction of the child will be rendered instrumental to the parents' own improvements, and by the regular observance of the Sabbath, independent of other amelioration, decency [,] cleanliness and moral propriety will be promoted.[13]

According to these regulations Fort Okanogan and Fort Colville now became centers from which the faith spread to other areas. This was "Bible Christianity" merely. Without priests, the Canadians and the Iroquois tried their best to teach the faith to their families and to the surrounding Indians. At the forts the officer in charge presided at Sunday services. The Bible was read, hymns were sung, prayers were said, maybe a talk was given. The Indian chiefs assembled their people to honor the "Great Spirit." Francis Heron in a letter to James Hargrave written from Fort Colville, April 1, 1831, speaks of the progress made by the Indians:

Every chief is parson of his tribe and I assure you hold forth to them in real Orthodox style — It is really a pleasant sight to see old and young of both sexes going to Church on Sundays with faces as long and no less sanctified looking.

. . . The Chiefs likewise perform family service morning and evening throughout the week — attends the sick and infirm, when he is no less fervent in offering up his prayers on their behalf to the great Master of

---

[13] Fleming, ed., *op. cit.*, 96.

Life, nor will one of these reverend gentry sit down to a meal without asking a blessing before he begins and returning thanks when he has done — Even the children [Indian] will not pick up the least trifle about the post, as they say if they steal they will be burned when they die. — They are indeed altogether the very best Indians I have ever seen, since this reformation has been wrought amongst them.[14]

The need for priests became a great problem and the Catholics inquired where to find them. The nearest bishop lived at the Red River Settlement. A Scotch Protestant gentleman, Thomas Douglas, known as Lord Selkirk, who owned about forty percent of the Hudson's Bay Company stock, obtained a grant of land along the Red River in present Manitoba in 1812, and started a colony of settlers from various countries. Lord Selkirk later applied to Bishop Plessis of Quebec for Catholic priests. One of the priests sent there was the Rev. Norbert Provencher who from 1816–1818 was the founder and pastor of St. Boniface in Manitoba. His position was raised to that of vicar-general of the Bishopric of Quebec in 1818. In 1820, on February 1, he became the vicar apostolic of Northwestern North America under the title of Bishop of Juliopolis *in partibus infidelium*. He was consecrated by Bishop Plessis at Three Rivers on May 12, 1822.[15]

Bishop Provencher was anxious for more information about the immense territory that lay to the west of his mission field. When on July 14, 1827, the botanist, David Douglas, on his return trip from the Oregon Country stopped at the Red River Colony, he was delighted to receive the visit of this Bishop and his priests:

> . . . They conversed in the most unreserved affable manner and made many inquiries concerning the different countries I had visited. I have some reason to think well of their visit, being the first ever paid to any individual except the officers of the Hudson's Bay Company. I am much delighted with the meek dignified appearance of the Bishop, a man considerably above six feet and proportionally stout; appears to be a man of the most profound acquirements seen only through the thick rut of his great modesty.[16]

---

[14] G. P. De T. Glazebrook, ed., *The Hargrave Correspondence, 1821–1843*, 71–72.

[15] Abbé J. B. A. Allaire, *Dictionnaire Biographique Du Clerge Canadian-Francais*, 453–454. Also: Chester Martin, *Lord Selkirk's Work in Canada*, Oxford Historical and Literary Studies, Vol. VII; George Bryce, *The Remarkable History of the Hudson's Bay Company*, 418–419; John Perry Pritchell, *The Red River Valley: A Regional Study*. For more detail on Bishop Provencher see also: Rev. A. G. Morice, O.M.I., *History of the Catholic Church in Canada*, I, 113–245.

[16] *Journal Kept by David Douglas*, 280. Also: Sir W. J. Hooker, *Companion to the Botanical Magazine*, II, 139.

The Hudson's Bay Company depended on the good influence of Bishop Provencher and showed its appreciation.[17]

The employees of the Company had to sign a contract of service, after the fulfillment of which they were free to leave. A Stephen Lucier had already paid for his transportation back to Canada, but circumstances prevented him from crossing the mountains. The Company did not like former employees to settle in the fur country, and in the case of Lucier, McLaughlin assisted him to settle on the east bank of the Willamette River, later called the French prairie. In spite of difficulties ("a man must have fifty pounds in order to be permitted to settle"[18]), the settlement of former Hudson's Bay Company men and their families in the Willamette Valley increased. As we will see later, baptismal and marriage records show that Okanogan and Colville Indian women had married Catholic employees of the fur companies at Forts Colville and Okanogan and later settled with their families in the Willamette Valley. These Catholic settlers urgently desired to have a priest in their midst. On July 3, 1834, and again on February 23, 1835, they sent petitions to Bishop Provencher. The Bishop wrote on June 6, 1835, to McLaughlin: "My intention is to do all I can to grant them their request. . . ."[19] At the same time the Bishop wrote a pastoral to his spiritual children in the Willamette Valley:

> I have received, most beloved brethren your two petitions. . . . Both call for missionaries to instruct your children and yourselves. Such a request from persons deprived of all religious attendance, could not fail to touch my heart, and if it was in my power, I would send you some this very year. But I have no priests disposable at Red River; they must be obtained from Canada or elsewhere. . . .[20]

He then exhorted the Catholic settlers to prepare their souls for Christ's teachings and pay more attention to their salvation. At the same time he sent catechisms. The settlers were full of hope and started building a

---

[17] Pritchell, *op. cit.*, 235. Simpson quoted: "Indeed it is to the Catholic Mission we are alone indebted for the safety of the Company's establishments and the peace of the Colony . . . as their followers . . . had made up their minds to seize the grain we had provided for the consumption of our Brigade." Bishhop Provencher received a yearly stipend of 50 pounds, and in 1831, 100 pounds, for the repair or rebuilding of the church from the Hudson's Bay Company. See: Fleming, *op. cit.*, 284–285.

[18] E. E. Rich, *The Letters of John McLaughlin From Fort Vancouver to the Governor and Committee* (First Series, 1825–1838) (HBRS, IV), 174.

[19] Rt. Rev. Joseph Norbert Provencher quoted by Most Rev. F. N. Blanchet, *op. cit.*, 22.

[20] *Ibid.*, 22–23.

church. Bishop Provencher informed Bishop Joseph Signay of Quebec about the calls for priests.

On February 28, 1836, by indult of the Holy See, the Columbia Country was annexed to the Vicariate Apostolic of Red River and remained so until 1843.[21] Bishop Provencher felt his responsibility. It did not take long to appoint the two first missionaries for the Oregon Country, but it took more than two years before the appointed priests, the Reverends Francis Norbert Blanchet and Modeste Demers, could start their dangerous journey from Red River down the Columbia River. The Hudson's Bay Company objected to giving the priests a ride in their canoes:

> Were we satisfied that the sole object of Missionaries were the civilization of the Natives and the diffusion of moral and religious instruction, we should be happy to render them our most cordial support and assistance, but we have all along foreseen that the purpose of their visit was not confined to those objects but that the formation of a Colony Of United States Citizens on the banks of the Columbia was the main or fundamental part of their plan, which, if successful, might be attended with material injury, not only for the Fur trade, but in a national point of view.[22]

Dr. McLaughlin in a letter to the Governor and Committee objected to the unjust policy based on suspicion of the Governor and Council of the Northern Department.[23] A free passage was given only under the following conditions:

> The governor and committee therefore agreed to give passage for the two priests, provided that they would induce the Willamette freemen to move to the Cowlitz and would promise to trade in furs and to trade exclusively with the Company.[24]

---

[21] Rev. Peter Jean De Smet, *Oregon Missions and Travels Over the Rocky Mountains,* 17 ff. Also: Most Rev. Edwin O'Hara, *Pioneer Catholic History of Oregon,* 14 ff.

[22] E. E. Rich, ed., quoting the Governor and Committee, in a letter dated November 15, 1837, to James Douglas, in *The Letters of John McLaughlin to the Governor and Committee* (First Series, 1825–1838) (HBRS, IV), CXXIV.

[23] *Ibid.,* 202–203. John McLaughlin to Governor and Committee, October 31, 1837: "10. I see by your 14th Paragraph that the Governor and Council of the Northern Factory have recommended to you not to allow a passage to the Two Catholic Missionaries. . . . I can see no injury that the Roman Catholic Missionaries would do the Hudson's Bay Company by being in the Willamette, but the reverse, they would prevent the American Missionaries acquiring influence over the Canadians. We stand high in the opinions of the Canadian Trappers, and Freemen in the Willamette, as a proof, we have made six hunts in the vicinity of the Settlement in California, and have not lost a man."

[24] John S. Galbraith, quoting Governor and Committee to Douglas, November 15, 1837 (HBC Archives A-6/24), in *The Hudson's Bay Company as an Imperial Factor,* 203.

Bishop Provencher gave his assent. This was at least an opportunity to have the priests travel to the Oregon Country. Further developments were in the hands of God. Simpson's letter to Bishop Signay furnishes a summary of the correspondence on this subject.[25]

Bishop Signay appointed the Reverend Francis Norbert Blanchet his vicar-general on April 17, 1838, and gave him jurisdiction over the territory lying

> . . . between the Rocky Mountains on the east, the Pacific Ocean on the west, the Russian possessions on the north, and the territory of the United States on the south.[26]

Special instructions for the priests as to their mission were also given in the same document. From this document we see that the Indians were considered first: the missionaries were specially sent to them. But the priests were to take care of the white population as well.[27] The whites

[25] O'Hara, op. cit., 25–26. Also: Blanchet, op. cit., 25. Simpson to Signay, February 17, 1838: "My Lord, I yesterday had the honor of receiving a letter from the Bishop of Juliopolis, dated Red River, 13th. October, 1837, wherein I am requested to communicate with your Lordship on the subject of sending two priests to the Columbia River for the purpose of establishing a Catholic mission in that part of the country.

"When the Bishop first mentioned this subject, his view was to form the mission on the banks of the Willamette, a river falling into the Columbia from the south. To the establishing of a mission there, the Governor and Committee in London and the Council in Hudson's Bay had a decided objection, as the sovereignty of that country is still undecided, but I last summer intimated to the Bishop that if he would establish the mission on the banks of the Cowlitz River, or on the Cowlitz Portage, falling into the Columbia River from the northward, and give his assurance that the missionaries would not locate themselves on the south side of the Columbia River . . . I should recommend the Governor and the Committee to afford a passage to the priests.

"By the letter received yesterday, already alluded to, the Bishop enters fully into my views and expresses his willingness to fall in with my suggestions. This letter I have laid before the Governor and Committee and am now instructed to intimate to your Lordship that if the priests will be ready at Lachine to embark for the interior about the 25th of April, a passage will be afforded them, and on the arrival at Fort Vancouver measures will be taken by the Company's representatives there to facilitate the establishing of the mission."

[26] Blancht quoted by Clarence Booth Bagley, ed., Early Catholic Missions in Old Oregon, I, 21.

[27] Sister Laetitia Mary Lyons, quoting Bishop Joseph Signay of Quebec in Francis Norbert Blanchet and the Founding of the Oregon Missions, 24–25. Also: Blanchet in Bagley, op. cit., I, 21–22:

"1. They shall consider their first object to be to regain from barbarism and its disorders, the savage tribes scattered over that country.

"2. Their second object shall be to extend their help to the poor Christians who have adopted the customs of the savages and live in license and forgetfulness of their duties.

"3. Persuaded that the preaching of the Gospel is the best way to obtain these

were not to settle south of the Columbia River. The Rev. Blanchet traveled in a canoe of the Hudson's Bay Brigade to Red River, where he stayed for thirty-five days before embarking for the West.[28] The young Reverend Modeste Demers had been a missionary at the Red River settlement since the preceding spring. Here he joined the Rev. Blanchet as missionary for the Oregon Country.

The first Catholic missionaries for the West embarked in one of the Hudson's Bay brigade canoes on July 26, 1838, at Norway House. They saw regions where a Catholic priest had never visited. At every stop the brigade made, the priests proved themselves true apostles. Father Blanchet mentions "one hundred and twenty-two" baptisms on the eastern slope of the mountains.[29] The Hudson's Bay Company brigade was transferred to a horse caravan for the last nine days of traveling from Jasper House to Boat Encampment, which they reached on October 13 in the evening.

Sunday, October 14, 1838, was a day of great significance for the "Old Oregon Country": On that day the first Holy Mass was said, at the Big Bend of the Columbia River.[30] This year only two bateaux were waiting for the brigade, when four were needed. The brigade was therefore split into two parties. One third of the travelers was left behind and it was decided that a boat would be sent from the next place. The missionaries arrived safely on the sixteenth at the House of the Lakes, which was under construction at the time. The boat was unloaded and sent back. It returned on the twenty-fourth half wrecked; of the twenty-six persons who had been in the boat, twelve had been drowned. An Indian express was sent to Colville to get more boats and to spread the news, while one boat was sent to the Dallas of the Dead to recover the bodies; only those of three children were found.

This enforced stay of eighteen days at the House of the Lakes brought

---

happy results, they will not lose a single opportunity to inculcate its principles and maxims either in their private conversation or their public discourses.

"4. In order to be as useful as possible to the natives of the country, they shall apply themselves as soon as they arrive to the study of the language of the savages and shall try after some year of residence to publish a grammar.

"5. They shall prepare for baptism as soon as possible the women who live in concubinage with Christians, so as to be able to substitute legitimate marriages for these irregular unions.

"6. They shall give special attention to the Christian education of the children, establishing to that end schools and Catechism classes in all the villages which they may have occasion to visit. . . ."

Fifteen other points were listed.

[28] Blanchet quoted in Bagley, *op. cit.*, I, 23.

[29] *Ibid.*

[30] *Ibid.*, 25.

the Catholic missionaries for the first time in contact with the Lake tribe. They found these Indians of "mild, peaceable character and well-disposed to receive the words of salvation."[31] Father Demers, in a letter to the Very Rev. Charles Felix Cazeau, vicar-general of the Diocese of Quebec written from Vancouver, March 1, 1839, says, among other laudable things about the Indians:

> These Indians desire nothing more than to know God and the religion that leads to Him; they anxiously long for the moment when a priest may come among them to teach them the holy truths and maxims of our divine religion. It was not without grief that these poor people saw the missionary leave them, and on our part we were not indifferent to the expression of their warm affection.[32]

During their stay at the House of the Lakes the missionaries performed seventeen baptisms, one marriage, and the burial services of the three drowned children.[33] The beginning of the conversion of the Colville tribes had been made.

On the sixth of November the missionaries arrived at Fort Colville. The news of their coming had preceded the priests; and the chiefs and some of their people belonging to five tribes — the Chaudieres, Sanpoils, Spokans, Pisscows, and Okanogans — were gathered to greet them. When they saw the boats coming, the Indians, including women and children, rushed to the shore to place themselves in a file to shake hands:

> All gathered together in a large house given to them for the occasion and waited in silence for the moment when we should speak to them. With what attentive eagerness they listened to the word of God, which being translated to them by the chiefs, acquired a new force and additional weight. We forgot nothing that was calculated to fortify them in the principles of the Catholic religion, thus, in a short time, we have scattered some of the seed of the divine word, and we have the sweet hope, that according to God's merciful designs it will bear fruit in this portion of the human family so long neglected. We easily can see what progress Christianity would make among tribes so well disposed.[34]

The missionaries baptized nineteen at Fort Colville. At Fort Okanogan where they stopped for twenty-four hours, they baptized fourteen.[35] The

---

[31] Blanchet quoted in Bagley, *op. cit.*, 25.

[32] Blanchet quoting Demers in Bagley, *ibid.*, I, 48.

[33] Carl Landerholm, transl., *Notices & Voyages of the Famed Quebec Mission to the Pacific Northwest*, 16 ff.

[34] Blanchet quoting Demers to Very Rev. Cazeau in Bagley, *op. cit.*, I, 28.

[35] Blanchet quoted in Bagley, *op. cit.*, I, 27. Also: AAS has a copy of the first volume of *Records* kept at Vancouver.

time was short, but the missionaries promised to visit the Okanogan and Colville tribes during the following year. Father Demers remarked about the Okanogan to Very Rev. Cazeau on March 1, 1839:

> We may say of them what we have said of those mentioned above; to make fervent Christians of them it would suffice to teach them the Christian doctrine. Nothing more is needed.[36]

It is interesting to note who were the ones baptized. Among "The Acts of Faith at Fort of the Lakes, on the Columbia" were: "B[aptism number] 128 — George Harren [Heron], baptized on October 17, 1838, son of Chief Factor Francis Harren [Heron]; B[aptisms] 129 & 130 — Isabelle McKay and William McKay, children of the postmaster of the Fort of the Lakes; B[aptisms] 131 & 132 Louis and Baptiste Soisanteplus, sons of a Lake Indian; B[aptism] 139, Marguerite Ptitchouegge, daughter of the Chief of the Lake tribe." The marriage performed was between John McKay, the postmaster,[37] and Josephte Boucher, a Catholic Lake Indian woman. At Okanogan are named four children of Jean Gingros, the postmaster, and Charlotte Skialks, Okinagan. In Colville nearly all those baptized were the children of engagees and Indian women. One baptized child was the daughter of Jacques Iroquois and Susanne Okanogan.[38] The time of grace had finally arrived for the Okanogan and Colville tribes. Those who wanted to become Catholics were on the alert. Distances meant nothing to them; they knew where to find the missionaries. Had they not near relatives in the Willamette Valley who had married Catholic men?

The first Catholic missionaries arrived at Fort Vancouver on November 24, 1838. Among the many people waiting for them were three representatives from the Willamette Valley, settlers who had sent out the repeated call for priests. They were the Catholics still alive from the Astor's overland party: Joseph Gervais, Stephen Lucier, and Peter Beleque.[39] All the Willamette people had been here, but because of the delay caused by the

---

"Actes faits au Fort des Lacs, sur la Colombie October 17–November 1, 1838, Baptisms 17, Mar. 1, Burials 3" (p. 13).

"Actes faits au Fort Colville sur la Riviere Colombie, November 7, 1838, Bapt. 19" (p. 15).

"Actes faits au Fort Okinagan, sur la Riviere Colombie, November 13, Bapt. 14" (p. 17).

[36] Blanchet quoting Demers to Cazeau, in Bagley, *op. cit.*, I, 49.

[37] A Hudson's Bay Company "postmaster" was a kind of chief clerk.

[38] M. Leona Nichol, *The Mantle of Elias*, 260–262. All church records used in *The Mantle of Elias* were translated from the originals by the author herself with permission of the Most Rev. D. Howard, Archbishop of Portland, Oregon. See 256.

[39] Sister Laetitia Mary Lyons, *op. cit.*, 19.

accident in the Columbia Dallas had had to go home. Later the missionaries came in contact with Michael La Framboise, the leader of the brigade of the south. He had arrived in 1811, with the ship, the *Tonquin*. Blanchet also mentions Louis Labonte as belonging to the Astor party.

As we have seen, Father Blanchet was forbidden by the Hudson's Bay Company to make the Willamette Valley his headquarters, but nobody could keep him from making a visit there. The first Holy Mass was said in the new church, January 6, 1839. After three weeks of instruction he baptized the twenty-five Indian wives, blessed their marriages, and baptized forty-seven children. The influence of the Catholic fur traders and of Catholic Hudson's Bay officials on the religious development of the Colville and Okanogan Tribes can be traced from the *Baptismal Records,* some of which we quote:

B. 9 — Francois Lavigneur, January 6, 1839. Francois Lavigneur, age 5 years. Natural son of Hyacinthe Lavigneur and Marguerite of the Colville Nation. Godfather: Joseph Gervais. F.N.B.

B. 13 — Basile Picard, January 6, 1839. Basile Picard, aged 6 years. Natural son of Andre Picard, a farmer, and Marguerite Okanogan. Godfather: Joseph Gervais. F.N.B.

B. 20 — Joseph Lonetain, January 6, 1839. Joseph Lonetain, aged 11 months. Natural son of Andre Lonetain and Nancy Okanogan. Godfather: Joseph Gervais. F.N.B.

B. 26 — Nancy Okanogan, January 16, 1839. Nancy Okanogan, aged 30 years. Godfather Etienne Lussier. F.N.B.

M. 4 — Andre Lonetain and Nancy Okanogan, January 21, 1839. Andre Lonetain of St. Constant, Canada, District of Montreal, a farmer, and Nancy Okanogan. Witnesses, J. B. Dupati and Pierre Stanislaus Jacquet. Legitimizing the following children: Henriette, aged 14; Catherine, aged 13; Angeline, aged 9; Joseph, aged one year. F.N.B.

M. 10 — Hyacinthe Lavigneur and Margueritte Colville, January 21, 1839. Hyacinthe Lavigneur of St. Genevieve, District of Montreal, Canada and Marguerite of the Colville Nation. Witnesses, J. B. Dupati and P. S. Jacquet. Legitimizing Noel, age 10 years; Jean Baptiste, aged 7 years; Francois, aged 5 years; Joseph, aged 6 months. F. N. B.

M. 11 — Andre Picard and Marie Okanogan, January 21, 1839. Andre Picard of St. Thomas, District of Quebec, Canada and Marie of the Okanogan Nation. Witnesses, J. B. Dupati and P. S. Jacquet. Legitimizing Jean Baptiste, aged 9 years; Basil, aged 6 years; Emelie, aged 17 years by another woman; Andre Regis, aged 3 years. F.N.B.[40]

⁴⁰ M. Leona Nichols, *op. cit.,* 263–264.

Vicar-General F. N. Blanchet began a new *Register of the Mission of St. Paul, on the Willamette,* on October 13, 1839. Here more Okanogan and Colville Indian relations are recorded. On November 11, 1839, Isabelle Boucher, aged 18 years, whose mother was Josephte from the Lake Indians, was baptized; we read of the marriage of Ignace Servant and Josephte Okanogan and of the legitimizing of seven children; of the marriage of Joachim Hubert and Josephte des Chaudieres and of the legitimizing of seven children; of more baptisms of teen-agers, Pierre Delard, 18 years old, whose mother was Lisette Okanogan; of Joseph Gingris, 14 years old, whose mother was Charlotte Okanogan, and so we could keep on and on citing further examples of the growth of Christianity.[41]

In 1839, while Dr. McLaughlin was in London, the Hudson's Bay Company removed restrictions on the priests staying north of the Columbia River.

The Vicar-General described the conditions he found in a letter to Bishop Signay, dated March 7, 1839.[42] The difficulty was to give the various Indian tribes a concrete means to understand the true historical significance of the only religion established by Christ Himself. They had to see in order to grasp abstract ideas and truths. Francis Norbert Blanchet conceived the idea of representing the forty centuries before Christ by making forty marks on a square stick, the thirty-three years of our Lord by thirty-three dots. The year 1839 was represented by eighteen marks and thirty-three points. Now he could show the creation, the fall of Adam and Eve, the promise of a Savior, His birth, His death upon a cross, the mission of the Apostles, and other truths. Soon this "Catholic Ladder" was further developed to show other aspects of the faith and was finally copyrighted by Archbishop Blanchet in 1859; it was five feet in length and two and a half feet in width.[43] Soon other denominations borrowed the idea and made "Protestant Ladders" in which the history of the Catholic Church was misrepresented.[44] This forced Father Blanchet to revise his

---

[41] Nichols, *op. cit.,* 288–289.

[42] Sister Laetitia Mary Lyons, quoting Blanchet, AAQ, *op. cit.,* 21: "The Indian tribes were numerous, scattered all over the country, speaking a multitude of diverse and difficult tongues, and addicted to polygamy and all the vices of paganism. The servants of the Hudson's Bay Company in active service in its twenty-eight forts for the fur trade, were in great majority Catholics; so also were the four families at Cowlits, and the twenty-six established in the Willamette Valley with their wives and children. Many of the servants and settlers had forgotten their prayers and the religious principles they had received in their youth. The women they had taken for their wives were pagans, raised in ignorance. One may well imagine that in many places disorders, rudeness of morals and indecency of practices, answered to that state of ignorance."

[43] O'Hara, *op. cit.,* 27.

[44] *Ibid.*

ladder to show that up to the sixteenth century all were Catholics. Then a branch grew out from the main stem and divided into smaller twigs. Beside we find the names of Luther, Calvin, Henry VIII.[45]

It took Father Demers only three weeks' study of the Chinook jargon in order to make himself understood by many tribes. The Colville and Okanogan tribes were waiting for at least one of the missionaries to come back. Father Demers embarked with the Hudson's Bay Company brigade on June 22, 1839. He left the boat at Walla Walla to make the rest of the journey to Fort Colville by horseback. Mr. Pambrun, in charge of Fort Walla Walla, had secured horses, as well as "a man of the Company to make the journey from Walla Walla to Colville, and a guide whom I was to find only after a day and a half of travel."[46] The guide proved to be treacherous and abandoned Father in the wilderness after three days. All of Sunday, July 7, 1839, was spent trying to find the correct direction. At last Father Demers resolved to stay alone in the wilderness and sent his companion back to Walla Walla for another guide. He had to wait all week in extreme heat, with only a knife and a small ax for weapons. On the next Saturday his companion arrived with a good guide.[47] They reached Colville a week later, on the seventeenth of July, and were greeted joyfully:

> A virtuous man by name of Brown had taught the Christian prayers to the natives during our absence. These poor natives gave themselves a joy inexpressible in making me acquainted with their progress in the prayers as well as in the catechism. One cannot tell the happiness of those men, starved for the bread of the divine word, when they had understood and retained some of the truths of our holy religion. What good would not a missionary do, residing among a people so perfectly docile to the graces of the Lord![48]

Father Demers stayed twenty-five days at Colville, during which time he baptized thirty-six children, heard a large number of confessions, and then gave orders for the coming mission. The missionary explained about the unjust policy of the Hudson's Bay Company which restored freedom to its engagees only at Montreal. One condition of their contract was not

[45] A photograph of an authentic "Catholic Ladder" thirty inches in length can be seen in Landerholm, op. cit., insert.

[46] Landerholm quoting Father Demers, op. cit., 32.

[47] Mrs. Helen Toulou's husband's grandfather was the faithful companion of Father Demers who went back to Walla Walla for provisions and another guide. This Louis Provost was married to Julia of the Lake Indians on July 31, 1845, by Father De Smet. From an interview with Mrs. Toulou, St. Mary's Mission, Omak, Washington, November 3, 1959. See: Baptismal Records of Old St. Paul's Mission, OPA.

[48] Landerholm quoting Demers, op. cit., 32.

to marry. Away from religious aid and overcome by passion, some men had yielded to unions with Indian women. Father could have easily succeeded in making these unions legitimate and in marrying them according to the laws of the Church, but Chief Factor McDonald remarked that "The missionaries had nothing to do with the employees of the Company."[49] The nearby Protestant missionaries had inspired prejudices against the two first Catholic priests by telling the Indians: "It is not ceremonies that save." They wanted to paralyze the work of the Catholic missionaries and for this purpose used slander.

But God does not bless such means, and Catholicism rises everywhere while overthrowing those contrivances raised by the hand of men to sap its foundations. *Portae inferi non praevalebunt.*[50]

Father Demers traveled from Colville to Fort Okanogan — a week's journey. At the fort he found a Mr. Robillard who had taught the prayers to the Indians, but the natives who had eagerly waited for him had finally gone hunting and fishing. Father Demers had lost a whole week while he was waiting for his new guide. The attitude of those who had stayed at the fort consoled him. He was able here as at Colville to induce the Canadians to break up forbidden unions. During the eight days of his priestly work he baptized ten Indian children and four Canadians. On the way back to Walla Walla he baptized another nine children and induced two natives to put aside the women they had taken contrary to God's law.[51]

At Fort Okanogan Demers had found a white Christian who gave scandal to the natives. This man had married three wives and tried by slander to lower the esteem the Indians had for the priest. For a long time following this period it will be a recurring complaint of the missionaries that the whites are giving bad example. In Okanogan, too, ministers were trying to induce the natives not to join the Catholic Church: "To borrow the weapon of vice in order to prevent nations from joining a religion presenting every virtue, is a method little certain of making proselytes."[52]

Archbishop Blanchet in his report for March, 1839, to March, 1840, mentions "73 baptisms at the Colville mission."[53] Sketch XX says: "One of the items sent to Quebec, Canada, from March 1840 to March 1841, was 164 baptisms by Father Demers at the Chinook, Cowlitz, and Colville mission."[54] Among the baptisms of note at Colville we read in the

[49] Sister Laetitia Mary Lyons, *op. cit.,* 40, quoting Quebec Archives.
[50] Landerholm quoting Demers, *op. cit.,* 33.
[51] Landerholm, *op. cit.,* 34–35.
[52] *Ibid.,* quoting Demers.
[53] Blanchet quoted in Bagley, *op. cit.,* I. 87.
[54] *Ibid.,* 100.

Baptismal Records:

B. 144 — Isaac Ogden, July 17, 1839. Isaac Ogden born last June. Natural son of Peter Ogden Esquire and Julie of the Spokane Nation. Godfather, Pierre Lacourse. Modeste Demers.[55]

Mr. Ogden was one of the chief factors of the Hudson's Bay Company. In 1840 there was a Colville mission from June 29 to October 1,[56] and "Father Demers gave a mission of nine days to the O'Kanagan Indians, on returning from Colville" in 1840.[57] The good news of the presence of Catholic missionaries had traveled from the Okanogans to the Yakimas, their neighbors to the south. In the fall of 1840, the Yakima chief, Harkely, made a trip to the Willamette mission with his family and some of his people. "After three weeks of instruction he returned home with a pair of beads, a cross, some pictures and a Catholic Ladder, and used to explain it to his people on Sundays."[58] The Okanogans were impatiently waiting for the missionary. Not all tribal members could be at Fort Okanogan. "A chief from Okanogan sent word to St. Paul asking what to do; that he was ready to come with his people next spring, if so recommended."[59] These old Indians bore sacrifices in order to learn their religion. Father Blanchet wrote to the Right Reverend Turgeon, March 18, 1841:

> Several savages of the Okanogan spent the winter near my chapel, received instructions and left this spring to return to their country. Crosses, rosaries, pictures, "Catholic Ladders" are much esteemed by these natives.[60]

Formerly the Yakimas were feared as the fierce warriors. Now the Yakimas, the Okanogans, and the Spokanes tell each other of the true faith.[61] The Colvilles were making progress. "The little chief des Chaudieres was an apostle among his people, with the Catholic Ladder in his hands since the departure of the priest."[62] Yes, more priests were needed for this big territory.

The vicar-general, Blanchet, had sent appeals for more helpers to Canada, but Governor Simpson would not allow any passages in the boats

---

[55] Nichols, *op. cit.*, 271.

[56] *Ibid.*, 272.

[57] Blanchet, *op. cit.* (1878 ed.), 122.

[58] *Ibid.*

[59] *Ibid.*

[60] Lyons, quoting Blanchet to Turgeon, *op. cit.*, 77.

[61] Blanchet, *op. cit.*, 126: "Harkely, the Yakima chief, who visited St. Paul last fall arrived at Cowlitz on January 25th, with some Indians from Okanogan, and a son of the Spokane chief, called La Grosse Tete. . . ."

[62] *Ibid.*

of the Hudson's Bay Company. Bishop Signay of Quebec, on April 13, 1840, writing to Father Blanchet expressed his concern about the impossibility of sending co-workers. He had received notice from Governor Simpson that the Company was not "disposed to favor the extension of the Catholic mission on the Columbia before being informed as to the progress which you have made.[63]

Dr. McLaughlin encouraged Father Blanchet to write to Simpson. In this long letter the vicar-general has many things to report that show progress. He reminds the governor that the most difficult work of the fur trade has always been done by Catholics who, exposed to the rigor of the seasons, have spent the best years of their lives in the service and have often lost them. It would not be just to refuse them "the consolations and the joys of life":

> Now prayers are recited, the Catechism is learned, the holy law of God has taken its empire, the moral code is put into force, decency reigns, vice is diminished. This, Sir George, is the good which the two priests have begun among the old and the new servants of the Honourable Company and among their wives and children.[64]

Besides the priestly services to the Canadian employees Father Blanchet mentions all the improvements among the many tribes.

When the Bishop was refused passage for more priests in the boats of the Hudson's Bay Company, he sent them by sea. It was only later when the Jesuits had already arrived that James Douglas told Governor Simpson in a letter that the Company had lost out.[65]

The first calls for priests came from the Willamette Valley, and the Canadian missionaries had answered these calls. At an earlier date

---

[63] Lyons quoting Quebec Archives, Simpson to Signay, *op. cit.*, 50.

[64] *Ibid.*, 54–55.

[65] Rich, *op. cit.* (Third Series, 1844–1846) (HBRS, VII), 184–185. Douglas to Simpson: "I think you did wrong, in throwing obstacles in the way of the Canadian Catholic Missionaries; instead of being restrained, they ought to be encouraged and allowed a free passage, in the Company's inland Craft, to any part of the District, they may wish to visit. The expense would be a mere trifle to the Company, while the accommodation would be a means of securing their good will, and moreover, such good offices keep them in a state of dependence on our assistance. It is the settled purpose of the Catholic Missionaries to establish in every part of the country; the Jesuits talk of pushing into New Caledonia in a year or two, and of all the Parties of Catholics I prefer Mr. Blanchet's people to them. The only way of preventing the intrusion of a foreign Priesthood, is to pre-occupy the field, by assisting those Missionaries, who have always, since they have been in the country, pursued their calling under the company's protection, a boon which they repaid by the most devoted attachment to our cause. You may rest assured that the prohibition of passages, has not in the least checked the activity of the Priests, in this quarter as they can perform their journies without our assistance, while we have incurred odium by the measure."

representative groups of Indians had been on their way to St. Louis to search for "Black Robes" to come to their tribes. It all had started when in 1816 twenty-four Iroquois Indians from the Caughnawaga Mission near Montreal had crossed the Rockies and settled among the Flatheads.[66] Here they were admitted into the tribe, married, and taught the Flatheads the Catholic faith. The leader of this group was Ignace La Mouse known as Big Ignace or Old Ignace. The Flatheads were taught the Sign of the Cross and other prayers; they were to keep the Sunday holy; they were to baptize those in danger of death. The need for "Black Robes" was felt intensely.

According to Father Palladino, Old Ignace suggested in council to send an expedition to St. Louis. Four volunteered and arrived safely in St. Louis. Two of them died there and the other two were never heard from.[67] Father Garraghan examines the different versions that were circulating about the tribal identity of the members of the first expedition. The Nez Perce were the neighbors of the Flatheads. One of the buried ones in St. Louis is listed as a Nez Perce Indian. The fact that the Indians wanted Catholic priests is without doubt established. They had no other contact except with the Iroquois and the Catholic Canadian trappers. Father De Smet and Father Palladino who knew the Flatheads are

---

[66] Blanchet, *op. cit.*, 3.

[67] Rev. L. B. Palladino, S.J., *Indian and White in the Northwest*, 11, quotes Bishop Rosati's letter of December 31, 1831, to the editor of the Association of the Propagation of the Faith: "Some three months ago four Indians who live across the Rocky Mountains near the Columbia River [Clark's Fork of the Columbia], arrived at St. Louis. After visiting General Clarke, who, in his celebrated travel had visited their nation and had been well treated by them, they came to see our church and appeared to be exceedingly well pleased with it. Unfortunately, there was not one who understood their language. Some time afterward two of them fell dangerously sick. I was then absent from St. Louis.

"Two of our priests visited them and the poor Indians seemed to be delighted with the visit. They made signs of the cross and other signs which appeared to have some relation to baptism. The sacrament was administered to them; they gave expressions of satisfaction. A little cross was presented to them. They took it with eagerness, kissed it repeatedly and it could be taken from them only after death. It was truly distressing that they could not be spoken to. Their remains were carried to the church, and their funeral was conducted with all the Catholic ceremonies. The other two attended and acted becomingly. We have since learned from a Canadian, who has crossed the country which they inhabit, that they belong to the nation of the Flatheads, who, as also another called Black Feet, has received some notions of the Catholic religion from two Indians who had been to Canada and who had related what they had seen, giving a striking description of the beautiful ceremonies of Catholic worship and telling them that it was also the religion of the whites. They have retained what they could of it, and they have learned to make the Sign of the Cross and to pray. These nations have not yet been corrupted by intercourse with others. . . ."

witnesses to this fact.[68] The Flatheads were waiting for "Black Robes" and did not welcome the Methodists, Jason and Daniel Lee. When in 1835, Marcus Whitman and the Rev. Samuel Parker came to Green River, the Flathead chief Insula was waiting. He was disappointed; these were no "Black Robes." On December 2, 1835, a second delegation, this time Ignace La Mouse and his two sons, arrived at St. Louis. They could speak French and were understood. The sons were baptized and Ignace went to confession and Holy Communion. No priest was yet available to be sent to them. The three arrived home safely.

In 1837 another attempt was made to reach St. Louis and petition for priests. Old Ignace went again with three Flatheads and one Nez Perce. He was on the way when, according to Father Palladino, Mr. W. H. Gray inspected the possibility of establishing a mission among the Flatheads. Gray's Party joined the Flatheads' delegation near Fort Laramie but at Ash Hollow about three hundred Sioux ordered the whites to stand apart. Ignace was clothed in civilian attire and ordered among the whites, but he did not want to abandon his friends. The Indians defended themselves bravely; all five perished in the struggle. When the news reached the Flatheads, two Iroquois volunteered to make a fourth attempt to secure "Black Robes." This time young Ignace and Peter Gaucher went searching for priests, joining some Hudson's Bay Company men. On the way they stopped at the Potawatomi mission at Council Bluffs and met Father Pierre Jean De Smet, a Jesuit priest, for the first time. Father told about this event:

> On the 18th of September last two Catholic Iroquois came to visit us. They had been for twenty-three years among the nations called the Flatheads and Pierced Noses about a thousand Flemish leagues from

---

[68] Garraghan, *op. cit.*, II, 244, mentions the Protestant mission propaganda resulting from the first visit of the Flatheads in 1831 in St. Louis: "In the *Christian Advocate* of New York appeared under date of February 18, 1833, a letter from G. P. Disoway enclosing another from William Walker, the Wyandot interpreter, describing his alleged meeting with the Rocky Mountain Indians in November, 1831. Further correspondence on the subject appeared in the same journal, which was soon sending out fervent appeals to the Protestant religious world to dispatch missionaries to the benighted savages of Oregon. The form which the incident of 1831 now took in the Protestant press was that the Indians had come to St. Louis in search of the Bible, the 'White Man's Book,' which, to their great disappointment, they failed to find. In this connection there grew up a myth that on the eve of their departure from St. Louis the two surviving members of the party were given a banquet, at which one of them made an address deploring their failure to meet the coveted book. No evidence of the truth of these statements could ever be found. Bishop Rosati's letter published in the same year the delegation came speaks about the sign language the Indians used. Nobody understood their language. How could they have made up a speech?"

where we are. I have never seen any savage so fervent in religion. By their instruction and example they have given all that nation a great desire to have themselves baptized. All that tribe strictly observe Sunday and assemble several times a week to pray and sing canticles. The sole object of these good Iroquois was to obtain a priest to come and finish what they had happily commenced. We gave them letters of recommendation for our Reverend Father Superior at St. Louis.[69]

The last delegation reached St. Louis. Bishop Rosati now wrote to the Very Reverend Roothaan, Father General of the Jesuits, requesting priests for these Indians. He spoke of the efforts the Indians had made in search of "Black Robes," of the planting of the faith among the Flatheads, of the four Iroquois who were still alive from the twenty-four that had settled among the Flatheads, and of the refusal of the Flatheads to accept any other denomination. The Iroquois would say to the Flatheads:

> These are not the priests about whom we have spoken to you, these are not the long black-robed priests who have no wives, who say Mass, who carry the crucifix with them.[70]

The Second Provincial Council of Baltimore in 1833 had placed the Indian missions of the Far West under the spiritual care of the Jesuits.[71] The superior of the Jesuits at St. Louis, the Rev. Father Verhaegen, wrote the Father General that he had promised the Indians priests who would come to them next spring. One of the Iroquois left to bring the good news to the waiting tribe while Ignace, who would accompany the priest, wintered in the vicinity of Fort Leavenworth. In a letter of April 21, 1840, to J. N. Nicollet, Washington, D. C., Father De Smet in telling how he had gone to St. Louis for supplies writes:

> During my stay amongst my colleagues the question came up of appointing one or two missionaries to accompany the Iroquois who had come with a request for some priest in the name of the Tete Plattes. As I had already the honor of advising you, their choice fell upon me. I started again from St. Louis on the 28th of March and arrived at West-Port on the 11th of April in time to fit myself for the mountains.

---

[69] Palladino, *op. cit.*, 27–28, quoting Father De Smet. Also: O'Hara, *op. cit.*, 48–49.

[70] Palladino, *op. cit.*, 28, quoting Bishop Rosati's letter to Very Rev. Father General John Roothaan, S.J. See also for the complete history of the beginning of the Jesuit missions of the Rocky Mountains, *ibid.*, 1–75, and Garraghan, *op. cit.*, II, 236–334.

[71] Peter Guilday, *A History of the Councils of Baltimore, 1791–1884*, 106.

I have purchased four horses and three mules. The caravan, I assume, will leave on the 1st of May under the direction of Captain Dripps, and of Messrs. Trap & Ledger.[72]

The appointment of Father De Smet, S.J., as a missionary for the Rocky Mountains had far-reaching significance for the Christianization not only of the Flatheads and neighboring tribes, but also for the Colvilles and the Okanogans and their related bands of Indians. When in the summer of 1840, Father De Smet made his exploratory trip and met the Flathead Indians at Pierre's Hole, he was told that two missionaries were already working among the Columbia tribes. He wrote to Father Blanchet and told him about his experiences with the Flatheads. After preliminary work he would go back to St. Louis to report to his superior and return the next year. Father Demers then in Colville heard the news that somewhere in the mountains missionaries had arrived. He wrote to these missionaries on August 6, 1840, not knowing Father De Smet was alone:

> Though I have not as yet the pleasure of knowing your names, I eagerly take the opportunity which is presented to send you news of the two poor missionaries of the Columbia, knowing that I am writing to Catholic priests, ministers of our holy religion, who have generously come to sacrifice themselves for the salvation of the savages. With what joy and contentment have I learned of your arrival among the Flatheads.[73]

News traveled comparatively fast in those days even without modern communication systems. Dr. McLaughlin related what he had heard to Governor Simpson.[74] Father De Smet returned to the Flatheads in 1841, accompanied by Fathers Gregory Mengarini and Nicholas Point and three Brothers. In a short time he had established St. Mary's mission about thirty miles up the Bitter Root Valley in Montana. The Flathead catechumens had been well prepared by the faithful Iroquois Indians. Before long many of the tribe were baptized.

In the meantime Father De Smet had received an answer from Father Blanchet and an invitation to come and bring more apostolic workers along. The letter from Father Blanchet, of September 28, 1841,

---

[72] Rev. Pierre Jean De Smet, to J. N. Nicollet, autographed original letter, Public Library, Spokane, Washington, Ms.

[73] CR, De Smet, IV, 1551, quoting Demers.

[74] Rich, op. cit., 261, quoting McLaughlin to Simpson: "The Revd. Mr. Desmit a Roman Catholic priest from Belgium came with the American party to their Rendez-vous. He then joined a party of Indians and went to the Flat Heads with whom he passed some time but returned to St. Louis from whence he is, it is said, to come back to the Flat Head this summer with several other priests. . . ."

congratulates the country on the arrival of the Jesuits, praises Dr. McLaughlin, "this noble hearted man," for his support and is sure that the Jesuits will receive his assistance; describes the work of the two missionaries, their problems, their needs, their successes. By now "the Catholic establishment of Willamette consists of nearly 80 families." Blanchet in this letter also speaks about the vexations encountered, the controversies created by members of so many sects.[75]

The Catholic missionaries most certainly did not push themselves into the picture; they were called for as we have seen by repeated requests, and it had been hard to answer these calls because of the shortage of priests and because of financial difficulties. The first serious challenge to the faith sown by the Canadians and the Iroquois came in May of 1836, when the Reverend Samuel Parker was on his way to visit Fort Colville. He was staying at a Nez Perce camp at the time. We will let him tell his own story:

The night of our arrival a little girl, of about six or seven years of age, died. The morning of the twelfth they buried her. Everything relating to the ceremony was conducted with great propriety. The grave was dug only about two feet deep. They have no spades, and a sharpened stick was used to loosen the earth, and this was removed with the hands; and with the hands they fill up the grave after the body is deposited in it. A mat is laid in the grave, then the body is wrapped in its blanket with the child's drinking cup and spoon, made of horn; then a mat of rushes is spread over the whole, and filled up, as above described. In this instance, they had prepared a cross to set up at the grave, most probably having been told to do so by some Iroquois Indians, a few of whom, not in the capacity of teachers, but as trappers in the employ of the fur companies, I saw west of the Mountains. One grave in the same village had a cross standing over it, which was the whole relic of the kind I saw, together with this just named, during my travels in the country. But as I viewed a cross of wood made by man's hands of no avail, to benefit either the dead or the living, and far more likely to operate as a salvo [sic] to a guilty conscience, or a stepping-stone to idolatry, than to be understood in its spiritual sense to refer to a crucifixion of our sins, I took this, which the Indians had prepared, and broke it to pieces. I then told them to place a stone at the head and foot of the grave, only to mark the place; and without murmur they cheerfully acquiesced, and adopted our custom.[76]

Where was Parker's courtesy and charity and what kind of Christianity

---

[75] De Smet, *Letters and Sketches With a Narrative of a Year's Residence Among the Rocky Mountains,* 230.

[76] Parker, *op. cit.,* 275–277.

did he want to teach? This was not the only instance when crosses, the symbols of the Christians' salvation, were broken.[77]

The Catholic priests knew psychology. Through long years of study they were prepared for their ministry; they knew how to adapt themselves to the outlook of and how to appeal to the senses of nature's children, the Indians. This understanding was often lacking in the Protestant preachers. We must not forget how much each soul won had cost the Catholic priest in prayers and self-sacrifice to bring down God's blessing on his work. Jealousy of the success of Catholic priests dictated the following letter written by Mrs. Whitman, the wife of Dr. Whitman, a minister among the Cayuse Indians:

> Romanism stalks abroad on our right hand and on our left and with daring effrontery boasts that she is to prevail and possess the land. I ask, must it be so? The zeal and energy of her priests are without a parallel and many, both white and Indians, wander after the beasts. Two are in the country below us and two far above in the mountains.[78]

The Whitmans even attacked the Hudson's Bay Company for supporting the Catholics and forgot all the services they themselves had received. Charles Wilkes from the United States expedition denies this accusation:

> The liberality and freedom from sectarian principles of Dr. Mc-Laughlin may be estimated from his being thus hospitable to missionaries of so many Protestant denominations, although he is a professed Catholic, and has a priest of the same faith officiating daily at the Chapel. Religious toleration is allowed in its fullest extent.[79]

The Colville mission was omitted from the schedule of Father Demers during 1841; Father De Smet was expected to travel there. De Smet left the Flathead country on October 28 to procure provisions and seed at Fort Colville. He arrived with his faithful companions, November 15, and remained three days at the fort. He spoke highly about the services of the Hudson's Bay Company officials.[80] Did this priest realize that the

---

[77] Blanchet, quoted in Bagley, op. cit., I, 111, mentions that Father Langlois had erected a cross in 1841. He found it had disappeared. It had been cut down by order of the Methodist preacher, Waller. Other instances are told by Father Blanchet. On Sunday they had a flag, with the sign of the cross on it, hanging in their place of assembly, and it had been cut down.

[78] Garraghan, op. cit., II, 267, quoting Mrs. Whitman. See also: A. B. Hulbert, Marcus Whitman, Crusader, 3 vols.

[79] Wilkes, op. cit., IV, 331.

[80] De Smet quoted by CR, De Smet, I, 356. "Wherever one finds the gentlemen of the Hudson's Bay Company, one is sure of a good reception. They do not stop with demonstrations of politeness and affability, they anticipate your wishes in order to be of service to you. . . ."

priestly functions he had established at Colville were to be continued by the Society of Jesus exclusively during nearly a century? He merely says:

Besides the instructions that I gave during mass to the Canadians employed at the fort, I had several conferences with the chief of the Skoyelpi or Kettle Indians, an intelligent gentleman, who invited me to come and evangelize his nation.[81]

During the forty-two days of Father De Smet's journey he baptized 190 persons, including 26 adults and those who were sick or extremely old.[82]

He had just come home to St. Mary's at the Bitter Root Valley when a young man of the Sanpoil nation arrived at the Flathead camp, and proposed to stay the winter among the Flatheads and to return in the spring to his nations. He introduced himself with these words:

I am a Sinpoil, my nation is compassionate. I have been sent to hear your words, and learn the prayer you teach the Flat Heads. The Sinpoils desire also to know it, and to imitate their example.[83]

---

[81] Par Le R. P. Pierre De Smet, *Voyages Aux Montagnes Roucheuses Et Une Annee De Sejour Chez Les Tribus Indiennes Du Vaste Territoire L'Oregon.* Letter to his Provincial, December 28, 1841, 214. Also CR, *De Smet,* I, 356–357.

[82] De Smet, *Letters and Sketches,* 192.

[83] *Ibid.,* 170. Letter to his Provincial, December 30, 1841.

CHAPTER IV

Father De Smet, the Mission Organizer

THE Colville Indians had not long to wait for a second visit of Father De Smet. Little did Father De Smet realize when he left his beloved St. Mary's Mission among the Flatheads that the coming events would start him on a career of momentous importance for the conversion of the Indians of the Pacific Northwest. From now on, his beloved Flathead Nation would need the help of other priests, and Father De Smet's magnanimity would embrace all the missions. No trip seemed too tiresome and no distance too great for his apostolic zeal.

The spring of 1842 had come suddenly and had transformed little creeks into roaring rivers and rivers into lakes from the fast melting of the mountain snows. This prevented Father from an overland journey to Fort Vancouver. He needed more supplies than Fort Colville could furnish. Also the problems of the mission work needed to be solved by mutual understanding and organization. The Canadian priests had faculties from the Canadian bishops and the vicar-general ruled in the Vicariate of the Columbia. Father De Smet was subject to his superiors and was in possession of letters patent from Bishop Rosati of St. Louis.

Father De Smet arrived at Fort Colville at the beginning of May. The boats were not ready until the thirtieth. This gave him time to devote his priestly zeal to all who needed him. He translated the prayers into the Indians language and instructed old and young. He baptized all the younger children who had not received this sacrament before at the hand of Father Demers. "The great chief and his wife had long sighed for baptism," Father tells us, "which holy sacrament I administered to them, naming them Martin and Mary. This chief is one of the most intelligent and pious I have become acquainted with."[1] Father

---

[1] De Smet, *Letters and Sketches,* 213–214.

De Smet records the administering of fifty-six baptisms at Kettle Falls.[2]

Father De Smet left Colville to vist the Okanogan Indians on the thirteenth of May in company with the interpreter, Charles, and Chief Martin of the Shuyelpi. Father's mule ran away and Charles nearly died on the prairie from running after the mule. After a few days of rest Charles recovered. On the way Father came to a Shuyelpi village where he baptized the babies and gave some instructions. The whole village accompanied him to the first Okanogan encampment where he was received with "greatest cordiality and joy." The chief was clothed in a shirt of horse skin with the hair outside, the "Mane partly on his chest and back." This party also joined Father De Smet. The news of his arrival had spread far and wide. From all the narrow mountain passes, he saw the people coming. They brought many sick Indians to be baptized because they knew already of the importance of this sacrament. The missionary was surrounded by more than two hundred horsemen, and another two hundred were waiting at their meeting ground. According to Judge Brown of Okanogan, Washington, this was the Indians' horse-racing grounds at Lake Osoyoos, in the Okanogan Valley, east of the Okanogan River. "The land is now in irrigated orchards and situated in the north half Section 27., Tp. 40 N., Range 27, W.W. M."[3] Father De Smet and the assembled Okanogans said night prayers together and the people listened attentively to Father's instructions. Chief Martin and the interpreter talked about religion far into the night. All the next day was spent in prayer, instructions, and hymns. Father De Smet wrote in his *Letters and Sketches*:

> I baptized 106 children and some old people and in conclusion named the plain where the consoling scenes occurred, the "Plain of Prayer." It would be impossible for me to give you an idea of the piety, the happiness of these men, who are thirsting for the life-giving waters of the Divine Word. How much good a missionary could do, who would reside in the midst of a people who are so desirous of receiving instruction, and correspond so faithfully with the grace of God.[4]

Yes, the Okanogans needed a priest for themselves. He would have plenty to do but such a great grace had to wait another forty-three years before it became a reality. Father left some regulations and gave some advice and departed from "this interesting people." He traveled for three days over mountains and through dense forests, today a matter

---

[2] De Smet, *op. cit.*, 224.

[3] Judge William Compton Brown, in an interview at Okanogan, Washington, February 6, 1960.

[4] P. 216.

of a three hours' ride in a car, until he was back at Colville.

The priest embarked on May 30 in Mr. Ogden's boat for the voyage to Vancouver. On the second day they came nearer the Okanogan Dallas where, informed of the danger ahead, Father asked to go on shore. While he was saying his breviary and walking along the rocky river feeling already sorry about having left the boat, a terrible accident occurred near what is now the city of Brewster. Their boat was suddenly stopped and the passengers could hardly keep their balance. They tried with all their efforts to row the boat but to no effect. Father De Smet stood helplessly on the bank and watched it happen:

> . . . They are already within the power of the angry vortex: the waters are crested with foam; a deep sound is heard which I distinguish as the voice of the pilot encouraging his men to hold to their oars — to row bravely. The danger increased every minute, and in a moment more all hope of safety has vanished. The barge — the sport of the vortex, spins like a top upon the whirling waters — the oars are useless — the bow rises — the stern descends, and the next instant all have disappeared. A deathlike chill shot through my frame — a dimness came over my sight as the cry "we are lost" rung in my ears, and told me too plainly that my companions were buried beneath the waves.[5]

As Father De Smet stood motionless and saw no trace of the boat, the whirlpool suddenly threw up the oars, the poles, the capsized barge, and all lighter articles. He saw the men struggling for their lives; five of them sank and never came up again. Father's interpreter twice reached the bottom of the river and after a short prayer was thrown upon the bank. One man seized the handle of an empty trunk and saved himself, and an Iroquois was holding on to Father's bed.[6] This accident brought another delay at Fort Okanogan where Father used the time for more instructions and baptisms.

He arrived finally at Fort Vancouver on June 8. Father Demers has

---

[5] De Smet, *op. cit.,* 219.

[6] Rich, ed., *op. cit.* (Second Series, 1839–1844), 57–58, quotes McLaughlin to Governor and Committee, June 24, 1842. "The brigade under the charge of C. F. Ogden accompanied by C. T. Manson reached this on the 8th Instant and I am sorry to have to inform you that one of the boats was swamped in the Dallas above Okanogan and five men were unfortunately Drowned. Canote Umphreville the Columbia Guide, P. Martineau, David Flett, Louison Boucher, Andre Arenhoniante, the Guide Canote Umphreville, was a Good faithful servant of 31 years standing in the Columbia. The furs were delivered in good order and with Mr. Ogden came the Revd. Father Desmet a Jesuit, who with two other priests and five lay Brethren has Established a mission on Bitter Root River in the Vicinity of Flat Head Post — the Revd. Gentleman is come for a few Agricultural implements which we can afford to sell him."

left a description of the touching scene of greetings between the saintly men, Father De Smet and Father Blanchet. Father Garraghan states that a letter from Bishop Signay of Quebec to Bishop Rosati tells of the matter discussed at this meeting: the erection of a special diocese for the Oregon Country. Bishop Signay further stated that in his opinion Father De Smet would be best suited for the office of bishop and that Father Blanchet had asked to be passed over. The Fifth Provincial Council of Baltimore in 1843 recommended the erection of a Vicariate Apostolic west of the Rocky Mountains and put Father De Smet's name first on the list of three choices. However, various reasons combined to make Father Blanchet the newly appointed bishop. Father Roothaan later wrote that it was at Father De Smet's request that Father Blanchet was chosen and that he refused to allow Father De Smet the title of "Vicar-apostolic of Oregon."[7]

Father De Smet left Vancouver with the Hudson's Bay Company brigade on June 30 in company with Father Demers who was on his way to the Caledonia missions.[8] How the two diocesan priests felt when the Jesuits, member of a religious order, entered the mission field is expressed by Father Blanchet in writing on October 28, 1842, to Bishop Signay: "I rejoice to see that this country is going to fall in regards to spirituals under the learned and enlightened direction of the Jesuits."[9]

Father De Smet in the meantime was on his way back to his beloved St. Mary's among the Flatheads and from there he would go to St. Louis. Great work lay ahead of him; the future of a spiritual kingdom, the kingdom of God in countless souls in the great Northwest, was at stake. Nearly every tribe had pleaded for "Black Robes." He needed priests, Brothers, Sisters, financial help, mission goods. Father Verhaegen in a letter to the Father General in which he asked for more priests

---

[7] Garraghan, *op. cit.*, II, 282, quoting Roman Archives.

[8] Landerholm, transl., *op. cit.*, 154. Father Demers in a letter dated December 20, 1842, tells Bishop Signay of his stop at Fort Okanogan when on route to New Caledonia: "The natives at this post, who had Reverend Father De Smet's visit last spring, were overjoyed to see me. They had even sent a messenger to meet us to inform me that a native dangerously ill was asking anxiously for the help of my ministrations. However I did not find him in immediate danger of dying, and I did not have enough confidence in his attitude to administer baptism to him. Experience has taught me many times, in the course of our missions, not to count too much on the apparent frame of mind of the natives. The Reverend Father De Smet, having baptized two of them in danger of death last year, those wretches, after recovering their health, live as before in polygamy. Fearing a similar downfall on the part of my sick man, I put him on probation. May God be pleased to make a Christian out of him. Before leaving these poor people I baptized twenty-eight children, whom the parents presented to me with an eagerness that inspired in me hope that the kingdom of God is near for those forsaken souls."

[9] *Ibid.*, 277.

for Father De Smet's missions told of the enthusiasm Father De Smet enkindled in the hearts of his fellow Jesuits. "All our Fathers burn with the desire of accompanying him thither next spring."[10] Father De Smet would not go back to his missions for the next two years. He could not send helpers without meeting the cost; this took him on a fund-raising tour from New Orleans to Boston. In 1843, Fathers Peter De Vos and Adrian Hoeken and Brother J. B. McGean were escorted for a while by Father De Smet on their way to the Rocky Mountain missions. When Father De Smet came back to St. Louis, more volunteers had arrived from Europe. Among them was Father Joseph Joset who became later the missionary of the Colville and Okanogan Indians for many years. Father De Smet gave his orders before he sailed for Europe. A mission among the Coeur d'Alenes was to be opened by Father Point. St. Ignatius Mission among the Kalispel Indians was founded by Father Hoecken in 1844. This mission was only two days' travel from Kettle Falls. Now some of the Colville and Okanogan Indians would go to St. Ignatius for instructions. This mission was for a short time the center from which the missionaries would visit the Colvilles and the Okanogans at the fishing place at the Kettle Falls. Chief Martin from the Kettle Falls Indians attended instructions at St. Ignatius Mission. He had come late and Father Hoecken was explaining the Sacrament of Penance. Chief Martin heard only a part of it. He went back to his tribe and told his people that the "Black Robe" had said that all would go to hell if they would not confess their sins. He had all members of his tribe line up for confessions which he himself heard. After each confession he ordered 20 lashes, 40 lashes, 60 lashes, and so on, the number being determined as he judged the seriousness of the guilt committed. It took all night to hear these confessions.[11]

Father De Smet knew how to interest the people of nearly all the main countries of Europe in his missions. Father Palladino mentions the reception Father De Smet received when presented to Pope Gregory XVI, who stood up from his throne to embrace the humble missionary. It was then that the Father General helped Father De Smet to be relieved of the burden of being named a bishop.[12] On the feast of St. Ignatius, July 31, 1844, the ship that brought Father De Smet and new

---

[10] Garraghan, op. cit., II, 278, quoting Fr. Verhaegen to V. Rev. Roothaan, November 1, 1842, Roman Archives.

[11] Joset, "St. Paul's Mission," The Joset Papers, Mss., OPA.

[12] Palladino, op. cit., 55. Father Palladino does not mention his sources of information, but we are sure that he had it from reliable quarters. When he wrote his first edition many of Father De Smet contemporaries were still alive. See also: Garraghan, op. cit., II, 290–296.

mission helpers from Europe around Cape Horn crossed successfully the treacherous bar of the Columbia River after having been in great danger. The missionaries had been sailing for eight months. Fathers Ravalli, Nobili, and Vercruysse belonging to this newly arrived group were destined by Providence to give their services later to the Colville and the Okanogan tribes.

Father De Smet wanted to reach the Flathead mission before winter in 1844. He had visited the Kalispel mission and attempted to reach the Flatheads but winter was too far advanced. He had to stay at St. Ignatius Mission and keep Father Hoeken company. Early in spring of 1845 Father De Smet made a trip to St. Mary's among the Flatheads and transacted some business at St. Ignatius Mission.

The year 1845 became a memorable one for the Colville and Okanogan tribes. Father De Smet went to Kettle Falls during the height of the salmon fishing. He found eight to nine hundred Indians gathered there and he wanted to spend the nine days before the feast of St. Ignatius with them. He caused a little "chapel of boughs to be placed on an eminence in the midst of the Indians' huts. . . ." The natives assisted with great attention at the three daily instructions. Father was greatly consoled as he tells us:

> More then one hundred children were presented to me for baptism, and eleven old men borne to me on skins, seemed only awaiting regenerating waters to depart home and repose in the bosom of the Savior.[13]

The eldest of these men, who was about one hundred years old and blind made a touching speech:

> My life has been long on earth, and my tears have not ceased to flow, even now I daily weep, for I have beheld all my children and early associates disappear. I find myself isolated among my own nation, as if I were in a strange land, thoughts of the past alone occupy me, and they are of a mournful and bitter nature. Sometimes I find consolation in remembering that I have avoided the company of the wicked. Never have I shared in their thefts, battles or murders. This blessed day joy has penetrated the inmost recesses of my soul; the Great Spirit has taken pity on me, I have received baptism, I return thanks for this favor, and offer him my heart and life.[14]

Some of the Kalispels were at Kettle Falls and served as singers for the celebration of the solemn Mass, which was followed by the many

---

[13] De Smet to V. Rev. Roothaan, S. J., August 7, 1845, in *Oregon Missions and Travels Over the Rocky Mountains, 1845–46,* 107.
[14] *Ibid.*

baptisms. Father De Smet is quite poetic in describing the religious ceremonies, the perfect order, joy, and harmony of the celebration and the beauty of the nearby falls. As always here were several tribes gathered in peace for the fishing, and the word of God was spread to several nations. It is remarkable how the native tried to teach each other the prayers and the truths they knew. From now on more definite missionary activities will take place at Kettle Falls and the future mission center received a name before it was built up:

> I gave the name of St. Paul to the Shuyelpi nation, and placed under the care of St. Peter the tribe inhabiting the shore of the great Columbia lakes, whither Father Hoecken is about to repair, to continue instructing and baptizing their adults.[15]

From Kettle Falls Father De Smet made his way to what is now called Chewelah. Here a number of half-breed families wanted to build a settlement. He named this station St. Francis Regis.[16] As we will see, a St. Francis Regis mission will become an important religious, cultural, and education center; but then it will be located between Kettle Falls and Colville.

Father Demers had written to the Rt. Rev. Cazeau on March 1, 1839, that at Fort Okanogan he had been informed that a great many Indians had settled a great distance from the Rocky Mountains toward the north. "A priest could do well among them. . . ."[17] Using the Hudson's Bay Company trail Father Demers had made very successful missionary excursions. From 1844 on, no diocesan priest would move along the big Okanogan Valley; all this work of Christianization would be left for the Society of Jesus. After the Indian Wars the Oblate Fathers would share the work. Father De Smet had promised to send missionaries into this promising region. In 1845, the zealous Father John Nobili, S.J., was sent to the upper Okanogans, the Shushwaps and other tribes in what is now Canada. In a letter written by Father Bolduc to "M. T." — probably Msgr. Turgeon, then the coadjutor to Bishop Signay, later the Archbishop of Quebec — October 24, 1845, we read:

> The R. P. Nobili, who left in June for New Caledonia almost died of starvation before arriving at Fort Okinakan. His colleague, the R. P. Ravalli, had almost drowned some days before, while ascending to Fort Walla Walla.[18]

---

[15] De Smet, *Oregon Missions*, 108.
[16] *Ibid.*, 110.
[17] Blanchet quoting Demers, in Bagley, *op. cit.*, I, 52.
[18] Landerholm, transl., *op. cit.*, 241–242.

There never was a missionary in the Northwest whose endurance of physical and moral adversities was not taxed to the utmost limit. Father Nobili and his companion had left the Willamette with three pack horses. A Hudson's Bay Company man traveled with them a few days and then left them stranded without provisions and without a tent; these he had taken along on his horses. Father Nobili nearly perished without food and drink until two Indians who had known him at Vancouver rescued him and his companion. The natives gave him an owl to eat, which they had killed shortly before.

Father Nobili stopped at Fort Okanogan and all along at places in the Okanogan Valley where the Indians congregated waiting for his priestly functions. His work was crowned with great success. Privations, disappointments, hunger, thirst, and cold were the price he paid for his many conversions. At the head of Lake Okanogan some Indians once stole all is belongings:

> Years afterwards Father Le June was informed that an Indian there was found wearing the Priest's cassock, and another had thought the Church vestments were suitable material for making leggings. But amends were made. In later years Father Le June blessed the church built by one of the Indians concerned in the affair.[19]

Father Nobili visited and instructed the Indians as far north as Fort Alexandria. Father De Smet, speaking of Father Nobili, wrote to Dr. McLaughlin, July 18, 1845: "Next summer or spring he is to return to make his report and I hope arrangements shall be made to establish a permanent mission in that region."[20] This mission was established among the Okanogans two days' travel from Thompson River. Father Nobili named it St. Joseph's Mission. It was located near the end of Lake Okanogan.[21]

A newly arrived priest, Father Goetz, from Europe became Father Nobili's companion. While Father Nobili traveled hundreds of miles in all directions to minister to the tribes, the newly arrived priest, not familiar with the language yet, was left alone for some length of time. It seems that the young priest was recalled and that Father Nobili was

---

[19] F. M. Buckland, "Some Notable Men in the Okanogan Valley," *First Annual Report of the Okanogan Historical and Natural Society* (September 10, 1926), 14–16. Father Le June was an Oblate Father stationed at Kelowna, B. C.

[20] De Smet to Dr. John McLaughlin, July 18, 1848, quoted by Garraghan, *op. cit.,* II, 329 (Missouri Archives).

[21] From extracts of Roman Archives, OPA. "De residentia Sti Joseph inchoanda 'ai confini gran lago D'Okanogan . . . al 50 degrees 40' di Lat. e 120 degrees 8' di long west ca Greenwich . . . Die 24 April, 1847, advenit at gran lago d'Okanogan."

for a time left alone in New Caledonia.[22] How this promising mission field was abandoned is told by Father Nobili himself to a fellow Jesuit in a letter:

> In May, 1847, I founded the first residence of St. Joseph's among the Okinagans, two days journey from Thompson's River, and resided there the following year with Father Goetz given me as a Companion. Then, I will not say for what motive, I was with deep sorrow snatched away from my dear Indians, in the midst of whom I had hoped to die, and then called South to the residence of the Flatheads.[23]

Father Nobili regretted greatly having to abandon seven thousand Indians and many catechumens and more than fifteen hundred neophytes. He wrote to San Francisco to Father De Smet asking him why he had left Oregon so quickly. The mission that yielded such good fruits never would have been abandoned if Father De Smet had remained in Oregon:

> . . . Well, Father Joset, as soon as he received the letter making him Superior of the Missions, recalled me from New Caledonia with all my baggage and ordered me to withdraw from the Residence of St. Joseph, which had been established at the foot of the Great Lake of the Oka-nagans; later he sent me as a companion there one of the Fathers recently arrived from Europe; finally, for the second time he wrote un-expectedly to me and my companion ordering us even under a precept of obedience to abandon Mission, Residence, Indians, and private effects to the care of Providence and return to the Rocky Mountains.[24]

Father General Roothaan wanted the mission continued but mail was many months and even years on the way. Father Joset had no fitting companion for this mission and in addition the doctor had declared Father Nobili unfit for missionary life. So ended what would have turned out to be a great early blessing for the Okanogans and related tribes.

Father De Smet later speaking about Father Nobili's life and death told of the terrible hardships undergone by the heroic missionary in the great wilderness:

> During his sojourn in New Caledonia, Father Nobili had to endure great privations. Through the course of one whole year, his only sub-sistence was a sort of moss or grass and roots. His chief food was horse-

[22] Rev. John Nobili to Father Goetz, "Two Old Letters," *WL* (18:52, February, 1889), 77–79. Also: Garraghan quoting Joset to Roothaan, August 2, 1850, Roman Archives, *op. cit.*, II, 329.

[23] Rev. Nobili quoted from a letter to one of his fellow Jesuits, by Rev. John B. McGloin, S.J., "The New Caledonia Years," *The Owl* (40:8, May, 1953), 6 ff.

[24] Nobili to De Smet, March 28, 1850, Missouri Archives, quoted by Garraghan, *op. cit.*, II, 330–331.

flesh, and often he was reduced to eating the flesh of dogs and wolves. What he suffered from cold, hunger, and other privations is only known to God.[25]

In September of 1845, Father Anthony Ravalli, S.J., a priest stationed at St. Ignatius, went from St. Ignatius Mission to visit the Shuyelpi Indians. He encouraged the Indians and helped them to build a chapel and a cabin for the priest. The missionary however was allowed to stay only one month. The shortage of priests was acute and he was needed elsewhere. The Indians around Colville had been much addicted to gambling and adhered also to their old superstitions. Chief Martin and his son Antony brought about a dramatic stop to the gambling of the tribe. Now left without a priest, the Indians again would frequent St. Ignatius Mission. A remarkable change came over the tribe, which was noticed by all who came to Kettle Falls. In 1846, Father Hoecken came to St. Paul's Mission and instructed and baptized children and adults.

During the winter of 1845–1846 Father De Smet was on a perilous journey. He had resolved to enter the Blackfeet country by way of the Canadian Rocky Mountains and make peace between the Flathead Indians and the Blackfeet. He had not been successful but found much missionary work on the trip. On his way down the Columbia River he met the Hudson's Bay Company brigade on the way to York Factory. Fifteen Kettle Falls Indians had been engaged; each had a pack with hundred and fifty pounds on his back. Captains Ward and Vavasseur were among the party; they praised the Indians for their honesty, civility, "their sincere piety and great regularity in their religious duties; every morning and evening, they were seen retiring a short distance from the camp, to sing . . . hymns, and join in common prayer."[26]

Father De Smet found twenty families of the Lake Indians encamped beside the lake. Most of the tribe had been converted the past year at Kettle Falls but these families had not been there. These natives were overjoyed when Father instructed and baptized them. Chief Gregory, who had been baptized in 1838, was especially happy to see all his people become Christians. Father De Smet described the Lake Indians as a poor people. He resolved to bring agricultural implements and seeds as soon as he would have the means to help them.

About end of May Father De Smet was back at Fort Colville. He found that the Indian nation had been instructed by Father Hoecken.

---

[25] De Smet to the editor of the *Preces Historiques, Brussels,* January 18, 1858, in *Western Missions and Missionaries: A Series of Letters,* 516.
[26] De Smet to Father Provincial, May 10, 1846, *Oregon Missions,* 205.

Proudly the Indians showed him their St. Paul's chapel. He writes:

> They had built, to my great surprise, a small frame church so much
> the more beautiful and agreeable to my eyes, at being their first attempt
> at Architecture, and the exclusive work of the Indians. With a laudable
> pride they conducted me, as in triumph, to the humble and new temple
> of the Lord, and in favor of that good people, and for their perseverance
> in the faith I there offered the august Sacrifice of the Altar.[27]

It was during Father De Smet's stay at Colville that Father Nobili
came from his Caledonia and Okanogan missions. About the Shuyelpi
Indians he had the following to say:

> Their nation numbers about 600 subdivided into various tribes. It is
> incredible what a change came over everybody after the first catechetical
> instruction of our Fathers. The commandant of the Fort (Colville) and
> all the other Hudson gentlemen are in amazement at it.[28]

Father De Smet went from Colville in one of the barges of the
Hudson's Bay Company to Vancouver. On the way he stopped at Fort
Okanogan where he baptized "forty-three persons, chiefly children." On
his way back from Vancouver he noticed that already "about seventy
metis or half-breeds" had collected at St. Francis Regis to settle permanently.[29] This is the last we hear for a few years of Father De Smet's
presence in the Inland Empire. His job from now on is to provide financial help from whatever source it might come for his Rocky Mountain
missions. He had established his missions; further developments lay in
the hands of other superiors. Father DeVos lists the fourteen missions
and stations in 1847.[30]

---

[27] De Smet to his Provincial, May 29, 1846, from St. Paul's Mission, Kettle Falls,
Oregon Missions, 220.

[28] Nobili quoted in Joset to Rt. Rev. Roothaan, March 18, 1848, in Roman
Archives quoted by Garraghan, *op. cit.*, II, 336.

[29] De Smet to his Provincial, July 26, 1846, *Oregon Missions*, 243.

[30] De Vos, S.J., "Newsletter," October 19,1846, in CR, *De Smet*, IV, 1564.
"The residence and church of St. Mary's among the Flatheads.
"The mission and church of the Sacred Heart among the Coeur d'Alene.
"The mission and church of St. Ignatius among the Kalispels.
"The station and chapel among the Chaudieres.
"The station and church of St. Francis Regis among the half-breeds between the
Kalispels and Chaudieres.
"A church built by the Indians at Stuart Lake, New Caledonia.
"A church built by them at Fort Alexandria, New Caledonia.
"A church built by them at Appatoka, New Caledonia.
"The station of St. Peter's, upper Lake of the Columbia.
"The station of St. Francis Borgia among the upper Pend d'Oreilles.
"The station of the Assumption among the Arcs a Plats.
"The station of the Immaculate Heart among the Kootenais.
"The station of St. Joseph's among the Okinagans."

The need for a permanent missionary at St. Paul's Mission became a necessity. Father Joseph Joset, S.J., on March 18, 1848, wrote to his Father General: "Everybody says the opening of a mission at St. Paul can no longer be delayed without great loss to souls." In April of the same year Father De Vos was sent by Father Joset as a missionary to Kettle Falls. In 1847, a better chapel and a residence had been built at this place. The early Christians at St. Paul's were fervent. The white people from Fort Colville gave good example and helped Father De Vos. The chiefs were at first vigilant, but then one of chief's daughters gave scandal and was not reproved by her father. The bad example of another of the chiefs ruined much of Father's work; his disappointments were severe and undermined his health. Father J. M. O'Sullivan, S.J., speaking about the *Journal of Father De Vos,* gives us an idea of the great amount of spiritual work done by this zealous priest:

1847 Baptisms: adult 0
            infant 28 (29 by entries)
       Marriages 0, Confessions 0, Communions 0, Burials 0[31]

1848 Baptisms: adult 64
            infant 42, total 106 (102 by entries)
       Marriages 31
       Confessions 200
       Communions 100
       Burials 4

1849 Baptisms: adult 172
            infants 45, total 217
       Marriages 66
       Confessions 1,900
       Communions 300
       Burials 25

1850 Baptisms: adult 25
            infant 50
       Marriages 12
       Confessions 2,100
       Communions 600
       Burials 27

1851 Baptisms by Fr. De Vos 33
            Fr. Vercruysse 25
            Fr. Joset 7, total 65[32]

[31] According to the *Joset Papers,* Mss., OPA, Father De Vos went to reside at St. Paul's in the fall of 1847.
[32] *The J. M. O'Sullivan Papers,* Mss., OPA.

From the number of baptisms in 1851, sixteen were adults. Many of the parents of the infants baptized were pagans. Marriages were performed right after baptism. Father De Vos was sent for reasons of health in 1851 to the Willamette Valley and was succeeded by Father Joset. At St. Francis Regis among the half-breeds many families had moved away. It was deemed advisable to have two Fathers at St. Paul's and from here visit St. Francis Regis in Chewelah occasionally. Father Louis Vercruysse therefore came to live at St. Paul's with Father Joset; in the years before he had been accustomed to visit Father De Vos. From his observations he could give a wonderful testimony about Father De Vos:

> Alone as he was for three years, everything changed. The Canadian employees of Fort Colville are no longer the same nor are the Indians of the locality and its environs. He is loved and respected and no longer makes use of an interpreter. Of all the missions, this is the one where most is done for the instruction of the Indians.[33]

Father Joset has left us interesting descriptions of the Mission of St. Paul's near the Kettle Falls of the Columbia. At first things went on as before. The French Canadians and Iroquois, former employees of the Hudson's Bay Company, had begun to settle in the valley. They came every Sunday and feast day to church and they helped to maintain the missionaries. The Okanogan Indians started to travel to Colville and several of their families were baptized. Then trouble started. Father Joset blamed the devil for sending a "dreamer":

> He had been dead for 6 days, said he, [and] had been to heaven, the ladder to which did not touch the earth. He spoke of Our Lord, of his horse, etc. He saw in heaven plenty of meat and salmon etc., etc. but the gist of all [was that] he had seen there the two chiefs who had given scandal.[34]

The superstitious Indians, especially the relatives of this man, were easily induced to believe this story. The chiefs told Father Joset that the Canadians and Ignace, the Iroquoi, believed the story. At the end, however, the dreamer had publicly to recant the story and his fraud did not do much harm as he later had to move away. St. Paul's Mission was visited by Dr. Suckley from the Stevens expedition.[35]

---

[33] Father L. Vercruysse to Father General Roothaan, quoted by Garraghan, *op. cit.*, II, 336–337.

[34] "Colville Mission," *The Joset Papers*, Mss., OPA.

[35] Dr. George Suckley, quoted in Isaac I. Stevens' report, *op. cit.*, 284–286. "Arrived at Fort Colville November 13. Near the falls is the mission of St. Paul established among the Kettle Falls Indians on the left bank of the Columbia about

In 1853–1854 a terrible smallpox epidemic swept eastern Washington. A man had brought the disease from the Sanpoel Indians and did not obey the missionary's command to stay away from the camp at Kettle Falls. Soon the infection had spread everywhere. The urgent need made a doctor out of the missionary and he saved hundreds of lives. Father Joset writes:

> There was no doctor in the country and no vaccine to be had; as the man was of a very good constitution, the father took the matter from him and inoculated first his wife and children, and everyone escaped the infection: the father had never done such a thing before . . . but a missioner in such circumstances must improvise himself a doctor.[36]

Camp after camp caught the sickness, which lasted almost a year and taxed the missionaries' time and strength. Father kept on working, inoculating, warning the people to keep warm and isolated. Those who followed his directions were saved, while others died. The whites, half-breeds, and squaws who lived in the valley and came regularly to church were all spared. Not one got the sickness. About sixty miles from St. Paul's was the abandoned house of the Presbyterian minister, which two families had made their winter home. They never came to the mission, yet they caught the pox. One of them, a Protestant, had been in the employ of the Hudson's Bay Company and Mr. McDonald, who felt sorry for the people, asked Father Joset to go there and offered to give him a companion and horses. Father brought the Last Sacraments to the sick Indian woman, baptized and inoculated the children; only the woman died.

Father Adrian Hoecken visited the Indian missions and in a letter to Father De Smet told him about Father Joset's activities:

> Father Joset, among the Skoyelpis, at the Kettle falls of the Columbia, had baptized a large number of adults and children. During the late

one mile from the Kettle Falls. I visited the mission establishment three times during my stay at Fort Colville. It is superintended by the Reverend Father Joset, assisted by one other priest and a lay-brother. Father Joset received me kindly. He is a Swiss and very gentlemanly and agreeable in his manners. To him I am indebted for such valuable information concerning this part of the country. The mission establishment consists of a chapel, a dwelling-house and several other buildings. There is no farm attached to it. The missionaries can obtain all they need from the Hudson Bay Company.

"The Kettle Falls Indians call themselves Squee-yerpe. The chief of this tribe is called Pierre Jean. He, with most of his followers, live in lodges around the mission. The number of this band is about 350. During the summer season the Indians from all the surrounding country congregate at this place to catch salmon. There are then 1000 at the falls."

[36] Joset, *op. cit.*

prevalence of the small-pox, there were hardly any deaths from it among the neophytes, as most of them had been previously vaccinated by us, while the Spokans and other unconverted Indians, who said the "Medicine (vaccine) of the Fathers, was a poison, used only to kill them," were swept away by the hundreds. This contrast, of course, had the effect of increasing the influence of the missionaries.[37]

The Jesuit Fathers did not have the same success with all the tribes who depended on St. Paul's Mission to Christianize them. Father Joset remarked that Chief Vincent of the Lake Indians had told him that:

> . . . in the mountains there is faith, at the lake it is half and half: in the prairie it is superstition or the old Indian practices and vices. It was lucky that the mission was established among the mountaineers: it made the work much easier and surer. The others were wont to domineer.[38]

Father Joset, an experienced missionary, does not belittle the power of the devil on a superstitious pagan people. He says that Father Giorda, S.J., "who by no means was a credulous man," told him positively that some gamblers had invoked the devil, who appeared to them in person. Father Joset had in his room a man who had been a great medicine man before his conversion. This medicine man used to take live coals in his mouth and blow fire out. Father Joset wanted to know how he got his "medicine." Father then reported the conversation:

> When I was about the age of my younger son (about 12 years) one of our dogs died: my father told me: take the dog on your shoulder and go out to look for medicine. I did so and went wandering on mountains: the first day I saw nothing. The second day evening I was at an old sweating lodge: the dead dog spoke to me and told me: "You will kill plenty of deer." The sweat lodge told me: "You will take fire in your mouth without burning yourself." "You were dreaming." "No, I was wide awake."[39]

Father Joset then adds:

> In this he might have easily been mistaken: being tired and hungry he must have had a very agitated sleep, and thought himself awake though really sleeping. It is in dream that they are ordinarily initiated: They see an animal, a deer, a bear, a snake who speaks to them, teaches them their peculiar air which they hum in sleep and afterwards, when awake: even these apparitions continue after they are baptized, and

---

[37] A. Hoecken to De Smet, October 18, 1855, in *Western Missions*, 302.
[38] Father Joset quoting Chief Vincent, *Joset Papers*, Mss., OPA.
[39] Father Joset quoting a medicine man, *Joset Papers*, Mss., OPA.

many times they come to see the missionary to know how to get rid of them.[40]

To show his power the medicine man let himself be tied as was the common practice among the tribes. First the man had his thumbs tied together, then his wrists, then his arms tied to the body, then his legs, and so on until he was not able to move any of his members. Somehow, singing or humming their power song they were suddenly loosed. Father Joseph kept on investigating these occurrences. Of another famous medicine man who had been converted he writes:

> I had never any medicine. "You lie" another Indian told him. "Indeed, I do not lie: I never had any medicine, but seeing that those who had no medicine were despised I falsely said that I had." The missionary insisted: "Still you used to have yourself tied and placed in the medicine lodge, and by singing you were suddenly loosed: who taught you that?" "Nobody, I tried and succeeded. The only thing I know is that as soon as I began to sing I became furious, and was loosed."[41]

These examples show that the missionaries had to fight against the very powers of darkness, against century-old superstitions which had been transmitted from one generation to the next. Father Joset told of another interesting incident that took place in 1870. On a tour visiting the Indians he ran out of provisions, and had to depend on that what the Indians could provide. This food caused him such severe colic that his companion was afraid that Father Joset might die. Shortly before Father had been asked by an old man for some tobacco; he had to refuse, because he had none. The old man, hearing of Father's condition, said: "It is the tobacco he refused me." Father arrived safely home but had another spell so severe that he asked to receive the Last Sacraments. The doctor had given up all hope. Hearing of Father's sickness the old man rejoiced and boasted of his great power that "was killing the blackgown":

> Next day he himself was sick, his belly swelled like a barrel, and the third day he died, the Indians saying that his spells had fallen on him.[42]

An incident that had far-reaching and degrading influence on the Indians around Kettle Falls, and gradually on all tribes classified today as the Colville Confederated Tribes, occurred when in 1854 two white men brought liquor into the Indian country and chose a location for its sale where the people coming from the valley passed as they were

[40] *Joset Papers.*
[41] *Ibid.*

[42] *Ibid.*

going to church. The settlers kept on going to Mass but found excuses to stay away from the afternoon services in order to frequent the saloon. Soon the Indians followed the example of the whites; even some of the influential chiefs started drinking. The population was still for the most part Catholic. People went to church on Sundays and kept their Easter duties, but the original fervor waned. In the same year Morel, an employee of Angus MacDonald, chief trader at Fort Colville, discovered gold at the Pend d'Oreille River.[43]

The year of 1855 was a memorable one. Several history-making events occurred whose consequences were far-reaching. On December 1, 1843, Pope Gregory XVI had raised Oregon Territory to a vicariate apostolic and had named the Rev. Francis Norbert Blanchet the first Bishop of the Oregon Country with the title of Philadelphia *in partibus,* which was changed to Drasa on May 7, 1844. At that time only twelve priests, ten of them Jesuits, were working in this immense mission field.[44] The Most Reverend F. N. Blanchet was consecrated as Bishop of Drasa in Montreal in 1844. From there he went to Europe to solicit funds and recruits for his vast vicariate. While in Rome he addressed a lengthy *memorandum* on Old Oregon to the Sacred Congregation of the Propaganda. In accordance with the conclusions of this document the Apostolic Vicariate of Oregon was divided into eight dioceses named as follows: Oregon City, Nesqually, Walla Walla, Fort Hall, Colville, Vancouver Island, and New Caledonia. For the time being the Holy See would name only three bishops for this ecclesiastical province of which Oregon City was the metropolitan see. The Most Reverend F. H. Blanchet was named the metropolitan; his brother, the Most Reverend A. M. A. Blanchet, was named the first Bishop of Walla Walla and was to take care of Colville and Fort Hall until later these places would have their own bishops. Father Demers was to become Bishop of Vancouver Island. This division included the territory between the 42nd and the 54th parallels. The Diocese of Walla Walla had just begun to exist when the

---

[43] George W. Fuller, quoting Angus MacDonald, chief trader at Fort Colville, *op. cit.,* 1941 ed., 304: "I took charge of Colville in 1853 and hinted at the golden geology of that country to our men. I had a little sack of dark sand given me by a friend in California, which I showed to our men. Morel had been cutting a large tree for firewood and felt dry. He went and drank freely with his mouth deep into the Columbia. He saw some black sand of the kind I showed him in my little sack. Pulling off his old hat, he put some of the gravel of the beach and water into it, managed to shake it enough to see several scales of gold, bigger and smaller than a pinhead, that remained in the hat after he poured the water out of it." MacDonald ordered some men to prospect and after a few days they returned with several ounces of fine gold from the mouth of the Pend d'Oreille River.

[44] De Smet, *Oregon Missions,* 46–48.

Cayuse War started. This was followed by the closing of the territory for settlement. Nominally the diocese existed, but the bishop could not live there. The Diocese of Walla Walla was suppressed later and its bishop transferred to the newly created bishopric of Nesqually; the districts of Colville and Fort Hall were made subject to the Archbishop of Oregon City. On June 29, 1853, at the recommendation of the First Plenary Council of Baltimore, held in 1852, the Columbia River and parallel 46 became the lines of division between the Dioceses of Oregon City and Nesqually from the Pacific to the Rocky Mountains.[45] The Bishop of Nesqually now had jurisdiction over the territory situated north and west of the Columbia River together with the whole district of Colville.[46] In was in 1855 that a bishop had first visited the later-named Colville Confederate Tribes at the Kettle Falls. Father Joset wrote to Father De Smet about this event:

> I hope that the holy Sacrament of Confirmation which many have lately received, will add still more stability to their good resolutions. The arrival of Monseigneur Blanchet from Nesqually, had been announced only a few hours before, yet notwithstanding that one half of the neophytes were absent on their hunting grounds, the zealous prelate gave confirmation to over six hundred persons. He expressed the greatest satisfaction at the flourishing condition of the missions, and the exemplary and Christian conduct of the Indian faithful.[47]

During the late summer and fall of 1855 the first real gold rush took place through the Colville Valley. This predicted the eventual doom of St. Paul's Mission because all kinds of people came into the territory and through their bad example gradually scandalized and demoralized the Indians. In 1857 Father Ravalli was appointed superior of St. Paul's Mission. One day he received an urgent call. A woman had had a quarrel with her husband and in a jealous rage had hanged herself to a tree with a lariat. Father cut off the lariat and freed the woman's neck, which was not broken. The body was still warm but no pulse at the wrist or at the heart could be found. She appeared to be dead. Father Ravalli stretched her on the ground and started to breathe into her mouth and to move her arms up and down applying artificial respiration. He kept on working for three quarters of an hour when suddenly her color started to change. Still Father kept on working on her; slowly the life came back. The Indians were astonished when

---

[45] F. N. Blanchet in Bagley, *op. cit.*, I, 3, 125 ff. Also Rev. Joseph Delannoy, *History of the Diocese*, Mss., AAS; Landerholm, *op. cit.*, 212; O'Hara, *op. cit.*, 149.
[46] Delannoy, *op. cit.*
[47] Joset quoted by De Smet to the editor of the *Precis Historiques*, Brussels, *Western Missions*, 200–201.

the woman started to breathe, first weakly and at intervals, then slowly and more regularly. Shortly after she opened her eyes and was soon up and around; she lived to be quite old. The Indians hereafter called Father Ravalli the "Great Medicine Man."[48]

Trouble had been brewing during the last years, and St. Paul's Mission, the earliest cradle of Christianity in the Inland Empire, felt the repercussions coming from depredations committed elsewhere. In 1853, the Territory of Washington had been organized. In the same year Governor Isaac I. Stevens had paid a two days' visit to Fort Colville and the congregated Indian tribes. He promised them the help of the government and peace with the Blackfoot tribe.

When, in the same year, Captain McClellan's expedition explored the Okanogan and Yakima Valleys, the members of this group were looked upon with suspicion. Ka-mi-akin, one of the Yakima chiefs, having assured himself of the intentions of Governor Stevens to buy the Indians' lands and to put them on reservations, was aroused to defend his land and to fan a deadly hate against the white intruders. He invited all the surrounding tribes and formed an Indian confederacy to defeat the whites. The Palouses, Yakimas, Skoyelpis, Okanogans, Spokanes, Coeur d'Alenes, Kalispels, Kootenais, and Flatheads entered the coalition.[49] In the Council of Walla Walla in 1853, Governor Stevens of Washington Territory and Superintendent of Indian Affairs, forced treaties on the Indians without granting them sufficient time to reflect. The governor's action aggravated matters and the powerful chieftains rode home in anger swearing revenge.

Governor Stevens then went to Montana to conclude treaties with the tribes there. He intended to make a treaty with the Colville Indians after his return. While still in the Blackfeet country word was brought to him of the Yakima uprising. He hurried back to Spokane where he had a council with the northern tribes at Antoine Plante's place on December 4, 1855. He promised the Colvilles to return for the treaty. The Catholic Colville tribes were peace-loving and showed their peaceful intentions:

> . . . The Colvilles furnished Stevens and his party with fresh horses to meet the obligation of immediate investigation. That was the last the tribe saw of Isaac Stevens, nor of the horses that were loaned to them. And so the treaty was never carried out for the Colvilles.[50]

Governor Stevens knew that the influential position of the Jesuit

---

48 Palladino, *op. cit.*, 56–57.
49 CR, *De Smet*, II, 731.
50 Mrs. Helen Toulou, *Manuscript Book*.

Fathers had far-reaching effects in keeping the Indians peaceful. This is expressed in a letter to Father Joset written on November 28, 1855, from Spokane Prairie:

> . . . I reached this place with Father Ravalli this evening, shall remain here a few days, and on Sunday bring into council the friendly Indians of the regions. . . . Tribes who have taken part in the war I do not wish to see. I desire your presence here at the earliest practical moment, and I trust you may reach this place [Antoine's] on Saturday, December 1st. . . . I am personally and officially under weighty obligations both to yourself and Father Ravalli; for your repeated good offices, and I shall bear testimony to the official services you have rendered me in the cause of humanity. I anxiously desire to prevent the spread of war contagion, and trust that the spirit of the disaffected may be confined almost exclusively to the Yakimas.
>
> Your friend and obedient servant,
> Isaac Stevens[51]

In the meantime bloody battles had been fought in the Yakima Valley and on the West Coast. The confederacy formed at the Grand Ronde Valley against the whites had in its plan simultaneous outbreaks among the various tribes to scatter the defenses of the whites. No white person was sure of his life after the Walla Walla Treaty where the Indians had been treated so unjustly; before, they had been friends of the Indians, who had treated the whites with great hospitality. Further outbreaks occurred in southern Oregon. Signals flared on the mountaintops to give information to the various tribes. Governor Stevens tried to make peace but without results. A. J. Splawn tells of differences coming up between the chiefs Ka-mi-akin and Ow-hi. Ka-mi-akin had been only partly of royal ancestry; now his leadership was contested. Ow-hi wanted to make peace for a while. This proved dangerous to the Palouse, the Spokanes, and the Coeur d'Alenes. Ka-mi-akin left with half of the warriors to sow the discord and hatred of the whites among these tribes of the Inland Empire. Two miners on the way to Colville were killed by Indians. An investigation attempted by Colonel Steptoe was thwarted by attacking Indians.[52] The war in the Inland Empire nearly ruined the missions that had been developed gradually with so much care and sacrifices on the part of the missionaries. Father Congiato, S.J., the superior of the Rocky Mountain missions, wrote to Father De Smet on November 29, 1855:

[51] Governor Isaac I. Stevens to Father J. Joset, S.J., Mss., OPA.
[52] For more detail see: Ray Hoard Glassley, *Pacific Northwest Indian Wars.* Also: A. J. Splawn, *KA-MI-AKIN: Last Hero of the Yakimas*, 21–101, and George W. Fuller, *A History of the Pacific Northwest*, 207–294.

All was going on wonderfully well when I was in Oregon; now all is on fire. The last tidings which I received from the Mission of St. Paul at Colville, inform me that your Indians express their horror for the excesses committed by the [other] Indians, and show no disposition to join them in the war.[53]

It was a hard task for the missionaries to keep the tribes peaceful in the face of the encroachments of the whites who were hungry for the lands which the Indians had occupied since time immemorial. Governor Stevens did not consult the Catholic missionaries before the Walla Walla Treaty about the best approach to win the Indians' friendship. But when he was in trouble he threw the blame unjustly on the Catholic missionaries.[54] He later changed his views however. In a letter written April 15, 1857, Father Adrien Hoecken tells about Father Ravilli's work for peace at St. Paul's Mission:

Father Ravalli labored as much as he could to pacify the tribes which reside to the west, namely: The Cayuses, the Yakamans, the Opelouses, [Palouse] etc. As our neophytes hitherto have taken no part in the war, the country is as safe for us as ever. We can go freely wheresoever we desire. No one is ignorant that the Black gowns are not enemies; those at least, who work among the Indians. . . . A few days since, Father Joset wrote me that Father Ravalli had already written to him several weeks before; "I fear a general rising among the Indians, towards the commencement of spring. Let us pray, and let us engage others to pray with us, in order to avert this calamity. I think it would be well to add to the ordinary prayers of the mass, the collects for peace.[55]

---

[53] Father Congiato, S.J., to De Smet, November 29, 1855, quoted by De Smet, Western Missions, 293–294, February 4, 1856, to the editor of the Preces Historiques.

[54] Hazard Stevens, The Life of Isaac Ingals Stevens, II, 229. From Stevens' report to the Indian Department, October 22, 1856. "In times of peace the influence of the Catholic missionaries is good in that quarter, and their good offices are desirable till some outrage is committed, or war breaks out. But since the war had broken out, whilst they have made every exertion to protect individuals, and to prevent other tribes joining in the war, they have occupied a position which cannot be filled on earth, — a position between the hostiles and the Americans. So great has been their desire for peace that they have overlooked all right, propriety, justice, necessity, siding with the Indians, siding with the Americans, but advising the latter particularly to agree to the demands of the former, — murders to go free, treaties to be abrogated, whites to retire to their settlements. And the Indians, seeing that the missionaries are on their side, are fortified in the belief that they are fighting in a holy cause. I state on my official responsibility that the influence of the Catholic missionaries in the upper country has lately been most baneful and pernicious."

[55] De Smet quoting Father Hoecken's letter from April 5, 1857, in Western Missions, 309.

Scenic view of the Colville Valley near Kettle Falls, Washington.

Okanogan River flowing into the Columbia River. On the peninsula at the left, Fort Okanogan was established in 1811.

Fort Okanogan. Original painting by J. M. Stanley of Steven's Expedition, 1853. (Courtesy of the Washington State Historical Society of Tacoma, Washington.)

Fort Colville. A close-up view as it looked in 1860–1861. (Institution of Royal Engineers, Chatham, Kent, England.)

Fort Colville and Valley of the Columbia with Indian settlements. (Institution of Royal Engineers, Chatham, Kent, England.)

Dr. John McLoughlin, the "White Eagle" of the West, First Chief Factor of the Hudson Bay Company from Fort Vancouver, U. S.

The old St. Paul Mission, built in 1847, and the priest's house as it looked when the mission was closed in 1860–1861 (Institution of Royal Engineers, Chatham, Kent, England.)

Scenic views of the Kettle Falls of the Columbia River. Now covered by Roosevelt Lake. (Courtesy of Department of the Interior.)

Lake Chelan as viewed from the summit of Bear Mountain. Lake Chelan State Park may be seen in the lower left foreground. On the upper right center is the city of Manson.

To construct a sweat bath was often a simple matter.

Babies were kept on a cradleboard that could be hung from the belly of a horse.

Annie Atkins, Menatchee Indian. (Courtesy of Chelan County Historical Society.)

Dress of the Colville Indians. The Charlie Leo Family.

Yut-huen-alks, sister of Chief Smitkin.

Mrs. Christine George, daughter
of Chief Seattle, wife of
Chief Coxit George.

Elizabeth Friedlander and her eighteen-year-old daughter, Isabel,
who was sold for six steers and four good horses by her stepfather.

Most Reverend Francis
Norbert Blanchet, first
archbishop of Portland,
Oregon.

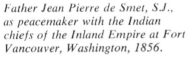

Chief Joseph Tonasket.

Father Jean Pierre de Smet, S.J.,
as peacemaker with the Indian
chiefs of the Inland Empire at Fort
Vancouver, Washington, 1856.

In 1858, Father Congiato, S.J., found it necessary to close St. Paul's Mission at the Kettle Falls. He had no efficient missionaries who would be able to cope with the difficult situation which had developed in that part of the country because of the gold rush and the threatening attitude of the Indians toward the whites. A great shortage of priests became apparent in the formerly great mission field of the Rocky Mountains. Several of the priests had been transferred to the California missions. The thirty Canadian families received the periodic services of priests who came from the only two Jesuit residences and missions that remained open, Coeur d'Alene and St. Ignatius Mission. Many of the Indians who had congregated at the Kettle Falls of the Columbia River were forced away to find their livelihood somewhere else. The whites had opened big fisheries at the mouth of the Columbia; as a result the fish could not swim up the river to spawn in such great numbers as before. The need for Father De Smet to come back and inspire new life into the missions which he had founded was felt by the Indians who had remained faithful. The following letter to Father De Smet is especially touching:

Father Smet, I am a poor savage. My name is Michael and I belong to the Nation of Skoyelpys, which the whites call the "Chaudieres." I have left my nation to follow the Fathers to whom I owe everything; first, the knowledge of God and the true religion, and then all the other instructions I have. They have taught me how to read and write, and more besides, for they have taught me to sing. They have taught me also to speak French. God has given me an excellent and pious wife. We are both quite young. We have learned the Christian Doctrine well and we have decided to consecrate ourselves to the spiritual and temporal good of our fellow countrymen. I know, Father, that you are a great friend of the Indians. I know also that, although far away from us, you never cease to do us good, and I thank you for it sincerely in the name of all the Indians. After having done us spiritual good, you are now doing us temporal good. In return we will try to do you spiritual good, by praying to the Great Spirit for you. I have learned from Father Congiato, Great Chief of all the Indian Missions, that you are thinking of coming to us. All the hearts of the Indians would be very happy at your visit. Come quickly, Father, come to see and console your poor children who love you so much. Your visit could perhaps bring back my nation to the right path. You know, Smet, that they are not behaving well. Gambling and whiskey have destroyed all the good that the Fathers did among them. The bad example of the Whites, who are looking for gold has ruined my poor nation; the Fathers have been obliged to abandon them. Only the Lake people continue to be good. My heart will be happy when

I learn that you pray for my poor nation. I bid you good Bye with all my heart. Thy Child in Jesus Christ, Michael, Skoyelpy Indian.[56]

In the fall of 1858, Colonel Wright allied himself with some Nez Perces in order to avenge the defeat of Colonel Steptoe in the Spokane country. At the beginning of September the battle of Four Lakes took place. "A Colville Indian chief had viewed the battle of Four Lakes with astonishment, and had dashed back to his people with the advice that they never fight the whites."[57]

Father De Smet had given his disapproval of United States Indian policy in a letter written in 1854:

If the poor and unfortunate inhabitants of the Indian territory were treated with more justice and good faith, they would cause little trouble. They complain, and doubtless justly, of the dishonesty of the whites. These banish them from their native soil, from the tombs of their fathers, to which they are devotedly attached, and from their ancient hunting and fishing grounds: they must consequently seek what is wrested from them, and build their cabins in another and strange clime. But they are scarcely at ease in their new abode when they are removed a second and a third time. With each successive emigration, they find their grounds restricted, their hunting and fishing places less abundant. Yet, in all the treaties, the agents promise them, on part of the President, whom they call their Great Father, protection and privileges that are never realized. Is it, therefore, astonishing that the savages give the whites the name forked-tongues, or liars?[58]

General Wright, too, needed the help of Father Joset to bring about an end to the hostilities and to have the tribes involved in the war assembled for the signing of a peace treaty. This treaty, however, was between a mighty foe and a weak, conquered enemy. Outside force could not develop peaceful attitudes and secure permanent peace. This delicate work was left for Father De Smet to accomplish. His influence among the many Indian tribes had come to the notice of the United States Government, which had made Father the intermediary peace officer between the Indians and the Federal Government on several difficult occasions. In 1852, Senator Benton had said that:

---

[56] Michael, a Colville Indian, to Father De Smet, October 28, 1858. Missouri Archives quoted by Garraghan, *op. cit.,* II, 338.

[57] R. Ignatius Burns, S.J., *A Jesuit in the War Against the Northern Tribes,* 44. Reprint from the *Records of the American Catholic Historical Society,* Philadelphia (LXI:1, March, 1950).

[58] De Smet to the editor of the *Precis Historiques,* Brussels, December 30, 1854, quoted in *Western Missions,* 214–215.

Father De Smet could do more for the Indians, more for their welfare and keeping them in peace and friendship with the United States than an army with banners.[59]

Father De Smet at the beginning of 1858, resigned his position as army chaplain in the Utah expedition, but the Secretary of War did not accept his resignation on account of the Indian wars west of the Rocky Mountains. Father was notified by telegraph to proceed to New York and embark there with General Harney for the Isthmus of Panama and from there to Vancouver. Arriving in Vancouver Father De Smet was asked by the commanding officer to go to the mountain tribes and establish peaceful relations with the government. Father was only too happy to see all his old friends among the Indians whom he had not seen for twelve years. He stopped at Walla Walla to visit the hostages of the war who were released at Father's request. He visited all his former missions and mentioned "a small portion of lawless Kettlefalls." He returned, April 16, 1859, accompanied by nine chiefs to Vancouver. Among these chiefs was Chief Dennis Zenemtietze, or Thunders-robe, of the Skoyelpi tribe from Colville. This chief and Chief Theodosius Kolasket had kept the Kettle Falls Indians from joining the war.[60]

While in Vancouver, Father De Smet wrote to Captain Alfred Pleasonton, on May 25, 1859:

> During my stay among the Rocky Mountain Indians in the long and dreary winter, from the 21st of November last until end of April, I have carried out, as far as lay in my power, the instructions of the general. I succeeded, I think, in removing many doubts and prejudices against the intentions of the Government, and against the whites generally, which were lurking in the minds of a great number of the most influential Indians. I held frequent conversations with the chieftains of the Coeur d'Alenes, the Spokans, several of the Skoyelpies, or Kettlefalls, and lower Kalispels, who had chiefly aided, particularly the two first mentioned tribes; in their lawless and savage attacks on Colonel Steptoe, and their war with Colonel Wright.[61]

The chiefs returned to their homes from Vancouver three weeks later with Father De Smet and remained peaceful. To protect the Indians from the encroachments of the whites Father De Smet had suggested

---

[59] Gilbert J. Garraghan, S.J., quoting Senator Benton *Chapters in Frontier History*, 171.

[60] De Smet, *New Indian Sketches*, 88; 131.

[61] De Smet, Chaplain of U.S.A., to Pleasonton, Captain, 2d dragoons, A.A. Adjutant General, May 25, 1859. *Excutive Documents No. 65. Affairs in Oregon, House of Representatives, Thirty-Sixth Congress, First Session*, 141–143. See also *ibid.*, Father De Smet's plan, 147–149.

a plan to isolate the Indians from the whites. He would have liked to see the Indians in a part of the country by themselves, where game and fish abound, where there would be enough resources to make a living, and where good agricultural land would be available. General Harney writing to General Scott mentioned this plan. The General then continues:

> The history of the Indian race on this continent has shown that the missionary succeeded where the soldier and the civilian have failed; it would be well for us to profit by the lessons its experience teaches in an instance which offers so many advantages to the white as well as the red man, and adopt the wise and humane suggestion of Father De Smet.[62]

Before we examine the repercussions of the Indian wars in the Okanogan Valley, we have to get acquainted with the history of a tribe not mentioned in early fur-trading relations but coming into prominence chiefly through its leader, Chief Moses. Often we read of the Isle de Pierre, the Sinkaieus, Sin-Kahyoush, Kawachkin, Columbia, and Moses tribes. Curtis names other related bands. The Sinkumkunatkuh were near the mouth of the sink of Crab Creek; above them were the Sinkolkoluminuh. "Then followed in succession the Stapisknuh, the Skukulatkuh, the Skoahchnuh, the Skihlkintnuh, and finally, the Skultaqchinuh, a little above the Wenatchee river."[63]

The most important of this group were the Skoahchnuh at Rock Island rapids, opposite the mouth of Moses Coulee. Their chief, Sokultahlkosum or Sulk-stalk-skosum, had been born during a partial solar eclipse. His name indicated, according to Judge Brown, "a piece split from the sun." The whites called him "Half Sun." He was considered head chief of all the bands named. Curtis mentions that according to his son, Qai-it-sa, Sulk-stack-skosum was a "rover and a fighter." He used to lead some of his people into the Missouri River plain together with Okanogans, Spokans and Coeur d'Alenes for the buffalo hunt. It was while there that he answered the challenge of a Blackfoot chief and met his death about 1847.[64] After the "Half Sun's" death his son, Quiltti-ne-nock, took over the leadership of the Columbias. He took part in the Walla Walla Council but did not sign. It had been agreed that the Sinkiuse and other tribes up the Columbia to the mouth of the Okanogan River should be placed on the Yakima reservation.

---

[62] General Harney to General Scott, Thirty-Sixth Congress, *op. cit.*, 140–141.

[63] Curtis, *op. cit.*, VII, 66 ff.

[64] Judge W. C. Brown, mimeographed copy of manuscript. Also: Theo H. Scheffer, "Chief Moses," *Spokesman-Review*, March 29, 1953, 8–9; Click Relander, *Drummers and Dreamers*, 178–181.

Quilt-ti-ne-nock and his younger brother, Moses, followed Ka-mi-akin's summons to help fight the whites in 1855. A stray bullet struck Moses, but he was not wounded. This made Moses believe he was invulnerable and a medicine man. Quilt-ti-ne-nock and his brother participated in fighting Governor Stevens' escort after the second Walla Walla Council had been broken off in 1856. Quilt-ti-ne-nock was killed in 1858 and Moses became the leader of his tribe. His influence among neighboring tribes became great; his hatred of the whites increased for a time.

In the spring of 1858, three miners on their way to the gold discoveries on the Fraser River were attacked north of Palmer Lake in the Okanogan Valley. One was shot; the others escaped. The Okanogan Hudson's Bay Company trail leads directly to the mines. In spite of dangers from the hostile Indians a group of a hundred and fifty miners, only partly armed, congregated for greater protection in Walla Walla and chose David McLaughlin as their guide. Scouts were appointed and always had to be in advance of the party. They had about 450 pack mules in their train, a special attraction to the Indians who were lying in wait to steal them. Moses wanted to avenge the death of his brother, Quilt-ti-ne-nock, who had been shot by a miner. He instigated his cousin, the Chelan chief, In-no-mo-secha, to help arouse the Okanogans. This chief in turn rode up to Chief Sarsapkin and won him over to take command of the attacking Indians in the canyon known today as McLaughlin's Canyon. The Chelan chief then went back to Old Fort Okanogan where he induced the miners to take the trail through the canyon. While the miners were on their way Sarasapkin's Okanogans and the Chelans were busy felling trees to trap the miners. Robert Frost's story in *Ka-mi-akin* relates that two hundred Indians engaged in the fight that followed after the careful scouts of the miners detected an Indian hiding in the rocks. The miners were able to take their horses down to the river and hide and fight Indian fashion. While some kept up the fight others would build rafts for crossing the river, which they accomplished during the night. They camped for several days to take care of their wounded and to bury their six dead. The Indians could be seen in groups walking off toward Chelan and the Columbia River.

The miners were on the way up the river to the camping ground which is Oroville today, where new trouble awaited them. They had taken an Indian as a hostage. During the night the Indians tried to dash through their camp and stampede the horses and free the hostage. The Indians did not succeed. During the next day the Indians were finally coaxed into the miners' camp by the half-breeds who could speak their language. The Indians came; Chief Tonasket among them. The miners gave the Indians presents and were not bothered any more. Mr. Frost noticed the fine-looking Indians.[65]

Mr. Guy Waring wrote about the commander of the Indian fighters whom he knew in later years:

> Sarsapekin, as I later learned, was a local chieftain who when young, had been an outlaw and a murderer of whites. He had killed several white men back in the fifties as they were on their way to the gold fields of British Columbia, and was highly respected and feared by his own people.[66]

Chief Sarsapekin remained a pagan. We will hear more about him.

Chief Tonasket was mentioned for the first time in the written records in connection with the Indians coming into the miners' camp. Authors writing on this subject where Chief Tonasket showed up with the good-looking Indians were not sure if Chief Tonasket or Chief Factor Angus McDonald stopped the fight. Records from the National Archives show that it was Chief Tonasket. At the council held at Osoyoos, July 3, 1870, with government officials, Tonasket made a speech in which he shows his attitude toward the white man. The following is a part of the speech:

> I never changed my views of the White Man; I never threatened one. When my people fought the Whites I was not here, when I heard of it I came and found that they were going to fight again, they were preparing to get their horses to fight some White men down below, I got on my Horse, took my Gun and when I got to the place I found the Whites and Indians with their guns levelled on each other. I rode between them and told them to stop, they put down their Guns and I told my Father I would fight against him if he molested the White Man who was going to dig Gold. I pitied the *Wearied Miner* and his *Hungry Horse* for he was afraid to go to the Woods for fear of a lurking foe, or to let his Horse graze for fear of its being stolen. My Father listened to me and laid down his Gun and his young men did the same, and from that time they have been at peace with the Whites.[67]

The miners were followed by the cattlemen driving cattle through the valley to the gold mines of British Columbia in spite of the danger of theft. Three years after the McLaughlin Canyon fight, Splawn witnessed

[65] A. J. Splawn, quoting Frost's story in *KA-MI-AKIN: The Last Hero of the Yakimas*, 107–115.

[66] Waring, *op. cit.*, 72.

[67] "Speech made by Tomaskut, Head Chief of the Okanogans at Council held at Soo-yoo-oos July 3rd 1870," *Records of the Bureau of Indian Affairs*, Washington Superintendency Letters Received, 1861–1874.

a scalp dance near Loop Loop Creek. Indian outlaws had stolen cattle and he was forced to shoot and wound an Indian. Here again Chief Tonasket appeared and gave the cattle drivers an escort of his men until they would be out of danger. Splawn mentions that he heard that Tonasket was a Catholic. Tonasket in his relation to the white man is always the honest, straightforward man of principles.

In spite of the fact that St. Paul's Mission at Kettle Falls was closed, Father Joset kept on administering to the Indians periodically. Mission life at St. Paul's was not all deprivations and adversities; it had its rewarding aspects too. Father Joset speaks of the good example of some of his boys whom he had instructed. One was an orphan boy who had been baptized Ignace by Father Joset and raised by him after his father had died of the smallpox. While on a sick call in 1860 Father Joset was informed that Ignace was living at the Okanogan River where he had a farm. Ignace was working like an apostle, "reproving the sinners, encouraging the good, baptizing the dying." Father Grassi gave permission to Father Joset to visit Ignace. Father Joset made the trip over the mountains while the snow reached even to his horse's belly if only he could instruct Ignace better. First only a few Indians assembled after Father reached Ignace's place. The others had scattered to look for food. Slowly, however, the people came in small bands. They stayed a few days until they had received the sacraments. Some were baptized. Those who had been baptized were prepared for and received confession and Communion. Father Joset found the Okanogan people in the best disposition. They told him that no priest had visited them since Father De Smet had baptized them in 1842. Chief Tonasket arrived as one of the last and Father Joset was fully satisfied with him. The only one who was "very kind and serviceable" but could not hear of abandoning polygamy was Chief Sarsapkin.

Father Joset had resolved to return to St. Paul's but, because his horse had strayed away, he was forced to stay. This was one of the many incidents in the lives of the missionaries where it might be said Divine Providence could be seen at work. Before the priest's horse could be found, news came that the brother of Chief Sarsapkin had accidentally shot himself in the knee and that he was bleeding badly. Father borrowed a horse and although he reached the wounded chief after the bleeding had been stopped, he did find that a little child in the camp had been bitten by a rattlesnake. He baptized her and then sent somebody to the nearest trading post for serum. Then the chief told him that another baby needed to be baptized. The Indian mother was alone after baptism in a lodge when the priest asked her for the names of the parents. He was told that the wounded chief was the father. "Are you baptized?" he asked. When she told him she was, he said: "And how is it that you, a child of God, are living with an infidel in polygamy. . . ?" "It was the will of my father," she replied. We know that among the Okanogans and related tribes the daughters of the families were sold to their husbands. Father Joset went to see the chief and gave him the following lecture:

> I knew well that you were not baptized and that you had several wives, still when I heard you were hurt, though I knew that you were not baptized, that you were a polygamist, I did not hesitate to come to you, and I spoke not one hard word. But now I must scold you for a very bad thing: that woman being baptized is a child of God, and you stole her from God her father, who is most unwilling that you should have her.[68]

The chief did not speak a word, and Father Joset never saw him again but he heard that very soon the chief sent away all his women, was instructed, baptized, married in the Church, and lived as a good Christian. He was given the name of Francois. He became instrumental in having his camp embrace the faith.

Gradually, from the early missions, especially from old St. Paul's Mission at the Kettle Falls, the influence of the teachings of the missionaries spread farther in the Okanogan, Middle, and Upper Columbia Valleys. Peace is a prerequisite for every growth. The Christian civilization as the foundation of culture and justice developed slowly as more peaceful years followed. Much arduous missionary labor still lay ahead. It had required the love and foresight of a Father De Smet to lay the foundations; it required many more men of vision and faith to build up these missions.

---

[68] *The Joset Papers,* Mss., OPA.

CHAPTER V

St. Francis Regis Mission in the Colville Valley

IN 1862, when Father Joseph Giorda, S.J., became the superior of the Rocky Mountain missions, new missionary zeal was enkindled. The old pioneer missions, among them St. Paul's at Kettle Falls, were reopened, and, later, new establishments were added. Father Giorda recalled former Rocky Mountain missionaries from the California missions and ordered Father Joset from the Coeur d'Alene Mission back to his former place of apostolic work, St. Paul's.

When Father De Smet made his last visit[1] to the Rocky Mountain missions in 1863, Father Joset was absent from St. Paul's. However, Father Joset in a letter to Father De Smet described in detail his work. This letter, written after Father Joset's return to St. Paul's gives us an important historical date not mentitoned anywhere else. It was in 1863 that the last church of St. Paul's was rebuilt and that St. Paul's again became the center from which the missionary activities to the many surrounding tribes were carried out.

We quote from Father Joset's letter, retaining, of course, as in all other quotations from this priest (as well as those of other foreign-born priests) his own idiom:

> Your reverence [sic] knows that I am at St. Paul's to reopen the mission. I have many excursions to make, among the Kalispels of the Great Lakes of the Columbia, among the Pend d'Oreilles of the Bay, on Clark's Fork, one of the main tributaries, among the Simpoils, the Okinagans — but the church to finish, the house to build, keep me often at Colville, to my great regret.[2]

[1] This visit must have been about September 26, 1863. Father De Smet reached Sacred Heart Mission, Coeur d'Alene, on September 18 and left again on the twenty-third. See CR, *De Smet*, III, 803.

[2] Joset to De Smet, quoted in CR, *De Smet*, III, 801–802.

He continues, that he was looking forward to the arrival of his companion, Father Joseph Menetrey, to share the abundant missionary burden. Father Joset had been in Walla Walla to buy his provisions and had just returned in time to bury two of his parishioners. He writes: ". . . tomorrow I go again to the new church, to try to push the work." The priest mentions the great number of parishioners — the middle of October he had registered the eighty-second birth. He is living in a tent, regulating his time by the stars and by the sun when the weather is clear. His many activities took up all his time. Beside the Christian tribes, Father Joset speaks about the "the Simpoils, the Tlakam, the people of the stone Islands." This is the first time that the Moses tribe, which later became famous, was mentioned by a missionary. It shows us that St. Paul's mission territory is widening. The missionary mentions his white parishioners whom he seldom sees, except on Sundays, unless he goes after them. Inspite of bad influences, however, he is happy about his good Christians:

> Although whiskey is making great ravages among the Indians, especially at Colville, still the Lord has preserved himself a goodly number untouched by corruption. With them it is always the same avidity to hear the word of life, the same eagerness to approach the sacraments.[3]

Father Joset expresses the need for priests in these words: "The little ones are begging for bread but there is none who breaks it for them." He prays and trusts in the divine goodness that old St. Paul's, once reestablished, will be able to give more priestly services.[4]

Indian Agent George A. Paige, in his first annual report on the Colville Indians, speaks about the influence of the Jesuit missionaries:

> The Colvilles — Though, as a tribe, they may be considered industrious and well disposed, yet there are among them several drunken vagabonds who can be induced to labor for no other purpose than to raise the means for the purchase of Whiskey. Drunkenness, however, prevails to a much less extent than among the Coast tribes, attributable, as I conceive, to the influence exerted by the two Catholic missionaries residing in the Valley.[5]

St. Paul's had a short-lived revival. The tribes appreciated the opening of their mission and for the next years showed progress in goodness. However, this progress was hampered and in danger of being ruined

---

[3] Joset to De Smet, CR, *De Smet*, III, 802.

[4] *Ibid.*

[5] George A. Paige, "Annual Report," Fort Colville, W.T., July 8, 1865, in "Report of the Secretary of the Interior," *Executive Documents, House of Representatives, Thirty-Ninth Congress, First Session,* 266.

by the scandalous example of the whites: miners, soldiers, and settlers who gradually wanted to push the Indians from the Colville Valley. On November 4, 1866, Father Joset writes again to Father De Smet:

> I think that I am in the most difficult situation of all the missionaries of the Mountains. The others have their neophytes more or less isolated and even far away from the contact with the whites and consequently less exposed to temptation. Here the neophytes find themselves constantly aroused by corruption and there are continuous calumnies against the missionary. Nevertheless a great many have not knelt down before idols. Our poor chapel is visited frequently. It has become too small.[6]

Father Joset then tells how solemnly the month of March was observed in honor of St. Joseph on whose feast day there were one hundred and twenty-one Communions. The great saint brought him at the end of the month nine unbelievers, whom he had never seen, asking to be baptized. Some families had spent Lent near St. Paul's in order to fulfill their Easter duties. Confessions lasted nearly all through Holy Week, and on Easter there was such a crowd that many could not find a place in order to attend a second Mass.[7]

The following year Father Joset speaks again about the progress made by the Colville tribes. The chiefs had united and, helped by their young people, had made all public disorders disappear. Three years before, the missionary had counted twenty-eight scandalous unions among the Lake tribe, but now only four were left, and these people were forced to leave the tribe. Gambling and sorceries were banished from the camps of the chiefs and there were fewer cases of drunkenness.[8] Fathers Urban Grassi and Joseph Bandini had in 1869 established a new mission about fifteen miles downriver from St. Paul's, which was not successful and had to be later abandoned.[9]

In 1859 a military post had been erected about three miles north from modern Colville and south of what is called today Mill Creek. This post changed its name from Harney's Depot to Fort Colville in 1860. It must not be confused with the old historic Hudson's Bay Company Fort Colville on the Columbia River. Across Mill Creek a settlement sprang up and was called Pinkney City after Maj. Pinkney Lugenbeel, the commander of the fort. According to Thomas I. Oakshott, from the approximately 290 soldiers at Fort Colville, 117 had been

---

[6] Joset to De Smet, November 4, 1866, in De Smet, *Lettres Choisies*, III, 228–229.
[7] *Ibid.*
[8] Joset to De Smet, February 26, 1867, *op. cit.*, III, 232–233 (translated by Sister M. Agathe, O.P.).
[9] File on St. Francis Regis Mission, no author, Mss., OPA.

born in Ireland.[10] The Catholic soldiers helped build the church of the Immaculate Conception near the fort, probably in 1862. Father Grassi realized that this church and St. Paul's at Kettle Falls were too near together to be served efficiently and economically. In 1869, he bought forty acres from a French Canadian and established the second St. Francis Regis Mission about halfway between Pinkney City and St. Paul's. This residence was built merely for the use of the Fathers from which they would depart on their missionary journeys.

The following quote is of great historical importance. We notice the difficulties some of the early busy missionaries had with the English language. Father Joset was a Swiss, many priests were Italians, others were Frenchmen who volunteered for the Rocky Mountain missions.

An entry in the *Diary of St. Francis Regis Mission,* May 11, 1870, tells about a missionary trip of Father Joset:

> Today about 10 o'clock Fr. Joset started for a missionary tour to the Okinagan and then down the Columbia River; purposed to remain at the Sanpoilshi at the home of their fishing the salmon, then come up the Columbia and be back to St. Paul's by the time the Spoielpi will begin their fishing at the Kettle Falls (St. Paul) completing his tour in a month and a half; taking for provisions: 100 lb. white flour, 20 lb. short., 20 lb. dry smoked meat, coffee, etc. He has been instructed to leave to Fr. Pandosi a chapel on the very division line, but to notify this to the same Father, that we may be certain that those Indians are attended to.[11]

According to this entry, Father Joset was on a missionary trip to the many bands of the Okanogan and Sanpoil Indians. He took advantage of the fishing seasons in order to meet the majority of the tribal members at their fishing centers. The missionaries had developed a certain routine round-trip route to accomplish as much as possible. The missionary was supposed to visit all the bands of Indians below the Canadian boundary. "On the very division line" between Canada and the United States very probably were the Inkameep Indians, as we will see. The Reverend Charles M. Pandosi, an Oblate priest, had moved from the territory of the Yakima Indians to British Columbia after the 1858 War.

On June 20, the entry in the *Diary* is as follows:

> Fr. Joset returned from his Missionary trip very well pleased with the disposition of the Okinakein, but displeased, though not discouraged, at the coldness of the Simpoilshi — he remained 3 weeks with the latter. He told me he wished to bring a boy from the Okinakein to remain in the house. I have acceded.[12]

---

[10] Thomas I. Oakshott, *Colville: City of Proud Heritage,* 5.
[11] *Diary of St. Francis Regis Mission,* May 11, 1870, Mss., OPA.
[12] *Ibid.,* June 20, 1870.

Father Joset gives a more detailed account of this trip to Father De Smet. Ignace, whom Father Joset had raised, had acted again like an apostle in the Okanogan Valley. At Father's arrival Ignace mentioned a woman who was about to die, living about eight miles from his place. Father Joset found her husband just returning from a great journey and both in excellent disposition. The man had been baptized in his childhood and needed only short instruction to be prepared for confession and Holy Communion; the woman was baptized and the marriage blessed. Then Ignace pointed to a father, mother, and three children, saying: "They have stolen their prayers; they never have seen a priest." Many years ago Father Joset had baptized the man's parents at St. Paul's. The priest wanted to know if the man knew his religion. The man answered by at once kneeling down, closing his eyes, and with real fervor reciting his prayers. Where had he learned them? Ignace had said he had stolen them. The truth was the man had used all the meetings with the neophytes to instruct himself in his religion. Ignace was chosen as godfather and named this Indian "Abraham," which seemed very fitting as he loooked like a venerable patriarch. The whole family was received into the Church.

The poor Okanogans were astonished that Father Joset did so much for them. This priest was then the only one who spoke the language of this tribe. The missionary administered the sacraments in seven different places. Whole families came to be baptized and even the pagan chief encouraged his relatives to see the priest. Father Joset had not too much to do to prepare the people; Ignace again had done his job well. The tribal members felt very keenly the need for a church and wanted to build one with their own money. Father Joset's wish would have been to have moving chapels, but this would have been an impossibility because of the lack of roads. No white settlements existed then in the territory. The Okanogans told Father Joset: "When the whites have to pass through this valley, they whip their horses in order to cross the country as fast as possible." Father Joset speaks about the difficulty of uniting the tribes.[13] Fifteen more long years will pass before the Okanogans can call a priest their own.

Scarcely had St. Francis Regis mission been reestablished when agitation for the removal of the Indians to reservations was stirred up again by the settlers who coveted the lush meadows and fertile fields of the Colville Valley. Father De Smet speaking about the Indians and their missions in the Inland Empire and of the white adventurers who made

---

[13] Joset to De Smet, October 6, 1870, in De Smet, *Lettres Choisies*, III, 281–284 (translated by Sister M. Agathe, O.P.).

use of every means "to get rid of the Indians or force them to move" had in 1870 this fatherly advice for his brother priests:

> If the missionaries effect real good among the savages, under the present circumstance, they will need a profound humility, a truly disinterested zeal, and above all a sovereign scorn for the judgments of men.[14]

The Indian agent, William P. Winans, had closed his annual report of 1870 by saying, that "The Upper Spokane, Calispels, Colvilles, Lakes, and Okanogans are Catholics. The Fathers reside with the Colvilles, and visit the other tribes during the year. They have no schools among them, but wish them."[15] Was it prudent to open schools while the Indian policies of the United States were so unsettled? The original Colville Reservation, created April 9, 1872, included the Colville Valley and therefore St. Francis Regis Mission. Three months later, July 2, 1872, the boundary was changed by President Grant to the north side of the Columbia River. This action excluded the mission from the land of the Indians, hampered the good work done at St. Francis Regis, and foreshadowed its eventual closing. The coming events, however, could not at that time be foreseen.

In spite of reservation policies and local politics, the Jesuit Fathers decided in 1873 to move the central location of St. Francis Regis Mission about three fourths of a mile nearer to St. Paul's. This became the third St. Francis Regis Mission.

Concerning the extensive landholdings of this new place that became the early property of the mission, Mrs. Helen Toulou, whom we mentioned before, gives us some information. The Jesuit Fathers at Kettle Falls had recognized the great influence of Chief Kee-Kee-tum-nouse of the Lake tribe and had converted his wives and children. The wives removed to other places and awaited the chief's decision as to which of the women he wanted to marry in the Church. The chief was baptized, lawfully married, and died shortly after. Then Chief Kin-kan-nouha, an early convert, became chief. He and his family were the aboriginal owners of what later became known as Ward, Washington. The property started from a small lake on the hill east of where the old cemetery of St. Francis Regis is now and extended to the Colville River. Chief Kin-kan-nouha had an agreement with the Jesuits that as long as the Fathers maintained a church and a Catholic school they should have the use of the land. If they abandon their missionary activities, then the

---

[14] De Smet quoted by CR, *De Smet*, III, 931.

[15] William P. Winans, "Annual Report of 1870," in "Report of the Secretary of the Interior," *House of Representatives, Forty-First Congress, Third Session, Executive Documents* I (Part 4), 490.

land would revert to its original owners and heirs if any survived, otherwise to the Colville tribe. Kin-kan-nouha saw a church and a convent established before he died. He had lived in a small cabin that stood where now the highway between Kettle Falls and Colville is situated. The chief had lost his sons through a smallpox epidemic but his nephew, the later Chief Bernard, survived. Before the chief died he had his nephew informed of the agreement reached with the Fathers.[16] The Colville Valley was at that time still tribal land.

We have seen that Old St. Paul's was too small for festive occasions. At the beginning of March in 1873, the Indians were busy loading the logs for the new St. Francis Regis Church. They were very eager to begin the church.[17] The building of the mission seems to have been like an anchor of hope that the Indians were to be allowed to stay in the Colville Valley. On April 17 of the same year, Father Paschal Tosi, one of the missionaries stationed at St. Francis Regis, was able to say Mass in this uncompleted new church. Father Diomedi, in his report of his missionary journeys in 1879, mentions that this church was ninety-five feet long and sixty feet wide.[18] Even the Indian agent seems to have been impressed with the size of this church. After stating that the Indians, with the exception of the Sanpoils, are peaceable and well disposed, and that they have made great advances in Christianity and civilization, he says:

> There are quite a number of thrifty farmers among them, and they show more disposition to work and make their living by the arts of civilized life than any Indians I have met with on this coast during a residence of more than twenty years. The Colvilles have this year built for themselves a large church of hewn logs, capable of accommodating nearly a thousand persons, and they take great pride in their handiwork.[19]

The year of 1873 was of great importance and had its historical significance for the Indian tribes of the Inland Empire. It was on May 23 that the saintly Father De Smet, the founder of the early missions, died. According to Fuller's study:

> Besides his constant wanderings over the western country during many years, he crossed the Atlantic nineteen times and made one voyage

---

[16] Mrs. Helen Toulou, *Manuscript Book;* also through interviews.

[17] *Diary of St. Francis Regis Mission,* March 10, 1873.

[18] Alexander Diomendi, S.J., "Extract From a Letter of a Rocky Mountain Jesuit Missionary," *The Indian Sentinel,* 1906, 28.

[19] John A. Simms, Special Indian Agent, "Annual Report for 1873," to General Milroy, Superintendent of Indian Affairs, Olympia, Washington Territory, in *House Executive Documents, Forty-Third Congress, First Session* (Vol. 4, Part 5), 683.

around the Horn and two by way of Panama. The total mileage of his journeys, at a time when travel was difficult, was from seven to nine times around the earth.[20]

Also in 1873, formal education for Indian children was introduced at St. Francis Regis Mission. The Indian agent reports that

> A day school for Indian children has been organized January 1, 1873, and placed under the instruction of Father Tosi, at St. Francis Regis Mission, in Colville Valley. The average attendance is forty-five. The progress made much exceeding my expectation.[21]

This school was discontinued March 31, because the families went to the root grounds. On September 20, 1873, four Sisters of Providence arrived at St. Francis Regis Mission to take over the school for girls. Some log cabins had been erected for temporary use by the Sisters.[22] Agent Simms reports:

> I have recently established a boarding and industrial school, as directed by yourself, and placed the same in charge of Sisters of Charity, the Catholic Fathers having kindly proffered the necessary buildings for temporary use of the school.[23]

When the boarding school was organized it was understood that the Indian Department would grant an annual appropriation of $5,000 for the Chehalis and Colville schools together. The Colville school had started on October 1, 1873, in charge of the Sisters of Charity. "The progress made was gratifying in every respect." Then on March 13, 1874, Agent Simms was directed to suspend the school as the allowance had been reduced to $1,000. However, the Sisters of Charity continued the school at their own expense. Agent Simms was hoping that the government would reimburse them. This was another occasion for the Indians to mistrust the government, as the agent tells us

> That was a severe blow to our educational prospects, and one which the Indians took very much to heart. They had taken great pride in the school and the progress their children were making, and they could not, or were not, willing to understand this sudden action of the Government, and all their grievances, real or imaginary were renewed.[24]

Mr. Simms closes his official account by congratulating the Indians under

---

20 Fuller, *The Inland Empire of the Pacific Northwest,* II, 101.
21 Simms, "Annual Report for 1873," *op. cit.*
22 *Chroniques de la Providence du Sacre Coeur Collville,* W. T. Mss., 1.
23 Simms, *op. cit.*
24 Simms, "Annual Report for 1874" *Executive Documents, Forty-Second Congress, Second Session* (Vol. 6, Part 5), 328.

his charge upon their continued improvements in leading morally good lives and in their growing zeal toward "Observance of their religious duties, more than three hundred of them having received the sacrament of confirmation at the hands of the Right Rev. Bishop of Nesqually during the recent visit."[25]

The agent's praise of the work of the Sisters and Fathers becomes still more pronounced in the 1875 report:

> Owing to the untiring devotion of the Sisters of Charity, who have charge of the boarding school, the progress made by the children in their studies is highly gratifying. Besides the branches ordinarily taught in primary schools, the girls are taught sewing, knitting, house-keeping, and to cut and make their own clothes. The boys saw wood and work in the garden, and have with the assistance of the girls, under the direction of their teacher raised sufficient vegetables for the use of the school.[26]

Mr. Simms then gives credit to the Jesuit Fathers and their influence in maintaining peace:

> The self-sacrificing devotion of the Jesuit Fathers to their flock renders the work of the Indian agent comparatively easy, and to their influence more than to any other are we indebted for the long peace that has prevailed on this frontier.[27]

The danger of closing the school was again averted in 1876, when on February 21, the Indian agent came to St. Francis Regis Mission to stop the school saying that the government gave no appropriation in that quarter. The Fathers, however, kept the school open. The very next day the entry in the *Diary* of the mission states: "The Indians help in cutting logs for the Sisters' new house."[28]

As professional educators, the Jesuits tried very early to establish a school in Pinkney City. There a county seat had been erected January 18, 1859, under the name of Spokane County, which name remained only four years and was then changed to Stevens County with the same county seat. Then, on January 19, 1864, Spokane County was annexed to Stevens County. The name of the country was not used until October 30, 1879, when it became an independent county with the county seat at Spokane Falls.[29] Father Militry, S.J., successfully petitioned the board

---

[25] *Ibid.*

[26] Simms, "Annual Report for 1875," to Hon. E. P. Smith, Commissioner of Indian Affairs, September 1, 1875, *The Report of the Commissioner of Indian Affairs,* 1875, 362.

[27] *Ibid.*

[28] *Diary of St. Francis Regis Mission,* February 21 and 22, 1876.

[29] Oakshott, *op. cit.,* p. 3.

of county commissioners for permission to open a private school. According to a report of the Indian agent, August 1, 1879, this school also was taught by the Sisters of Charity. The report states in part:

> The boarding school established in December last has been in charge of the Sisters of Charity, and the progress made by the scholars is satisfactory in every respect. . . .
>
> The Colville school, in which forty scholars are being boarded, clothed, and educated by the government, is also in charge of Sisters of Charity, and has also been conducted with the same satisfactory results; the great proficiency of the scholars in their various studies greatly surprised the large number of citizens who were present at the recent commencement.[30]

The agent in the same report praises the eagerness of the Indians to have their children educated and regrets the largeness of the number of children who could not be admitted for want of money. Not only the children profited by education, as the agent tells us. He visited the farms near the mission and along the Columbia River and noticed the good fencing, the many acres under cultivation and the comfortable cabins. The Lake Indians had constructed a small chapel, eighteen by twenty-five feet, with a board floor and a cabin for the priest's use when he visited them.[31] This showed clearly the educational influence of the Jesuit Fathers not only on religion and morals but also on the practical and civilizing aspects toward self-support and dignity of work.

Father Urban Grassi, S.J., became superior of St. Francis Regis Mission in 1876. Fathers called upon to teach had to have their teaching certificates from the county superintendent of schools. A Mr. Rickey observed:

> During the incumbency of Mr. Hofstetter, Father Grassi, a Catholic priest, came to the county seat to take a teacher's examination from the superintendent. The father made his mission known to Mr. Hofstetter. "Well," said the superintendent, "You know how to teach, don't you?" The priest replied that he thought he did, but that he believed it was customary for the superintendent to ascertain the fact before the teacher was allowed to enter his duties. "Well, you must know more about school matters than I do." "I do not know that I do," replied the father. "If you hold to that assertion, Father Grassi, I cannot issue you a certificate to teach."[32]

---

[30] Simms to Commissioner of Indian Affairs, August 1, 1879, in *Annual Report of the Commissioner of Indian Affairs to the Secretary of the Interior for the Year 1789*, 141.

[31] *Ibid.*

[32] Mr. Rickey quoting Hofstetter and Father Grassi in *An Illustrated History of Stevens, Ferry, Okanogan and Chelan Counties*, Richard F. Steele, ed., 174.

Father Grassi then changed his approach and finally admitted that he was better informed in school matters and had a better education than the superintendent of schools. Whereupon he received his certificate without examination.

The report of Indian Agent Simms for 1881 says that

> A large school building 60 x 40 feet was built during the year by the Jesuit Fathers at the Colville Mission for the better accommodation of the schoolboys, who are under the constant supervision of the male teacher, under whose direction they are making satisfactory progress.[33]

An anonymous author in an article, "The Missions of the Rocky Mountains in 1881," stated the reasons why the boys were taught later by men teachers and by the Jesuit Fathers:

> This school supported at Government expense, was under the charge of Sisters of Charity, but they were unwilling to keep the boys, and as the agent was dissatisfied with the management, and there was danger that the school might fall into secular, and perhaps Protestant hands, we have been obliged to take charge of it. The Sisters have a flourishing school for girls, with fifty boarders, supported by the government.[34]

While the Yakima and Wenatchee Valleys experienced the disquietude, the excitements, and the insecurity of their white settlers during the Nez Perce War, Colville Valley was a haven of peace, mainly because of the influence exerted by the Jesuit Fathers and the Sisters of Charity through the education and the guidance given to the Indians, as the agent himself asserted:

> This agency is the only one within a radius of three hundred and fifty miles where the aid of the military has not been invoked either to supress hostilities or to prevent an anticipated outbreak, and during the two wars that have occurred — that of the Nez Perces and of the Bannacks, in 1878 — not an Indian was disaffected, or left the agency to join the hostiles.[35]

The charity of the Providence Sisters merited outstanding praise of the new agent, Mr. Waters:

> During last winter the measles made sad havoc among the children, and many from want of proper care and attention died. At one time at

---

[33] Simms, "Annual Report for 1881," in *Annual Report of the Commissioner of Indian Affairs to the Secretary of the Interior for the Year 1881,* 158.
[34] Anonymous, "The Missions of the Rocky Mountains in 1881," *WL* (12:1, 1883), 53.
[35] Simms, "Annual Report for 1882," *op. cit.,* 1882, 152.

the Colville girls' school, 27 were sick; but owing to that loving care and devotion of the Sisters not a case was lost.[36]

Reading through the *Chroniques* of the Sisters we learned that they sent the healthy Indian girls home and kept the sick ones to be nursed back to health, while the Sacred Heart Academy for white girls kept its daily schedule and not one white girl caught the sickness. The Sisters "stormed heaven" for help and used the common means of prudent prevention, cleanliness and fumigation to arrest the spread of the sickness.[37]

Truth is objective; it cannot be interpreted subjectively. The same holds from goodness as it is done in human society. It does not matter who does the good, the main thing is that it is done. Our modern age has come far in developing real democratic interrelationships and appreciations among men of different denominations. We know that this situation did not prevail in early mission history. The new agent showed his humane and upright character when he acknowledged the good that was being done at St. Francis Regis Mission:

> Much hard work has been undergone and money spent by the Jesuit Fathers to erect these buildings for school purposes, and they ought to be (partly at least) reimbursed by the Government. I am a Protestant, but I must testify to the unswerving love and devotion that the Jesuits have for these schools. How much labor is expended by them in rescuing these children from the vices and miseries of the camps will perhaps never be known, but in the end, they will receive the mandate "Come up higher."[38]

According to the 1885 report a new school building had been erected, this time for the girls, at the expense of the mission. The pupils were given board, clothes, and tuition at the expense of the government of $108 per year per pupil, which was much less than the cost per pupil in the government's own schools.[39] The third St. Francis Regis Mission and its vicinity was later called Ward, Washington, and had its own post office. Mission authorities wanted to honor the young promising missionary, Thomas B. Ward, S.J., who had died in 1902.[40]

---

[36] Sidney D. Waters, "Annual Report, August 12, 1884," to Commissioner of Indian Affairs, *House Executive Documents, Forty-Eighth Congress, Second Session, 1884–1885* (Vol. 12), 204.

[37] *Chroniques,* 1884–1885.

[38] Waters, "Annual Report, 1884," *op. cit.*

[39] Waters, "Annual Report to Commissioner of Indian Affairs, 1885," in *Annual Report of the Commissioner of Indian Affairs to the Secretary of the Interior for the Year 1885,* 184–185.

[40] Courtesy of Mr. Van Peterson, S. J., in an interview with Rev. Paul Sauer, March 10, 1961. Also: *Catalogus Defunctorum Prov. California, S.J.*

Now let us follow the missionary and pastoral work done at St. Francis Regis Mission. The *Diary* under August 14, 1875, has the entry:

> Fr. Vanzina goes to St. Paul, where he will remain a while attending to the Indians, who are fishing.

Under August 24, we read:

> Fr. Tosi in the morning goes in buggy to St. Paul to take Fr. Vanzina home.[41]

Evidently old St. Paul's was still used temporarily during the fishing season. Gradually it fell into disrepair. The Indians who since time immemorial considered Kettle Falls their most important fishing center were gradually robbed of their rights until there were no fish and no Indians.

As formerly hundreds of Indians congregated at the Kettle Falls, so now these people, proud of the new St. Francis Regis Church which they had built, made this mission their place of union with all the neighboring tribes. Colorful tribal assemblies took place especially during the solemn feast days of the Church. Father Diomedi left us a description of how these were organized. The Okanogans and the Kalispels would send a messenger a day ahead saying that at a certain hour they would arrive at the church. Then the chiefs of the Kettle Falls tribes would notify their people to be ready to receive their friends. At the appointed hour when the incoming tribes came into sight of the mission, they would fire a salute which was answered from the plateau in front of the church and this salute continued as the horsemen advanced toward the mission. The Colville Indians bearing their flag would leave the church in double rows for the reception. The visitors would dismount about three hundred yards away from the church and tie their horses to the fences. With the chief in front they too would form a double row which dissolved into single line when they met the Colville tribes. The lines would pass each other and each would shake hands with the members of the incoming tribe. Then all would go into the church where they were greeted and given instructions as to the order to be observed.[42]

The *Diary* of the mission for the year 1874 tells us that for Corpus Christi, May 23, over one thousand Indians were assembled and that the three Fathers needed three days to hear all the confessions. The Lake, the Kettle Falls, and the Okanogan Indians are specially mentioned.[43] For Corpus Christi of 1876, we find the following entries:

---

[41] *Diary of St. Francis Regis Mission*, August 14 and 24, 1875.
[42] Diomedi, S.J., *WL* (32:2, 1893), 255–256.
[43] *Diary of St. Francis Regis Mission*, May 23, 1874, Mss. OPA.

May 10.   The Okinakein arrived about 350 altogether.

May 13.   The Kalispel Spokane came altogether and were met by the Okinakein and Skoilpi down the Mill.

May 19.   The Okinakein left the Mission altogether.[44]

How the Indians prepared themselves and how they celebrated the feast of Christmas is told by Father P. G. Guidi, S.J. About the middle of December, 1874, a group of Indians gathered around the church, coming from distances of ten, twenty, or even eighty miles in spite of the cold. The Jesuit Fathers inaugurated the first Forty Hours' Devotions three days before Christmas in 1874, during which the chiefs forbade all kinds of amusements and all unnecessary business. The Indians prepared themselves for the high feast by keeping their hour of adoration, while the priests were busy teaching the meaning of the Sacred Liturgy, training the altar boys, rehearsing the sacred songs, visiting the old and the sick in the camp, and administering the sacraments.

As the first signal for midnight Mass was given a mighty fire was enkindled on top of the hill opposite the church. At the second signal the Indians fired a salute. Then all the people filed in orderly procession into the spacious church singing a appropriate song. Father Guidi writes:

> High Mass began, the Indians forming the choir. I preached a short English sermon for many whites who were present, and we had four hundred and fifty communions. At the pressing request of our good people, an Indian went around after the Credo, taking a collection for the church, and he got from the Indians twenty-eight dollars, which in the following days were increased to seventy dollars — indeed a considerable sum for this poor flock.[45]

The Archdiocesan Archives of the Diocese of Seattle, Washington, preserve Father Tosi's census of the Catholic population depending for spiritual care on St. Francis Regis mission in 1877:

Recensement dans les Missions des R.R.P.P. Jesuites Par Rev. P. Tosi Oct. 1877 Missions des Indiens

		Eglise	Nombre de catholiques
Colville Indians	catholic	St. Francis Regis	750
Lakes Indians	cath	St. Paul	300
Schewile id.	cath		130
	protestant	45	

---

[44] *Ibid.*, May 10, 13, 19, 1876.

[45] P. G. Guidi, S.J., to Father A. Romano, S.J., January 22, 1875, *WL* (IV:2, 1875), 178–179.

Colville Mission

Okinakein id.	cath	1	St. Mary	530
		30		
Upper Spokane	cath	1	St. Michael	230
	infidels	90		
Lower Spokane —	cath			
snetotis	protestant			60
	protestants and			
	infidels	40		
zegzeges	cath			20
	protestants and			
	infidels	40		
Columbia Indians				
simpoilshi	inf.	120		
Nepelem	cath.			35
	inf.	40		
Chelence	inf.	60		
Simpikneusi	cath.			260
	inf.	45		
	non-Cath.	590	Cath.	3371
Whites Colville Valley	cath.			35[46]

This census shows that by 1877 all Sanpoil and Chelan Indians were still pagans; all Colville and Lake Indians were Catholics; the Moses tribe is not mentioned yet.

The missionaries traveled from St. Francis Regis Mission to the different tribes two or three times during the years and also on special calls. They never knew into what situations they would come, what dangers they would face. They needed their presence of mind to adjust to a given condition. The experiences of the missionaries are therefore most interesting. Father Diomedi related his experiences during a winter's excursion from St. Francis Regis Mission to the mouth of the Okanogan River and from there through the Okanogan Valley to Lake Osoyoos and into the Similkameen Mountains. At the foot of the hill where St. Francis Regis Mission is located there was during Father Diomedi's time an Indian settlement which extended along the Columbia River for several miles. For this particular trip, the missionary left his home mission on December 2, 1879. He knew that the roads were dangerous and that his trip in this season would take about three to four months. He needed a companion and therefore asked a good Indian guide by the name of Edward if he would have pity on the poor Indians who never see a priest and be his companion. Edward first was hesitant, then went home to see if his wife had provisions. He returned after three days fully prepared. Then Father assembled his provisions, which consisted of a sack of flour, some pounds of bacon, tobacco with which to pay the

[46] Archdiocesan Archives, Seattle, Washington (henceforth cited as AAS).

ferryman on the Columbia River, his Mass kit, the always handy buffalo robe, and two blankets.

Father had to take the lead wherever Indian settlements could be seen, for according to Indian custom the guide should follow; Edward therefore followed the priest leading the pack horse. One and a half miles' journey from the mission the travelers entered the dense wood of pine and red fir. After six more miles an Indian came and told Edward he wished Father would stop at his house. He felt ashamed to talk to the priest. Three months ago this man had gone to town and the whites had tempted him to drink; in a fight that followed he had wounded his own friend. Even after satisfaction was made, this man was despairing and did not want to show himself in public. The priest had warned the Indians to stay away from the town of the whites. Father visited the man and encouraged him to attend the mission that the priest was going to give in a little chapel near the Columbia River "which had been built in the year 1878 by a chief of the Sempuelsh."[47] The next morning, seeing that Father's horse was lame, the grateful man lent his own horse to the priest.

Father kept on traveling along the Columbia River inviting all the people on the way to come to the chapel the next morning. He himself covered twenty miles' distance that day. He was warmly welcomed by the Sanpoil chief. After supper the problems of the chief's people were the subjects of the conversation. The chief asked Father Diomedi to stay away from one L.P. The priest reports:

> You know that L.P. sometime ago became dissatisfied with his wife and accused her of a crime to the chief of the Sgoielpi last summer. We had our court and found her innocent; yet he insisted that we should have punished her. From inquiries made we found out that he had been anxious for us to condemn her, because this would have made her appear as guilty before the people and thus have furnished him with a pretext for killing her. So the chief went to see you and you said that it was not lawful to punish an innocent woman. This made him angry against you and in his wrath he swore to kill you.[48]

---

[47] This chief of the Sanpoil was most probably Chief Barnaby. A report of Indian agent, Rickard D. Gwyder, August 31, 1888, names two Sanpoil tribes. "Barnaby is chief of the Upper San Puells. His country extends from Rogers Bar, on the Columbia, to Kettle Falls. His people number 100 males and 90 females. They are very poor, and are willing to be helped. In that they differ from the San Puells under Sko-las-kin. They also differ in religion, being Catholics. *Report of the Secretary of the Interior, House Executive Documents, Fiftieth Congress, Second Session* (Vol. 11), 1888–1889, 222.

[48] Diomedi, S.J., "Extract From a Letter of a Rocky Mountain Jesuit Missionary," *op. cit.,* 31.

Next morning after the services Father called a man named Timothy and said: "Let us go to see L.P. and his gamblers." They had a three-mile horseback ride down the Columbia. About thirty yards from the gambling lodge Father stopped and sent his companion in to call them out. The gamblers and L.P., however, did not have the courage to face the priest. Timothy was sent in again to tell them that Father was waiting for them in L. P.'s house. Finally they came. Father's account continues:

> There were about fourteen or fifteen of them sitting on the floor, and they surrounded me, with L.P. just in front of me. Standing in their midst and addressing L.P., I said: "Now here I am, alone, without arms, surrounded by your men; get up, take your bow or your revolver and shoot me." For a moment there was silence, then he got up and said: "Yes, that was my wish and I had sworn to kill you, but now my mind is different."[49]

Father Diomedi then lectured them; all of them, except L.P., followed him to the church. For five days mornings and evenings Father preached to them; all showed signs of repentance. About fifty people went to confession and Communion. With the help of the chief good order and morality were restored. L.P. now was isolated and had to stop gambling.

The priest and his guide traveled thirty miles the next day to the mouth of the Spokane River which they wanted to cross at that place. Under no circumstances and not for any money would the Protestant Indians who had their camps there ferry them across. "Never," said a woman, "The priest is our deadly foe, never." As they were standing there not knowing what to do, Father Diomedi saw an Indian chasing a horse. It happened to be L.P.'s brother. This man knew that some relatives owned a canoe some miles down stream. He helped the stranded ones to cross the same night.

More trouble was in store the next day. Father and his companion now entered the territory of the Lower Sanpoil Indians, whose headquarters were around White Stone. They found five lodges of these Indians; one contained a little store. Here lived a white man who had married an Indian woman, a member of the "Dreamers." Father Diomedi wanted to buy a kettle in which to cook his flour as his was leaking, but the Dreamer woman abused him with insulting language. When Edward lost his patience and told the woman to shut up, Father decided that it would be best to leave.

They traveled several miles and camped at White Stone, where the snow was fourteen inches deep. They removed the snow from a spot and

---

[49] *Ibid.*

set up their tent for the night. After a good supper they made themselves as comfortable as possible. Early the next morning they started to cross the Big Bend country of the Columbia. It was about forty-five miles to any of the willow thickets. After about three hours they were caught in a heavy snowstorm which shut out all landmarks and covered the trail. Camping was impossible; the tent would be blown away by the wind, and fuel could not be found on the open prairie. Edward thought that the river must be on their right side. Finally they came upon a deer trail which helped them guess the direction of the mountains. Toward evening they became aware that they were about four miles from the Columbia River near the mouth of the Sanpoil River. They had traveled more or less in circles that day.

Edward wanted to go to Kolaskan's camp and ask for somebody to take them across the Columbia. His proposal was not carried out, because Kolaskan was the prophet of the Dreamers. Edward then listened to Father Diomedi's version of the beginning of the Dreamer worship:

> Kolaskan is a poor Wretch who has greatly deceived his own people. He is a dreamer who sometimes shuts himself up in his tent and allows no one to see him. Then he comes out and tells the people that he has had a revelation from heaven during his seclusion.
>
> The revelation he had a few years ago was this: There will be a great flood all over the earth; all human beings shall be destroyed, but the Sempuelsh Indians shall be saved, if they do what he commands them. Then he told them to set to work and build a large boat in which they were to take refuge as soon as the flood began, which would be in the course of eight years from the time of his revelation. The people began to saw lumber with a whip-saw and had prepared about three thousand feet for the building of such a boat. He endeavored to persuade some Catholics to do the same; they informed me and I spoke several times to the people to caution them against such nonsense. Then he began to preach against the priest and the Catholic religion, and excited his own people so much that at present it is impossible to do anything with that tribe, nor is it safe for a priest to go among them. When Father Vanzina went to visit them, Kolaskan, crippled as he was, took a knife and tried to strike him while he was preaching, seeing which, Father Vanzina jumped on his horse and rode off.[50]

Rather than waste time with the Sanpoils, Father Diomedi decided to keep on traveling along the Columbia River where there might be some pagans willing to listen to the Word of God. They reached the military camp "Okinagan" after two more days, where the commanding

---

[50] *Ibid.*, 35–36.

officer invited the travelers to stay at the camp. Father declined the invitation in order to be available for the Indians. He continued his trip and found some lodges of pagans from the Moses tribe, among them a dying child. Father Diomedi visited twice the next day but the father of the child thought he could not give permission for his child to be baptized, as there were no Christians at all in the Moses tribe then. Moses would be angry with him. The priest stayed and kept on visiting the child. Finally, on Christmas Eve, he received permission for the baptism. Thus the first child of the Moses tribe became a Christian. Edward served as godfather. Six days later the priest was informed that the child had died.

The inclemency of the weather increased with high winds and severe temperatures. Father Diomedi and his guide were still on the way to the Okanogans. Most of the priest's work was on the opposite side of the Columbia River. To add to the trouble, Father's fever returned. About the twenty-eighth of December he felt better, however, and decided to continue the journey. After six miles of traveling they came to a place on the Columbia where six soldiers were hauling wood. They helped Father to cross the Columbia River which was full of floating ice.

After six more miles Father Diomedi reached the former Hudson's Bay Company Fort Okanogan. Here he found about 500 wild Indians from the "Sinkensi, Tecoratum, and a part of the Mitgavi tribe." The Indians were still full of superstitions sixty-five years after the first contact with the white man. It was here that Father Diomedi observed the spirit dance. The dances started around Christmas and were prolonged throughout the winter, the dancers passing from one camp to the next. The tent for this purpose was erected on a conspicuous place in the camp and was made four or five times as large as the other tents. Father estimated that the tent he saw was about thirty feet in length and twenty in width. Poles were driven into the ground and skins or canvas stretched around them; the top was left open. About three or four fires were prepared in the center and the "dancing floor" was covered with soft pine needles upon which were spread blankets and buffalo robes.

The young Indians were clothed about the waist, the rest of the body was painted and adorned with beads; eagle feathers encircled the heads. Nmosize, the chief of the Chelans, was there to direct the dance. First, all had supper; then the old people and children were excluded from the dance tent for want of room. Now the dancers took their places and stood so packed that it would have been impossible to move; only the upper part of the body was moved up and down from the knees; the arms were raised and the thumbs were touching the shoulders. During these movements the dancers would watch the entrance; they could hear in the distance the humming of a tune without words by the medicine man. As he came nearer, the dancers would try to imitate the tune of this "spirit man," which took only a short time; amid confusion and loud streaming the medicine man went around the tent pretending to look for the entrance while another man interpreted to the people the messages the medicine man had received from the world of the spirits. Finally, the medicine man entered and all "turned toward him as hungry wolves upon their prey," barking like angry dogs. The medicine man then commanded silence and shook his medicine bag in which his charms and his "spirit" were. A sick man was then slipped into the tent and the medicine man shook his charm, or "somesh," over him, spat upon him, rushed at him, grasped his throat, and nearly choked him. Then he blew into the patient's mouth as if to breathe into him the healing spirit. The sick man was now so excited and "his hair stood on end as if charged with electricity." He began throwing dirt at the onlookers and used the foulest language until he fell down exhausted.[51]

Nobody came for services the next day when Father Diomedi rang his bell. When he sent his guide to call the people to come, the ten Catholics who had taken part in the spirit dance came and other pagans and Chief Nmosize. "Last night was for the devil, let today be for God," said the priest. But Chief Nmosize became angry, saying:

> Go away from my land; you always come here to reprove us for our customs. Your Americans spent New Year's day worse than we did. I saw them drunk and still drinking, quarreling and fighting. You are worse than we are, and yet you come here and urge us to become Christians.[52]

Father Diomedi then told the chief that those who spent New Year's Day as the chief had described it either were no Christians or they did not live up to their religion; hence no blame could be thrown upon the Christian religion. The chief then asked for Father's buffalo robe, which he did not get. Father Diomedi wanted to talk to the people, but again the chief interfered:

> I will not allow you to talk to them; nobody asked you to come here; we do not want your religion; we follow that of our forefathers. You heard we learned from our fathers who were a noble and glorious people. If we follow their example, we shall be as they were. And you have come

---

[51] Diomedi, S.J., "Sketches of Modern Indian Life," *WL* (32:3, December, 1893), 353–378.

[52] Diomedi, S.J., "Extract From a Letter of a Rocky Mountain Jesuit Missionary," *op. cit.*, 38.

here to tell us that these customs are bad that we should give them up. You are an imposter.[53]

Again the chief tried to trade Father's buffalo robe for two horses and wanted the priest to be discredited in front of the people, but Father lectured him. Finally the missionary told the chief that he had no time left for idle talk and that he would go, but next summer he would come to Chelan and build a chapel. (This he did while the chief was absent. He baptized two persons and made many friends. The chief upon his return set fire to the chapel.)

Chief Kolossasket had listened to the Chelans chief's angry speech. He felt sorry and told Father Diomedi: "These people are bad, they do not want the priest, come to see us, we are nearly all Catholics." By now it was the fourth of January; Father was about two hundred miles away from his home mission; his provisions were low and his horses were getting thin. He still was a hundred miles from his destination — the Similkameen Indians. Father Diomedi traveled for twelve miles along the Okanogan River and arrived safely at the Mitgavi camp. He was expected and made welcome and comfortable. There were seventy people, nearly all of whom were Catholics. The priest could only stay over Epiphany, 1880, for three days, but these days were filled with work as he tells us:

All day long, between my instructions, men and women filled my tent to learn how to baptize children in danger of death, or when the Ember-days would fall, or when Lent would begin, or what kind of work should be avoided on Sunday, and what was allowed.[54]

These people felt sorry to see the missionary leave them, but they helped him to cross the Okanogan River, which was partly frozen.

The roads were choked with snow; Father's fever returned again; quinine did not have much effect. Another twelve to fifteen miles were covered on the first day. More snow began to fall the next day and a severe windstorm followed. They made camp, tying their tent to some willow brushes. On the other side of the river they saw some rye grass sticking out above the snow; they went there with the horses. Father Diomedi and Edward had to stay another day at this camp on account of Father's fever and dizziness. The priest was too exhausted to stay on the horse and the animals refused to face the storm. The next day they lost their way and finally camped in a gulch of the Similkameen Mountains; the hills on the east were covered with bunchgrass. Father

[53] Ibid., 39.
[54] Ibid., 40.

fed his horses some flour and then let them loose to graze, But they, scenting the approaching storm, disappeared in the distance.

The tent was erected in a pine grove. Another heavy snowfall came during the night; all trails had disappeared. The guide went all day looking for the horses; he came back at night crying. Seeing Father suffering with fever, he said:

> Father, you are already a dead man; our horses have disappeared, leaving no trace behind; the cold is intense, our provisions are nearly gone and we are very far from the nearest Indian house.[55]

Father consoled him and told him of God's help. "I am ready to die," said Edward; "I thought of this when I started, and I am glad to give up my life for the sake of Christ and for the salvation of the Indians." As he prepared supper he kept on repeating: "Poor priest, you must die." The next day Edward did some scouting to get their bearings. He returned in the evening and told Father he thought they were about thirty-five miles from Chief Francois' place and that it would take him three days to reach it. He would leave next morning. Then he baked the rest of the flour into three little cakes. Father insisted that he take two of them for the trip.

The next morning Edward made his confession and said that he was ready to die. He fastened an ax and two blankets to his shoulders; then asked Father's blessing. He grasped Father's hands and said: "I leave you alone, but if God helps me I will come back for you; otherwise we shall never hear of each other again, but my heart is good."[56] Father was overcome with emotion as he watched his faithful guide disappear from view.

Two more days and the Chinook wind blew over the Similkameen Mountains. When the water started flowing through his tent the priest realized that he was encamped in a creek. As fast as he could he removed his belongings and his tent to a new location. Then he lay down completely exhausted. Meanwhile Edward was traveling on the ice of the Okanogan River and reached in two days Chief Francois' place. Father Pandosi, the Oblate priest, who had a mission seventy miles from the place where Father was waiting, was told to be ready for Father Diomedi's funeral. Chief Francois first prepared provisions, had his wife bake bread, took his best horses, and early next morning they were on the way riding fast. They found Father late in the evening, made him as comfortable as they could, and urged him to eat. Next morning

---

[55] *Ibid.*, 43.
[56] *Ibid.*, 44.

they left for Francois' place which they reached in the evening. The news had spread and Father found about forty Indians waiting for him at Francois' place. He gave them a short instruction and prayed with them. The next day Father was able to say Mass at Francois' home, where twelve persons received Holy Communion. Then the Okanogans spread the news that on Sunday there would be Mass at Michael's place. This Indian had built a special comfortable room next to his house for the priests. The generous Okanogans brought so many provisions for Father Diomedi that he was able to take only half of them for the journey back. About fifty received Holy Communion at Michael's place. The people acted very considerately in order to spare Father's strength and nurse him back to health. About a week later Father was able to start the trip home to St. Francis Regis Mission. There was most certainly nothing romantic about Father Diomedi's missionary trip.

Father Diomedi praised the progress made by the Okanogans:

> If we would have had means to establish a mission and school among the Okanogan, they would by this time hold the foremost rank among civilized Indians. What a pity that some generously disposed persons cannot be found to supply this need and thus enable the missionaries to go on with their work of Christianizing and civilizing such a large number.[57]

Father Diomedi's wish was to be fulfilled five years later. The importance of St. Francis Regis Mission, according to Father Diomedi, was that it had been the advanced post for Christianizing the Sanpoil and the Okanogans, "the northern Okanogans and the Similgami have all been gained." Pagans were still quite numerous between the Colville mission and the Yakima mission. The fruits of the dangerous journey were: three adults and five children baptized, two hundred fifty Communions, and about three hundred confessions.[58]

In his *Sketches,* Father Diomedi described how horse gambling was practiced among the Okanogans. Once while Father Diomedi was among this tribe an Indian without saying anything to the priest staked and lost Father's saddle horse. The winner wanted to ride off with the horse when Father intervened and called the gambler a thief. Only by warning him that he would call the Catholic chief to give him a flogging did Father get his horse back. The Okanogans would gamble away a horse part by part. They would start with one foot, then with the other and so on until the whole animal was gambled away. This often took all night and was accompanied by yelling and screaming.

[57] Diomedi, "Sketches of Modern Indian Life," *WL* (32:3, December, 1893), 373.
[58] *Ibid.*

Gambling was a seasonal occupation practiced mostly by married men. When the Indians fished for the white salmon at the mouth of the Okanogan River sometimes as many as a thousand Indians were gathered. During these days they would amuse themselves with horse racing and at night they would sit at their stick games and gamble, with all their possessions at stake. The unmarried men were kept from gambling by the fact that nobody would give his daughter in marriage to a gambler.

Father Diomedi also told of another encounter with Chief Nmosize of the Chelans. The priest once was preaching against polygamy when this chief stood up and objected:

> You come here to destroy us. Our polygamy is the inheritance which we have received from our forefathers. They were a glorious people and had large numbers of hunters and fishermen and never knew what starvation was. In war, they were strong and defeated their enemies because they were many soldiers. You come among us and persuaded some of my people. They keep only one wife and have few children. Our hunters and fishermen are disappearing and in the case of war we shall have no soldiers. This is the evil of your speech.[59]

To break customs that had been in existence hundreds of years must have had its hardships for these children of nature.

The old baptismal records of St. Paul's at Kettle Falls and later of St. Francis Regis Mission show the great amount of spiritual work done at these missions and the big territory that depended on them. The records also contain the names of many heroic priests who gave their lives in order to plant Christian civilization in a great part of our Pacific Northwest. Many of them are still gratefully remembered by the old people. The following are the number of baptisms and the names of the Fathers that administered them from 1852 on. Previous ones have been quoted:

1852	Fr.	Vercruysse	85	1876	Fr. Guidi	18
1853	"	"	109		" Tosi	10
	"	Joset	54		" Grassi	23
1854	"	"	34		" Giorda	3
	"	Vercruysse	95	1877	" "	8
1855	"	"	45		" Vanzina	30
	"	Joset	19		" Tosi	5
1856	"	"	15		" Grassi	52
	"	Vercruysse	43		" Diomedi	4
	"	no name	3	1878	" Diomedi	20
1857	"	Vercruysse	61		" Vanzina	29
	"	Joset	19		" Canestrelli	3
	"	Ravalli	10		" Grassi	58

[59] *Ibid., op. cit.* (32:2, July, 1893), 237–238.

1858	"	"	14		"	Caldi	2
	"	Vercruysse	49	1879	"	Diomedi	30
	"	Pandosi	1		"	Vanzina	29
	"	Fabini	1		"	Canestrelli	20
1859	"	Pandosi	9		"	Joset	5
	"	Joset	43	1880	"	"	23
	"	Vercruysse	33		"	Grassi	29
1860	"	Joset	55		"	Vanzina	9
	"	Pandosi	1		"	Cataldo	8
1861	"	Joset	84		"	Canestrelli	27
1862	"	"	99		"	Diomedi	24
1863	"	"	115		"	Giorda	1
	"	Giorda	10	1881	"	Canestrelli	12
1864	"	Joset	72		"	Cataldo	9
	"	Menetry	7		"	Grassi	19
1865	"	Joset	72		"	Caruana	8
	"	Giorda	1		"	Joset	4
1866	"	Joset	64[60]		"	Tornietti	2
1867	"	Tosi	1	1882	"	Canestrelli	53
	"	L. Van Grop	3		"	Caruana	46
	"	Joset	51		"	Tornietti	13
1868	"	"	40		"	Joset	1
	"	Tosi	5		"	L. Van Gorp	1
1869	"	"	1	1883	"	Caruana	35
	"	Bandini	16		"	Tornietti	5
	"	Grassi	4		"	Canestrelli	28
	"	Vanzina	35		"	Joset	4
	"	Joset	13		"	Folchi	14
1870	"	"	47	1884	"	"	43
	"	Grassi	34		"	Canestrelli	19
	"	Tosi	11		"	Joset	9
1871	"	"	19		"	Schuler	2
	"	Grassi	5		"	Grassi	3
	"	Vanzina	14		"	Robaut	2
	"	Giorda	9		"	Cataldo	1
1872	"	"	20	1885	"	Ruellan	2
	"	Vanzina	14		"	Folchi	16
	"	no name	5		"	Robaut	17
	"	Tosi	19		"	Grassi	107
1873	"	"	25		"	Canestrelli	20
	"	Guidi	81	1886	"	"	16
	"	Vanzina	5		"	Robaut	12
	"	Giorda	3		"	Folchi	7
1874	"	"	1		"	Filippi	22
	"	Guidi	81	1887	"	"	11
	"	Tosi	11		"	Diomedi	1
	"	Vanzina	5		"	Folchi	8
1875	"	Tosi	15[61]		"	Mackin	11[62]
	"	Vanzina	16		"	De Rougé	3
1876	"	Vanzina	17				

---

[60] *Baptismal Record of St. Paul's Mission*, Book II, OPA.
[61] *Liber Baptizatorum in Missione S. France. Regis Colville* (*St. Paul's*), OPA.
[62] *Ibid.*, Book III, OPA.

The priests having the greatest number of baptisms were mostly on missionary journeys to the Okanogan country, as records indicate. From 1887 on there is a marked decline in baptisms registered at St. Francis Regis because St. Mary's Mission, Omak, Washington, had its own establishment by then.

If the boundaries of the Colville Reservation had not been changed and St. Francis Regis Mission had been on the reservation, the founding of St. Mary's Mission, Omak, might not have become an urgent matter. The letters of the missionaries stressed more and more this necessity. The big territory needed to be divided and other centers of faith and education established on more central locations for the Indians. The need for more priests and missions was suggested by an anonymous writer thus:

> This Mission should be divided into three: — Colville, with three Fathers and three Brothers; Okinagan with two Fathers and two Brothers; and the Band of Moses, with two Fathers and two brothers.[63]

On September 10, 1901, Father Caldi, in a report to his Father Provincial about his work of the past year, named the white and the Indian settlements in his charge and gave us some interesting historical data. For instance: Colville was then a town of about six hundred persons. The missionary went there from St. Francis Regis mission by train every fourth Sunday. The church was adequate; the congregation consisted of about one hundred Catholics, half of them from the surrounding country. Some of the Catholics were negligent and Father had difficulty in getting some of them to bring their children for baptism. There was also the Apostolate of Prayer with a membership of twenty-five. A new altar was built in that year for $150 and Stations of the Cross installed. Catholics who lived seven or eight miles away were visited by the missionary.

Every first Sunday of the month the priest visited Northport, a city of about 1200, mostly men, thirty-five miles from the mission. The town had a small but beautiful new church with an adjacent room that served as sacristy and as living quarters. Only about eighty persons came to Mass even though about half of the population was then Catholic. The priest went to the workshops of the smelter, mixed with the workers, and encouraged them to come to church. These were mostly young people who had been away from the Church for a long time. Father

---

[63] Anonymous, "The Missions of the Rocky Mountains in 1881," *WL* (12:1, 1883), 53.

Caldi realized the need for a resident priest. Surrounding the city were many Catholic farmers who had forgotten much of their faith.

Another mission parish, Republic, a town of 2500 inhabitants, was surrounded by many small communities of miners. The church was little more than a shack. The priest's trip to Republic, because of bad roads, required two days in winter and one in summer. The work there, however, was gratifying. The ladies had a good Sunday catechism school. Some people came to church from a distance of more than twenty miles; almost all the miners were Catholics. Again Father Caldi regretted that these people had the priest among them only two days per month. The Protestant people in Republic and in Curlew were aware of the sacrifices that were needed for the priest to come there, and were very courteous to him.

Father Caldi made a visit every second month to Curlew, then a settlement of about sixty people with many others living in the valley that stretches between Curlew and Republic. The place had a small church for the Indians. Catholics were on the increase; many who pretended not to have any religion were in reality fallen-away Catholics. Nearly all who came to the church were half-breeds from the valley of Curlew, Kettle River, and Toroda Creek. They were good farmers and diligent in their duties toward the Church. Many, however, got drunk often. In all directions from Curlew were Indian settlements. Father Caldi tells of visiting a bed-ridden woman who had not seen a priest for three years. Out of gratitude she left him ten dollars when she died.

Barnaby, another mission in charge of Father Caldi during 1900–1901, which he visited every other first Friday, was twenty-five miles from St. Francis Regis Mission and gave excellent prospects for the future. Besides his regular visits he made extra trips for sick calls and for baptisms. Over four hundred Indians participated in the Corpus Christi procession of 1900. On his regular visits Father Caldi could stay only one day at Barnaby, because he had to be in Colville the first Sundays. Often he had to travel more than fifty miles on one day, especially when sick calls were involved. Father Caldi complained that many young Indians had taken to heavy drinking.

On the first Friday of every second month, Father Caldi took care of Pia, a place eighteen miles from his home mission. Here was a large church for Indians and half-breeds who had good homes and were very religious. About eighty to ninety people attended the services, often coming from great distances.

In his report the priest mentions Kettle Falls, a little village with only three Catholic families, where Mass was celebrated once in awhile in homes, where the people of the surrounding area would gather. The territory to the left of the Columbia River for about thirty miles from Kettle Falls was then occupied by white people. All this territory was at the time included in St. Francis Regis Parish.

Often great sacrifices were asked of the missionaries in attending to the sick. Father Caldi tells of being away from the mission when a sick call was received by telephone. The young man who received the call in town forgot the address and made a mistake about the name. The old Father Superior started out on horseback and carrying a lantern to inquire at the different post offices about the location of the sick persons. The call had come from Daisy, twenty-five miles away, about 6 o'clock. It was a rainy winter evening, the way lay among the mountains, and when the priest arrived, after midnight, he was too late; the sick one had died one hour earlier. The priest fainted from fatigue, but after a two-hour rest started back again.[64]

The relations between the Indians and the white settlers who had pushed the Indians across the Columbia River and had taken hold of age-old possessions of the Colville and the Lake tribes, the bad example of the whites, and the traffic in liquor prompted the Fathers to discourage the Indians from coming to St. Francis Regis Mission. The greatest feast of the Indians, Corpus Christi, was already being celebrated at the Barnaby mission in 1892, "in order to bring about more friendly relations in the northern part of the reservation."[65]

Father Edward Griva, the successor of Father Caldi at St. Francis Regis Mission, tells in his 1903 letter to his provincial the reasons for the decline of the mission:

> They [the Indians] come to St. Francis Regis Mission only two or three times during the year, at Christmas, Easter and Corpus Christi. The rest of the time they attend services at their churches which are located in two little stations named Pia and Barnabee. I go there once every two months and sometimes one Sunday a month and I stay there two or three days according to Father Superior's permission.
>
> In general the Indians do not like to come any more to this principal mission, because now it is more convenient than it was years ago and above all, they are more exposed to the temptation of drinking whiskey, whereas at home they would not be tempted.
>
> Another reason also for not wishing to come here, is because they all own a small farm and any time they go away with the whole family, some of their possessions have been stolen, and this they have learned

---

[64] "Lettera del P. C. Caldi, S.J., al R. P. Provinciale, 10 settembre 1901, *LDPT*, 92–101 (translated by Louis Botter, Spokane).

[65] *Diary of St. Francis Regis Mission*, June 16, 1892, Mss., OPA.

at their own expense. The same was experienced last year by the old Chief Long Aleck, who came here on Palm Sunday. When he returned home he found that all his money was stolen (over hundred dollars), and now he does not like to leave the house anymore.[66]

The year of 1904 saw the abandonment of the famous "Christ Dead Procession," as the *Diary* tells us:

> April 1, 1904, Good Friday
> Services began at 7 o'clock — Fr. Filippi celebrant, Fr. Mc M. deacon, and Mr. Condeyre subdeacon. At 3:30 Fr. Filippi had the way of the Cross and spoke to the Indians; at 7 o'clock it had been arranged to have the procession, but Fr. Filippi abandoned the idea, because white albs, red flannel capes and coifs, relics of the past, could not be furnished to the Indians who were to carry the bier. — He preached instead.[67]

The *Historia Domus of St. Francis Regis Mission,* Ward, Washington, April 11, 1908, to February 16, 1912, lists all the many missions, chapels, and developing parishes that owe their foundations and buildup to the Jesuit Fathers coming from St. Francis Regis mission:

St. Francis Mission	Ferry Co.	In Okinagon Co.
Colville †	Danville	Lafleur †
Marcus †	Republic †	Oroville †
Boyd †	Curlew †	Molson †
Bossburg	Barnaby †	Chesaw
Orient †	Hallcreek †	Nighthawk
Pia, little Mission	Rogersbar †	Loomis †
Northport †	Nespelim	Tonaskat †
Niggercreek †	Daisy †	Indian Church †
Onion Creek	Bissel	Ind. Church in B.C. †
Kettle Falls	Hunter †	Cusick (Kalispel Ind.)
Arzina	Fruitland	
	Spokane	Jumpoff †
		Spokane Res. (St. Joseph) †[68]

A few important historical events at St. Francis Regis mission might be noted here: a gristmill and a sawmill were built between 1875 and 1880; a larger church, started in 1877, was completed in 1881. Most Reverend Aegidius Jumger, Bishop of Nesqually, visited the Colville

[66] Rev. Edward Griva, S.J., "Lettera del P. Edoardo Griva al R. P. Provinciale, St. Francis Mission, Meyers Falls, Wash.," 22 July, 1903, *LPT* (1904), 124–129.
[67] *Diary of St. Francis Regis Mission,* June 16, 1892., Mss., OPA.
[68] *Historia Domus of St. Francis Regis Mission,* III, Mss., OPA. Crosses after certain names appear in the original manuscript and probably stand for chapels or Churches existing then.

Valley the first time on May 25, 1880. On Christmas morning of 1888, the second big church burned down. A third one, which was completed for Christmas 1911 by Father Fletcher, was leveled by fire at the beginning of June, 1938.[69]

Let us now retrace our steps and follow the later educational developments at the mission. Old school reports show that the far-away-living Okanogans were as eager as the Colvilles to avail themselves of the opportunity to have their children educated. In the reports for 1893 and 1894 appear the names of twelve children from the Okanogan tribes. The author has spoken with several old people who received their education at St. Francis Regis Mission, where the Fathers had their school for boys, and at the Sacred Heart School of the Sisters of Providence at the same place, where the girls had a separate school.

Owing to the unjust reservation policies of the United States government, the school and the church attendance showed a marked decline in the 1890's. An entry in the *Diary* of the mission for August 30, 1891, tells that the average attendance at the school was forty-two girls and twenty-one boys and that the schools had government contracts for seventy. On July 27, 1892, we are told that the new contract was received for sixty-five children only and that the Fathers received word that several children who formerly attended St. Francis Regis Mission schools had gone over to the agency school. The *Diary* notes that Chief Barnabi of the Upper Sanpoel Indians was boasting about the quality of the government school near Bonaparte Creek, close to the present town of Tonasket, Washington. Chief Tonasket of the Okanogans had requested this school for his people, as we will see. On October 2, 1902, the schools at St. Francis Regis Mission opened the new school year with only fourteen boys and twenty-seven girls in attendance. Mission school contracts were outlawed by Congress in 1896.[70] Every year after that the government contributed twenty percent less than the year before until after five years the mission schools had to depend completely on charity. The boys' school at St. Francis Regis closed September 1, 1908; another attempt was made to reopen, but lack of funds and other factors contributed to its discontinuance.

The girls' school of the Sisters of Providence was generally more prosperous than the school for boys of the Fathers. The Sisters also had a private school for white girls, called Sacred Heart Academy. Standards were a far cry from what they are today, but this was the pioneer age in

---

[69] See: *Diary of St. Francis Regis Mission and Historia Domus* for the years mentioned.
[70] Rt. Rev. J. B. Tennelly to the author, December 15, 1959.

the West. Girls who had completed their eleventh grade were given teachers' diplomas. With the closing of the mines during 1913–1914, the enrollment of white girls dropped. The 1917–1918 *Chronicle* entry mentions that from forty-three Indians enrolled thirty-two remained at the close of the school. Enrollment declined further during the following years. Father Griva wrote the last sad news about the earliest educational center for Indians and white in the Inland Empire. "The Sisters left the mission on the 30th of July, 1921."[71] They had done heroic self-sacrificing work during the nearly seventy-five years of the existence of the Sacred Heart School of St. Francis Regis Mission in the Colville Valley.

Gradually a very active diocesan clergy grew in numbers and was able to take over many parishes that had seen hard beginnings by the Jesuit pioneers. Many old Indians and white people gratefully remember the many benefactions and spiritual graces received at St. Francis Regis Mission. The mission is merely a huge farm today with an extensive cemetery on the hillside, its history written on tombstones, while Old St. Paul's at Kettle Falls has been restored by the Reverend Paul M. Georgen in 1939. It is one of the old historic landmarks of the state of Washington.

[71] *Historia Domus of St. Francis Regis Mission,* July 30, 1921, Mss., OPA.

CHAPTER VI

Fighting a "Peace Policy"

THE Indian missions of the Inland Empire that had been built up by the Jesuit Fathers with such great sacrifice were once in danger of coming under the control of non-Catholic denominations. Congress had forbidden, in 1870, the placing of army officers in civil positions. The secretary of the Board of Indian Commissioners, Vincent Coyler, of New York, suggested to President Grant that the management of Indian reservations be given to members of the different denominations. The President then, on December 5, 1870, sent this message to Congress:[1]

> Indian agencies being civil offices, I determined to give all the agencies to such religious denominations as had hitherto established missionaries among the Indians and perhaps to some other denominations who would undertake the work on the same term — that is, as missionary work. The Societies selected are allowed to name their own agents, subject to the approval of the Executive, and are expected to watch over them and aid them as missionaries, to Christianize and civilize the Indian, and to train him in the arts of peace. . . .[2]

The policy sounded just and would have resulted in a more peaceful attitude on the part of the cheated Indians, but Coyler had made his distribution of agencies according to geographical regions and not according to missionary work done among the tribes by the different denominations. Then Secretary Cox wrote to the denominations asking them to take over their respective regions and reservations. The Catholics never received a letter. On February 11, 1871, Father De Smet wrote to Father

[1] For a thorough study of this subject see: Rev. Peter J. Rahil, *The Catholic Indian Missions and Grant's Peace Policy,* 69.

[2] President Ulysses S. Grant, "Second Annual Message," December 5, 1870, *Messages and Papers of the Presidents,* IX, 4063–4064.

120

D'Aste, S.J., about a meeting of the Board of Indian Commissioners with the representatives of the various denominations, where Father alone as a private person represented the vast mission territories the Catholic Church had Christianized:

> I have been called to Washington by the Secretary of the Interior where a great council has been held on Indian affairs in general. I then learned that forty-three Indian stations were to be divided among different denominations in the various sections of the country inhabited by the Indians, of which only four are assigned to the Catholics, viz. one in Dakota (the mission we intend to establish in the spring among the Sioux), one in Mexico, another in Montana (Flathead), and a fourth in Idaho. In the whole of this affair the Indians have not been consulted as to the religion they desired to belong to.[3]

Father De Smet had given all the information that concerned the missions in Montana and Idaho, but he was not sufficiently informed as to the number of Indians converted, schools and churches built, etc. He asked for statistics and hoped "upon the information given, the Government may and will modify its plan of Christianizing and civilizing the Indians."[4]

Father De Smet's writing showed that originally the Colville reservation was not allotted to the Catholics. The constitutional right to choose their religion was denied to the Indians. Father De Smet had in the meantime obtained the statistics from Father Giorda, S.J., and had sent them to Commissioner Parker, but this document was ignored. Father De Smet's many services for the United States government in the matter of peace were forgotten by the very officials of the same government. They lacked even the courtesy to answer his letters. It is a historical fact that the Catholics of the United States generally have been tolerant and broad-minded toward members of other denominations. Mr. Harvey, agent at Colville, was not a Catholic; however, he did his duty as a Christian. The Fathers wanted him to stay.[5]

There were repeated protests from Archbishop Blanchet of Portland,

---

[3] Father De Smet quoted by CR, *De Smet,* IV, 1335–1336.

[4] *Ibid.*

[5] De Smet to Honorable E. S. Parker, Commissioner of Indian Affairs, March 27, 1871, in CR, *De Smet,* IV, 1430. "At Colville the Kettle Falls Indians number 600 Catholics. The missionaries of said section attend the Spokane [*sic*] Indians, who number 300 Catholics. The former Agent, Mr. Harvey, though not a Catholics, aided the missionaries in their effort to promote the welfare of the Indians and was highly popular and beloved by them. They beg that he may be reappointed. His successor among the Spokanes gives no satisfaction, neither to the missionaries nor to the Indians. The chief in his effort to prevent the spread of licentiousness among his people, was threatened with jail. The Lower Kalispels number 403 Catholics, the Okinagans number 107 Catholics; the Snaiclist number 229."

Oregon, to the Secretary of the Interior, Delano, but the policy of the government was not changed. At about the same time appeared the Spalding lies blaming the Catholics for the Whitman massacre that started the Cayuse War. This was more than twenty years after the occurrence and stirred much ill will toward Catholics generally. A complete refutation of Spalding's statements was later made by a Protestant, William I. Marshall.[6]

Father De Smet was invited to the second meeting of the Board of Commissioners, January 11, 1872, but since he was then in Europe, he could not attend. Leading responsible Catholic bishops were completely ignored; they were not represented. After this meeting the Catholics were given the charge of 17,000 Indians on seven reservations. The tribes, later named by the government "Colville Confederated Tribes," were this time under Catholic supervision.

The Reverend Peter J. Rahil in his study of this situation quoted the *Catholic Review* correspondent who made an investigation. This man arrived at a total of 106,911 Catholic Indians and only 15,000 Protestant Indians; yet the Protestants were given thirty-six agencies and the Catholics only six. Nearly 90,000 Catholic Indians were placed under non-Catholic control and domination.[7]

The Catholic Church had contributed over half of the funds spent on missions, yet the antagonism was so great that:

> The entire Board of Indian Commissioners threatened to resign if Grant appointed a Catholic to the body, whereupon the President promptly backed down.[8]

Much politics was connected with the corrupt Indian Department. Many denominations were not eager to accept the work on the agencies. Rahil's quote of the report of the Board of Indian Commissioners for 1873 showed that thirty-three agencies were unfilled.[9] Rahil also quoted from a letter of Father De Smet:

> Men presented for Indian agents by the religious bodies must favor the re-election of Grant, else they would not be confirmed by the Republican Senate.[10]

---

[6] William I. Marshall, *The Long Suppressed Evidence Concerning Marcus Whitman*, 2 vols. Also: Edward Gaylord Bourne, "Non-Catholic Historians Demolish Legend," in *Essays in Historical Criticism*, 144 ff.

[7] Rahil, quoting the *Catholic Review*, New York (November 1, 1873), *op. cit.*, 105.

[8] *Ibid.*, 108.

[9] *Ibid.*, 113.

[10] Rahil, quoting De Smet to Archbishop Blanchet, *ibid.*, 63.

Even after the allotment of the Colville Reservation to the Catholics and the appointment of Special Indian Agent Simms, the care of the Indians was not without interference. The agent wrote in his report of September, 1874:

> At the last term of the United States district court held in this [Stevens] county the grand jury called the attention of the judge to the fact that the Catholic Fathers were in the habit of marrying Indians without their [the Indians] having first procured a marriage license, and advised that they be notified to discontinue the practices, as contrary to statute. The fathers at once called upon the judge and informed him that if such a rule was to be enforced here they would abandon their mission and leave, as war would certainly follow for which they wished in no way to be responsible.[11]

The judge then ruled that no notice should be taken of the complaint of the grand jury for the present. The Fathers had blessed marriages many years previous to any existence of civil authority in the West; in addition, the Indians were subject to their own tribal laws and were angered about the unjust reservation policies of the whites. Only the Fathers helped them to remain peaceful.

While the Indians belonging to the Colville Reservation were now guided by Catholics, the neighboring Indian tribes on the Yakima reservation were not. In 1848, Chief Kamiakin had asked for Catholic priests for his people. The Oblate Fathers had answered that call and built a mission chapel at the Athanum, near the present Yakima, Washington. During the Yakima War, Father Pandosi had buried a keg of powder to keep it from the Indians.[12] This was found shortly after and the priest's intentions were misinterpreted; the mission of the Athanum was burned by soldiers. In 1865 Father L. N. St. Onge started again the work among the Yakimas and was assisted by Mr. J. B. Boulet, the later Monsignor Boulet of Ferndale, Washington. Five years later the Jesuits took over the Yakima mission and had great success. Then Indian agent, James H. Wilbur, a Methodist minister, moved into the agency. Father Parodi, S.J., who had firsthand experiences wrote to his provincial about the change under Wilbur:

> . . . When he arrived, there were 500 Catholic Indians; in a few years he perverted 300 of them. The government gave to such an agent all financial means to build a house for every Indian family and to furnish them with

---

[11] Simms, "Annual Report of September 1, 1874," op. cit.

[12] For more about the Oblate Fathers see: Rev. George M. Wagget, "The Oblates of Mary Immaculate in the Pacific Northwest of the U.S.A.," in Etudes Oblates (6:1, Janvier-Mars, 1947), 7–83.

all the tools needed to cultivate their lands. The agent though was furnishing the needed things only to those Indians who were willing to become Methodists and in so doing he attracted 300 of them.[13]

The repercussions from the unjust discriminations against the Catholic Church and its members living on the Yakima Reservation could be felt among the neighboring Okanogan and Colville tribes. They became the talk of the countryside. Chief Moses, although a friend of Agent Wilbur, did not want to settle on the Yakima Reservation. Was it on account of the narrow-minded religious policy of Agent Wilbur?

Agent Wilbur forbade the Catholic priests entrance into the Yakima Reservation to visit and administer the sacraments. Frequently he even forbade parents to take their children outside the reservation to the Catholic church for Mass and instructions.

Lieutenant James M. Smith was ordered to substitute for Agent Wilbur while the latter was absent from the Yakima Reservation. He observed the injustice and wanted more Christian fairness practiced. We quote excerpts from his 1870 report:

> More than three-fourths of these Indians are professedly Catholics and adhere with peculiar devotion to that sect. There are two meeting houses on the reservation. At present religious services are held on alternate Sabbaths, conducted by native Protestant preachers. I would respectfully recommend that one be set apart for the use of the Catholics, the other for the Protestants. . . .
>
> . . . J. H. Wilbur not only forbade Catholic priests to come upon the reservation, threatening them with arrest and confinement, but adopted stringent measures to prevent the Indians from attending worship at the mission chapel of that sect just beyond its boundaries. This restraint of their religious liberty was always the occasion of great discontent among the Indians. . . .
>
> As a general fact I have observed that those pertaining to the Methodist Church are well supplied with such material, and I may say, well to do in most respects; whereas those adhering to the Catholic faith have little or nothing. . . .[14]

President Grant's policy to give to the denominations who converted the Indians the administrations of the agencies had been called "Grant's Peace Policy." There was nothing peaceful about this policy in action.

---

[13] Rev. Louis Parodi, S.J., to Father Provincial, April–September 1902, *LDPT*, 1902, 65–66.

[14] Lieutenant James M. Smith, United States Army Agent, to Colonel Samuel Ross, U.S.A. Superintendent of Indian Affairs, Olympia, W.T., August 31, 1870, in "Report of the Secretary of the Interior," *Executive Documents 1, House of Representatives, Forty-First Congress, Third Session* (Part 4, Vol. 1), 485–497.

The religious intolerance finally reached its climax when in 1879 Congregationalists wanted to enter James McLaughlin's Catholic Devil's Lake Agency and were forbidden to enter by Commissioner Hayt on account of the wrong interpretation of this policy. The Catholic Church always realized that successful work for the Indians could be done only if its missionaries were free to enter any reservation. Under President Hayes, in 1881, finally full religious freedom was given to the Indians.

Wilbur continued his policy on the Yakima Reservation between 1870 and 1882, then he was replaced. In spite of his hostility the Catholic faith had grown from this center in the West to the tribes along the Wenatchee, Columbia, and Okanogan Rivers mainly through the efforts of the Jesuit Fathers.

CHAPTER VII

These Lands Are Ours

A hundred years or so of governmental direction of the Indian, sometimes by cajolery, frequently by warfare, and occasionally by rational and fair treatment, has produced a being who is still a child in his understanding of our ways, our philosophy, and our knowledge of the necessity for "hustling" for what is desirable. That century of experiment and exploitation has ultimately effected this: it has placed about the Indian and his property sufficient restrictions to prevent him from being officially robbed, and it has secured him an inheritance that is just sufficient to make him an unproductive loafer — unless he happens to be an individual of such strength of mind that he is the mental superior of his white neighbor.[1]

THESE poignant observations of a man of long experience in work for and with the Indians, James McLaughlin, were the outcome of an imprudent and unjust United States reservation policy.

It was quite late in the nineteenth century when the United States government became concerned about the Indians of Eastern Washington and then it was for the sake of "land robbery." On March 2, 1853, Washington Territory was separated and ceased to be a part of "Old Oregon." Control over Indian Affairs in this new territory was vested in the governor, serving *ex officio* as the Superintendent of Indian Affairs. Another Act of Congress, March 3, 1857, changed this status again and appointed for the two large territories only one Superintendent of Indian Affairs for Oregon and Washington, Isaac Ingall Stevens, the governor and *ex officio* Superintendent of Indian Affairs. Stevens was succeeded by Superintendent James W. Nesmith for Oregon and Washington Territories, June 2, 1857. This arrangement lasted only four years, after which the

---

[1] James McLaughlin, *My Friend the Indian*, p. 261.

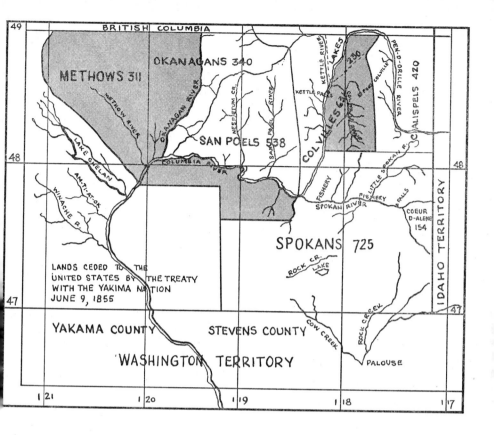

territories were divided again for the administration of Indian Affairs, and William W. Miller was appointed the new Superintendent for Indian Affairs for Washington Territory. In June, 1874, the office of Superintendent of Indian Affairs in the territory was abandoned for lack of funds. "During the twenty-one years from 1853–1874, eleven Superintendents had charge of Indian Affairs in Washington Territory."[2]

This gives us an idea of the unsettled Indian policies of the United States before and after the Civil War. It is a fact that not all Indian agents, superintendents, and commissioners were appointed because they loved the Indians and wanted to help these people to adjust themselves when confronted with the white man's civilization. Rahil quotes Representative James Garfield, later President Garfield, who made this statement in 1869:

---

[2] James R. Masterson, "The Records of the Washington Superintendency of Indian Affairs, 1853–74," in *PNQ* (37:1, January, 1945), 31–37.

No branch of the national government is so spotted with fraud, so tainted with corruption, so utterly unworthy of a free and enlightened government, as the Indian department.[3]

The greatest civilizing agent of the Indians in eastern Washington was not the United States government; it was the Catholic Church through the Jesuit Fathers. These pioneers taught the first principles of personal property values by teaching the Indians to build their homes, to plant their fields, to be self-providing. Although the Jesuits were as yet unable to reach all the tribes permanently on account of shortage of priests, those tribes living nearest to the missions profited greatly by the teaching and the example of the missionaries. Since the establishment of the military Fort Colville in 1859, the military commander acted as an "overall supervisor" over the surrounding tribes. It was only in 1865, that George A. Paige was ordered to Fort Colville to take charge of Indian affairs. He mentioned the great influence of the Catholic missionaries.[4] The Colville tribes were at that time well acquainted with farming. William P. Winans, who was appointed Indian farmer in 1870, speaks about the progress of the Indians in his first report:

They have 31 farms, with 1,621 acres under fence, and 751 under cultivation; they have sown this year 414 bushels wheat, 311 bushels oat, 203 bushels potatoes, 15 bushels peas, 22 bushels corn, and 69 pounds garden seeds, using in cultivation the above, 35 plows, 28 cradles, and 77 hoes; and some have in stock 602 horses, 85 cattle, and 379 chickens.

Some have cabins to live in, and barns to put their grain in, but they mostly live in lodges. There being mills in Colville Valley, they have their wheat and corn ground for consumption, these mills are a great help in encouraging them to farm. The Indians at the mouth of the Colville River have vegetables in the market for sale before any of their white neighbor. I purchased early in July peas, carrots, beets, onions, cabbages, etc.: and they are the only ones that have so far successfully cultivated the tomato, the frosts not troubling them as early as those living further up the valley.[5]

The mission garden and fields had served as examples. The repeated changing of reservation boundaries by the national government ruined

---

[3] Rahil, quoting James A. Garfield, *op. cit.,* 22.

[4] George A. Paige, "Annual Report," July 8, 1865, *op. cit.,* 226.

[5] William P. Winans, "Annual Report, September 1, 1870," in "Report of Sml. Ross," Brevet Colonel United States Army, Superintendent, to Hon. E. S .Parker, Commissioner of Indian Affairs, "Report of the Secretary of the Interior," *Executive Documents 1, House of Representatives, Forty-First Congress, Third Session* (Part 4), 488.

this early attempt of the tribal members to establish themselves and their families on a more secure economic basis.

The Homestead Act of 1862 was one way in which the land was taken away from the Indians and over seven million acres annually disposed of. Soon land-hungry adventurers, gold diggers, and military men, who wanted to stay and settle down, were looking for land in the "wild West." Means had to be devised to avoid clashes between Indians and the whites and to protect the rights and the property of the Indians. So it came about that Indian reservations were created to isolate the Indians until they would be able to join their white brothers, to compete with them in the pursuits of life. But instead of protecting the rights and the property of the Indians the opposite occurred.

The unjust and shameful treatment of the Indians in order to occupy their lands was based on a materialistic philosophy that failed to see in the Indian a person consisting of body and of soul who would have in-alienable rights like any of his white brothers. The following ideas of Joseph S. Wilson, Commissioner of the General Land Office, gives us an example:

> In regard to the right of the soil it was settled in the case of the United States vs. Rogers (4 Howard, 567), that the Indian tribes are not owners of the territories occupied by them. These are vacant or un-occupied lands belonging to the United States.
>
> In the case of Johnson vs. McIntosh (S. Wheaton, 543), it was held that the Indian tribes were incompetent to transfer any rights to the soil, and that any such conveyance were void *ab initio,* the right of property not subsisting in the grantor. The right of making such grants was originally in the Crown, but by the treaty of 1783 it was surrendered to the United States.
>
> . . . the General Government has the right to terminate the occupancy of the Indians by "conquest or purchase," Does this involve the right of forcibly dispossessing them of that occupancy? This issue has never yet been presented. . . . In our acquisition of Indian territory, and in reduc-ing the wilderness to civilization, we may, through consideration of policy rather than of abstract right, continue to avoid the question.[6]

The commissioner then speaks about the reckless temper developed by the Indians as a result of privations of abundant subsistence and the intro-duction of physical diseases. He closes his remarks about the Indians by

---

[6] Jos. S. Wilson, Commissioner of the General Land Office, to The Honorable Secretary of the Interior, in "Report of the Secretary of the Interior," *Executive Document 1, House of Representatives, Forty-First Congress, Third Session* (Part 4, Vol. 1), 24–26.

saying: "They are daily diminishing in numbers, and at no remote period they will be among the extinct races of men."[7]

All the tribes belonging today to the Confederated Colville Tribes had no treaty whatsoever with the government. They had lived since time immemorial in these valleys near their streams and mountains, near their hunting and fishing places and close to their root-digging grounds. How can we blame them if they were attached to their ageless lands?

Government officials wanted to sound out the wishes of these Indians and had several meetings in June–July, 1870. They contacted Qua-tal-i-Kim, head chief of the Sanpoils and Nespelems at a council held at the mouth of the Sanpoil River, June 26, 1870. The following is the chief's anwer:[8]

I am a child in knowledge, I have listened to what you have said. There are three things you have spoken of: First, — You want our numbers; second, — You desire to know if we have any religious instruction or wish to have any; and third, — You want to know what our wants and wishes are. The first, — I understand: the Second, — I partly understand; but the Third, — I don't understand at all. I don't understand why you want to know what we wish or what we desire. Do you think we will accept anything from the Government? The Agent at Colville has had Potlatches and sent us word to come and get Blankets, Calico, and Shoes, but we never have gone, or have we accepted or received anything from the Government, and we never will, we have plenty to supply our wants, we have Horses and Cattle, and when we need anything we have money to buy it. It is out of pity that the Superintendent desires to know of us, so that he can help us? We need no pity, all we desire is to be left alone, we don't want the assistance of anyone. We want to live just as we are, not desiring to have our mode of living changed at all, or be interfered with. Our land is a grazing land, not suitable for white man. *They* want farming land, therefore I don't fear them settling on it. As to the Second,— We have no religious Instructor. We desire one. We would like to have a protestant clergyman sent among us, religious instruction is of more importance than all things else. We live but a day here, but our life hereafter is for ever, therefore we should have instruction for the longest life first, after that we can see to the comfort of our bodies. We have always been friendly to the Whites. When the Spokanes and other tribes around me were fighting the Whites, I kept my men at home, forbidding them to go near any of the war parties under pain of punishment. You see by this I've always

---

[7] Wilson, to Secretary of the Interior, *op. cit.*

[8] The Documents from the National Archives in Washington, D. C., are of utmost importance in the study of further developments. We have decided to quote completely these lengthy speeches of the chiefs.

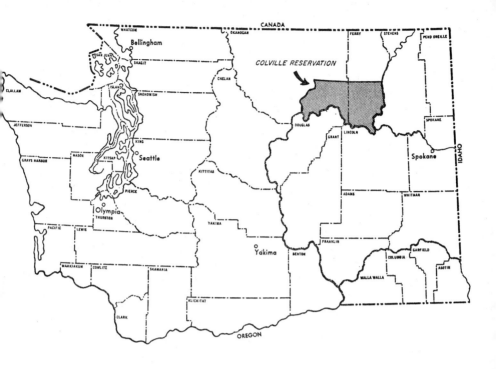

been friendly to the Whites, and I always desire to be so. As to giving the Superintendent our numbers, that is not necessary, we are already numbered. The Chief of us, "God," has numbered us and no man shall number us. I have spoken.[9]

Then Pok-pok-o-Kine or Mr. Wilson spoke in his own behalf and said:

I am alone among my people. They don't see what is for their good. Years ago I was a friend of the Whites for during the War I saved the lives of three White Men, when they were pursued by the Isle de Pierres, and told the Indians that they would have to kill me and walk over my dead Body, before they killed the White Men that were in my lodge. For thus placing my life in danger to save the three White Men, I desire three things. Viz, A Preacher, A Doctor, and A Teacher, and any other assistance that the Superintendent may think will better the condition of the people around me.[10]

Then the government officials went to the mouth of the Okanogan

---

[9] Speech made by Qua-tal-i-Kim, head chief of the Sanpoils and Nespelems at a council held at the mouth of Sanpoil River, June 26, 1870. *Records of the Bureau of Indian Affairs*, Washington Superintendency Letters Received, 1861–1874 (henceforth cited as *RBIA*).

[10] Speech made by Pok-pok-o-Kine (Mr. Wilson), June 26, 1870, *RBIA*.

River where the Moses Indians were assembled in a council on June 30, 1870. Chief Moses was known for his oratory and for his anti-Catholic propaganda. All these chiefs had several wives; therefore they preferred Protestant clergymen. Chief Moses wants to have one too:

I am ignorant, you are educated, therefore you are older in knowledge than I, but I wish to speak my heart as a child speaks to its father, and by so doing I speak for the whole of my tribe. If I am foolish and I mislead my people, I am like an untamed colt, If I am wild, my tribe will follow my example. The White Men are numerous I know not all their Chiefs. You Agents all say that you are sent by the Superintendent, and each one speaks differently so that my heart is divided towards you. If I only knew that the same Superintendent sent you all I would have but one heart. You speak well to the Indians perhaps your heart is good and you want to help them. The Agents are mixed, some good and some bad; you and Harvey are the only two that have spoken alike to me. Your people don't exactly treat my people right, if you tell them not to molest me I would be glad. Whenever you make your people listen to you, I will make mine listen to me. My people will not molest nor trouble the Whites unless they are first molested by them. I say let me alone and give me what is good for me, and I will take it. What you have spoken is good and has already gladdened the hearts of some. I am pleased at your coming among us and at what you have said, and I ask you to tell me if what you have said is true, if so I will believe you. The Priests and Protestant Ministers came among us long ago and the Indians learnt to pray and they were glad, but they are ignorant of religion now, it being so long since they were here. Both Catholic and Protestant Indians pray, they are all badly treated by the Whites. The Indians don't receive any better treatment from the Whites on account of their religion, they treat Christians and Heathen alike. The Indians think they do right to pray but when the Whites see them assembled for worship they mock them; and treat them the same as they would a band of fast Horses, they drive them off; then the Indians cease praying, that is why our hearts are troubled. We sometimes think that if there was a just God he would not suffer us to be thus mocked at, although it is a long time since we stopped praying. We know there is a God who watches over us and we want to learn more of him and wish you would send a Protestant Clergyman and School Teacher among us to instruct and enlighten us. The White Man is the cause of our sorrow, they don't think of our future happiness when they scatter us and take out our gold from our lands. We think religion will do us good, but even while I pray, my heart tells me that the Whites will come and drive us out of our Country. I fear the ruin of my people is coming. I don't speak this personally to you, but to the Superintendent and Government. But to you I say try and get Religious Institutions established among us. But whenever the Government tells me to remain peaceably at home in my own Country, that there they will protect me, I will be thankful, but the way the White Man has talked and threatened me heretofore it appears to me that he wants to take my Country and send me to parts unknown. I don't expect always to live but when you, White, and Me, a Red Man die, we shall have to give an account of ourselves before our Maker, "God," who is our supreme Chief, and if we lie it will be hard on us at the judgment day. Now you tell me to fence and cultivate my land and after a time the Government will give me a deed for it and then it will be mine. My parents gave birth to me, here, and I fancy that this is my country. Your country is where you were born, it is far away, but White Men have a nose like a good Hunting dog, and smelt mine at a great distance and came and found it pleasant. I look upon you as Guests but you treat me as though I were yours, by that treatment I suspect you want to deprive me of my country and take it as your own. I wish we could have one country, one land, and be one people. I want to be friends with you and share my lands with you. I don't prevent you from building and settling in my country. My people have fenced some of the tillable land and are cultivating it. What is not fenced you are welcome to, but it appears to me that you think day and night about me, and puzzle your brains to find out where to place me. I sleep comfortably and don't trouble myself about you but I invite you to come and stay and settle with me. There is room enough for all. Let me remain in my own Country and I shall die contented.[11]

From the mouth of the Okanogan River the officials went to Lake Osoyoos and there heard Chief Tonasket's talk which we have partly quoted in relation to stopping the McLaughlin Canyon fight. We continue:

I, To-nas-Kut, fancied I was [good] medicine for I saved the lives of my people by my advice, for the following Spring the Soldiers came, and would have killed all my people if they had not followed my advice. When the soldiers came and encamped here, I went and saw Capt. Archer, who asked me "What do you want? Do you want to fight?" I said, "No," I live peaceably at home and you White Men can go where you please." Capt. Archer then shook hands with me and said "Thank you." "I did not come to fight but to make peace." From that time we were friends and he said to me, "I want you to look after your people and make them do right"; and I went hand in hand with Capt. Archer in governing my people, and I gave up all evil doers to justice even when they were my near relatives, those whom I pitied. If any White Man kills any of my people I want you to bring him to justice. If my Brother kills a White Man I will deliver him to you, and if your Brother

[11] Speech made by Moses Se-qua-tal-coo-sum the head chief of the Isle de Pierre Indians at the council at the mouth of the Okanogan River, June 30, 1870, RBIA.

kills one of my people I want you to deliver him up to the Officers for punishment.

From the time I saw Capt. Archer in 1859 I was made the Head Chief of the Okanogans, and I am so to this day and by my doing what is right to the Whites and treating them as my friends I am never afraid of being driven out of my country, for my heart never troubles me. I never listen to Indian Reports, I tell all my old men to be of good cheer because I have never harméd the Whites; *that is* what gives me a stout heart. All the Indians think, what shall I say to the Agent, I say "Do what you think is best for me." I have hidden nothing from you. I have told you all I have to say. For the sake of my children I want all you can do for me. I want a Church, a Catholic Priest, a School House, and Teacher, to be instructed in Mechanical Trades, and then we can make our own Plows, build our own Houses and live independent of the Whites who have been so kind to us; we want to be able to supply all the wants of our own people by our own hands. I have spoken.[12]

The last chief to give a talk was Weeh-ah-pe-Kun or Kis-a-wee-ligh, subchief of the Okanogans. His speech is especially touching for it tells us how the incoming whites were undermining the authority of the chief and of the Indian parents. They were degrading the moral life of the Indians generally, that had been on a high level among the aboriginal Okanogans:

Before we saw the Whites we only knew our Fathers and listened to them because we had no other to look up to. When the Whites came among us we could not keep our children together, they would follow the White Man's example, and from them they learnt wrong. The very Indian Boys that work for the Whites are the ones that steal from them and bring us all into trouble. These young men learn the value of money and, being the White Men's adopted children, they learn to murder and to rob. They don't respect their Chiefs. I am pleased to hear you say the Chiefs must be obeyed. When you see my Boy working for the Whites, ask him "Did your Father send you?" if he says no, send him home, for when he comes home at night I will say to him "My son, I am thirsty, go and get me some water to drink," and he turns around and says: "You d——d old b——h, pay me for my trouble." All this they have learned from the Whites. When the Whites come to our camp the first thing they do is to steal our Wives and Daughters, and when I tell them to go away, and ask my Wife and Daughters to stay with me, the Whites abuse, threaten, and G——d d——m me, and take my daughter to prostitute to their passions, when I follow their examples and do the same to my fellow Indian, I get into trouble, I get my head broken, and

---

[12] Speech made by Tonasket, head chief of the Okanogans at a council held at Soo-yoo-oos (Osoyoos), July 3, 1870, *RBIA.*

punished by my Chiefs. You don't punish the White Man for the same conduct I am guilty of, I get punished for doing what they taught me. You tell us to stop drinking and not get drunk; the White Man makes and gives us Whiskey, and then takes our Women from us; the Indians are poor and ignorant but they don't deserve such treatment from the Whites. If they want to better our condition let them stop bringing Whiskey in our Country.

You are the only Agent that has ever assembled our people together and spoken to them for their good. You have given us good advice, and tell us to adopt the habits of the Whites; when we see them drinking and get drunk, we follow your advice, by doing the same as they do; you must send better White Men as Teachers than those that live around us now, if you want us to better our condition by adopting their habits. If you find any of your people running off with our Wives and Daughters, take them and put them in jail. The same God made us both and if a White man does wrong he should be punished as well as the Red Man, for God is just. He does not regard color. I dig roots, and catch fish. God so willed it. If I do wrong, Kill some one, and am hung for it, it is God's will. You say you are sent by the Superintendent to learn about us, to help us for our good, I am glad. I will do all things to help the conditions of my people. If you say that hanging me will better the conditions of my people I will be satisfied to die. We have but one God, for all men. You and I will appear before the same judge, therefore I want religious Teachers sent among us, we want all the help we can get to be better and wiser here, and prepare ourselves for that long life that is to come. We want to be more comfortable and happy and would like to be assisted with Agricultural Implements and instructed how to use them. Some are fearful about their land I do not fear being driven out of my land, if I do right, but if I do wrong I fear. This land is but a Camp, we stay for a night, for all die and reach their destination. I have spoken.[13]

Generally, all the chiefs interviewed wanted to be left alone. All, except the Sanpoil and the Nespelems, wanted to learn about the better things the whites could give, but also their eyes were keen enough to see that the interviewers wanted something in return. Future treaties were forbidden on March 3, 1871, by the Indian Appropriation Act.[14] Henceforth the whites

[13] Speech made by Wee-ah-pe-Kun or Kis-awee-likh, subchief of the Okanogan, July 3, 1870, *RBIA*.

[14] Provided that hereafter no Indian nation, or tribe within the Territory of the United States shall be acknowledged or recognized as an independent nation, tribe, or power with whom the United States may contract by treaty: provided further; that nothing herein contained shall be construed to invalidate or impair the obligation of any Treaty heretofore lawfully made, and ratified with any such Indian tribe, or nation." *Senate Executive Document 452, Fifty-Seventh Congress, First Session, 1901–1902* (Serial No. 4253). *Indian Affairs: Laws and Treaties*, V. 1, Comp. & ed. by Charles J. Kapler, 8.

would call their business transactions for acquiring the Indians' lands an "agreement."

Winans, the Indian farmer, whose official duty was to represent and help the Indians, and who had sent the 1870 report on the industrious Colville Indian farmers, had the following year already changed his attitudes toward his charges. He seemed more concerned about the "property" of some white people which they were gradually taking from the Indians than about the age-old property of the Indians which was transgressed upon by some crooked whites. He reports in 1871:

> There is fear that the encroachment of settlers on lands that the Indians consider their own may cause a collision between them and a general war ensue. . . . I would also state, judging by the actions of the Indians last spring, on the rumor of a withdrawal of troops from Colville, that it is my belief that the lives and property of the settlers in this vicinity would not be safe without military protection; a majority of the Spokane, San Poels, Okanogan, and Colvilles were anxious to appropriate the property of the settlers to their use and benefit; they made no effort to conceal their intentions. . . .
>
> In view of these facts, I believe that the continued occupancy of Fort Colville, by the military is our only security against an Indian war, until these tribes are placed on reservation.[15]

The most important document concerning the Colville Confederated Tribes reads as follows:

Department of the Interior, Office of Indian Affairs,
Washington, D. C., April 8, 1872.

Sir: I have the honor to invite your attention to the Necessity for the setting apart by Executive order of a tract of country hereinafter described, as a reservation for the following bands of Indians in Washington Territory, not parties to any treaty, viz:

The Methow Indians numbering	316
The Okanogan Indians numbering	340
The San Poel Indians numbering	538
The Lake Indians numbering	230
The Colville Indians numbering	631
The Calispel Indians numbering	420
The Spokane Indians numbering	725
The Coeur'd'Alene Indians numbering	700
And scattered bands	300
Total	4200

---

[15] Winans, "Annual Report," September 1, 1871, to General T. J. McKenny, Superintendent of Indian Affairs, Olympia, W.T., *Executive Documents, House of Representatives, Forty-Second Congress, 1871–1872,* 709.

Excluding that portion of the tract of country referred to found to be in the British possessions; the following are the natural boundaries of the proposed reservation, which I have the honor to recommend be set apart by the President for the Indians in question, and such others as the department may see fit to settle thereon, viz: Commencing at a point on the Columbia where the Spokane River empties into the same, thence up the Columbia River to where it crosses the forty-ninth parallel north latitude: Thence east, with said forty-ninth parallel to where the Pend d'Oreille or Clark River crosses the same; thence up the Pend d'Oreille or Clark River to where it crosses the western boundaries of Idaho Territory, the one hundred and seventeenth meridian west longitude; thence south, along said one hundred and seventeenth meridian, to where the Little Spokane River crosses the same; thence southwesterly with said river, to its junction with the Big Spokane River: thence down the Big Spokane River to the place of beginning.

The papers hereinbefore referred to are respectfully submitted herewith.

Very respectfully, your obedient servant,

T. A. Walker, Commissioner.

The Secretary Of The Interior.[16]

This document was signed on April 9, 1872, by President U. S. Grant. So far the Colville Indians were satisfied, because their ancient homes in the Colville Valley had been included and their St. Francis Regis Mission was about in the center of the ancient lands of the Lake and Colville Nations. A storm of protests from the about sixty white settlers, half of whom had Indian wives, reached Washington, D. C. Mrs. Toulou told the author that a Mrs. Meyers went to the military fort in order to gather signatures, which she sent to President Grant, asking him if he thought all these white people now had to move.[17] We were not able to verify this but, as we will see, a special investigation committee blamed the Meyers for injustice done to the Indians. Without any further investigation Grant changed the boundary line of the reservation on July 2 of the same year:

It is hereby ordered that the tract of country referred to in the within letter of the Commissioner of Indian Affairs as having been set apart for the Indians there named by Executive order of April 9, 1872, be restored to public domain, and that in lieu thereof the country bounded on the east and south of the Columbia River, on the west by the Okanogan River, and on the north by the British possessions, be and the same is hereby, set apart as a reservation for said Indians, and for such other Indians as the Department of the Interior may see fit to locate thereon.[18]

[16] T. A. Walker to Secretary of the Interior in *Executive Orders Relating to Indian Reservations From May 14, 1855 to July 1, 1912*, Washington, D. C., 194.
[17] Mrs. Helen Toulou in an interview.
[18] *Executive Orders*, p. 195.

While Indian treaties were made the Indians were at least allowed to speak their mind, and they also had to sign the treaties. The Colville Confederated Tribes, who had done a great service to the United States Government by remaining peaceful and friendly to the whites, were not consulted. After the boundary lines of the reservation were changed, not quite three months having passed, nobody dared even to tell them of this fact. This new reservation took away the Indians' age-old fishery at Kettle Falls by pushing the Indians on the other side of the Columbia River and into the mountains. Winans, who had been largely responsible for the unjust transaction of excluding the Colville Valley from the reservation by seeking his own personal gain and by giving in to some white agitators, gave his reasons why the first reservation was not satisfactory in his last report of September, 1872:

> First, it was too small for so many Indians; the country mostly mountainous, it did not contain sufficient grazing area for their horses and cattle; secondly arable land being nearly all occupied by whites who had been settled on it for ten years or more, it would necessitate their removal before Indians could occupy it.[19]

In the struggle for their lands the Colville Indians did not hesitate to write directly to the President of the United States.

> To The President of the United States
> We Colville Indians, named Skielpi, hear so much talk about our own expatriation from our lands that makes us very sorry. When Colonel Watkins invited us to Spokane Falls to have a talk about our lands we made the agreement that we should have for our residence, as well for other children, six miles of land along the Columbia. Now we are told by the Whites that we must expatriate. We thought that such an agreement should have never been changed, and we shall never be the first to change it.
> Our land is very dear to us, and though we are very poor people we think we can have our rights as well as any one else. We have already been despoiled of the best grazing country, and have no place wherein we might cut hay; we are bound to sow it to winter our cattle and our horses. We have our villages, houses, farms, and mission on this side [the east] of the Columbia; if we must expatriate we shall never be able to build them up again and the little progress in civilization we made already will be lost. The Whites love their land, and we do not love our less. What we want is the title to our land — very poor for American settlers — but good enough for us.

---

[19] Winans to R. H. Milroy, Superintendent of Indian Affairs, Washington Territory, September 1, 1872, "Report No. 71," in *House Executive Documents, 1872 to 1873, Forty-Second Congress, Third Session* (Vol. 4, Part 5), 740–741.

. . . And now we must expatriate, we shall be utterly ruined. Expatriation is one of the causes of our disappearance; and famine will follow and discouragement. We have six or seven Whites in our land; we would see them out altogether, because it is not safe for us to have them in, and much less for our women. The Whites take our wives, and go to a man called judge, and we can never have them back again, and so their Indian husbands have to remain single for all their life. This is the only benefit we get from them. . . .[20]

This letter was signed by the chiefs: Kinkanakua, Charles and Joseph Cotolegan. Needless to say the appeal did not receive any consideration.

Many kinds of dishonest means were used to force the Indians to cross the Columbia River. Then in 1873, the Catholic agent, John A. Simms, took over Winan's job at the Colville Agency. This honest official reported the various complaints of the Indians, and of all who were concerned about them, to Washington, D. C.; whereupon a special commission was named to investigate the matter. It happened that R. H. Milroy, superintendent of Indian Affairs for the Territory of Washington, was on his way to Colville when he heard about the presence of special Commissioner Shanks in Lewiston, who was then invited to come along to Colville to meet the different tribes in council. In their reports neither had much good to say about the character of Winans.

Milroy's report mentions that of the sixty settlers of the Colville Valley, about half had Indian wives (that meant that half of the settlers belonged to the tribes because the children according to law take the blood and race of the mother). He mentions further that the improvements made by the whites were generally small but they would mean much to the Indians. He stated that the government had been deceived "as to the true state of affairs." The Okanogans and the Lakes needed the lands set off for the second reservation, as agricultural lands were scarce there. The Colvilles did not want to take the land away from these tribes who lived west of the Columbia and their wives and children most certainly would have to starve on such unproductive soil. They asked the government to enlarge the reservation. It was pointed out that these tribes "are strongly under the influence of the Catholic Fathers."[21]

Special Commissioner Shanks's report from Colville, August 14, 1873, shows the sad conditions of the Indians living in the Colville Valley and that these were either fostered or aggravated by the Indian farmer,

---

[20] Historicus (Rev. George Weibel, S.J.), quoting the Colville Indians, "Fifty Years of Peaceful Conquest," *Gonzaga Magazine* (5:7, April, 1914), 351.
[21] R. H. Milroy to Hon. E. P. Smith, Commissioner of Indian Affairs, October 20, 1873, "Report 62," *Executive Documents Forty-Third Congress, First Session, 1873 to 1874* (Vol. 4, Part 5), 664–665.

Winans. The meeting took place on August 12, 1873, near the old Hudson's Bay Company fort at Kettle Falls. Indians and whites and Winans himself were present. We quote Shanks's observations:

1. All these people are peaceable, quiet, and industrious, and express a loyalty to the United States Government, as simple, confiding, and faithful as children.

2. They are divided into Catholics and Protestants; the majority of the latter are Presbyterians; and are very zealous in their faith respectively. In the aggregate the Catholics largely outnumber the Protestants.

3. Their agent, John A. Simms, is a Catholic, and the Indians, irrespective of faith, have confidence in his integrity, and speak well of him.

4. They all, irrespective of religious faith, condemn their ex-agent who immediately preceded Simms, one Park Winans, a merchant of Colville.

5. All these Indians desire a permanent reservation, schools, churches, etc.

6. They generally labor either on farms of their own, of which there are a considerable number, or for others, which is the general rule. Many who had farms before the recent influx of whites, have sold their farms to whites and now work by the day for a living.

7. The whites have encroached on the Indians very much, and are continuing to do so.

8. In these encroachments their late agent, P. Winans, was a principal and participant, and still continues to be their exponent and principal operator. He was a partner in a trading-house dealing with the Indians, while [he was] agent, from which whiskey was given to secure bargains in furs, which is the principal trade in that locality. And when the reservation was set off east of the Columbia River, he concealed that fact to the Indians, and busied himself to have it changed to the cold, dry highlands west of that river, where white men have abandoned the country after trial, and failed to farm owing to frost and other difficulties in the way.

9. The reservation has been by interested, and in many ways unscrupulous men, relocated from east to west of the Columbia River; and from the advantages of the salmon fisheries on the Spokane and Columbia to west of the Columbia, only coming to the west bank of the stream, and that without any privilege of fishing in that river, literally robbing the Indians of their country and their food.

10. There are numbers of white settlers in the Colville Valley, where the Indians are now, the Indians not having been removed west of the Columbia under the late unjust assignment of reservation, and I hope never will.

11. These whites are the same persons who procured the change of reservation and are not entitled to any sympathy, as they obtained an unjust order against the Indians, knowing that the new reservation was

unfit for habitation, and avoiding it themselves, procured an order that gave them the Indians' homes, and drove the Indians where they would not reside themselves.

20. It would be expensive, troublesome, dishonorable, and wicked to drive these people away from their homes, where they have lived from time immemorial, to give place to cunning men who have supplanted them and procured the action of the Government against them.[22]

The chiefs had plenty to complain about the whites. Antoine, chief of the Colvilles, stood up in council and told the government representatives:

> We want you to take our part; the liquor is coming up to our knees; we tie our people up for drinking, but the whites do not tie or punish their people for selling liquor to Indians. I wish you who come from Washington would take our part and stop this selling liquor to us.[23]

We can imagine how these conditions hampered the spiritual work of the Jesuit Fathers who were teaching the Indians the white man's religion and yet the whites themselves did not live up to the principles of Christianity. They would marry Indian women according to the simple Indian custom of living together and would break up these unions whenever they wanted, leaving wives and children unprovided for and unprotected. Chief Antoine challenged the whites in the presence of the Commission:

> I want you to take pity on us and help us; bad white men have taken twenty of our squaws from us, and when they have born children to them, the white men take all the property and leave the squaws and children. They leave no property or food for the squaw, mother or children. When I want to get my daughter or my sister from these white men they will not let me have her, and when I ask them to marry our women who they took, they would refuse to marry them, but would keep them in sin; what shall I do?[24]

Antoine even addressed some of the squaw men directly, who were living in adultery and had connections with former agent Winans. One of them was a certain Smith, who wanted the agency. Winans had permitted some bad Indian women to keep places of "ill-fame at Colville, near his place of business. . . ." The good white people stated the same facts and Winans could not deny any of these accusations. Winans had concealed the boundaries of the first reservation from the knowledge of the Indians until he could manipulate the change.

---

[22] J. P. C. Shanks to Hon. T. W. Bennet and H. W. Reed, Gentlemen of the Special Commission, August 14, 1873, *Executive Documents, Forty-Third Congress, First Session, 1874 to 1875* (Vol. 4, Part 5), 529–530.

[23] *Ibid.*, 531.

[24] *Ibid.*

About Mrs. Meyers, who had worked with Winans to have the reservation changed, Shanks wrote the following:

> The Facts are these: Myers [sic] and his wife reside on one hundred and sixty acres of land in what was the reservation, and which they aided to change, (I have been on the place), while Myers has possession of another 160-acres tract, including the old Hudson's Bay Mill property; so the wife claims one, and the Husband the other. Such are the fraudulent actions of these pursuers of the Indian of Colville Valley. I have seen Myers, his wife and home. . . .[25]

The sorry fact remains that in spite of the investigations of the injustices committed against the Colville tribes, President Grant did not have the honest courage to straighten out the wrong and restore the Colville Valley to the tribes. Indians and whites lived side by side in the Colville Valley as before, with the difference that the Indian agent observed that the Indians were becoming negligent in fencing their fields, fearing to be pushed away from their possessions. The Indians' consolation was that their mission and mission schools were still in the valley and were now at the height of their success. The *Diary of St. Francis Regis* mentions on June 17, 1878, that word was received of a general council for the purpose of a permanent locality for the Indians belonging to the Colville Agency. This meeting had been transferred to August 10 of the same year.[26] The agent's report for 1883 still mentions that in comparison the number of the Indians residing on the reservation was small and that those who were living on the east side of the Columbia River took little interest on the reserve. We can readily imagine with a little insight into our human nature how this prolongation of future insecurity must have been harmful to the Indian character in general and how badly it must have affected his outlook on life.

Not only the whites of the Colville Valley but also the settlers seeking homesteads in the Wenatchee, Entiat, and Chelan Valleys and in the Big Bend country kept on encroaching upon the Indians' ancient lands. By executive órder of April 19, 1879, President R. B. Hayes created the Moses or Columbia reservation.[27] Prior to 1879 there was great unrest among the settlers of the Okanogan, Wenatchee, and Yakima Valleys. The influence of Chief Joseph's War and the Bannock War precipitated many lawless acts of violence. Moses had been involved in earlier outbreaks

---

[25] Shanks to Bennet, *op. cit.*

[26] *Diary of St. Francis Regis Mission,* June 17, 1878, Mss., OPA.

[27] R. B. Hayes, "Executive Order" in "Report of the Secretary of the Interior," *House Executive Documents 1, Forty-Sixth Congress, Second Session* (Vol. I, Part 5), 323. See also: Charles J. Kappler, ed., *Indian Affairs: Laws and Treaties,* I, 904.

and was not trusted now, especially in connection with the Perkin's murder, of which he was innocent. He was arrested but through the interference of Agent Wilbur protected. In 1877 tribesmen from all directions were on the way to meet Moses. A. J. Splawn, who investigated, found about six hundred and fifty lodges pitched on the Wenatchee plains. Chief Joseph's scouts kept on coming and leaving, trying to induce the other tribes to join him in the war. The Chelans, Okanogans, and Sanpoils were among the camping tribes. Moses gave as explanation that he had no intention of joining his cousin Joseph in the war. He kept the excited tribesmen in the camp for three weeks under guard and did not let them go until the war fever had subsided.[28] It is said that through the diplomatic and prudent action of Chief Moses another war was prevented.

The care of Moses for his tribe had not been without heartaches as the following letter of Moses to General Howard indicates:

I, Moses, chief, want you to know what my tumtum [heart] is in regard to my tribe and the whites. Almost every day reports come to me that the soldiers from Walla Walla are coming to take me away from this part of the country. My people are excited and I want to know from you the truth so that I can tell them, and keep everything quiet once more among us. Since the last war [Nez Perce] we have had up here rumors that I am going to fight if the soldiers come. This makes my heart sick. I have said I will not fight and I say it to you again and when you hear white men say Moses will fight tell them 'No.' I have always lived here upon the Columbia River. I am getting old and I do not want to see my blood shed on my part of the country. Chief Joseph wanted me and my people to help him. His orders were many. I told 'No, never.' I watched my people faithfully during the war and kept them at home. I told them all, when the war broke out, that they must not steal. If they did, I would report them to Father Wilbur [the Indian agent at Simcoe].

It is time for us to begin spring work. We all raise lots of vegetables, and wheat and corn, and trade with Chinamen to get money. I wish you would write me the truth, so that I can tell my people that they may be contented once more and go to work in their gardens. I do not want to go on the Yakima reservation. I wish to stay where my parents died. I wish you would write to me and send your letter by the bearer of this, and be sure I am a friend and that I tell you the truth.[29]

Moses was sent to Washington, D. C., and there in 1879, his special reservation was granted him. Before that date the Sinkiuse had no home; they had been driven during the wars from their ancestral lands. The

---

[28] Splawn, *op. cit.*, 340–342.
[29] O. O. Howard, Major-General, quoting Chief Moses in *My Life and Experiences Among Our Hostile Tribes*, 350–351.

Moses reservation was bounded on the east by the Okanogan River, on the west by the Cascades, on the north by Canada and on the south by Lake Chelan and the Columbia. Mr. John Cleveland told the author that while Chief Moses was in Washington he was named the head chief of the Okanogans. Mr. Cleveland saw the document with the gold seals stating Moses' chieftainship.[30] Chief Moses himself had nothing to do with the Okanogan tribes and was therefore very much resented by the real Okanogan chiefs. The territory of the Columbia reservation was also considered a part of the primeval possessions of the Okanogans, and Moses and his people were for some years considered as the intruders.

The regions of the Similkameen and Osoyoos were settled quite early by ranchers and miners who voiced their protests. Others wanted to work in the mines there. Moses was called during the summer of 1881 to Fort Spokane and was induced to relinquish the upper ten-mile strip of his reservation where ore had been found. Moses replied: "If the whites wish to work the mines, they can pay me."[31] About the same time Lieutenant Thomas W. Symons had been sent to make an examination of the Upper Columbia River and the adjacent territory. He mentions the dispute about the mines:

> There is a great deal of good land along the Okinakane River and in its vicinity, and good mines are known to exist. Some mines were discovered and were claimed and worked before the reservation along the river was set apart for Chief Moses and his people. Disputes have arisen between the miners and the Indians in regard to the right of the former to pursue their work. This has been the subject of a recent decision at Washington, that those mines which were discovered before the reservation was set apart belong to the discoverer and owner who must not be interfered with in working them.[32]

Symons visited the camp of Indians at the mouth of the Okanogan River. "Cleanly looking squaws" were cooking, making moccasins or gloves, or were mending clothes, while the "fine fierce-looking bucks" were either gambling or were making arrows and fishing spears. He wanted to start a conversation with them but these Indians were "cold and surly" and regarded him with suspicion."[33]

Then on February 23, 1883, President Arthur restored to the public

---

[30] Mr. John Cleveland, in an interview at St. Mary's Mission, Omak, Washington, August 12, 1960.

[31] Moses quoted by Click Relander, *Drummers and Dreamers*, 195.

[32] Lieutenant Thomas W. Symons, "Report of an Examination of the Upper Columbia River and the Territory in its Vicinity in September and October, 1881." *Senate Executive Documents, No. 186, Forty-Seventh Congress, First Session.*

[33] *Ibid.*

domain a strip of land fifteen miles wide along the Canadian boundary. Through this action Moses became alarmed reasoning that if the government could take a part of his land without his permission they would take away the rest of the land any time they wanted. He took his people and went back to the region around Moses' Coulee.[34] General Miles then summoned Chief Moses to Vancouver and, in 1883, sent him with other chiefs to Washington, D. C., where they signed the wrongly called "Moses Agreement":

In the conference with chief [sic] Moses and Sar-sarp-kin, of the Columbia reservation, and Tonaskat and Lot, of the Colville reservation, had this day, the following was substantially what was asked for by the Indians:

Tonasket asked for a saw and grist mill, a boarding school to be established at Bonaparte Creek to accommodate one hundred pupils (100), and a physician to reside with them, and $100 (one hundred) to himself each year.

Sar-sarp-kin asked to be allowed to remain on the Columbia reservation with his people, where they now live, and to be protected in their rights as settlers, and in addition to the ground they now have under cultivation within the limits of the fifteen mile strip cut off from the northern portion of the Columbia Reservation, to be allowed to select enough more unoccupied land in Severalty to make a total to Sar-sarp-kin of four square miles, being 2,560 acres of land, and each head of a family or male adult one square mile; or to move on to the Colville Reservation, if they so desire, and in case they so remove, and relinquish all their claims to the Columbia Reservation, he is to receive one hundred (100) head of cows for himself and people, and such farming implements as may be necessary.

All of which the Secretary agrees they should have, and that he will ask Congress to make an appropriation to enable him to perform.

The Secretary also agrees they should have, and that he will ask Congress to make an appropriation to enable him to purchase for Chief Moses a sufficient number of cows to furnish each one of his band with two cows; also to give Moses one thousand dollars ($1,000) per annum during his life.

All this on condition that Chief Moses shall remove to the Colville Reservation and relinquish all claim upon the Government for any land situated elsewhere.

Further, that the Government will secure to Chief Moses and his people, as well as to all other Indians who may go on to the Colville Reservation, and engage in farming equal rights and protection alike with all other Indians now on the Colville Reservation, and will afford him

[34] Judge W. G. Brown, manuscript. Courtesy of Mrs. Katie Lacey, Osoyoos.

any assistance necessary to enable him to carry out the terms of this agreement on the part of himself and his people. That until he and his people are located permanently on the Colville Reservation, his status shall remain as now, and the police over his people shall be vested in the military, and all money or articles to be furnished him shall be sent to some point in the locality of his people, there to be distributed as provided. All other Indians now living on the Columbia Reservation shall be entitled to 640 acres, or one square mile of land, to each head of family or male adult, in the possession of ownership of which they shall be guaranteed and protected. Or should they move on to the Colville Reservation within two years, they will be provided with such farming implements as may be required, provided they surrender all rights to the Columbia Reservation.

All of the foregoing is upon condition that Congress will make an appropriation of funds necessary to accomplish the foregoing, and confirm this agreement; and also, with the understanding that Chief Moses or any of the Indians heretofore mentioned shall not be required to remove to the Colville Reservation until Congress does make such appropriation, etc.

H. M. Teller
Secretary Of The Interior
H. Price
Commissioner of Indian Affairs
Moses [his X mark]
Tonasket [his X mark]
Sar-sarp-kin [his X mark][35]

This "Moses Agreement" was ratified July 7, 1884, and $85,000 appropriated to carry out the provisions of this act.[36] The four bands: the Skoahchnuh, the Sinkolkoluminuh, the Stapisknuh and the Skukulatkuh went with Moses to the Colville Reservation. They numbered five hundred and twenty-one in 1910, excluding those who received allotments outside the reservation.[37] A special reservation was set aside for the Spokane Indians by Executive order of President Hayes, January 18, 1881.[38]

The Colville reservation now comprised an area of approximately 2,886,000 acres and was bounded on the south and east by the Columbia River, on the west by the Okanogan River, and on the north by the

---

[35] Kappler, *op. cit.*, II, 1074.

[36] "Report of the Secretary of the Interior, 1884," *House Executive Documents, Forty-Eighth Congress, 1884 to 1885, Second Session,* Vol. II, 45.

[37] Curtis, *op. cit.*, VII, 68.

[38] *Executive Orders*, 207.

Canadian boundary. Indian Agent Hal. J. Cole tells about the reluctance of the tribes to give away still more of their ancient lands:

Colville Commission — On May 1, 1891, the Commissioners consisting of Hon. Mark A. Fullerton, Hon. J. F. Payne, and Hon. W. H. H. Dufur, appointed to treat with the Indians residing on the Colville Reservation, visited the Colville Agency, and a few days later met a number of the Indians in council at Nespilem, and presented to them some proposals for purchasing a portion of the reservation. The Commission had to talk to the Indians two or three days before any agreement could be reached. The Okanogan tribe was the first to sign. Then came Moses and his band of Columbia, and next Joseph's band of Nez Perces. The San Puell tribe and the Nespilem tribe were bitterly opposed to the treaty, and not one of them signed. They said they had never asked any favors of the Government, had accepted none, and simply desired to be let alone. The Commissioners closed their labors on May 23, 1891, opposite Marcaw, on the reservation where the Colville and Lake tribes signed the treaty.

By the term of the treaty, the Indians agree to sell 1,500,000 acres, or about half of the Colville Reservation, and the Government agrees to pay the sum of $1,500,000 for that Portion of the reservation ceded, in five annual installments of $300,000 each.[39]

By the Act of July 1, 1892, the north half of this reservation was restored to public land and 1,500,921 acres taken away from the Indians. Before this area was opened to be settled, 660 Indians were allotted 51,653 acres, about 80 acres per person. The land then left — 1,449,268 acres — was opened for settlement on October 10, 1900. Each homesteader had to pay $1.50 per acre plus the regular fee which was to be placed in trust for the benefit of the Indians.[40] The land had been taken away from the Indians under the condition that the United States would compensate for it and buy it. Congress declined to ratify the agreement of May 9, 1891, because of the stipulation contained in it that payment for the land be made in five equal installments of $300,000 each. Instead it passed the act of July 1, 1892. The Colville National Forest was created out of the area ceded in the north half in 1892, when by Presidential proclamation, March 1, 1907, 869,570 acres were set aside. On March

[39] Hal. J. Cole, "Annual Report of 1891" in "Report of the Secretary of the Interior," *The Executive Documents of the House of Representatives for the First Session of the Fifty-Second Congress, 1891 to 1892* (Vol. 2), 443.

[40] Walt Horan, Congressman, "History of the Colville Reservation," in *Hearings Before the Subcommittee on Indian Affairs of the Commission on Public Lands, House of Representatives and the Committee on Interior and Indular Affairs, United States Senate, Eighty-First Congress, First Session on H.R. 2432*, Serial No. 19, p. 7.

4, 1927, an additional area of 2880 acres were added to the Colville National Forest.[41]

In 1896 the northern half of the reservation was opened to mineral entry and in 1898 the rest of the south of the reservation was opened for the same purpose. Now many lawless white people swarmed over the Colville Indian Reservation disturbing again the peace of the Indians. The agents' reports mention several times that many white people used their mineral entries only to secure land titles. This brought about a special investigation by representatives of the Land Office. In many cases patents had been issued and the Department of Justice had to interfere to restore these nonmineral lands. Old newspapers of Stevens County tell of the propaganda made to secure more white people for their county. The Index of the *Colville Examiner* for June 17, 1911, states: "1,340 acres in Colville Indian Reservation fraudulently taken as mineral lands . . . will be returned to Reservation as Indian property."[42] Indian Agent Captain Webster, a close friend of Father de Rougé, complained in a 1905 report that the opening of the reservation to mineral entry has brought a train of evil in its wake. Towns have been built on placer mining claims, and all sorts of businesses excepting that of mining are carried out. The saloons are now in the heart of the reservation and the federal judge has decided that no law was transgressed by carrying liquor across the reservation in order to reach the mining claims. From these saloons the liquor is given secretly to the Indians and no judge will try such cases on Indian testimony alone. Crops are raised and garden-truck farming carried on openly on the fraudulent mining claims.[43]

Every unrest and dissatisfaction among the Indians had its repercussion in the work the Jesuit missionaries were doing. Without their presence, encouragements, and wise counsels the Indians most likely would have banded together and tried to chase the unlawful intruders from their lands. It is in this sense that the Indians and the whites of the Colville Reservation owe perpetual gratitude to the Jesuit Fathers and their missions.

Enough land had been taken away from the Confederated Colville Tribes, but the government of the United States and unscrupulous

---

[41] Hon. Harry P. Cain, "Pertinent Facts Concerning the Colville Reservation in the State of Washington and the Indians Belonging Thereto," speech in Senate of United States, Friday, July 4, 1952. *Congressional Record, Proceedings and Debates of the Eighty-Second Congress, Second Session,* 220755–44328.

[42] *Index of the Colville Examiner,* 190, Je. 17, 11, 1:3, 201.

[43] J. McA. Webster, Indian Agent, "Report, June 30, 1905," in "Annual Reports of the Secretary of the Interior," *House Executive Documents, Fifty-Ninth Congress, First Session* (Vol. 19), 355–356.

white settlers were still land-hungry. They sent Indian Inspector James McLaughlin to force another agreement from the Indians. James Mc-Laughlin had been Indian agent for many years; he loved the Indians, but here he was told by the government what to do. According to the testimony of Chief Jim James at the hearings, the Indians were taken separately and told if they would accept the allotments they would then receive the payment of the $1,500,000 for the north half of the reservation which the United States government had not paid yet. Chief James and many of the elder leaders did not sign.[44] This so-called McLaughlin Agreement ceded, granted, and relinquished to the United States all title, right, and interest of the diminished Colville reservation. An allotment of eighty acres should first be made for every man, woman, and child. The cession by the Indians of the surplus land left was conditioned on the fact that they will be compensated by the United States for the approximately 1,500,000 acres they relinquished in the north half of the reserve. Much discussion and dissatisfaction with this last stipulation made the Indian leaders of the next generation feel that their grandfathers "were betrayed by the Government probably through erroneous interpretation . . . payment for the north was contingent on the Indians signing away" their last land.[45]

The lengthy McLaughlin Agreement stated in detail how much money the Indians should receive from the $1,500,000 for the different purposes and what amount was to be put in trust under the guardianship of the Secretary of the Interior. Per capita payments from the income and proceeds from their reservation were left to the discretion of the Secretary of the Interior. What made the Agreement seem completely invalid are the three hundred fifty signatures which the Indians said was not a majority of the adult population of the Confederated Tribes.[46] Mrs. Helen Toulou, in a copy of the McLaughlin Agreement, has identified the tribal affiliations of the signers, and counts twenty Nez Perce Indians. She maintains that the Nez Perce were at the time of the agreement prisoners of war; so she feels that the document is invalid.

If we consider how these agreements were forced from the Indians we feel outraged about this national injustice done to a minority group. We heard that Congress failed to ratify the first agreement on account of the $1,500,000 to be paid to the Indians. Again, after the McLaughlin Agreement had been forced from the Indians, Congress accepted the terms of the McLaughlin Agreement without the paying of the $1,500,000 from

---

[44] Chief Jim James, "Testimony Before the Subcommittee on Indian Affairs," *Eighty-First Congress, First Session on H.R. 2432,* Serial No. 19, 15–16.

[45] Cain, "Pertinent Facts," *op. cit.,* 31.

[46] Congressman Walt Horan, "History of the Colville Reservation," *op. cit.,* 7.

the first sale. The poor Indians had recourse to court action begining in 1894. The $1,500,000 was finally paid under court procedure but now the Indians had to pay $60,000 attorney's fee.[47]

Great injustice was done by white settlers to the Chelan Indians. After the Columbia Reservation had become public domain, some Indians were free to have their allotments there and later it was provided they could have their patent in fee simple. Some of the prominent Indian tribal families were molested, their homes ruined, their wives and children chased away by crooked "land sharks." Frank M. Streamer wrote the following letter to General Howard, August 20, 1890, as Chief John Wapato dictated it to him:

> Wapato John — Lake Chelan speaks: My people are taken from their homes and carried to the Colville reserve, and they are citizens and pay taxes. The soldiers surveyed out their lands and they lived on them in accordance with the treaty. Now some of them [whites] filed on their lands to hold them, as they were told that the Yakima land office did not know of the surveys made by the agent from Washington and the soldiers. So white men have filed on our allotted lands, and great trouble I have. Tell Gen. Howard that I paid Seventy Dollars taxes to Okanogan County, and that the special agent from Washington City, said I should not pay any taxes, as I was a Washington City Indian by treaty of the Moses reserve. Now three of my Indian people are robbed of their farms, and I will go next, I am afraid.
>
> I want to know from General Howard and Washington, if their treaty is true, or whether the Chelan Indians must leave their age-old farm-homes and obey the Colville Indian Agent Hal. Cole, or obey the treaty made at Washington City with Chiefs Moses Su-cep-kin, Tonasket, and Lot. The whites now survey the lands, and then, drive us away, and the soldiers help them.
>
> The Wenatchee Indians want to know what has become of the Col. Wright-Lt. Archer-Samew treaty, granting them an Eight mile square reserve from Mission creek to Wenatchee Falls in 1856 which the Indians lived on, and is now settled upon by whites, and a few Indians, who had to pay for their homesteads thereon $22.00 a piece, when they should have them free, as the reserve was theirs. Another survey made for reserve by General Gordon, a special agent in 1887, further up in the mountains, where a bear could not live, and now that is stolen, and the Wenatchee Indians are very poor, yet they fought for Colonel Wright and Washington City.
>
> Now we are told we must all go away to the Colville reserve and

---

[47] Hon. Hugh Butler, speech in Senate of the United States, January 22, 1951, in *Transfer of Title to Certain Lands to the Colville Indians, Washington*, 936530–38519, 4.

lose all our farms, and by and by, lose the Colville reserve, and forget where we belong, and who owns us, and whether we ever had a good father or mother or whether we are only Coyotes to be shot at, and coralled like cayuses.[48]

Some changes in the General Allotment Act were made by the act of June 25, 1910. The Indians could receive now either 40 acres of irrigable land, 80 acres of nonirrigable land or agricultural lands, or 160 acres of nonirrigable grazing lands. A vast amount of land of the Colville Reservation is nonproductive.

It was only in 1914 that the allotment rolls were closed. Settlers had looked over the best land sites before that time. The *Colville Examiner* on April 29, 1911, carried the notice that "during 30 days ending April 30, 90,000 prospective settlers came to the Pacific Northwest."[49]

The United States Indian policy and especially the McLaughlin Agreement destroyed the tribal economy of the Confederated Colville Tribes and the incentive to work in many of its members. Under the early guidance of the Jesuit Fathers and their schools, many Indians had learned to improve their tribal and individual property. We have seen how the Colvilles had made progress in their family holdings without special allotments. This constant uprooting from tradition, from their homes, from tribal authority created a different Indian character than the free aboriginal Indians had shown.

McLaughlin himself condemns the United States Indian policies as the following quotations show:

What he is, the white man made him — for in the Indian of today there is very little trace of that high spirit and cheerful independence which marked the aborigines.[50]

. . . the Indian has been made the object of speculative persecution by every white man who felt that he needed what the Indian possessed.[51]

The younger people have little pride in ancestry and no care for the future. The older people have neither ambition nor hope — beyond the next payment. They are utterly listless of the passing of time, except as it brings a payment nearer, and are much given to the cheaper amusements of the whites and the inane dances of their ancestors. Fifteen years of annuity drawings has made of a people that was struggling to the surface by personal effort, a set of paupers in chancery.[52]

[48] Composed by Chief Wapato, written by Frank M. Streamer, August 20, 1890, to Major General O. O. Howard, *Streamer Letters, Streamer Papers*, Mss., AWHS.
[49] The *Colville Examiner*, "Index," April 29, 1911, 254.
[50] McLaughlin, *op. cit.*, 260.   [52] *Ibid.*, 398–399.   [51] *Ibid.*

They will be stripped of their farms, as soon as they are patented, by their more thrifty neighbors. Then, perhaps, they will go to work in order to eat.[53]

Many of the Indians, especially the chiefs, had before the McLaughlin Agreement been great stock raisers with hundreds of cattle and horses. They would help by their contributions to maintain the Indian missions. After the Indians became uprooted from their tribal possessions and their individual holdings they became in many instances poor. The white neighbor was allowed to buy enough acres to increase his profits while the Indians became poorer as the years went by. How should they divide the land given them per capita after a new generation with more people on the allotment grew up? It became more and more a burden to keep the Indian missions open and to maintain them through charitable gifts given.

---

[53] McLaughlin, *op. cit.,* 398–399.

CHAPTER VIII

A Mission Center on the Reservation Is Needed

WE MENTIONED the early call for priests from Chief Kamiakin of the Yakimas and how Stevens' treaty-making and the Indian wars had destroyed the hope of early Christianization of that tribe. We also know that the Jesuits took over the care of the Yakima mission in 1870. Father St. Onge left during June of 1871, after having acquainted Father Joseph Caruana, S.J., with the Yakima language. The *Diary of St. Francis Regis Mission* states under date of May 13, 1871:

> Today Fr. Grassi and B. Compopiano started for Yakama, with Kolosaskat and an Indian send here by Fr. ——————— from the Yakama. They had taken for provisions 160 lbs flour, 36 dry meat and a few dry salmon.[1]

The Okanogan tribes were now visited from St. Francis Regis and from St. Joseph's at the Athanum. Definite attempts were made to win over the tribes which hitherto had still been pagans: the Methow, the Chelans, the Wenatchees, and other related bands. Father Urban Grassi became the traveling missionary who was on the way most of the time, fording rivers, climbing mountains, transversing valleys and canyons.

We owe to Father Grassi some of the most interesting missionary letters. In one of them, dated October 4, 1873, Father Grassi tells Father Cataldo some of his experiences with the Simpesquensi, who belonged to the Wenatchee tribe. They lived some hundred miles north of Yakima, almost buried in the mountains. Years ago they had been visited by the Oblate Fathers from Yakima mission and later by Father St. Onge. They numbered about three hundred souls and had quite an influence on three

---

[1] *Diary of St. Francis Regis Mission,* Mss., OPA (May 13, 1870).

smaller neighboring bands. Father Grassi had heard about their Chief Patoi, who possessed the entire confidence of the tribe:

> He makes them keep holy not only the Sunday but the Saturday also; he has banished all sorts of sins from his camp, and makes his people assemble frequently for common prayer.[2]

When Father arrived at the camp the people were at prayer and he had to wait. After this Father was received with great honor. Chief Patoi had his tribe line up in two rows facing each other and Father then had to shake hands with everybody. Then Chief Patoi made a speech expressing his joy over the visit of the priest. The people then were dismissed and Father took possession of an empty hut. After awhile, Father went to Patoi's lodge and told him the purpose of his coming, whereupon the chief rang the bell to assemble his people. After such a courteous welcome Father did not expect to have difficulties. Patoi, however, had Father repeat the purpose of his coming to the whole tribe and then rebuffed and humiliated him in the presence of all. The reason: "The Blackgowns by abandoning his tribe had renounced their right over them." Chief Patoi refused to point out to Father those who were Christians. The missionary had recourse to silent prayer and went back to his empty hut where he was visited by some of the tribe. He taught whatever he could to those who came.

Then one evening Patoi rang the bell near Father's hut and assembled the people so that all could hear what he had to say to the missionary. "If God did not like our prayer, how could we have become so good as we are, for I do not think that we have become so good of ourselves." Father then praised the chief and explained that if they were so good with the little they knew, they would become like the first Christians if they would accept the entire prayer which he had come to teach them. Chief Patoi then told of an apparition he had four months before during the night. He became more friendly after Father assured him that there was nothing wrong with his apparition. A conference was then allowed in the presence of the people and Father's mission was accepted provided he would stay during the winter with the tribe. Then those who were baptized were introduced.

Father Grassi visited this tribe again as he had promised. While he was staying at the camp an epidemic broke out. Five medicine men were busy about the sick and the dying. Only after they all had tried their incantations was the missionary allowed even to visit the afflicted ones.

---

[2] Father Urban Grassi, S.J., to Father P. C., October 4, 1873, *WL* (III:1, January, 1874), 70.

He tried in vain to dissuade them from their sorceries about which he remarked in his letter to Father Cataldo, "Sorcery is practiced by them to so great an extent that most of the men have some satanic spell or other about them."[3] Father then explained how these medicine men procure this satanic spell:

> One will go rambling alone in the woods, abstaining from food and drink, for ten, fifteen or even twenty days, until at last from sheer exhaustion, he falls into a state of senselessness. Then, whether in trance or waking he does not know, the *genius loci* appears to him and asks him if he wishes to be lucky in something or other, such as fishing, hunting, trapping, or the curing of diseases. On the man's answering in the affirmative he becomes the bondsman of his visitor, from whom he receives a badge. It may be a feather, or a clam, or a ring of the rattlesnake. This badge which they call *somesh*, they preserve with religious care and, to doctors especially who are supposed to have the most powerful spell, it is a very rich source of revenue.[4]

Father Grassi using great prudence and a heavenly patience was able slowly to win over more people from the Simpesquensi tribe. Patoi himself, forty-five years old, was baptized on April 5, 1874. Six of his children had received baptism three months earlier. It was a happy Easter day when baptism was followed by a Christian marriage and many of the tribe followed the example of the chief. Father Grassi was able during the year of 1874, to baptize 186 persons, to perform the blessing of 28 marriages, to give Christian burial to 10 adults; he recorded also the death of 39 babies who had been baptized. Uapto John (Wapato John) is often mentioned as assistant at christenings and marriages.[5] (Chief Wapato was the grandfather of Dr. Paschal Sherman, Washington, D. C., one of Father de Rougé's former honor students.)

When Father Grassi's letter to Father Cataldo was published in the *Woodstock Letters* the curiosity and interest of his fellow Jesuits was aroused. They knew that Father Grassi was not the man to believe in stories. We know that our Lord had to drive out the devil who had entered into persons and had made his hell in them; and that the power of the devil in a pagan world was great.[6] The fellow Jesuits wanted Father Grassi to investigate further into the true story "about the talisman which the medicine men are said to receive from the evil one." In a letter written from St. Joseph's Mission at the Athanum, on May 26,

---

[3] Grassi to Cataldo, *WL* (3:3, September, 1874), 214.
[4] *Ibid.*
[5] Historicus (Father George Weibel, S.J.), "Fifty Years of Peaceful Conquest," *Gonzaga Magazine* (5:4), 185–186.
[6] See Matthew 4:24; 8:23–33; Mark 1:39; Luke 4:41; etc.

1874, Father Grassi tells about the results of his investigations. He had come home from his latest missionary trip. A medicine man who had been converted some months ago had come to confession, after which Father questioned him about how he received his *somesh*. His story follows:

When I was a boy about twelve years of age I began to ramble alone on the mountains in search of a *somesh*. One day — it was the fifth that I had passed without having eaten or drunk anything whilst walking on the side of a mountain — I heard a great noise as if a mountain had fallen on the one where I was. I stopped in dismay, when I heard a human voice calling on me to approach. Immediately I hastened towards the place whence the voice had come, when upon raising my eyes, I saw at a distance of about fifteen steps a very beautiful young man covered with white feathers. He was, indeed, a splendid sight to look upon, and whilst I was gazing . . . at him, without approaching any nearer to him, he told me not to fear, that he was a dweller in another world far away from this, but that he had leave to go and come at pleasure. He held in his hand a bow and arrow which he showed to me saying that he meant to give them to me as he wished me to become a valiant in hunting. Having said this, he threw the bow and arrow on the ground; other things, too, he told me, which I have now quite forgotten. At last he said: "Well I am going away now, but I shall see you again," and he disappeared from my sight. Then I went up to the spot where he had thrown his bow and arrow, but there was nothing to be seen. I looked all around among the trees, trying to catch another glimpse of him, but in vain. I understood however, what he meant. So I went home and made myself a bow and plenty of arrows; and from that day my aim has been unerring.

About one year after, whilst I was again traveling in search of a *somesh*, I heard the voice of a man that had called me, and upon looking up, I saw a bear. I was very much frightened and began to look around for the man that had called me. Then the bear with precisely the same human voice, spoke to me and said: "Approach and be not afraid. I am a bear, a brute which you can kill with your arrow. You will in fact, kill me, flay me and eat my flesh. Now I wish to teach you how to cure certain diseases — he mentioned what they were. You will apply your hands as I do. Look — There was a stick there and, whilst he spoke, he put his paw upon it. Now, continued he, shoot me." Immediately I shot him dead, flayed him, ate a part of his flesh, took his paw for a *somesh* and went my way rejoicing.

Some two years later I was walking on the mountains when I heard the pici — a bird very common in these parts. I looked to see him, but saw instead I very beautiful boy, white and feathered and like in every respect, save the size, to the one whom I had seen before. Near him was a rattlesnake and the boy told me how to cure the bite of the reptile. "Kill that snake," he said, "and take the tooth for a *somesh*." I was afraid to stir, when, suddenly, the boy disappeared and the *pici* pounced upon the rattlesnake and killed him. Then I saw nothing more but the dead snake. I cautiously approached and, finding him really dead, I took out his poisonous tooth and went off.

Then Father Grassi continues:

> The evil one shows himself very frequently to our medicine men and speaks to them through wild geese and caiotes [coyotes]. Usually he teaches them a song which they take good care to sing during their incantations. By the application of the hands I believe that magnetism is taught them; and that they have worked cures thereby, not only upon Indian patients but upon white ones also, who had been given up by other doctors are incontestible facts.[7]

Father Grassi built for these Indians the first primitive mission log church in that country. When Father de Rougé was called there years later he found this chapel had instead of a roof a tent stretched over the walls, as we will see. This camp was about ten miles west of the Columbia River and about eleven miles west of Wenatchee on the Wenatchee River.

Father Parodi, stationed for a time at Yakima mission, wanted to visit the other camp of Wenatchees. He was not well acquainted with the Wenatchee language and knew that only a few Indians spoke the Yakima language. He induced Chief Patoi to accompany him and act as interpreter. The chief, however, came only once. Father Parodi told this to Father Grassi, who in turn asked about the subject Father Parodi had discussed:

> Sorcery! 'Oh, you made a mistake; Chief Patoi is a staunch sorcerer.' The Indians had got a large picture of the Samarian woman talking with our Lord. The father explaining this picture made our Lord say: "You have stolen 5 men already, and the man you keep is not your husband."[8]

The Indians were silent and looked at each other in amazement. Father Parodi had used the Indians' own language only with opposite meaning. The Indian men seduced the women; they "stole a woman." Father Parodi had been sure that this was a good subject.

Father Parodi and his companion once entered an Indian house where they saw a picture of hell which somebody must have given to the mission. His companion inspected the picture and then said: "No Indian has gone into Hell." The painter had put only white people in hell.[9]

Father Grassi speaks about the Intialicum and the Indians living there; it is understood that they were the Indians of the Entiat Valley.

---

[7] Grassi to Father Valente, S.J., May 26, 1874, WL (3:3, 1874), 214–216.
[8] Father Louis Parodi, S.J., *Memoirs,* Ms., OPA.
[9] *Ibid.*

They had their camps about sixteen miles away from the Chelans. In a letter to Father Giorda, November 10, 1874, he mentioned three camps which were a number of miles apart, each having its own chief. An epidemic had carried off almost all the younger generation, and the earthquakes, the sunken ground, and the broken mountains had taught them the necessity of prayer. Here too Father Grassi made the observation on the power and the appearances of the devil. The evil one had appeared in several instances to the various chiefs in the guise of the missionary wishing to show them how to pray. One of the chiefs had been formerly in the service of a white man in Oregon whom he asked about the good prayer. The white man himself did not practice any religion but told the Indian that he was convinced the Catholic missionaries taught the good prayer. This chief showed great joy when Father Grassi entered his camp; the chief was instructed and baptized. The devil had appeared to him "clothed as the missionary." "The chief asked him if he were the Blackrobe. 'No,' but that he was a messenger sent from heaven to teach him the prayer."[10] The chief did not want to have anything to do with him, so the devil left and perverted five or six of the other chiefs of the small tribes living in that region. Father Grassi tried his best to convince these chiefs of their error but without success. One of them was especially satanic "and the horrible blasphemies he vomited declared him a worthy disciple of such a master."[11]

Here Father Grassi had to fight the demon himself, not just ignorance or superstition. It was hard work to win these souls and Christianize these natives where the chief had all kinds of clever arguments to discredit the missionary in the presence of the people. He had not taken into account the saintliness of the good Father and his extraordinary degree of patience and perseverance. Sometimes a chief would promise the priest that he would receive baptism at the next visit of the missionary and then would be completely perverted when the missionary arrived again. But not only the devil tried to obstruct the work of the Catholic missionary. Father Grassi complained about white people who instill doubt into the Indians by ridiculing the priest and who misinterpret the life of privations the priest is leading and attribute low and sinful motives to the missionary. But in spite of all the difficulties Father Grassi had little by little baptized nearly all the members of the tribe. He had proved himself a perfect teacher; he composed a little catechism of the most important doctrines the recitation of which took only about

---

[10] Grassi to Father Joseph Giorda, S.J., Superior of the Rocky Mountain Missions, November 10, 1874, Ms., OPA.
[11] Ibid.

a half hour. He had taught hymns to the song-loving Indians and had instructed and drilled the more gifted persons to ask questions and act as teachers in his absence.[12]

Great difficulties awaited Father Grassi as he attempted to convert the Chelans. They had poor little camps on the Columbia River, winter quarters five or six miles from there on the river Mitgan near to a tribe of the same name. Here was another fishing center of the surrounding tribes. When Father Grassi wrote this letter, he had visited the Chelans three times, all in the same year, 1874.

During the spring season Father Grassi had arrived on the opposite shore of the Columbia. The chief of the Chelans was not at home and nobody dared to take the missionary across the river. Two boys, whom he had instructed and baptized the winter before, finally came and took him across. Father pitched his tent and shortly after Chief Ninusize of the Chelans arrived. There was no greeting for the priest; the chief showed his displeasure but others came timidly to welcome Father. In the evening Father rang the bell and the Indians filled his tent, but no male adults came. Only after darkness had set in did Ninusize call Father to his wigwam where he had gathered his men. Father was asked various questions but due to difficulties in the Chelan dialect he was not able to answer effectively. This took nearly all night. Father Grassi was to leave next morning; he promised to learn the Chelan language better and then would visit the tribe at the summer camp at Mitgan.

The red salmon season was nearly over before Father Grassi could reach the Chelans the second time. The people he met on the way had warned him not to meet Ninusize, that he would be beaten by him. This chief had made trips into the surrounding country looking for baptized people and making them give up prayer and throw the medals and the crosses which they were wearing away. Father's companion was afraid to cross the Mitgan River where the Chelans were, but Father Grassi stayed on his horse, crossed over, and went directly to the chief's camp. He found the tent filled with people and Chief Ninusize was unwilling at first even to shake hands. Father tells us about this meeting:

> With a ferocious face he asked me savagely whether I had been sent from Washington: I answered, "No," but I had been sent from God; a little after he said, that he had never killed a white; then stretching himself out, he took a lad who was near me and suggested words insulting to the missionary, which the [boy] repeated in a loud voice.[13]

The Indians wanted to make fun of Father and of holy things, but the

---

[12] Grassi to Giorda, *op. cit.*   [13] *Ibid.*

experienced missionary knew how to deal with ridicule on the part of
these primitive people. The chief's son-in-law wanted Father to baptize
a magpie; this brought a lecture on the difference between the soul of
a brute animal and a human soul and of the ingratitude of the latter.
While he was still talking, a bell rang for prayer and Father Grassi
went with the people to a large prayer tent in which the people were
kneeling or sitting facing the outside. An old medicine man led the
services; first they had a short exhortation and then they recited all together with great devotion a short prayer. The whole service did not
last longer than seven or eight minutes. Father asked the Indians who
had taught them that prayer. An old Indian told him: "Old Blanchet."
Father inquired further and was told that it was only after the earthquake that the Chelans had wanted to pray. They did not know how
to pray until a very old woman said a short prayer in Chinook which
Bishop Blanchet of Portland had taught her thirty years before. They
translated it into their language and since that time said it. After prayer
Father went back to his companion on the other side of the river; and
the next morning returned to the camp of the Chelans. Father Grassi
stayed three days, and mornings and evenings gathered the Indians for
prayer and instructions. He received many visits from Chief Ninusize
who was still discontented at the last visit. On the morning Father wanted
to leave, the chief told the missionary that he did not like his prayer and
that he did not wish the priest to come again among the Chelans.
Father Grassi knew how to appeal to the chief's pride. He told him
that he had always showed himself as a man with a head; once he
would understand the doctrine he would teach other chiefs. Then the
chief started a two hours' conversation, after which he felt displeased
that Father would leave now after he had begun to win the chief's
heart. The chief wanted him to stay on. But Father Grassi promised
to see him at the fishing of the white salmon.

On the third visit to the Chelans at the fishing center where the
Okanogan and the Columbia Rivers meet, called by the Indians Stlakam,
Chief Ninusize was again full of distrust:

> I have found out [the chief told the priest] that after your departure
> from Mitgan you went to Nisquali, and that you told the chief of the
> Americans that you had tried again to win over the Cilans, but that if
> you had not succeeded, he would have sent soldiers to bind me and lead
> me away from my land. It was with some difficulty that I showed him
> that this was a calumny against the Blackrobe.[14]

Father Grassi went again with the people to their prayer tent and

---

[14] Grassi to Giorda, *op. cit.*

was invited by the chief to speak. The missionary gave morning and evening instructions before their short prayer. On the third day he told the audience that he would like to say his prayer too. Many accompanied him and the chief remarked: "Now I have no longer two hearts with you, Blackrobe, but one. I do not think that it will be difficult for me to send away one of my wives and to give up gambling."[15] On the fourth and the fifth days the chief assisted in gathering the young men for instruction. All went well until the fifth day when "the mother of Mussus, the Pentarcha of these tribes," arrived. The old woman did not like it that the children of the chief were learning their prayers. That evening a famous medicine man of Stlakam, one of those visited by the devil, a relative of the chief, raised his voice against the Black Robe and spoke "like an obsessed all night." The next day "Joksters" wanted to bother Father Grassi but his tent filled suddenly with people who loved him. The priest baptized two women after Mass on Sunday. He had just completed the sacred ceremonies when the son of the chief came and spoke against those who love baptism and said that God had given them their land, and that the Black Robe, under the pretext of teaching them the prayer, was the precursor of the whites who would come to hunt them from their land. Father Grassi later went to the prayer meeting where first the medicine man had spoken. The priest cleared away the doubts and inspired new confidence in the Black Robe on the part of the Indians. The missionary was ready to depart on a certain day when Chief Ninusize came to tell him that he was thinking of sending the two baptized women away fearing disorders might break out. Father reminded him of his duties as the chief to prevent that and promised to come again and again to the Chelans until all would be instructed and all, who wished, be baptized. He saw the men assembled and went to shake hands with all of them. A day's journey from there Father Grassi baptized two more Chelans. Thus his record for the three visits and the hundreds of miles traveled through the wilderness was four baptisms.[16]

Father Grassi was too active to have much time for letters; therefore historians appreciate greatly the few he has left. Another precious one was written to his superior on June 29, 1876. Father Grassi had been again with the Chelans who this time showed much pleasure at seeing him. They kept on repeating: "Alas, we shall not see you again for another year!" The missionary told them that even if they are not yet baptized, they could baptize their babies when the babies were in danger of death and so too adults in the same danger who were

---

[15] Grassi to Giorda, *op. cit.*   [16] *Ibid.*

repentant and wanted to be baptized. They very eagerly learned the formula and the manner of doing it.[17] Gradually the Chelans became converted, and Father Grassi could count for certain on the friendship of the chief. One of the priests reported that when he contacted this chief after Father Grassi had been transferred, he was not allowed to preach. The chief maintained that Father Grassi was his only friend, that only he could do in his land as he pleased.[18] Future success with the Chelans was assured by the work of Father de Rougé. The little catechism and the prayers translated into the Chelan language by Father Grassi were used to great advantage by other missionaries.

From the Chelans, Father Grassi went to the Mitgan tribe where he baptized the chief, Kolosaskat, his wife, and others. This chief had the previous spring observed the coldness of the Chelans toward Father Grassi when he was among them. He had been at Stlakam the year before in the fall, too, and was touched when he saw how ungrateful the Chelans were for all the solicitude and the instructions Father gave them. The chief then began to dispose himself for baptism and asked the priest to stop in his country on the way back to the Skoelpis. The two Chelan chiefs had done all they could to dissuade the Mitgan chief from becoming a Catholic. Chief Kolosaskat became one of the faithful guides for the missionaries.

Father Grassi had eight miles to walk from the Mitgans to the mouth of the Okanogan River. Here he found a boat and started to cross the stream; however, the boat overturned and Father fell into the river. The missionary and the pilot by tightly clinging to the boat reached shore. The second attempt at crossing was successful. Several miles upstream were some Okanogans waiting to have their babies baptized, but Father heard about it only later.

The next stop was with the Nespelem Indians. The camp Father saw consisted of about thirty people. These Indians did not show any hostility to the priest. Nearby was a numerous Canadian Catholic family who wanted Father Grassi to stay with them a few weeks, but he could manage only two days. The missionary also visited the Sanpoel tribe. At that time their old chief was still alive but was absent, so was the "man of prayer," Skolaskan; the others did not dare to say much. Skolaskan had his people cut wood for the second ark to save them from the flood that was to come as Father Grassi told his superior:

I saw the wood being cut and I also saw a large pile of lumber. There

---

[17] Grassi, letter to Father Superior, June 29, 1876, Ms., OPA.

[18] Anonymous, *Notes on Father Grassi*, Mss., OPA. See also: Anonymous, "Obituary," *WL* (19:2, June, 1890), 266–270.

seems no doubt that the devil has talked to him, but it also seems beyond doubt that a much more important issue is what he can get for himself. He said to a white man . . . "You see that I am a cripple and unable to make a living in any other way."[19]

Skolaskan made the people pay for his dreams with horses and cows, which he sold and thus provided for himself.

Father Grassi was made superior of St. Francis Regis Mission in 1876. Now other priests would serve the Okanogan and Chelan tribes. We mentioned Father Diomedi. During the winter of 1877–1878, Father Grassi was administering again to the tribes of the Okanogan country. His missionary zeal resulted in forty-five baptisms, fifteen of them adults and the rest children; he also blessed twelve marriages.[20]

From 1880 on we hear more about this "Apostle of the Okanogans and the Chelans"; he was back on the job. Again he tells his superior, who now was Father Cataldo, about his missionary experiences. Here Father Grassi gives us another historical sketch of the Sanpoil Indians, their "prophet" Skolaskan, their dreamer religion, and their influence over neighboring tribes. Father Grassi names the "Zaszages, Simpoilschi, Nespilim and the Suipakein" Indians who had been under the influence of Protestant missionaries in 1838. After these missionaries left the Indians retained little of their doctrine; yet the Indians harbored a deep sentiment of hatred, fear, and suspicion against the Catholic missionaries. Father Grassi had some years before sent Father Tosi to the Zaszages. Chief Garry from Spokane heard about it and sent a messenger with the order that they should wait a few days before accepting the Catholic prayer. Later visits of the missionary brought the answer: "If you had been first to come to us, we would now belong to you."[21]

Father Grassi reports that Father Joset had been well known to the Sanpoil Indians. Once a deputation of seven or eight Indians from that tribe came to him and invited him "to give the Catholic prayer to the tribe." Father talked to them about religion, gave each one a name which they kept, and promised to come to their country next spring if they would come for him to guide him there. The leader of this expedition died and no one ever came.

Quite of few years later, one of the Indians from the Sanpoil tribe fell sick of some nervous disease from which he suffered for two years

---

[19] Grassi to Father Superior, June 29, 1876, Ms., OPA.

[20] Historicus, quoting Father Grassi, "Fifty Years of Peaceful Conquest," *op. cit.* (5:7, April, 1914), 354–355.

[21] Grassi, letter to Father Cataldo, S.J., April 19, 1881, Ms., OPA.

and was left crippled for life. He said that he had visions of Paradise, and that he had received messages for the people:[22]

> That the Catholic missionaries had been envoys of God up to that time, but as they had entered into friendships with the Whites, the Lord had now cast them off, and had chosen him to let them know the will of God, and be saved; that God was angry and commanded him as a second Noah, to build an ark, in which all the new believers were to be rescued from the deluge, which would overwhelm the world after eight years.[23]

The greater part of the tribe believed him. The eight years were soon over but there was no sign of the deluge. Then a second revelation told him that he had first to build a church and then an ark. Skolaskan was greatly venerated by his people. His name was second to God only and Jesus and Mary were invoked as intercessors. Father Grassi found that the religious code Skolaskan taught was a mixture of Catholic and Protestant doctrines. He happened to visit this tribe once when the people were all assembled and Father went with them to their prayer meeting. The "prophet" had not given Father permission to preach, but he had not reckoned with the zeal of this missionary to save souls. The priest started with praising the little that was good and then taught something of the Divinity of Jesus Christ and the necessity of baptism. Skolaskan listened for a while and then stopped him, telling him that he had talked long enough as he had no permission to talk. He did not deny that baptism was good but the tribe was not prepared for it.

From the Sanpoils Father Grassi passed on to the Nespelems. These Indians were very pleased to see the missionary but remarked that if the chief would receive baptism they would all imitate him. The chief happened to be a staunch believer in Skolaskan's revelations and strictly opposed to the Catholic religion. Then the priest went on to the Suipakein Indians where he entered a deserted hut. The Indians came and greeted him respectfully and Chief Suipakein gave Father the neighboring house that had windows and a door. Seven or eight Christians were among this tribe, who by the reception of the chief became encouraged to come forward to shake hands with the priest. Father Grassi had been two weeks with this tribe when they sent as spokesman to him one of those who had been baptized. He told the priest that he had stayed long enough; they had all gone to confession so he could leave now. Suipakein did not want to be baptized. But Father was eager to learn what revelation Suipakein had received. Then this "Dreamer" told the history of

---

[22] We quoted Father Diomedi's version of the story already.
[23] Grassi to Cataldo, April 19, 1881, Ms., OPA. Also: *WL* (11:1), 65–66.

the creation, the deluge, the life of our Lord. Father praised him; so far nothing was wrong. A few days later Suipakein declared publicly he wanted to give up his dreams and wished to be baptized, but nobody believed him. Later his fervor diminished. Father Grassi saw him again after two years; he was still the "Dreamer." Father Grassi had contemplated building a chapel and a small house on this place during the fall of 1880. It was the same story: the Indians did not trust the missionaries on account of the reservation policies practiced by the United States government. They believed

> that if the missionaries were allowed to erect a dwelling place in their country other white men would come and [it] would end by taking possession of all their lands, as they had done elsewhere.[24]

This shows that Father Grassi realized the necessity of erecting a mission somewhere among the Okanogans and related tribes. The "Annual Report" of the Indian agent, Simms, for 1881, after repeating the yearly praise of the work of the Jesuit Fathers, whose large church at Colville was nearing completion, tells about the missionary zeal of Father Grassi trying to convert the Sanpoil and Nespelem Indians:

> Special efforts are being made by the reverend fathers to induce the San Poel and Nespelem Indians [Dreamers] to embrace a Christian life, and with that view, the Rev. U. Grassi, "without scrip or staff," spent the whole of last winter, the most inclement known for several years, among them, cut off entirely from all communication with his mission and white settlements for five months. His success has induced him to take measure for the early establishment of a permanent mission in their vicinity.[25]

Father Grassi was contemplating having a school for the Indian children somewhere in the Okanogan Valley when in the fall of 1880 he left the Suipakein Indians. He had traveled down the Columbia River for twenty-five or thirty miles to meet the Indians at Stlakam while they were fishing. There he heard that Moses and other chiefs were gathered to wait for the government official, who was to ask the Indian chiefs to send their children to an industrial school in Oregon. Father Grassi crossed the Columbia and cautioned the Catholic chiefs not to surrender their sons; the Catholic priest was not allowed to enter these schools once the children were there. He told Moses and the other chiefs that it was his

---

[24] Grassi to Cataldo, S.J., April 19, 1881, Ms., OPA.
[25] Simms, "Annual Report for 1881," in *Annual Report of the Commissioner of Indian Affairs to the Secretary of the Interior for the Year 1881, 159.*

intention to build a small house in that neighborhood, and that then I
should have their sons taught to read and write. Moses approved the
plan, but afterwards added that the government had granted the land
to him, and, consequently he could not dispose of it for a school-house
or a place of prayer.[26]

Father Grassi had left the place when he heard that several days
later the government official had been at the mouth of the Spokane
River and called the chiefs to meet him. Only Chief Moses answered
the call and had the courage to refuse sending the children there, "saying
that the Catholic priest would take charge of them." The official was
very angry and talked for quite a while against the priest. He threatened
Moses that he would accuse him before the authorities and that he
would be punished if by next spring he would not have surrendered
the children. Moses was frightened but he returned without promising
to send the children.[27] Reading some of these accounts one wonders who
were the "savages," the Indians or some of the whites.

Further mission news from Father Grassi speaks of the many "Win-
akes" (Wenatchees) in Father's tent wanting to learn the truths of
Christianity, of several baptisms, of confessions dating a long time back,
of much spiritual work to be done. Father Grassi would like to have a
companion; this would be a great consolation and much more good
could be done.

Father Caruana informed Father Cataldo of the immense mission
territory and the constantly increasing work due to the coming in of the
white settlers. Then he made some suggestions:

> . . . two other Fathers, or at least one, should have charge of the
> Winashes as far as the Okanogan inclusively, and they would spend the
> greater part of the year traveling from one place to another. Their
> residence could be fixed near the boundary of the Reserve, on this side
> of Lake Chelan, at Natelve, as Father Grassi thinks that to be the best
> place for such a purpose.[28]

It was easy for anyone to ask for priests but it was very difficult
to supply them in a new country that had as yet no vocations. Still a
few years had to pass until the first priest ordained in the Rocky Mountains was ready for work. In the meantime Father Grassi would continue
to travel up the Okanogan Valley into British Columbia and down again
back to the Wenatchees, ministering on the way to all who called on
him. On the place where today St. Mary's Mission, Omak, Washington,

---

[26] Grassi to Cataldo, April 19, 1881, Ms., OPA.
[27] *Ibid.*
[28] Rev. J. M. Caruana, S.J., to Father Cataldo, *WL* (11:3, September, 1882),
269–270.

is located Father Grassi spent a whole winter in a tent. It was he who selected the place for this mission that was to become the only one to survive to the present.[29]

We don't know if it had been in the Omak Creek Valley or at another place. Once Father Grassi was not able to cross the mountains during the winter; he had to stay with the Indians. The missionary had a sack of flour, a pot of lard, and a pound of salt; the only item on his menu was pancakes. Once while traveling with Father Cataldo, Father Grassi baked pancakes on the way. "Father Cataldo was not through with one when Fr. Grassi had eaten half a dozen." It is said that Father Grassi could stand hunger for days but when he got something to eat he could do justice to it.[30]

Father Joseph Caruana, S.J., making the journey in 1883 from St. Francis Regis Mission back to St. Joseph's Mission, Yakima, has left a day-by-day account of his travels and missionary work while he traversed the country. Reading over his notes one is reminded of the fervor of the first Christians during the time of the Apostles. News was spread throughout the Okanogan country that a Father was on the way. Father Caruana went from camp to camp and gathered a rich spiritual harvest. He mentioned in his *Diary* on September 5, "The chief's reception was so hearty that I decided on remaining here over Sunday." This was Chief Tonasket; other chiefs started to arrive. On September 6, Father wrote: "We have now four big chiefs here." On September 9, a Sunday, Father has the following entry:

> 17th Sunday after Pentecost. I sang Mass at Tonaskat's. There were many people here from all sections and tribes, from the Smilkamein, from Yokontichin, from the Okanogan, from above and below the international boundary, and from the Sgoelpi. Yesterday and today I heard over 200 confessions and gave 150 communions; baptized Joseph Silpize and Mary Cecilia Snimpize, both of the Smikamein tribe, and revalidated their marriage. Chief Gregory and his wife Susan stood for the converted people.
>
> This was indeed a time for spiritual rejoicing but also for a good deal of bodily fatigue and weariness as I was all alone for the work of which there was an abundance.[31]

Father Caruana stayed overnight at Chief Ignace's. Chief Ignace became Father's escort to the great fishery at the mouth of the Okanogan River. Father stayed a few days for instructions and the Indians availed

---

[29] Father Etienne de Rougé, S.J., *St. Mary's Mission,* Mss., OPA.

[30] Parodi, *Memoirs,* Mss., OPA.

[31] Historicus, quoting Father Caruana, S.J., "Fifty Years of Peaceful Conquest," *op. cit.* (5:8, May, 1914), 415.

themselves of the opportunity to receive the sacraments. Father Caruana is full of praise for Chief Ignace who was very much respected among the Okanogan tribes and was therefore influential in spreading Christian ideas among the Indians. Also Julia, the wife of Chief Cotolego, is mentioned as doing excellent work among the women. About Chief John Wapato the missionary said: "I found deep faith and respect for the missionary, at the same time an inquisitiveness that baffles description." Father Caruana finally arrived at the Yakima mission toward the end of September.[32] He had seen again the pressing need for a missionary who would solely care for the Okanogan Valley.

Father Parodi tells about the proper names given by the Indian to their missionaries:

> Father Grassi was left handed, and so they called him Wakachal. He was well pleased and in some letters he signed his name Wakachal. Milkakain was the name of Fr. Giorda, because his head was round like the moon. Kutene'-us is the name of Father Caruana, because he is a big fat man. Kawskin is the name of Father Cataldo, because he broke his leg.[33]

From 1884 to 1885 Father Grassi was again doing his priestly work in the Okanogan Valley. Grandma Zacherle from Disautel, Washington, told the author that in those years it was considered a great grace by some Indians to have a priest at their deathbed. Often the missionary seemed to have had the guidance of his guardian angel. Mrs. Zacherle was a small child when her grandmother was in her last agony. Pauline happened to see Father Grassi riding by at some distance. She called her mother who would not believe the child but was happy when Pauline ran and called the priest. The old grandmother was then able to receive the Last Sacraments before she died.[34]

Father Grassi was in danger of death more than once while traveling. He had converted some Sanpoil Indians and was therefore hated by the rest of these "Dreamers." They were looking for an opportunity to kill Father. One day Father Grassi needed to cross the Columbia River and offered some gift to one of these Indians if he would paddle him to the other side. The Indian accepted the offer in good spirits, knowing that Father Grassi was not able to swim. When the two were near to the opposite shore the Indian suddenly upset the canoe and then swam to the shore. Father Grassi held on to the canoe and was carried by

---

[32] Caruana quoted by Historicus, "Fifty Years of Peaceful Conquest," *op. cit.* (5:7, April, 1914), 354–355.

[33] Parodi, S.J., *Memoirs,* Mss., OPA.

[34] Mrs. Pauline Zacherle, interview at St. Mary's Mission, Omak, Washington, November 8, 1959.

the current, through God's providence, into shallow water.[35] In spite of this attempt on his life, the saintly missionary kept on visiting the Sanpoil again and again sowing the seed of faith into stony soil.

Hundreds of Indians were converted by Father Grassi. For the Chelans he had built a log chapel, as Father de Rougé tells us. His mission for the Wenatchee, later called "Old Mission," became important through Father Grassi's attempt to show the Indians the rudiments of irrigation. "Father Grassi turned a small stream of water flowing to the river from the mountain, over a small garden patch and planted a few seeds which he had brought with him into the country."[36] He had very good results. The white settlers later realized what irrigation could do when they saw the productive gardens of the Indians. But as always, when the Indians had something good, the white men wanted it.

The place where Riverside, Washington, now stands on the Okanogan River was formerly an Indian camping ground. Once Father Grassi came on horseback and stopped there for the night. It happened that the Indians had a gathering for the Chinook dance in the same lodge and the medicine men were officiating. The Catholic Indians asked the priest later how he felt to be in such a lodge. Father had retired to a corner and said his prayers. Maybe the devil was not quite so powerful that night. The medicine man Swipkin was later converted.[37]

According to an anonymous fellow missionary, who wrote some important notes on Father Grassi, the success of Father Grassi was the fruit of his continual prayer and his close union with God. He was known to spend the greater part of the night in prayer. When on missionary trips through the wilderness Father was nearly always speaking with God, and his companion often did not dare to speak and disturb his recollection. Father Patrick Savage tells the following after describing Father Grassi's trip to Goldendale:

I have not been able to get a picture of Father Grassi, but an aunt of mine, Sister Rosinda, tells me she always thought he resembled a picture of Pius IX which hung in the pioneer home of my grandfather, John J. Kenny. In his home Grandfather had a chapel, complete with statues and an altar which he himself had built. It was here my parents were married in the early 70's by Father Grassi.[38]

[35] Anonymous, *Notes on Father Grassi*, Mss., OPA. Also: "Obituary," *Woodstock Letters* (19:2, June, 1890), 267–269.

[36] Richard Steele and A. P. Rose, ed., *History of North Washington: An Illustrated History of Stevens, Ferry Okanogan and Chelan Counties*, 671.

[37] Mrs. Pauline Zacherle, in an interview.

[38] Father Patrick Savage, S.J., "How Are Things in Okanogan?" *The Calumet*, n.d.

Old baptismal records of St. Mary's Mission show one hundred and seven baptisms administered by Father Grassi during part of the year 1884–1885. To a great number of persons he had been through the years God's instrument for the beginning of the life of grace in their souls. The old Indian people in the Okanogan Valley still gratefully remember him as their spiritual father, as the trailblazer for another great Indian missionary, Father Etienne de Rougé, and as the one who selected the place for the only permanent Catholic mission boarding school in the state of Washington, St. Mary's Mission, Omak, Washington.

CHAPTER IX

The Birth of St. Mary's Mission

THE so-called "Land of Liberty," the United States, did not always guard the religious liberty of every one of its citizens. It took many years for the development of the real democratic spirit. A study of the Congressional Records for the years of the late 1890's shows a serious flare-up of anti-Catholic propaganda right in Congress. The subject of the heated controversies was the Catholic Indian schools. Indian Commissioner John H. Eberly defended the work of the Catholic Church when he declared:

> . . . that the Catholics have contracts for the greatest number of pupils is not due to discrimination in their favor, but to the fact that they have expended larger sums of money than any other denomination in the erection of school-buildings and in the establishment of schools, and therefore have been enabled to accommodate more pupils under contract.[1]

A footnote on the same page gives information concerning Catholic expenditures on mission schools:

> The Bureau of Catholic Indian Missions reports that it expended $115,000 for Indian school buildings and furnishings during the fiscal year ended June 30, 1887, and that the whole amount invested by the Catholics in such buildings is about $1,000,000.[2]

This controversy lasted several years. The defender of the Catholics during the Fifty-First Congress, Senator Teller, made this observation:

---

[1] John H. Eberly, Commissioner of Indian Affairs, "Schools Contracts With Bureau of Catholic Indian Missions," in "Report of the Secretary of the Interior," *House Executive Document 1, Fiftieth Congress, Second Session* (Part 5, Vol. II), xv.

[2] *Ibid.*

Mr. President, there has been a good deal of complaint, I know, in the country that the Catholic Church had monopolized a large part of the educational facilities for Indians. I have no particular affinity with the Catholic Church. All my connections and all my teachings and associations have been the other way. I have observed, though, that the Catholics have been the most successful educators of the Indians of any people in this country.[3]

During the Fifty-Sixth Congress, Senator Vest told the anti-Catholic opponents that he was reared a Protestant and expected to die one, but that he had not the slightest sympathy with people who believed that an Indian child should be raised an "utter unbeliever, an idolator" rather than be educated by "the Society of Jesus or in the Catholic Church." Senator Vest was a member of the Committee on Indian Affairs and as such examined the existing Indian schools. He had the highest praise for Jesuit education.[4]

St. Mary's Mission is especially grateful to Senator Vest for the following remarks:

If I have ever done anything in my whole career in this chamber of which I am sincerely proud, it is that upon one occasion I obtained an appropriation of $10,000 for an industrial school at St. Ignatius, in Montana. A few years afterwards, in passing through to the Pacific coast, I stopped over to see that school. They heard I was coming and met me at the depot with a brass band, the instruments in the hands of Indian boys, and they played without discrimination Hail Columbia and Dixie. They had been taught by a young French nobleman whom I had met two years before at the mission, who had squandered the principal portion of his fortune in reckless dissipation in the salons of Paris and had suddenly left that sort of life and joined the company of Jesus and dedicated himself to the American missions. He was an accomplished musician, and he taught these boys how to play upon the instruments.[5]

[3] Senator Teller, quoted in *Congressional Records: Containing the Proceedings and Debates of the Fifty-First Congress, First Session.* Also Special Session of the Senate, xxi, 7651.

[4] "I wish to say now what I have said before in the Senate, and it is not the popular side of this question by any means, that I did not see in all my journey, which lasted for several weeks, a single school that was not doing any educational work worthy the name of educational work unless it was under the control of the Jesuits. I did not see a single Government school especially these day schools, where there was any work done at all. . . .

"Mr. President, the Jesuits have elevated the Indian wherever they have been allowed to do so without interference of bigotry and fanaticism and the cowardice of insectivorous politicians who are afraid of the A.P.A. and the votes that can be cast against them in their districts and States. They have made him a Christian and above even that have made him a workman able to support himself and those dependent upon him." See: *Congressional Record Containing the Proceedings and Debates of the Fifty-Sixth Congress, First Session* (Serial No. 356, xxxiii, 3884–3886).

[5] Senator Vest quoted, *Congressional Record, op. cit.,* 3886.

This young French nobleman was Father Etienne de Rougé, later the founder of St. Mary's Mission. The heated debates in Congress continued until 1896, when Congress outlawed any financial help for private Indian schools. So it came about that Father de Rougé had to build his St. Mary's Mission School under the most trying circumstances. "The mission school never received a dollar from federal funds."[6]

Father de Rougé was born on January 28, 1860, in the Chateau des Rues, in the Commune of Chenille, France, the son of a French count. He entered in 1876 the College of the Jesuits at Le Mans, France, and in 1879, the novitiate of the same order at Angers. Anticlerical laws forced him to leave his homeland and he volunteered for the Rocky Mountain missions. When in 1881, the young Count de Rougé was on his way to the United States, he found himself in company with the French delegation sent to the centennial celebration of the surrender of Yorktown by Lord Cornwallis. Count de Rougé stayed for some time in Woodstock College, near Baltimore, Maryland, and then as a scholastic was stationed at St. Ignatius Mission, Montana. In 1882, he was ordained subdeacon by Archbishop Seghers.[7]

The Jesuit community at St. Francis Regis Mission in the Colville Valley must have eagerly awaited, during the years of preparation for the priesthood, the arrival of the day on which the first priest would be ordained in the Rocky Mountain area. The shortage of priests was acute. Father Grassi was to go to Spokane to supervise the building of the new Gonzaga College and the new priest de Rougé was to take over the care of the various tribes of the Upper Columbia and Okanogan valleys. The entries in the *Diary of St. Francis Regis Mission* show that the Fathers followed the movements of the priest to be. First mention of Father de Rougé's name was on December 22, 1884, when he arrived at Spokane Falls. On April 13, 1885, the future priest is mentioned as being with the Kalispels. On June 3, 1885, the entry reads, "de Rougé arrives at Colville." The subdeacon must not have stayed at Colville; on September 22, of the same year, the entry tells us that he arrived at Spokane Falls to be ordained "pro diacone Sacerdoto." On September 30, we are informed that the Deacon de Rougé left for Helena to be ordained a priest on October 3, 1885, by Bishop Brondel. There was no time for vacation and celebrations at St. Ignatius Mission, Montana, where the young priest had served as a scholastic. The very next day on

---

[6] Rt. Rev. J. B. Tennelly, Director of the Bureau of Catholic Indian Missions, to the author, December 15, 1959.

[7] Oliver de Rougé, Chenille France, to Father Vandewaale (*sic*), May 4, 1923, Mss., OPA. Also: file on St. Mary's Mission, OPA.

the third of October, as the *Diary* tells us, Father de Rougé arrived as a priest in Colville. Then he had a few days of preparation for his future mission work. There is a note of great joy in the *Diary* entry of finally having a young priest available. "Next Sunday [11th] sing the high Mass assisted by Fr. Canestrelli diac. et fr. Robaut, subd. Dinner as big as possible for the new priest." Finally under October 15, we read, "Fr. de Rouge starts for the Simpoelshi to strive to build a church among them."[8]

The young missionary was on the way to fulfill his life's ambitions, a life of heroic utter self-forgetfulness. We shall follow this missionary, priest, teacher, doctor, builder, and man of every trade, as a part of Washington state's history unfolds itself. Let us do justice to one of its most noble pioneer citizens, to a planter of Christian civilization whose name should be in every history book of our great state.

The date of arrival of Father de Rougé in the Okanogan Valley is not known. Did he have a companion over the two mountain summits? Or did he cross and recross the Kettle River many times? Later letters will tell us about the hardships endured by these crossings. From the *Baptismal Records* we know that by the middle of November he had started his priestly functions. On the place where two years later two fruitmen, Ellis and Forde, planted their orchards, today called Ellisforde, Father Grassi had a half-completed log cabin. Father de Rougé finished this building and erected a small chapel in the fall of 1885. More he could not do as the cold season was advancing. Near the place of his first temporary residence the Okanogan River went into a bend; the Indians, therefore, called the place Hull-kees or Schall-kees, meaning "going around the bend."[9] It had always been a great gathering place for the Okanogan Indians. According to the Bottomleys at Oroville, Washington, the first church at Ellisforde had a dirt floor, a sod roof, and walls of logs. Tule mats were placed on the floor.[10]

In a letter dated March 21, 1886, to Very Reverend Father Joseph Cataldo, S.J., who was then the Superior General of the Rocky Mountain Missions, the young priest writes: "You have heard from me at Christmas time and since then I have visited all the Indians from the whole Okanogan

---

[8] See: *Diary of St. Francis Regis Mission*, Mss., OPA, for the dates mentioned in the text. The two priests mentioned, Father Canestrelli and Father Robaut, were fellow Jesuit Fathers then stationed at St. Francis Regis Mission. Both had come over from Italy to serve in the Rocky Mountain Missions.

[9] Narcisse Nicholson, who has lived at Schall-kees during a great part of his long life, sent a written account of the early history to the author during the fall of 1960.

[10] Maggie and Charles Bottomley, in an interview with Mrs. K. Lacey, Oroville, March 15, 1960. Courtesy of Mrs. Lacey.

valley."[11] Then Father de Rougé enumerates the spiritual work he has already done and how he has gained ground:

> On Ash Wednesday we had more than 100 Communions and not one without [the person's] having been to confession 3 or 4 times before. Also I have been able to verify the good that has been done in many of them. . . . The Indians spent 4 days at the Mission before the feast. They had 40 hours devotion and Catechism several times during the day and a Highmass on the day of the feast.[12]

Then Father continues to say that two Oblate Fathers had come to their mission on the other side of the line and had celebrated Ash Wednesday thirty miles from his place. He does not give the name of these priests or where they came from. Very probably they were fellow religious of the good Father Pandosi who had established a mission near what is today Kelowna. The Oblate Fathers also had established a mission at Kamloops, British Columbia, in 1879. Thirty miles from Father de Rougé's place might have been the mission church of the Inkameep Indians which during the following decades was visited by Father de Rougé. The young priest tells Father Cataldo that this visit was extraordinary and that he believes that in the future the number of Indians meetng at his place at Schall-kees will be even greater.

> Thus the Indians wish to build a large chapel and they are speaking much about it. It would be necessary to have a Brother to help them direct their work with them. Okanogan Mission is arranged better and a brother is able to live there from now on.[13]

Father de Rougé says that it is impossible to do anything without a "Brother coadjutor." During the missionaries' first winter in the Okanogan country he had found a man lost in the snow who stayed with him without being paid. Father complains about the wages demanded by the Indians. "With a brother one could have a garden, chickens, and live and do the work of the house and the church." Then the priest brings out the reason why he did not build a church among the Sanpoil Indians. He could not abandon the Okanogans and establish himself at Nespelem, for it is not enough that the Indians be baptized and left to themselves. The Nespelems could be visited and cared for from the Okanogan Mission. For the tribes of Joseph and Moses, humanly speaking, there is little to be done. Father makes the suggestion that if he had

---

[11] Father de Rougé to Very Rev. Joseph Cataldo, S.J., March 21, 1886, Mss., OPA (translated from the original by Sister Mary Cunise, O.S.F.).

[12] Ibid.

[13] Ibid. Narcisse Nicholson and others have told of a long three-room cabin Father de Rougé had built at Schall-kees.

a young Catholic man from Lapwai, who knew the dispositions of the Indians, this would help to attract the Nez Perce to his cabin.[14]

The *Diary of St. Francis Regis* again tells us that on April 9, 1886, "Fr. de Rougé with B. Malony started to Okinagan."[15] In a letter to Father Calaldo, May 9, 1886, Father spoke about the hardships endured on this missionary journey. He had now returned to Okanogan after having been a few weeks at Colville. The trip had been hazardous as the waters were high and the roads bad. Without a good little Indian whom he had picked up on the road they would never have been able to advance. Father's companion had been too lazy to get him out of difficulty.

> The poor child has shown marvels of valor in saving us embarrassment, and in spite of sixteen years he was worth more than many men of forty. When it came to crossing the river . . . he did not hesitate and started out with his axe searching for a trunk of a tree. He found it . . . a trunk which projected into the water, and with three strokes of the ax an oar was shaped, and Abraham . . . was soon safe on the other side.
>
> A half hour later . . . he had found a canoe and recrossed the stream. In the meantime the brother prepared the supper.[16]

This supper consisted of a baked mixture of flour and water. In the dugout all the goods had to be loaded that Father had brought along for his new mission. Everything was done at night in order to save time. They arrived at the Okanogan Mission after a week of travel. The priest was able to say Mass only twice during this time as the weather was bad, but he was happy that none of his provisions were ruined. His only regret was that "we did not suffer more for the good God and for the salvation of souls."

The missionary had arrived at the abandoned mission on Friday evening before Palm Sunday. The next day the Indians assembled and all week they were camped in the vicinity. Father gave a retreat; the evenings were spent in chant classes and catechism. The Indian men worked to erect a big cross for Good Friday and prepared the wood for the bonfires. An Indian plowed Father's garden and the women offered to plant his potatoes.

All during Holy Thursday until midnight there was perpetual adoration before the depository which Father had constructed in the room

---

[14] De Rougé to Cataldo, *op. cit.*

[15] *Diary of St. Francis Regis Mission*, April 9, 1886, Ms., OPA.

[16] De Rougé to Cataldo, May 9, 1886, in *Missione Della Provincia Torinese Della Compagnia di Gesu* (translated by Sister Mary Cunise, O.S.F.), 87–88. Original manuscript in OPA.

This picture of St. Paul's Mission, near Kettle Falls, was taken in 1905. The last building was erected by Father Joseph Joset, S.J., in 1863. In 1939 the building was restored for the centennial which celebrated the coming of the first priests in Kettle Falls in the years 1838–1839.

St. Francis Regis Mission, about 1912. Left: The Sacred Heart School for Girls of the Providence Sisters. Center: St. Francis Church. Right: St. Francis Regis School for Boys.

Sacred Heart School. Sister Mary Raymond's class in 1915.

Early progress in civilization. Shown is an early wedding picture of Annie Francis and Alex Antoine in white man's dress.

The first Indian visitors to the St. Francis Regis Mission in white man's dress.

Okanogan Valley's first bishop, Right Reverend Aegidius Junger, D.D.

The second bishop to visit the Okanogans, Most Reverend Edward John O'Dea, D.D.

From left to right: Chief Coxit George (George Lahome), Sam Lahome (George's brother), Veracostchien from Nespelem, Chief Louie Timentwa, Chief Dick Aeneas.

Okanogan chiefs: Long Jim, Charley Swimpkin, Louie Timentwa. Sitting: John Louie, Chief Smitkin.

Long Jim lived near Manson. (Courtesy of Chelan County Historical Society.)

Portrait of Long Alec, painted by Caroline Orr. Long Alec was a chief of Colvilles on the north half. His granddaughter, Marceleine Nelson lives at Curlew.

COLVILLE CHIEFS

Chief James Bernard, Colville Tribe

Peter Wapato, a Menatchee Indian, lived near Manson. Son of Madeleine and Chief John Wapato. (Courtesy of Chelan County Historical Society.)

Chief Moses of the Columbia Tribe.

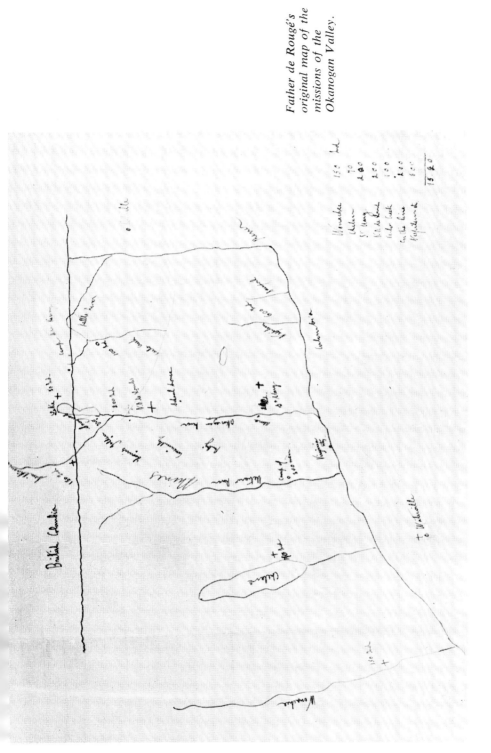

Father de Rougé's original map of the missions of the Okanogan Valley.

St. Mary Mission, built in 1887. First public chapel in the Omak Creek Valley. Chief Patoi (Patomve) of the Wenatchees.

Father de Rougé monument on the Mission grounds.

William Hill standing before a shrine he built near Omak Creek.

The first set of mission buildings — as they gradually grew, piece by piece. The first church standing is at the left.

The second building of the first set.

The rear view of the first church standing.

Girls' school (left) and school for white girls (right).

The college building of St. Mary's Mission decorated for dedication in 1915.

College building dedication ceremonies, 1915. Bishop Schinner, Chief Smitkin, Chief Baptiste, Father de Rougé, S.J.

adjoining the chapel. At midnight he sent the Indians away in order to rest. On Good Friday at midnight the whole front of the mission was illuminated by eight bonfires. A procession went out of the chapel and in the midst of these bonfires the Indians raised the big cross and saluted it with "endless chants, 'O good Jesus, you my love.'" Father gave a sermon and the cross was planted the first time on the banks of the Okanogan River. Father had many conversions while he continued the retreat.

On Easter Sunday evening there came a call from Chelan in the person of a "young infidel," asking Father to see his dying brother who had asked for baptism. A brave Indian gave Father a spirited horse and next morning, even while the Indians were still camped around the mission, Father and his companion were galloping across the plains. Soon he had struck up a friendship with his companion. Arriving during the evening at the cabin of the dying man, he found that grace had prepared more souls: all three brothers asked for and received baptism. These men straightened out the marriage of their mother, and the whole family returned to God. The dying man received his first Holy Communion two days later; furthermore, Father was able to baptize some children who had long been refused this grace by their parents. An old sorcerer abjured his superstitions and an old woman was baptized. This brought the number up to eleven baptisms. Father de Rougé attributed this blessing to the "good Sisters de la Nerrie who during Holy Week prayed for us." The Indians promised to attend the services three weeks from then in the chapel built by Father Grassi at Chelan and to visit the Okanogan Mission for the feast of Corpus Christi.[17]

A letter written the previous day to Father Canestrelli confirms the report of his eleven baptisms and his resolve to visit the Chelans after three Sundays. It also contains remarks significant to the history of St. Mary's Mission, Omak, Washington.

> Halfway on the road [to Chelan] the Indians are giving me a house which I have bought . . . they [will] pay for their chapel. For a long time Father Grassi desired a chapel there and the medicine men had opposed. This time the affair was done too quickly for the wicked tongues to take part. This place is at the spot where the road to Catarre joins the road to Okanogan. There is always a numerous camp there and many are not baptized. There the father will be able to become fixed in his home and to spend on certain occasions one or two quiet weeks. This will be a place where I will be able to do as much good as here. In that same camp the baptized Indians are very good to the father. Even the Indians from Metgan can come to Mass as the Indians from Metgan often camp

---

[17] De Rougé to Cataldo, op. cit., 87–88.

only 12 miles [from] where they spend the winter. It is there that I visited them during the last winter.[18]

Apparently, buying the log house was all Father de Rougé did during 1886 concerning his new St. Mary's Mission.

Father de Rougé did not stay at the Okanogan Mission but went into the different camps to say Mass in private homes. He contacted the Indians wherever it was convenient. Guy Waring, one of the early white settlers, was present when Father de Rougé said Mass in Chief Sarsapkin's home during the summer of 1886. It was early in the summer and the Indians passed word around that the priest was coming. Waring was not a Catholic but he had acquired a great respect for Father de Rougé and his work. He expresses his respect eloquently:

> He was about thirty years old, short and unimpressive in stature. Kindness however, radiated from his eyes and he spoke in a soft mellow voice which converted somehow all that he said into a kind of poetry. His mind was always upon his mission there in the West, which was to find some goodness in the Indian's nature and in time, to bring it out.[19]

Waring tells of one of the greatest tributes paid to the young missionary by a white settlers with whom Father had once stayed overnight.

> He was not one of the ordinary kind; intent on yellow-legged chickens, like the Protestant missionaries they sent out here; far from it! I don't believe he ever thinks of what he eats or where he sleeps. His mind is always focused on others.[20]

Waring says there were about twenty settlers, squaws, and half-breeds in Sarsapkin's place when Father de Rougé had the services there. The people sat on the floor or on wooden boxes. The real pagan, Sarsapkin, sat in front close to the priest, listening respectfully. The sermon lasted nearly an hour and had as its subject Joseph (San Susep), all delivered in the Okanogan Indian language, of which the priest was a master.

> The priest's soft, plaintive voice was a sensitive musical string, which rose and fell in beautiful rhythms and cadences, and the people listened in silence throughout.[21]

During the first years of Father de Rougé's ministry to the Okanogan and Columbia tribes, he came back occasionally to St. Francis Regis Mission in the Colville Valley. He would stop sometimes at the home of Emil Toulou, a Frenchman and the father-in-law of Mrs. Toulou.

---

[18] Father de Rougé to Father Canestrelli, May 8, 1886, *MDPT*, 86.
[19] Waring, *My Pioneer Past*, 143.
[20] *Ibid.*
[21] *Ibid.*, 144.

He was an honored visitor also at Sacred Heart Academy, as the girls' school at St. Francis Regis Mission was called. Here he felt at home among the French-speaking Sisters.[22]

A letter of the missionary to Father De La Motte, S.J., a fellow Jesuit, dated July-August, 1886, tells about the terrible dust storms that sometimes visited the Okanogan Valley. Father had come back from Colville one week before the feast of St. Ignatius in 1886. His mission home was all upset. A big dust cloud had come down from the sky at the beginning of June and had lasted two months. The dust went into houses and everywhere and made animals and humans suffer. It irritated the skin and caused scabs to form; and it brought with it blindness and tears. Incredibly, in addition, mosquitoes filled the air and bothered everybody. Finally men and animals fled to the mountains.

With the help of his companions Father started to put his house in order and to get ready for the feast of St. Ignatius. The priest still had a week before the feast, so he went to the other side of the Okanogan River, the former Columbia Reservation, which had just been opened for settlement in 1886.

> My intention was to visit the little colonies which slowly populated the country. I put up a petition to the Secretary of the Interior to help against the intruders who come to sell whiskey to the Indians, without faith and without law.[23]

The whites took advantage of the Indians and gave them whiskey in exchange for their horses and cattle. Father tells us: "The drunken Indians are like devils; they break and kill and scare."[24]

The Indians came to the priest in great numbers and because it was the season for outside work they could stay only two days. The thirtieth of July they had confession, prayers, catechism, and, during the evening, Benediction. On the feast day there were a high Mass, a sermon, and another sermon and Benediction during the afternoon. In between services Father was consulted, gave advice, and dispensed medicine. After all the Indians had left, Father stayed to visit the white people the next day.

This was followed by a missionary journey which started on August 2, and was to last thirty-eight days. It was quite a job to prepare for such a trip and Father enumerates all the articles needed. He had as a companion, Ignatius, an intelligent Indian boy, nineteen years old, who

---

[22] Mrs. Helen Toulou, in an interview at St. Mary's Mission, Omak, Washington, November 9, 1959.

[23] De Rougé to Father De La Motte, July–August, 1886, *MDPT*, 92. Also: original manuscript in OPA (translated by Mrs. Scarpelli and Mrs. Victor Rocca).

[24] *Ibid.*

wanted to see cities. Father de Rougé promised him that he would have his wish fulfilled if he would go with him. Father's day-by-day report tells of Christians who were eager to see a priest: August 10, he was in Father Grassi's chapel at Chelan; August 16, he had to stop with a Catholic Indian family on account of suffering from fever and headaches. He forced himself to keep on traveling in order to reach Ellensburg, where he rested and where he met Father Louis Parodi. The next day he was on his way to Yakima where he stayed one and one-half weeks until his fever went down. Here he met Father Garrand, another fellow Jesuit. But now he could not find his boy Ignatius. To the Okanogan Mission the distance was 200 miles, to Colville 300. Father returned to Ellensburg and there met Ignatius again who had come from Yakima on foot. On September 9, Father de Rougé was back at his Okanogan Mission at Schall-kees.[25] We assume that he visited his place at Omak Creek. The *Diary of St. Francis Regis Mission* tells us: "Today arrived here from the Okanogans Fr. de Rougé. He was far better than I expected and will start very soon for the Kalispels."[26] The zeal of this missionary seems to have been without bounds.

Father de Rougé came back to St. Francis Regis Mission from Chewelah where he had gone to see if he could visit the Kalispels on October 21, and left for the Okanogan Missions during November of the same year.[27] Apparently he wintered in his log house at Omak Creek. He had stated that this place had a more central location in relation to the surrounding tribes during the winter, especially the Catholic Mitgan tribe. Father Caldi tells about Father de Rougé's first winter:

> The first winter among the Okanogans was one of real missionary life. There was no building but a log house without a floor, window or chimney, and unfurnished. A few sticks with some wild straw spread on them for a mattress and blankets placed on the straw served for a bed, a few boards for a table. A room added to the log house became a chapel.[28]

The missionary now had to divide his time between the two mission stations, Ellisforde, which he called Old Okanogan Mission, and St. Mary's Mission on Omak Creek. The Shall-kees mission seems to have been the more important one before Father's return from France in 1889. He had started a school at this place even before he moved to Omak Creek. Father de Rougé was a born educator and teacher and knew

---

[25] De Rougé to De La Motte, *op. cit.,* 94–95.
[26] *Diary of St. Francis Regis Mission,* October 17, 1886.
[27] *Ibid.,* October 21 and November, 1886.
[28] Rev. Celestine Caldi, S.J., "The First Christmas Among the Wenatchees," *The Indian Sentinel,* No. 1 (Winter, 1929–1930), 2.

that he could not implant a Christian civilization without education. The education of the Indians, young and old, started with the first contact he had with them. Mr. Edward Derrickson of West Bank, British Columbia, was one of the early pupils in the first "boarding school" at what is now called Ellisforde.[29] There was no floor in the church then, only grass around which the sides of the church were built. The children used the church as sleeping quarters, wrapping themselves in blankets. The *Inland Empire Catholic Messenger* states that Father de Rougé used the log chapel as a school, where he "imparted secular and religious instruction to local Indians, and some white children, among whom were Charles and Gus Bottomley."[30]

On March 7, Father de Rougé was back at St. Francis Regis and on the ninth he went "down to Spokane Falls to have a talk with R. P. Cataldo about the things in Okinagan, and came back on the 26th."[31] He left on the same day for his Okanogan Indians.

The year of 1887 was a memorable one for St. Mary's Mission. The little log house was falling to pieces; a substantial and larger chapel was needed. The archives of the Oregon Province of the Society of Jesus contain a booklet that gives information on the former St. Mary's High School. Father de Rougé here gives a résumé of its beginning at Omak Creek:

> Chief Ignace and Chief Smitkin had come into touch with a good father over at Colville and were in sympathy with Christian teaching while many of their people, their medicine men in particular, were terribly opposed to the coming of the white priest with his teaching of God and civilization. Thus it was that Chief Smitkin offered a place on his tribal possession near his wilderness home, thereby giving slight protection and encouragement to the religious pioneer whom he believed had come to settle among the Redmen for their salvation and benefit.[32]

Several people have made the remark that this valley along Omak Creek had been a gathering place for the superstitious practices of the Okanogan medicine men and that even Chief Moses who had resided across the Okanogan River on the Columbia Reservation and who was now admitted to the Colville Reservation made serious difficulties. It was all right for the Father to come and go but not to settle there.

---

[29] Mr. William Hill, former student of St. Mary's Mission, in an interview at Spokane, June 16, 1960.

[30] *The Inland Empire Catholic Messenger*, II:4 (January, 1929), 71. Also: interviews of Charles Bottomley at Oroville, Washington, by Mrs. Katie Lacey and the author, 1961–1962.

[31] *Diary of St. Francis Regis Mission*, March 7 and 26, 1887.

[32] De Rougé, *St. Mary's High School*, OPA.

Even Chief Smitkin could not make an end of the difficulties when he declared: "This is my land." Mr. Jerry Buber of Puyallup, Washington, who was at the mission school from 1904 to 1914, wrote to the author:

> When Father first got there the Indians were going to kill him. One of the Indian chiefs stopped Chief Moses from doing that. I didn't see it; Father told us about it.[33]

Father Joseph Balfe, S.J., informed the author that Father Dillon had told him that a group of chiefs and medicine men came up from the mouth of the Okanogan River to the Omak Creek Valley to kill the "Black Robe."[34]

Formerly this valley had been the hiding place, also, of quite a group of Indians under Chief Moses. They had been split away from the rest of the tribe for some time and had settled around Omak Lake, probably to avoid meeting the soldiers in case Joseph was defeated. They thought the soldiers might look for others involved in Chief Joseph's War.[35]

This valley was a little pagan kingdom, and it was not surprising that all hell seemed to be loose to prevent Father de Rougé from settling there. "Deputations of medicine men and dreamers were sent to discourage the Father and make him leave the country.[36] The affair reached its climax while the log chapel was being built.

> Chiefs Ignace and Smitkin, together with a few followers assisted Father to get out the logs and put up the first building while the medicine men of the tribe held a remonstrance meeting on the creek a short distance away to decide whether or not they would let the white man stay among them.[37]

It is further stated that while this council was going on near the banks of the creek, a child fell into the rushing waters and was washed downstream. The Indians looked on helplessly, while Father de Rougé jumped into the swift waters and rescued the child.[38] Inquiries as to the truth of this statement, not found in the Oregon Province Archives, were answered in the affirmative.[39] This action of Father de Rougé was decisive; he was not only allowed to stay but asked to stay. The Indians love

---

[33] Jerry Buber, letter to the author, November 11, 1960.
[34] Rev. Joseph Balfe, S.J., in an interview at St. Mary's Mission, July 10, 1961.
[35] Anonymous, "St. Mary's Mission," *The Spokesman Review* (July 7, 1946), 5.
[36] De Rougé, *St. Mary's Mission 25 Years Ago and Today,* Mss., Archives of the Sisters of the Blessed Sacrament (henceforth: ABSS).
[37] De Rougé, *St. Mary's High School,* OPA.
[38] Anonymous, *op. cit.,* 5.
[39] Francis Favel, secretary of Father de Rougé, heard the story from Father himself, interview, May 22, 1960, St. Mary's.

their children; Father's action convinced them that the priest wanted
only to help them.

Just above St. Mary's Mission there is quite an opening in the rocky
hill that resembles a cave. No reference is made to it by the missionary.
The front wall was built up with flat rocks that can still be seen lying
in a pile. Former pupils of St. Mary's stated that this cave was completely closed up and had a wooden door on one side. An altar was
there many years ago. The general rumor has it that Father de Rougé
went to the cave for the sake of security when the medicine men
threatened him in the early years of his missionary life. He might have
used the cave, too, in order to have some privacy when he wanted to
say his prayers and be alone with his God. Mrs. Maggie St. Peters,
who died in 1964 at the age of ninety-three years, definitely stated that
Father de Rougé lived in that cave. Mrs. St. Peters had lived in a log
house near St. Mary's Mission for quite some years during the early
times.[40] Harry A. Van Coelen, Portland, Oregon, who attended St. Mary's
School from 1905 to 1908, was one day sent up to the cave to repair it,
to replace some rocks that had fallen off in front, leaving a hole. This
indicates that Father had a certain attachment to the cave and wanted
to keep it intact.[41] Mrs. Edna Dignan, the former Edna Verdier, who as
a white pupil attended St. Mary's from 1911 to 1914, still remembers
that in those years the cave was still closed up. A holy-water font was
there and a statue of the Blessed Mother above the font. It was a small
shrine.[42]

An annual report of Indian Agent Rickard D. Gwydir, written in
longhand on November 24, 1887, to the Hon. J. D. C. Atkins, Commissioner of Indian Affairs, Washington D. C., mentions Father de
Rougé's two chapels as the only ones then on the reservation:

> The Colville Indian Mission was begun previous to the year 1843
> but is not on any reservation. There are two chapels on the reservation
> built for the accommodations of the Indians west of the Columbia River,
> one near Omak Lake, the other 20 miles south of "Lake Osooyes" [sic].
> They are rude log houses with dirt roof and only erected that the
> visiting priest might have a place to celebrate services in.[43]

As the Indian agent very seldom visited the less accessible regions of
the reservation he was not informed that these two primitive chapels

[40] Maggie St. Peters, in an interview in her home, Omak, May 1, 1960.
[41] Harry A. Van Coelen, in interviews at St. Mary's Mission, May 8–11, 1960.
[42] Mrs. Edna Dignan, letter to the author, April 15, 1961.
[43] Rickard D. Gwydir, Indian Agent, to Hon. J. D. C. Atkins, Commissioner of
Indian Affairs, Washington, D. C., November 24, 1887, Ms., NA, Record Group
75.

were the beginnings of the first permanent mission centers in the Okanogan Valley and that on both places there were also accommodations for the Father to stay.

Father Grassi had started to convert the Wenatchee tribe. Half of them had been baptized when the old Chief Nraamelt came to the Okanogan mission to ask Father de Rougé to come and visit his people. Chief Nraamelt told the priest that many medicine men were a hindrance to the conversion of his people; every one of them had at least two wives. Father de Rougé went and found, near the banks of the Columbia River, the primitive chapel probably built by Father Grassi. It was "a roofless log chapel on the top of which a tent had been placed for protection against the sun and the rain." A deputation of Indians told Father that a woman was dying and that the medicine men had performed their superstitious actions over her. The father of the dying woman came and asked the priest to see her, but Father acted indifferent to his request. The man was disappointed and went away; but he came again: "She is dying; will you come and see her?" Father de Rougé again showed his indifference. The man stood still and then tried again: "She wants you, she is dying."

> "I am not going," said the priest. Soon other Indians came and asked him to go. "Call those who wanted the medicine men and let them see her," he replied. A few relatives came in and made excuses. "Well," said the priest, "The best thing for you to do is to call the medicine men of the country and have them help the woman to die quickly."[44]

We can imagine the effects of such strong speech. It shows that Father de Rougé knew Indian psychology. He waited; after a long silence one came up and asked him to go to see the dying woman. This was followed by strong rebuke from Father for those who had taken part in the superstitious rites. After many promises not to use superstitions anymore the priest finally consented to go to see the woman. Everybody thought she would die that night, but Father de Rougé asked the Indians to pray that she might be able to receive Holy Communion the next day. The whole camp passed the night praying and singing hymns. In the morning the dying woman was taken into the chapel and after Holy Communion felt better and could walk with a stick. She lived two more weeks, a fact which made a strong impression on all the Indians.

Father used another method to stop gambling. The first action during the week-long mission was to rid the Indians of the instruments of gambling:

---

[44] De Rougé, "The Conversion of the Wenatchee," *The Indian Sentinel*, (1912), 42–44 (no number).

After Mass, the priest, knowing that all these Indians were gamblers, said: "Now, my dear Friends, all must go home immediately." They looked up in wonder as to what he meant. They all had camped in order to be a few days at church, and could not understand the order. "Yes," said he, "You are all gamblers, you must go home at once and bring me, right away, all your cards and gambling bones." After a while hardly any one could be seen in the camp.[45]

An old man was allowed to stay but promised to give his cards and gambling bones to the priest on the way back because the man lived too far away. All the Indians were back in the evening; one after the other entered the chapel and threw his cards and gambling bones on the floor until there was quite a pile of them.

Father's next action concerned the ones who fostered all the superstitions, the medicine men. They received a strong rebuke and were lectured, after which one of them came in and said that he would stop his ritual. He had two wives; soon he sent one away and others followed his example. After Mass the Indians had a public meeting at which time they all arose and solemnly promised to make an end to their pagan rites. Then baptisms were administered and marriages were blessed; now the whole tribe belonged to the Church.[46]

The priest knew that age-old practices that had permeated every phase of the Indians' living could not be abandoned in a short time. It was a strong temptation for these children of nature to attend the winter dances and Chinook dances of the medicine men. Father de Rougé tells us about these dances:

In the winter he [the medicine man] would call the people to his dances, oblige them to throw in a sacrifice . . . blankets, clothing, provisions of all kind, saddles and money. Out of this he would not forget to get a good share at the end of the feast. The south wind had to answer the prayer and come to hurry up the coming of the spring. All the Indians were afraid of the medicine man, no one would refuse to come to his call. If sick, they were sure to experience their [sic] vengeance which was driving them to their graves. There was no other remedy than to call for another medicine man hoping that the power of this one would be stronger than the power of the other, and would offer him anything of their poor property to be cured by his superstitions.[47]

Winter had come in the land of the Wenatchees, the time of the dances. The old chief Nraamelt forbade the superstitions; nevertheless, a woman and her family had gone to Chelan for the dances. This woman

[45] De Rougé, "The Conversion of the Wenatchee," *op. cit.,* 43.
[46] *Ibid.*
[47] De Rougé, *St. Mary's Mission 25 Years Ago and Today,* Ms., ABSS.

was stricken during the dance and started to spit blood. Father de Rougé was then in Colville but left for his Okanogan missions early in February.[48] He had to cross the Kettle River several times on the ice, once finding it necessary to spend an hour freeing his two pack horses from a hole in the ice. The provisions were ruined, but the young priest arrived safely at Chief Smitkin's camp at Omak Creek. It was here that a messenger called him to Chelan where the superstitious woman was dying. Father found her all covered with blood which she had been spitting now for a month. She was unconscious and unable to take food. The priest remarked to the surrounding infidels that this was the punishment for her disobedience. He administered Extreme Unction and told the Indians to call him if the woman should regain her senses. Then he traveled seven miles to visit the Catholic Indians. He was recalled to Chelan the next day. The woman made her confession, regained her health, and was still living in 1912 when Father published the story, and she has never gone back to a dance.[49] To save this one soul, Father de Rougé had traveled many days during that icy winter when no roads existed.

The Indians had no news of Father's coming; therefore only three hundred natives were waiting at Schall-kees for the ceremonies of Ash Wednesday. They had the Forty Hours' Adoration. Then Father went back to the Chelans and to the Wenatchees, where the Indians were happy to see him. Here he helped to organize the first police force in the upper Columbia and Okanogan Valleys. He speaks about much fruitful work and of good cooperation on the part of his Indians in Wenatchee, in Chelan, and in the Okanogan Valley:

> There we got up in each tribe 10 policemen to help the chiefs. All the cards and gambling bones were brought to me in the church and burned. Then I said the first mass in the new Simponskneuchi chapel — very nice and all built up by the Indians. They bought lumber, paint, doors, windows and everything themselves. In Chelan the Indians are buying lumber to finish their own chapel and build up a room beside for the father.[50]

Another great surprise awaited Father de Rougé when after a month on the Columbia he came back to Schall-kees. Here the Okanogan Indians had wanted a larger chapel and in his absence had hauled lumber. Father tells us:

---

[48] This incident told in Father de Rougé's letter to Father Cataldo, Colville Mission, "Mars 20," apparently was written in 1888. He mentioned the first Mass in the new Wenatchee church which had been built in 1888, Ms., OPA.
[49] De Rougé, "The Conversion of the Wenatchee," op. cit.
[50] De Rougé, letter to Cataldo, March 20 (1888), Ms., OPA.

I got a good carpenter at once and Saturday before Palm Sunday the bell was in the steeple to call the Indians who enter the new church (40 x 20). That evening all Indians of Columbia about 3 or 400 arrived in a block. The Okanogans received them with shaking of hands and salvo of guns. 700 Indians were in camp from Palm Sunday to Easter Sunday and they went away Thursday after Easter. I had about 12 baptisms of adults and 8 marriages. The whole day of holy Thursday adoration. Friday night procession with innumerable fires around the place. A big cross was brought on the shoulders to the grave ground. On Easter high mass was sung by all Indians as one voice.[51]

The Indians, in addition to building the second church at Schall-kees, had collected $100 for their new church. The handshaking ceremony and shouting, "Let us meet again . . ." ended the departure of the tribes. Father de Rougé wrote this mission news from Colville where he had gone to see Father Grassi and where he expected an answer from Father Cataldo. The Columbia Indians wanted to send their children to school. Father de Rougé wrote, "I am going back to bring the children here after a few weeks."[52] Some Okanogan children attended St. Francis Regis Mission School before St. Mary's had been organized.[53]

The old Indians still remember the large Ellisforde church of hewn cottonwood logs and of boards. The second church had a "puncheon floor [hewn logs] and tule mats on the floor. It had no benches."[54] According to Louis Pierre, Father de Rougé had the help of a Brother; both living in the long three-room cabin beside the church.[55]

It is difficult to trace the name of the church at Schall-kees. Father de Rougé drew a map of this vast mission territory. His first mission at Schall-kees, which he later called "Old Okanogan Mission," was marked by a cross and the name "N. de Lourdes."[56] A financial statement sent to the bishop shows that he spent $350 "At former station of Our Lady of Lourdes" in 1890.[57] Father de Rougé very often ministered to the Indians in the vicinity of Chopaka by Loomis. Local Indians point to the fact that Father de Rougé very probably built the Chopaka church. This church at Chopaka is named also Our Lady of Lourdes. The indications are clear on Father's map; he must have meant the church at Schall-kees. Chopaka is on the other side of the Okanogan River and was

[51] De Rougé, *op. cit.*

[52] *Ibid.*

[53] St. Francis Regis Mission, *School Reports,* 1892–1893, Mss., OPA.

[54] Mrs. K. Lacey, in an interview with Suzette Teobasket, March 15, 1961. Courtesy of Mrs. Lacey, Osoyoos, B.C.

[55] Louis Pierre of Vernon, B.C., in an interview at St. Mary's, April 20, 1961.

[56] Original map of Father de Rougé, OPA.

[57] De Rougé, *Financial Statement,* 1890, Ms., ADS.

built about 1892 or 1893.[58] Narcisse Nicholson thinks that the Ellisforde church built by Father de Rougé was named Saint Joseph's.[59]

Narcisse Nicholson, who has lived near the church at Schall-kees nearly all of his long life, remembers how Father de Rougé tried to appeal to his primitive spiritual children:

> It took quite a bit to convince the early day Indians. Father de Rouge was quite an artist and would draw pictures of what the bad Indians were like, when they gambled he drew pictures of Fire & Brimstone & of snakes winding around them & the devil hovering over them & showed some of them with horns & what would happen to the unbelievers. They were large wall size pictures.[60]

The Indians called Father de Rougé "Sapp-ee," and still give him that name when talking of him, but nobody seems to know the meaning of the word. Sapp-ee made sure that no one was sleeping while he preached, and he appointed some men to help him keep order. The Indian policemen he appointed were strict; on the camping grounds there were certain rules to be observed and there were strict rules especially in the church. Charley Swimptkin was a church policeman; with a long sharp stick he would try to keep the Indians attentive. Drunken Indians were tied up to trees and were not allowed to come into the church:[61]

> Father de Rougé would have the Indians from the Canadian side camp North of the church, in order as they came, & the Indians from this side camp south of the church, in order as they came, & then he would call the Indians to line up . . . and shake hands as they went by [each other] & then go into the church.[62]

Not long after the church in Schall-kees was built Father de Rougé blessed a piece of ground that is still used today as the Catholic cemetery. Some markers go far back to the early times of the mission. Father stopped the old custom of the Indian burying the dead in the shale or other loose rocks on the hillside above the present cemetery.[63] An earlier blessed graveyard was in Tonasket where in former times an Indian village had existed. When later the whites settled down in Tonasket, they just leveled the ground and built houses on top of the graves. The area from

---

58 Mrs. K. Lacey, in an interview with Mr. Paul Loudon, March 15, 1961. Father de Rougé stopped at the Loudon place at Loomis on his missionary trips; they had better accomodations for horses. Courtesy of Mrs. Lacey.

59 Mrs. K. Lacey, in an interview with Narcisse Nicholson, March 15, 1960.

60 Narcisse Nicholson, Ellisforde, *Remembrances*, Fall, 1960. Also: interviews at Ellisforde and at St. Mary's Mission, May 10, 1960; September 12, 1960; July 15, 1961.

61 *Ibid.*

62 *Ibid.*

63 *Ibid.*

the hospital to the park was the graveyard which probably was blessed by Father Joset or by Father Grassi.[64]

Miss Margaret Bottomley, whose parents settled at Oroville in 1884, says that the first tame flowers she ever saw were at Ellisforde where Father de Rougé had a little rustic garden. His mother had sent him the seeds from France. Miss Bottomley's father worked on the original church. She remembers that some time after 1888 her mother took Father de Rouge's suit and turned it for him, because it had gotten so shiney and shabby. Maggie had to help her mother pull the threads.[65] Father most certainly needed a "better look" before he went back to France to make his tertianship in 1888–1889.

An early settler, Mr. Fries, reported some of the talks he had with the Indians about Father de Rougé. One Saturday morning of May, 1888, Mr. Fries saw bands of Indians passing his house; all were dressed in their best clothes. He found out that they were on their way to the mission. The next day an Indian family visited him: man, wife and daughter. The following questions and answers were recorded:

> Why are you and your family not with the rest of the Indians at the mission, Mountas? I don't like the priest.
> Is the priest a bad man?
> Perhaps, perhaps not.
> If you are not sure whether he is good or bad, what has he done to you?
> A long time ago, there were not many priests here, but many Indians. The squaws gave birth to many babies. Then the priest came. The squaws almost stopped having babies. The Indians died. Soon there will be no more Indians.
> Do you believe that priests are to blame? Yes, I believe so.[66]

Then Mr. Fries says the Indians did not like it that there were more deaths among them since the priests had come. But the Indians did not realize that with the priests the traders had come also. The Indians did not know how to use coffee and other foodstuffs. "They would load their stomachs and finish off with a long drink of whiskey." This kind of diet proved especially harmful for the pregnant mothers. The Fathers had done all in their power to stop certain trading activities and had tried to elevate and educate the Indians.[67] Mr. Fries continues the interview:

---

[64] Mrs. Mary Therese Pierre, in an interview at St. Mary's, April 5, 1961.
[65] Miss Maggie Bottomley, in an interview with Mrs. Lacey, March 15, 1961. Also with the author at Oroville, July 13, 1961.
[66] Ulrick E. and Emil B. Fries, *From Copenhagen to Okanogan*, 150.
[67] *Ibid.*

Mountas, You don't like the priest. Does the priest like you?
No! Some time ago the priest came to my house and asked me to go
to the mission to partake of Holy Communion. I said to him, "No, I
don't go to the mission to take eat with the Lord." The priest got very
angry with me . . .[68]

Father de Rougé's last entry in the *Baptismal Records* for 1888 was
on May 10th, and the first after his return from France was on April
21, 1889.[69] During the time of Father's absence, Father Parodi twice
visited the Okanogan and Upper Columbia tribes. After leaving Ellensburg
he had spent a year in California. Now he was told to visit the Okanogan
missions. The Okanogans had a language of their own and were very
particular about being instructed in this language. Although they understood the Calispel and Chinook Indians, they were insistent about using
their own Okanogan dialect. Father Parodi knew only enough of the
Okanogan language to be able to hear confessions. For preaching, he
had at his disposal twenty-eight sermons composed by Father Grassi in
the Okanogan Salish language. The Indians delighted to hear these very
instructive sermons. Father Parodi had with him Father Giorda's catechism
and prayers in the Calispel language. Knowing that the Okanogan Indians would not like religion explained in Calispel, Father Parodi looked
in Father de Rougé's house, where he found a catechism written in
Chinook by Bishop Blanchet. Father Parodi, thinking that this language
was spoken by all the Indians in the United States, and not caring if
the Okanogans were scandalized, took the book along to church. He
started to teach in Chinook. It did not take long before the chief
approached, saying: "Away with that language; we talk that language
transacting business and trading with white people. We never speak
Chinook in the church."[70] Father Parodi then asked a half-breed, Pion,
to translate Father Giorda's catechism into the Okanogan language; it kept
Pion busy all day. The next day Chief Antoine wanted Father to translate
a letter into the Okanogan language, which Father Parodi was not able
to do. When the chief told the half-breed Pion about it, he was surprised and said, "Yesterday I taught him the language from morning
to night."[71]

The *Diary of St. Francis Regis* for September 6, 1888, records that
"Father Filippi went to visit the Okinagan accompanied by the Chief

[68] Fries and Fries, *op. cit.*, 150.
[69] *Registrum Baptizatorum in Ecclesia Stae Mariae apud Okenakanos*, Book I,
44–45.
[70] Parodi, *Reminiscences*, Mss., OPA.
[71] *Ibid.*

Smitkin."[72] This entry indicates that Chief Smitkin of the Omak camp was eager to have a priest attending his people again and came to Colville to ask for one. It seems that Father Parodi was then at Schall-kees and Chief Smitkin was not aware of it. Father Filippi went on his way to the Okanogans with Smitkin; he had received an order from Father Cataldo to visit the Okanogan Valley as far down as Chelan during Father de Rougé's absence. He had to travel over 200 miles "crossing rivers, forests, mountains and 7 miles trails winding in the back of steep mountains above the Columbia river between rocks and pine trees. The Indians call it the 7 devils trail."[72] At Smitkin's camp Father Filippi was told that another Father was at the Okanogan Mission. He hurriedly rode there and found to his great surprise Father Parodi whom he had not seen since his novitiate years, 1873–1875. He embraced him "so hard as to cause him stop breathing." Father Filippi then decided to take Father Parodi along to Colville.

The Indians saw that Father Filippi's horse would be unable to re-cross the mountains and that Father Parodi, who had come by stage, had no horse. They consulted Chief Smitkin, who gave Father Filippi a young and strong horse and he urged his wife to give Father Parodi her own horse. But the wife wanted money, which Father Filippi gave her. Two Indian guides and an Okanogan boy from St. Francis Regis Mission School accompanied them toward Colville. On the way the travelers had to ford the Kettle River eleven times, but in five days they were back at St. Francis Regis Mission. The *Diary of St. Francis Regis* for October 9, 1888, says, "Fr. Filippi came back from Okinagan with P. Parodi after a month of absence, and very much pleased with his visit to these poor people."[73]

While Father de Rougé was in France, the Okanogans had to cele-brate Christmas without a priest. They were told to keep the feast as well as they could. Chief Smitkin from the Omak camp of Okanogans wanted to do something special. On his return from a trip he had brought along calico and a clock. With the calico he covered the logs of his small chapel. After the Indians of the camp had supper they all sat around the clock on the floor of the log chapel. When the clock showed that it was midnight, they arose, marched around, then knelt down and said all the prayers they knew and sang all their hymns.[74]

At the beginning of February, 1889, Father Parodi was on sick calls.

[72] Parodi, *Memoirs*, Mss., OPA.

[73] *Diary of St. Francis Regis Mission*, October 9, 1889.

[74] Rev. Celestine Caldi, S.J., "The First Christmas Among the Wenatchees," *The Indian Sentinel* I (Winter 1929–1930), 2. The heading of this article is mislead-ing. Smitkin was chief at Omak, not of the Wenatchees.

One call came from Fort Spokane, the other from Chelan. He left Colville on February 5 and traveled first to Spokane and from there another 128 miles to Chelan. After several days of travel Father and his companion lodged in a house where a girl had consumption; next door to her a man had pneumonia, and Father Parodi himself was stricken with malaria. He heard the confessions of the two sick persons. He was too ill to get up the next morning to ride the remaining thirty miles to Chelan. The Indians were eager to help him to get to Chelan twenty miles down the Columbia in a canoe; from here Chief Wapato John would send a wagon to carry him the last ten miles to the lake. Some young braves rode ahead to tell this to the chief. Father Parodi rose at nine o'clock to fix the altar. He heard the confessions of twelve Indians, said Mass, and gave the consumptive girl Holy Communion as Viaticum. The year before she had received her first Holy Communion from Father de Rougé. Out of fine brush the Indians made a sort of chair in the boat for the priest to rest in while two Indians, one at the head and the other at the stern, paddled the boat. They did this with such speed that they arrived at Chelan at four o'clock. There were wagon tracks but no wagon, and so they started to walk. After a mile, the sick Father was unable to move further. Happily the wagon arrived and this made it possible for Father Parodi to reach the chief's place before dark. He had been on the way twelve days for a sick call. Magdalene, the chief's wife, made a good supper for him, and he then heard the confession of the sick man. Close to the chapel Father Grassi had built a primitive "shanty" for himself. There Father Parodi made a fire and baked a supply of hosts. The next morning there were fifteen Holy Communions, at which time the priest also gave the Last Sacraments to the sick man. The Indians, hearing that a priest was at Chelan, came from all directions, even from Wenatchee, forty miles away. Wapato John took up a collection from the hundred and thirty Indians present and gave Father thirty-eight dollars.

The priest could hardly believe what he saw next. A band of Indians came on horses. They had traveled thirty miles bringing the consumptive girl who had received Viaticum, and the dying old man. The sick persons wanted to have more grace before their death. Tents were erected near the church while Father heard the confessions of the two. When he wanted to bring them Holy Viaticum the next morning, he was astonished to see two women leading the girl and two men the sick old man. He had to turn and go back to the chapel where these two heroic Indian souls received their Lord for the last time. Father later anointed them. The girl died two days later and the man a month afterwards.

Now Father Parodi had to make a choice; the Wenatchees had built a church and they wanted him because Father de Rougé was still in France. Wentachee being nearer, he first went there and promised the Okanogans to come later to the Omak camp and to Schall-kees. At Wenatchee the chief took up a collection which made the sum of Father's money nearly a hundred dollars. He sent the money to Benziger Brothers of New York, and the Indians, later, "were crazy for joy" when they opened the box and found all kinds of glittering candlesticks for their poor churches.

Chief Antoine of the Okanogans had come to Chelan to be Father Parodi's companion for the trip to St. Mary's Mission. Every two or three days the poor Father Parodi would suffer an attack of the fever. Chief Smitkin's place was still twenty-five miles distant when Father had to stop in an Indian house. The next day the Chief came with a buggy and brought Father to Alma City which was later called Okanogan. At that time it consisted of three buildings, a store, a livery barn, and a hotel with a stage office. The owner, Mr. "Pat" Cummings, did not belong to any denomination, according to Father Parodi. As we shall see, he was supposed to belong to the Catholic faith. His wife, Alma, was a Jewess. Father was so ill that he was forced to spend fifteen days in their home, being most kindly cared for by Mrs. Cummings. She was the only person who had quinine, the specific medication for malaria. When Father recovered sufficiently, he went across the Okanogan River to an Indian house to give the Indians an opportunity to have a Holy Mass. Cummings was also the owner of the ferry boat which provided portage across the Okanogan River to the Colville Reservation. Smitkin was told to send a riding horse to meet the priest. At the same time Father Cataldo had just sent six bottles of Mass wine. When Father Parodi was ready to leave and asked for his bill, Cummings said, "Father, I am well pleased to have you here, come whenever you wish and make yourself at home."

Father Parodi arrived at St. Mary's Mission, Omak. The chapel had only the damp ground for a floor. Not until eleven at night did Father Parodi finally finish hearing confessions. The next day was Easter Sunday. He did not want to sleep in an Indian lodge, as some of them were vermin infested, but tried to sleep on the damp chapel floor. The Indians came the next morning to the chapel and peeped in, but Father did not move. At ten o'clock the priest resolved to try to say Mass. After that he would go to bed. Before he attempted to say Mass he wrote a letter to Father Cataldo saying that he should send a priest to the Omak mission, as "I am going to die." Of the fifty-six Indians who had

wanted to go to Holy Communion only twenty-two received because of
the late hour; however thirty-four had stayed without breakfast. After
Mass Father went to bed again. Chief Smitkin killed a young deer and
his wife roasted two slices from it, which Father forced himself to eat.
His evening meal consisted of two trout. Father then felt that he was
getting better. He put double mats on the ground and used double
blankets for covers and had a good night. The next morning he was up
and around and asked Smitkin to have a horse ready. He wanted to
go to the Okanogan Mission at Schall-kees.

The United States government had built in the same year, 1889,
the school for Chief Tonasket's people on Bonaparte Creek.[75] There
Father Parodi had to stop and use the superintendent's bed. He was
there two days under a doctor's care when one morning another sick
call came. He was rushed nineteen miles to a woman with a serious
snake bite. The superintendent of the school then took Father to the
Schall-kees Mission where they saw a black-clad gentleman waving his hat.

> They thought he was Father de Rougé come back from France,
> but then they saw that he was Father Monroe. He had been sent by
> Fr. Cataldo to assist the dying Father at Okanogan; had been at Alma
> and told the dying Father was at Smitkin and there was told the dying
> Father had gone to the school house. At the school house he was told
> that the dying father had a sick call. Father Monroe then went to the
> Mission and the dying Father was not there.[76]

Father Monroe stayed at the mission eight days. Father Parodi had
no attack during these days but on the same day that Father Monroe
left, which was in the morning, Father Parodi had another attack in
the evening.

Father Parodi then prepared the things needed for the Corpus Christi
procession. He went to the forest and shaped four handles for the canopy
to be used during the procession. All was in readiness when the Indians
arrived from all directions.

The Wentachee chief and about a hundred of his tribe were first.
Then Father had to march through the line to shake hands. He experienced a shaking spell while doing this, but the Indians were not aware
of it. The tribes arrived one after another and Father Parodi was
occupied for days hearing the many confessions. On the feast he had
over two hundred and seventy Indians in the church and about fifty
outside the church. The missionary had been busy all morning hearing

---

[75] Report of the Secretary of the Interior," House Executive Documents, Fifty-
First Congress, First Session, 1889–1890, II, 283.
[76] Parodi, Memoirs, Mss., OPA.

confessions, preaching, saying Mass, distributing Holy Communion to about three hundred people, and now it was noon when he finally wanted to have his breakfast. But it was not until he had baptized three Indian babies in succession that he could go to his room for something to eat. In his room he found six sets of dirty dishes to be washed, left there by six chiefs. Not one of the cooks had thought of Father Parodi; he ate some cold meat and warmed-over coffee.

The Corpus Christi procession took place during the afternoon, through a lane the Indians had made days before by planting trees on both sides.

> There were 9 squaws that had lost one eye, and two more were blind altogether. The two blinds, to keep straight in line took hold of the gown from behind another squaw. With great sorrow they were separated by the Indian soldiers. The Indians in procession were screaming in their own language; the Father holding the Bl. Sacrament under the canopy was singing in Latin [sic.]. It took one hour to make the turn in the prairie.[77]

Back in church another sermon and Benediction followed. Then Father Parodi went to bed without eating.

He left the Okanogan Mission the next Monday and arrived during July in Spokane and then went to Colville. In his jovial manner Father Parodi recorded that he had been on a sick call from February until July.[78]

The Indians were waiting for the return of Father de Rougé. According to the *Baptismal Records,* he must have been already at the Omak camp. From now on Ellisforde or Schall-kees will be only of secondary importance and the Valley of the Omak Creek will be the social center for many decades to come.

---

[77] Parodi, *op. cit.*
[78] *Ibid.*

CHAPTER X

He Helped to Preserve the Peace

IN 1889, Father de Rougé returned to his log chapel and to Chief Smitkin's camp at Omak Creek. He was full of new missionary enthusiasm after his tertianship, another year of ascetical training. His plans were ready; he would build a mission dedicated to the Mother of God, that would become a haven for Indians and whites alike. He would transplant European culture and schooling to his favored spot in the Okanogan country. From here he would visit the camps of the Indians and of the many whites who gradually settled at points on the east side of the Okanogan River. This would be his central location for a school and for big gatherings on the high feast days. Smaller chapels and churches would be built hundreds of miles distant from St. Mary's Mission where he could say Mass and minister the holy sacraments to those who could not come to St. Mary's. He knew it would take time, heroic patience, utter selflessness and self-sacrifice. He was prepared to pay that price. Besides the costs that only his personality could pay, he needed financial means to carry out his plans. He wrote to friends:

> I built myself a log hut at St. Mary's in the first place. Then I went to France in '88–89 on my tertianship and begged, borrowed, and stole money from everyone I knew to get capital to erect a better building.[1]

In 1889 he erected a little house and chapel "to take the place of the log chapel at St. Mary's."[2] Then Father de Rougé could say, "We

---

[1] De Rougé quoted by Mrs. Nellie Picken, "St. Mary's Mission Serves Young Okanogan Indians," *The Spokesman Review,* (January 1, 1956), 12. Original letter probably burned at the mission.

[2] De Rougé in *Historia Domus* [n.d.], Ms., OPA.

now have a fairly good mission house on Omak Creek."[3] However, the sum of money from France was not in such amounts as the rumors that were circulated would indicate. Gradually Father attracted the Indians that did not belong to Smitkin's camp. They came from far distances and this made it necessary to build more log huts and little houses, which the Indians called "church houses." Old photographs show several of these church houses on both sides of the Omak Creek. Many old and sick people would wait in these little houses until God would call them to their eternal home. Here they could attend daily Mass when Father was home; here the priest visited them. In nearly every interview the author had with the old Indian people, she was told that Father did good service as a doctor. His pills and medicine cured many. No regular doctor was easy to reach and Father de Rougé was equipped for emergencies.

Only patient and persistent work could gradually make the Indians give up calling on the medicine men. Father de Rougé saw the influence of the medicine men as a major hindrance to civilization. The Indians were afraid that the medicine men were able to send sickness and death; and these quacks made the Indians pay to keep them from being sick. Father de Rougé repeatedly expresses his displeasure at this belief in the power of the medicine men as being the principal obstacle in teaching Christian culture to the Indians:

> The missionaries always had trouble to stop these superstitions which have not yet disappeared. They [the Indians] will not use medicine or call doctors, but will, first of all, call the medicine man. These of course, have to get several horses, saddles, blankets or money to do their work and cure. Even though reservation laws forbids these things, very little has been done to stop them.[4]

It was Father's ability to treat the sick successfully and his loving sincerity that made the Indians aware of how much he was concerned about their spiritual and corporal well-being. Gradually, but very slowly, his prestige grew and that of the medicine men declined.

Over and over old Indian people have told the author proudly, "He ate with us." Father de Rougé, the son of a count, whose estates in

---

[3] De Rougé quoted by Mrs. Nellie Picken, *op. cit.* Also: De Rougé in Annual Report of 1890 to Rt. Rev. Bishop O'Dea, Ms., ADS. Father spent $932 for the new church, $136 for the bell and freight, $120 for furniture and statues and $260 for his building and lodging. He received "Private alms from France, or the Society of $909.50."

[4] De Rougé, S.J., "Father De Rougé Among the Indians," in *History of North Washington,* Richard F. Steele, ed., 861–862.

France were taken care of by sixteen gardeners,[5] became an "Indian" among the Indians in order to raise them to a higher level. He would travel hundreds of miles during the next years in all directions to find souls who needed help. He would camp with the Indians, sleep with the Indians, and pray with them. The first years at St. Mary's he had no regular school during the summer months; this gave him time to visit the summer camps of the various tribes. He, himself, gives us an idea — in his own words — of the big territory he had to traverse in saddle and canoe:

> This little Okanogan Mission is a great mission if you look at the map. To give you an idea of it . . . if we start from the center here at St. Mary's you have 100 miles to Wenatchee south west, 80 miles to San Poil east, and 70 miles to the line of B.C. [British Columbia]. At Wenatchee we have 160 Indians, at Chelan 115, at St. Mary's 210, at Okanogan 200 [Ellisforde]. Besides the camps of infidels at Nespelem and San Poil where we have about 900 or more Indians, among them 100 Catholics, we have also two camps right across the B.C. line; it is not our mission but these Indians are coming here and we have to go there for sick calls as they have no other priest and one camp has about 215 and the other 90. Now all these figures have been lately well calculated and are making quite a population around us.[6]

The Indian tribes were able to congregate at St. Mary's only on high feast days: Christmas, Ash Wednesday, Holy Week and Easter, Corpus Christi, and the feast of St. Ignatius. Then they would camp around the mission for a week or so. Between these feasts Father de Rougé had to visit them and be ready for sick calls. This meant that Father was most of the time on the way traversing mountains and valleys exposed to hunger and thirst, to wild animals that were then still roaming the country, and to all kinds of weather.

The first years of Father de Rougé's work among the Okanogan and Upper Columbia tribes were filled with various kinds of adventure. We mentioned the danger to his life on account of the hate of the medicine men. The country was overrun on all sides by the incoming whites, miners, farmers, and traders. Echoes of former Indian wars, of soldiers stationed at Chelan, of unjust reservation policies were filling the air. The heart of the missionary suffered because of the cruelties and sometimes deaths inflicted on his beloved Indians. Two Indians had been killed on account of the whiskey traffic at Chelan in 1886.[7] Even if the stoic faces of the

---

[5] De Rougé to Sister M. Michael, O.P., one of the former Lady Missionaries of St. Mary's, interviews.
[6] De Rougé, St. Mary's Mission, Mss., OPA.
[7] Emil Fries, *op. cit.,* p. 325.

Indians did not betray their thoughts, discontent and unrest among them was growing. The root of the evil lay in the forced abandonment of their homelands. Long Jim, the hereditary chief of the Chelans, counseled his tribe not to accept any allotment after the Moses agreement had stipulated either an allotment or a move to the Colville Reservation.[8] Long Jim rightly contended that the land upon which they lived had belonged to them; it was their original property right to keep it. Father Grassi and Father de Rougé had worked hard to convert these Indians and before Father de Rougé left for France they had started to complete Father Grassi's church and make other improvements on Father's cabin. It had been hard for these Indians to convince themselves that the Jesuit Fathers had nothing to do with the United States government and that they were sent by God and not by the "White Father" in Washington.[9] Now the soldiers had been ordered during May of 1890, to drive these Indians from their homes and gardens and to take them to the Colville Reservation.[10]

How could Father de Rougé teach the Indians the white man's religion if the lives of the government officials and other white men showed that they did not practice Christian principles of justice? No culture and civilization can be planted in an atmosphere of distrust and war. Disagreements among the United States officials in administering justice between the white man and the Indians aggravated the spirit of uneasiness. Pokamiakin, a guilty wild Indian, feared by whites and Indians alike, had finally been caught by Sheriff Allison under the most difficult circumstances but illegal ones. He was brought to trial and was thereupon cleared by Attorney M. B. Barney. The whites had caught him in order to make an example out of him. This action had far-reaching results and serious consequences in that it made the whites distrust court procedures and influenced them, therefore, to take justice into their own hands.[11]

In October of 1890 two well-known freighters, Mr. S. S. Cole and Mr. Wilkinson, disappeared, and the rumor that they were murdered spread over the countryside. Cole's wagon and horses were found but no trace of the men. Rewards were offered for the recovery of their bodies and for the arrest of the murderers. Indian Johnny and a boy named Steven had been witnesses to the murders. The murderers had suspected Wilkinson to be in possession of a great amount of money;

---

[8] Charles J. Kappler, *Indian Affairs: Laws and Treaties,* II, 1074. See: "Moses Agreement."

[9] Father Urban Grassi, Letter to his Provincial, Father Joseph Giorda, S.J., November 10, 1874, Mss., OPA.

[10] Emil Fries, *op. cit.,* 325 ff.

[11] *Ibid.* See also: *Glimpses of Pioneer Life (Okanogan Independent,* 1924), 78.

they had murdered him on the Colokum Creek road and pushed his wagon over the steep bank so that it could not be seen from the road. On the way back the murderers took the life of Cole. Soon the story circulated and gossip did the rest to name Indian Johnny and Steven as the two perpetrators of the crime. Johnny was killed by Deputy Sheriff Lee Ives while resisting arrest. Later the decapitated body of Cole was found. The people were enraged and wanted Steven arrested. He was asked to give himself up. Mr. Fries quotes Richard M. Price, United States deputy marshal and justice of the peace at Ruby:

> On January 4, 1891, at the east end of Omak Lake, I met Steven by appointment through Smitkin's niece Nancy. . . . I took him to the Mission and the Indians gathered around him and tried him from an Indian's standpoint of law. He admitted that he was a witness with Johnny to the Cole murder, but that the real murderer was a Nez Perce Indian.[12]

Price could do nothing with Steven as a witness as long as there was a warrant for him for murder in the first degree. He took him to jail; he was given a hearing and U. S. Commissioner George S. Hurley decided that Steven had a right to bail, which was fixed at $1,000. Steven had given himself up on condition that he would be allowed bail. Before the bail could be collected the news of Steven's arrest had traveled far and wide through the Okanogan country. All the whites were convinced that Steven was the murderer. A reprint of the *Ruby Miner,* January 13, 1891, which appeared in 1936 under the heading: *Indian Scare 35 Years Ago,* brings a summary of the following events:

> Last Thursday morning twenty horsemen swept silently and swiftly through the town of Ruby. The soft white snow muffled the sound of their horses' hoofs and the slumber of the camp was not disturbed by their movements. . . .
> Arriving at Conconully, the party called on the jailer Thos. Dickson, and forced him to admit them into the steel cell where the boy was confined. The boy was taken from there and Dickson locked up in his place. . . .
> A large tree standing by McGillivary's fence was the gibbet and upon this, with gutteral groans upon his lips and the agony of death in his heart, the miserable being was quickly hung.[13]

Steven was only fifteen years old and the son of the prominent medicine man, John. The executioners, who had been organized at Alma, quickly dispersed after the lynching. This vigilante committee acted on the grounds that the same lawyers and court officials who freed Pokamiakin would clear the murderer of Cole.

---

[12] Fries, quoting Richard M. Price, *op. cit.,* 329.
[13] "Indian Scare 35 Years Ago — Okanogan Called For Troops," *The Ruby Miner* (Jan. 13, 1891), reprint. Courtesy of Mr. F. A. De Vos, Soap Lake, Wash.

Then followed what was called the Indian Scare of 1891. The body of Steven was placed in a coffin, loaded on a bobsleigh, and one George Monk was ordered to bring the body to the reservation for burial. On the way he met Chief Smitkin and two other Indians who were on their way to Conconully to post bail for Steven. Not only was the cruel lynching a terrible offense in the eyes of the Indians but George Monk by sitting on Steven's coffin offended them further. The Indians greatly honored their dead and this act by Monk outraged even the primitive Indians. Monk was held up twice by hostile Indians, and Chief Smitkin needed all his influence to persuade them to let Monk pass on. At Smitkin's place, where the Indians assembled, Monk received a hostile welcome. He wanted to return but Smitkin kept him back and protected him with his own person. He told General Curry later, "I slept with him myself that night under my blanket, and in the morning took him to Cummings."[14] On the way back to Cummings' Ferry, the present town of Okanogan, the old chief and Monk barely outdistanced the hostile Indians.

In connection with the Indian scare, editor Richard F. Steele in an article written during Father de Rougé's lifetime, tells the following:

> Father de Rougé was one hundred and fifty miles away. On his arrival home an old Indian came to the mission at full speed and said to him: "You are just in time; last night the Indians had a big meeting and determined to go and kill some white men. But some one came in and said, 'The father is home.' It was sufficient; the Indians dispersed and plans for summary vengeance were abandoned.[15]

But before they dispersed they had the whole countryside in an uproar by their threatening attitude toward the whites. For days they nourished their hate at the bier of Steven and they danced day and night. "Finally the priest subdued their excitement long enough to have the body buried in the Catholic cemetery at Omak Lake."[16] The dancing ended and fifteen braves were sent to the Dakotas to help stir up hatred against the whites. They were amply provided with necessities. The Okanogan Indians had been influenced by the "Messiah craze" that had then traveled west from the Dakotas.[17]

---

[14] A. P. Curry, Chief Smitkin quoted in *Report on the Indian Troubles in Okanogan Country* to General R. G. O'Brien, Adjutant General, N.G.W. Olympia (Spokan Falls, Jan. 24, 1891), mimeographed copy. Courtesy of Judge Brown, Okanogan.

[15] Richard F. Steele, ed., *op. cit.*, 488.

[16] *The Ruby Miner*, reprint.

[17] James McLaughlin, *op. cit.*, 183–198. Messiah Craze told to James McLaughlin by One Bull, a nephew of Sitting Bull, who repeated the preaching of

The *Ruby Miner* continued to say that now the braves were looking for Pokamiakin to lead them against the whites, but Pokamiakin now "experienced religion":

> This feeling was manifested in Puck [the chief's nickname] about two weeks ago. He had heretofore killed several white men, assisted many of his own dusky brethren to their hunting grounds, and evidently did not fear man, God, nor the devil.
> But Puck got religion. The bucks want him to lead them against the Boston, but his religious convictions compel him to abstain.[18]

During the first days of the unrest Mayor George J. Hurley and his councilmen sent a petition to Governor Charles Laughton at Olympia, asking to be supplied with arms and ammunition. Old Indian fighters said that "the signs are serious. The probable force of Indians we may have to contend with will be about 400 bucks. The number now collected is about one hundred fighters."[19] General Curry was then ordered to proceed to the Okanogan country with a supply of arms. Arms were delivered to Lincoln, Douglas, and Okanogan counties. Curry then helped to form an independent military company at Conconully and gave them hints about military drill. On January 20, 1891, the General held a meeting on the Colville Reservation with Chiefs Smitkin, Antoine, Aeneas, and about seventy-five of their men. Father de Rougé was instrumental in bringing the Indians together; he also served as interpreter. The influence toward good of the Catholic Church was expressed by Chief Smitkin to General Curry:

> I am but a poor man, and not a great chief. I and my men work for

---

Kicking Bear. "My brothers, I bring to you the promise of a day in which there will be no white man to put his hand on the bridle of the Indians' horses; when the red man of the prairie will rule the world and not be turned from the hunting grounds by any man. I bring you word from your fathers the ghosts, that they are now marching to join you, led by the Messiah who came once to live on earth with the white men, but was cast out and killed by them. I have seen wonders of the spirit-land, and have talked with the ghosts. I traveled far and I am sent back with a message to tell you to make ready for the coming of the Messiah and return of the ghosts in the spring. . . .

"Take this message to my red children and tell them as I say it. I have neglected the Indians for many moons, but I will make them my people now if they obey me in this message. The earth is getting old, and I will make it new for my chosen people, the Indians, who are to inhabit it, and among them will be all those of their ancestors who have died, their fathers, mothers, brothers, cousins and wives — all those who hear my voice and my words through the tongues of my children. I will cover the earth with new soil to a depth of five times the height of a man, and under this soil will be buried the whites, and all the holes and the rotten places will be filled up" (pp. 188–189).

18 *The Ruby Miner*, reprint.
19 *Ibid.*

the Church, and the Church teaches us to be good and behave ourselves and give up drinking . . . He was glad that we came and sorry at what had happened. . . .[20]

One Indian after another, when called upon, told the general that they meant no harm for the whites and that the rumors had been false; even Pokamiakin and Doc John, the father of Steven, assured the general of their peaceful intentions. Klappallaten then told the general that he had come a long way to see him and urgently besought him to stop the selling of liquor to the Indians. Chief Susapkin then arose and said:

> There is no wrong to be feared from the Indians. Who is it from the white people that say the Indians want to fight? Letters have been sent telling that we are going to war, but we knew nothing about it.[21]

On his way back, the general met with a committee of citizens and told them the result of his council with the chiefs and their men. General Curry then wrote down his conclusions after he had examined the case:

> That the Indians maddened by the hanging of their comrade Steven, determined to get even with the whites and made many threats; that they sent runners to the British Columbia Indians, the Kettle River Indians and also to Joseph and Moses' bands asking for assistance in case of an uprising; that the former bands Kettle River and British Columbia, promised substantial aid; that Moses and Joseph both declined to take part but failed to denounce and discourage it as they should have done. Those upon whom they depended and who had promised them assistance in case of outbreak would number from three hundred and fifty to four hundred. This action, however, was confined entirely to the younger class and did not meet the approval of the older ones nor their local chiefs. The prompt action of the state authorities and the best council of the older men and chiefs, aided by the priest and the Indian farmer prevailed. . . .
>
> Liquor was the cause of this trouble, and such is the case with nearly every trouble in the country. I cannot speak too highly of the work done by the priest, Father de Rougé. . . .[22]

Only God knows how this Indian Scare would have ended without the great influence of good Father de Rougé.

---

[20] Curry, *op. cit.*
[21] Curry, *op. cit.* Susapkin was the old chief of the Similkameens.
[22] *Ibid.*

CHAPTER XI

Gradual Development of a Huge Parish

IN ORDER to be of more help to the widely scattered members of his spread-out parish territory, Father de Rougé had seen the need of having mission churches at different localities where he could say Mass, administer the Sacraments and, if time permitted, stay a week or so to instruct his parishioners.

The Wenatchee Indians needed two churches. One camp of this tribe resided on the Wenatchee River, the other had winter quarters on the Columbia River about eleven miles west of present Wenatchee. The first place had been visited by the Oblate Fathers while they were stationed at the old Yakima Mission. We mentioned that Father de Rougé directed the building of the new Simponskneuchi Church in 1888.[1] This church had been built on Louie Judge's land and was called "Mission" for many years. The name "Mission" was changed to "Cashmere" in 1904.[2] Father George Weibel studied the old records and reported that all the "Simpesquensi" baptisms that were entered in the *Athanum Mission Baptismal Records* were administered at a St. Francis Xavier Mission.[3] The exact spot of this early mission is unknown. The Simponskneuchi were the Indians ruled by Chief Patoi.[4] The second camp of Wenatchee Indians under Chief Nraamelt was about ten miles south of Wenatchee near the Columbia River. We mentioned the roofless log chapel over which a

---

[1] De Rougé to Cataldo, March 20, 1888, Ms., OPA.

[2] W. F. Hill and Francis Favel, in an interview at Spokane, June 30, 1961. These gentlemen were early students of Father de Rougé; Francis Favel as his secretary accompanied the missionary on his trips.

[3] Historicus, "Fifty Years of Peaceful Conquest," *op. cit.* (January, 1914, 5:4), 185.

[4] Grassi to Cataldo, *WL* (January, 1874, 3:1), 68.

tent had been placed when Father de Rougé found it in 1887.[5] A second church was erected there by Father de Rougé. The exact date is unknown. This place later was called Malaga and is still in existence. Mr. Favel accompanied Father to this place.[6] On Easter, 1886, when Father de Rougé answered a sick call to Chelan, he mentioned the chapel built by Father Grassi.[7] It was built on land given by Chief John Wapato near Manson on Wapato Point, and had living accommodations for a priest. It was later renovated.[8] These were the three Indian churches of Father de Rougé situated toward the southern end of his parish territory. A grass fire destroyed the old Indian church at Wapato Point, October 28, 1953.

Other Indian churches were built near the opposite boundaries of Father de Rougé's big mission territory. We mentioned the church of the Inkameep Indians, probably built 1869–1870.[9] Father de Rougé had this little church marked on his pencil map as belonging to his care.[10] Father Parodi mentioned Chief Gregoire and fifty men coming for Corpus Christi to the Schall-kees church.[11] The successor of Chief Gregoire, Chief Baptiste George, was often at St. Mary's Mission on high feast days with his tribe. A photograph taken on the occasion of the dedication of the second church at St. Mary's in 1915, shows this chief carrying the canopy for Most Reverend Bishop Augustine Francis Schinner of Spokane.

The old mission church at Chopaka was in all probability built by Father de Rougé, according to Mr. Paul Loudon of Loomis. The Loudon place had better accommodations for horses, therefore Father would stop here on his way to Chopaka. Mr. Loudon places the date of the erection of this church in 1892–1893.[12] No other priest was then in that region. Suzette Teobasket, daughter of Chief Sarsapkin's daughter, Julia, on the Similkameen reserve, verified the statement by saying, "Father de Rougé used to come there a lot."[13] An interview with Mr. John Beal of Loomis resulted in a definite statement that Father de Rougé had built the church at Chopaka.[14] The same church is still there.

[5] De Rougé, "The Conversion of the Wenatchee," *op. cit.*, 42.
[6] Hill and Favel, interview.
[7] De Rougé to Cataldo, May 9, 1886, *op. cit.*, 87–88.
[8] *Ibid.*
[9] *Diary of St. Francis Regis Mission*, May 11, 1870.
[10] De Rougé, original map, OPA.
[11] Parodi, *Memoirs*, Mss., OPA.
[12] Mrs. Lacey, in an interview with Mr. Paul Loudon, March 15, 1961. Courtesy of Mrs. Lacey.
[13] Suzette Teobasket, in an interview with Mrs. Lacey, March 15, 1961.
[14] John Beal, in an interview with the author at Loomis, July 16, 1961.

It was orginally built of logs, then was shiplapped, and now it is plastered.[15]

In the care of his Indians Father de Rougé did not spare himself. He would cross the two mountain chains and visit the tribal members that lived in the Kettle River Valley. There he would say Mass in a big house that belonged to Long Aleck who was not only the owner but also the "bellboy." When time came for Mass, Aleck, who had no bell, would go out of the house and holler so loud that everybody could hear him. "He would get so excited and got so much kick out if it, he would always wind up shooting his six-gun off into the air."[16] *The Indian Sentinel* of January, 1917, mentioned that Father de Rougé built a church at "Kettle River."[17] About 1885, Chief Tonasket and a part of his people left the Okanogan Valley and settled in the Kettle River Valley. Shortly before his death in 1891 he had promised Father Filippi that he would build a church near where Curley is located today. He had selected the place for the church and had shown the priest where it would stand. Then he had two eye operations in close succession and died before he was able to erect the church. His son Joseph was made chief and he told Chief Urpaghan of Colville to notify the priest that he did not like to see the missionary at his place. "In old times the Indians were happy and free, dancing in the wood like deer, the Priest came to preach hell, and the Indians became miserable."[18] Nobody will listen to him if he comes and speaks "strong." Father Filippi soon had another sick call from Okanogan. Joseph was absent but Father had to stay another week because he found work in the Indian camp. When Joseph returned the Indians told him that Father "spoke very mildly."

> Joseph met the Father, shook hands, and joined the Indians going to instruction. On the last day, there was a meeting and Joseph decided to build the church planned by his father. The church was built, and afterwards the railroad was built too with the depot close by. White settlers built a town, called Curlew near the church.[19]

The church was built under the direction of Father de Rougé. Mr. Joe Somday of Curlew said that Father de Rougé made rounds about that time. Mrs. H. T. Nelson, from Curlew, stated that she was a very

---

[15] The author saw photographs of the early church and of the present one at Chopaka in Mrs. Lacey's album.

[16] Mrs. K. Lacey, in an interview with Narcisse Nicholson, Ellisforde, March 15, 1961.

[17] Rev. Celestine Caldi, *The Indian Sentinel* (I:3, January, 1917), 37–38. "Father de Rougé built churches in Waterville, Chelan, Wenatchee, Republic, Loomis, Similkameen and Kettle River."

[18] Parodi, *Memoirs*, Mss., OPA.

[19] *Ibid.*

small girl when Father de Rougé said Mass after the first church was completed. The first church stood near Long Aleck Creek.[20] This church was ruined by a storm when a tree fell on it in the early 1900's. It was still there when Father Caldi took charge in 1900–1901.

Father de Rougé would say Mass in the Turoda Creek Valley at Jimmy Lynch's place. Often the services were in the open country where a big rock or a tree stump served as altar and wild flowers, green boughs, and God's trees made up the decorations. Father would stop at Wauconda and say holy Mass at the home of Harry Van Brand.[21] The author saw a photograph where a tent had been erected as a chapel with the front open. It was a most beautiful forest scene, trees on all sides, some fallen ones serving as seats. The people attending numbered about forty; some were kneeling devoutly, others showed through behavior that they did not quite know what sacred meaning was hidden in those mysterious services. Mrs. Lilian Brady remarked that Father de Rougé would sometimes say Mass in her grandfather's house near the Okanogan River at Schall-kees. This was William Peone's place.[22]

The opening of the reservation for mineral entry had brought prospectors, miners, businessmen and all kinds of unsettled people into the Okanogan Valley. These in turn were followed by the cattle and sheep men. Still Father de Rougé was the only priest available for the growing population. He became the Father for all; no matter what color or creed, his services and good counsels were sought and appreciated. It is an outstanding fact in Okanogan mission history that St. Mary's Mission, its founder and his successors, never had to experience any small-mindedness or unjust remarks from members of other denominations. They all appreciated the self-sacrificing lives the priests were leading and the immense good that was done at St. Mary's Mission and in its big mission territory.

Father Grassi baptized the first white child, Mary Bottomley, in November, 1885, in Oroville.[23] Father de Rougé was then starting his missionary work among the Okanogans and we can rightly assume that the saintly trailblazer, Father Urban Grassi, introduced the newly ordained Father de Rougé to the Okanogan Indians and the few whites. From 1885 to 1907, Father de Rougé would make missionary trips to Oro, as Oroville was then called. In the early years he celebrated Mass at the Driscoll residence on Driscoll Island, one mile from Oroville. He also used

[20] Mrs. H. T. Nelson Curlew to Mrs. Lacey, July 12, 1961.
[21] Favel, interview at Spokane, June 30, 1961.
[22] Mrs. Arthur Best, in an interview at St. Mary's Mission, August 14, 1960.
[23] Rev. Denis A. Cronin, "Oroville and Missions," *Inland Empire Messenger"* (II:4, January 1929), 71.

Hamischi's residence and the Desmond's store for that purpose. In 1905, Mrs. Francis Brown Driscoll built the priest's house and donated it to the parish.[24]

When the Columbia reservation of Chief Moses had been declared public domain in 1886, the country on the east side of the Okanogan River became dotted first with tents and gradually with growing mining towns. Some miners and settlers had been there earlier. Names such as Ruby, Conconully, Golden, Chesaw, Loomis, bring many memories to old timers. The primitive unsanitary conditions caused many plagues and deaths at first. In connection with the later unveiling of a statue of Father de Rougé, Mike Leahy remembered assisting him during the plague at Loomis:

> It was my extreme fortune to meet Father de Rougé, and under the circumstances of that meeting, I can truthfully say that there never has been a man that I was more grateful for the chance of seeing.
>
> I can see him yet coming through that door; that kindly smile on a bronze countenance that had seen many kinds of weather; that straight healthy body that had walked and rode horseback many, many miles that he might be of comfort to folks in need; that friendly Christian atmosphere that he brought with him to give what physical comfort he could to those who were dying, and to prepare the souls of humans such as myself so that they might meet their God, and give an account of how they filled their little niche in the short space of time that is called life.
>
> It was in the years 1891 and 92 that a terrible typhoid epidemic swept over the Loomis country, and I happened to be working in Loomis. Nobody seemed to be able to avoid it. There was very little medical care in the country, and even if there had been more, they wouldn't have been able to quell the disease because of the lack of knowledge of that subject at that time among rural doctors.
>
> The homes were filled with sick cases, and the little hospital in Loomis that could only hold 30 patients was taxed to its utmost. I finally came down with the disease. I had to wait a short time for someone to die so that I could have their bed, but at the rate they were going, I didn't have to wait long. I remember that out of the 30 that were in the beds when I went in, 25 died.
>
> In the meantime the late George Loudon asked Father de Rougé, who was many miles away, to come to the hospital. Traveling in those days was very slow and tedious, consequently it took quite a long time for the word to reach the priest, and for him to come. Waiting, — waiting — and each night listening to the chanting of prayers, and the singing of "Nearer My God To Thee" as they gave one after another back to the earth and to their God. It is rather a peculiar feeling lying on a cot with all the pain and fevers of that terrible disease, watching for a door to open — waiting, hoping, and praying that its opening would reveal the

---

[24] Cronin, *op. cit.,* 71.

man I wanted to see. Praying that it would open to let him in before it opened to let me out. Can you realize why memories came back to me when I saw his name again?

Father de Rouge finally came. He did all he could for me, and gave me the last sacraments of my Catholic faith. But I guess my time had not come yet for I was one of the five to live. Father de Rouge went about his work in a kindly and generous manner, trying to help everybody no matter what faith they professed. He was a great and noble man and I shall never forget him because after all it is not how big a niche you have occupied, or where that niche happened to be located that counts. The things that finally add up to a big total is how you filled that niche, and the good you have done while you occupied it. So all I can give to that man who gave so much and so freely is an Irish "God bless you." Some day I shall visit his memorial and like the statue that stands there now, I shall remember when he stood over me representing and supplying all that I hoped for — with the crucifix of his dying Saviour in one hand and the other extended in benediction and blessing.[25]

Father de Rougé did the same for his white parishioners as he had done for his beloved Indians: he built churches for them. In 1896 he built a church in "Loomistown," as Loomis was called then, for the miners.[26] The church at Loomis had a floor in it, was built of 1 by 12's and had a lumber roof and benches.[27] It was dedicated to St. Michael the Archangel. Loomis was then a thriving little town called by some people "Rag Town." Gold and silver mining made it grow rapidly until the decline in the price of silver in the late 1890's that forced many miners to settle down as cattlemen.[28] Loomis became the stopping place of Father de Rougé when he was on his way to the northwestern end of his immense parish territory. In places where there was no church, Father de Rougé would say Mass in homes as he did for his Indians. The former county seat of Okanogan, Conconully, did not have a Catholic church. The Dillebaugh Hotel, where the owners were Catholics, served for this purpose. At Nighthawk, old Indian Edward's ranch and Dan Mulcahay's cattle ranch were honored by having Father de Rougé as guest. The wilderness of Palmer Mountain and the Wannacut region and innumerable other places were traversed by the saintly missionary on foot and on horseback when all was still primeval beauty and when

[25] Told by Mike Leahy and written by Lawrence Leahy, "Father de Rougé Described as Mike Leahy Knew Him," in *The Wenatchee Daily World*, (January 30, 1926). Father de Rougé's statue was unveiled January 6, 1962. See: Article in *Northwest Progress* (January 8, 1926).

[26] Rev. Denis A. Cronin, "Oroville and Missions," *IECM* (II:4, January, 1929), 71.

[27] Mr. Paul Loudon, in an interview with Mrs. Lacey.

[28] Lewis A. Runnels, letter to the author, January 19, 1961.

there were still also primeval obstacles to travel. We saw the mountainous regions traveled by Father de Rougé and can imagine how exhausting the visits must have been. No boundaries existed in the care for souls. His zeal to work for the honor and glory of God and to be of help to any soul who might look for the administrations of a priest drove him far up into Canada. The Similkameen Mountains and the country around Hedley were frequently the goal of his missionary journeys.[29] Catholics and non-Catholics alike showed veneration and respect for this completely self-sacrificing priest whose every movement betrayed refinement and nobility, and who so often appeared on the scene when he was most urgently needed.

Father de Rougé studied the development of his surrounding territory and found another mining town in the making. Eureka, later called Republic, had its beginning on February 21, 1896, when with the opening of the north half of the Colville Indian Reservation, the first mining camps developed and later more substantial log buildings were erected. Among the early miners there were quite a few Catholics. Once a month Father de Rougé would travel over the mountains, about seventy miles one way from St. Mary's Mission, to offer Mass at Republic in different private homes. A frame church building was erected in 1898, according to Mary Louise Hesse. This church was on what is now Keane Avenue, between Sixth and Seventh.[30] The "Building Record of Spokane Diocese, 1838–1938," names the year 1896 for the building of the first church in Republic.[31] Reverend F. C. Dillon's *Annual Report for 1898,* mentioned that "The Republic Church is advanced enough to say Mass in."[32]

The old baptismal records of St. Mary's Mission, Omak, Washington, contain the record of a number of baptisms from Waterville. Father de Rougé considered the Big Bend country as belonging to his parish. He visited there as early as 1890. During the months when he was able to surmount the difficulties of transportation the priest would say holy Mass once a month either in the home of Joseph Brockman or in the John Kelly bakery. Soon money was collected and a church started under Father de Rougé's direction in 1892. The missionary used this church for religious services when only the outside was completed. When the cold season arrived the members of the parish united to plaster and

---

[29] Francis Favel, in an interview.

[30] Mary Louise Hesse, "History of the Immaculate Conception Church, Republic, Wash.," in *A Short History of the Catholic Church in Ferry County,* 2.

[31] Rev. T. Pypers, "Building Record of Spokane Diocese, 1838–1938," in *Centenary and Silver Jubilee Souvenir Book for Spokane and the Inland Empire,* 49.

[32] Rev. F. C. Dillon, S.J., *Annual Report for 1898,* Ms., ADS.

furnish the church.[33] The missionary mentioned in his *Annual Report of 1903* that he was in charge of two churches at Chelan, one for the Indians and one for the whites.[34] St. Francis Church for the whites was probably erected during 1902. It was built in about the same style as the present church at Ellisforde. Previously Mass had been said in John Walsh's home.[35]

A mountain road leads from Riverside along the mountains until it meets the Tunk Creek and continues through the valley for many miles. Leaving behind a beautifully forested area and then high cliffs on both sides of the road, we suddenly see an immense expanse of various mountain pastures. High up in these mountains Father de Rougé would travel to bring the consolations and the sacraments of the Catholic faith to the families living near their cattle ranches. A swift rider would notify the families of the coming of the priest and they would gather in one of the homes: John Figlenski, Art Schmidt, Mrs. Ernest Stowe, Theodor Tedra, and Gus Fuhrman.[36]

Father de Rougé was especially devoted to his Indian parishioners. When he was in France in 1888–1889, his many friends there wanted to know more about his apostolate among the Indians. He described the Northwest as being many times larger than France. He wrote in his account in 1890, that Father De Smet's writings are now out of date and could not be consulted anymore; they would give false ideas. Father de Rougé also condemns the judgments passed on the "poor of God." Civilized man did not show pity and compassion.

> Is he a Christian who speaks when an American tells you coldly: "The best Indian is a dead Indian"? The American believes that it is a glory for his country to have pushed the Indians to the last frontier, and an honor to have made him almost disappear.[37]

Father told his friends that the Indians of the Northwest are both naturally good and gentle. The Indians did not think of revenge and of doing harm to the white men who had invaded their country. The kindly Father de Rougé becomes outraged when speaking of degraded white men:

---

[33] Rev. Arthur Joda, "St. Joseph's Church, Waterville," *IECM* (January, 1929), 74.

[34] De Rougé, *Annual Report of 1930 to Rt. Rev. O'Dea*, Ms., ADS.

[35] Favel, in an interview.

[36] Mr. Ed. Figlenski, in an interview at Tunk Valley, July 13, 1961. Also: Francis Favel, an interview.

[37] Le pere Etienne de Rouget [sic], "L'Indien du Nord Quest. Recit D'n missionnaire de montagnes rocheuses," *Les Etudes*, XLIX (1890), 470–500 (henceforth: De Rouget, *op. cit.*).

The white man has not presented himself as a protector, he has declared himself immediately as an enemy; he has not come as a civilizer, but as a killer, neither respecting any right or virtue; a robber and immoral, sounding the words of civilization and peace, and seeking only war and debauchery. Thanks to the so lamentable examples and to the conduct, with such corruption, the character of the Indians lost its native qualities and took on defects of its invaders.[38]

Then the experienced missionary talks about the natural virtues of the Indian, especially his hospitality. Anyone who appears at the lodge of an Indian is received as if he were his best friend. He is cordially introduced and the women hurry to prepare something good to eat, while the men offer a smoke. Then the stranger has to tell the things he knows. This is their newspaper and their opportunity to carry on trade and other business. A shelter for the night is provided and when the stranger departs he has to bring messages to the next camp. The Indians do not accept pay for these services but expect to be treated in like manner if they should one day pass the lodge of the stranger. Many lost whites have been saved from starvation and death by the Indians. The ungrateful whites have in turn served the Indians alcohol. The traffic in alcohol is watched but with "negligence." The authorities often collaborate with the guilty:

> Once carried away by drunkenness, the Indian is very difficult to correct, and becomes terrible. It is the moment waited for to speculate on [to trade for] his possessions. It [drunkenness] makes him trade a horse for a small flask of the brandy; that which costs no more than a dollar is retailed to him at a price twenty times dearer; the merchant makes him pile up his furs very high before delivering to him the thin bottle which will be its price.[39]

Father de Rougé knows that the Indians need guidance and that they are subject to the "weaknesses of humanity." They need direction and should be wisely counseled and will thus arrive at great virtue. Then the Indians will be docile as children and will live according to good judgment. Often Father has been surprised by the "wisdom of his [the Indian's] profound reasoning." It is true that the Indian generally is not enterprising. He uses his arms only for hunting and does not know how to cultivate fields. He was the master and the lord of "the most beautiful country in the world; he can live without work." Nature provided for him. It was a painful transition from the life of a hunter to that of a farmer and the nature of the Indians cannot be changed too quickly. It is an injustice not to take account of his aspiration for a nomadic life. "The civilized Indian

---

[38] De Rouget, *op. cit.*
[39] *Ibid.*

is very industrious, and he has the zeal for work: his farm house, his herds, their products are marvelous proof of the intelligence of his activity."

Father de Rougé then tells about the Indian's practical and intellectual pursuits: his bark canoes that can stand the most rapid currents, his talent for design manifested in his clothing which show his original taste, his skill in training wild horses. Indian children sitting side by side with white children have often taken the first place in schools:

> I have had a class for many years, of the youth of the mountains, white children mixed with the young redskins, and quite often I have seen the redskin learn all his letters in two lessons, and know them so well that he was able afterwards to take his book in his hand and teach the young white children seated around him.[40]

The Indians will not be inferior to other men if given a religious and moral culture; therefore they need the care of the missionary.

Next Father tells his friends about the respect of the Indians for authority and calls this "A mark of true and excellent character":

> The chief of the tribe has the power of a king; a hereditary power which exists among most of the tribes, fundamentally there is no exception in this practice. This is a paternal authority; I was going to say Patriarchal. It is rare that the chief punishes; when there is a fault, the guilty is called; and the chief by his speech alone ought to convince him. Won over by the Picturesque and original eloquence of the chief, the criminal submits and atones for his fault.[41]

The whites have destroyed this respect for authority by giving bad example through insubordination and in obeying only when force is used. The whites knew how to break the union of inferiors with their chiefs. When the Indians depended on the chiefs for the defense of their rights, some chiefs were seized. The Indian agents worked to make the individual Indians independent and destroyed authority within the tribes. They substituted themselves for the chiefs but were not able to inspire respect; so they had to rule by fear. How can the Indians respect representatives of the government who make promises and do not keep them?

Father de Rougé's great love for the Indians is especially expressed when he speaks about the religious concepts the old Indians had:

> Intelligent by gift of God, respectful through tradition, the Indian is still very religious in character. From time immemorial, he has believed in God, the Creator and calls Him "He who has made. . . ." The Catholic savages still tell us the story of this or that white haired old

---

[40] De Rouget, *op. cit.*
[41] *Ibid.*

pagan who prayed saying: "My Creator, I do not know where you are, but I pray to you."[42]

The Indians say grace before meals knowing that it is God who gives the food. They still go and pray on the mountain tops to be near "him who made." They would fast several days in order to obtain a favor, even that of becoming a sorcerer. Even if it led to superstition, Father de Rougé could see in this the clear idea the Indians had of God and of the need for prayer. The Black Robe was received with respect and confidence in the Northwest. He had only to sow the seed into the prepared soil. The true religion has changed the naturally upright hearts of the Indians into Christians:

> The work of the civilization of the Indians could then have been accomplished without the shedding of their blood. The cross and not the sword was more needed for these natures open and entirely ready to embrace the Catholic truth.[43]

Whites have by their conduct tended to destroy the influence of the Black Robe; also by preaching contradictory religions, falsehoods, errors. And not having succeeded in winning the Indian, they have left them nauseated and lost forever to the true faith.

Father de Rougé then relates some stories of unjust Indian wars and of outright killing of innocent Indians in some parts of the United States. He quotes General Harney speaking before a government committee: "I have lived on this frontier fifty years. I have never known an example of a war between us and the Indians, in which the tribes were not within their right."[44] Father is justly incensed about the attitude of the United States government toward the Indians, who were considered enemies of the land. The republican government is "covered with infamy and blood." It seemed necessary to force the Indians to live on reservations where lumbering and pasturing of flocks were no longer permitted them. Father de Rougé speaks of Indian agents who are changed every time the political party is changed, and if one is among them who was good to the Indians he receives no thanks. The priest writes of the injustice he has witnessed:

> I have seen Indians living outside the Reservation from whom whites have taken by force, fields and property. Driven from their patrimony with the whole family, they drew away in order not to resist by force: they were counting on justice which they were going to appeal to the agents. They wait yet for their complaints to be made right.[45]

---

[42] De Rouget, *op. cit.*
[43] *Ibid.*
[44] De Rouget, quoting General Harney, *ibid.*
[45] De Rouget, *ibid.*

After such injuries it is no wonder that the Indians do not love the whites and are defiant. Sometimes matters are pushed to extremes and murders are committed. But this is sure: if an Indian kills a white man he is pursued and hanged, often without a trial; if the white man kills an Indian, most of the times he goes unpunished.

After enumerating all the injustices done to the Indians, Father de Rougé closes his long account on Indian problems by referring first to President Grant's Peace Policy, under which the Indians were not even allowed to choose their own religion and the Catholic priests were driven away from the mission fields which they had founded. He gives credit to the more enlightened United States government of his time which helped the missionaries to maintain their schools through contracts with the government.

Father de Rougé himself, when he was ready for his school, was excluded from any contract. These accounts written to his friends in France show us how deeply he understood the Indian problems of his time and how only he knew they could be solved. His solution was a thorough Christian education. He would give his boys such an education that they could be the equals of the whites and would be able to compete with them on equal terms while pursuing their future work.

The *Catholic Directories* for the years 1890 and 1891 mention Father de Rougé and one brother as being present at the Columbia and Okanogan missions. Father Parodi tells us that Father de Rougé had been absent from St. Mary's Mission for a few months. Father Cataldo had no priest available to replace him and therefore sent Brother Gasper Occhiena, S.J., who could speak the Indian language. The Indians liked the Brother who was teaching them the Catechism and prayers and who would conduct funerals. They were only sorry that the Brother had no power to forgive sins and could not give them Holy Communion.[46]

Father Parodi had to act again as Father de Rougé's substitute during March, 1892. He was looking for a guide to the Okanogan country when an Indian offered, for the sum of ten dollars, to bring him to St. Mary's Mission and from there to Chelan for another ten dollars. The guide had not been of much help, but the Okanogan chief took up a collection on Sunday to pay the guide. This Indian went in great haste to the store and bought a "new outfit for the upper half of the man." Then he started to persuade Father Parodi not to go to Chelan, because the people said that Father de Rougé would go there on his way back from his trip. The reason was that this Indian wanted to earn fourteen dollars instead of only

---

[46] Parodi, *Memoirs*, Mss., OPA.

ten by plowing somebody's field, which would have enabled him to buy a fourteen-dollar blanket.[47]

Father de Rougé had many faithful and noble Christians among his Indian parishioners. They had learned by the heroic example of the priest whom nothing could keep from visiting his flock. It was their turn for self-sacrifice, hunger, and cold when Christmas happened to be stormy and icy and the good old people traveled a hundred miles, often on foot, in order to attend the Christmas Midnight Mass at St. Mary's Mission. One of these bitterly cold seasons was in 1892–1893. Two feet of snow on Christmas Day was followed by a blizzard that lasted four days. Mr. Fries, carrying the mail, was delayed in crossing the mountains from Sunday until Thursday. When he did get across he found Methow George and others in the Chiliwist Indian camp. They had attended Christmas services at St. Mary's and were prevented from going farther. Mr. Fries was then accompanied by Methow George who knew where Mr. Fries had his lunch box hidden. Mr. Fries stated, "I had let a few Indians know where my box was hidden but I had never told any white people. Never did the Indians break the confidence I had shown and pilfer the box."[48]

The year of 1893 was another memorable one for St. Mary's Mission. During the feast of Corpus Christi, Most Reverend Bishop Aegidius Junger, the second Bishop of the Diocese of Nisqually, visited St. Mary's Mission. This was the first time that a bishop ever set foot in the Okanogan Valley. For many tribal members this was their first contact with a bishop. Bishop Junger encouraged the Indians to build a schoolhouse.[49] The Indians living near Schall-kees and farther up the Okanogan Valley had been informed that the bishop would come to their church. Since they wanted to see the bishop, not only hear him, they had built a high platform. Next morning all the place in front of the church was underwater from the flooding Okanogan River. What to do? The men carried the heavy bishop through the knee-deep water and put him down dry on the platform.[50] In an article written sometime in January, 1899, Father de Rougé states: "Bishop Junger was the first Bishop here and had nearly 300 confirmations. Bishop O'Dea came also and had 100 confirmations."[51]

Father de Rougé had prepared to celebrate the feast of Corpus Christi

---

[47] Parodi, op. cit.

[48] Fries and Fries, op. cit., 201.

[49] De Rougé, "St. Mary's Mission, Omak, Washington," in History of North Washington, Richard F. Steele, ed., 488.

[50] Pierre Louie, Vernon, B.C., in an interview at St. Mary's Mission, April 20, 1961.

[51] De Rougé, St. Mary's Mission, Mss., OPA.

in 1894 at Schall-kees. There he had a bigger church available for the crowds that would gather especially for this feast. The roaring floodwaters of the Okanogan River inundated overnight the place where the church was situated. Four of the young men lifted Father onto a buggy and pulled him across to higher ground.[52] The year of the flood was also the year of an earthquake. The quake came while Father de Rougé was holding services in his church at Schall-kees. Mrs. Arthur Best's maternal grandmother happened to be in church at the time and remembers that Father ordered the people to leave. He was afraid the building would fall on them.[53]

In 1894 the red and white parishioners of St. Mary's Mission nearly lost their beloved pastor. Mrs. Helen Toulou was attending St. Francis Regis Mission School for girls, at that time called Sacred Heart Academy of the Sisters of Providence. She was twelve years old at this time. One morning early in 1894, a strange priest came to say Mass. This priest happened to be Father de Rougé. The French-speaking Sisters seemed sorrowful; they sent all the children to the chapel during the following days to say the Rosary for this Father that he might be able to stay at St. Mary's. Father de Rougé was supposed to be transferred and had pleaded with his superior to let him return to his beloved Indians. He had learned their language to perfection and "could make the Indians feel ashamed speaking their language."[54] It was in the fall of the year when heavy, deep snow covered the mountains. In spite of this Father de Rougé went back to his mission with a heavy heart. Would he be allowed to stay?[55] In the *History of North Washington* we read:

> . . . at one period a few years ago it was decided to remove Father de Rougé to another missionary field. To this the Indians vigorously objected; circulated a number of petitions and so seriously did they protest against such a course that he was permitted to stay.[56]

The relationship of the Indians with their missionary was of such a nature that no higher authority existed for them. They loved Father de Rougé and considered him as belonging to their tribe; so perfectly did the priest stoop down to them in order to raise them up to the Christian level of culture. These old faithful Indian people knew their catechism and lived accordingly. They knew what was going on during Mass. Father

---

[52] Narcisse Nicholson, *op. cit.*, Mss.

[53] Mrs. Arthur Best (formerly Lilian Brady), in an interview at St. Mary's Mission, August 14, 1960.

[54] W. F. Hill, in an interview, June 30, 1961, Spokane, Wash.

[55] Mrs. Helen Toulou, in an interview at St. Mary's Mission, November 9, 1959.

[56] Richard F. Steele, ed., *op. cit.*, 488.

de Rougé had translated the most important prayers into the Okanogan language and had it printed in booklet form in France. It contained a short catechism, prayers before and after Holy Communion, the mysteries of the Rosary, the *Memorare,* a consecration to the Sacred Heart of Jesus, the Way of the Cross, nineteen other prayers, the most important prayers of the Mass as the *Gloria,* the *Credo,* the *Sanctus,* the *Agnus Dei,* and others; also the Benediction hymns in Latin, the Baptismal ceremonies and the ceremonies and prayers of Extreme Unction in Latin and Indian. The front page had the inscription:

A.M.D.G.

I SMEMEIS, I NKAUMEN

I SNKUENZIN

L OKENAKAN NKOLKOELTENS

Preces in Linguam Indorum Okenakan Versae

A. P. De Rougé, S.J.

Printed 1442, Paris, Imp. G. PICQUOIN, 54 Rue De Lille.[57]

The old Indian people told the author that when they were still children attending St. Mary's Mission School. Father de Rougé would not allow them to pray or sing in English in the presence of old people. They had to use the Indian language so the old people would not feel out of place. Father de Rougé tells of an old Indian woman who saw a white house in a dream, many years ago, on the spot where the mission is now. A voice told her: "Do you see this house? It is a church, one day you will see a church built here." How many times did she speak about that dream that had become a reality![58]

While Father de Rougé was gradually organizing his large parish territory and was building churches for Indians and for whites at faraway localities, he did not neglect his place at Omak creek. It is difficult to trace the building program of the first set of buildings. The Indians had built a schoolhouse at their own expense as Bishop Junger had asked them to do. When in 1897, the government school at Tonasket burned, Father de Rougé sent over a team of horses and a sleigh to bring the Friedlander children to the mission. These were Sam, Herman, William and their sister Millie, now Mrs. Arcasa. At that time the school was in full session and accepted only boys; Millie had to live with her mother's cousin, Mr. and Mrs. Smitkin (Chief Smitkin). The parents of the children came from Ferry County for the celebration of Christmas and took Millie Friedlander home. In June of the following year the children were sent to St. Francis Regis Mission for further education.[59]

---

[57] Original in OPA., also at St. Mary's Mission.
[58] De Rougé, St. Mary's Mission, Mss., OPA.
[59] Mrs. Arcasa, Nespelem, to the author, undated. Also: interviews.

Mrs. Zacherle mentioned that Father de Rougé had in early times an old Brother as a companion who had been formerly at the Ward Mission. He could hardly move around but did the cooking for Father when he was alone. They just called him Brother Jack. A widow, Mrs. Mary Lambert, who lived where East Omak is now, came and washed for Father de Rougé. This full-blooded Indian woman would mend his clothes and patch his stockings and "was like a mother to him."[60] Mrs. Caulfield remembers how Father de Rougé told about one of his cooks in the early boarding school. Henry Aim had mixed the yeast and flour for the bread and forgot to watch the dough until it had run over on the floor. So he closed the door and started to clean up. Soon there was a knock on the kitchen door. "Who is there," called Henry. "The Father." But Henry did not want to be disturbed. "I don't care and if you be the Pope of Rome, you can't come in."[61]

The exact date when the winter school was started at St. Mary's is not known. Father de Rougé had started a little boarding school Schall-kees and we assume that he continued this winter school at St. Mary's Mission in order to teach religion to the children of the camp. From 1889 on, after his return from France, Father de Rougé seems to have spent the winter months with his flock at St. Mary's. He now had better accommodations. He still periodically made the trip back over the mountains to visit St. Francis Regis Mission for various reasons, one being that he was subject to his superior there. Then he would visit the Sisters' school and give the girls one of the delightful "Punch and Judy" puppet shows. Mrs. Florence Quill still remembers how perfectly he could imitate the different voices of the puppet characters.[62]

Father de Rougé wrote during January, 1899:

> In order to be able to teach and prepare for first communion we have a kind of a little school all the winter. The parents, Indians and whites, give the things necessary for the children's food and clothing, sometimes money, and with the little help from our kind Bishop we can get along. The Indians have built a good house where the children are under the care of an Indian family; there is a kitchen, a bedroom for the boys and two rooms upstairs. We teach school in our chapel and the children are also quite a little help to us; besides, winter is a hard time to be out and it keeps us busy and makes the place lively.[63]

This is the last time that Father de Rougé speaks of a winter school only.

---

[60] Mrs. Pauline Zacherle, in an interview at St. Mary's Mission, May 22, 1960.

[61] Mrs. Audrey Caulfield, quoting Father de Rougé, in an interview at Spokane, September 30, 1961.

[62] Mrs. Florence Quill, in an interview at Omak, August 22, 1960.

[63] De Rougé, *St. Mary's Mission,* Mss., OPA.

He continues that if in time he could have Sisters at the Mission he could have a "good school for white children for many have asked us for it." The missionary then quotes Father Garrand, who had visited the place a few years before and remarked, "Here is not holy poverty, but it is holy misery." Thanks to God's providence he is not so poor but that a good brother would be the "resurrection" of the Mission. The Mission property then consisted of a little garden, a few chickens, two cows and three horses. Father then gives us a clue as to when the first regular church was built:

> Our buildings are pretty small, our chapel is altogether too small and we can make no ceremonies of any kind in it. An alms have been promised and this part of the business will be settled soon. I hope before next summer to have a good chapel up. The chapel now will become what it was intended first to be: parlors and rooms.[64]

This would indicate that the old church was built during 1899. A financial statement to Bishop O'Dea in 1899 shows that Father de Rougé received $1,000 from France for the new church. The report of 1900 shows that he spent an additional $105 on the church.[65]

Chief Smitkin, Chief Ignace or Aeneas and other faithful Indian friends helped Father build the first church and most certainly helped him also to add different sections to the other buildings. Photographs of the first mission buildings show the gradual growth of the institution according to the means available. There is no unity of design or architecture, but a certain resemblance to the homes of the French nobility can be seen in the towers that were added. The first set of mission buildings grew up in the years between 1889 and 1907. Drawings and photos show us that the first mission center consisted of two main buildings with several additions and that the first church, built in 1899, stood directly adjacent to the school buildings.

By 1899, Father de Rougé had his parish well established. Most of his churches had been built; his parishioners were instructed in the fundamental truths; his winter school would now grow into a regular educational institution, and he had a helper organization which was functioning smoothly. His Indian people were devout and were a credit to his zealous labors. The missionary tells us:

---

[64] De Rougé, *op. cit.* Father de Rougé's description of his Mission is undated. He mentioned that the "mission will be sanctified in a few days by the last vows of Fr. Nicholson," which occurred on February 2, 1899, and enabled us to date Father de Rougé's writings.

[65] De Rougé, *Annual Reports of 1899 and 1900,* Mss., ADS.

Today is the beginning of the 40 hours. It is very edifying to see our Indians accepting their marked hour of adoration, and the watchmen changing them every hour. Most all of them stay on their knees on the floor all the time. Going out of church after the hour of adoration, they go again to the calvary in front of the building to say some prayers, and from there to the grave yard.[66]

So grew slowly but securely, through the personal sacrifices of Father de Rougé, a great mission center that was to have a great future.

[66] De Rougé, *St. Mary's Mission,* Mss., OPA.

CHAPTER XII

Influential Indian Chiefs

THE patriarchal system of tribal government ruled the life of the tribe as a whole. What concerned the entire tribe, or was considered so, depended either on the judgment of the chief alone or of the chief and his council members. Religion had always been a tribal matter among the Okanogan and Colville tribes. The old pagan superstitious rites concerned the tribes as a unit; the chief would be the leader in the pagan rituals. If he held on to the old inherited practices that were handed down from one generation to the next, most of the time the whole tribe would follow his example. If he happened to be converted to Christianity, his influence would be of vital importance for the conversion of the entire tribe. Often an infiuential chief would inspire neighboring chiefs to embrace the Christian faith. Every year there were certain times reserved when the friendly tribes would meet each other for the sake of games or races, for business and exchange of goods and for the fishing and root-digging.

In this sense old St. Paul's Mission, Kettle Falls, was situated near one of the greatest meeting places of several mutually friendly Indian tribes and was of utmost importance for St. Mary's Mission in the Okanogan Valley, that was established a generation later than St. Paul's. Father de Rougé would have been unable to accomplish all the good he did without this early influence that was slowly spreading along the Okanogan Valley. The early baptisms at the House of the Lakes in 1838, where among others the daughter of the chief of the Lakes was baptized,[1] was the beginning of the great influence the chiefs would assert. When the first missionaries, Fathers Blanchet and Demers, were met by the chiefs of five nations at

---

[1] M. Leona Nichols, *The Mantle of Elias.* See the copy of the church records, 260–262.

Colville in 1838,[2] these chiefs had to make their decision either for or against the Catholic faith.

Father De Smet, as we have seen, reports about the conferences he had in 1841 with the chief of the "Skoyelpi or Kettle Falls, an intelligent gentleman, who invited me to come and evangelize his nation."[3] This Father De Smet did in the year following, 1842, when he baptized Chief Martin and his wife, Mary, and performed fifty-six baptisms in all.[4] Now Chief Martin was to become an apostle for the conversion of the Okanogans and Father De Smet had done some preliminary work for his later fellow Jesuit, Father de Rougé. Chief Martin of the Kettle Falls nation accompanied Father De Smet to the Okanogans when they had their big meeting near Lake Osoyoos during May of 1842. There Chief Martin kept on talking and explaining religion far into the night and Father De Smet, as we have seen, was able to baptize 106 children and some old people.[5] These baptized persons were about the age of grandparents when Father de Rougé came upon the scene. It was Chief Martin who kept on asking for a priest to be stationed right at Kettle Falls and who kept on visiting St. Ignatius Mission in order to learn more and instruct his tribe and others. Without the establishment of St. Paul's Mission, in which he was indirectly responsible and from where the circuit-riding priests would travel to points in the Okanogan Valley and spread the Catholic faith, St. Mary's Mission, Omak, might never have been born.

Another very influential chief had been Chief Kee-kee-tum-nouse, a chief of the Lake Indians. We know that a major obstacle to the chiefs' embracing Christianity had been polygamy. This chief set the example, dismissing his wives, who were all converted, and embracing the Catholic faith, which allowed him only one wife.

Father De Smet also mentioned Chief Gregory of the Lakes who had been baptized in 1838 by Father Blanchet, and "who had not ceased to exhort his people by word and example. . . ."[6] After speaking about the Lake Indians, their industry and peaceableness, the Indian agent speaks about their chief:

> Gregoire, their head chief, is about eighty years old, is of low stature, and is hale and hearty. He has always been a staunch friend of the whites, and is an honest, straightforward man; his tribe honor, respect and obey him. . . . Their principal place of rendezvous is the Hudson's

---

[2] F. N. Blanchet, "Sketch V," in Clarence B. Bagley, ed., *Early Catholic Missions in Old Oregon,* I, 28.

[3] CR, *De Smet,* I, 356.

[4] De Smet, *Letters and Sketches,* 213–214.

[5] *Ibid.,* 216.

[6] De Smet, *Oregon Missions,* 216.

Bay fort, which is built on their land. They are Catholics, and want teachers to instruct them in reading and writing.[7]

This shows us how their faith became to them the foundation of civilization and of culture.

A famous Chief of the Colvilles was Kin-kan-nowha, who gave the land on which the third St. Francis Regis Mission was built. He played the important role of host to all the tribes that came to St. Francis Regis for the celebrations of the big feast days. We mentioned that the Okanogans camped at St. Francis Regis, before they had their own mission. We see the interrelationship of the three missions: St. Paul's, St. Francis Regis and St. Mary's on Omak Creek. The friendship of the Colville, Okanogan, Lake and other related tribal chiefs helped the Jesuit Fathers considerably in the spreading and deepening of the Catholic faith.

Winans speaks of "Kin-ka-now-kla, the Salmon Chief," who distributed the salmon among his own and the different tribes that assembled at Kettle Falls:

> He together with the subchiefs Antoine, So-ho-mie, Que-cem-te-kum, and Coo-loo-sas-kut, exert a powerful influence over their tribe for their good, and to keep them so disciplined that they are quiet and peaceable among themselves and are friendly to the whites; they punish all offenders with the whip, having ten steady young men at their command to bring evil-doers before them.[8]

This chief's influence waned with advanced age and then in critical circumstances when a tribesman was executed because he had perpetrated a crime while under the influence of intoxicants, "at the advice of the Fathers the old Chief Kinkanakua was asked by the tribesmen to resign. . . . Then Joseph Cotolegu . . . a man of remarkable strength of character and integrity, was chosen, as head chief. . . ."[9] He checked gambling, drinking, and other disorders and broke up illicit connections among the Indians.

Two subchiefs, Chief Orphan and Chief Bernard, aspired for a time for leadership after the old Chief Kin-ka-nowha's death. After Chief Orphan's death, Chief Bernard proved himself a fine Christian leader. Bernard was the nephew of Chief Kin-ka-nowha. He was a friend of the priests, a good organizer and unifier, a conscientious and Christian man. Mrs. Helen Toulou tells about the attitude toward the non-Catholic Nez

---

[7] William P. Winans, quoted by Samuel Ross, Superintendent of Indian Affairs, Olympia, to Commissioner of Indian Affairs, Washington, D. C., September 1, 1870, in Report of the Secretary of the Interior, *Executive Documents 1, Forty-First Congress, House of Representatives, Third Session* (Part 4, Vol. I), 489.

[8] Winans quoted by Ross, *op. cit.*, 488.

[9] Historicus, "Fifty Years of Peaceful Conquest," *op. cit.* (V:8, May, 1914), 410.

Perce tribe, which was absolutely not welcome on the Colville Reservation. We mentioned that in early times the Nez Perce had been the enemies of the Okanogan Tribes. The Confederated Colville Tribes, as they are called by the government, had a tribal meeting at which some important officials from Washington, D. C., were present. A group of white people together with members of the Nez Perce tribes wanted Coulee Dam to be named Chief Joseph's Dam:

> Naturally, we Colvilles opposed their choice of name. The opposite faction detailed Chief Joseph's nobility, how he and his followers fought for Indian rights, how he and his followers suffered defeat, because of the cowardliness of tribes living in this area, and how brave he was when taken prisoner by U. S. troops, how he was exiled, living a life of sorrow. . . .[10]

After they had made Chief Joseph the hero, Chief Bernard asked to speak. He met some sneering looks from the Nez Perces as he was introduced as the chief of the Colvilles. There happened to be a priest present and Chief Bernard used the occasion to name the priest as the cause of the Colville tribe's never having shed the white man's blood:

> It is true that I cannot boast or exhibit scalps taken in defense of my lands, nor can any of my tribe say they have spilled the blood of our white brother, although our rights are invaded.
> Pointing to the priest, he said, 'Ladies and Gentlemen, there is the cause. Because of him and his kind, I and all the members of my tribe can hold our hands and say that they have shed no man's blood for something that God only created and is meant to be shared by all. I bless him and the day the Black Robes were sent. Because now' (holding out both hands) he said, 'See, they are clean of human blood. And if I must kill to hold my country, I'll be a coward; not of men [am I afraid] but I am afraid to offend God. I thank you.'[11]

Coulee Dam was then settled on as the name. Chief Bernard was often seen at St. Mary's Mission together with other chiefs assembled in council. Father Edward Griva, S.J., in his *History* often mentions Chief Bernard as choir leader.

When in 1860 Father Joset visited the Okanogan Indians he spoke reproving words to Chief Francois, because he had been living with a Christian girl in polygamy. This chief became converted, sent his wives away, and was then instrumental in his camp's conversion.[12] The same Chief Francois found Father Diomedi, in January, 1880, lost and ill in the Similkameen Mountains, and nursed him back to health.[13]

---

[10] Mrs. Helen Toulou, manuscript book.

[11] *Ibid.*

[12] *Joset Papers,* Mss., OPA.

[13] Diomedi, "Sketches of Modern Indian Life," *WL* (32:3, December, 1893), 354 ff.

Chief Francois' brother was Chief Sarsapkin of the Moses Columbia Indians, whose home ranch was in Loomis. Father de Rougé said Mass in his home and was politely listened to by the chief, but polygamy barred the way to conversion. This chief later took on a sneering attitude toward Christianity. Narcisse Nicholson wrote that Sarsapkin came to the church at Schall-kees only to make fun of the others. Father de Rougé had a large cross in front of the church and asked the Indians to kneel and kiss the cross as they went by. All did so with the exception of Chief Sarsapkin, who tied his horse to the cross. Some young men then scared the horse, who broke his reins and ran away. Father de Rougé would ask Chief Sarsapkin to take off his feathers before he came into the church, but the chief would refuse and become angry.[14] Chief Sarsapkin died as he had lived, a pagan. On his way home from a drinking feast he had to be tied down to his horse. His son, Pete, also under the influence of alcohol, pushed the horse and his rider down over a steep rocky precipice causing the chief's death. The Indians placed a cross at the foot of Chief Sarsapkin's grave — "apparently so that the old heathen, as he lay in the ground, could look forever at the symbol of salvation."[15]

A chief who lived up to his Catholic faith, during the McLaughlin Canyon Fight in 1858, was Chief Tonasket, as we have seen. Through the following years when the country was invaded by more miners and cattlemen, it was Tonasket again who kept the Indians quiet and protected the lives of the whites traveling through the Okanogan Valley. The Inkameep Indians, who owned the first little church as a tribe in the 1870's, were part of Tonasket's tribe which preferred to stay in the Okanogan Valley when Chief Tonasket moved his family and all his herds to the Kettle River region near the location of the present town of Curlew. The Okanogan Mission, as the church at Schall-kees was called, as well as the two cemeteries, at Schall-kees and at Tonasket, was built on land given by this chief. The chief is often mentioned as sponsor in baptisms administered by Fathers Grassi and de Rougé.

According to Judge William Compton Brown of Okanogan, Washington, Chief Tonasket's home ranch and wintering place was on the east side of the Okanogan River, directly across from where Oroville is today. This had been a favorite gathering place of the Indians for horse races and

---

[14] Narcisse Nicholson, written account to the author. Also: an interview at Ellisforde, July 15, 1961.

[15] Guy Waring, *op. cit.*, 250. The new monument in Loomis has the inscription "Sarsapkin, A Chief of the Moses Columbia Indians." Looking at the white cross on top of the monument, the author had to think of Waring's statement. Sarsapkin's wife Margaret and other members of his family were converted. Old attendance records show that during Father Caldi's time Ellen Sarsapkin was a student at St. Mary's Mission, June 30, 1920, Mss., SM.

games. On the level grounds of the same land the meeting with Father De Smet had taken place in 1842; his so-called "plain of Prayers." This property was sold by Tonasket late in 1884 to Hiram F. Smith, known as Okanogan Smith, and to Mary Manuel, his wife, the daughter of Chief Manuel.[16]

When in 1883, General W. T. Sherman was on a journey to the western states, Chief Moses and Chief Tonasket were also on the same train returning from Washington, D. C. The General was received at Osoyoos, B. C., on August 12. The report of his journey tells about the afternoon reception:

> During the afternoon the General was called upon by Tonaskat and a large following of his people. He is a respectable looking oldish man, resembling in appearance a Louisiana Creole planter. He is said to be quite wealthy in cattle and farms.[17]

Chief Tonasket wanted progress in civilization among the Indians. He, in spite of not having been fortunate enough to have schooling, asked the government to have a school erected where Tonasket is now; it was built but burned in 1897 and was never replaced. Tonasket was a progressive farmer who bought machinery and was one of the first Indians to provide hay for his cattle. In the fall of 1890, Mr. Carr, then Okanogan county auditor, made a trip all along the Canadian boundary and came into a great gathering of the Simil-kameen and Tonasket tribes. He met Chief Tonasket, who was in favor "of opening the reservation, alloting lands in severalty, freer intercourse with the whites and more general adoption of their customs."[18]

Father Parodi tells that one afternoon in November, 1890, an Okanogan Indian was seen inspecting the Colville Mission barn, the orchard and the garden. He came to the priest's house and wanted Father Filippi to come to his place to give the Last Sacraments to his dying daughter. It was Chief Tonasket whose place at the Kettle River Valley was fifty-three miles away from St. Francis Regis Mission. Father had been at Chief Tonasket's place two weeks before where the suffering girl was a means of edification for all who saw her. Father Filippi went and, after administering to the girl, taught the workmen and the children catechism after supper. Chief Tonasket was present and was all attention. Later he addressed the priest:

---

[16] Judge W. C. Brown, mimeographed manuscript. Courtesy of Mrs. Lacey.

[17] John C. Tidball, Colonel, aide-de-camp, brevet brigadier-general, Washington, D. C., October 27, 1883, "Report of Journey Made by General W. T. Sherman in the North-West and Middle Parts of the United States in 1883." *Forty-Eighth Congress* (Vol. I), 235.

[18] Henry Carr, quoted by Richard F. Steele and Arthur P. Rose, ed., *op. cit.*, 862.

Father, I kept away from the Church these last eight years, but I couldn't help it; I am half blind and the Okanogan Church is 50 miles distance. I met the Father sometimes, but he never says Mass in the house. I will do a good thing; I will build a church right here near by, I have already selected a lovely spot, the best of all my land, and that will be the location for the Church. Tomorrow I will take you in there; it is only a quarter of a mile from the house. When the church will be ready I will send for you four or five times a year. In winter I will send a wagon. It is too hard for you to ride 53 miles.[19]

Chief Tonasket planned to build a room for Father beside the church and Alexis' wife nearby would be able to prepare his meals. In his hospitality, Chief Tonasket wanted to assure Father that he had a sufficient supply of meat for his priest guests. He had sheep, cattle, pigs, and chickens, and as a change he could have deer. "Now, Father, if you please, I will be ready for confession in half an hour." After Mass the next morning Father Filippi looked over the church site and went back to Colville.

About a month later the Fathers heard that Chief Tonasket had gone to Spokane to have an eye operation which was not successful. The second operation failed and Chief Tonasket went home to die. On the way he stopped at St. Francis Regis Mission to receive the sacraments. Four days later the Fathers received the news that the great chief had gone to his eternal reward while he was still forty-seven miles away from his home.[20] This was at Marcus where his camp had been waiting for him during the spring of 1891; he was about seventy-one years old.[21] Mr. Henry Nelson, Curlew, great grandson of Archibald McDonald, chief factor of the former Hudson's Bay Fort Colville, was mainly responsible that the memory of this great chief was honored by a monument bearing the inscription:

CHIEF JOSEPH TONASKET
1822–1891
HE PROVED HIMSELF A STRONG AND ABLE LEADER.
AND ALTHOUGH HIS WAS NOT AN INHERITED
CHIEFTAINSHIP HE WAS OFFICIALLY RECOGNIZED AS
CHIEF OF THE OKANOGAN INDIANS IN ABOUT THE YEAR
1858. HIS WHOLE LIFE WAS A SERIES OF
ACCOMPLISHMENTS FOR HIS PEOPLE.[22]

A very devoted helper of Father de Rougé, the former government guide and ex-chief of the Okanogans, Chief Ignace commonly called

---

[19] Parodi, *Memoirs,* Mss., OPA.
[20] *Ibid.*
[21] Judge Brown, manuscript.
[22] From a photograph of the monument. Courtesy of Mr. William F. Hill, Spokane, who attended Father de Rougé's school from 1904 to 1912.

Chief Aeneas, had originally been located with his band of Okanogans west of the Okanogan River. He was unable to restrain the impetuosity of the younger generation of his tribe who considered the incoming whites as intruders. Chief Aeneas had always been a friend of the whites. Rather than give in to the fight-loving young warriors, he severed his relation with his tribe and moved into what became known as the Aeneas Valley. This location is next to Bonaparte Valley.

Chief Aeneas was one of the great benefactors of early St. Mary's Mission and took an active part in having the Mission established. He and Chief Smitkin assisted Father de Rougé in building the first log chapel on Omak Creek while the medicine men objected, thereby protecting the life of the missionary. Chief Aeneas would travel far distances to attend holy Mass even in his advanced age. When he was present he would pass the collection box or more often his hat around for that purpose and he always put in a substantial sum, often a $100 bill. "The rest of the Indians would say that he is just showing off."[23] Many good old Indian people told the author that Chief Aeneas was very sincere. Before St. Mary's existed Chief Aeneas could be seen at the gatherings at St. Francis Regis Mission. This chief later married Margaret Brady. The name of Chief Aeneas is often mentioned as sponsor in baptisms. He is also still remembered for his mastery in speechmaking.[24]

Chief Antoine of the Okanogans lived in the Antoine Valley northeast of Tonasket; his name occurs often in the *Diary of St. Francis Regis Mission*. He often served as a guide and companion for Father de Rougé during the strenuous trips across the mountains during the first years of the existence of St. Mary's Mission. At that time all the supplies still had to be shipped across the mountains. Chief Antoine had two wives: one was Ellen — whose Indian name was "All-in," the other was Katherine. When Father de Rougé told him that he could have only one wife, he chose Katherine. "All-in" later married Baker Jim and became a great leader in praying and singing in the Okanogan Mission.[25] Chief Antoine took care of the Indians below the Canadian line after Chief Tonasket left for the Curlew region. Antoine was described as a big man with long hair. It was he who objected when Father Parodi used the Chinook language in church.

Chief Martin Swimptkin "was not exactly a chief" but ruled the Indians around what now comprises East Omak. "He used to police the grounds on big feast days."[26] Another minor chief who was very cooperative and

---

[23] Narcisse Nicholson, written account.
[24] Hill and Favel, interviews.
[25] Narcisse Nicholson, interview.
[26] Mrs. Therese Swimptkin, interview at St. Mary's, May 28, 1960.

helpful during Father de Rougé's time was Chief Louie Timentwa of Monse. Pauline Zacherle stated that this chief went hunting and fishing to help Father to provide for the school.[27]

Loup Loup George, Katar George, George Lahome, and Chief Coxit George are the names for the same man. After he broke a leg he was called Coxit, which means "broken." Coxit George was a faithful Moses Indian chief who came every Sunday and feast day to St. Mary's Mission to attend holy Mass. When still a pagan, he possessed three wives, a situation Father de Rougé told him was against the law.[28] The chief had the courage to dismiss the wives and then married one who was an Indian princess, the daughter of Chief Seattle. Father de Rougé baptized the chief and then blessed his Christian marriage. Chief Coxit George was always bestowing his benefactions of various kinds of St. Mary's Mission. Owing to the possessing of herds of thoroughbred horses and cattle he was quite wealthy. While we were visiting the queenly widow of Chief Coxit George, she praised the goodness of her parents. "Father helped the sick and the dying and baptized sick babies." Asked about how Chief Coxit George helped the Mission, she replied in broken English, "He helped to buy the St. Mary and our Lord," meaning the statues in the church. The old people keenly felt the lack of formal education needed to make themselves understood by the whites. "No school — no good." It must have been quite a hardship on these old Indian people when there was no priest available any more who understood their Indian language. The grave of Chief Coxit George in the Katar cemetery bears the inscription: "Coxey George, 1850–1922, 72 yrs."[29] Christine later married Sam George one of the right-hand men of Father de Rougé.

Chief Alexander Smitkin — his family name was formerly spelled Smetaken — is considered the most important chief in relation to the establishment of St. Mary's Mission. Father de Rougé mentioned that during the spring of 1886 he "bought" a cabin from this chief. He did not take it as a present; he wanted to make sure that superstitious chiefs and medicine men could not too easily interfere with his rightfully acquired property. A simple addition to this cabin became Father de

---

[27] Pauline Zacherle, interviews.

[28] Hill and Favel, interview.

[29] Mrs. Christine George, interview, at Katar, May 3, 1960. The nobility and dignity of her bearing were outstanding. From the *Omak Chronicle*, July 28, 1960, 2. "Funeral mass was Saturday at St. Mary's Mission church for Christine J.. George, 82, a daughter of the famous Chief Seattle. Mrs. George died July 20 in the Omak hospital. Burial was in the Katar cemetery. She was born June 20, 1878, at Ellensburg. She went to Seattle as a small child. In 1894 she married Coxey George. They lived on the coast until invited by Chief Joseph to move to the Colville Reservation."

Rougé's first chapel. It stood on the "left side of the road toward Omak Lake, near Smitkin's house, about fifty feet away and was built out of logs. It was still there in 1916–1917, but falling to pieces. Father de Rougé stayed at first with Smitkins."[30] The second chapel "built by Father de Rougé, Chief Smitkin, and Chief Aeneas was across the creek from the Mission."[31]

Chief Smitkin did all in his power to help Father to establish his mission. Through the following years the chief with his men hauled the logs and the lumber for the other buildings that were to be erected. The first school and church were built with his assistance. He was the protector of the missionary during the first years until slowly the priest's influence and prestige grew. To be sponsor for many baptisms and to be Father De Rougé's companion was a great honor to him. It would be nearly twenty-five years until the allotments of the south half of the Colville Reservation would be given to individual persons. The land along Omak Creek belonged at that time in great part to Chief Smitkin and to his relatives. He freely gave his land to the Mission, but did not see the difficulties of later years until the Jesuits were able to acquire the land in the name of the Society. On big feast days Chief Smitkin was a gracious host to the many tribes camping around Omak Creek. Each time the chief would have one of his many steers killed and divided among the Indians of the camp.

Along the wall of his chicken house, Chief Smitkin had buried his fortune in glass jars. There were two and a half rows of them filled with gold pieces. When Joe Thomas cleaned the chicken house he struck a jar and decided to explore further. When he discovered more jars he covered them again and told Smitkin, "I ran into your cash; somebody could go away with it." The next day when Joe Thomas came back, Smitkin had moved the money. Nobody knows where he buried it. Shortly after this incident Chief Smitkin stopped at Joe Thomas' cabin where he suddenly felt sick. His sons were called and Paul came first. As Smitkin started to talk to Paul the other son, Louie, entered the cabin. Louie had not been good to his father. Chief Smitkin remained silent and death came before he was able to reveal the place where he had hidden his money.[32] Chief Smitkin died on the twenty-ninth of July, 1919.[33] This chief who had done so much to transform the pagan valley into a Christian land lies buried in the cemetery of St. Mary's Mission without any marker whatsoever on his grave. His friend, Father de Rougé, had died three years before. How

[30] Mrs. Florence Opel (Bernier), interview at Seattle, June 4, 1960.
[31] Mrs. Christine George, op. cit.
[32] Johnny Louie, interview at Disautel, January 30, 1961.
[33] Courtesy of Mrs. Yvonne Adams, granddaughter of Chief Smitkin.

Father de Rougé appreciated his faithful helper can be seen in the following lines:

> The Indian chief here is Alexander Smetaken. He has quite a fortune in cattle and horses and the finest land on the Reservation. His house is half a mile from the church. Every morning, snow or rain, burning sun or wind, he is at Mass and in the evening at prayers. He is a perfectly good Catholic and of course the best friend of the mission.[34]

The power and influence of the medicine men were decreasing, yet occasionally they still caused great difficulties. Even the good Chief Smitkin fell once more a victim to superstition. The daughter of Chief Smitkin, Madeleine, was suffering from tuberculosis. Father de Rougé had told the chief that there was no hope. Chief Smitkin, in desperation, called the medicine man, who first wanted to be paid in horses and saddles. Madeleine Smitkin died January 28, 1909. After the burial Chief Smitkin wanted Father de Rougé to help him to get his horses and saddles back from the medicine man. Father was not successful. Two days later one of the squaws who hated the medicine man was driving a wagon and two horses near the Mission. The medicine man just then came up the road. The horses became frightened and raced away up the hill where they were caught. The woman, who had fallen from the wagon, was not quite conscious when the medicine man came up the road. Looking at her he said, "See, I sent my spirits out."[35]

Judge Brown of Okanogan told the following story to several people. Father de Rougé came to him on several occasions asking him to do something against all the superstitious practices of the Indians. The Judge could not find any laws in his books pertaining to the matter and could not stop the Indians' superstitious rites. Once an Irish priest came to visit Father. The subject of conversation was again complaints concerning the superstitious Indians. The Irish priest then remarked with a twinkle in his eyes: "Father, we have tried to root out superstition from the Irish for 2000 years and have not succeeded. Yet, the Irish are good Catholics."[36] This settled the matter.

Chief John Wapato, one of the noblest and most influential chiefs of the Chelans, and other chiefs living far from the Mission would gather their people in the little mission churches nearest to them and would direct the prayers to be said, the hymns to be sung, and on ordinary Sundays would give a talk to the people on the fulfillment of their Christian duties.

[34] De Rougé, *St. Mary's Mission,* Mss., OPA.

[35] Van Coelen, interview.

[36] Judge W. C. Brown to Father J. Balfe, S.J., October 24, 1959. Also several publications bought the story,

Father de Rougé had taught them how to keep the faith alive. Only on high feast days were those tribes able to come to St. Mary's Mission.

Two good people still much remembered were Captain Jim and Okanogan Mary. The influence of Captain Jim came not from chieftainship but from upright character. But even at that, Father de Rogué did not have an easy task in converting him from polygamy. Mrs. Fries records a visit from Captain Jim, who wore his hair cut short and was a friend of the whites. The Captain had been a scout for General Crocker during the early years. Mrs. Fries quotes a dialogue between her husband the the chief:

> You got squaw?
> No, I have a white wife — she is in the kitchen.
> Me got two squaws. Priest not like me got two squaws. Me no care.
> I agree with the priest. You are not like white man if you have two squaws. I think you better get rid of one.
> One squaw not enough. They do lots work.[37]

Captain Jim still had his two wives while he was policeman at the Tonasket government school. But gradually he was converted. He was often seen at St. Mary's Mission and in all kinds of weather. This old Captain's home was a dugout somewhere in present Okanogan. During a social gathering a few years ago old-timers recalled Captain Jim and old Mary:

> He was a fine old Indian. I never knew him to take a drink of liquor. I remember some of us kids came by one morning as he and old Mary were sitting down to breakfast. Captain Jim asked us to eat with him but we had already eaten. He and Old Mary bowed and said grace before they ate. I've never forgotten that.[38]

Father de Rougé was not able to convert four of the chiefs who wielded great influence throughout the Okanogan Valley while he was building up his Mission. Chief Long Jim of the Chelans, living later in Monse, condemned the Catholic Church. "His belief was that the Black Robes were followers of Judas who betrayed Christ." He was converted on his deathbed through the instrumentality of Mr. John Cleveland, one of Father de Rougé's former honor students.[39] Father Caldi gave Chief Long Jim the Last Sacraments.

Chief Long Jim might have been influenced by Chief Skolaskan of the Sanpoil Indians. Skolaskan, the founder of the Dreamer religion, was

---

[37] Fries and Fries, *op. cit.,* 303.
[38] Harley Heath, quoting Graves, "Life Was a Lot of Fun in Early Okanogan," *The Okanogan Independent* (October 30, 1957).
[39] John Cleveland, interview.

sowing hostility and opposition to Father de Rougé's missionary efforts. Early missionaries had experienced his defiant attitudes. Because Father de Rougé was residing on the Colville Reservation, he was made to feel the hate of the Dreamers personally. The priest tells about this "Dreamer":

> The religion of the dreamers had been started by a liar, who Died and went to heaven where God revealed him his religion. Coming back to life, he proclaimed that his followers would be the only ones to be saved from hell, and from the abuses of the coming white race to their country; he forbade them to have anything to do with any other religion or with any government officer. He built then a log-house chapel and established himself high priest. Prayers were taught as well as songs and ceremonies for the burials, all revealed in dreams.[40]

Nearly all the Sanpoil country as well as Nespelem was under the sway of Skolaskan. He had his own police force, his own jail, and administered justice according to his own interpretation. Finally the United States government made an end to his autocratic rule by giving him a ride to McNeil's Island and by keeping him there without trial or a hearing. After two years he was sent back to his people, but declined further to be their leader and his religion died out.[41]

Another chief, who was originally against Father de Rougé's settling at Omak Creek, Chief Moses, created quite a disturbance at the Colville Indian Reservation. The Nespelem and the Sanpoil claimed that

> Moses had sold his country where he first lived that he sold the reservation that was set apart for him [Columbia Indian Reserve] without consulting the Indians resident thereon; sold it for money to buy

---

[40] De Rougé, *St. Mary's Mission, 25 Years Ago and Today*, Mss., ABSS.

[41] Henry Covington, tape recording on Chief Skolaskan, made by Mr. Cull White. Courtesy of Mr. White. See also Griva: *History*, 153. Father Griva gives the following information about Chief Skolaskan, Corpus Christi, May 30, 1918: "I must not fail to relate the baptism of one old man. He was very old and crippled so much so that he could not work and was always carried to the church. On that day he had to be carried to the communion rail. He was considered as a prophet. Many years ago, before any priest had gone to the Colville Reservation, he was telling the people, a man all dressed in black will come among you and will teach you who is the Great Spirit and will teach you what you must do to be good and go to heaven. You must listen to him you must learn what he will tell you. Then he told them: time will come when the Columbia river will rise so high that it will overflow your land and you will have to go away from here. For this reason I have built a big boat and when this will happen if I will be still alive I will take you all in my boat and will bring you all to Canada. Some years after he had said these words Father De Smet came to the Colville reservation and other Fathers came also and the prophecy of Mr. Kullaken who was the man who had made the prophecy was fulfilled." Father Griva must not have known Skolaskan's former "prophecies" and how the men "dressed in black" were treated by this "prophet."

whiskey and to gamble, and that he will be as ready to sell their country for more money when the time comes and the white man wants it.[42]

The Okanogans and their chiefs also felt cheated when Moses was named "Head Chief" of the Okanogan tribes by high officials in Washington, D. C. He was placed on the Columbia and later on the Colville Reservation. The agitation lasted quite a few years; Father de Rougé's influence kept the peace among the Okanogans, but he was as yet powerless with the self-made chief of the Sanpoil Indians.

"We have recorded knowledge that 'Moses had for a time attended the mission school of the Spaldings at Lapwai, when a boy.' "[43] We are unable to ascertain if he was named Moses in baptism or was baptized at Lapwai.[44] Chief Moses, the great diplomat, often played a double role: for and against the Catholic Church. Father Parodi related a conversation he had with an Indian about marriage:

Father, I know some Indians have two wives . . . and Moses the great chief has three wives. He had some dispositions to become a Catholic and was taken by two Jesuits to the Catholic bureau in Washington for examination. Fr. Brouilett at the head of the bureau asked him: Moses are you disposed to renounce superstitions? Yes, I am. Moses, will you help the missionaries in their ministry to baptize the children of your tribe, and teach the Catholic religion among your Indians? Certainly I will. Moses, will you keep only one wife and send away the other two? No sir, I cannot, and he took up his hat and went out. I met Moses in Okanogan and he said he kept three wives to work on his farm and in the house. If he had to take women to work for him he would have to pay them, whilst his wives work for nothing.[45]

Mrs. Helen Toulou stated that at great gatherings of the tribes during the early years Chief Moses would wail because the land was taken away. He blamed the Black Robes for making the Indians too docile so they would not object and fight for their lands.[46] Frank M. Streamer, always making himself the advocate of the Indians, copied the following letter addressed to the Indian Agent D. Gwydir, Camp Spokane, September 22, 1888, into one of his *Messenger Books*. The original letter seems to have been sent to Sam Miller, Esq., on August 21, 1888:

---

[42] Sidney D. Waters, in "Annual Report of the Commissioner of Indian Affairs to the Secretary of the Interior for the Year 1885," 183.

[43] Theo. H. Scheffer, "Good Land 'O Moses . . .," *The Spokesman-Review* (March 29, 1953), 9.

[44] For the sake of historical accuracy this history should have been written thirty years earlier.

[45] Parodi, *Memoirs,* Mss., OPA.

[46] Mrs. Helen Toulou, interview.

Dear Sir:

Chief Moses is in trouble regarding the report that the priests are persecuting his people, because they refuse to become Catholics.

Will you please let me know if there is any truth in the matter, as Moses fears it will lead to trouble. He wants his people who are Catholics to remain that way, but not to use force with those who do not wish to be Catholics. He desires you to write him a letter on the subject; an early answer will be greatly appreciated by me.[47]

We are not able to shed more light on the subject. Suffice it to say that nobody ever could be made a member of the Catholic Church without his own consent. A procedure by force would be invalid according to the laws of the Church.

Indian Agent Gwydir reported that Moses had promised to stop drinking himself, and show a good example to his people, but in his opinion he never would as long as he could obtain whiskey. "He is opposed to the Catholic religion. I think his objection dates to the fact that the priests informed him that he must give up one of his wives, he having two."[48] At least he now had one wife less. When in the fall of 1890, the tribes congregated at the Lake Osoyoos horse racing tracks, "Chief Moses was present and made a speech urging industry, sobriety and morality."[49] How much more effective might Chief Moses' influence have been if he would have lived a Christian life. We wrote to Mr. A. De Vos asking if Chiefs Moses and Joseph ever had been at the gatherings at St. Mary's Mission. Mr. A. De Vos answered in the affirmative. "Am sure chiefs mentioned in your of Aug. 14/60 attended services at the Mission. They

---

[47] Frank Marion Streamer, *The Streamer Papers, Messenger Book I*, 60, Mss., AWHS. Frank M. Streamer, appointed a notary public, January 21, 1882, for the county of Yakima by William A. Aerrell, governor of the Territory of Washington, wrote countless letters to high government officials and persons of influence, always made the Indians' troubles his own, but wanted the Indian Department to pay him. About his first visit to the Omak Mission he wrote: "The next day [October 17, 1893] I went over the rock trails of the Omack Mountains and came to the Smithkin ranch at night and stayed in William Jim's tent near the Church of Father de Rougé, who . . . had gone to the Wenatchee Church at Mission Creek . . . The Indian woman gave me a good warm bed and a good supper — such as they had. They are very poor and have no tea, coffee or sugar and very little flour. Their men are close followers of the priest, and have no time to make hay or bread when the sun shines warm. They, it seems, propose to starve themselves into Heaven, and deny the food of farm and garden which God gives to his loving people," Vol. II, 360. On April 24th, 1894, Streamer was invited by Father de Rougé for dinner. Book III, 227. Streamer later spent some time in a mental institution.

[48] Gwydir, "Annual Report of 1887," *Report of the Secretary of the Interior, House Executive Documents, Fifty-Seventh Congress, First Session, 1887* (Vol. II, 1887), p. 288.

[49] Henry Carr, quoting Chief Moses, *op. cit.*, 862.

all marched in parade in full regalia. I say this."[50] Chief Moses died March 25, 1899, at Nespelem, Washington. The inscription on his monument states that he was born in 1829 and that he was seventy years old when he died.[51]

Slowly Father de Rougé was able to count more baptisms from the Moses tribe. He wrote:

> A father would be needed to visit the Nespelem district, 40 miles from here. There also a part of 45 acres is to be put aside by the government for a church. There Indians are getting . . . converted [and] every year we baptize some and last Easter the most prominent chief was baptitzed . . . here in our church.[52]

According to the baptismal records this prominent chief was Chief Joseph Moses, the nephew of Chief Moses, then the ruling chief of the Moses tribe. He became a member of the Catholic Church on March 22, 1913, together with two women from the Moses tribe.[53] Mr. John Figlenski remembers that he was altar boy on that day.[54] Two of Chief Joe Moses' children had been baptized years before his own conversion. This chief was often at St. Mary's Mission, even when Nespelem had its own church. Chief Smitkin's wife was Chief Joseph Moses' sister.[55] This chief died on December 23, 1924.[56] The last living wife of old Chief Moses was Catholic and was buried by Father Griva, June 2, 1937.[57] Mary Owhi Moses had been Chief Owhi's favorite daughter Kamola whom Moses married after the death of her sister Hi-o-li-saw.[58] Many of Chief Moses' people are Catholics today.

There were some similarities between the language of the Sinkaiuse or Moses Indians and the Okanogan language when in 1885 Moses moved his people to the Colville Reservation. No similarities existed between the Nez Perce and the Okanogan languages when Chief Joseph and the part of his people not accepted at Lapwai were located near Cousin Moses at Nespelem on the same reservation. The Indian Agent Gwydir needed the presence of troops to quiet the opposition of Skolaskan and his

---

[50] Mr. A. De Vos, letter to the author, November 4, 1960.

[51] See: Moses Cemetery, Nespelem, Washington.

[52] De Rougé, *Historia Domus*, Ms., OPA (n.d., dated according to content and comparison with baptismal records).

[53] *Baptismal Records of St. Mary's Mission*, II, 117.

[54] John Figlenski, interview at St. Mary's Mission, October 16, 1960.

[55] Johnny Louie, interview.

[56] See: Moses Cemetery, Nespelem, Washington.

[57] Griva, *History*, 339. "In the course of that week I performed the burials of the 2 oldest women of the reservation. One of them was Mary Moses . . . who was about 118 years old.

[58] Splawn, *op. cit.* (1958), 487.

Sanpoil People.[59] These Nez Perces came as prisoners of war on a reservation that had been the home of the peaceful Okanogan and Colville tribes, who considered this a disgrace. The Colville Confederated Tribes were then for the most part Catholics with the exception of the Sanpoil and many Nepelems, while the incoming Nez Perces were pagans, bringing Smohalla's Dreamer religion into the Colville Reservation. These Nez Perces did not settle down peacefully; they still hoped to be able to return to their stolen homes in the Wallula country. It is understandable that these people as a rule did not want to have anything to do with the whites after they had been greatly abused by them. Often the so-called Christians had acted like savages and the Indians like gentlemen. No wonder that there were so few conversions among them for the first twenty years. The Nez Perces did not want to work during the first years and the agent's complaint about this might have had its roots in Smohalla's doctrine:

> My young men shall never work, for men who work cannot dream, and wisdom comes from your dreams. We will not plow the ground, for we will not tear our mother's breast. We will cut no hay, for we dare not cut off our mother's hair.[60]

Chief Joseph's band had been asked at Wallula if they wanted to be Christians and go to Lapwai or retain their tribal worship and go to the Colville Reservation. Yellow Wolf was quoted as saying: "Religion had to do with where they placed us."[61] The predominently Catholic population of the Colville Reservation was considered more tolerant and broadminded than their former friends at Lapwai. It was the influence of Father de Rougé and other missionaries who preceded him that developed peaceful attitudes even toward enemies, for this is Christ's teaching on brotherly love. We mentioned that the Nez Perces had been the ancient enemies of the Colville Confederated Tribes.

Chief Joseph himself had attended school at Lapwai and had been baptized there. During the Cayuse War he and his father went back to their old homes and their old religion. It might not be too well known that quite a number of the Nez Perces were Catholics in early times. The fur traders had awakened in them the desire for Black Robes.[62] One of the first delegations to look for priests in St. Louis in 1831 and who died there was a Nez Perce.[63] Father De Smet had visited them

[59] Gwydir, "Annual Report for 1887," *op. cit.*, 288.

[60] Russel Blankenship quoting Smohalla, *And There Were Men*, 49.

[61] L. V. McWhorter quoting Yellow Wolf, *Hear Me My Chiefs!* 541.

[62] Blanchet, *op. cit.*, 60.

[63] See Bishop Rosati's letter of December 31, 1831, to the editor of the *Association of the Propagation of the Faith* in L. B. Palladino, S.J., *Indian and White in the Northwest*, II.

and had quite a number of baptisms.[64] Father Cataldo and other priests had visited them from the Coeur d'Alene Mission. Chief Joseph is quoted in a council with a special government commission at the Nez Perce Agency in Lapwai:

Question: Do you want schools and school-houses on the Wallowa Reservation?

Answer: No we do not want schools or school houses on the Wallowa Reservation.

Question: Why do you not want schools?

Answer: They will teach us to have churches.

Question: Why do you not want churches?

Answer: They will teach us to quarrel about God, as the Catholics and Protestants do on the Nez Perce Reservation, and other places. We do not want to learn that. We may quarrel with men sometimes about things here on earth, but we never quarrel about God. We do not want to learn that.[65]

Agent Monteith on the Nez Perce Reservation had refused to let the Catholic Nez Perces have a church on the reservation and had shown himself hostile to the Catholic priest. No freedom of conscience was allowed by him to the Catholic Nez Perces, who numbered approximately two hundred souls. Chief Joseph had leanings toward the Catholic faith. It is an historical fact that the Catholic Nez Perces did not want to go to war. While the Nez Perces were gathered for council the "Treaty Nez Perce from the Catholic Mission and elsewhere packed up and departed. They foresaw the outcome of the council."[66] Concerning Chief Joseph, Father Cataldo, S.J., said:

. . . He promised to act peacefully, and try to have the others do likewise, and said that when the trouble was over, he would settle down and become a Catholic.[67]

While on the Colville Reservation Chief Joseph was always very respectful toward Father de Rougé. Chief Looking Glass had been killed during the war of 1877 and Chief Joseph honored his memory by keeping his two wives. This may have been the reason why he did not become a Catholic. Chief Joseph, Hin-Male-Too: Thunder Rolling in the Moun-

---

[64] CR, De Smet, I, 338–39.

[65] Chief Joseph quoted in "Report of J. B. C. Shanks, T. W. Bennet, and H. W. Reed," House Executive Documents, Forty-Third Congress, First Session (1874), 531.

[66] Chester Anders Fee, Chief Joseph: The Biography of a Great Indian, 123. Also: The Cataldo Papers, "Nez Perce History," Mss., OPA.

[67] Cataldo quoting Chief Joseph, Ibid. Also: R. Ignatius Burns, "The Jesuits, the Northern Indians, and the Nez Perce War of 1877," PNQ (42:1, January, 1951), 50–51.

tains, died September 21, 1904. His body rests in the Nez Perce Cemetery at Nespelem where on June 20, 1905, a monument was dedicated to him.[68] A few of the Nez Perces have in the course of time become Catholics; the majority holds on to the "Dreamer" worship.

The chiefs knew that they needed united action so that their complaints would receive attention in Washington, D. C. In the fall of 1908, the following chiefs had a meeting at Omak: Long Jim, Charley Swimptkin, Louie Timentwa, and Alexander Smitkin. Johnny Louie served as interpreter. They complained that they lost too many boys who were fighting and killing each other when drunk. Judge Pendergrass in Conconully was visited and he was asked to help prevent the selling of liquor to Indians. The Judge wanted $1,500 to go to Washington and see the proper authorities. Chief Smitkin contributed $1,000 and the others paid the rest. Judge Pendergrass went to Washington, D. C., in May, 1909, and came back in the fall. Then the chiefs all went to Conconully to hear the answer from the President. "The Indians did have no right to go into the saloon and drink over the bar. They would send out dry squads to help to stop it." The squads came and stopped it and Father de Rougé felt very happy with the result.[69]

Among nature's noblemen who were very influential and cooperative were the chiefs of Lower British Columbia. Chief Nicola and his tribal members were allowed to stay in their country. A big, beautiful lakeside reserve was theirs given them by the British government, which followed a wiser Indian policy than was ever experienced in the United States. Chief Nicola married one of his daughters to Francois and made him chief of Penticton. Francois was succeeded in 1909 by Chief Gabian and he in turn by his brother Edward. Chief Edward was Maria Houghton Brent's grandmother's brother.[70] The Penticton chiefs with their people met their tribal relations at Schall-kees and at Omak Creek on the big feasts of the Church. The Inkameep Indians, formerly under Chief Tonasket, had a very good Chief Gregoire who is mentioned in 1886 as coming to the first mission church at Schall-kees; later he camped with his people at St. Mary's Mission. After his death in 1907, Baptiste, who had married Gregoire's daughter Cecile, was appointed chief and continued to hold a place of honor and respect among his people, because he lived his religion. Father de Rougé would often stop at the Inkameep church for services when on the way to the northern part of the big parish.

---

[68] See: Nez Perce Cemetery, Nespelem, Washington.
[69] Johnny Louie, interview at Disautel, January 30, 1961.
[70] Maria Houghton Brent, *op. cit.*, Mss. Courtesy of Mrs. Lacey.

Former students of St. Mary's Mission school remember Chief Loup Loup from Malott wearing a derby hat and seven shirts all outside his pants, each one a little shorter and of a different color. He is described as having been of medium height, his hair in braids, never saying anything to anyone but Father de Rougé, and then he spoke in Indian. At the Holy Thursday ceremonies of washing the feet, he was one of the honored ones always occupying a front seat.[71] Charley Swimptkin from Omak is often mentioned, also Louie Judge from Cashmere, as Father de Rougé's devoted helpers. In charge of immediate church activities as ushers in church and taking care of orderly processions were, among others, Jack Carden and Alexander Nicholson. The last named gentleman still did his duty in his advanced age. He would slowly walk to the communion rail and see that the children observed order and respect when receiving their Lord. Mr. Nicholson was dressed in his ceremonial sash as usher when lying in state before burial.

The tribal leaders were either a great help or a great hindrance to Father de Rougé, according to their attitudes toward the Catholic faith. No good Indian leader could for any length of time exclude himself from the common council of the chiefs who met with Father de Rougé to discuss tribal problems that needed correction. This council of the chiefs met at St. Mary's Mission when the Indian bands camped there. This must have been a very colorful event; the chiefs were all dressed in their finest regalia, braids hung down in front. They sat high on horseback and formed a circle.

These chiefs had quite an organization where every little detail of the camping order was regulated. Every tribe had its camping place. The poles for the tents were left at the Mission; it was a matter of minutes to erect an Indian village. Indian policemen were constantly on duty, day and night. Church policemen saw to it that no drunkards, medicine men, or people married outside the church entered. This rule was later somewhat mitigated. The chiefs would hold places of honor in the front row on the right side, while the women prayer leaders had the front row of the left side reserved. Some of these good women chieftainesses were: Matilda Wapato, Elizabeth Friedlander, Cecille Antoine, Agatha Francis, Louise Michel, Rosalie Yat-ha-nolx Batoi, and Yut-huen-alks, the sister of Chief Smitkin. The ushers wore special ceremonial sashes and were proud of their duties. Offenders were brought before the chief, this becoming a regular court procedure. Special herders were named to watch the horses. At nine o'clock at night, the curfew bell gave the signal to go to rest and no visiting in other tents was allowed. Father de Rougé's

---

[71] Harry Van Coelen, interview at St. Mary's Mission, May 8–11, 1960.

prudent and harmonious relations with the Indian chiefs was a vital factor in his attempt to Christianize and civilize the tribes.

On May 23, 1961, the mourning Colville Confederated Tribes paid their last tribute to Chief Jim James of the Sanpoils, the last of the chiefs. He was devout, helpful, and a splendid example of active Christian living. To fulfill his Sunday duties he would walk all the way from Keller to Nespelem with his elderly wife in his very advanced age. At most of the funerals at St. Mary's Mission he could be seen addressing his people. During November of 1958, when the question of supporting St. Mary's Mission came up at the Council meeting, Chief Jim James made the following remarks:

> I think that we could not do any better than to support the school at St. Mary's Mission, because there are many children that have no home or parents that are taking care of theirs. It might mean less beer for some of us, but we are doing the right thing to support a school that takes care of our orphans and children.
>
> It used to be that they took the children away, off to other parts of the country where we could not see them, and some we never saw, because they died.[72]

The author was fortunate to be able to visit the aging and ailing chief about five months before his death. He repeated to us his appreciation of St. Mary's Mission:

> St. Mary's Mission has done immense good in its long history for all the tribes that came from every direction, especially on Corpus Christi, Easter, Christmas, and other big feast days. I am very old now and I still go there when I get a chance. We need St. Mary's Mission as a home for those who have none and where the children learn their religion, because nowadays they don't care learning religion. The influence of St. Mary's Mission is carried back into the homes of the children. Even the children that have a home need St. Mary's Mission for the many things needed in life, especially how to take responsibilities.[73]

An era has closed. The patriarchal rule of the chiefs belongs to yesterday's history and the rule of elected Council members has replaced it. The white man has tried to destroy tribal life and in doing so has removed prematurely the very factors of progress in faith and morals and in other civilizing pursuits.

---

[72] Chief Jim James, quoted by Mrs. Helen Toulou, interview.
[73] Chief Jim James, interview with the author, January 28, 1961, at Keller, Washington.

CHAPTER XIII

Growth of the First Educational Institution in the Okanogan Valley

FATHER DE ROUGÉ mentioned several times that through all the years he had tried to have a little "winter school" in order to teach the children their religion. This school was opened for the children of the surrounding area during the months that Father had the time and could be at his mission. It would be a mistake to assume that Father de Rougé, the born educator, taught only religion. As we have said, he had the prayers and hymns translated into the Okanogan Salish language and printed in booklet form in France. The Okanogans and other related tribes never had a written language. This emphasized the necessity of teaching the Indians first to read the alphabet in order that they might learn to read their own language. Interviews have shown that as early as 1886, Father de Rougé was teaching his neophytes how to read and write at his first mission at Schall-kees.[1] Narcisse Nicholson said that at that time Father de Rougé had a brother who planted a little garden and cooked for the children. The school at Schall-kees was then not only Father de Rougé's first boarding school but the very first school in all the Okanogan country for hundreds of miles in all directions.

We have seen that when the Friedlander children were brought to St. Mary's Mission, the school was in full session. Narcisse Nicholson attended the Omak Creek school during the years 1899–1900. Only big boys were then enrolled and the program of studies contained, besides religion, useful secular subjects, such as the three R's and organ and band music. Narcisse learned how to play songs on an old organ.

[1] Charley Bottomley, interview at Oroville, July 13, 1961. Mr. Bottomley, then 84 years old, was one of the first pupils at the boarding school in Schall-kees.

Father de Rougé was an accomplished musician and used this talent to develop the Indian love for melodies and rhythms. When Narcisse was there only one long building was on the premises. It was adjacent to where the first church stood. Kitchen, bedrooms, classrooms, and parlor were under one roof.[2] Lewis H. Runnels who attended St. Mary's Mission school during 1901–1902 found that the institution had grown into two different buildings. The kitchen, dining room, assembly hall were on the first floor, and dormitories on the second floor in another building that had to be reached by going over a backyard. The teachers then were Gade Riley and Father de Rougé.[3]

Mr. Richard Hirst reached the Mission on Omak Creek in 1901 by freight team from the Columbia River, and he then went along the shores of the Omak Lake. At that time there was a road which in the course of years has been washed into the Lake. Mr. Hirst reported that all the region around the Mission was in its original wilderness and that trees and underbrush were everywhere. Besides the Mission buildings he saw many cabins which had hand-hewn floors; also many tents were pitched on the place. Many people had moved closer to the Mission in order to give their children a chance to attend Father's school. The Indian people were "very nice" to Mr. Hirst. He was sent by Father to an Indian woman who had bread. Mr. Hirst still remembers Father's remarks, that he guarantees that the bread baked by this woman was clean. The stranger wanted to buy two loaves but this gracious Indian lady did not accept pay for it. Quite a few children were around. Father de Rougé's hospitality was extraordinary; this too served as practical schooling for his students. The future settler was shown the exact spot where he could ford the Okanogan River.[4]

Enormous sums of money are needed to build up an educational institution and to keep it in existence. The following letter is the first one Father de Rougé wrote to the Catholic Bureau of Indian Missions in Washington, D. C. It is dated December 15, 1900, and is transcribed just as he wrote it:

> I have a mission of about 800 Cath. Indians and 600 Infidels. This mission center is here at St. Mary's and I have 100 miles west, 60 North to go, 70–80 miles East. In this immense territory you cannot see your people but once in a great while. Hence have to attend to children for 1st. Communions, etc. without a school to gather them. All over the country public schools are gathering our Indian children and already they are getting used to it because we do not look after them properly.

[2] Narcisse Nicholson, interview at Ellisforde, July 14, 1961.
[3] Lewis Runnels, interview at Tonasket, July 14, 1961.
[4] Mr. Hirst, interview at St. Mary's Mission, January 27, 1961.

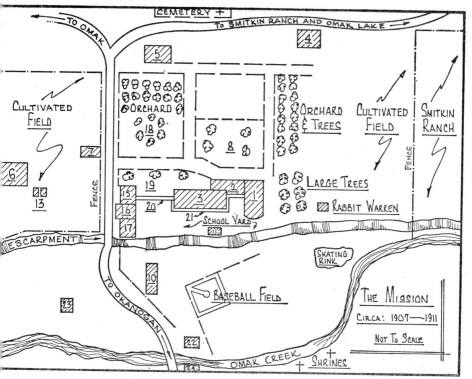

1. Church; 2. First floor — offices and reception rooms; Second floor — boys' dormitory; 3. First floor — classrooms; Second floor — boys' dormitory; 4. Convent — school for girls; 5. Infirmary; 6. Barn; 7. General mercantile store of a French-Canadian Irishman, Mr. Corrigan; 8. Lawn and flower beds, upper field — a vegetable garden; 10. Fieldhouse open on one side for basketball and gymnastics; 11. Carbide producing plant for gas illumination; 13. Pig feeding enclosures; 15. First floor — dining rooms and kitchen; Second floor — rooms and dormitory and farmhand quarters; 16. School auditorium and theater; 17. First floor — carpentry and taxidermy shops and museum; Second floor — guest rooms; 18. Large trees planted in a circle*; 19. Lawn, flower beds, and shade trees; 20. Sidewalk connecting buildings and leading into dining rooms; 21. Porches leading into church; 22. Private residence; 23. Private residence; 24. Site of first low chapel.

* There were cherry trees in fields 8 and 18 but I cannot precisely place them.

NOTE: Buildings 4 and 5 were not up when I first went to the Mission. There was no girls' school then. Buildings and fields are approximate and are not drawn to scale. The main boys' school began to come down in 1911 or 1912.

I have tried all these past years to have a school with the little self-help given by our good and kind Bishop O'Dea. I have buildings enough to keep 30 boys now while we should have 100 children. This year we started fine. I have a good teacher and a cook depending for their wages on $600 promised to me by Right Rev. Bishop if he would get the same alm from the Commission as he got last year. Besides these wages it was left to me to provide the best I could, the food, wood, light, books, washing, and the general running of the school, also with the little help of parents that at least try to give the clothing. I have no support, and have for myself and my mission to depend on charity. Often I have no masses. A few days ago a letter comes that our Right Rev. Bishop having not received his expected allowance from the Commission can only give me $250. I had to call the teacher that night and tell him to be ready to leave. Yet in the same time I asked him to wait a few days and let us see if Providence would not come and save our school. I have been here twenty years among the Indians without many things necessary to life. If we do not look after a school here our mission will be ruined, these long years passed here will be lost. I should even build more for more boys, and should have already long ago here sisters for the girls.[5]

We quote this lengthy letter to help correct the wrong notion that Father de Rougé as a count had "Princely Dowry" to build up his St. Mary's Mission. As we will see, his family helped substantially in the upkeep of his mission, but the greatest source of help was the charity of Mother Katherine Drexel.

Divine Providence must have inspired the Reverend Director of the Catholic Indian Bureau to send Father de Rougé's letter to Reverend Mother Katherine Drexel.[6] This generous Mother in turn sent it to Bishop O'Dea together with a check of $340 and the first gift of Mother Katherine saved the Mission and was to be followed by innumerable benefactions up to 1936. Mother Katherine, a very prudent lady, did not spend her money carelessly, as the following letter to Bishop O'Dea shows:

The enclosed letter was sent to the Bureau for Catholic Indians & sent to us. We have made out a check to the order of Rev. E. de Rougé for $340. It may come too late to save the dismissal of the teacher. If so, I have asked the Rev. Father to return it. We are devoted solely to the education of Indians and Colored, therefore, we beg that you see

---

[5] De Rougé, letter to Catholic Bureau of Indian Missions, Washington, D. C. Ms., ADS.

[6] See: Katherine Burton, *The Golden Door: The Life of Katherine Drexel.* Mother Katherine Drexel was born November 26, 1858. She was the daughter of Francis Drexel, a rich banker of Philadelphia. Her parents always had been very charitable to the poor. Katherine made the aquaintance of Bishop Marti of the Dakota Territory and of Father Joseph Stephen of the Catholic Indian Bureau, Washington, D. C., who had come to enlist the interest of the Drexel girls in the Indian missions. She had been left a great fortune after her father's death which she resolved to use for the poor neglected Indians. Pope Leo XIII encouraged her to be a missionary herself. In May, 1889, she entered the convent of the Mercy Sisters in Pittsburgh to learn the religious life, make her novitiate, and to be enabled to found her own congregation, the Sisters of the Blessed Sacrament for Indians and Colored. She was a great and noble benefactress of these two minority groups. She died March 3, 1955, ninety-six years old. (A good many statements by Katherine Burton in the *Golden Door* concerning the Dominican Sisters at the Mission are incorrect.)

that every cent, be spent for the Indians alone. Rev. E. de Rougé is also a stranger to us & therefore should you doubt that the Rev. gentleman expend the money injudiciously, I beg you kindly to return the note addressed to him, to us, otherwise, to mail it to him.[7]

In appreciating Mother Katherine's contribution let us not overlook money values sixty years ago and today. We were not able to locate correspondence between Mother Katherine and Father de Rougé for the following four years.

In 1902, at the invitation of Father de Rougé, the Reverend Th. M. J. Pypers visited the Mission. The then pastor at Davenport required three days to reach St. Mary's, for the transportation was difficult: railroad, open stage, and ferry. On the reservation on the west side of the Okanogan River, at Malott, an Indian had the father's team and buggy waiting and conducted him to the Mission, where the "noble Father de Rougé" gave him a hearty welcome. It was the season before the feast of Corpus Christi and the visitor had ample opportunity to observe firsthand the missionary and his flock.

Every Indian on arrival would first come up the little hill on which the Mission was erected to greet the priest. They followed Indian customs and entered without knocking at the door. Father de Rougé had a large tobacco can where the men and the old squaws helped themselves before they left. Then the Indians would pitch their tents and tepees and the young priest found it "as interesting as watching a circus spreading its big canvas for a show." By evening the landscape was changed by the presence of an Indian village. Father de Rougé only once was "peevish with a visitor." It was a pagan who was drunk and entered Father's office. "The padre didn't utter a word, but rose, tapped on the window and motioned to an Indian boy to come over. He quietly told him to get the marshal." Silence was not disturbed even when the Indian policeman entered Father's room; pointing to the culprit sufficed.

> Quick as lightning the marshal grabbed him by the collar of his coat and the seat of his pants and threw him bodily out of the door, where he sprawled headlong into the dust. Such muscular Christianity caught me by surprise and I quickly stepped over to the window to watch further developments.[8]

The marshall then lined up the boys and girls and the young men and maidens and let them pass in line before the drunkard, who had been

---

[7] Mother Mary Katherine Drexel to Most Rev. O'Dea, Bishop of Nisqually, then having the seat of his immense episcopal territory at Vancouver. Letter of February 1, 1901, Ms., ADS.

[8] Rt. Rev. T. M. J. Pypers, "On a Visit," *History of St. Ann's Parish, Spokane, Washington, 1902–1941. And Stories from the Big Bend Missions, 1901–1906,* 78.

tied with his back to a pine tree. The young people pointed fingers of contempt and ridicule at the poor sinner. Then five strong men on horseback helped the man on his own horse and rode off with him several miles distant from the Mission. He was asked to come back after the feast to apologize, which he did. The poor man then "looked like a whipped dog."

Father de Rougé used the time well during a Triduum before the feast to give his Indians as much as possible. They were called several times during the day to early Mass, sermons, instructions, evening devotions, rehearsals; and they showed their earnestness and their reverence so clearly that Father Pypers was greatly edified. "Not a word was said from the time they left their tepees until they returned." They would fold their hands as they entered the enclosed church grounds and would pray.

Father Pypers commented on Chief Smitkin who was not only a good orator but also a generous host. The chief had his home there but pitched his tent right among the people and gave them a treat on the first day. Some young men were sent to round up some of the chief's cattle and returned in no time chasing the animals in front of them.

> The horsemen galloped to their chief for orders and at a signal from him, pulled their rifles from their saddle bags, motioned to each other and fired, and the pick of the band dropped dead amidst the loud cheers of the spectators. In no time the beautiful animals were butchered and distributed to the Indians, but the first and choicest cuts went to their Blackrobe and his guest.[9]

The priestly visitor made some delightful observations on dear old Mrs. Pauline Zacherle. At that time she was enjoying the best of health and was newly married. Her husband was a German boy who had been a lay brother with Father de Rougé for some years.[10] Pauline had been very devout during her girlhood and had wished to become a sister. Her mother, however, violently opposed her; she forcibly removed the crucifix from Pauline's neck. In her desperation and sorrow Pauline consulted Father de Rougé, who, to solve the predicament, finally suggested "that as her mother was insisting on her getting married, and Pauline was not in love with any man, perhaps she should marry this brother."[11] Maybe Father saw that the brother had other inclinations also. Pauline stated that she had been taken to the Ward Mission when seven years old and had stayed there for about eleven to thirteen years,

9 Pypers, *op. cit.*, 80.
10 Nicholson, interview.
11 Cull White quoting Mrs. Isabel Arcasa, Nespelem. Courtesy of Cull White.

and "had a good time there." She learned to play the organ. When she was sick Father de Rougé doctored her. She seemed to be pleased with the choice of husband for her.[12] Father de Rougé married Pauline to John Zacherle in 1901.

One afternoon Father suggested that his visitor watch Pauline who was directing the choir and was practicing Gregorian Chant for the Sunday Mass with a group of young Indians. "She wore modern clothing and a big black shawl about her shoulders. Her actions and her speech showed her convent training." Pauline seems to have waited for just such an opportunity to speak to the visiting priest. Carefully she inquired if perhaps he could write German, and her face became radiant when he said that he could. She wanted a letter written to her husband's mother. The husband probably was not able to write.

> Pauline was the first to suggest that the letter should begin with a word about their marriage, that she had married him because he was such a good Catholic, hoping thereby to make better Christians of her own people. And, of course, it was to be written down that they were married in St. Mary's Church by their beloved Blackrobe, the saintly Father de Rouge. Fritz [John] . . . was more interested to let his mother know how many acres of land they owned and about their stock and crop. . . .[13]

On Corpus Christi, Indians and whites, Christians and pagans filled the church of St. Mary's. The Catholics received their Lord in Holy Communion during the early Mass; later the High Mass was to be celebrated by Father Pypers. The Indian ushers, wearing their ceremonial sashes of office, directed the men to the epistle side and the women to the gospel side. The gallery was filled with the mixed choir of younger Indians and Pauline was at the organ with her papoose tied across her back with her black silk shawl.

> Be it said to the credit of these Indians that their singing was truly praiseworthy, due to the untiring efforts of the priest and the persevering practice of Squaw Pauline. I only wished that my people of the nearby Big Bend Mission could have heard them. My white parishioners would have learned a lot from these Indians.[14]

All had not been quite perfect, however. When Father Pypers used his "full bass voice" to sing the *Dominus Vobiscum,* after the *Gloria,* he "scared the papoose who let out a war whoop, two octaves higher, that

---

[12] Pauline Zacherle, interviews at St. Mary's Mission, May 22, 1960; November 15, 1959.

[13] Pypers, *op. cit.,* 86.

[14] *Ibid.*

almost raised the roof." Pauline had to move her shoulders right and left to rock her baby into being quiet.

Another experience was in store for Father Pypers. The local chief and the leaders of the visiting tribes met on the second evening in Father de Rougé's office for a serious conversation. They wanted the new priest to preach to them on the feast day; Father Pypers excused himself saying that he did not know their language. Chief Smitkin told the visiting priest that this problem was easily solved; he could use any language he wanted and their Black Robe would be the interpreter. The chiefs left "happy as children who have had their wish." Father Pypers then asked Father de Rougé what he wanted said about the Blessed Sacrament as this was the feast of Corpus Christi. The missionary suggested that Father Pypers use what he had preached about lately and add a few words about gambling, drinking, and quarreling in the family. But this was Corpus Christi; it was more appropriate to speak about the feast. The subjects suggested by Father de Rougé were needed more. however, as the priest had these Indians only a few times during the year.

Father Pypers prepared himself to talk about drinking, gambling, and home life. When the feast day came there stood two preachers at the altar, Father Pypers at the gospel side and Father de Rougé on the epistle side. It was a back and forth, "first I then he" performance, the interpreter always having the last word. Finally Father Pypers began to "waver." "The interpreter was getting the upper hand. He knew what I was talking about but I couldn't figure out a word of what he said." Finally it was all over and the congregation seemed to be relieved. Chief Smitkin told Father de Rougé after the services that the visiting priest had been far too strict, but the missionary thanked Father Pypers, remarking that from now on his own words would have greater effect.[15]

The attitude of the Indians toward the whites was expressed on the closing Sunday as Father Pypers was talking to a group of English-speaking Indians. Suddenly white people joined them. Father immediately observed that "right then and there they closed up like clams and hardly a 'yes' or 'no' could I get out of them." When the white were gone and Father asked them for their reasons for acting like this, one of the Indians said:

> Silence is golden when they are around. If we speak their language they'll report us to the big Chief the President, and they'll say that we are civilized, and then we won't get any more money from the Government.[16]

Had it not been for an experienced and calm Indian boy Father Pypers

---

15 Pypers, *op. cit.*, 86.
16 *Ibid.*

would have lost his life on the return trip from St. Mary's Mission. Floodwaters of the Okanogan River had swept away the primitive ferry at Malott. Father's companion from the Mission tied his horse to a tree and found a boat; crossing the river they were caught in a strong current. Only the presence of mind of the boy calling to Father "pull, pull!" saved them. The postmistress who had been watching thought that this might be the end of both. When discussing it later the Indian boy said "that he felt perfectly safe, as there was a priest with him."[17]

Father de Rougé's educational center at Omak Creek was slowly growing into a town. In January, 1903, a post office was established and the little town was allowed to take the name of Omak from the nearby Lake "Omache."[18] Previously the address had been: Mission, Okanogan County. Mr. Octave Corrigan, or as his tombstone has it "Carrignan," owned a ranch in partnership with his brother located below the present town of Omak. They had settled there after the Moses Columbia Reservation had been opened for settlement in 1886. Mr. Octave Corrigan sold out and opened a store at St. Mary's Mission where campers could buy their supplies. The children liked the store; Octave was very generous with his candy and made little profit. This man would spread out his blankets on the counter and go peacefully to sleep at night. Later he could afford to build a little addition for a sleeping room. When there was no business he would help Father de Rougé with the work to be done at the Mission. Often he would haul goods for him. Corrigan's store stood about halfway between the present kitchen and the church. The store owner later moved his store to East Omak when this settlement grew.[19]

During September, 1903, Father de Rougé was answering one of Father Cataldo's letters. The answer shows us his progress and the gradual growth of his parish and also of his educational work:

> The amiable letter of V.R. has overfilled me with consolation, and I can not refuse the desire in it expressed, that I may give some news about our Mission.
>
> First, the region assigned to us is an immense one and the Indians are more numerous than elsewhere. We have about 800 Catholics and 500 infidels all people scattered, on one side about 80 miles and on the other 100 miles from the residence; therefore not all can come to Mass on Sunday. We have to rove around by horse from one tribe to another if we want to do some good; although on the solemn feasts we are con-

---

[17] Pypers, *op. cit.*

[18] *Second Annual Progress Edition, Okanogan County* (*Okanogan Independent*, 1958), 1.

[19] Mrs. Zacherle, interviews.

soled to see 300–500 Indians camped around the church. There are also white people here and there and 400 of them are Catholics.

In our district there are 5 chapels and 2 more are in the process of being built, but they are not enough for the needs and we should have 2 more among the infidels. They are very well disposed and, if I had the time to instruct them there would not be the need to wish for conversions. The Lord of the harvest will send laborers. . . .

Among other things I teach the children; this is only to prepare them for first Communion, because it would be impossible to get them ready otherwise. It is an extreme difficulty to see them often, once they go back to their homes. To my sorrow I see all over schools . . . without religion, attended by a generation which will be irreparably perverted and that will never be sincerely Catholic.

By the mercy of God our schools enjoy a high esteem and, because the white children come to them . . . the Indians believe that they are good for them also. Last year we had only thirty pupils, but should have a hundred. It is true that we are living in great poverty but the occasions are not rare in which we can touch with the hand the delicate solicitude of the Divine Providence towards us. This gives us courage and keeps us contented.[20]

The *History of North Washington* is another source that acquaints us with Father de Rougé's school projects as they were around 1903. The schoolhouse which the Indians had built had become too small and a larger one had to take its place. (This must have been there when Narcisse Nicholson attended in 1899–1900.) Two departments were created at the school, one for whites and one for Indians. Father de Rougé had by this time introduced higher education at his mission school. Beside the elementary subjects, Latin, Greek, higher mathematics, bookkeeping, typewriting, music and art were taught. St. Mary's Mission's famous brass band had then eleven pieces.[21] During the Christmas season the whole population of the countryside, Indians and whites, would assemble at St. Mary's Mission for the solemn religious services and the fine classical entertainment for which Father de Rougé was famous. For the plays he would sew the costumes for his pupils and dress them up himself. Some of his students still tell of the roles they played in Julius Caesar and other classical plays. All through Father de Rougé's time, St. Mary's Mission was the home of the fine arts and of the sciences. The Mission had the first high school and the first junior college in this part of Eastern Washington.

The teacher with the highest qualifications at the school was Father himself. He personally taught Latin and Greek for many years. From

---

[20] De Rougé to Father Cataldo, September 26, 1903 *LDPT*, (1904), 129–130. (Translated by Mr. Louis Botter, Spokane, Wash.)

[21] Richard Steele, ed., *op. cit.*, 488.

1901 to 1906 Mrs. Pauline Zacherle was a faithful helper of Father de Rougé. She taught the three lower grades and played the organ and taught some of the boys how to play the organ. Her husband, John, was the cook. Pauline still gave a helping hand occasionally after they had moved away from the Mission.[22] Two of the first qualified teachers Father de Rougé engaged were Mr. Peter J. Lawless from Toledo, Ohio, and Mr. Leonard R. Savage from Detroit, Michigan. Both had been graduates of Detroit University. Who would not remember some humorous events from his happy school days? One day, Frank, a white boy, came howling to Mr. Savage, with the complaint that another boy had hit him. "Where did he hit you?" the teacher asked. "Between the woodshed and the kitchen."[23] About 1905 Father de Rougé hired an old gentleman, a Mr. Parr, for various purposes.[24]

Mother Katherine Drexel had kept an eye on St. Mary's Mission. We can trace the further development of Father de Rougé's institution through the letters he wrote to his great benefactress. On January 4, 1905, Father wrote:

> Thanks very much for the $40 for masses; it is quite a help to me. All I get goes to my children, and it is double good work for those who send masses. Your letters are a great consolation as I know how you are devoted to the Indians. I have 50 children and hope one day to be able to accommodate more. As I wrote to you I got a check from you for $90. I hope I did not misunderstand you when you wrote you would give me enough to pay two teachers and a cook for my children, each one $30 per month. I had, besides, to take a third helper and teacher, as in a boarding school so much help is needed. I have only seculars and they cannot be treated as religious and be too crowded of work, yet they are, and I have to help all I can to give them a little free time. The good Bishop sent me only $300 this fall which will not even pay our food this term.[25]

Father de Rougé continues to say how grateful he is for the promised help. Now he is hopeful of taking more children into his school next year when he might acquire two Christian Brothers from France. He would need four. Father de Rougé shares his joy with Mother Katherine that he was able to baptize four of his grown children on Christmas. He feels a certain relief now that Mother Katherine will pay the wages, but a big burden is still left on his shoulders. He asks her if she could

---

[22] Mrs. Zacherle, interview.

[23] Hill and Favel, interview.

[24] Harry Van Coelen, Portland, Oregon, interviews at St. Mary's Mission, May 8–10, 1960. Also: Hill and Favel, interviews.

[25] De Rougé to Mother Katherine, January 4, 1905, Ms., ABSS.

not give his address to some benefactors to help him build some more for his children.

Mother Katherine did nothing without consulting the proper authorities, especially if the benefactions would entail big sums. She wrote to the Right Reverend George De La Motte, S.J., then Superior of the Rocky Mountain Mission on the twenty-second of January, 1905, for further information concerning Father de Rougé and his mission. Father De La Motte replied on January 31, 1905, that Father de Rougé deserved the "praises that are bestowed on him, so far as zeal and self-denial are concerned." He told her that Father had worked nearly twenty years among the Okanogans and had learned their language perfectly and he had done much good also among the whites that came into the country, and now he had started a little winter school and kept it open from October until Easter. His only resources were:

1. the money left him by his parents, two or three thousand dollars, I think,
2. a yearly sum of five or six hundred dollars given him by the Rev. Bishop of Nesqually,
3. a few alms collected by him, and the produce of his farm.[26]

But Father De La Motte had his doubts. He was not sure if Father de Rougé would use the money for white children and if he would use the money "as economically as he should."

At times, it has appeared to me that he was going beyond his means, and undertaking too much. As he is far away, in an out of the way section of the country, and traveling a great deal, he has scarcely been visited by his superior, and this accounts for my ignorance in which I am concerning the two points in question. I intend to visit him this spring and I shall then answer your question with a better knowledge of the case.[27]

Another "thank you" letter from Father de Rougé to Mother Katherine is dated February 10. He thanks here for a second check of $90 and expresses appreciation for her precious words of encouragement. He had sent her a little album of his mission so she could picture the place and its problems. Father de Rougé never wrote a letter to Mother Katherine without humbly asking for prayers. He has trouble with his teachers and will have to make some changes. He tells Mother Katherine:

... it is hard to get good men for the work. I do not suppose you would know a gentleman who would for the price we give come here and devote himself to the education of these children. I am not so sure now to be

---

[26] Rt. Rev. George De La Motte, S.J., to Mother Katherine, January 31, 1905, Ms., ABSS.
[27] Ibid.

able to get brothers and even if I would get them I would need a man for the . . . English . . . and Latin.[28]

Father De La Motte wrote a detailed account of his trip to St. Mary's Mission in his *Diary*. He reached Wenatchee on May 12, 1905, at 1:30 a.m. and arrived at Brewster at 5:00 p.m. He was not able to board the steamer *Enterprise,* which was running during May and June from Brewster to Riverside and was stopping at Alma, now Okanogan. The steamer had left that morning and could not make a round trip because it had too much freight. Father De La Motte continued his trip on the 13th by stage to Alma and from there by rig to St. Mary's Mission where he arrived at 5:15 p.m. The next day he visited the Mission, gave the boys an instruction and had a nice entertainment during the evening. He left the Mission on the 15th at 2 p.m. for Alma. He "told Father de Rougé he c' [sic] have a girls' day school in Indian parlor. Try to secure teacher."[29]

This was not merely a winter school teaching only religion that Father De La Motte found in session during the middle of May. He saw that girls needed education as well as the boys and offered his help.

Father De La Motte was eager to let Mother Katherine know the results of his investigation and visit to St. Mary's. On the 17th of May when he had arrived at Seattle he wrote:

> I have visited good Father de Rougé's Mission in Okenagan, and I hasten to send you the results of my visit. I have been more than pleased with all I have seen. Fr. de Rouge has truly done wonders. The spiritual results are excellent, and are evidently due to supernatural intervention: they are the fruits of holy poverty and abandonment to God's Providence. With very scanty means, Fr. de Rougé has built a very creditable little school house, where he keeps 40 boys. Each of every dollar he has received in the past ten years, he has drawn a hundred cents; nothing was lost. Necessity has taught him to apply to the Indians themselves for assistance, and he has succeeded better than any other father in doing so. They clothe their children, and help here and there besides, in hauling wood for instance. Fr. de Rougé is very prudent, and knows how to wait when means are not forthcoming.[30]

The second half of Father Da La Motte's long letter brings home to us the importance of the problems discussed with this great benefactress. On the solving of these depended the future success of St. Mary's Mission as an educational institution:

> Now, Reverend Mother, allow me to suggest how you could help the good father substantially. I intend to obtain for his school the services

[28] De Rougé to Mother Katherine, February 10, 1905, Ms., ABSS.
[29] De La Motte, *Diary*, 33, Mss., OPA.
[30] De La Motte to Mother Katherine, May 17th, 1905, Ms., ABSS.

of two Brothers of . . . a French community that are now dispersed. I have these brothers in several missions already where they do well. For each Brother, I must pay $250.00 per year to the Mother house; said money defraying all expenses, clothing, transportation, and so on. If you could give the father or me $500.00 every year, this would be a great help. Moreover, I have strongly urged the father to start a Day school for the Okenagan girls that live in the neighborhood. He could use his parlor for that purpose. We will have to look for a teacher. I may obtain 2 Ursuline nuns for that work, and we would like to be able to offer a little compensation of $10.00 a month to each Sister, or $20.00 if we use a lay teacher. I may be asking too much. In that case, dear Mother, please, do what you may think best in the Lord, and we will trust, to Divine Providence for the rest. Fr. de Rougé will need some more assistance to improve the dormitories; but I trust I may be able to obtain funds for that purpose from some other quarter.

Father de Rougé has a few white boys in his school, who are a help to the Indian boys; but these white boys pay for their board. In a word, Reverend Mother, all my doubts I had concerning the managements of Fr. de Rougé's school have been solved. He is a hard worker, and very skillful. It is a pleasure for me to recommend him to your charity, for every cent he receives is well spent.[31]

Truly, Father de Rougé could not have had a better recommendation from his superior. It is to be deeply regretted that Mother Katherine's correspondence with Father de Rougé was not preserved and protected. It was either destroyed or was burned in 1919 when the so-called College burned. Here were two saintly souls inspiring each other; two souls that had the same goals, namely, the education and care of the neglected Indians. How precious must have been Mother Katherine's encouraging letters! Father de Rougé in turn told her of his difficulties, his needs, and his many projects. While many of Mother Katherine's benefactions were handled through the Catholic Indian Bureau in Washington, D. C., the help given to St. Mary's Mission was always attended to by Mother Katherine herself.

Mother Katherine answered Father De La Motte's letter on May 23 and promised to give Father de Rougé "$500 for two Brothers, $30.00 a month for a cook, and $20.00 a month for a lay teacher or two Ursuline nuns who are to teach the Okanogan girls." Father de la Motte thanked Mother Katherine on June 9, 1905, for this generous offer of help. If two Brothers would take over the teaching they would take the place of the two seculars for which she had paid this year. The two teachers were as "good as could be desired, but the main trouble with seculars is that we can never be sure to keep them. They have a future to provide for. . . ."

---

[31] De La Motte to Mother Katherine, May 17, 1905.

Mother Katherine had inquired about the Congregation of Brothers Father De La Motte wanted for St. Mary's Mission, as no doubt in some of her other missions, she needed them too. Father de la Motte tells her that

> . . . their Congregation is a model one. They were founded in Britanny (France) by the holy Father Lamennais (brother of the unfortunate apostate of the same name). This Father de Lamennais will soon be upon the altars. The brothers are about 2000 now, mostly all Britons (Britons are the best part of the French nation, without the least doubt, steady, thorough, full of faith). Their formation is splendid. They join the order very young, and I know it for certain that less than 5% leave the order. . . .[32]

Father de Rougé received a check of $650 from Mother Katherine in the meantime. He had the children pray especially for this kind Mother's intentions. She had asked him about his plans for the new school year. He tells her of his hopes to get the Brothers, but that he still needs to keep one of the seculars for $30 per month. If he could not get the Sisters, he would have to engage a lady. He urgently requests Mother Katherine to pray with him that he might have Sisters next year and asks her to pray for his boys. He soon would let them go home; "may their guardian angels take care of them till they come back and keep them from sin."[33]

This last point "to keep them from sin" was so important to Father de Rougé that in his constant struggle to provide for the needed food for his students he did not hesitate to keep the boys in school another month, even if it meant more sacrifices to himself and many more begging letters. The fourth of July celebrations were quite wild adventures

---

[32] De La Motte to Mother Katherine, June 9, 1905, Ms., ABSS. "They are formed to teach boys of the poorer classes, and have a number of parochial schools. They also have a few boarding schools and some industrial schools. Their success in moulding characters is marvelous in France and all French colonies. Of this I am certain. Their only drawback in this country comes from the English language. It is so very hard for French people to acquire a pure English pronunciation. I have four years ago secured 15 of their young men and given them a whole year of study in one of our Missions. They have picked up the language with amazing rapidity, but their pronunciation has remained defective. It is true that they had little facilities to acquire it. Their Brother General has sent a number of them to Ireland, and founded quite an establishment somewhere in the State of New York; and I think that the young men who will have passed through either of these places will have a good pronunciation; but I am not sure of it. In a word, Reverend Mother, I do not hesitate to recommend these good Brothers to you for your noble work, if the Brothers are given sufficient facilities to acquire a good English pronunciation. In point of talent, devotedness, and religious spirit, they are the best Brothers I know of.

[33] De Rougé to Mother Katherine, June 2, 1905, Ms., ABSS.

during pioneer days. Father's former students have told how he kept them in school until the overflowing spirits of frontier merrymaking were somewhat subdued.[34] Quite a few children stayed at the mission during the summer months. Father always had some orphan boys or children who had no home for whom he tried to substitute as father and mother. Mrs. Pauline Zacherle saw Father de Rougé sewing quilts with his own hands for two of the orphan boys who were there during her stay at the Mission. She wanted to take this work, but Father replied, "Oh no, I can do it myself."[35]

The annual reports of Father de Rougé to Bishop O'Dea give important information about the development of the school at St. Mary's Mission:

> 1896 — $12 are received for the school
> 1897 — 12 boys and 10 girls attended the school
> 1898 — $229.30 expenses for the school
> 1899 — 17 boys and 4 girls attended the school
> 1900 — 10 boys and 5 girls attended the school
> 1901 — 25 boys and 5 girls attended the school
> 1902 — $500 expenses for the school
> 1903 — 31 boys and 10 girls attended the school
> 1904 — 41 boys and 12 girls attended the school
> 1905 — 40 boys and 10 girls attended the school
>   4 teachers paid $750
>   Mother Katherine contributed $270
> 1906 — 53 boys and 13 girls attended the school
>   Mother Katherine contributed $1,170
> 1907 — 50 boys and 9 girls attended the school
>   Mother Katherine contributed $2,110
> 1908 — 39 boys and 18 girls attended the school
>   Mother Katherine contributed $1,670
> $700 expenses for girls' school
> 1909 — 50 boys and 49 girls attended the school
>   Mother Katherine contributed $2,989
>   Catholic Bureau contributed $2,754
> $1,000 expenses for girls' school
> $1,000 expenses for new church
> 1910 — 63 boys and 37 girls attended the school
>   Mother Katherine contributed $4,925
>   Catholic Bureau contributed $ 459
>   Schools contributed $ 696.50[36]

Mother Katherine read Father de Rougé's letters carefully. She knew how to glean from his words some undercurrents of his thoughts and

---

[34] John Cleveland, interviews at St. Mary's Mission, 1959 and 1960.
[35] Pauline Zacherle, interviews.
[36] De Rougé, *Annual Reports, 1896–1910*, Mss., ADS.

needs, to read between the lines. Another check for $90 arrived when Father had least expected it. He writes:

> May God almighty reward you as we pray and ask Him to do. You speak kindly again about the dormitory — it will take a new building, very urgent. The first floor being a room for the little ones and [the] top for the dormitory. This building will cost me about $600, with the furnishings of beds, etc.[37]

Mother Katherine had asked him about his plans for taking more boys into his school.

In the meantime Father de Rougé had another inspiration. He tells Mother Katherine on August 16, 1905, that after he had written the thought came to him that, if she agrees, this $600 could be used to build a house for the girls. He will have two Sisters this fall and today he has started the carpenters on a house 30 x 18 feet.

> It is all I can build for them now. They will not be able to take the girls till I can get some money to build. They will have to come to my parlor to teach the girls of the camp and of course many girls will not have the benefit of the school till I can take them in. So, dear Mother, it would be a fine way to use the money A.M.D.G.[38]

This tiny house became later the beginning of the girls' school.

We were not able to discover any mention by Father de Rougé himself of the arrival of the long expected Brothers. Father D'Aste's *Diary* mentions that two Lamennais Brothers left for St. Mary's Mission on September 5, 1905.[39] Harry Van Coelen remarked that the first Brothers arrived September, 1905, and were replaced the following year. Father de Rougé was not on good terms with them.[40] Francis Favel affirmed this and said that Brother Barnabee had been his teacher during that year. When asked why Father de Rougé had difficulties, Mr. Favel stated that Brother Barnabee had formerly been a French army man and was very determined.[41] Nobody seems to remember the name of the smaller brother.

Father de Rougé did not expect Mother Katherine to do all the charity for his mission; he explored various means to raise money. His boys were quite a help to him. They would take the telephone directories of diverse cities and mail thousands of mimeographed letters asking alms for their school. Once some boys considering this quite an adventure, signed

---

[37] De Rougé to Mother Katherine, June 19, 1905, Ms., ABSS.
[38] De Rougé to Mother Katherine, August 16, 1905, Ms., ABSS.
[39] Rev. Jerome D'Aste, S.J., *Diary*, September 5, 1905, Mss., OPA.
[40] Van Coelen, interviews.
[41] Favel, interview.

their names as "Buffalo Bill, Sitting Bull, Big Bull" and other glamorous names, a practice which Father de Rougé soon discouraged.[42] To have their own post office and to do the work connected with it gave Father de Rougé's boys some practical lessons in civics.

A letter of February 23, 1906, informs us that Father's school increased its enrollment to 42 Indian children and some whites. The educator says that he needs the white children to teach the Indian children how to speak English. We have seen how careful he was in the presence of the old Indian people; he wanted them to feel at ease at the Mission when speaking their language. Now Father observed how only gradually English came to be spoken around the place. He remarks, "All are surprised to see how my Indian boys speak English."[43] Gradually, as more white people came to the Mission, Father would preach in both Indian and in English.

The same letter states that the missionary has engaged a special teacher for the whites and that he also asked a lady to teach a few girls of the camp until Sisters would take over.[44] This places the beginning of the special education of the girls in the school year 1905–1906. The first three girl pupils are still proud of the event; they were Mrs. Lilian Brady-Best, Mrs. Josephine Carden-Marchant, and Mrs. Agnes Robbinett from Monse. It was a great privilege in the great pioneer territory to have a school for the children, especially the girls. Therefore, the families were glad to make the sacrifice and move nearer to the Mission during the school year. The classroom was only two doors from Father's office. Old Mr. Parr was one of the teachers; Mrs. Pauline Zacherle taught the first three grades. The girls went to Mass, then home for breakfast; they came back to school at nine o'clock; at 11:30 they went home for dinner; from 1:00 to 4:00 they were in school again. At four o'clock Father de Rougé would go with the girls to church to say the Rosary and night prayers and then the girls were dismissed. Father de Rougé was very strict in permitting absolutely no mixing of boys and girls. Mrs. Best gave the names of fourteen girls who attended the Day School: Nancy Whitmore, Josephine and Caroline Carden, Madeleine Smitkin, Harriet Snowjacks, Alice and Ida Ingrim, Christine Jewt, Martha Alex, and a certain Mathilde. After two years of school attendance Father de Rougé wanted Mrs. Best to continue her schooling at St. Francis Regis Mission's Sacred Heart School.[45]

---

[42] Van Coelen, interview.
[43] De Rougé to Mother Katherine, February 23, 1906, Ms., ABSS.
[44] Ibid.
[45] Mrs. Lilian Brady-Best, interview at St. Mary's, August 14, 1960.

Father de Rougé traveled and visited his extensive parish territory during vacation time. He kept a lively interest in the problems of his dear parishioners and they in turn would look forward to seeing him again at his Mission. Many of his old Indian people would put white men to shame who consider themselves good Christians. There was a certain magnanimity and nobility of heart in the Indians not found too often among whites. An example of this was Mrs. Matilda Wapato, the mother of Dr. Paschal Sherman, one of Father de Rougé's honor students. Mrs. Wapato was called to attend the murder trial of the son of her husband's brother who had shot Mrs. Wapato's husband in the year of 1905. A dispute about family property had caused the attack. Mrs. Matilda Wapato made a sudden end of the murder trial, yet her grief must have been profound:

> Suddenly she stepped down from the witness chair and faced the jurymen . . . with tears coursing down her cheeks, she spoke and gestured eloquently — 'Me man dead. He go setting sun. He go up there. Hang him by neck — ' and she pointed at Ignatius, who was on trial, 'Make him die. Would this second die bring back my boys' father? Hang him by neck you acurse him before God. Me no like that. Me no like my family defiled before God. No good. Me witness no more.[46]

Even while traveling the priest was occupied with his mission school, as a letter of July 16, 1906, shows us. He was rereading a note his superior had sent him the previous year telling him that Mother Katherine had promised $20 a month for a lady or two Sisters. Before Father De La Motte left for Europe he had written to Father de Rougé "to make all arrangements and be ready for the Sisters for this next term." But, Father de Rougé writes: "Dear Mother, $20 a month will never support the school for girls." The Sisters were supposed to come last year but they did not; Father would have to take ladies.[47]

More history is told in a thank-you letter writter by Father de Rougé to Mother Katherine during August of the same year:

> May the souls saved be your crown in heaven. I will have a lamp burned before the Blessed Sacrament for your intentions for nine days. This will be anyway a little present in return. I am looking every day for an answer from the Ursulines, if they cannot accept I will take another teacher. I have two fine brothers now ready to start school. I should have . . . 100 children but the means are short.[48]

---

[46] Mrs. Matilda Wapato quoted in "Death of Paul Wapato Brings to Light History of Indian Family," *The Wenatchee Daily World,* [n.d. and n.p.].
[47] De Rougé to Mother Katherine, August 6, 1906, Ms., ABSS.
[48] *Ibid.*

The priest makes no mention anywhere of the first two. Brothers. Now the second two had arrived and Father is satisfied, mentioning "two fine brothers." These were Brothers Celestine and Rene; later additional help was given by Brother Hypolite. All three of them were excellent teachers and musicians. Brother Celestine, an expert taxidermist, started a museum. The first animal exhibited was a seagull from Omak Lake. Soon the Indians became interested and brought all kinds of rare animals and birds to be stuffed.[49]

Father de Rougé had a hard time gathering his children for the beginning of the school year. The love of freedom in the Indian boys was strong. Often the Indian police would have to be sent to bring the stragglers in. Everybody and everything was disinfected; for two weeks the dormitory would smell of the carbolic acid. Father saw to it that both Indian boys and white boys kept their hair short; he himself would clip it.[50] Narcisse tells that when he went to school at St. Mary's, one day there came two big fellows from Wenatchee who wore braids. One of them put up quite a fight with Father de Rougé but finally sacrificed the braids.[51] These were some of the jobs the Count de Rougé had to perform.

Father de Rougé had returned August 29, 1906, from one of his missionary journeys that had taken longer than a week. He was tired and exhausted but happy to find another precious letter from Mother Katherine that showed so much interest in his Mission. He complains to this good Mother that the Sisters have not written to let him know about their coming. He is starting his day school for the girls anyway next Monday and has the old gentleman to teach them. He is also corresponding with a lady to come and take over. Mother Katherine most probably had asked him to state what he would need.

> What would be the most important help for me to support the Indian children this season as I have so much trouble to do it. Anything you feel to do for them to feed them the whole year and buy things necessary as books, music instruments, clothing, blankets, chairs and other furniture, would be the most practical. If I say this so freely, dear Mother, it is because you asked me.[52]

Father de Rougé would like to build a boarding school for the girls, when he gets permission. For the present they are day students. Yet, he wished to build a house for them where they would be under the super-

[49] All the former students are full of praise for the three Brothers and their teaching. The boys were proud of their museum; this was expressed in every interview.
[50] Van Coelen, interview.
[51] Nicholson, interview.
[52] De Rougé to Mother Katherine, August 29, 1906, Ms., ABSS.

vision of an Indian family and not wandering all over the camp. This would be a start toward the regular boarding school. Father then had some happy news to convey to his benefactors: "The agent was here and told the Indians that this was the best school in the country and that he was not saying this because he is a Catholic as he is not."[53]

Sister Mercedes had sent a check for $270 in the name of Mother Katherine. Father thanks her for it and says that all his fortune had been $25 when her letter arrived. He needs to buy winter provisions, books, and fire wood. "I have made many improvements this season with all I could save and yet my buildings will be full."[54] These improvements were rather extensive in the direction of added space. He had three teachers in addition to Mr. Parr for the girls. The expanded high school and college program needed classrooms, a museum, a music room, a special section for the smaller boys. Before the Brothers had come, Father had the roof of the school building removed, replaced the stairs and built another complete story in order to have dormitory facilities for the whites and for the Indian boys on the second floor.[55] Thus the first set of buildings grew slowly piece by piece.

Father de Rougé never was free of financial trouble as long as he lived. His was a life of constant struggle to build up and to maintain his school for God's poor Indians. It seems that the difficulties coming up challenged the spiritual forces of his soul and that in this way the problems he had to solve and the obstacles he had to overcome became a source of new energy, courage, and complete trust in God's Providence.

John and Pauline Zacherle, the cook and the teacher, had to leave their jobs to take care of their growing family. Father de Rougé now had teachers but no cook. He had to take a Japanese for the purpose and pay him $45 monthly. The priest wrote Mother Katherine that he is sure she will save him again and he is so thankful that she understands his situation so well.

> Some days I feel so bad not knowing what will be next, that I cannot sleep at night. But Providence is good. I have yet to beg much and try to make the ends meet. I . . . wrote several letters but so far no answer. Its the work of God and sure He will see to it. Yes, we will pray for your intentions and the boys will offer 9 Holy Communions for you. I could not give anything to the Brothers yet . . . as I have no money. We had a bad crop this year, as I had no farmer last year of the season to attend to things the proper way.[56]

---

[53] De Rougé to Mother Katherine, August 29, 1906.
[54] De Rougé to Mother Mercedes, September 27, 1906, Ms., ABSS.
[55] Van Coelen, interview.
[56] De Rougé to Mother Katherine, October 10, 1906, Ms., ABSS.

Father stresses again at some length the problem so dear to his priestly heart: how to keep his boys out of temptation. He asks Mother Katherine if she will pray for a boy who is so much troubled by the temptations of the devil. "Help me to save his soul." This boy is one of the best of his school and will spread good influence if he stays at the Mission; also his brother gives much trouble to the family. "The father is an infidel white man, or rather, the stepfather, but he likes me and tries with me to save the boys. Let us pray for his conversion."[57] These were half-breeds and would be a fine credit to Father's school. The oldest tells the priest that this is his last year at the Mission. "He must be saved, and should not even leave this place at all, even when possible, but as long as he is here he is a holy boy." Father de Rougé considers Mother Katherine as his helper in saving the souls of his boys. He asks her: "Pray for me, that the courage does not fail me. That I may be holy myself to sanctify the others." Father is thankful for the good news from his former student Louis Runnels. He "was so sorry to see him go."[58]

This anxious care for half-breeds expressed by Father de Rougé had its historical foundation. Mr. Cull White told the author that when other church societies came slowly into the Okanogan Valley, they looked with disdain on white men who had married Indian women.[59] Some very respectable men, such as George W. Runnels (Tennas George), the father of Louis Runnels, who was respected by Indians and whites and was very active in the early mining business, sent their children to the East rather than have them looked upon with contempt because they were only half-breeds.

Carlisle had opened its door to the Indian youth of various tribes and its agents made propaganda trips to the West. The children of Indian parents often were taken away without the free consent of their parents. These government agents knew how to intimidate the people and how to make attractive promises. Quite a few children from the Colville Reservation attended school either at Carlisle, at Chemawa, or at the government school, Fort Spokane. To the great sorrow of their parents some of the children never returned from the East. Carlisle had been more or less only an industrial school, while at St. Mary's the academic subjects were stressed also. Responsible men finally saw the injustice done to Indian parents and to their offspring as can be seen in a report of the Commissioner of Indian Affairs:

The idea of bringing East the entire 30,000 red children now in school

---

[57] De Rougé to Mother Katherine, October 10, 1906.

[58] *Ibid.*

[59] Cull White, interview at Spokane, January 7, 1961.

and of educating, civilizing, and settling them in the East is a fantastic dream which has not been and can not be realized. A fair trial of twenty years has been given this theory, and the paucity of results is amazing.[60]

Mr. William Hill as a boy had attended the Fort Spokane School. He was supposed to be in the third grade. When he left there, he knew as much as when he entered: the alphabet up to the G. He had to start the first grade at St. Mary's Mission and ended by graduating from college two years after he left St. Mary's.[61]

Mr. J. P. Trodden, formerly from Chesaw and now living in Bellingham, attended St. Mary's Mission School with his brother from 1905–1907. His mother had been the school cook during the first year. We give some excerpts from his letter:

> I remember an Indian (Chief Smitkin) who lived near the school and had donated part of the land for the school. His son Paul went to school with us. I remember the Chief taking off his coat and joining us boys in a football game, several times and wearing his Buckskin Moccasins, he could outrun all of us. . . . When Father de Rouge went on trips it was with buggy and team of horses. We had a 17 piece band and I was a member of the band and one of the youngest. . . . The present City of Okanogan was called Alma and the County Court House was at Conconully. The City of Omak had not been born yet. . . . Mail addressed to us was to St. Mary's Mission, Omak, Post Office, Wash. The Indians came for Mass from miles around and I still can remember the older ladies had a kind of singing Chant at Church. . . . The learning I received there surely helped me in later years and I have many memories of Father de Rouge. . . .[62]

On April 21, 1907, Father de Rougé again thanked Mother Katherine for two checks he had received. He is still waiting for Sisters to come and has just returned from a week of missionary journeys.[63] Father is worried about his girl's school; he may have to let the girls go. "It seems impossible to get sisters after I built a fine little house for them last year."[64]He asked for prayers for the girls. "Let Holy Providence see about these girls." The educator had his hands full with his boys and he is building more for them.[65]

---

[60] Francis E. Leupp, "Report of the Commissioner of Indian Affairs," Annual Report of the Department of the Interior, Fiscal Year Ending June 30, 1904, *House of Representatives, Fifty-Eighth Congress, Document No. 5, Indian Affairs* (Part I), 33.

[61] Hill, interview at Spokane, September 18, 1960.

[62] J. P. Trodden, Bellingham, Wash., to the author, August 22, 1960.

[63] De Rougé to Mother Katherine, April 21, 1907, Ms., ABSS.

[64] De Rougé to Mother Katherine, to Mother Mercedes, July 11, 1907, Ms., ABSS.

[65] *Ibid.*

As he writes to Mother Katherine again on August 28, he tells her all his worries and all his money troubles. The kind and understanding Mother had firsthand experience in mission work. How precious must have been her letters and encouraging words! Father writes:

> Sure I thought Holy Providence will not abandon me, all I do is not for me, but for the souls. Anyway discouragement was coming, and if it was not the good of the souls of these boys, (I know they would be entirely lost), I do not know what I would have done.[66]

Father had not paid his farmer since spring; he enumerates his debts; he has not eaten any meat all summer in order to save. He never went for a vacation. Now he should buy provisions for the winter. He had trouble again with the cook, who now receives $50 per month.

Then follows some more consoling news. Father intends to take some girls as day students later. He had tried to send some of them to the Sisters' school at Colville, but the Sisters wrote that they could not take more. Now the Jesuit educator concentrates upon the school of older boys. "If we keep boys only till 15 or so," he writes, "and then not take them back, it is to abandon them at the worst time of their age." He tells how happy the boys were to be back and how they love their school; how he plans to level the baseball ground and do other things to attract his boys. He hope to buy more musical instruments, "but first we must live."

Father continues to speak about all the work to be done at a boarding school. The two Brothers each have a class and teach the music. They take turns also in supervision day and night and they are very busy. Mr. Parr, the old gentleman, will have to take over the care of the little boys; besides he is in charge of the clothing. Father is trying hard to hire a woman to care for the clothing but has not been successful. He teaches some classes also and does some prefecting, besides caring for the parish and many other things.[67]

The need for women's help became more and more apparent. Children need mothers wherever they are. Father de Rougé knew that if he wanted to raise the status of the women and of family life on the reservation he needed a school for the girls and women to teach them not only as day students but in a boarding school. The training in more civilized home-living and housekeeping could not be accomplished by teaching the girls and then by sending them back into the tepee. Also women's hands were needed to take care of the altar linens, the washing, mending, and sewing.

---

[66] De Rougé to Mother Katherine, August 28, 1907, Ms., ABSS.
[67] *Ibid.*

Harry Van Coelen was Father de Rougé's companion when in August, 1907, the priest made a trip which resulted in finding a woman, Mrs. La Londe, who in December of 1907 became the first of his woman missionaries. They went first to Riverside on a two horse team. About a half mile below what is today Tonasket, a Mr. Perry had a store, a saloon, and a ferry. They went across the ferry and proceeded north and stayed overnight at a farm house, probably belonging to people by the name of Hone. Father and mother slept in the kitchen, three girls and a boy climbed a ladder and slept in the attic. The bedroom was reserved for Father and his companion. The next night they arrived at Favel's place, about fourteen miles toward Republic, where they stayed for three days. Everywhere Father came he gave the people an opportunity to receive the sacraments. From here they went to a trader's place somewhere in the mountains and stayed one night. They climbed the hills near Kepling and came upon a little cabin belonging to Mrs. La Londe. She must have known of the priest's impending visit for she was cooking a chicken. She let the travelers have the cabin by themselves. Next morning quite a few people came to Mass, which Father said on top of a sewing machine. After breakfast our wanderers went to the log house of the Poitras. The two girls there were Mrs. La Londe's nieces, Agnes and Edna, who joined her later at St. Mary's Mission for some time.

After administering for three or four days to the people of the hills they returned to Riverside and stayed in the front room of a merchant's house. Here Harry made the acquaintance of bed bugs and exchanged the bed for the floor while the dead tired "Count de Rougé" slept with the bugs.[68]

What a relief it must have been when Mother Katherine's check for $630 arrived. The work of Father de Rougé was highly appreciated by the early community leaders. Father remarks to Mother Katherine, "I have the great blessing that all our civil authorities are so kind to me and anxious to help me."[69]

Father de Rougé would give his boys experiences to prepare them for later life by taking them along to larger cities. Most Reverend Bishop O'Dea regretted that he was not able to visit St. Mary's Mission to administer Confirmation. He was busily preparing for the dedication of his cathedral which he hoped might be in September, 1907.[70] Francis Favel values happy memories of the time when he was allowed to accompany Father to Seattle for this event.[71]

[68] Van Coelen, interviews.
[69] De Rougé to Mother Katherine, September 12, 1907, Ms., ABSS.
[70] Most Rev. O'Dea to De Rougé, March 20, 1907, Ms. copy, ADS.
[71] Favel, interview.

Mr. Van Coelen told the author how hard it was when no ice boxes and freezers existed to preserve the meat for so many people. All had to be either dried or salted. During the winter of 1907 Father de Rougé wanted to make an ice house. The boys had to haul the ice from Omak Lake and place it in one of the root cellars they had along the hill. It did not work; the ice melted when spring came.[72]

Looking back over the long years since 1885, Father de Rougé could see outstanding accomplishments in the field of education. At a time when many white settlers were not able to have their children attend school, either because there was no school or the distance was too great, Father de Rougé already had a kindergarten, an elementary school, a high school, and a junior college for his Indian boys. The incoming white settlers considered themselves fortunate if there was a place for their boys in Father de Rougé's school.

This mixing of races of God's children, this give and take exchange of two different cultures, an aboriginal culture with natural virtues and a Christian one with supernatural virtues, practiced first of all by Father de Rougé and instilled into his students, became an inspiration for the Okanogan Valley, eastern Washington and a great part of British Columbia. The population of the surrounding country for hundreds of miles would eagerly watch for news from the Mission, their only social and cultural center for many years. They shared in the fruits of the careful education given Father de Rougé's boys when on Church feasts, not only their religious needs were satisfied, but also their intellectual and social needs in the form of concerts, plays, and games.

By 1907, Father de Rougé's first set of buildings was so far completed and his school for the boys was well established. The arrival of Mrs. La Londe and her two nieces in December brightened his outlook for building a boarding school for girls. A happy Christmas present was waiting for him at the end of 1907, an annual pension from his mother of 8600 francs for the Mission. Father De La Motte put two limitations upon its use: that it be used for the Indian boys exclusively, and only with the consent of the "Superior of Colville or of the general Superior."[73]

---

[72] Van Coelen, interviews.
[73] De La Motte, S.J., *Diary*, Mss., OPA.

Ladies Catechists Missionaries of St. Mary's Mission

IN A letter written January 21, 1908, Father de Rougé thanks Mother Katherine for promising to take care of the "ladies teachers." But he notices that she has not mentioned paying for the old gentleman who is now "at the head of the general washing and takes care of the little boys." Otherwise the two Brothers would have too much to do. Then Father tells Mother Katherine of the arrival of the first Catechists, Madame La Londe and her two nieces:

> You can begin your payment from Dec. if you want as the ladies came in Dec. I am anxious to get some more, and will try to get some who would give their lives to the mission, but will I succeed? I have them enrolled already in the sodality of the Catechists of the institution. This is my plan as I can not get sisters. May Holy Providence send me help, I should have ten in place of two, and if I can get some as sisters it will not cost so much. I am sure your good prayers will help me much in the enterprise.[1]

Now that Father de Rougé has ladies to help him, he intends to make an end of the day school for girls. The school term of the girls had started late in the year of 1907 as he had said. St. Mary's Mission Day School for Girls existed only during the years of 1905–1908. Gradually boarders were accepted. To be able to achieve his objective in making a complete separation between the school for boys and another for girls only, Father needed a schoolhouse that would serve as a boarding school. He had built a little two-room house in 1905 when he had expected the help of the Ursuline nuns. This small building stood at a distance from his boys' school at the foot of a very rocky hill. Through the following years several additions were added.

---

[1] De Rougé to Mother Katherine, January 21, 1908, Ms., ABSS.

On February 18, 1908, Father de Rougé already had four loads of lumber for his boarding school for girls, lumber purchased with money collected from the people who had settled in the valley.

> The plan is to build 50 by 26, as a wing of a building to be going on later on. For the present it would be divided in two rooms downstairs, and dormitory and room for the Catechists upstairs. The little house now, 30 by 18 would be divided in kitchen and dining room.[2]

Father de Rougé knew that he could not accommodate all of the girls who would ask for admittance; he intended to take twenty girls only for the beginning. He would need, in addition to the first building, a laundry and "outside buildings and sheds." According to his means he would go ahead with his plans. He needed a special department for his little boys, and women to care for them. He had to take the little boys in order to keep them away from the government schools where parents, who did not care for them, would place them. "Not one from the tribes around ever came back from the government school and can be called a Catholic now." He says, "I have also to try to get Ladies to teach and try to have them as Catechists, that is at a small pay. . . ."[3] On the same day when he wrote to Mother Katherine, Father also thanked Sister Mary James who had sent $525 in the name of Mother Katherine.[4]

Father de Rougé applied to Catholic papers and magazines, especially to *Extension,* to publish his need for Lady Catechist Missionaries.[5] Quite a few responded to the call. The applicants were received under quite rigorous conditions by Father de Rougé:

> After 45 years of age as a rule one should not be admitted. Exception may be made in case of extra good qualities of spirit or talent, such as music teacher, good cook, or perfect good health. . . .
> It would be no use to apply if one is sickly, has to be under special treatment, use extraordinary medicines all the time or not able to be depended upon for the house work.
> No one can expect exception to the rule as to food except in some special case as it may happen to anyone and any place. The applicant must give a plain account of her health before [being] admitted. . . .
> Once here no one must have excuses not to be able to do this or to do that. In case of doubt, a doctor's certificate or statement could be sent.[6]

---

[2] De Rougé to Mother Katherine, February 18, 1908.

[3] *Ibid.*

[4] De Rougé to Sister Mary James, February 18, 1908, Mss., ABSS.

[5] Sister M. Michael, O.P., the former Madame Foster, interviews in Spokane, Wash.

[6] De Rougé, *Applicants as Catechists Missionaries to St. Mary's Mission,* mimeographed copy, OPA.

He goes into detail about the duties of the women helpers: They are to take complete care of all the needs of the children — their food, cleanliness, clothes, health, and industry.

A questionnaire of twenty-four inquiries had to be answered by each applicant. Besides this an agreement had to be signed.[7] Further instructions told what each of the Catechists had to bring (the priest's English is, as usual, characteristic):

> Let each one bring the clothing she has. Do not bring useless things, which overload the trunks. Trunks cost much especially on the stage. Bring clothing enough to last quite a while, (say two years.) Bring black to make two dresses, veils, and long coat. A black shawl. Bedding enough for winter, 4 changes of sheets, pillow cases, towels, and napkins. If you are afraid to have too much baggage, you can as well buy these things here as soon as you arrive, and save extra baggage charges. If you have a few spoons, forks and knives, just as well bring. If one is poor let her bring what she has.[8]

All these prerequisites show that Father de Rougé did not have in mind the founding of merely a group of lay apostles. The applicants too thought they were entering a regular convent not only with its sacrifices but also with its privileges. Former Ladies Missionaries told the author that they were never told that they were greatly astonished when they learned that they were not entering a regular community. It seems to us, we regret to admit, that Father de Rougé merely used this approach in order to obtain cheap workers for his mission.

Father de Rougé's correspondence with Bishop O'Dea of Seattle shows that the Bishop was not in favor of founding a community. On September 12, 1908, Father de Rougé started this correspondence about the coming of Sisters:

> I just got a letter from Sister Gertrude, Dominican Tertiary, 310 Pleasant Ave., New York, who with 5 sisters seems very anxious to come here. She gives for reference Right Rev. Bis. Cusack, Aux. Bis. 142 E.

---

[7] De Rougé Agreement, mimeographed copy, SM. "In the event of my acceptance in the Society of the Lady Missionaries of St. Mary's maintained at the St. Mary's Mission, Omak, Washington, by the Pioneer Educational Society, of the Reverend Jesuit Fathers, I agree that aside from the home and shelter furnished me, that I will not claim compensation for any services performed while a member thereof; that I will persevere in the vocation I am seeking to the best of my abilities, that I will acknowledge and accept the authority of the Superiors in charge of said Mission and Society, including their authority to dismiss members as its interest may require. I agree that should I not persevere in my vocation, I will not ask to have my fare to St. Mary's Mission reimbursed. I shall pay my traveling expenses back home."

[8] De Rougé, To Applicants Catechists Missionaries Coming to St. Mary's Mission, mimeographed copy, OPA.

29 and Rev. D. J. McMahon, D.D. 239 E. 21, their spiritual director.
Now before to make any application which I will not make till I hear
from the sister again to know exactly with what conditions they would
come here, I like to know in order to save time, if your Lordship would
have any objections to their coming, or would willingly accept them. . . .
As soon as the sister writes, if everything is satisfactory to the superiors,
they will then make the regular application. I will kindly ask your Lordship not to go to any trouble about it till I hear from the sister.[9]

September 16, 1908.
    I will send to your Lordship the letter of the sister in question. Rev.
Father Superior writes that it is all in your Lordship's hands, and if you
approve of their coming, he is satisfied.[10]

September 24, 1908.
    I hope everything will be alright, as it is a shame to see here all the
girls abandoned for such a long time . . . all to whom I applied refused
to come for a reason or another. . . . some sisters are very particular
to get so much a year, and here I could not give them enough to satisfy
them. Sister Gertrude seems well disposed and full of courage, and I am
in a hurry to know what can be done as the bad season will come soon,
also the school term is started. . . .[11]

September 25, 1908.
    Thanks for the letter. . . .
    They have signed they will do all kinds of mission work such as cook-
ing for all, washing, mending etc. for all boys, girls, teachers etc. That
they do not ask for any compensation for their work or so much per
capita. That they recognize the property and buildings not to be theirs,
but to belong to the mission.[12]

September 26, 1908.
    I got yesterday a letter from Right Rev. Bis. Cusack, and according
to his letter Sister Gertrude and her companions are not sisters, and
would come as simple pious ladies, yet Sister Gertrude has been a sister
and is highly recommended. In that case they may simply join if they
want . . . the Catechists. . . . It was my plan, not being able to get sisters,
to try some pious ladies. If such is the case after your Lordship has also
the answer from Bishop Cusack, the situation is much simplified, and I
will write to them that it is well understood that this is the condition with
which they come.[13]

October 2, 1908.
    I am anxious to get a letter from your Lordship . . . but are they Sis-
ters or not? If they are not sisters, regular sisters, I . . . [hope to have]
them as simple teachers, pious ladies, ready to do the work.[14]

---

[9] De Rougé to Most Rev. E. J. O'Dea, September 12, 1908, Ms., ADS.
[10] *Ibid.*, September 16, 1908, Ms. ADS.
[11] *Ibid.*, September 24, 1908, Ms. ADS.
[12] *Ibid.*, September 25, 1908, Ms. ADS.
[13] *Ibid.*, September 26, 1908, Ms. ADS.
[14] *Ibid.*, October 2, 1908, Ms. ADS.

On October 9, 1908, Father de Rougé wrote another letter to his Bishop, while on a missionary trip to Wenatchee and urged him to answer and to admit the Sisters.[15] On October 16, 1908, another letter followed asking for permission to call the Sisters.[16] Father de Rougé seemed to be completely disappointed when he answered the Bishop on October 26, 1908:

> . . . I had the hope to have found a solution, in the question of these sisters from N. Y. to save our mission here and save the children, and it is a bitter deception for me. I must say that I feel more and more discouraged. Yet I do not pretend to criticize any action of your Lordship. I will propose to them to come as they are: simple ladies to work as teachers.[17]

The succession of urgent letters shows us that Father de Rougé considered his plan of having his own Sisters of paramount importance for the build-up and continuance of St. Mary's Mission. There is no doubt that he had the best of intentions and only wanted to have the work done for God's poor, the Indians.

What happened in the meantime with the Sisters' convent? A letter of June 2 informs us that the workman had to stop building until more funds could be made available. The building so far consisted of little more than a framework.[18] Father de Rougé asked Mother Katherine, on October 8, if she would be kind enough to help him as she had done before. Besides other problems he would like to fix up two rooms at least for the new Sister and the girls.[19] He renewed his petition on November 13. Then he tells Mother Katherine the news about his Ladies Catechists Missionaries:

> As they cannot be approved by the Bishop, who refused to approve them, they have accepted to come and join my Catechists, and will come as pious Ladies Catechists and be here about the 21st of the month. The Catechists have already about 15 girls in school this term. I have done the best I could to try to fix the new convent and furnish two rooms for these poor ladies. We are making little rooms with curtains, etc. and try to have them warm for winter.[20]

Father then keeps on asking for some financial help to make the Sisters more comfortable. The little house still needs so many items but he cannot "cripple his boys' school for the convent." The Catechists came with

[15] De Rougé to O'Dea, October 9, 1908, Ms., ADS.
[16] Ibid., October 19, 1908, Ms., ADS.
[17] Ibid., October 26, 1908, Ms., ADS.
[18] De Rougé to Mother Katherine, June 2, 1808, Ms., ABSS.
[19] Ibid., October 8, 1908, Ms., ABSS.
[20] Ibid., November 13, 1908, Ms., ABSS.

such courage, "do not ask for compensation, etc., yet, I will have to give them so much per month, even if little, so that we have clear understanding."[21]

Even the public considered the new Madams of St. Mary's Mission full-fledged Sisters as an announcement of their arrival in one of the county's newspapers shows:

> Okanogan, Wash., Nov. 20.
> The new Catholic convent at Mission, seven miles east of here on the Colville Indian reservation which has been erected under the direction of Rev. Father de Rougé, to be run as a part of St. Mary's Mission and school, is ready for occupancy and yesterday six sisters of charity arrived from New York to engage in their work here.
> During the last four years the Christian Brothers have been directing the boys' department at St. Mary's, but this is the first time that the sisters have entered the Okanogan field. The sextet is headed by Sister Gertrude, who has already founded several institutions, the last one being for the Italian settlement in New York.[22]

Mother Katherine had sent another $700 to the hard-pressed Father de Rougé for which Father thanked her on December 1, 1908. Mail service was not too regular, therefore mention is made again of thanks for a check that had arrived in June. The priest hopes that Mother Katherine has received his letter. Joyously now he tells his benefactress about his new Sisters; he had not received them as seculars:

> What a fine little community are these 6 sisters! . . . and just a nice number, with the three I have we are well provided and all are at work at once. It is a miracle of grace, the immense sacrifice they made, and had to make, as they could not be approved as sisters, was the means the Sacred Heart used to bring them here. Have many prejudices against them from high quarters, but I do not think I was wrong to let them come. I only wish you could see them! Well, they have put aside their costume of dress, and taken a very simple one as Catechists Missionaries.[23]

The missionary had told these "secular Sisters" to "keep in private their rule and obligations before God and their conscience." All were happy and not tired from the trip.[24] Great faith and a courageous missionary spirit were needed by these newcomers to St. Mary's. Their convent consisted of a room with only building paper over the rough boards; each one had a bed surrounded with white curtains which had

---

[21] De Rougé to Mother Katherine, November 13, 1908, Ms., ABSS.

[22] Anonymous, "Convent Opens at Mission, Marks Entrance of Sisters of Charity in Okanogan Field," November 29 (1908, newspaper clipping in OPA, no name of newspaper).

[23] De Rougé to Mother Katherine, December 1, 1908, Ms., ABSS.

[24] Ibid.

been sewn by Father himself; another room had one table and shelves of boards and a chair for each. This was all. Now Father intended to buy beds for the girls who had slept on the floor, Indian fashion, until now. He also needed to build up his schoolroom and the dormitory. The school term was too advanced to take in more girls, but he hoped to be ready for the next year. Mother Katherine had made a most generous offer again to keep the girls' school at St. Mary's Mission going.

> With what you promise, as long as you live, that is . . . $15 per month for each of the first three ladies, and $100 for the children for the term, as they came in, I will be able to support the other ladies.[25]

Father de Rougé calls Mother Katherine "Our Providence." This convent school, consisting only of rough boards as walls, must have caused great sufferings from cold during the icy winters of the Okanogan Valley. To give all of his subjects the spiritual strength needed for their lives of toil and sacrifice, Father gave all the children and the teachers a retreat soon after the arrival of the Ladies Catechists.[26]

The need for Sisters and the need of the convent were expressed in a brochure published around 1909:

> St. Mary's Mission devoted to the spiritual, moral and educational welfare of the Indians, is a Roman Catholic institution, the only one in a district, extending 100 miles north and 200 miles south, and 150 miles to the East and West. Although it has been in existence for years, and Rev. E. de Rougé, S.J., has devoted to it all his means, time, energy, and the zeal . . . nothing as yet has been done for the training of the young girls.
>
> Through the Rev. Father's untiring efforts, the co-operation of two [and later of three] Lameney [sic] Brothers was secured, and St. Mary's High School now gives a solid and religious education to about 50 boys. But alas, when the young man is thus prepared to meet the dangers of the world and to establish a family and a home, he finds no one worthy of his character and moral standing. The Indian girls are naturally prone to evil, to vice and to drink. At ten, the child is already, in many instances, a confirmed drunkard, too lazy to work.
>
> Only a day or two ago, two children were brought to this Mission, who had been abandoned by their Mother and sold for $100.00. It is to help such as these, kind friends, that we appeal. Three devoted Catechists have for the past year taught a small girl's school and sheltered 7–10 borders, who slept on the floor for want of beds, and lived and labored in two rooms measuring 12 x 18 and 6 x 12 ft.
>
> In a response to an urgent appeal from the good Father, which appeared in different missionary papers, six Mission workers from New York volunteered their services and have joined the humble noble band of "Three." In provision for their coming, two large rooms were added

---

[25] De Rougé to Mother Katherine, December 1, 1908, Ms., ABSS.
[26] *Ibid.*

to the lowly Convent, so that one dormitory now shelters the 9 Ladies Catechists (such is the name adopted in these parts) and 15 Indian children who sleep on serried rows in temporary beds on the floor. The attendance in the schools was doubled the first week, but alas; the bare plasterless walls, the boarded windows and many other such details, tell of the pressing needs of the Mission. We want a suitable dormitory for the boys and girls respectively, more school accommodations and the necessaries of life in sufficient quantities, that we may not refuse a single applicant. Who will respond to this appeal by becoming a yearly member of our Guild? Surely, He who promised to reward even a cup of cold water given in His Name, will abundantly repay the alms given to bring under Catholic influence, the many girls who are in such great peril of eternal death.

And who has a better claim upon your charity, than the natives of our free and glorious land. But to make our work a success, our means must enable us to compete to advantage with the Government Schools, in order that the Indian parent may find at St. Mary's not only the educational advantages equal to the Public School system, but in addition the pearl beyond all worth; the love and knowledge of God's divinely revealed truth. Address

The Directress of the Ladies Catechists
St. Mary's Mission,
Mission P.O., O'Kanagan [sic] Co., Wash.[27]

Mother Katherine most probably was worried about the primitive buildings that housed the Sisters and the girls as we can guess from Father's answers to Mother Katherine, March 5, 1909. He thanks her for the letter and then says: "Of course we [will] need better buildings here and especially for the convent when I can get the sisters or ladies for the girls." But Father had more projects in mind. "Later on if we are to build for the girls I may let you know." In the meantime another check of $672 arrived from the always generous Mother. She had told him that from now on she would send the tuition for the children every quarter. Father, when thanking her, tells her of his new building plans; he wants to add "as much as we have now" to the convent. Then he speaks about his Madams, as they were called at the Mission, admitting that they suffered a great deal from the cold the previous winter:

These ladies are fine and the Superior is certainly a saint. I hope in May to get two more from the east. Our winter was very hard, very cold, all froze, and we have to haul water for a while yet which makes a great extra work this season.[28]

---

[27] Madame Gertrude Clark, *St. Mary's Mission* (brochure). Preserved by Mrs. Frank Mechtel, Wenatchee, in whose family Madame Mayr later lived until her death.

[28] De Rougé to Mother Katherine, March 11, 1909, Ms., ABSS.

More definite plans for the enlargement of the convent are revealed in the missionary's letter of May 4. He speaks of his "fine Ladies Catechists" who take care of the girls and the little boys. They started with a half-finished building and endured many privations during the winter. He hopes that Providence will come again to his aid as he starts "today" a new addition to the building that will make the whole structure 100 by 26 feet "with a little house on one side for the laundry." The girls are using the hall for a classroom while the others "are piled up in a small room where the teacher cannot put her desk." The kitchen serves as dining room for the children as well as for the Ladies. The new addition will consist of two classrooms and a dormitory for the little boys and it will take still another addition to accommodate everyone. Father de Rougé then mentions again the hard winter of 1908–1909. All the potatoes had frozen and he even had his fields plowed over and reseeded. That would mean a poor first crop and not enough to keep the few cattle over the next winter.[29]

The second addition was built; again there was only money enough for rough boards for the walls. Francis Favel, Father's secretary, writes on October 11, 1909, that the girls' school was crowded:

It is only too bad that the buildings are incompleted. The Sisters will have to pass another hard winter as the building is not yet plastered and Father cannot afford to do that work this fall as he is laying the foundation of the new church, which is much needed. The Indians are settling more around the Mission and on the feastdays the old church is crowded to its utmost.[30]

Father had sent many letters asking support but only a few had brought results. The inhabitants of the Mission will start another novena to end with the feast of St. Margaret Mary and they will not forget their greatest benefactress.[31] This promise of prayers and novenas nearly always was the closing remark of every letter that went from the Mission into the outside world. It is clearly to be seen that without Mother Katherine's financial help there would not be a St. Mary's Mission today; it would have ceased to exist.

The foregoing pages have shown us under what conditions the Ladies Catechists Missionaries had to start their school and apostolic work at the Mission. Not every Madam could stand the rigors of the climate in such a primitive dwelling and the hard work under such austere conditions. Many came and many went again. Desperately in need of help,

---

[29] De Rougé to Mother Katherine, May 4, 1909, Ms., ABSS.
[30] Francis Favel to Mother Katherine, October 11, 1909, Ms., ABSS.
[31] *Ibid.*

Father de Rougé sent more articles to the Catholic magazines. He was more demanding also in his letters to applicants; he did not want them to be disappointed. Many had answered the call but many did not come. He still let the applicants believe that this was a proper religious convent:

> It is a life of real sacrifice, not of pleasure, it is work and not a home for a person of age, and it is also a rule to observe at least for the good order of the house, as mostly in any well organized convent. Never will I send letters encouraging very much, as the call must come from God, Who alone can give the vocation.[32]

Father de Rougé's missionary Sisters must be ready for any work: to help the cook or to teach the children. There "is no difference for the one who has the spirit of the Missionary. The Ladies Catechists Missionaries must be a brave band, ready to do anything. . . ." The Ladies Catechists Missionaries will follow a simple rule:[33]

> Half an hour Meditation, half an hour visit to the Blessed Sacrament; half an hour spiritual reading and Examens at noon and at night; annual Retreat, special instruction every week. Everyone must be very punctual and exact for all the exercises of the house as well as for the work.[34]

Of from Father de Rougé's group of Ladies Missionaries not one had learned the religious life as a postulant or novice in another community. Sister Gertrude with all her fine qualities had been only a Dominican tertiary. She is the only one buried at St. Mary's cemetery from the first group of six who came from New York. The former students still remember how she fainted in the church. Madam Gertrude Clark died of tuberculosis while Father de Rougé was absent from his Mission. He had given her the Last Sacraments before he left; she had to be buried without a priest.[35] Hers had been a heroic life; she died in the prime of her life, at forty-four years.

Father de Rougé expected the Madams to be not less self-sacrificing than himself. His Lady Catechists had no privacy in their personal mail. The following is the signed agreement to that effect:

> November 1, 1910.
> All mail matters is understood to be under the supervision of the Superiors of the Mission, who have the right to retain or deliver any mail or express matters, coming from any source whatever.
> After three months this rule will be enforced or changed if not satisfied.

---

[32] De Rougé, *To Ladies Applicant as Catechist Missionaries*, mimeographed copy, OPA.
[33] *Ibid.*
[34] *Ibid.*
[35] John Figlenski, interview.

Signed: Madam Vallero   Hickey   LaLonde
        Conaty   Mayr   Nilan
        Sheehan   McGroth   Cunningham[36]
        Cooper   Woodhedger

From the Madams who signed, only Madam La Londe died at St. Mary's, April 23, 1926. All the others left. Miss Mary Mayr found a home and another apostolate at Wenatchee with the Frank Mechtel family. Earlier the nieces of Madam La Londe, the Poitras girls, had married. One of them married the mission carpenter, Ernest Middleton, a convert.

Father de Rougé had his Sisters make vows for six months and then if they wished they renewed them. He composed a special formula for this purpose:

> I Sister ——, servant of Jesus Christ, although unworthy, but full of confidence in the Divine grace under the protection of the Blessed Virgin, of all the Holy Virgins in heaven, and of the holy Women in the Gospel, who serve Our Lord and the Apostles, consecrate and devote myself with all heart and soul to the service of Jesus Christ, especially in Missionary work, and Vow to follow Him in Poverty, Chastity, and Obedience for six months. I promise obedience to my Superiors, whoever they are appointed over me, at any time and to support them in everything. I promise obedience to follow the rules of our Society and devote myself according to my ability to the greater glory of Jesus. O Mary, my loving Mother, help me as thy child, direct me in the service of Jesus that I may serve Him worthily and please Him during life, and after death have the happiness of praising Him and loving Him for all Eternity.[37]

During the first years the vows were made publicly in the presence of the boys;[38] in later years they were renewed privately.

On January 5, 1910, Father de Rougé writes to Mother Katherine that with the boys he now has over a hundred children. The Ladies Catechists are "doing admirable work," and he wonders if he will be able to build for them. He has hope that Mother Katherine will help again. There are still no plastered walls in the convent. The dormitory for the Ladies is also used in part by the pupils. He plans another wing to the present building.[39]

This means that when his new addition takes shape Father will have only slightly more than half of his project completed for the girls in its most primitive form. Father has eleven more ladies interested in coming, ten from the East and one from California. All were not likely to appear but some would and he felt that "God Almighty wanted this

[36] Original Ms., OPA.
[37] De Rougé, *Formula of Vows,* Original Ms., OPA.
[38] Hill, interview.
[39] De Rougé to Mother Katherine, January 5, 1910, Ms., ABSS.

work to go on." Some of the ladies who left may have been responsible for an article in a New York paper stating that they "could only expect the worst kind of food." One new prospect sent Father this article and asked to be admitted; whereupon the priest concluded that "she must have courage."[40]

Father de Rougé encountered the full measure of critical situations in the course of developing his Mission center. Tuberculosis, trachoma, and smallpox, the main killers of the Indian race, did not retreat before the doors of St. Mary's Mission. On February 3, 1910, the missionary reports that he intends to build an infirmary, where two of his Ladies Missionaries will find plenty to do.

> Just now we have a smallpox scare; one started at the convent. Let us hope it is the first and last. So you see, dear Mother, I have my crosses and troubles. The poor Sisters are quarantined, and they received 2 days Communion at the door of the church outside, [standing] almost in the snow . . . it was very impressive and pious. Looked like the time of persecution.[41]

Two weeks later a letter brings the dreadful news of more smallpox at the convent. Mother Katherine and her Community are asked to pray that the "heavy cross will be taken from us by the Sacred Heart." Then Father continues:

> The dear, holy Directress has taken (as usual) all to herself even sacrificing the consolation of mass and H. Communion. She is really good and holy. At once, money or not, I have started carpenters at work to put up a house to separate the cases. How many will we have? God knows.[42]

This directress was Madam Gertrude Clark.

Not all of Father's letters seemed to have reached their destination. He hoped that Mother Katherine had received the quarterly report on school attendance according to which he received the quarterly allowance from her. Father de Rougé had not quite recovered from a sick spell. The constant attention needed by building projects and the need of money drained his strength and endurance. His former students remarked that he always had money troubles. Often he could not pay his helpers. This may have been a reason why the Lamennais Brothers were recalled. Father writes to Mother Katherine:

> I have to make room as the poor Ladies are in the same dormitory with the little boys. I have to give them more boys as we are going to

---

40 De Rougé to Mother Katherine, January 5, 1910, Ms., ABSS.
41 *Ibid.*, February 3, 1910, Ms., ABSS.
42 *Ibid.*, February 19, 1910, Ms., ABSS.

lose the brothers. Did you get all their news? My only hope is in the Ladies to save the mission girls and little boys.[43]

The new addition to the convent was to cost about $1,000 or more. Soon the work would start. New Ladies Catechists were supposed to arrive next month and Father had no room for them; yet there was so much for them to do. Furniture consisted so far only of rough benches.

Mother Katherine kept on sending her quarterly checks and a word of encouragement with them. Father thanked her and remarked about the many families wandering all over the reservation looking for land allotments. Many families would be near the Mission, which was to become an important center. The priest expected new Ladies again this week; he had to let some go of their own will; others he had to send away. He needed still more Catechists and has many applications. He writes confidentially to Mother Katherine: "I do not pretend to establish a congregation of sisters now. Let God see to it in the future if it is His will. It is the only way, the only remedy for me in the present situation."[44]

The same subject is stressed again on May 5, to Mother Katherine:

> . . . we do not pretend to make a new foundation of Sisters, but are simply Catechists Missionaries, this is the name. If I did not start this, where would I be? What would become of the mission? Just now as we are going to lose all the brothers in our mission? The only thing left would have been to close here.[45]

His Ladies were to again save the mission. That fall was to be the twenty-fifth anniversary of his coming into this region. Father reflected seriously that in all these years he had not been able to do something for the girls. Now he had nine good catechists.[46]

Another addition to the convent had gone up during the late months of spring in 1910, but "it will not be enough for the future." Father de Rougé is grateful for the growth of the building and considers it "like a miracle"; he had started with nothing. Father then gives some spiritual advice to Mother Katherine and to her community who have the same goal, the care of the neglected Indians. It reflects his own striving for perfection:

> Let us all be united in the thought to save the poor Indians, and to obtain all the conversions possible. For this we must all be really self-sacrificed and persevere in our great vocation, and obtain more vocations

---

[43] De Rougé to Mother Katherine, March 17, 1910, Ms., ABSS.
[44] Ibid., April 25, 1910, Ms., ABSS.
[45] Ibid., May 5, 1910, Ms., ABSS.
[46] Ibid.

for the work. It is not enough to have been called by our Lord, but all must become perfect instruments, correct the defects in the way and have courage, not give up for trifles, and look out for the devil who tries to stop us, and indeed succeeds too often.[47]

In his November letter Father speaks about the wonderful work done by the Catechists: they visit the people, especially the sick and are trying to organize a sodality of the mothers of families. The girls are not so numerous this year because false talk has been spread against the Madams' school. "Of course I had to let go one or two, as it is very hard to get only good ones at a distance, even if I make it very hard in the conditions to come here."[48] This coming and going with its restlessness among the Madams and their pupils probably created all the talk against the school. We have to remember that the building for the Catechists and the girls still consisted only of rough boards.

We have seen that on account of the smallpox cases Father had started in February of 1910 a separate house. This was the beginning of his hospital. He mentioned this building again in his November letter. "We have started an infirmary and are building on it; it is also a great work. It could become quite an extensive work, but I will go slowly at first."[49] Some registered nurses were among the Ladies Missionaries most of the time. They were able to give professional service like in any other hospital of the nation. One of the nurses was Madam Joanna Blake, a very intelligent and capable Sister. On the way to St. Mary's she had thrown her nurse's diploma out of the railroad window. She did not want to be a nurse at the Mission, but she was called again to duty for the sick. She was also a good typist and served later as Father Caldi's secretary.[50] She is one of the few who died at St. Mary's Mission — after sixteen years of faithful service.[51]

The former Madam Riedmiller, afterward named Sister M. Rose Francis, O.P., shortly before her death in 1944 wrote to Mrs. Monda, Wenatchee, about the early times at St. Mary's Girls' School. She reports about very hard beginnings. Father de Rougé spoke the Indian language very well and could start successfully in the boys' school while the Madams did not have this advantage. They were not understood by the homesick Indian girls. The Indians disliked white people and the Madams at first had to teach the children English word for word before they could give them any lessons in school. It was very hard to

---

47 De Rougé to Mother Katherine, June 30, 1910, Ms., ABSS.
48 *Ibid.*, November 6, 1910, Ms., ABSS.
49 *Ibid.*
50 Sister Mary Michael, O.P., interviews.
51 See mission cemetery.

make the girls acquainted with another way of living. The parents watched the white women handling their girls. If the fingernails were cut or if there were any deviation from their age-old customs trouble followed.

Before the Sisters came, the words "please" and "thank you" were not known. Very slowly the children overcame their fear and their mistrust of white people and became especially friendly to the missionaries.

> After they could speak English they were very proud; they told us how much they loved us, and when school closed in June they cried because they had to leave us for a few months. Every two weeks we changed their work as an Indian cannot do the same work too long. The girls loved to help to take care of the church.[52]

The girls had only grade school from the primer to the eighth grade. They made the grades with ease after the English language had been mastered. Often parents would not send their children to school, using the excuse that they were too young. Many started school when in their "teens," twelve, thirteen, fourteen, or older. Later a rule was made that the children should start school at the age of eight.

The children were never allowed to be idle because they got into "mischief and worked at a trade we called stealing, as to them what was yours was theirs, and what was theirs, was their own." The Ladies Catechists taught the children "how terrible it was to steal and how it displeases the Great Spirit when people steal. It did not take long until they quit this bad habit." The children were very sly, a trait which required strict supervision. Government officials told the Sisters that a great change had taken place after the Catechists came. From a concept of communal ownership to that of individual ownership must have been quite a step for these children of nature.

Beside the ordinary school subjects the girls were taught how to sew and mend, cook and bake, darn stockings, and do fancy work. They learned how to keep house, wash and iron, and plant a garden. Every Thursday and Sunday would be half free days for walks and picnics; then they were marched in strict ranks, the bigger girls having charge of smaller ones. Sister Rose Frances felt her great responsibility in supervising about sixty children on an outing. All could swim like fish and would not come out of the water until they were nearly exhausted.

The children were not allowed to have guns and knives during the school term as they were too handy with these weapons. Once a full-blooded child was corrected at table and pointed a fork at the Sister. The Ladies Catechists were not allowed to whip the children. They cor-

---

[52] Sister M. Rose Francis, O.P., to Mrs. Monda, Wenatchee, September, 1944, Ms.

rected them with kindness and had great success. Even the adult Indians were influenced through the kindly remarks of the Catechists. For instance, the men were induced to carry the burdens which formerly the women had carried.[53]

It can be imagined that when the number of pupils grew, Father de Rougé had a hard time to feed them all in spite of gardens and fields. Mrs. W. J. Dignan, the former Edna Verdier, who, as a white girl, attended St. Mary's Mission, remembers that the children were always hungry. They had a diet of dried salt cod and plain boiled vegetables, no milk, no butter, little sugar, and plain bread. The girls would be happy if they were allowed to have their picnics with Madam Mayr whom they all loved. Then Mattie George would be their leader and she would always know what was good to eat. She knew where to find fresh-water clams and fish and how to roast them. Madam Mayr always tried to make the girls happy. Once, when the fish were roasted, she told them in broken English, "The eyes you shut and make a wish." Then to the surprise and delight of the girls she produced a bag of stale bread from beneath her cape and proceeded to distribute large hunks of it.

Mrs. Dignan remembers how Madam Mayr seemed to be always out of favor with the other Madams. She could scarcely speak English and was "usually given the jobs the others did not want." The girls called her their favorite Sister who was always kind and patient. Her habit was of coarse material; the coif and other white parts were hand made out of flour sacks.[54]

Mrs. Josephine Carden-Marchant, a former pupil of the girls' school, remembers the girls taking turns learning how to bake bread for the whole mission population. They learned how to make their dresses, and when the girls left the Mission, they were good seamstresses. Each big girl had four little girls to take care of in the morning. Mrs. Marchant remembers being in charge of Mattie Grunlose, the daughter of Chief Coxit George, who cried every morning when her hair was combed. Since traveling was primitive, it was hard to go home and the children had to stay at the Mission from the beginning of the school year until Easter. Many would not see their parents all year.

The separation between the Boys' School and the Girls' School was complete. Each school had its own household and its own cook. The boys had to wash their dishes, each one at his place; dishwashing bowls

[53] Sister Rose Frances, O.P., to Mrs. Monda.

[54] Mrs. W. J. Dignan, reminiscences to the author, fall, 1960. The students of the boys' school stated that they had simple wholesome food. A photo of a group of girls with Mrs. Dignan as pupil does not show them to be undernourished. It cannot be imagined that the children continuously had the diet mentioned by her.

were placed at the head of the dining table and passed along. The girls, likewise, did their dishes. The laundry was washed in the Sisters' house and two or three boys had to help in washing the boys' clothes. This was the only contact the boys had with the convent. When the students went on walks boys and girls would go in different directions and were never without strict supervision. The boys who had sisters in the convent would, twice during the month, receive permission slips from Father de Rougé to visit with them in the parlor of the covent. They were usually allowed fifteen minutes or sometimes a half hour of mutual visiting. Then most of the time they did not know what to say and just looked at each other and giggled.

The girls could not even look at the boys when they went to church on Sundays. Huge big bonnets were then in style and the girls thought some of them were specially made for them. They reached out quite far in front and looked like horse blinders; the girls called them "our blind-folds." "If we would look around we would get into trouble; we could only look straight ahead."[55]

Mrs. L. Morris, the former Celestine Moomaw, remembers that when she attended the school from 1910–1912, the convent had a tiny chapel with the Blessed Sacrament. All girls went daily to the unfinished church for Holy Mass.[56] Later a beautiful big chapel in the so-called new college was used by all during the winter months. The entrance to it in the rear of the house was used.

Father de Rougé's "board house" for the girls and Catechists that had been built under such urgent and miserable conditions nearly fell a sacrifice to flames when in 1911 the baking of the bread caused a chimney fire. All the population of the mission was alerted. The girls stood with their Sister Catechists along the fence of the wall saying the Rosary, while the boys, Mr. Corrigan, and Mr. Middleton formed a bucket brigade. Only with the greatest efforts was it possible to extinguish the flames.[57]

Father de Rougé received an important letter that concerned his Ladies Catechists Missionaries. On October 4, 1912, Bishop O'Dea of Seattle wrote:

Please, inform me what religious community of women, if any, you have engaged in work at the mission. The Holy See requires the Bishop to render an account of the communities in his diocese, and I would be pleased to know from you if the sisters in your charge are professed nuns,

---

[55] Mrs. Josephine Carden-Marchant, interview at St. Mary's, May 28, 1960.
[56] Mrs. L. Morris, interview at Brewster, Washington, August 23, 1960.
[57] John Figlenski, interview.

and of what community or communities, and if they are there by permission of their lawful superiors.[58]

The answer was simple as far as Father de Rougé was concerned:

> In answer to the letter of your Lordship asking "what religious community is engaged here at the Mission, (if any)?" will say: That no religious community is engaged here, or no professed nuns of any kind.
>
> The ladies here in charge of the girls, of the little boys and of the hospital are seculars. I have simply enrolled them as Catechists, or Mission helpers under small wages: They sign . . . a paper in which it is said that: they understand that the Ladies Catechists do not mean to form a religious congregation of any kind, but to be simply Catechists, who give their lives for the Missions as long as they like for the sake of the souls of the Indians and poor settlers. . . .[59]

For the sake of historical accuracy we can say that such a "paper" never was signed by the Ladies Catechists and there never were small wages. On the contrary, those who had money were induced to will it to the Mission.[60]

The Diocese of Nisqually changed its name to that of Seattle in 1907. In 1913 a part of this diocese was incorporated into the newly formed Diocese of Spokane. The Mission in the Okanogan Valley now came under the jurisdiction of the first Bishop of Spokane, the Most Reverend Augustine F. Schinner. Bishop Schinner visited St. Mary's for the first time during 1914. This brought new hope to Father de Rougé who would like to have his secular Catechists made real Sisters. The following letter shows his first approach to the new Bishop:

> Many thanks for the great kindness shown to us all here, and especially to the convent. Everyone keeps a warm feeling for your Lordship here and asks God Almighty to send many blessings on your Lordship and the diocese.
>
> Would your Lordship object if I would allow for the present at the convent, little vows of devotion, say for one year, quite in private, for each one who may be admitted, simply subject to the confessor?
>
> Would your Lordship object, if the beads were added, which by humility so far were not given to carry?[61]

Bishop Schinner answered November 19, 1914:

> In answer to your letter of the 13, inst. would say that you have permission to give the persons mentioned the vow "of devotion subject to the

[58] Most Rev. O'Dea to De Rougé, October 4, 1912, copy, ADS.
[59] De Rougé to Most Rev. O'Dea, October 8, 1912, Ms., ADS.
[60] Sisters Mary Michael and Mary Ann, O.P., interviews.
[61] De Rougé to Most Rev. Augustine F. Schinner, Bishop of Spokane, November 13, 1914, Ms., ADS.

confessor," and also to add the beads. I think their service deserved some recognition.[62]

Father de Rougé told Mother Katherine, "The Bishop was so pleased with all that he will do all he can for the community and we had the first vows at Christmas."[63] However, the Ladies Catechists Missionaries were never approved by the Church. It is a praiseworthy undertaking to give one's life to God by becoming a lay apostle, but the status of the Ladies Catechists Missionaries should have been cleared from the beginning with full knowledge of the Ladies themselves. It would have saved some embarrassments later when Sisters who thought they were Sisters left the so-called convent or were dismissed.

Nevertheless, a group of zealous and self-sacrificing lay apostles kept the Mission going, as we will see, through very hard times until the Poor School Sisters of St. Dominic, Kettle Falls, Washington, took over on July 2, 1936, and the remaining three Ladies Catechists Missionaries then entered the real convent of the Dominican Sisters.

Father de Rougé set down for the Bishop the following facts about the Ladies Catechists Missionaries, giving a summary of his organization:

In December, 1906, the Ladies Catechists Missionaries were regularly organized with a Religious Rule and following a daily routine similar to the community life in Convents. Since their organization there have been not less than ten at a time. They now number thirteen. Four postulants are expected this fall. At the present time there are on the list for consideration about sixteen applications. They have a Directress and Assistant Directress who constitute the Consultors of the Father. The Father is the Superior. The Rule followed by the Ladies Catechists Missionaries is formed after the Jesuit Rule.

Almighty God has blessed their work in a manner visible to all. The few rooms in which they started their work have now grown into the four Houses or departments under their supervision: The Convent, The Hospital, The Home for the little boys and the School for White girls now ready to be opened.

The average number of girls received during the year is forty. They are carefully trained in all things that relate to Domestic Science and are given an education which will in time form them into good Christian women.

The number of little boys received during the year and under the care of the Ladies Catechists Missionaries is about twenty-five.

The patients received at the Hospital averages about sixty annually and are under the constant care of the nurses among the Ladies Catechists Missionaries.

In addition to the foregoing duties which they have gladly assumed

---

[62] Schinner to De Rougé, November 19, 1914, Ms. Copy, ADS.
[63] De Rougé to Mother Katherine, January 22, 1915, Ms., ABSS.

they take entire care of the Church, washing and keeping in perfect order the altar linens and vestments. They make all the Altar Bread. By their careful watchfulness the Lamp of Sanctuary burns incessantly. At all times the altar is kept in perfect order and neatness. On occasions of great festivals no pains are spared to make the Church most beautiful and attractive, as the Indians and many others on those occasions come to the Mission from distances of many miles. They are always pleased with the display of candles and flowers that adorn the altar.

Their labors are still not ended. The washing for the entire place is done by the Ladies Catechists Missionaries. They do all the laundry work for the Father and the teachers, the large and the small boys at the Mission. They do all the washing for the Hospital and with the exception of the clothes for the girls, which they themselves wash, all the washing for the Convent. When the washing and ironing are completed, the clothes before being returned to their respective places are mended and put in order.

In many other ways, too, the Ladies Catechists Missionaries make their presence felt, and their influence felt. Many white settlers desiring their children to receive the Sacraments but not in a position to leave them here at the School all the time, bring them here to receive instruction. These children on such occasions remain sometimes a week at a time.

Were it not for the Ladies Catechists Missionaries the Mission would have been forced to close, long ago. It would not be possible anywhere in this territory to secure the help of such services as are rendered by the Ladies Catechists Missionaries, for the payment of money of the wages represented by their services would be beyond the financial ability of our poor Mission to meet. Even if regular Sisters had been called here, their Congregation would expect a sum of money which also in the past it would have been impossible to pay.

A point to which careful attention is called is the fact the Government has established Government Schools, their transportation paid, clothing and everything being offered to attract them, such as dances and the light modern gaieties. The time has now arrived when a great many of these Indian children desire to be equal to the Whites and far too many have enrolled in these Protestant Schools. Once there they are forever lost to the Church and it is plain to be seen that allowing only such an education out of Catholic schools, and the fact of being taken away from the country must mean the rapid destruction of Catholicity and the work of the first Missionaries who labored for so many years. . . .

For the same reason it was necessary to build a hospital here. At any moment Government Doctors and Inspectors were calling with the idea of excluding from our school as many children as possible, under the pretext of sickness or disease. Those children being sent to the Protestant Sanitarium Schools are also forever lost to the Church. When it was discovered that they were thus draining our schools the Father started a hospital where the Ladies Catechists Missionaries can take care of and save the souls of these delicate and sickly children. In any event no Catholic hospitals exist within two hundred or three hundred miles of the Mission.

The Doctors of the country have already sent here many patients. It is a remarkable fact that most of these are men and especially men who were fallen-away Catholics but through the good influence of the Ladies Catechists Missionaries they have received the last Sacraments and would never have done so otherwise.

Under such circumstances have the Ladies Catechists Missionaries come to St. Mary's Mission, knowing that they are sacrificing their lives and their health, receiving in return not a munificent salary but simply their clothing and food, some of them even buying their own clothing in order that they may not be a burden upon the Mission. Notwithstanding the fact that they are not a recognized Congregation uncertain as to their future, deprived of the benefits of vows, they have in the past braved all these trials for the sake of this great work, trusting in Providence for whatever might happen later on.[64]

Without the assistance of these women, it would have been impossible to keep the Mission open. By helping to raise the status of family life of the Indians through the education of the girls, the Ladies Catechists Missionaries contributed immeasurably to the spreading of Christian civilization and culture among the Indians of the Okanogan and Upper Columbia Valleys.

---

[64] De Rougé to Bishop Schinner, n.d., Ms., ADS.

CHAPTER XV

Climbing Toward the Peak

WHILE Father de Rougé was building his girls' school bit by bit and having trouble in establishing his convent, he could look with satisfaction on the progress his boys were making. He had a group of highly intelligent boys who were eager to study and who were his joy and his consolation. No sacrifice seemed too great for the educator if he could help his boys. He wrote on June 2, 1908, "We had a fine school this term. All the big boys are speaking of coming back. Only one left us."[1] During 1908, Father's letters to Mother Katherine show that he is preoccupied with the Madams and their school, but once in a while he mentioned his good boys. "I think all the boys will offer Holy Communion every day of the novena."[2] The school opened again in September, 1908, with 39 boys; more were to come. Father Ketcham of the Catholic Indian Bureau, Washington, D. C., had visited St. Mary's Mission, and had promised to pay for 17 boys.[3] Now besides the help from Mother Katherine for the girls and for the building of the convent, Father has the assistance of the Bureau of Catholic Indian Missions. This, however, depended on the generosity of people, whose contributions to the Indian Bureau varied from year to year.

We were told by Harry Van Coelen, who attended St. Mary's from August 1905 to April 1908, that he once saw that Father de Rougé's "was really mad." Father came into the yard and told old Mr. Parr that the French government had seized the money belonging to his mother, which she had willed to him. Harry heard Father repeating, "They can't do this; they can't do this."[4] We have seen that the use

[1] De Rougé to Mother Katherine, June 2, 1908, Ms., ABSS.
[2] Ibid.
[3] Ibid., October 8, 1908.
[4] Van Coelen, interviews.

of this money had been granted Father at the end of 1907. Harry also remembers that Father always wore his cassock. When asked why he wore it all the time the "Count" answered that his trousers were worn out underneath.[5] The priest was absolutely poor; he gave his very last cent to his beloved Indians.

During Harry Van Coelen's time the order of the day at the boys' school was as follows:

6 o'clock up, no heat, as fast as possible into clothes
6:30 Breakfast, mush, bread, fried potatoes, coffee, never fruit
7:30 to Church
8:00 to classroom
9:45 Recess
12:00 Dinner, boiled potatoes, meat gravy, etc. The food that time was good.
12:–1:00 free time
1:–4:00 back to school, except the days when Father had a special project
4:–5:30 Chores — Kerosene lamps to be taken care of, about 50 of them. The Indians brought the logs down from the hills. The boys had to saw them, split them, fill the wood boxes all over the place, except in the dormitories.
5:30–6:00 Supper
6:00–8:30 Study time

Then Father would come to tell stories or in later years the boys would go to Father's office for that purpose. Father would pick the boys for the story characters. He always stopped when the story was most interesting and the boys looked forward to the continuation next evening.[6]

Father de Rougé was a strict disciplinarian. Like every experienced teacher he knew that deportment and subject matter grades are interrelated. Deportment grades ranged from 1–5. "5 stood for perfect, 4 was permissible, 3 was bad, 2 and 1 or 0 were followed by an immediate investigation; 0 or red 0 was dynamite."[7] The Brother teacher would take charges against these boys and Father acted as both juror and judge. Father wanted his boys to take advantage of every chance to get an education. He would come up noiselessly behind them, point to a mistake with one hand, and slap the careless student with the other. There was no time for play if the schoolwork was not done.

Besides the weekly checks and reports the Jesuit educator had inaugurated a healthy system of competition for class honors. The students with the highest averages in all high school and college subjects were

[5] Van Coelen, interviews.
[6] *Ibid.* Also: John Cleveland and others, interviews.
[7] *Ibid.*

rewarded at the end of each school year. Many alumni of old St. Mary's have proudly recalled how greatly honored they felt when during a public ceremony the orchestra would play and then each outstanding student would be called to come forward to receive his award from Father in the form of various gold and silver medals.

The boys had to help to prepare and store food for the long winter months. During vacation time and after school hours all who were present at the mission had to help to peel apples, slice, dry, and pack them in sacks which were stored under the stage in the old auditorium. The good apples, potatoes, carrots, turnips, and other edibles had to be brought into the root cellars along the hill below the boys' schoolhouse. The Mission had some of its own grain; it did not own at that time enough land to be completely self-supporting. The boys helped in every way; Harry Van Coelen even had to bake the altar breads and when the Madams arrived, he showed them how to do it.[8] Harry Buber, now living in Puyallup, had to help the hired man milk the cows, of which there were about twenty-five.[9]

The orchards, gardens, and parks were irrigated with water from the "Squant," the falls of Omak Creek, where the boys had built a dam to collect the water. Since metal pipes were not available or they were too costly in this part of the country, square wooden ones were constructed and laid all the way from the falls to the Mission for domestic purposes. It was many years before these flumes could be replaced by metal water pipes. Various irrigation ditches helped water the soil and served as a demonstration to future Indian farmers. Did the pioneer missionary have a vision into the future of his Mission and see the difficulties his successor, Father Celestine Caldi, S.J., would experience, when a white man settled above the falls and diverted nearly all the water onto his own property?[10] We found the original of Father de Rougé's water claims filed with the County Auditor on March 16, 1905. This shows us again that Father de Rougé had foresight and organizing talent. The first "State Water Code" became law on January 6, 1917.[11]

Father de Rougé had written to Mother Katherine, "I am anxious to level our baseball ground."[12] This must have been quite a job considering the otherwise hilly surroundings. This level area served many purposes.

---

[8] Van Coelen, interviews.

[9] Harry Buber, interview and letter to the author.

[10] Rev. Celestine Caldi, S.J., "Disputes about Water Claims," *The Caldi Papers*, Mss., OPA.

[11] De Rougé Water Claims, Ms., SM. Also: Robert H. Russel, Assistant Supervisor, Division of Water Resources, Olympia, to the author, June 1, 1960.

[12] De Rougé to Mother Katherine, August 28, 1907, Ms., ABSS.

The boys would open the dam and flood the ground in wintertime. The below-zero temperatures of the earlier Okanogan winters did the rest and the boys had their ice skating rink.

Good Mother Katherine probably wanted to know the problems of the Mission again. When speaking about his needs Father pointed out that mattresses, tables, musical instruments, books, and many other things would be welcome. Then he refers to the needs of his science laboratory:

> I am planning also a room with instruments of Physics to give the boys a good and useful recreation and put our school above the level of the humble public schools all around us. The people should see that here we can teach more than the other schools.[13]

Harry Van Coelen remembers the curiosity aroused by the chiefs when seeing the many strange instruments and gadgets in Father's science room. Brother Celestine knew much about physics; he had all kinds of electrical equipment for demonstration. Once he invited all the chiefs to hold hands, connected the electricity and "made the sparks fly out of their hands. They never wanted to have anything to do with that thing." Then Brother took one of the chiefs and had him stand on the electric stool which itself was on glass, and then started hitting him with a rabbit skin. He then asked Chief Smitkin to touch him with his finger. "A long tongue of fire came out." Brother Celestine then took half globes and used the vacuum pump to hold them together. The chiefs were asked to try to pull the half globes apart. Then Brother Celestine took the globe, turned the knob to release the pressure, which they did not see, and the two half globes lay in his hands.[14] Maybe these superstitious chiefs really thought that there were spirits in Father's laboratory.

Father de Rougé replaced the kerosene lamps with carbide lights. The second Japanese cook of the Mission once let the carbide gas burn all night in his room. The boys took the burner off and filled it with soap.[15] This Japanese cook must have felt out of place at a Catholic mission. When this cook would hear church hymns and organ play he would dance. He told the boys, "Man comes from the monkeys." "Not all men come from the monkeys, only the Japs," the boys would tell him. He would boast to the boys that the Japs would conquer the United States after they had conquered China.[16]

The Jesuit educator was constantly trying to raise the standards of his boys' school. He remarked to Mother Katherine that when the reserva-

---

[13] De Rougé to Mother Katherine, March 5, 1909, Ms., ABSS.
[14] Van Coelen, interviews.
[15] *Ibid.*
[16] John Figlenski, interview.

tion was opened it might be hard to urge the Indians to attend the mission school unless they saw the superiority of his school. The country would then be filled with people. Father was looking for a piano which he felt he needed at once; and he figured the cost of repairing the old building.[17]

In his next letter Father speaks about his troubles but at the same time tells of his great encouragement over his good boys. "Our big boys are doing fine, and take great interest in their school, the contrary of so many others in other places." His boys have formed a club on their own initiative to advance the education of their tribes. They have prepared speeches and had already called a meeting with the chiefs to stress the importance of education and to interest them in bringing all the children to St. Mary's Mission to be educated. The students were daily communicants and they belonged to the Sodality of the Blessed Virgin. One of the boys had suggested having a mission banner; everyone contributed from the little they had and now they have $35 for it. If the boys continue the way they are now, Father de Rougé says, success really will come. The boys will be able to deny the false charges that to educate Indians will be a fruitless task. The boys felt the challenge put to them and can in this way do more good than the priest could accomplish in many years. Then as so often, Father is asking again that Mother Katherine should pray for his boys that God may keep the temptations of the world away from them.[18]

It seems that Father was never out of trouble. The second addition to the convent, consisting only of boards, had just been erected when Father discovered the old building could not be repaired; he had to start all over again to build another boys' school. He had thought that his first set of buildings would last a few years when, in 1907, he had made the last improvements. Now four important building projects needed his attention simultaneously: a convent and girls' school, a hospital, a new church and a new boys' school. The missionary tells the bad news to Mother Katherine:

> The old school house for the boys was put up at the time I had no means, and put up for a time, now we discover it is dangerous and the dormitory upstairs not safe. I will have to try and hope in Holy Providence to start at once a new building but when shall we be able to finish it? It is the same for the church as the two schools now nearly fill it up, and there is no more room for the Indians inside. I got both permissions for building and now what will the Sacred Heart send me?[19]

[17] De Rougé to Mother Katherine, March 5, 1909, Ms. ABSS.
[18] *Ibid.*, May 4, 1909.
[19] De Rougé to Mother Katherine, August 28, 1909, Ms., ABSS.

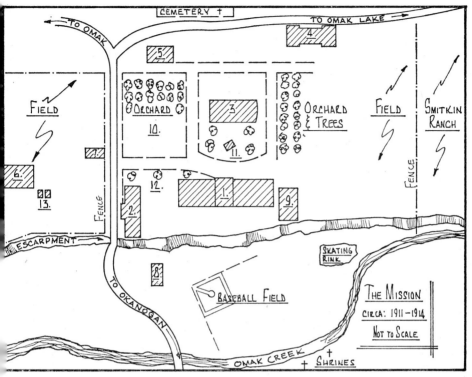

1. **Boys' school** (destroyed by fire in 1919); 2. Old building used mainly for employee quarters and storage; 3. New church; 4. Convent and girls' school; 5. Infirmary; 6. Barn; 7. Site of Corrigan's store (torn down — Corrigan removed to Omak); 8. Old field house; 9. New gymnasium; 10. Trees planted in circle cut down; 11. Bandstand; 12. Lawn; 13. Pig feeding enclosures.

"The building of the new church was uneventful. I and some boys together with a teacher named N. C. H. Smith dug the foundations on our own measurements but the carpenters and masons found our digging to be out of line so we had to re-dig the foundations. When the frame was completed, it was seen that the steeple, though built with the longest lumber available, looked stunted. In order to get the proper proportions it was necessary to add additional lumber of the same length to the half-way point of the structure. Sister Katherine Drexel of the wealthy Philadelphia Drexel family, was a never failing benefactor of the Mission. How much she contributed to the building program, I don't know. Considerable money was raised too through letter writing campaigns. Some of the boys used to write many of the letters in long hand." (Fr. de Rougé's note).

We should not forget that Father de Rougé still had quite a large mission territory to visit besides taking charge of all the problems at home. He had the best cooperation from the Lamennais Brothers who had the boys well in control; the schedule would be observed as rigorously as if the Superior himself were present. Father de Rougé has succeeded in blending the second group of Lamennais Brothers, who had come in 1906, together with his grown-up boys, into a closely-knit unit, who had the interests of their Mission at heart. This was their home, their school; the priest was their beloved Father whom they saw sacrificing himself for their welfare. His problems would be also their problems.

Toward the girls and the Sisters, Father was very reserved. Sister M. Michael told that she never saw him shake hands with a girl. Nobody was supposed to address him if they should meet him on the grounds; a simple nod of the head became the standard greeting.[20] With the exception of the few faithful Madams, the majority of the Catechists felt isolated. They considered themselves merely the needed cheap workers. It would have saved Father de Rougé much trouble if he had used a more congenial and prudent approach, and made the girls' school and the Ladies Catechists another unit with whom he could share some of his problems and listen to an occasional suggestion. By listening to them he would have enabled them for one thing to fulfill a psychological need. These ladies had only their companions with whom to share their views in that very isolated spot. They were not recognized religious and most certainly had not the vocation to lead a Trappist's life. In addition, they had come from big cities into a wilderness.

A completely different spirit prevailed at the boys' school. Teachers and boys became active helpers in raising funds for their Mission projects. Once, while Father was on a missionary trip, they sent a report on all the boys to Mother Katherine. Mother Katherine paid for the girls after Father had sent a report with their names, degree of Indian blood, days attended, etc. Perhaps the boys felt they were left out. Father wrote to Mother M. James:

> Many thanks for your kind letter and check. If a report of the boys was sent, it was that the reports were sent in my absence by the teachers and they made a mistake.[21]

He repeats to Mother M. James what he had written to Mother Katherine, that he intends to build a new church. The old church then will be used for a part of the school building, because the boys' school is too small also. He has written many letters begging for money; and he asked Mother James to contribute a little help toward meeting the building costs:

> The bad season comes quick, and I wish I could cover the church, and perhaps work inside during the winter. God knows what I will be able to do. The good Mother is doing already so much for me, but she is able. I am sure she would not refuse a little, even a little would be of help.[22]

---

[20] Sister M. Michael, O.P., interviews.   [22] *Ibid.*
[21] De Rougé to Mother M. James, October 15, 1909, Ms., ABSS.

In the building of his second church Father de Rougé had very enthusiastic helpers in his big boys. They were busy digging the trenches for the foundation, hauling rocks on a wagon, taking orders from the carpenters and acquiring many useful skills for later life. How many times former students have pointed to the church, the only building still kept up from Father's time, and told the author, "I helped build that church." The church was erected largely by volunteer help of carpenters who could not work steadily on the project. Some of the men who helped were: Ernest Middleton, Paul Stahl, Bill Byars, Victor Gengro, Francois Desautel, and George Wanicut. The building lumber came from Oroville by steamboat. Other lumber was hauled from Conconully and closer places. Good old Grandma Zacherle told how she sewed muslin strips together day and night for under the laths, which were used in the frames of the walls.[23]

Some old Indian people told the author that the first new church did not look the way it is now. Nobody seemed to know just what was different until the author found a photograph of the church made in 1913. Visitors coming from Kamloops, B. C., have stated that there are great similarities between the churches at St. Mary's and at Kamloops. Former students remember inquiries made by Father de Rougé about the Kamloops church, before he made his own plan, which was in the form of a straight cross. The back of the main altar was so constructed that it could be used as a kind of a sacristy with a dressing table, drawers and cupboards for the vestments. The main altar had been in the first church; now it was enlarged for the new church.[24]

Mrs. Florence Bernier Opel remembers when the church was built and the carpenters tried to raise the cross and the bell up to the steeple:

> In those days they did not have the modern cranes to hoist heavy things like they do now and they had to do it by hand. I can still see Father de Rougé standing with his hands clasped behind his back and cautioning the men to be careful not to fall.[25]

Francis Favel and other workers in Father's office sent thousands of letters in all directions begging money to complete their church. Letters went to New York, Boston, Washington, D. C., Syracuse, Pittsburgh, Dawson City in Alaska, and others.[26] The bell of the second church is a piece of history of St. Mary's Mission. It had served the first house chapel and had been shipped from Milwaukee to Omak in 1890. Through the decades it had pealed for the glamorous gatherings of the tribes in the

---

[23] Mrs. Pauline Zacherle, interviews.
[24] John Cleveland, Francis Favel, William Hill, interviews.
[25] Mrs. Florence Bernier Opel, Seattle, to the author, April 18, 1960.
[26] Favel, interview.

Omak Creek Valley; it had given the signals for their religious and social gatherings. Every phase of the daily order from morning until night was regulated by this bell. It also served to announce the end of the earthly sojourn of many good old Indian people and accompanied them by its tolling to their final resting place.

John Cleveland wrote in his *Reminiscences* of his student days at St. Mary's that it was always somewhat of a mystery to him how and where Father got the money for the buildings and how he could carry on his school. "It must have cost a lot of money to feed all of us, who in most cases, did not pay tuition or for board and room."[27] A written permit from Bishop O'Dea to "solicit aid along the Columbia River," reveals that Father de Rougé tried all means available.[28] Some help toward completion of the church was received from the Extension Society, as correspondence shows.[29]

The following information is from Mr. F. A. De Vos, former owner of the *Omak Chronicle:*

> Fr. de Rougé remains one of the most cherished memories of early days of the wife and myself in the Okanogan country. This man was a true Christian in every sense of the word. More than this, he willingly, and cheerfully, gave not only all the substance of his share of a large French estate, but his whole life for the betterment of the Indian youth and all others, old or young, regardless of faith, color or state of sinfulness.
>
> When personal resources were all expended, the Father had my little Omak Chronicle print shop make several thousand circular letters which were mailed to France. Our local banker informed me his first mailing returned a bit over $4,000.00. Do not remember how many times this was repeated.[30]

No matter how urgent the work to be done, be it helping build the church or the new school, Father de Rougé never allowed it to interfere with schoolwork. Nobody was to be called out of classrooms, especially during morning hours. However, Father knew how to decide what kind of education would be necessary in each individual case. Intellectual pursuits always came first for his gifted students. Others needed more practical training or, on account of health, needed outdoor life. Harry Green was a tubercular boy whom Father employed outdoors; he seldom saw the inside of a classroom and got well. John Figlenski also was kept outdoors much of the time.[31]

---

[27] John Cleveland, *Reminiscences,* December 5, 1960, Mss.

[28] Most Rev. O'Dea to De Rougé, November 4, 1909, Ms. copy, ADS.

[29] De Rougé and O'Dea: correspondence, January 7 and 19, March 10, 1910, Mss., ADS.

[30] F. A. De Vos to the author, fall of 1960.

[31] Cleveland, Favel, Figlenski, interviews.

Father de Rougé found a letter at home when he returned from a nine-day missionary trip. It was from Mother Mary James promising help from Mother Katherine after the New Year.[32] As Christmas drew near Father addressed Christmas wishes to Mother Katherine. He is so grateful for all she has done and hopes soon to be able to build more for his convent.

> It is crowded and far from being comfortable. Just now I am working on the new church, and as soon as we can use it, we will fix the old one for the department of the large boys. God knows how I will get out of all this and when . . . having nothing for it.[33]

The year 1909 had brought another big loss for Father's large mission territory: the second church at Schall-kees, now Ellisforde, which had been built in 1888, burned down. Mr. Narcisse Nicholson, whose home had burned and who was living with his family in the church while his new home was being built, says that it happened during the summer months.

> It was believed the fire was set by one of the Haley Brothers John or Lou, out of vengeance because previously I had been deputized to help catch the Haley Brothers for rustling cattle and had trailed them almost to Republic before they were caught. Some of the old Indians warned me that Lou Haley was going to kill me. I and my family barely escaped because the fire started in the middle of the night.[34]

The question might arise: why did Father de Rougé go through all the trouble to preserve his schools, which consequently resulted in so many worries? Why did he not send the Catholic Indian children to government or public schools? The best answer may be found in the encyclical of Pope Pius XI, "Christian Education of Youth":

> Christian education takes in the whole aggregate of human life, physical and spiritual, intellectual and moral, individual, domestic and social, not with a view of reducing it in any way, but in order to elevate, regulate and perfect it, in accordance with the example and teaching of Christ.
> Hence, the true Christian, product of Christian education, is the supernatural man who thinks, judges and acts constantly and consistently in accordance with right reason illumined by the supernatural light of the example and teaching of Christ; in other words, to use the current term, the true and finished man of character.[35]

Our studies and observations warrant the statement that Father de Rougé was two thirds successful in reaching this goal of a truly Christian edu-

---

[32] De Rougé to Mother Mary James, November 1, 1909, Ms., ABSS.
[33] De Rougé to Mother Katherine, December 19, 1909, Ms., ABSS.
[34] Nicholson, written account.
[35] Pope Pius, XI, "Christian Education of Youth," in Gerald C. Treacy, S.J., ed., *Five Great Encyclicals*, 65.

cation. Those of his students who completed their junior college training under his guidance became upright Christian leaders in civic affairs ready to compete with their white brothers in every way on equal terms.

The Colville Confederated Tribes had been essentially devout in their primitive life. Their former pagan ceremonies, fasts and even superstitious practices had dominated all their secular affairs. They had adhered rigidly to their customs. The acknowledgment of a Supreme Being, of a "Great Spirit" was the foundation upon which the "Black Robes" built the essential doctrines of Christianity. Father de Rougé and other fearless priests before him knew how to respect the belief of these Indians and use their knowledge for building up a Christian culture. Advancement in religion went simultaneously with development in all modern branches of education and civilized endeavors. Slowly and patiently Father de Rougé accomplished a real transformation from aboriginal and semicivilized living to the modern standards of their white brothers. In many instances ethics and morals of his Indians were on a higher level than those of many whites.

With many building projects going at the same time and the continuous financial difficulties, Father's buildings were not to be completed for some years. On February 3, 1910, the missionary wrote to Mother Katherine: "The church is going slow, but I hope we will be able to use it for Easter as it will be. It will not be cold then."[36] Father has difficult times but he has no debts so far:

> As far as bad news we are losing the Christian Brothers, all called away from our Indian Missions. Will I then have to return to seculars for my big boys? More expenses and more troubles? . . . It was Providential to get these Ladies join my idea of Ladies Catechists Missionaries; otherwise I would have to close the school.[37]

All the following letters of the great educator to his benefactress express his anxiety for his boys' school. Brothers Celestine, Rene, and Hypolite had been very much loved and respected by the boys. All three were expert educators, played with the boys in their band and knew how to inspire perseverance in studies. Brother Celestine was especially gifted in any subject matter as all former students agree. He was a fine mathematician and the creator of their museum, the pride of their college. These Brothers had helped to raise the standard of the school to the level of the junior college. We can understand Father's fears and worries as time drew near for the Brothers' farewell. John Cleveland is still full of praise for the three Christian Brothers:

---

[36] De Rougé to Mother Katherine, February 3, 1910, Ms., ABSS.
[37] *Ibid.*

These Brothers were the best teachers that were at St. Mary's. They were undoubtedly highly educated and the method of teaching was unsurpassed. — I know I learned more, made faster progress in all my studies under their teaching than under any teacher since.

In the fall of 1907, Bro. Celestine asked the students if any of them would like to play in the band. George Rinehardt, Paschal Sherman, and I raised our hands. I had no idea what was in store for me in learning to read and play music. I thought I would immediately get an instrument and start blowing — but no. Brother Celestine started to teach us the fundamentals of music.[38]

For two months there was nothing but "blackboard music." Then Brother would give John a sheet of music and a baton and ask him to tell the class all about the written music. John Cleveland, in later years, when he was a cornet soloist, was grateful for the Brother's teaching. The band, at that time, had over twenty instruments.

All informants agreed that Father's health was always delicate. He ate "like a bird." Frequently he had stomach pains. When traveling he would order eggs and then often insist that they be eaten by the boys. They all wondered how their Father could exist. All his worries in connection with his building projects, his teaching activities, the direction of the many missions and the immense sacrifices asked of him in this huge mission territory could have broken the health of a much stronger man. The priest remarks to Mother Katherine: "I wrote to you a short note the other day being sick. I am not quite well yet."[39] This missionary had no time to be sick.

Maggie St. Peter told the author that around 1910–1911, Father de Rougé was again ordered transferred. The Indians saw him crying; his whole love was with them and their souls. The chiefs again assembled and pleaded their cause successfully against the transfer. The old people could not speak English; it was only Father de Rougé who could administer the sacraments to them and teach them in their native tongue.[40]

The new church was used for services the first time at Easter, 1910. Father told Mother Katherine:

Easter! We have our new church full, yet [the building is] not half finished. Fine Easter yet — I could not preach having a bad cold and lost my voice for over one week. 7 Baptisms, 2 marriages so far, some returns of [after an absence of] 20 and 27 years to the sacraments. I am so busy that I am pretty tired, yet will not omit to thank you for the two checks arrived.[41]

---

[38] Cleveland, op. cit.
[39] De Rougé to Mother Katherine, March 17, 1910, Ms., ABSS.
[40] Maggie St. Peter, interview.
[41] De Rougé to Mother Katherine, March 27, 1910, Ms., ABSS.

The first marriage in the new church was that of Francis Favel, the former secretary of Father de Rougé.[42] John Cleveland, who now took Favel's place, accompanied Father to Seattle during the vacation months of 1910. They stopped at the College of Our Lady of Lourdes, where Father was able to plead successfully for Brothers. Mr. Cleveland remembers the telegram which was sent to Belgium to the Brother General: "Brother Adrian and Brother Aldridge ready to save school at St. Mary's Mission." While in Seattle Father de Rougé stopped at Lowman and Hanford. He picked out the side altars he wanted from the catalog; later these were shipped from some place in France around Cape Horn. John Cleveland says that this trip to Seattle was his first sight of a big city with its trolley cars and its hustling activities.[43]

The Brothers of Our Lady of Lourdes from Ostaaker, Belgium, arrived a month after school had started. This was the third set of Brothers but the second Congregation. Brother Adrian was teaching the lower grades and Brother Aldrige was prefecting. Mr. N. C. H. Smith helped with the teaching; Father mentions him in his letter to Mother Katherine. Now, besides his many other responsibilities, Father has to do much of the teaching of the college subjects himself. On November 6, in his characteristic style, he writes again to Mother Katherine:

> We have quite a school again, and Holy Providence has sent me help after much trouble. I got some brothers from Seattle. Brothers of Our Lady of Lourdes, Belgium. I had a very critical time to pass, as the school was started and I had nobody to help me, except a man from around here, not even a Catholic. But I was waiting every day for an answer from the Brothers and could not engage double help. Even now they could not give me yet the first teacher, and I hope he will soon come. All our large boys stay fine with the school and are quite advanced, two years more and two half breeds will be able to graduate in the regular college course as any white boy of the states. . . .
>
> I will have to build the school for the boys soon, and even am getting ready to get some material, as the old house is going to ruin fast, and hardly safe any longer. The foundations are rotten and the wall is giving in. We have no room anyway enough.[44]

During the fall of 1910, Father de Rougé looked back over his twenty-five years of work among the Colville Confederated Tribes and among the first settlers of his immense parish territory. He does not dwell on all his accomplishments: the spreading of the faith in so many growing communities, the sick he has healed, the comfort and instruction given, the feeding of the hungry, the Christian civilization and culture he has

---

[42] Favel, interview.
[43] John Cleveland, interviews.
[44] De Rougé to Mother Katherine, November 6, 1910, Ms., ABSS.

planted; he does not count all his personal sacrifices as pioneer of a higher culture who slowly had transformed all who came in contact with him. Rather, his thoughts are with all that still needs to be done. He wrote a summary of the history of his Mission, the language of which seems to have had some editing — probably for printing:

> Twenty-five years have passed. Now on the spot where the religion of superstition and dreams was in full strength, is the Mission of St. Mary, with its new church half finished, the convent of the Ladies Catechists Missionaries also to be completed, a new school for the boys to be erected with a building able to accommodate all. . . . The devil has to retire and give place to Christ. . . . The religion of the dreams is a thing of the past. The Mission had nearly 10,000 Holy Communions last year. . . . The medicine men are trying yet their superstitions, but their power is passing. If only help would come: first more courageous Ladies Catechists and secondly means to build, the situation would be saved.[45]

On December 7, 1910, Father de Rougé wrote an urgent letter to his Bishop. The two Brothers he secured in Seattle had been sent temporarily. The General of the Brothers now wrote that before he could make any arrangement with Father he would need the consent of the Bishop according to their constitutions. He hopes that the Bishop will have no objections. "If I would lose the Brothers, all I could do would be to close here, as no seculars will take an interest in the Indians. We have now nearly 100 children in school."[46] Bishop O'Dea wrote to Brother Bruno, Superior of the Brothers at Seattle:

> Please inform your Superior General that I hereby grant permission to establish a new Foundation of your Congregation at Mission, Okanogan County, Washington, for the instruction and care of the Indian children of that Mission.[47]

The Brothers were allowed to stay for the time being, but Father de Rougé was never able to secure the help of Brothers for the higher education of his boys. He had to secure laymen, whose salaries added to his worries. In spite of the added cost, Father always stressed the necessity of having the best teachers for his school. A Mr. Luergermiller taught the high school and college subjects from 1911–1912. A Mr. Mullen came in the fall of 1911 and left in January, 1912. Mr. W. E. Courtney succeeded him as an excellent coach in all kinds of sports.[48]

The successor of Brother Celestine in the music department was Professor John St. Onge, a well-known musician. Through the kindness of Right

---

[45] De Rougé, *25 Years and Today*, mimeographed copy, ABSS.
[46] De Rougé to Most Rev. O'Dea, December 7, 1910, Ms., ADS.
[47] Most Rev. O'Dea to Brother Bruno, December 23, 1910, Ms. copy, ADS.
[48] John Cleveland, *op. cit.*, and interview.

Reverend Abbot Raphael Heider, O.S.B., of St. Martin's College, Olympia, where Mr. St. Onge died as an Oblate of St. Benedict on May 11, 1936, we were able to copy St. Onge's own record of study and teaching:

Study

4 years	— Christian Brothers, Brother's College, L'Islet, P.Q., Canada
2 years	— St. Joseph's University, Nemramcvoh, N. B. Canada
2 years	— Dominion College of Music, Montreal, Com.

Teaching

2 years	— College of Notre Dame, Montreal, Can., 1900
2 years	— Farnham's College, 1901–4, Farnham, P.Q., Cn.
6 months	— Brunswick, Main, U.S., 1904
3 years	— St. Mary's Mission, 1911–14
14 years	— St. Martin's College, Lacey, Wash., 1914–28.[49]

While at Lacey St. Onge further attended courses in the different branches of music during some of the summer months. He was holder of a state certificate for piano and violin (Washington State Public School), and a certificate from the National Academy of Music, New York, 1922. When St. Onge wrote his record he had been conductor of orchestra and band music for twenty-six years. Even if St. Onge perfected his music education while at Lacey, this record shows us that Father de Rougé did not employ just any teacher he could find, even if the general standards for teacher's education were at that time much lower than they are today. When applying for a new teaching position at St. Martin's January 16, 1914, St. Onge stated that he needed a change.[50]

A letter to Mother Katherine on February 1, 1911, gives more information about the little hospital Father had started in 1910:

> I have built lately a little hospital, or the start of one, to try to save our tubercular subjects, and not to have to send them home where they [are sure to] die. . . . There is so much to be done for the glory of God. . . . I have a good doctor a protestant, at my disposition [sic] and he is anxious to help me. The agency sanitarium proved a failure and they gave it up. I want to buy a few things that help the examination. . . . I should say Microscope. . . . We have now three rooms and a pantry-kitchen and upstairs, we can have any time two more rooms. The first floor is all occupied already.[51]

Informants have mentioned the multiple cases of tuberculosis that existed especially among the Indians and partly among the whites during the early 1900's and later in the Okanogan country. No medical care and

[49] John St. Onge, *Record of Study and Teaching*, Ms., Archives of St. Martin's Abbey, Olympia, Wash.

[50] St. Onge to Rev. Father Superior, January 16, 1914, Ms. Also: interview with Rt. Rev. Abbot Raphael Heider, O.S.B., Olympia, Wash.

[51] De Rougé to Mother Katherine, February 1, 1911, Ms., ABSS.

The new sanctuary as it looked in 1913.

General view of the growing Mission in 1913.

Level place for ice skating.

The first hospital as it looked in 1913. The only place for hundreds of miles to receive medical attention.

Father de Rougé on sick calls.

*The second set of Chris-
tian Brothers: (standing)
Brother Rene, Brother
Hypolite; (sitting):
Brother Celestine.*

*Corners of the
famous museum
made by one of
the Brothers.*

The track team.

The baseball team.

Two honor students: Paschal Sherman and John Cleveland.

How the first typewriters looked in the the Okanogan Valley.

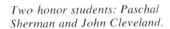

The band, under the direction of Professor St. Onge, provided entertainment for socially starved pioneers who came from hundreds of miles' distance.

The school band under the direction of Brother Celestine.

Mrs. Christine George bestowing her benefactions to Father C. Caldi, S.J.

Chief Coxit George and wife, great benefactors.

Narcisse Nicholson identifies pictures.

The Nicholson beauties: Agnes and Christine.

Father Edward Griva, S.J.

Mother Mary Bonaventura Groh, O.P., took over the charge of the Mission in 1936.

Mother Katherine Drexel, 1905–1936, St. Mary's greatest benefactress.

Corpus Christi procession to the cemetery.

The Dominican Sisters who were at the Mission in about 1938.

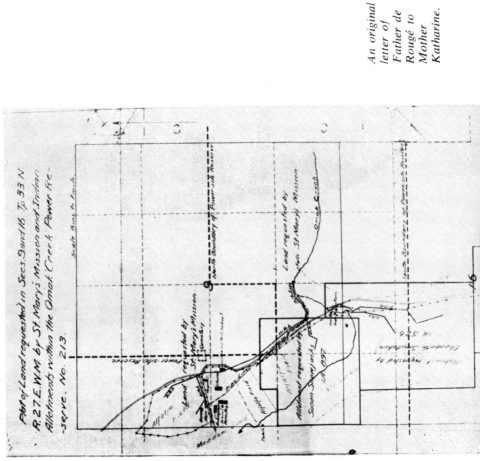

Plat of Land requested in Secs. 9 and 16 Tp 33 N R. 27 E WM by St. Mary's Mission and Indian Allotments within the Omat Creek Power Reserve. No. 213.

ST. MARY
MISSION P.O.
OKENAGAN CO. WASH.

Feb 8 13

Rev. Mr. M. Katharine
Reverend Mother

Many thanks for the church just arrived — I wrote but mail and I had not want ... to say — Thanks God I have a man now ... arrived who seem to be a fine teacher I let us hope for the ... in situation of our ... men. We pray for you all on ...

Yours ...

P. d. Rougé ...

An original
letter of
Father de
Rougé to
Mother
Katharine.

no facilities to care for so many patients were available. Tubercular children were sitting in the classrooms among the healthy and were sleeping in the common dormitory. There were absolutely no means of isolating the cases and even the little hospital was always too small to meet the needs in spite of several additions. Father de Rougé had always been a doctor for bodies and souls to the Indians and they considered him as such. It is understandable that a great percentage of tubercular people could be found at the Mission, hoping to receive help from the priest. How extensive could have been the social work of this missionary if the United States government would have given some financial assistance for this work.

We were told that most of the people buried in St. Mary's cemetery during that period died of tuberculosis.[52] The yearly reports of the Commissioner of Indian Affairs in regard to the Indians' health are appalling.[53] Of special interest are the statistics in regard to the Colville Confederated Tribes:

Colville: Population 2,425
Births 80
Total Deaths 70
     under 3 years 24
     due to tuberculosis 16
Indians examined for disease 533
     found with tuberculosis 75
           Trachoma 226
Estimated having tuberculosis 285
Estimated having trachoma 1,503
Housing: permanent, Families in 584
     Tents, tepees 6
     Houses having floors .... 532[54]

---

[52] John Figlenski, interview.

[53] Cato Seels, Commissioner of Indian Affairs, to the Secretary of the Interior in *Reports of the Department of the Interior, for the Fiscal Year Ended June 30, 1913.* (Administrative Reports in 2 Vols., Vol. I, Indian Affairs), 5–6. "I find the health conditions among the Indians are deplorable. Under the jurisdiction of this bureau there are approximately 25,000 Indians suffering from tuberculosis. Available Indian hospital facilities for all these patients, adults and children, will not exceed 300 beds. During the fiscal year, 1,905 Indians were reported as having died from tuberculosis. This is probably not more than 75 per cent of the total number of Indians who have died from this disease during the fiscal year. Of the whole number of deaths reported from the various reservations, 32 per cent were due to Pulmonary tuberculosis, as against 11.2 per cent due to the same disease occurring in the registration area of the United States. The death rate among Indians is 32.24 per thousand, while the Census Bureau gives 16 per thousand in the registration area of the United States.

[54] *Reports of the Development of the Interior for the Fiscal Year Ended June 30, 1914.* (Administrative Reports in 2 Vols., Vol. 2, Indian Affairs, Territories), 123.

For many years St. Mary's Mission hospital was the only hospital available in the Okanogan county. This big mining county with its 5000 square miles was then too poor to have regular welfare service. No roads and bridges existed; it took time until taxes could be collected. The pioneers had first to establish themselves and to assure a livelihood. It was solely the duty of the county commissioner to look after the poor. Mr. Shamway, a store owner from Omak, called on Mr. Robert Picken, then the County Commissioner. He took him to St. Mary's Mission to see Father de Rougé. In an agreement consented to by the other two county commissioners, Robert L. Wright and Albert C. Gillispie, Mr. Picken made a deal with Father de Rougé to take some old bedridden miners into his hospital. These old miners were isolated in their mountain cabins with nobody to care for them. Now Father de Rougé had a little income from his hospital and served the County of Okanogan with his hospital facilities.

Mr. Picken described Father de Rougé as "the sharpest man I ever met." He could look people right through, was simple in speech and made people feel at ease. He had wonderful eyes, a nice, smooth and high-pitched voice and was a gifted speaker."[55]

Letters written during the spring and summer of 1911 show that Father de Rougé was now building his big school for boys, the so-called "College." He says, "I would have started a year sooner, but I had my hands full with the building of the convent, which is not even finished at all inside. Now they will have to wait their turn, and I must go to work for my boys."[56] Again the boys eagerly helped to haul the rocks for the foundation. By now they had acquired some carpenter skills in building. By the middle of March Father had four loads of lumber ready. He complained about the bad roads which make the hauling of building material so difficult. This year he can build only half of the building; he still intends to use one of the old buildings for kitchen and dining rooms, which will be inconvenient for winter. He tells Mother Katherine who had asked about the cost, that he had saved $1,000 and would need about $3,000-$4,000 more. Even while he is starting his new "College," the educator reveals more of his plans. More laboratory supplies for teaching physics and a gymnasium are needed. He admits, however, that his strength is slowly decreasing.

It is hard for me to have so much to do all the time, build and build all the time, having taken this spot with nothing, not even a room. I am

[55] Robert Picken, sen., interview at Tonasket, July 12, 1961.
[56] De Rougé to Mother Katherine, March 13, 1911, Ms., ABSS.

getting less strong every year, but I am willing to stay to the last, except holy obedience calls me to another place. 25 years here now.[57]

We can imagine that Father was alarmed when public schools for the Indian children were planned by the government. He informs Bishop O'Dea about it:

> I am just told in confidence that the Agent is planning to build three little public schools around us. Of course this would be the ruin of the work here for so many years. . . .
> There is no need for such little schools around as each one would get only a few children, not enough to make a school, while it would drain our [school] out.[58]

When Father writes to Mother Katherine again on May 6, his carpenters are working on the second floor. The part of the building under construction is 108 feet long and contains two classrooms, a washroom, and music room. Upstairs he plans one dormitory and rooms for the Brothers. He still keeps one of the old dormitories.[59] The boys' school was built by the "Word Brothers of Conconully."[60]

Father de Rougé was always very grateful to Mother Katherine. A monthly novena for the benefactors called down God's blessing on her and her Sisters. The promise of prayers was expressed in every letter he wrote her. When Mother Katherine was in deep sorrow over a death, Father read her letter to the assembled children. She was their Mother on whom everything at the Mission depended. We quote from Father's letter:

> In the morning all have been requested to offer . . . Holy Communion for the soul of the dear lady, such an example of self-sacrifice and charity . . . will see to have as you ask, her name on a tablet with the date of this day, as a perpetual remembrance of the help of the Blessed Virgin whose instrument she was made to help us.[61]

In his July communication with Mother Katherine, Father expresses his joy that the new building "will be a credit to the Indian Missions. Everybody is admiring it . . . little by little we finish the inside . . . your name will never be forgotten at St. Mary's."[62]

Mr. John Cleveland related his experiences during a memorable trip he had with Father de Rougé during the fall of 1911. Father wanted

---

[57] *Ibid.*
[58] De Rougé to Most Rev. O'Dea, April 25, 1911, Md., ADS.
[59] De Rougé to Mother Katherine, May 6, 1911, Ms., ABSS.
[60] John Cleveland, *op. cit.*
[61] De Rougé to Mother Katherine, May 25, 1911, Ms., ABSS.
[62] *Ibid.*, July 27, 1911.

to induce some of the Wenatchee Indians to send their children to St. Mary's Mission. The first stretch of the trip to Okanogan was made by mission team and wagon. There a Mr. Rodeymeyer took the travelers in his automobile to Waterville. Travel by car was difficult; there were no graded and surfaced roads and highways, only trails and wagon roads. Another man was needed to accompany Mr. Rodeymeyer. The party had two flat tires before they reached Brewster. It was dusk when they crossed the Columbia on the central ferry. Mr. Cleveland said, "I almost shook my teeth out chattering from the cold ride when we reached the pastor's house at Waterville about 10 o'clock that night." The priest was expecting his guests and had roasted jackrabbit ready.

The parish wanted to buy a car for the Waterville pastor and the car dealer was eager to demonstrate a car by giving our travelers a ride. They went down a steep canyon and had to cross the Columbia River at Orondo Ferry. They had reached the opposite shore when the ferryman asked them to get out of the car while the dealer drove it up the steep bank. Then came the nearly fatal accident. Mr. Cleveland tells about it:

> I got off the left hand side, climbing over the ferry railing. Fr. E. de Rougé, S.J., was behind me, but when I heard a splash I turned around and he was gone. . . . In an instant his black hat came to the surface. I grabbed it then; it seemed minutes before Fr. E. de Rougé, S.J., came up. I grabbed his coat collar but he was too heavy to lift up on the ferry platform. . . . There were four men beside the Father. They got him out, helped him up the bank incline and into the waiting car. About what was said is hard to remember, only the ferry man said, "Father, you didn't lose your pipe." Fr. E. De Rougé, S.J., had plunged into the water and came out with his pipe in the mouth. This incident is the most memorable incident in my life, to save Father from drowning.[63]

At a distance from the ferry was a house where the kind people gave Father dry clothes. The travelers reached the parish in Wenatchee and, because Father had injured his back, they stayed there a few days before they went on to Cashmere. A faithful helper of Father de Rougé, Louie Judge, was waiting at the railway station at Cashmere with a team and a buggy. About two days were spent at the Cashmere mission church.

Father and his companion then traveled back to Wenatchee and from there on the steamboat to Brewster. Here they took a horse drawn stage to Okanogan. The boys at St. Mary's heard about the accident at the Orando Ferry and called John Cleveland "The Savior of the Father."[64] Father de Rougé mentioned this accident to Mother Katherine in a letter of October 20, 1911. "I made a long trip of 100 miles to try to get some

---

[63] John Cleveland, *op. cit.*, and interviews, 1959 to 1961.
[64] *Ibid.*

of the Wenatchees, but could get only very few. I fell in the Columbia and had a narrow escape from drowning."[65]

St. Mary's Mission was for many years the only place where music-loving pioneer people could receive musical training. Mrs. Robert Fancher of Tonasket, the former Wanda McMillan, lived at Tunk Creek. When she was fourteen and fifteen she rode horseback to the mission, staying there overnight to take piano lessons. She did this for two summers when she was fourteen and fifteen she rode horseback to the Mission, staying were given at the Mission if asked for. Father seems to have supervised the activities of his Mission very closely. Mrs. Fancher related, "Father de Rougé came in and listened to my playing. After a while he said, "Young lady, if you are going to ride that far, you should practice to make it worthwhile." Mrs. Fancher said that a Lady Catechist taught her in a whitewashed room.[66]

During the summer months of 1911, some plastering was done at the convent, as Father tells Mother Katherine. His Ladies had lived for three winters in their "board house, which would now be warmer."[67]

Various problems of St. Mary's are stressed in Father's Mission news to Mother Katherine during November. The girls' school now has forty Indian girls and more should be coming. The missionary is corresponding with the Indian agent to ask him to send several poor girls to the Mission. There are sixty-three Indian boys at the Mission; more are still coming. Father is forced to buy all the food this year as the crop was a failure and he sees a hard winter ahead. His new building is filled and he intends to complete as much of it as his means will allow.

> I stay . . . in the old building, which is terribly cold, and even got out of my office to make a dining room for the boys as it was too cold for them to go outside to the old building, and besides I am taking it down to use the material for the work on what we start again.[68]

Father then states that all the big boys are back in school and this stimulates the educator to do still more for them. Some day he would like to have laboratories for the different branches of science. "It is wonderful how they take to this, and how it excites them to stay with their education. . . ."[69] Father de Rougé wants his boys to be the future leaders of their tribes.

The missionary then makes special mention of the Nespelem and the

---

[65] De Rougé to Mother Katherine, October 20, 1911, Ms., ABSS.

[66] Mrs. Robert Fancher, interview at Tonasket, July 11, 1961. Courtesy of Mrs. Nellie Picken.

[67] De Rougé to Mother Katherine, October 20, 1911, Ms., ABSS.

[68] Ibid., November 27, 1911.

[69] Ibid.

Sanpoil tribes. "The infidels are coming to the church little by little easy enough, only they live so far it is hard to attend to them." Then follow some evil forebodings. "All this work makes me old, and I get tired easy now."[70] He is only fifty-one years old.

As the end of the year of 1911 draws near Father writes again to his benefactress. He points out that his students had a very poor Christmas owing to the loss of two packages which were sent to him but never arrived. He has one hundred and thirty people to feed every day now. Spiritually his subjects are advancing; he had a fine midnight Mass and a great number of Communions. He has some men at the Mission over the winter and he is taking down the old building for material.[71]

During the past years great building programs have been started at St. Mary's Mission. Father's plans are far from being completed. Long strides have been made in the field of higher education for the Indians. Greater numbers of souls have been won from paganism. Yet, this great missionary has no time to rest on his laurels. He is climbing toward the peak. Will he ever reach it?

---

[70] De Rougé to Mother Katherine, *op. cit.*
[71] *Ibid.,* December 28, 1911, Ms., ABSS.

CHAPTER XVI

Father de Rougé and the Land Question

AS WE have seen the Colville Confederated Tribes had to suffer greatly, like other Indian tribes, from the unjust and corrupt United States Indian policies. The story of the struggle for their ancient homes, hunting grounds, fishing places and root gathering domains would fill a volume. We merely indicated important points. Many volumes were filled with the multiple laws concerning Indian lands, agreements fulfilled only by the Indians and utterly disregarded by the United States government. The Colville Confederated Tribes never had any treaty with the United States, although they had been willing to have a treaty. They trusted that sound judgment would prevail among such United States officials as would be sent to the Indians for this purpose. They knew that they were wasting land by having merely a food-gathering economy; they were willing to learn the white man's use of the soil. The lack of wisdom in dealing with the Indians, the want of reciprocal concessions, the infringement and disregard of their rights as human persons have been a national disgrace.

The spirit of unrest, insecurity, alarm, and distrust of government officials and finally of every white settler had spread through the Colville Reservation when in 1885 the French Count Etienne de Rougé, S.J., had been sent to work among them. These tribes had formerly been known to be extremely friendly, helpful, and hospitable to every white stranger that crossed their country. Just two years before his coming to the Okanogan country, a strip of fifteen miles along the Canadian boundary was restored by President Arthur to the public domain without consulting the Indians. Then in 1884, the Moses, Tonasket, Sarsapkin Agreement was ratified, which made the Columbia Reserve public domain.[1]

---

[1] Kappler, *op. cit.*, II, 1074.

Much bitterness among many of the Okanogan bands and their chiefs resulted. Then in 1892, the north half of the Colville reservation was restored to the United States, thereby depriving the Indians of more than one and a half million acres.[2] If Father de Rougé would have stayed at Schall-kees, his first place of missionary work, the same would have happened to his mission as it did in 1872 to St. Francis Regis Mission in the Colville Valley; it would have been again outside the reservation boundaries. Again the Indians were called upon to give their last land before their allotments were decided through the most unjust McLaughlin Agreement. Father de Rougé was in the region and was aware of all these infringements on his Indian people. For him their problems were his own problems. All through the years while he was building up his Mission center, from the early 1890's to his death, he was concerned about the unjust United States reservation policies. How many times did he see his people uprooted from their homes and possessions. How could he teach them agriculture and the white man's ways of economics if all his work was undermined? What incentives are there for a more civilized living if every time the white man sees some improvements in homesteads and fields he looks with land-hungry eyes on the possessions of the Indians?

By June 10, 1910, the population of the Confederated Tribes consisted of the following number of individuals:

Columbia Moses 521
Colville, South Half 413
Lake and Colville 294
Nepelem 45
Nez Perce (Joseph's Band) 97
Okanogan 538
Sanpoil 189
Wenatchi (non-reservation) .... 66[3]

The last named tribe, the Wenatchi Indians, especially experienced their missionary's help in securing justice. Governor Stevens' treaty ratified by the Senate on March 8, 1859, and proclaimed on April 15, 1859, granted in Article 10 a special reservation "at the forks of the Pisquouse or Wenatshapam River, and known at the Wenatshapam Fishery. . . ."[4] A

[2] Walt Horan, Congressman, "History of the Colville Reservation," in Hearings before the Subcommittee on Indian Lands of the Committee on Public Lands, House of Representatives and the Committee on Interior and Insular Affairs, United States Senate, Eighty-First Congress, First Session on H.R. 2432, Serial No. 19, p. 7.

[3] Robert C. Valentine, Commissioner of Indian Affairs, in Reports of the Department of the Interior For the Fiscal Year Ended June 30, 1910. Vol. II, Indian Affairs, 56.

[4] Louis Judge, "Wenatchee Indians Ask Justice," WHQ (16:1, January, 1925), 20,

complaint, dated January 3, 1910, shows that this reservation never had been set off. White settlers came and made use of the Indians' land. Agent Lynch surveyed a region some thirty miles farther away and considered the Wenatchees as belonging to the Yakima Reservation. The Yakimas ceded this reservation which did not belong to them for $20,000, to be used for an irrigation system that benefited solely their own lands.[5] The Wenatchee families were landless and homeless. They rightly refused to belong to the Yakimas. A photograph taken by Father de Rougé himself and treasured by Mr. and Mrs. Louie Morris of Brewster, shows a group of Wenatchee children then attending the mission school. This picture was sent by Father de Rougé to responsible men plus the necessary information about the injustices done to this tribe.[6]

United States surveying parties stayed for a time at the Mission and were helped and entertained by the missionary and his boys. Some of the boys served as interpreters. Respect for civil authority on one side and the love of justice and charity toward his parishioners on the other made Father de Rougé serve for many years as the intermediary between the government and his Indians. John Cleveland wrote that

> On or about 1910 and later when the Federal Government was setting up its initial tribal Indian rolls for the purpose of determining the eligibility of Indians for Allotment of lands, the Superintendent, Captain Mc. A. Webster and his chief clerk, later his succesor, J. M. Johnson, were at conferences on several occasions with Fr. E. de Rouge, S. J., to secure the names of Indians eligible for enrollment. Fr. E. de Rouge, S.J., acquaintance among the Indians and his Baptismal Records were of great assistance to the Indian Agent. In return the Indian Agent gave every assistance possible to the Father as he needed — such as policing the camp grounds during Feasts, etc.[7]

The Confederated Colville Tribes adopted many tribesmen and their families into their tribal union. Under the supervision of Indian Agent Captain Webster and the sponsorship of Father de Rougé, they assembled at the mission to vote on the adoption.[8] About 1911–1912, United States Representative Valentine was for several days in conference with Father de Rougé and the Indian tribes on the matter of allotments. This was one of the largest gathering of Indians within memory. Many problems were straightened out under Father's prudent guidance.[9]

---

[5] *Ibid.*

[6] Mr. and Mrs. Louie Morris, interview at Brewster, August 23, 1960. (Both had attended St. Mary's.)

[7] Cleveland, *op. cit.*

[8] Mrs. Arthur Best, interview at St. Mary's Mission, August 14, 1960.

[9] John Figlenski, interview.

Father de Rougé did not imitate other western missionaries by settling on the Indians' land without asking their permission. He had been invited by Chief Smitkin and the tribes he served. The generosity of Chief Tonasket had provided the land at Schall-kees; at Omak Creek, Father de Rougé bought the little cabin and later Chief Smitkin donated from his own land the grounds for his mission center. Our missionary never transgressed against the property rights of the Indians. Whatever he cultivated in fields, gardens and orchards was for his beloved Indian children. He was holding the lands by right of gift, and he had the cooperation of the Indian chiefs in building up this land. When later the land was allotted in severalty the lands belonging to the Mission became subject to the General Allotment Act.[10] Let us not forget that the Jesuit Fathers took care of the Indians and taught them before any Indian Department was properly organized and many years before the government had sent even an agent to the Reservation. Even then the Indians of the Okanogan Valley for some decades hardly had a chance to see the agent.

In spite of all the heroic work done by Father de Rougé, it took many years, even under his successor, Father Caldi, to acquire the lands that belong today to the Pioneer Educational Society, Washington.[11] On December 1, 1905, the south half of the reservation was ceded to the government and the Indians surrounding the mission lost their age-old possessions. Father de Rougé wrote in alarm to the Bureau of Catholic Indian Missions, Washington, D. C., to ensure proper representation by the authorities. The director of this Bureau, the Reverend William H. Ketcham, wrote then the following letter to the Commissioner of Indian Affairs:

One of our missions, comprising church and school known as St. Mary's Mission, is located near Omak, Washington, on the Colville Reservation. As that reservation is soon to be opened, we greatly desire that a sufficient amount of land be set apart for it. I am informed that the Agent has "4 miles" of land to dispose of for agency buildings, schools, etc., and that it is his wish to devote "one mile" of this land to St. Mary's Mission. I do not understand just what is meant by "one mile of land, but I presume the expression will be intelligible to you — I am only quoting from information that has been furnished me. This, of course,

[10] See: "Public Law, No. 61, Act of March 22, 1906, Chap. 1126," *The Statutes at Large of the United States of America From December, 1905 to March, 1907* (Vol. 34), 80–82.

[11] Through the courtesy and generosity of Dr. Paschal Sherman we were able to come into possession of photostatic copies of the correspondence carried on with the Indian Department throughout the years concerning the acquired lands of St. Mary's. The originals are preserved in the National Archives, Washington, D. C. The scope of this work does not allow us to copy them all.

would not mean "one mile" of good land, as it would be impossible to secure this quantity in one place on account of the broken and rocky character of the country. It is desirable, however, to have an ample acreage for school and church purposes, for camp grounds for the large Indian meetings which occur at intervals, and also for the keeping at a sufficient distance undesirable white settlers who may, perchance, get possession of lands adjoining the mission property.[12]

The answer of the Commissioner stated that Agent Captain J. McA. Webster, from the Colville agency was then in Washington, D. C., and that he had referred to Section 7 of the Act of Congress approved March 22, 1906 (Public N. 61), authorizing the sale and disposition of unallotted land in the diminished Colville Reservation:

> That any of said lands necessary for agency, school, and religious purposes, and any lands now occupied by the agency building, and the site of any saw mill, gristmill or other mill property on said lands are hereby reserved from the operation of this Act: Provided, That all such reserved lands shall not exceed in the aggregate three sections and must be selected in legal subdivisions, conformable to the public survey, such selection to be made by the Indian Agent of the Colville Agency, under the direction of the Secretary of the Interior and subject to his approval.[13]

The Commissioner further stated that the Agent meant one square mile of land, or a section, which he would be willing to recommend should be set aside to the Mission for religious and educational purposes. The Mission then had in use about 80 acres of land. As the reservation then was not yet surveyed no allotments could be made. The Office of Indian Affairs, in addition, "does not commit itself to any quantity of land in excess of 160 acres, which is the amount usually allowed.[14] We readily see that the mentioned acreage would by far be insufficient for the Mission's needs; the cemetery area and the camping ground alone had about half of this allowance.

Captain Webster writing to Father de Rougé on February 3, 1909, advises him to select the land now occupied and make up the balance of six hundred forty acres in some other place, but no individual Indian land should be taken without his or her voluntary consent. Captain Webster then speaks about the intentions of the government Reclamation Service to irrigate 2600 acres of land on the great flat principally south

---

[12] Rev. Wm. H. Ketcham, Director of the Bureau of Catholic Indian Missions, Washington, D. C., to The Commissioner of Indian Affairs, Sept. 28, 1906. *Records of Bureau of Indian Affairs,* Classified Files, Portions of 19461/10-816.2. The National Archives Record Group No. 75 (henceforth: NA).

[13] C. F. Larrabee, Acting Commissioner, to Rev. Ketcham, November 2, 1906. Ms., NA.

[14] *Ibid.*

of Omak Creek. This land would not be available.[15] Besides the irrigation project, a power plant was for a time contemplated on the falls of the Omak Creek and a great part of that land was excluded for allotment.

Father de Rougé's friend, Captain Webster, had long expected Father's application for the lands on which the Mission is located but he had not received it. He assured the priest of his cooperation:

> You may be sure that I will do everything within my power to protect the interest of your Mission, for you have done a great and noble work during the past twenty years, and deserve the utmost consideration at the hands of the government.
> Of course I cannot promise favorable action so far as absolutely to prevent the development of the full power of Omak Falls and their vicinity, but I trust that I can do much in preventing its being entirely taken away from you.[16]

As advised to do, Father de Rougé sent his application and a map showing the location and acreage he wanted directly to the Commissioner of Indian Affairs with the following explanation:

> The Mission being in a very narrow place between rocks, has very little good land for cultivation . . . [therefore some] land around has to be saved to have a place for Indian camp, at times such as winter for parents to winter near the school, and church meeting days. I have selected a place at a certain distance, in [the] hope to be able to make of it a School farm in the future to train our boys. . . . We have here nearly one hundred Ind. children going to school and our number is augmenting, the Mission has erected many buildings, and we are building yet, we support our school at the cost of about $6,000 per year.[17]

On April 4 of the same year, Father de Rougé addressed a letter on the subject to Mr. J. M. Johnson, who took the agent's place while the latter was in Washington, D. C. Father had the land surveyed during the winter. This application and the data of the survey were sent to the Catholic Bureau of Indian Affairs, but the Bureau that time did not present them to the Commissioner of Indian Affairs. Father de Rougé also let Mr. Johnson know that the Mission did not want to claim any land at Schall-kees, since all the buildings were burnt down.[18] We can imagine Father's worry that, as the years went by, he was still not the owner of the land on which he was making extensive improvements.

Some actions finally were taken during June, 1910. The Commissioner of Indian Affairs recommended to the Secretary of the Interior that the

[15] J. McA. Webster, Captain and United States Indian Agent, Fort Spokane, Miles P.O., Washington, to Father De Rougé, February 3, 1909, Ms., OPA.
[16] Webster to De Rougé, December 10, 1909, Ms., OPA.
[17] De Rougé to Commissioner of Indian Affairs, January 27, 1910, Ms., NA.
[18] De Rougé to J. M. Johnson, Agency, Fort Spokane, April 4, 1910, Ms., NA.

following tracts be set aside for the use of the Mission. He gives the exact location of the 240 acres of land; then he adds his explanations:

> Father de Rougé has for many years maintained on a tract of land nearby a Mission School for the Indians of this and other reservations, and needs this additional land for use as a model farm and to enable him to give agricultural training to the pupils of St. Mary's Mission. The 240 acres has not been allotted and is not claimed by any Indian, and the Superintendent advises that it is not needed for Government purposes.[10]

Commissioner Valentine quotes again the Act of March 22, 1906, that limited the land to be used for agency and mission purposes to three sections. More instructions follow:

> In view of the extent of the work already accomplished by this mission and the desirability of its continuance, it is respectfully recommended that the Superintendent of the Colville Reservation be authorized to set apart the tract above described for the temporary use and occupancy of St. Mary's Mission. . . . with the understanding that no right, title or interest in the lands so set apart shall in any way vest in the said mission or any of its representatives . . . other than the right of temporary use.[20]

Captain Webster was informed of this on June 24, 1911, and told that no action had been taken toward the setting apart of the other tracts of lands wanted by Father de Rougé. The allotting agent had been instructed not to make any promises until further orders.[21] Inquiries of Senator Pointdextor with regard to a patent for the Mission land shows that all 400 acres requested by Father were along the Omak Creek and all the land with the "exception of a single 40" had been withdrawn, November 13, 1911, because of powersite possibilities. Besides the 40 acres Father now had the use of the 240 acres about three miles west of the mission for farm use.[22]

Two years later the surveyors were at work in the Omak Creek Valley trying to bring order and agreement among the claimants of the land. Father de Rougé did not want the five acres of the Indian Susan Snowjack which had been set aside among the forty acres of church lands. Instead he requested the camping grounds where the Indians' cabins and tents were set up on feast days.[23] A second letter on the same day concerns

---

[19] R. W. Valentine, Commissioner of Indian Affairs to the Secretary of the Interior, n.d. signed by First Assistant Secretary, Frank Pierce, June 11, 1910, Ms., NA.

[20] R. W. Valentine, op. cit., NA.

[21] Commissioner Valentine to Captain Webster, Colville Agency, June 24, 1910, Ms., NA.

[22] Bent E. Hielborn, Secretary of Senator Pointdextor, to Father De Rougé, April 23, 1912, Ms., OPA.

[23] Clair Hunt, Special Allotting Agent, to the Commissioner of Indian Affairs, April 30, 1912 (Church Lands, St. Mary's Mission), Ms., NA.

itself with the claim of old inherited lands by certain Indians which were within the powersite withdrawals.[24] The mentioned allotments of Susan Snowjacks, Elizabeth Smitkin, and John Abraham were later acquired by the Mission under Father de Rougé's successor.[25]

Superintendent Johnson had been asked to secure more information about St. Mary's Mission for the Commissioner of Indian Affairs. Johnson visited the Mission on August 28 and 29 and obtained the following information from Father de Rougé:

1. The capacity of the school is as follows:

   Dormitory: Girls, 60   Boys, 130
   Classroom: Girls, 84   Boys, 188
   Mess Hall: Girls, 40   Boys, 70

   The above capacity is in accordance with the measurements applied to Government schools in conformity with the Indian school rules.

   The school has an enrollment of 108 Indian pupils and an average attendance during the fiscal year 1912 of 88.49.

2. The minimum age at which pupils are received is 6 and the "maximum" 18, although there are each year a few pupils under the minimum and over the maximum.

3. During the fiscal year of 1912, 10 white boys and three white girls were enrolled. Four of these were charity pupils and the other nine paid a total of $475.00 for tuition.

4. No fixed tuition is charged but the parents are urged to pay what they can. During the year there were paid out of individual Indian bank accounts in behalf of Lee Cover $5.00 per month for five months or $25.00; Susan Abe nine months at $5.00 or $45.00; Jermiah Burbar four months at $5.00 and six months at $10.00, a

---

[24] Clair Hunt, to Commissioner of Indian Affairs, April 30, 1912 (Land-Allotments-Powerside withdrawals), Ms. NA. (Portion of 9834-1910 Colville, File #313, Record Group 75.)

[25] Correspondence between Superintendent Upchurch of Collville agency and Father Caldi, S.J., Mss., OPA, 1921–1923. Father Caldi had been the leaser of the Snowjacks and the Smitaken allotments before he acquired the Snowjacks allotment. Madame Blake received the Elizabeth Smitkin allotment on her name; she had offered a higher bid on the land than had Father Caldi. As the Madames were not informed about their status concerning the vow of poverty (the community not being approved by the Church), so Madam Blake had to give this property to the Mission. She paid $4,705.00 and received the Patent in Fee No. 901698, issued April 4, 1923, from Superintendent Upchurch. Father Caldi acquired Allotment S-879, Susan Snowjacks, for $3,500, February 16, 1922. Father Caldi reported that the Mission had bought both properties. See: Historia Domus, 1922–1923. "Praeia dui indica 115 acres et 75 acres emit Mission nostra aqua copiae causa $4705 et 3500. Missioni praedia sunt contigua," Ms., OPA. Translation: "The foregoing to indicate our mission has bought 115 acres and 75 acres to have an abundance of water for $4,750 and $3,500. The land is adjoining the mission lands" (faulty Latin).

total of $80.00. Three intermarried White men contributed a steer worth $40.00 and two full-blood Indians contributed Meat to the value of $25.00.

5. There are employed eight, and sometimes nine, instructors for the boys, four for the girls, and three for both boys and girls, altogether a total of fifteen.

6. The School buildings are situated on the NW/4 of the SW/4 of Section 9, except the school hospital which is located on the SW/4 of the NW/4 of Section 9, Township 33 north, Range 27 E., W. M.

7. The church is located on the NW/4 of SW/4 of Section 9, Township 33 North, Range 27 E., W.M.

8. There have been irrigated about 60 acres of land situated in the SW/4 of NW/4 and the NW/4 of Section 9, Township 33, Range 27 E., W.M.

9. Fuel has been taken from both the lands requested and from tribal lands but no timber has been used for building purposes.

10. A total of perhaps 1,000 cords has been used for the Mission and the School, part of which has been furnished by the Indian under contract and part cut by the pupils and by labor employed by the school. This cutting has extended over a period of approximately twenty-five years since the church was first established. The Mission used one hundred cords of wood in 1912. There is no record in this office that authority has ever been asked or granted.[26]

The correspondence with the Office of Indian Affairs shows clearly the immense patience needed by Father de Rougé and the great amount of "paper work" for which the Indian Office was known. According to the last paragraph of Mr. Johnson's information the attitude of the government toward private Indian schools can be gleaned. Instead of appreciation and of financial help, these officials expected to be asked for permission when Father de Rougé by hard work transformed the underbrush wilderness into a place of beauty and of culture. Many Indians seem still today wrongly informed about contributions of the government to St. Mary's Mission.[27] Some even consider the priests and sisters to be working for them out of free charity on an equal basis with the government.[28]

Mr. De Vos wrote to the author that Chief Smitkin insisted that the Church should have the title to the land to ensure continuance of the mission. Senator Wesley L. Jones was asked to lend his help. Mr. De Vos says that it was his

----

[26] J. M. Johnson, Colville Agency, to Commissioner of Indian Affairs, September 25, 1912, Ms., NA.

[27] Receipts from Superintendent Upchurch to Father Caldi, December 13, 1921, show that Father Caldi had to pay the Government for wood cut on tribal land and that he had to pay 3.00 per head of cattle for grazing permit.

[28] One of the high school Indian girls told the author last year: "You guys took our land away."

pleasure to escort the Senator on a personal visit to the Mission to confer with the Father and Smitkin. The work being done under such primitive conditions greatly impressed the Senator.

When the Senator asked the Father what he hoped to accomplish in his life time he got this reply: "If I can succeed in establishing just three young Indians who will carry on for the benefit of their race I will die happy." My question, as a newspaper publisher was: "Father, have you picked these lads, and off the record, would you name them to me?" These lads were Paschal Sherman, John Cleveland, Sr., now Monse, and Francis Favel.[29]

The land question became more and more pressing for Father de Rougé. The Secretary of the Interior kept on quoting the Act of 1906 which limited the lands that may be set aside for agency, schools, and religious purposes to three sections of land or 1920 acres. Not only St. Mary's Mission but also smaller mission sites on the Colville Reservation needed land allotments; there were camping grounds needed at Nespelem, Rogers' Bar, at the "Little Mission" or at Barnaby and at the Lynx Creek or Hall mission. The allowed acreage for the entire reservation simply was not sufficient. Prospective white settlers were roaming all over the land. Formerly the chiefs had large herds of cattle, now they were too poor to help the missionary. If Father would not succeed in enlarging his land holding and having it patented, his Mission would be in danger, because he would not be able to support and feed all his children. Once the white settlers would claim the land it would be lost to the Mission.

Even the allotting agent, Clair Hunt, was concerned, as a letter to the Honorable E. J. Cannon shows.[30] This gentleman was not a Catholic but he had seen "The high character of the missionaries . . . and the excellent results of their work. . . ." He stated:

> If all the surplus land is opened and the amount reserved for agency, school and religious purposes is limited to three sections the church is likely denied the land imperatively needed for its Mission work. The Church really should have a larger amount than it has selected. Besides a few small tracts at various points used as the sites of little mission churches, there is at Fr. D'Rougé's mission on Omak creek, a grain field, Alfalfa meadow, large orchard, gardens, as well as large herds of well bred cattle. By these means the Indian pupils at the Father's school are instructed in farming and stock raising and it is of the utmost importance that the work is not hampered. This instruction costs the Government nothing and certainly they should have ground to stand on while they are carrying on a purely charitable work.[31]

---

[29] De Vos to the author, Ms.

[30] The Hon. E. J. Cannon was a well-known attorney and was Dean of the Law School at Gonzaga.

[31] Clair Hunt to Hon. E. J. Cannon, Spokane, March 9th, 1915, copy, OPA.

As the correspondence in the National Archives shows there was still more "paper work" to be done before the Pioneer Educational Society[32] could claim the land. Representative Valentine and Senator Jones finally were successful in having reserved some 300 acres of mission land, in addition to the land already set aside, as acreage not available to white settlers. This setting aside of the land only assured the continuance of the work when the reservation was to be opened. A patent in fee was finally issued to the Pioneer Educational Society on November 18, 1924, for sixty acres; twenty additional acres were given to the forty on which the mission buildings were situated.[33] Besides acquiring the Snowjacks, Abraham, and Smitkin allotments, the Mission bought 230 acres for $150 from Mr. Joseph Yung who had been working at the Mission as carpenter and butcher from 1917–1924.

Father de Rougé himself never had the happiness to know that the mission lands were secure for the future. Yet, it was during the very years that he was struggling to secure the title to the land that he built his second Mission center. It most certainly required a strong faith and confidence in divine Providence.

---

[32] Corporate title of the Jesuit Fathers.

[33] See: *Map on Mission Lands* in NA. Also: map from the County of Okanogan concerning mission lands, and copy of map showing the lands at St. Mary's Mission.

[34] Joseph Yung, interview at St. Mary's Mission, October, 16, 1960.

CHAPTER XVII

The Huge Parish Is Divided

NOT only was St. Mary's Mission center growing but the country that belonged to St. Mary's Mission parish as well. Gone was the time of the fur traders. The early gold discoveries in various places in the Okanogan Valley and in British Columbia had started many settlements which had been gradually increasing through the years. Many of the settlements now had gradually developed into towns and cities. The era of the miners was followed by those of the "cattle barons" and the sheepmen. Then came the farmers, the fruit growers, and the lumbermen. The spiritual work of Father de Rougé increased as the number of immigrants multiplied.

All that is today the County of Okanogan on the east side of the Okanogan River was formerly included in the Columbia or Moses Reservation. This was opened for settlement in 1886 through the Moses, Tonasket, and Sarsapkin Agreement which relinquished the land to the United States, as we have seen. As more settlers took up homesteads it became necessary to establish law and order more effectively. This huge territory had been included in Stevens County, and the early settlers had to travel as far as Colville, the county seat, to have legal matters taken care of. In January, 1888, the formation of Okanogan County took place and the first meeting of the county commissioners occurred on March 6, 1888, at the first county seat, the mining town, Ruby. This seat was changed to Conconully after the election.[1] The boundaries of the newly formed county extended as far as the Wenatchee River. The lower part of Okanogan County was formed into Chelan County in 1899; in the same year Ferry County was organized.[2] After the north half of the Colville Reservation was declared public domain a still greater influx of

---

[1] *First Annual Okanogan County Progress Edition* (Vol. 1, 1957), 14 (The Okanogan Independent Press).

[2] C. H. Heffelfinger and George A. Custer, *The Evergreen Citizen*, 233.

miners and settlers into the Okanogan County took place. Between 1870 and 1880, the Territory of Washington increased its population from 23,955 to 75,116.[3] When on September 8, 1883, about sixty miles from Helena, Montana, near Deer Lodge, the last spike was driven to connect the eastern and the western sections of the Northern Pacific Railroad, still more rapid settlement and development of the West began.[4]

Father de Rougé had to use quite primitive means of traveling for many years. Transportation through the Okanogan Valley developed slowly as the old Indian trails became the rough wagon roads. Overland transportation had been by means of the saddle horse, the team and wagon, the stagecoach, and, during the winter months, the bobsleigh. Pioneers tell of icy winters and high snows when Father de Rougé went all the way to Wenatchee on a little sled. Traveling became somewhat easier when steamboat transportation replaced small hand-rowed boats. During early summer of 1881, the small steamer, *Chelan,* was giving service below Wenatchee. From 1888 on, the famous steamer, *City of Ellensburg,* made regular trips between Wenatchee and Riverside, when the water was high enough on the Okanogan River. Smaller steamers, the *Nixon,* the *Enterprise,* and the *Bureau* were added to take care of the increasing need for transportation of people and cargo to the developing Okanogan Valley.[5] Instead of Republic and Colville, Riverside now became the supply station for the Colville Reservation, for St. Mary's Mission, and for the settlements.

The increase in population in the Okanogan County can be compared in two reports. Lt. Francis R. Shunk made an examination of the Okanogan River in 1894. He then listed five towns in Okanogan County: Virginia City (within a mile from the present Brewster); Ruby, with a population of "several dozen"; Conconully, with a population of 200 to 300; Loomistown (Loomis) with about 150 to 200 people; and Oro (Oroville) with about 100 people.[6] The *Okanogan County Directory* for 1910–1911 gives the population of the county for the year 1910 as 15,000.[7] We were not able to ascertain what percentage of the population was Catholic. If we consider that St. Mary's Mission parish territory in early times embraced Okanogan County, Chelan County, parts of Ferry and Douglas Counties, plus a part of British Columbia, we can imagine the terrific work load put on the shoulders of Father de Rougé.

[3] Dorothy O. Johansen and Charles M. Gates, *Empire of the Columbia,* 343.
[4] Harold E. Barto and Catherine Bullard, *History of the State of Washington,* 146.
[5] J. S. Whiting, "Historian Tells of Steamboating," *The Wenatchee Daily World* (April 29, 1959), n.p.
[6] *Ibid.*
[7] *Chelan, Douglas, Grant and Okanogan Counties Directories, 1910–1911,* 324.

Soon the clamor for railroads could be heard everywhere in the Okanogan Valley. It took forty-six hours by steamer from Wenatchee to Riverside. During the winter the crew had to break the ice with dynamite. After the Great Northern Railroad had created in Seattle the western terminus of a transcontinental line in 1893, a complex of local lines gradually developed. For Okanogan County the nearest railroad depot for many years was in Wenatchee. In 1914 the first railroad through the Okanogan Valley, a work train, was put in operation; by 1915 the general public had its railway transportation. Many immigrants from various nationalities had been working for some years on the new railroad line through the Okanogan Valley. Among them were many Catholic Italians who called on Father de Rougé for priestly services. Truly the need for more priests became daily more urgent as the new railroad connections induced more settlers to come to Okanogan County.

As soon as more Jesuit priests became available they were sent by their superiors to take charge of regions which were farthest from St. Mary's Mission. Republic and Curlew and other smaller places in Ferry County received in fall of 1898, a new missionary priest in the person of Father F. C. Dillon, S.J., who succeeded Father de Rougé in that area.[8] The new priest would travel on horseback and later by stage from St. Francis Regis Mission in the Colville Valley. Father Celestine Caldi, S.J., was the traveling priest during 1900–1901. Father Edward Griva, the zealous and much beloved Indian missionary, took over on January 17, 1901.[9] At Curlew, Father would say Mass often at the house of Joe Somday. "They were good Catholics and would hardly ever miss a chance to receive the sacraments."[10] Father Griva would also visit the settlements of Toroda, Danville, and Ferry, formerly in charge of Father de Rougé. The *Historia Domus* from August 15, 1903, says: "Fr. C. Caldi came here during the week to take the place of Fr. Griva, who will go to his tertianship in the beginning of September." Father Caldi was to take care of Republic, Northport, Curlew, Inchelium, Hunters, etc.[11] On big feast days the Indians from these places would still congregate at St. Mary's Mission. According to the *Historia Domus,* Father Caldi became a resident priest in 1908. Under date of Saturday, August 1, we read: "Father Caldi goes to South Half to take residence there." More

[8] Rev. F. C. Dillon, S.J., *Financial Statement for 1898,* Ms., ADS. Also: Marie Louise Hesse, "History of the Immaculate Conception Church, Republic, Washington," in *A Short History of the Catholic Church in Ferry County,* 2–3.

[9] *Historia Domus of St. Francis Regis Mission,* January 17, 1901, Ms.

[10] Griva, Rev. Edward M., S.J., *History of the 50 Years of My Missionary Life Among Indians and Whites from July 1894 Till the End of September 1944,* 25, Mss., OPA.

[11] *Historia Domus,* August 15, 1903, Ms., OPA.

explanation is given two days later. "Monday 3, All Fathers return except Fr. Caldi, who stays for good. . . . Every month he will spend 2 weeks in South Half, and 2 weeks for Republic, Curlew."[12] Under Father Caldi's direction Father de Rougé's church at Republic was replaced by a bigger one in 1913. A new church had been started at Curlew in 1906.[13] When the Diocese of Spokane was established and more diocesan priests became available, the Jesuit Fathers asked Bishop Schinner of Spokane in 1915 to have Republic served by diocesan priests.

Father de Rougé ministered to his parishioners of Waterville and surrounding stations until the spiritual affairs of that area came under the direction of Father J. H. Colin, who came in September, 1903, from his headquarters in Wenatchee. In March, 1906, Father Joseph Luyten became the first resident priest of Waterville.[14] About 1916, the first church built by Father de Rougé was sold and a new one started at a different site by Father Schramm.[15]

Father Luyten from Waterville also took care of the church for whites at Chelan which had been started and nearly completed by Father de Rougé. The financial statement for 1906 shows that St. Francis Parish was still paying its debts for this new church.[16] We see how slowly the mission territory of Father de Rougé became smaller. However, he did not give up the care of his beloved Indians at Chelan and at the Wenatchee mission. As long as these Indian tribes were located and allowed to stay at their ancient possessions he would visit them occasionally at St. John's at Manson; he also would travel farther down to Mission, later called Cashmere, and to Malaga. After 1910, Father de Rougé had to stay more at St. Mary's Mission on account of the school. He had to teach, as the three Christian Brothers had been recalled. Tracing Father de Rougé's mission work through succeeding numbers of yearly *Catholic Directories,* we find that the 1912 *Catholic Directory* first mentions that at Lake Chelan, St. John's was a mission belonging to Waterville.[17] Old St. John's at Manson was consumed by a grass fire on October 29, 1953.

While visiting the Chelan and Wenatchee Indians, Father de Rougé

---

[12] *Ibid.,* August 1 and 3, 1908.

[13] Rev. T. Pyers, "Building Record of Spokane Diocese," *Centenary and Silver Jubilee Souvenir Book,* 50–52.

[14] "Cheney and the Big Bend Missions in Eastern Washington," *The Inland Empire Catholic Messenger* (Tenth Anniversary number, Vol. II, January 1929, No. 4), 35. (Henceforth: IECM). Also *Baptismal Records of St. Mary's Mission* show the early baptisms from Waterville.

[15] Rev. Arthur Joda, "St. Joseph's Church, Waterville," *IECM* (January, 1929), 74.

[16] Rev. Joseph Luyten, *Financial Statement for 1906,* Ms., ADS.

[17] *Catholic Directory,* 1912, 719 (The Wiltzius Company).

would stop along the Columbia and Okanogan Rivers at various growing settlements of white settlers. The good Catholic people felt honored whenever the priest said Mass in their homes. The *Catholic Directories* of 1903–1906 mention that Father de Rougé was in charge of a station called Bruster.[18] This name was anglicized to Brewster in 1906.[19] In his 1907 *Annual Report,* Father mentioned a place called "Nrumag."[20] Considerable changes in St. Mary's Mission boundaries occurred in 1907. Father Luyten now was responsible for priestly services at Brewster. Besides being pastor of Waterville and Chelan, this priest also traveled to Bridgeport, Winthrop, Twisp, Orando, and some smaller stations. The *Catholic Directory* for 1913 names for the first time a church of the Sacred Heart in Brewster,[21] which was dedicated by the Most Reverend Bishop Schinner on June 29, 1915.[22] Places where Father de Rougé had services during 1908 were: Old Mission (Ellisforde), Tunk Creek, Nespelem, Omak, and Murray's Settlement.[23] Murray's Settlement developed into a place called today Malott in the Okanogan Valley.[24] This place enjoyed the services of the Jesuit Fathers coming from St. Mary's Mission for quite some years. Services were in homes; there is no Catholic church, but the place has its own cemetery.

Let us trace further developments of Father de Rougé's big parish near its northern boundaries. *The Molson Independent* of October 12, 1906, announced that "Rev. Father de Rougé, of Omak, will conduct mass at the homestead of Miss Lucy LaLonde, near Kipling, next Sunday, October 14th."[25] The *Historia Domus of St. Francis Regis Mission* recorded: "Since June 1907, places visited by Fr. Couffrant or Fr. V. D. Velden: 1. Oroville — twice a month, about 125 miles from here, new church 30 x 60. 2. Molson — once a month about 125 miles from here."[26] The Archives of the Oregon Province of the Jesuit Fathers preserve a copy of the deed where lots 5 and 6, Block 60, were given to the church at Oroville from George W. Hardenburgh, Harney P. Home, and Lucy A. Home. It is dated August 22, 1907. This deed is re-

[18] *The Catholic Directories,* Series 1903–1906 (The Wiltzius Company), "Okenagan Mission."

[19] *Ibid.,* 1906, 464.

[20] De Rougé, *Financial Statement for 1907,* Ms., ADS.

[21] *Catholic Directory,* 1913, 685.

[22] *Book of Dedications,* Mss., ADS, 55.

[23] De Rougé, *Financial Statement for 1908,* Ms., ADS.

[24] Mrs. Audrey Caulfield, interview at Spokane, September 20, 1961.

[25] *The Molson Independent* quoted by D. E. Wood and others, in *Okanogan Highlands Echoes: Molson-Hill-Chesaw Community Study,* n.p. Also: De Rougé, *Financial Statement for 1906,* Ms., ADS.

[26] *Historia Domus, St. Francis Regis Mission,* June 27, 1904–April 10, 1908 (1907), Mss., OPA.

corded November 16, 1907.[27] Father Griva mentions that Father Van der Velten was the builder, while others maintain that Father Couffrant started the church at Oroville. James C. Lynch accompanied Father Van der Velten on his trip to solicit funds for the church, which was started in 1908. Father Edward Griva traveled to Oroville by train from Colville on September 5, 1913.[28] This trip started his missionary work in the northern part of Father de Rougé's parish for the next few years. Father Griva completed the church at Oroville and had side altars and other improvements made.[29] Bishop Schinner blessed the Church of the Immaculate Conception at Oroville on October 4, 1914.[30] Father de Rougé seems to have been called to Oroville or went there for priestly functions when he met Father Griva at the end of August, 1914. The latter writes about their meeting as follows:

> There I met Father Stephen de Rougé. I was glad to meet him for I had not seen him even since 1899 when he and I were going to visit the Indians in the Yakima country and were working in the field picking hops at Moxee and along the Athanum creek. On the 27th of August I went to his mission for the first time and stayed there one day, then I went back to Oroville.[31]

On September 9, 1913, Father Griva had first services at the Indian settlement Inkameep, B. C. He found a small but nice church there which was all filled with people whenever Father would go there after the first Sunday of each month. Chief Baptist was a good leader for his people; he would always send somebody to Oroville to bring Father to Inkameep.[32]

Sixteen miles north of Oroville was the town of Molson. Here the people of Chesaw, Bridesville in British Columbia, and others would attend services in Parry's Hall before they had a church whenever Father de Rougé would visit them. Father Couffrant had built a church there in 1910. Father Griva took care of the parish and the whole surrounding country from 1913 to about 1915. He found at Molson only the walls, the floor, and the roof of a church. He had an addition to the church built which consisted of a sacristy and of a room for the priest. An altar, pews, and other furnishings had to be acquired. In the meantime Mr. Lawless offered his house for personal services to the priest.[33]

27 *Books of Deeds Okanogan County,* p. 574, quoted, OPA.
28 Griva, *History,* 109, Mss., OPA.
29 *Ibid.,* 99.
30 *Book of Dedications,* 54, Mss., ADS.
31 Griva, *op. cit.,* 107.
32 *Ibid.,* 85, 86.
33 *Ibid.,* 86, 99. Also: Rev. Denis A. Cronin, "Oroville and Missions," *IECM* (January, 1929), 70–71.

Father Griva became a great helper to Father de Rougé in many ways and is still very well remembered by Indians and by whites. We quote the building record he left of the churches he either completed or built entirely, which gives us an idea of his life's work:

```
 1 — 1898 — finished the ch. at  White Swan
 2 — 1899 — built  the  ch.  at  Moxee
 3 — 1900 —   "    "            Prosser
 4 — 1901 — (Fr. Parodi at Mabton)
 5 — 1902 — I finished ch. at  Northport
 6 —  "   —    "    "         Marcus
 7 —  "   —    "    "         Pia  (Kelly Hill)
 8 —  "   —    "    "         Barnabee
 9 — 1904 — had ch. built at  Lodge Pole
10 — 1906 —   "   "    "      Polson
11 — 1907 — built "           Ronan
12 — 1912 — prep. blg. Ch. of Sacred Heart — San Jose, Cal.
13 — 1913 — finished ch. blt. Oroville — Fr. Vanderwelten [sic]
14 — 1913 —    "     "   at  Molson — Fr. Couffrant
15 — 1914 —    "     "       Ellisford — blt. De Rouge
16 — 1914 — built    "       Tonasket
17 — 1916 —    "     "       Nepelem
18 — 1917 —    "     "       Keller
19 — 1918 —    "     "       Monse
20 — 1920 — built St. Michael ch. at Inchelium
21 — 1923 —    "   chapel at Fort Belknap Agency
22 — 1924 — finished ch. along Milk river
23 —       [built ch.]        Cusick
24 —       finished ch. of St. Joseph at Ford,
                       Spok. reserv.[34]
```

John Cleveland has stated that there were no divorces among the Indians and no broken homes during the time of Father de Rougé. Mr. Cleveland saw how the chiefs were holding court to straighten out family difficulties and to bring wife and man together again. All this because Father de Rougé was the driving force behind it.[35] Now with more churches and priests available not all the Indians were known to the new priests. The Indians started to imitate the white man's vices. Father de Rougé had heard about an unlawful marriage of Martin Swimtaken and wrote Bishop Schinner that the culprit was not even sorry about it:

> This man Martin Swimtaken is doing much harm, holding meetings with the Indians to have me sent away from the reservation. . . He is a

---

[34] Griva, *Building Account,* Ms., St. Mary's Mission, Omak, Washington (henceforth: SM).

[35] Cleveland, interview; also: *op. cit.*

general disturber, has several times written against the Agent. . . .

Of course some are ignorant and fools enough to listen to him. They have been making their dances of superstitions even if they had promised you to stop, and we have a general little upset which with the grace of God we will have to overcome.[36]

Thanks to Father de Rougé's harmonious relations with the chiefs, he was able to induce them to assemble for a court meeting to straighten out this public scandal. He asked Bishop Schinner for a document that would show that the marriage was null.[37] Bishop Schinner then stated the facts:

When I was in Oroville, on the occasion of Confirmation, an Indian couple called in the sacristy and desired to be married. Fr. Griva acted as interpreter. Upon my question they assured me, as I understood it, that the man had never been married, and that the woman was a widow. They were then married by Father Griva. Naturally, if as is stated now, the woman's husband was still living, the marriage was contracted fraudulently, and both the man and the woman must be barred from church, until they have made amends for the scandal, and have given evidence that they will lead a good life.[38]

Martin Swimtaken was later converted and is buried at St. Mary's cemetery.

According to the *Catholic Directory,* the Catholics at Loomis were served still in 1909 by Father de Rougé.[39] Then other Jesuit priests took over. Father Griva found the church at Loomis in a "miserable neglected condition." In 1915 Father Thomas Ewing Sherman, S.J., the son of General Sherman, became the first resident priest of St. Michael's Church at Loomis. The priest had suffered a mental breakdown. His idea was to establish a Catholic Colonization Society. He wanted to bring immigrants from Chicago and other big cities to the West and establish them at Loomis. He had acquired the land for the undertaking before Bishop Schinner knew of his plan. The Colonization Society was a failure; however the priest stayed at Loomis until 1919.[40] This little town has no Catholic church today.

The town of Conconully had suffered a disastrous fire in 1892; then came the depression of 1893. The gold-seekers slowly became lumbermen and cattlemen. When the town was bypassed by the railroad it gradually became a ghost town. The Catholics moved to other localities.

---

[36] De Rougé to Rt. Rev. A. F. Schinner, February 17, 1915, Ms., ADS.
[37] *Ibid.,* March 28, 1915.
[38] Rt. Rev. Schinner to De Rougé, n.d. (copy) of Ms., ADS.
[39] *The Catholic Directory,* 1909 (The Wiltzius Company), 606.
[40] Rev. Joseph Thomas Durkin, S.J., *General Sherman's Son,* 225–227.

Today it is growing again as a tourist center. The same fate happened to the mining town of Ruby where once about one thousand miners worked. We were unable to trace the date of the last services of Father de Rougé in these dying towns. Other localities where Father Griva took over were Nighthawk, where he stayed at the house of Mr. Cormely; Bridesville, at the house of Mr. Dumont; Myncaster, at the house of Mr. Methow; and Chesaw, at the house of Mr. Catabin.[41] Under the direction of Reverend Joseph Sondergeld, St. Ambrose Church at Chesaw was built and dedicated on July 6, 1919.[42] As too few Catholics lived there for the maintenance of the church, it was later dismantled.

About midway between Oroville and Tonasket is situated Father de Rougé's former Schall-kees. Around 1911 the place was named Ellisforde after James E. Forde, George H. Ellis, and John Isenhart. These men incorporated the Ellisforde Orchard Co.[43] After the fire burned the second church in 1910, Father de Rougé had services in homes. When the north half of the Colville Reservation was made into public domain, he did not want to claim the land because now he was established at St. Mary's Mission. The Indians, however, wanted their old extensive cemetery preserved. A seven-acre tract was later reserved for the Indians. In 1913 the third church, this time a much smaller one, was built on a new location near the cemetery under the direction of Father de Rougé. Leading Indian builders were Andrew Day, George Tilletson, and Paul Antoine. It is significant that here was the site of Father de Rougé's first church and that here he started his last one. Father Griva completed this church and is responsible for its altar, benches, communion rail, and bell tower. The work was all completed in April, 1915, when Father Griva was able to say the first Mass in the little church.[44] The church at Oroville still has the statue of the Blessed Mother which had been at Ellisforde. Today this little church is still a reminder of hard and primitive beginnings, of the colorful religious festivals once celebrated in this valley. The great white cross made from rocks lying on the side of the hill remains. Visible from great distances it served once as both an invitation and a guide. The exterior of the little church still looks inviting, but looking through some broken windows one sees the dust of neglect that has settled on altar, pews, and organ. The date on the markers of some graves in the cemetery show the age of the Mission — the early 1880's.

[41] Griva, *History,* 99, 100, 104.

[42] *Book of Dedications,* 56, Mss., ADS.

[43] *First Annual Okanogan County Progress Edition* (Vol. 1, 1957), 11 (The Okanogan Independent Press).

[44] Griva, *History,* 123.

Where Tonasket is now there was once an Indian settlement and camping grounds. It became state-owned land after the north half was taken from the Indians. Here were great areas of pasture lands over which the cattlemen and the sheepmen were fighting. Mr. Arthur Lund, then a banker of Riverside, brought about a mutual understanding between the quarreling factions. He bought 320 acres of land at $10 per acre and formed the Bonaparte Land Company. Mr. Lund became the president; T. C. Dodge was vice-president; the stockholders were C. E. Blackwell, Clay Fruit, William Henderson, and Arthur Lund. The next year they laid out a town, which was the beginning of Tonasket. Bob Picken became the salesman for the lots. To attract a railroad, the company gave twenty acres to the Great Northern Railway Company and bought forty additional acres. The city developed, especially after Arthur Lund opened a bank at Tonasket in 1913.

The Catholic pioneers called on Father de Rougé for priestly services and on feast days would camp at St. Mary's Mission. Mr. Lund remembers that once he accompanied Irene Dillebaugh, a Catholic, and Sam Nelson, a non-Catholic, to the Mission. Sam wanted to marry Irene; the party had to stay overnight and sign the papers next morning. It was before Christmas and the weather was cold. The men rolled themselves in blankets and slept on the floor of the waiting room. "Sam slept and I kept the fire going."[45]

Soon Father Griva visited the Catholics of Tonasket and had services either in the hotel of Mrs. Schimneck or at the house of Mr. John Hone.[46] A few more visits and plans for a new church were under way, as Father Griva tells us:

5th October, 1914.
On the 5th the Bishop and myself went to Tonasket to see how the church work was going on. We took dinner with the father of Mr. Lund. As during the conversation we came to speak about the cornerstone the father of Mr. Arthur Lund offered to buy the cornerstone. This is a nice piece of marble with the inscription of the title of the Church that was to be dedicated to Our Lady of the Rosary. Here I must not fail to mention that Mr. Arthur Lund, the President of the National Bank in Tonasket donated 4 lots for the church. This was the greatest donation that I received from the people of this town. Mr. Lund deserves very great credit for though he is not a Catholic, yet he took very great interest in Catholic work.[47]

---

[45] Mr. Arthur Lund, interviews at Tonasket, October, 1960; July, 1961.
[46] Griva, *History*, 97.
[47] *Ibid.*, 109. Mr. Arthur Lund has remained through the many years one of St. Mary's Mission's good benefactors. For seven long years our Sisters had been mixing the dough for the bread of the entire Mission by hand when one day Mr. Lund

The church was built by Father Griva in 1914 and was situated on the hill near the forest service house. In 1929 a bigger church was built on a more central location. This place of worship again became too small and was enlarged only recently. The extremely civic-minded Mr. Arthur Lund is also the "builder" in Tonasket of St. Martin's Home for the Aged, the Dominican Sisters' Convent, the new St. Martin's Hospital, and the Medical Center.

The pioneer Okanogan County most certainly was in need of more churches and of more priests. Often Father de Rougé would complain about the loose living, the bad example of some whites and how they took advantage of his poor Indians. Among them were whiskey peddlers, cattle rustlers, horse thieves, gamblers, and others. Once a sheepherder brought to Father de Rougé a book of checks from Arthur Lund's bank. He was bragging: "I have a mine." He wanted Father to write a check for $5,000, claiming that he had a mine. What promises he made to the priest is not known; but Father let him wait while he sent a messenger to the bank. The messenger brought the information that there was not a penny in the bank for this sheepherder.[48]

Father Griva's work substantially decreased the area of St. Mary's Mission parish territory, even if Father de Rougé was still often called to assist the sick and the dying when Father Griva was busy elsewhere. The *Litterae annuae* tell us about the places Father Griva had to visit during 1914–1915:

> Father Griva administered the following churches in Okanogan County: Immaculate Conception in Oroville, St. Michael's in Loomis, Sacred Heart in Molson, and Most Holy Rosary in Tonasket — these were especially for the whites. For the Indians, however, there was St. Anthony at Ellisford. Besides that, he built and constructed the church of the Most Holy Rosary for the Calispel Indians near Cusick; he had the responsibility of the Church of St. Ann at Pia, North Half; he preached at St. Joseph's near the Inkamip Indians, B.C. and at many other stations.[49]

Riverside, about halfway between Tonasket and St. Mary's Mission, was in its heyday from about 1900 to 1914, because it was the terminal during those years for steamboat transportation. F. J. Cummings, who had started Okanogan in 1886 with a general store, moved to Riverside

---

happened to see the hard work of the Sisters, and as a result he bought the great mixer which is still in use. The children ran when "Uncle Ole" came. He always had something to distribute.

[48] Arthur Lund, interview.

[49] *Litterae annuae a die Julii 1914 as diem 1. Julii 1915*, St. Francis Regis Mission, Ms., OPA.

in 1898 and opened his store there. He added a livery barn for stage horses and a boarding house. His former wife was Alma Kahlo, who had left him and married Captain Hanson from the riverboat. A widow who had two children was cooking and taking care of the household. Mrs. Audrey Caulfield, one of the children, told the author, that when Cummings wanted to marry her mother, Father de Rougé had to write to New York for dispensation; the first wife had been unbaptized. The second Cummings marriage took place on January 4, 1897. Father de Rougé was often a guest at Cummings when he was on the way to his missions. Mrs. Caulfield remembers Father de Rougé as a very gentle man. Once she asked him about the propriety of going to dances. She received this answer: "My friend, if you go to a dance or any kind of a festival you may go as long as you are not ashamed of Jesus seeing you there."[50] Gradually Riverside developed; it had the first telephone line in the valley when in 1903 public-minded citizens connected Riverside with Synarep. It acquired a bank and a newspaper. There was a heated controversy when Riverside, Omak, Conconully, and Okanogan vied with each other for the county seat in 1914. But Riverside never had a Catholic church; Father de Rougé wanted to keep St. Mary's Mission as his center and expected the people to come there.

Father de Rougé wrote to Mother Katherine on August 28, 1907, "The name of the P.O. now is simply Mission, Okenagon Co., Wash."[51] This indicates that the town of Omak was born in 1907 with the original name of the mission post office. Informants have stated that the people of Omak wanted to have the name "Omak" and asked Father de Rougé for it. Ben Ross, "the Father of Omak," must have seen future possibilities in the development of the surrounding country, when in the fall of 1906 he laid out twenty acres of his farm in twenty-five-foot lots and then in January of 1907 filed the plat for a townsite. He sold the lots cheaply and soon a little town grew.[52] By 1915 there were only nine Catholic families living at Omak.[53] The building of a Catholic church and school took place in 1938, under the direction of Father Raymond Riedner. However, the most cordial relations existed between the people of Omak and Father de Rougé. On feast days Catholics and many non-Catholics were at the Mission. One of Father's friends, Mr. F. A. De Vos, the former owner of the *Omak Chronicle* already mentioned, had this to say:

[50] Mrs. Audrey Caulfield, interview.

[51] De Rougé to Mother Katherine, August 28, 1907, Ms., ABSS.

[52] "Cities" Founder Platted Avenues Across Alfalfa," *The Omak Chronicle,* Fall, 1957. Also: "Ben Ross Started Omak," *Annual Okanogan County Progress Edition* (Vol. 1, 1957), 55.

[53] Rev. J. M. Van de Walle to Rt. Rev. Bishop Schinner September 20, 1915, **Ms.,** ADS.

Not being members of your church, my early day connections, and friendship with the father, and his helpers, seemed odd to our Omak friends but the wife and I had lived at Oroville, always doing a lot of camping, horseback riding and became acquainted with the B.C. tribes before moving to Omak. Then, as Owner of the *Chronicle*, the Mission was one of my best customers for printing and we still camped, rode, became acquainted with the local Indians, liked and enjoyed the special Mission services, the Father and his good Sisters.

When we came to Omak, before the railway was completed in 1913, the *Chronicle* had the only local phone that was connected with the Mission and the Indian Forestry service and the Father depended upon us to transmit his messages and announcements, up and down the valley, to his people, even to the B.C. Tribes.[54]

The citizens of Omak appreciated the high standards in music and sportsmanship of the Mission boys and were an enthusiastic audience at musical and sporting events.

St. Mary's had the first school band in central Washington and I am quite sure in the entire state. A most clever French musician, St. Onge, did wonderful work with the youngsters. We all marveled where the Father found the second-hand instruments and how well his band leader repaired them and taught the kids to make such good music. Mrs. De Vos taught primary in the Omak school for several years and she always delighted in telling how one year none of her white youngsters could carry a tune but the little Indians were truly great. They loved music.

Omak was fortunate, and it paid our town handsomely to be friendly with the Mission, because the Father was always glad to have his band play at our celebrations. He also let his baseball, basket ball and foot ball teams play at Omak but Okanogan and Riverside were off limits for Mission Indians as these latter towns had saloons and Omak was strictly Dry, so dry in fact, that our druggist did not carry even one "Patent" Medicine that contained alcohol, and the Omak citizens made it a point to keep liquor away from the Indians, young or old. John Cleveland, Paul and Louie Smitkin played on Omak's baseball team and, travelling up and down the valley with these lads, I can vouch they never went astray. . . .[55]

The big feast days were still celebrated at the Mission even if now other priests were working in the great territory and more churches were available nearer by. Mr. De Vos speaks of Corpus Christi:

In those days, the annual celebration of Corpus Christi was a real event. Between 700 and 800 Indians always attended and the services and processions were truly marvelous and impressive. I can still see colorfully dressed Indians forming at the church and seriously stopping at the various stations along the trail down along the creek.[56]

[54] De Vos to the author.
[55] *Ibid.*
[56] *Ibid.*

Mr. Cumming's place, founded in 1886, and originally called Alma, experienced a little controversy about changing its name to Pogue in 1906. The discussion ended when thirty-nine of the forty-one present voted during the end of November, 1906, to give it the name of the county: Okanogan.[57] The city was incorporated into a fourth-class municipality in October, 1907.[58] In 1914 it won the vote for the county seat.

As the roads at that time were very primitive and the Catholics of Okanogan were not willing to spend too much time traveling to the Mission, they decided in November of 1910, to write to Bishop O'Dea of Seattle that they were willing to purchase the land for a church. The Bishop informed them that they should consult Father de Rougé:

> I am pleased to inform you, in reply to your letter of November 15, 1910, that I believe it advisable for you to consult the Rev. Father de Rougé, at Mission, relative to the purchase of property and the erection of a church in Okanogan, as the place is in his jurisdiction and will necessarily be attended by him for some time to come. If the Catholics of Okanogan and the Rev. Father decide upon building a church in that locality I would advise all concerned to erect a building to cost not over two thousand dollars for the present needs and to arrange it that it might serve later for school purposes.[59]

This letter started quite a controversy between Father de Rougé, Bishop O'Dea, and Father's Okanogan parishioners. Father de Rougé's greatest concern was over the temptations his Indians would be exposed to during vacations of his Indian children, especially the whiskey traffic and the bad example given. How many times had he written to Mother Katherine that the vacation is coming soon and that he begged her to pray that God may keep his flock from sin. The priest tells his Bishop what he thinks of the town of Okanogan:

> The town of Okanogan has been at all times the place where whiskey is sold to the Indians, they hold there horrible meetings, races and others, where the main thing is to get the Indians and sell them whiskey and make them drunk, then get all the money they have. All the towns voted dry, but Okanogan is the only one which kept the traffic, and gives us plenty of trouble. The Ind. Agent and his subagent here have done all they could, several arrests have been made, detectifs [sic] were sent, and plenty of money has been spent to try to stop the selling of Whiskey to the Indians. . . . We expect another detectif [sic] any day to try more work. Okanogan has been the ruin of the Mission work. The fourth of

---

[57] Harry J. Kerr, *A History of Okanogan*, 11.

[58] William C. Brown, "Struggle for Recognition Frame of Okanogan Story," *The Okanogan Independent* (Golden Jubilee Edition), 1.

[59] Most Rev. Bishop O'Dea to John J. McCauley, November 29, 1910, Ms. copy, ADS.

July every year we do not know what to do, as it is the beginning of the vacation of our children, and the first thing is to see the parents take them to this town, the mothers as well as the fathers drunk, and the children, boys and girls, all mixed up in the crowd. We had terrible scandals of course, the subagent of the reservation has been almost driven away from Okanogan, some speaking of killing him, on account of [his opposition] to the selling of whiskey to the Indians. . . . Gambling is organized in town for the Indians on the days of meetings, and races, and money put up to encourage them to gamble.

Now we do not feel much like having a church in such a place for a while, till the people would prove to be a better example to the Indians. The people besides look more at a church there as a business proposition than anything else, as to helping me they do not care at all about that, in fact the greatest number is not giving me anything.[60]

No doubt, Father de Rougé had generalized matters too severely and had not taken into account the upright people every town has. Maybe the overworked priest had already too much to do — at the time he was building a new church at the Mission. He had a department for white children, and he wanted the people to come to the Mission. The Bishop's reply shows the concern of the "good shepherd":

I think it advisable for you to continue the work of erecting a church at Okanogan, provided, the people there pay for the same, as you will then be in a better position to labor among the faithful in that community, and to militate against the vices and occasions of sin you mention. I do not believe you can better conditions by leaving the field to the vicious element, but by being there you can best preserve the parents and the children from the vice and scandal you see frequently there.[61]

The matter of building a church in Okanogan now rested for quite some time. To anyone reading this history it will seem obvious that it was nearly an impossibility for Father de Rougé to attend to building more churches outside his Mission. He had more then one hundred children to feed, to guide, to teach, and to provide quarters for. The state of his health grew poorer. On November 12, 1913, Bishop O'Dea wrote that he was informed that about three hundred Catholics in and about Okanogan were able and willing to support a priest. He asked for information of the exact conditions of these missions and he wanted to have Father de Rougé's opinion about stationing a priest there.[62] Father answered that he did not want the people in Okanogan to think that he was in the way of their getting a priest. "Soon the Railroad will be completed

---

[60] De Rougé to Most Rev. Bishop O'Dea, Bishop of Seattle, January 31, 1911, Ms., ADS.
[61] Most Rev. O'Dea to De Rougé, February 4, 1911, Ms. copy, ADS.
[62] *Ibid.*, February 4, 1911.

from Wenatchee to Oroville and then maybe a Father will be able to travel more easily and visit all the places along the R.R."[63]

Meanwhile the little church was being built. A letter from S. G. Novits of Okanogan in February, 1914, informs Father de Rougé that in accordance with the request made by Father Luyten from Waterville they had taken up a subscription for the support of the pastor. He enclosed the signatures and pledges of sixteen parishioners from the supposed three hundred Catholics who promised to pay nearly $300 annually.[64] Father de Rougé looked over the list with little enthusiasm. Some of his comments were: "Very poor — large family; poor Catholic — never goes to church; has large family, many debts, never any money"; etc. He sent the list to Bishop O'Dea who answered that he had given it some consideration and had his doubts that the good people of Okanogan would be able to support a priest; but if he could find a priest who would be able to work under such conditions he would gladly appoint him to Okanogan.[65] In order to have the church completed, the Extension Society was asked to contribute to the building fund, which it did. Father Luyten would occasionally help Father de Rougé and say Mass in homes in Okanogan during 1912–1914.

White children who had no priest in their locality had to be brought to the mission to be prepared for their first Holy Communion. The parents either had to camp at the Mission with their children for two weeks or the children had to be admitted as boarders. The real reason why Father de Rougé objected to having Okanogan made a parish was given to Bishop O'Dea in a letter dated March 21, 1914:

Sure I have no objection to anything, about a father to come in the country, only would say: We must keep a little territory around the Mission for our own support, especially from now on, and 2 priests 7 miles from each other in the country is too much [sic]. I would rather have another located either at Chelan, Brewster, or Oroville. My own feeling about it should never prevent your Lordship to do anything. . . . [I am looking to the future:] Omak will be a very good center . . . if later on a church is needed for the white Catholics. . . . [Besides.] The reservation will soon open, and a parish or mission must be started towards Nespelem, 40 miles from here.

Lots of white people will fill the reservation. Mission must have a district for the future. In the same time it would be good to have a father travel on the road between Chelan-Oroville. I am told Fr. Griva has Oroville and Tonasket, so the north is attended. Okanogan and Omak are only 7 or 8 miles from here and the church here is sure good enough

---

[63] De Rougé to Bishop O'Dea, November 15, 1913, Ms., ADS.
[64] S. G. Novits to De Rougé, February 26, 1914, Ms., ADS.
[65] Bishop O'Dea to De Rougé, March 18, 1914, Ms. copy, ADS.

for them if they want, in the same time if a father is on the road he can visit these places. Would it be better to give the whole line to one father from Oroville to Chelan [that] is not for me to say or judge. I would not be in a hurry to locate a father in Okanogan on account of reserving arrangements for the future, and keeping a territory for the Mission after having done here so many expenses. Who will [come] after me? how will he be supported? We must leave him something. Anyway anything and every thing is satisfactory to *me*, but it is not *me*.[66]

This is the last correspondence of Father de Rougé about the parish of Okanogan. During the year 1915, Father J. M. Van de Walle, a good friend of Father de Rougé, helped out during his absence by coming from Wenatchee, where he was stationed. He answered a letter from Bishop Schinner of Spokane about the appointment of a priest who would reside at Oroville and would take charge of Okanogan. Oroville then had 23 good families, a little church nearing completion.[67] On September 20, 1915, the same priest writes again:

I had endeavored to get the Omak people to come to Okanogan, but in vain. If I had stayed I would have said the 1st Mass at Omak and the 2d at Okanogan, which distance is only four miles. A few weeks ago I learned that Omak has 9 Catholic families; Father de Rouge states that they come to Mission; alas, only 2 families go, so I understand. I wish that the next priest would take care of Omak, he could perhaps say Mass in the house of Mr. Porter. . . .[68]

According to this letter we know that by this time the new priest residing at Oroville had not yet arrived. Father Van de Walle continues in the same letter:

Father de Rouge was absent on the 2d Sunday, but I helped him, gave Holy Communion at Mission at 6 o'clock, drove to Okanogan where I said Mass at 9 o'clock, preached and instructed the children; I reached the Mission at 11:30, sang Mass and preached.[69]

Parishioners often did not realize the sacrifices a priest had to undergo by serving more than one parish. If Father de Rougé had this Sunday schedule he would not get a drink of water from midnight on until after the last services. Only Father de Rougé could feel what this meant for his weakened condition.

By September 21, 1915, the church at Okanogan was under roof and ready for plastering.[70] Okanogan became a mission of Oroville only

---

[66] De Rougé to Bishop O'Dea, March 21, 1914, Ms., ADS.
[67] Rev. J. M. Van de Walle to Bishop Schinner, September 20, 1915, Ms., ADS.
[68] Van de Walle to Bishop Schinner, September 20, 1915, Ms., ADS.
[69] *Ibid.*
[70] Most Rev. Bishop Schinner to Rev. E. B. Ledovina, Vice-President of the Extension Society, Chicago, September 21, 1915, Ms. copy., ADS.

for a short time. In 1915 Father P. C. Tritz became the first resident pastor of St. Agnes Church at Okanogan; and Oroville, Brewster, Pateros, and the entire Methow Valley were taken care of by this priest.[71] Gradually more churches were built and more parishes established for the whites in the former immense parish territory of St. Mary's Mission.

Many of the whites now had at least monthly services, but not so the many scattered bands of Indians. The United States Indian policy of the Colville Reservation was such that many different tribes were now more or less centered around Nespelem and Inchelium and other smaller settlements. The Colville Confederated Tribes had been generous in adopting tribesmen who had no home. Even the sons of Chief Kamiakin, the last chief of the Yakimas, were living on the Colville Reservation at Nespelem. Slowly the ice had been broken and members of the Moses tribe followed each other in asking Father de Rougé for baptism. Only at great intervals was the priest able to travel the forty miles on horseback and attend to them. Faith needs to be nourished and deepened, and it is not surprising that in many instances there were now baptized Christians who practiced many pagan superstitions. Father de Rougé had often stated the necessity of establishing a parish at Nespelem. Again Father Griva was chosen to be the builder.

The *Historia Domus* mentions on September 12, 1915, "Accordingly Fr. Griva will be stationed at Nespelem."[72] He had arrived at his new place on September 7, 1915.[73] The Indians there then numbered about 500. "Almost all the Nespelem and Moses Indians have been baptized, but the Yakima and Nes Perces are for the most part still pagan," wrote Father Griva. Each tribe had its own peculiar dialect;[74] the priest had first to learn the Moses' language.[75]

The beginnings at Nespelem were like the ones at St. Mary's, full of hardships and very primitive. Father Griva did not have a place to stay and to sleep. Chief Nespelem George was very kind and gave him meals and a bed. On September 8, Father said the first Mass at the house of David Peon. On Sundays Mass had to be said either in the schoolhouse or in Condon's Hall. Winter was coming; for the time being Father Griva built himself a little 10 by 14-foot cabin. It served as bedroom, kitchen, and chapel all in one. Father de Rougé wanted Father Griva to take care of the spiritual affairs of the children of the Mission

---

[71] Rev. G. Feisst, "St. Agnes Church, Okanogan," *IECM* (January, 1929), 30.
[72] *Historia Domus, St. Francis Regis Mission,* September 12, 1915, Mss., OPA.
[73] Griva, *History,* 131. Also: Griva. "A Brief Account of the Missions of the Sacred Heart at Nespelem," *WL* (48:2, 1919), 210.
[74] Griva, *History,* 137, 131.
[75] *Ibid.*

in addition to his work at Nespelem. During December, 1915, Father therefore preached a triduum for the Sisters and the children of St. Mary's Mission. While at the Mission he tried to learn more of the Moses' language from Father de Rougé. As Father Griva had no church yet in Nespelem, he helped Father de Rougé at St. Mary's Mission during the big Indian gatherings before the feast days.

Many mines had been operating around Nespelem. It was thought that a big house could be erected that would serve as a hospital for the miners and be at the same time the priest's residence. The first Mass in this house was celebrated on May 21, 1916. At the same time the building of a church was under way. Mother Katherine contributed $1,000 for this purpose. Mass was said in the unfinished church on June 18, 1916.[76] Bishop Schinner dedicated the church in Nespelem on June 7, 1917. It was named the Church of the Sacred Heart.[77] This big church was later leveled by fire. A beautiful new Church of the Sacred Heart at Nespelem was completed in 1963–1964, through the efforts of Rev. Gordon Keys, S.J., and very mission-minded Miss Mary Milla.

Two more mission churches were built by Father Griva. The Indians in the San Poel Valley had used a small building as a church which had been dedicated under Father Caldi on October 26, 1916.[78] Father Griva did not like the location so near the river and the little church was too small and damp. A new Church of St. Rose was ready for Mass on November 1, 1917, and dedicated May 31, 1923.[79] Father also built the first church at Monse, situated on the reservation side of the Okanogan River on the hill near Chickencreek. This was blessed by Bishop Schinner on September 9, 1918.[80]

The Katar Valley near Omak Lake had formerly quite a settlement. Here was the home of Chief Coxit George, St. Mary's great benefactor. Father Griva took charge of this station also; there was no church, but there was a Catholic cemetery, where he once conducted the funeral of Sam George and tells of an old Indian custom that is still partly in use today:

> After the people went back to the house I saw something that I had never seen before, nor after. Everything that was in the house was given away so that every Indian who had attended to the burial received something. In the evening absolutely nothing was left in the house and the poor wife of Sam with her 4 children had to go to the house of her father-in-law, Coxee George.[81]

---

[76] Griva, *History*, 138 ff.
[77] *Book of Dedications*, 56, Mss., ADS.
[78] *Ibid.*, 54.
[79] *Ibid.*, 57.
[80] *Ibid.*, 56; also Griva: *op. cit.*, 157.
[81] Griva, *op. cit.*, 149.

During November of 1918, Father Griva was recalled to St. Francis Regis Mission in the Colville Valley. With the responsibility of all other Indian missions of the Reservation, except St. Mary's Mission, he was not able to see his former parishioners more than once every three months. St. Mary's Mission again had to bear the additional burden for some years. The Indians were reluctant to call on diocesan priests for the administration of the sacraments; they wanted "Black Robes" who spoke their language.

We have seen how Father de Rougé's huge parish was divided. There was no time for him to go fishing for fish; he had only time to fish for more souls.

CHAPTER XVIII

Until the Heart Stood Still

IT SEEMED that Father de Rougé had a forewarning of an early death. While his large parish territory gradually changed its boundaries, he intensified his work at St. Mary's Mission center. He drove himself to complete his plans, but in order to do so, he again needed the help of Mother Katherine. A succession of letters in the beginning of the year 1912 shows that he was in great need. Mother Katherine was to him his only refuge. He reminded her that in addition to the girls he also had sixty-one boys. Father Ketcham from the Catholic Indian Bureau was unable to help him for quite some time. He told his benefactress that "in France we had no crop and my brother was unable to help me for several months, so I have nothing left to pay my bills now. I expect your kind check soon."[1]

The generous Mother had helped again and Father told her how welcome her check was. He had put the money to good use. "Anyone who will come after me, will find, I hope, the place fixed, and will never have to pass [through] what I passed [through], having started here with a piece of bare ground." Then Father continued asking Mother Katherine to pray for his Mission and especially for his young men, whose future he regarded as so important. Father still needed many things to make his school a success. He named the building of shops and the plastering of the convent.[2] Here Father de Rougé stated again the most important need of the Indians: education — higher education for the leaders of the people. If they want to compete with their white brothers only higher education can give them the means to do so.

A precious little letter of Mother Katherine survived the fires or the willful destruction:

[1] De Rougé to Mother Katherine, January 25, 1912, Ms., ABSS.
[2] *Ibid.*

Upon reading your letter about the number of girls that should be in school, we arranged to pay for 40 pupils during 1912 instead of 30, if you can get enough to make an average of 40 per quarter. The allowance is at the rate of $25 per capita for the Quarter.[3]

This letter arrived most probably toward the end of January or at the beginning of February, 1912. Under date of February 6, Father thanked her:

Many thanks for your kindness and charity announcing that you will support more girls in our school.

May God Almighty bless you as I ask Him to do, and after all He is the only One who knows how to reward. Pray for me and these poor children.[4]

We found a part of a letter written by Father de Rougé wherein he complains that the Indians are not generous anymore:

. . . in some places they will make a small collection at the end of a visit of the priest to a tribe. Yet many will give not even for masses. They will divide all the property of the dead Indian, spend as much as several hundred Dollars in a meeting for big dinners in honor of the dead and not give a cent for the priest, and some are never proud enough if the priest ask them to do something for them. Not only this. You will hear some talk against collections taken in church and think that the priest should live on fresh air.[5]

Father de Rougé had problems again with his teachers. The two Belgian Brothers had difficulty speaking English. They were so different from the beloved Lamennais Brothers, even in dress. The boys did not like the little skullcaps they wore. Boys are usually quick to take advantage of the shortcomings of their teachers. One of the Brothers received the nickname "Baldy." These Brothers could not compete with the former teachers in talents and popularity. Father remarks to Mother Katherine:

I hope we will have good brothers for the next term; the General was here and promised me a good teacher. . . .[6]

In another letter Father de Rougé speaks about the visit of "Major McLaughlin" to his Mission. This was Indian Inspector James McLaughlin, the author of the McLaughlin Agreement. This missionary hopes that the visit of this official might bring better regulations for his Indians. He also

---

[3] Mother Katherine to De Rougé, undated, Ms., OPA.

[4] De Rougé to Mother Katherine, February 6, 1912, Ms., ABSS.

[5] De Rougé to his Bishop, only last part of letter, showing Father's handwriting preserved, Ms., ADS (n.d.).

[6] De Rougé to Mother Katherine, April 22, 1912, Ms., ABSS.

reports that he is trying to do some plastering at the convent; "it is so cold in winter."[7]

Great headaches were in store for Father de Rougé during the summer months of 1912. A foolish half-breed came back from the government school at Tacoma and tried to induce some of Father's boys and girls to leave the Mission. The priest was greatly consoled when the parents of the students stood faithfully by him and did not permit their children to go. Father sent one of his secular teachers on a trip to arouse interest in his Mission. He was so successful that now twenty more children "who were away from the Church and all Catholic schools, are coming soon."[8] The teacher was probably Mr. Smith, not a Catholic. The *Historia Domus of St. Francis Regis Mission,* September 12, 1912, records, "A certain Mr. Smith came from St. Mary's mission to canvas for boys for Fr. De Rougé's School."[9] Before St. Mary's Mission was operated, some Okanogan children attended St. Francis Regis Mission school; now St. Mary's Mission is making efforts to enlist the children of the Colville Tribes.

More trouble was brewing for the educator. The Brother General did not keep his word to send another good Brother teacher. Father was trying so hard to keep high educational standards but again he has to report, "I have to use seculars now, as the brothers have been taken away. It is quite a trouble for me to start again with new people."[10] One of the new people was a Mr. Mullen, an excellent teacher; Mr. McClain taught art and penmanship. He would also coach the baseball team until in 1913, when Mr. W. A. Courtnay took over. There seems to have been a succession of men teachers during the last years of Father's life. A Mr. William Ganon came in 1914.[11] Mr. Chris C. Smith, who attended St. Mary's from 1913 to 1916 as a day student, recalls the following teachers: Mr. Lurkenmiller, Mr. Yell, Mr. Watson, Mr. Noll, and Mr. Walker. Mr. Smith is of the opinion that the last three named became priests later on.[12] Other informants had the same opinion but we were never able to prove the point. Rumor has it that Father de Rougé planned to have his own priests' seminary in order to supply his mission with workers, but the Bishop was against it.[13] The *Historia*

[7] De Rougé to Mother Katherine, July 24, 1912, Ms., ABSS.

[8] *Ibid.,* September 21, 1912.

[9] *Historia Domus of St. Francis Regis Mission* (Book III), September 12, 1912, Mss., OPA.

[10] De Rougé to Mother Katherine, September 21, 1912, Ms., ABSS.

[11] Cleveland, interviews.

[12] Chris C. Smith, questionnaire.

[13] Compare: De Rougé to Mrs. Wilhelmine Coulbaugh, December 22, 1915, Ms., OPA (quoted at the end of this chapter).

Domus of St. Francis Regis Mission, under Thursday, July 23, 1914, has the following entry: "Today a young man [Mr. Yell] arrived from New York, on his way to Fr. de Rougé, who engaged him. By a mistake of the conductor he was left here. But continues his journey tomorrow."[14] This indicates that Father tried to obtain teachers from wherever he could get them.

Gradually more and more day students sought admission in St. Mary's Mission School. Mr. Smith gives the number of students while he was there as "about 130 boys and 110 girls."[15] Father de Rougé himself gives a lower number. Perhaps in reports to Mother Katherine and to the Indian Department he only enumerated the Indian children of his boarding school. The author saw a photograph showing one of the Madams supervising a group of small boys. The ages appeared to be about those of kindergarten and first and second grades. Father de Rougé never asked or expected his Ladies Catechists Missionaries to teach and take care of older boys in spite of his pressing needs. One of the Catechists, however, would give private piano lessons. To help him with his missionary work, Father de Rougé had quite an organization of lay apostles from among the Indians, who were able to exert a quite powerful influence over their tribal relations by being very respected persons and an inspiration to others. They were carefully chosen by the priest. One of them was Mrs. Maggie St. Peter, whom we mentioned.

> Maggie Keogan St. Peter of Omak, who died recently at the age of 93 years was one of a group of 12 men and 12 women who as members of Our Lady's Sodality pledged their assistance to Father de Rouge in his efforts at St. Mary's Mission. They taught Catechism in English and Indian, instructed Indians in the English language, helped at religious ceremonies and aided the sick and needy. Of the original group there is now only one survivor, Pauline Zacherle.[16]

In his September letter to Mother Katherine, Father mentioned that the agents were starting to better supervise the health of the Indian children and to transport them to government sanitariums. This forced Father to enlarge his hospital. He wanted to prove to the agencies that he was able to take care of his own sick children.[17] In connection with the hospital Mr. De Vos has some interesting items to tell:

> To add a bit to the Mission's income, a hospital was established and a contract made with the County to take over what was known as the "County Poor Farm." For several years there was a patient, who was

---

[14] *Historia Domus,* July 23, 1914, Mss., OPA.
[15] Smith, questionnaire.
[16] Mrs. K. Lacey to the author, March 15, 1963.
[17] De Rougé to Mother Katherine, September 21, 1912, Ms., ABSS.

a very bad "oldster" named Uncle Dan Sullivan, an old prospector we had known at Oroville. Can't remember how many times the Father phoned: "Mr. De Vos, Uncle Dan has run away again, can you round him up. I have an Indian and a rig on the way to bring him back." The old chap always headed for the Chronicle with a sad tale of how badly he was being treated and how he could get no liquor. He always trudged the almost five miles to town on foot and often the Indian reached the shop ahead of Uncle Dan, who had heard the team coming and hid in the brush while it rolled passed. The old chap finally broke down and told me he had, in earlier life sinned against the Church, that he knew he was still a member, but too stubborn to confess. One Day I had a call from the Father that Uncle Dan was asking for me to come and see him as he was very ill and not long for this world. My saddle horse made a quick trip and my last visit with Uncle Dan was a real delight as he wished to tell me he had made his peace with God and wanted me to thank Father and the Sisters for caring for such a bad old man.[18]

Mr. De Vos recalls how the first hospital was "a very simple affair" and how he helped unintentionally to make the "first advanced improvements." The Wenatchee Chamber of Commerce made a trip up the Okanogan Valley — about thirty businessmen in seven or eight Model T Fords. All that Omak had to show was the Mission which was situated some five miles east over a very rough dirt trail. We let Mr. De Vos tell the story:

It had been arranged to "Shanghi" this crowd, get them on the way to the Mission, and I was to phone the Father they were on their way and follow in the last car well equipped with shovels, axes and chains to assist the weak ones. By the time we were almost within shouting distance of the Mission, I was the most unpopular citizen in that part of the country as these city chaps had never traveled such a road, or labored so hard to get to any destination. The good Father saved the day, and I am sure my hide. An Indian lad had been stationed at the brow of the last hill. When he spotted the first car, he ran back to the Church. As the cavalcade rounded the rise and saw the church, the band struck up a lively tune and the entire assembled school broke into a welcoming song. A bountiful lunch followed, hardships were forgotten, good spirits revived.

Inspection followed and when we entered the hospital a good doctor asked the Father where he got the small amount of equipment and why the place could not be modernized. "No cash," was the answer. "Hey fellows," broke in the doctor, "Let's do something for the hospital. I am about to refurnish my office with new stuff and I am going to give my present equipment to the Father, how about some of you chaps throwing in some of yours?" The ice was broken, cash and equipment worth well over $500.00 was pledged and really arrived later. Despite a tough trip back to Omak, my standing was fully restored.[19]

---

[18] Mr. De Vos to the author.
[19] *Ibid.*

It would have been a great calamity for St. Mary's Mission and many other places if our Lord had called Mother Katherine to Himself during the fall of 1912. The money which she inherited from her father, and which she so generously spent for God's poor, was only hers as long as she lived. Father de Rougé most certainly could not have maintained his Mission and completed his many building projects without the help of this good Mother. A storm of prayer went up to heaven when it became known that she was sick. Father wrote to Mother Mary James:

> At once I have posted all over the schools a novena to start at once, all to offer the 9 H. Communions, to renew the intention before each class, to offer at the Convent the Holy Hour, to have a lamp [burning] the 9 days at the altar of the Blessed Virgin. . . .
> . . . Be sure to drop me one line once in a while. . . . We could not be without news.[20]

While Father de Rougé was absent from the Mission, the Ladies Catechists inquired about the health of Mother Katherine, for she was their Mother also as she maintained them.[21] Father de Rougé expressed his joy at the news of some improvement in the health of his benefactress.[22] Mother Katherine, however, was not out of danger and the population of the mission kept on offering prayers for her complete recovery.[23] Mother Katherine's health became again one of the petitions of the Christmas novena. On the last day of 1912, Father de Rougé wrote to Mother Katherine. "My last minutes tonight before the end of the year . . . for you and to thank God Almighty to have saved your life for His people, His poor."[24]

By February 5, Father hoped that Mother Katherine was quite well. He started again to tell his problems; he had to send away a teacher and had trouble finding a replacement. He just has not enough money. Government schools were now attracting attention and Father wanted to build as soon as the snow was gone and to keep on improving his school buildings. The children then would have no reason to stay away from the Mission. Then Father explained that he had difficulty securing a teacher for only $30 a month; even the cook received $45 per month.[25] Three days later the priest seem to feel relieved. "Thank God, I have a man now, just arrived who seems to be a good teacher. Let us hope for the success and the salvation of our young men."[26] In a "thank you"

---

[20] De Rougé to Mother Mary James, October 5, 1912, Ms., ABSS.
[21] Ladies Catechists to Mother Katherine, October 15, 1912, Ms., ABSS.
[22] De Rougé to Mother Mary James, October 18, 1912, Mss., ABSS.
[23] *Ibid.,* October 29, 1912, Ms., ABSS.
[24] De Rougé to Mother Katherine, December 31, 1912, Ms., ABSS.
[25] *Ibid.,* February 5, 1912, Ms., ABSS.
[26] *Ibid.,* February 8, 1912, Ms., ABSS.

letter to Mr. James Monaghan, the great pioneer of the Inland Empire, Father enumerated more of his needs:

> I thank you very much for the $10 so kindly sent. I am sure you are bothered by many besides myself, and of course you have to limit your donations. At the same time be sure of all my gratitude. You know as well as I do that this country here is new, and has been long a wild country, we have now many Catholics around, and it is hard to do something for them, it is no use in our days to build half and half for the comfort and even a little more, as people are very particular and it requires more expenses than really I can make. In the same time much good is to be done, even the day before yesterday a girl 16 years old came to the parlor asking me to take her at the convent as her parents had abandoned her. This is only one instance among so many all around us. The good Lay Catechists who are in charge, are in great poverty, they have only one dormitory as children have in school, and when one is sickly at night the others have no rest after a hard day's work. I am so anxious to build and give them a little more comfort. On the right, on the left I can only see work to be done, and it is almost impossible to get alms here for my work. I wrote many letters, and work hard at my desk this time of the year being not well myself and no more able to travel as I used to do, but all this brings very little. I was almost ashamed to write to you, but I know you are good and you would not refuse, this is the way good people are abused once in a while. . . .[27]

During the next years Father de Rougé, the perpetual builder, completed his building projects slowly, one after the other. The band and the team became famous throughout eastern Washington. The Indian name for the Omak Creek falls was "Squant." This became the name of the second team while the first team was named St. Mary's. Mr. Chris C. Smith still remembers one of the yells:

> Hoya, Hoya Sacca rah,
> Omega, Omega, Sis, boom bah
> M-I-S-S-I-O-N, Mission
> St. Mary's, St. Mary's
> Rah, rah, rah![28]

Mrs. Bernier Opel wrote to the author:

> The mission at that time had a very large attendance and had the best ball team in the Okanogan country. They traveled to other cities to play ball and Father de Rougé was the most enthusiastic booster of them all. When they played at the Mission on big church days such as Easter, the people would stay for the game and the hillside was a mass of living humanity. Father would toss out the ball and tell the team to play, and play they did.[29]

27 De Rougé to James Monaghan, Spokane, October 25, 1913, Ms., OPA.
28 Smith, questionnaire.
29 Mrs. Florence B. Bernier Opel, Seattle, to the author, April 11, 1960.

Father de Rougé knew how to appeal to nature's children. He used the European approach which had come down through the centuries from the Middle Ages, when all living was more God-centered. He made the whole man serve God. In order to more easily raise the hearts of his parishioners to God all of the human senses had their part. He wanted the altars always beautifully decorated; the church music was drilled to perfection; banners were carried in processions; candles, Japanese lanterns, and fires were used for evening processions to the cemetery; the band played soft music; several shrines were erected along Omak Creek. May devotions were solemnized outside before the shrine of the Blessed Mother, which the boys had erected. On Good Friday, the famous "Christ Dead Procession" to the cemetery took place, when mighty fires were enkindled along the path to light up the darkness. Men were taught to adore and praise God by walking, singing, and praying, by using body and mind and all that nature could give in the service of God. The old European custom of firing a salute to the Eternal King on certain festive occasions in Catholic countries was also practiced by Father's Indians. Mr. Chris C. Smith, a white boy, tells us his experiences:

> I was nearly scared to death the first Midnight Mass I attended at the Mission. The Church was packed with people, women on the left and men on the right. I was standing with a group of men, most of them wore their hair in braids and they would amuse themselves by picking at my hair or ears and when I would look around they would just ignore me and look straight ahead with a very stern look on their face, and at the Elevation, there were three men at the door of the church with rifles, which they fired in unison with the bells rung by the servers at the altar, I thought that was no place for a white boy.[30]

Mr. Smith told also that when Father taught the boys to serve at the altar he wanted them to lift the edge of his vestment when he went up the steps to the altar. Some boys were a little clumsy and Father turned around and said, "Some of you kids pinch my leg and some pull my socks."[31]

Funerals were solemn occasions where the bell tolled at intervals one minute apart. Mr. John Figlenski remembers a funeral where four caskets stood in the church at the same time. A husband and wife, another member of the same family and another person had been poisoned by drinking wood alcohol; they were the victims of bootleggers.[32] It was on such occasions that Father de Rougé thundered his "fire and brimstone" sermons. When the funeral procession arrived at the cemetery the caskets

---

[30] Smith, questionnaire.
[31] *Ibid.*
[32] Figlenski, interview.

were usually set down at the shrine of the Sorrowful Mother. Here more prayers were said. After the burial all would file past the grave and throw a little earth into it as is the custom in Europe. Harry Van Coelen remembers a funeral where the relatives had brought the body all the way from Wenatchee, a distance of more than one hundred miles. Such a distance could not be covered in one day, and the heat was terrible. The body of the dead person had been wrapped in a blanket. At the graveside the woman wanted to have her blanket back; Father de Rougé had to use some energetic words to dissuade her. Another funeral was from Nespelem and took place during an icy winter while there was a snowstorm. When the men wanted to lower the casket into the grave they found that the grave was too small. Father told them to put the coffin in half standing.[33]

Father de Rougé's *Historia Domus* for 1913 gives us a vivid picture of the activities going on at his Mission:

> Every year we have a retreat for the schools from 4- [?] Days. Before the great feasts, especially Easter, we have a Mission for all the people preached both in Indian and English. Every month we have a novena for our benefactors, and . . . an instruction every day during the 9 days. Also Benediction of B.S. We have the Sodality of the Blessed Virgin Mary with office, etc. Also a club or association with meetings to interest them in their studies. . . . Many practice the daily H. Communions in the Mission. The offerings for the Apostleship of Prayer . . . [regularly] average 30,000 per month. We have 110 children enrolled in our two schools. Three secular teachers for the boys, and Ladies Catechists for the girls. The two schools are separated by the church in the center of the grounds. Mother Katherine Drexel is now supporting the school for the girls. The Catholic Bureau sends a little contribution for the school of the boys, but it is far from supporting the school's needs.
>
> The first and old building was falling to the ground and condemned, little by little and every year doing a little more according to our little means, we have a large and substantial building going on, and already partly occupied by the boys. Every year also we improve the grounds by leveling, scraping, plowing. The government had promised a section of land, and we hope to get the patent some time. This will make a very valuable property for the Society. . . . The white population is also increasing and many white Catholics are scattered all over the country. White children begin to attend our schools, come to be prepared for 1st Communion, etc. . . .[34]

Great flu epidemics ravaged through the Okanogan country during World War I. They started when during the winter of 1913–1914 the snow

---

[33] Van Coelen, interviews.

[34] De Rougé, *Historia Domus of St. Mary's Mission* [1913], Omak, Wash., Ms., OPA. In the same document Father mentions the baptism "of the most prominent chief from Nespelem." This took place in 1913 according to the *baptismal records* and enabled us to date this *Historia Domus*.

was deep and all transportation stopped; these epidemics lasted until 1918–1919. John Figlenski and other courageous young men on horseback attempted to visit the sick people in their scattered mountain cabins. In some places they found some dead and others sick; these young men did whatever they could for the suffering people. The cats were so hungry, there was the possibility they might try to eat the dead; therefore whenever they saw cats they shot them.[35] Many of the good old Indian people died during these years. The situation was so serious that the agency had to erect a pesthouse at Nespelem. Father de Rougé's hospital was filled. It was in times like these that the old Indians reverted to their age-old superstitions and the medicine men became prominent again. The use of the sweathouse and the cold plunge killed many people.

Doctors were scarce and often miles away, so Father de Rougé used his medical skills and vaccinated many people for smallpox. Mrs. A. H. Caulfield remembers how this was done. The arm was washed and scraped until it showed red spots. In the meantime a piece of bone, which had been made pointed and sharp to serve as a hypodermic needle, was boiled and then the serum applied under the red spots of the skin on the arm.[36] Often Father's little bell could be heard during the night when he would bring the Last Sacraments to the dying. These calls for a priest would often come from great distances. He had to teach every day and also had to supervise his building program. The priest could not drop all his responsibilities and go whenever a call would come. In one instance Father Griva had to come from St. Francis Regis Mission for a sick call to Chief Antoine.[37]

A letter of April 17, 1914, informed Mother Katherine that now Father was working on another addition to the convent and that he was again enlarging his hospital.[38] Soon vacation time would be here and Father de Rougé had made his plans for a big missionary trip. In spite of all the work to be done at St. Mary's Mission, no distance was too great for the priest if the call came during vacation time. This time he answered a call to the West Coast. Father de Rougé reported about this trip:

> The tribe of the Suiattle Indians, numbering 125 members, is just now divided into two; one part lives on the Scaget and the other on the Suiattle River. Some years ago a family of this tribe came to the Wenatchee tribe, and I baptized them there. Later on they left and returned among their own, where they undertook to convert their people. I had promised to go and baptize them if they asked for it. Last winter the old

---

[35] Figlenski, interview.
[36] Mrs. Caulfield, interview.
[37] *Diary of St. Francis Regis Mission,* February 12, 1914, Ms., OPA.
[38] De Rougé to Mother Katherine, April 17, 1914, Ms., ABSS.

man Urban Silrue wrote to me to come. I made arrangements with the Indians to have someone meet me at Sauk, the nearest station, who should conduct me to their quarters.

On coming out of the train I saw that . . . nothing whatever of what had been arranged was done. It was necessary to stay the whole day and wait till the next, when a wagon of goods brought me to the crossing of the Sauk River. Beyond there is no road and the only way of traveling is by horseback or on foot. Soon after my arrival at the Sauk hotel an old Indian presented himself, Captain Moses, baptized long ago by some Missionary on the Sound [Puget Sound], but he had never had a chance to do any more for his religion. As he could speak Wenatchee, I was at home with him. He gave me all the information possible about the trip and I learnt that only half the tribe could be reached this time in the mountains, the other half being on the other River.

The next morning we started. The trip, about ten miles on loaded wagon over what is called a road, was anything but comfortable for an old man. At the bank of the river no house could be seen, and we had to camp under the sky, with one or two Indian blankets. Eleven miles of mountain climbing was before me. As it was or seemed too much for me either by foot or horse, I sent word to old Silrue to have him bring the Indians to the river and camp there. On Sunday I said Mass on an altar improvised from boxes left by packers. At last the old man arrived, but I was informed that I had to continue my journey, if I wished to see the Indians. There were both old and sick people to attend to, and these could not come nor be abandoned. So I had to make my way on foot. My path lay for seven miles through beautiful woods in the shade of pines and firs and cedars towering many of them to a height of over 100 feet. Many streams were crossed and hard trails traversed where the foot of a missionary had never been set before. After seven miles a boy came with horses, and I made the remaining four miles on horseback. We finally arrived at the place of gathering. The Indian houses are made of boards split from cedar trees and fastened to poles. They are very dirty. Old Silrue had gone ahead to tell the people of my coming. A white boy, Tom Porter by name, of Omak, got me a tent ready. The Indians began to gather at once. The next day all were present, and Captain Moses' party with my valise, containing the necessaries for Mass, had also arrived.

Though they have adopted names of the whites they do not mix with them, do not drink and are very good. Sometime ago Captain Moses went to Olympia and requested the Governor to see about their land before it would be all taken up by the whites, the big lumber concerns making away fast with the timber land. A party of government surveyors are now with them and allotments of 80 acres to each head of the tribes are to be made. This will bring the reunion of the whole tribe and they will all live together again.

The language is a very special one, but happily old Silrue and Captain Moses could speak Wenatchee, and a few more could understand it. I wrote down the prayers and a few other things, but the Wenatchee prayers were adopted as the time was short. Captain Moses acted as interpreter and discharged his office with zeal. He and Silrue were admirable in the assistance they gave me and harangued their pepole repeatedly to help me all they could. We started instruction at once and stopped only for meals. Midnight found us still together and none asked to retire.

When the time came after three days of instructing all without a single exception gave in their names for baptism. Fifty-one were baptized and thirteen couples married. A few, as Silrue's family remembered having received baptism when very small, and went to confession. It was about noon when the ceremony closed. A feast followed and I headed the banquet table which was on the ground. The entire tribe was of course present. The day was beautiful and all were as happy as they could be. Plenty of salmon was caught in the trap during the night. A man like Captain Moses is served with a whole salmon and I can assure you he knows how to use his hands far more artistically than a knife and fork. The next morning they attended Mass with great devotion and made their first Communion. I spent considerable time in teaching all how to baptize so that now no child will die without baptism. They wish to build a chapel for prayers on Sundays and to bring their dead to before burial. All my pictures, scapulars, and beads were quickly given away, and I promised to send some more by mail to Sauk. The separation was sad after such a good meeting. They are anxious to have a priest see them and requested me to come again next year. While returning I found a man about 100 years old who remembered being baptized on the Sound in his younger days. I got what confession could be obtained and left him absolved. There is no doubt but the other part of the tribe will follow the example of their more fortunate brethren.[39]

According to the old baptismal records all these baptisms and marriages of the Suiattle Indians took place on July 15, 1914.[40]

On October 16, 1914, Father de Rougé wrote to Mother Katherine that he was expecting the Bishop to come the thirty-first to confirm about 100 to 150 people if he can get them together.[41] The *Book of Dedications* gives us the year as 1914, when, on November 1, 104 persons were confirmed at St. Mary's.[42] In the same letter Father told Mother Katherine about his missionary journey to the Coast:

> Did I write to you that in July I made a long trip in the wilderness of the Cascades and baptized 51 Indians and married 15 couples? These

[39] E. de Rougé, S.J., "The Conversion of an Indian Tribe," *WL* (44:1, February, 1915), 35–38. [All the members of this tribe have the family name of "Moses" as the baptismal records show. We could only place them after reading Father de Rougé's article. Members of the Moses family at Nespelem did not know about these baptisms. We were able to date this event from the baptismal records and from Father's letter about Confirmation.]

[40] *Baptismal Records*, St. Mary's Mission (Book II), 129–142, Mss.

[41] De Rougé to Mother Katherine, October 16, [1914], Ms., ABSS.

[42] *Book of Dedications*, Mss., ADS.

poor people had never seen a priest. It is almost impossible for me to attend to them as they are so far and in such wild mountains, but if no one will go I will try again once more in spring.[43]

A great joy was in store for this restless and completely dedicated missionary, when the Very Reverend Richard Gleeson, S.J., Provincial of the Jesuit Fathers "of Montana, California, Oregon, Washington, Idaho, Upper and Lower Alaska," visited him at St. Mary's Mission. On the feast of St. Francis Xavier, December 3, 1914, Father Gleeson saw it his duty to write to Mother Katherine to thank her for all the good she had done. At the same time he told her his impressions and what was going on at St. Mary's Mission:

I am a stranger to you but not to the grand work you have done for the poor Indians and Colored people these many years. I have been making the Visitation of our Indian Missions in the Northwest and I wish to thank you for the help so generously accorded to them by you. May God bless you for it most abundantly here and hereafter.

I am just visiting the saintly missionary, Rev. E. de Rougé, S.J., for 31 years working among the Okinagan along the Columbia, and here at St. Mary's, Omak, for 28 of them. Up to a few months ago the nearest railroad was 36 miles off. During the early years he endured incredible hardships and built up his Mission alone. He had a companion in some 2½ years intervals.

I was certainly surprised and edified and consoled when I saw the fruit of his labor and sufferings and prayers. He came without a cent and lo! he has a fine establishment. He has a body of devoted women — Ladies Catechists and I was deeply moved at their single-hearted devoted zeal for the Indian children. They have 37 Indian girls and 25 Kindergarten Indian boys. They have grown into quite a community and Father has built them and his Indian girls a beautiful home. He has added a Hospital and the beginning of a school for white girls. He has a fine school for boys and keeps the larger boys when he can, even to 19 and 20. He has done much of the teaching himself and still teaches. He has 39 Indian and 17 white boys and has a museum and science room which astounded me. He wished to keep his boys from Carlisle and Cushman. One of them graduated from Lacey, O.S.B., last year, all his preliminary work had been done here. I saw his credits last month and they average 94 and he ranged 1st with another in the entire College. [This was Mr. W. H. Hill, now in Tonasket.]

Father de Rouge is of noble French family and loves the Indians and knows their language perfectly. He has a deservedly great influence over them.

I am leaving here today and I wish to share with you my happiness. The dear Father tells me you are a devoted and generous friend of his

---

[43] De Rougé to Mother Katherine, October 16.

dear Indian children. These mornings nearly all of them received Holy Communion and they are virtually all daily Communicants.[44]

Mother Katherine kept on sending the quarterly checks. Father de Rougé thanked her on January 22, 1915, for the last one received. Then he asked her to pray for the first directress of his Catechists, which was Madam Clark. "We need a miracle to save her. She has prayed as hard when you were sick." Then follows mention of the hospital again:

> Our little sanitarium is going on, but it is a hard thing to convince the Indians that it is good for their children to come to it. They are afraid of an hospital, and sure it must be filled with the ghosts of people who died there.[45]

Quite a few letters written during 1915 show Father's concern about the existence of his hospital. As he was against the people of Okanogan having their own church, so he was against the people of Oroville having their own hospital. This time Father Griva was involved. The people of Oroville had desired to have their own Catholic hospital. Thereupon, Father Griva wrote to Bishop Schinner asking him where he could find Sisters to take charge of a hospital. The Bishop recommended Mother Scholastica, a Benedictine Sister. Father Griva wrote to her to come to Oroville. She arrived on February 7, 1915. Together they went looking for a location. A meeting in the office of Dr. Lewis with representatives of the town closed with the agreement that until the new hospital would be built, the Sisters would take care of the hospital Dr. Lewis had. On May 31, 1915, Mother Scholastica, Sister Antonia, and a nurse, Miss Chulte, arrived at Oroville and took charge of the hospital.[46]

Reading about the hospital project in the newspaper, Father de Rougé became alarmed and wrote to Bishop Schinner:

> When Rev. Father Provincial came here he told me that he would not approve of this plan as we are started here already in this work and something *so near,* only two hours by train, is bound to hurt us very much. . . .
> After Mother Katherine dies, the main support if not the only one will be our hospital, it is the reason why I started it, to leave a support here later well established. The Indians are no support and what will we do here for a living? We have right along patients from around Oroville and Tonasket and we will lose. Only so few already. Okanogan has a hospital, too. Three are too much [*sic*] on a few miles of the R.R.[47]

---

[44] Very Reverend Richard A. Gleeson, S.J., to Mother Katherine, December 3, 1914, Ms., ABSS.

[45] De Rougé to Mother Katherine, January 22, 1915, Ms., ABSS.

[46] Griva, *History,* 119, 124.

[47] De Rougé to Most Rev. Schinner, February 28, 1915, Ms., ADS.

Bishop Schinner replied that Father Griva had written to him before the Bishop traveled to the East. At the same time he had received an application from this Benedictine Sister. When he returned he found that the Sisters had already established themselves. The question is simply, shall the Sisters take charge or shall it be a non-Catholic institution. The Bishop does not believe that he can cancel what has been started and thinks that both the hospital at the Mission and the hospital at Oroville will serve a good purpose.[48]

Father de Rougé then makes a special request. He does not want to go against the Bishop's will, but the arrangements are bound to hurt the mission. Could the Oroville hospital be induced not to accept county patients, the old and the poor? "While I do not care for myself, I must watch and try to leave after me a supporting mission, or it may be closed."[49] The Bishop answered that this may be a way out of the difficulties. He will see what he can do but the outcome rests with the county officials.[50]

The subject was brought up again at Father Griva's visit to the Mission on June 24, 1915, when Father Griva assured Father de Rougé that the hospital in Oroville would not accept Indians.[51] When on September 4, 1915, Father Griva received his transfer to Nespelem, he thought that the hospital at Oroville might have something to do with it.[52] At the beginning of October, Father de Rougé informed the Bishop that two Catechists were sent away from the Mission and that another one followed and that they are at the hospital in Oroville.[53] This hospital was closed in 1916.

Father acquainted Mother Katherine with conditions in his home country during the First World War. "I have four nephews in the war, and I recommend them to your good prayers. My brother and my sister have converted their homes into hospitals."[54]

The want of financial assistance and the fight to keep charitable organizations interested was a recurring problem and has remained one up to the present time. The director of the Catholic Indian Bureau, Father Ketcham, a friend of Father de Rougé, had to convey the unpleasant news that all the money for Indian missions had been divided and St. Mary's Mission had been left out for 1915. Father was not to worry Mother Katherine as she was overburdened already, but he should write to the directors at Baltimore.[55] Father asked Bishop Schinner to write for him:

48 Most Rev. Bishop Schinner to De Rougé, March 3, 1915, Ms. copy, ADS.

49 De Rougé to Most Rev. Schinner, March 6, 1915, Ms., ADS.

50 Schinner to De Rougé, March 9, 1915, Ms. copy, ADS.

51 Griva, History, 126.

52 Ibid.

53 De Rougé to Bishop Schinner, October 2, 1915, Ms., ADS.

54 De Rougé to Mother Katherine, January 22, 1915, Ms., ABSS.

55 Very Rev. Wm. H. Ketcham to De Rougé, February, 1914, Ms., ADS.

What will become of us if I have to be without help for the whole year? The allowance was small enough already. I used to get some private alms from France, but now for more than one year I can get absolutely nothing, and will not for perhaps some years, as we are ruined in France now.[56]

In his letter written to Very Reverend E. R. Dyer, St. Mary's Seminary, Baltimore, Father de Rougé saw only one way if help did not come — he would have to close the school:

I will have to give a vacation at once to the school and, if nothing is in view, I will not recall the children. I already notified the teacher that he should look for another place, but once gone it will not be easy to get another in case we could keep on, so it means a total disorganization. I should be notified long before Oct., if then I may be sure to reopen, to make arrangements. As long as nothing else can be done, it means to close, that is all I can see.

It is a hard blow for an old man.[57]

On April 23, Father de Rougé wrote to Bishop Schinner that Father Dyer had promised that the payment for the boys would be made.[58]

The Bishop of Spokane had inquired about coming to the mission on the feast of Corpus Christi in 1915. Father answered that he does not know which is best, to come or not to come. He would like to give his Indians a lesson, many of whom had gone back to superstitions and some to drinking. Perhaps a little scolding from His Excellency might help. Corpus Christi is too early this year, he said, and the parents who come to the feast want to take their children home, something that would break up the school.[59] The missionary suggests that the Bishop come later in June as he is not prepared for the Bishop's coming at this time. Bishop Schinner then gave permission that the feast of Corpus Christi be celebrated at the Spokane Reservation.[60]

The year of 1915 saw the completion and the enlargement of the church of St. Mary's Mission as it still stands today. Father wrote on April 5 that they "had a grand Easter, the church was too small and we decided to extend the sanctuary."[61] When after Easter Father asked his Indian parishioners to contribute toward enlarging and plastering the church, they responded wholeheartedly: "everyone donating no less than $5 and many $10."[62] The Bishop was happy to learn about the generosity of the people

[56] De Rougé to Bishop Schinner, March 4, 1914, Ms., ADS.
[57] De Rougé to Very Rev. E. R. Dyer, March 12, 1914, Ms., copy, ADS.
[58] De Rougé to Bishop Schinner, April 23, 1914, Ms., ADS.
[59] *Ibid.*, March 12, 1915.
[60] Bishop Schinner to De Rougé, March 21, 1915, Ms. copy, ADS.
[61] De Rougé to Bishop Schinner, April 5, 1915, Ms., ADS.
[62] *Ibid.*, April 27, 1915.

and expressed his pleasure to come and dedicate the church.[63] One of the reasons why Father de Rougé did not want the Bishop to come earlier might have been that his church was not completed. Father later wrote to His Lordship that "June 25th will be alright to all here and I hope we will be able to complete the plastering to have the church blessed."[64] The church was blessed on June 25, 1915, and dedicated to the "Assumption of the Blessed Mother."[65] On the same day the new "College" building and other building projects were blessed. It was a great day in the life of the zealous Father de Rougé. A new milestone had been reached, but this was not the peak. Besides the dedications there were fifty-seven Confirmations.[66]

A booklet printed by the *Omak Chronicle* press to advertise St. Mary's Mission High School, gives us an idea of the growth of this institution when all the surrounding country was still in its pioneer stage:

> Started originally as a school and religious place of worship for the Indians, the Mission of today has developed into a wonderful church center and educational institution for both natives and whites, where the equipment of learning is not surpassed in this part of Washington. The school has grown and kept pace with the country, in fact ahead of it, and when the reservation is opened for white settlers they will find here a school in which they will be delighted to have their youth educated as the training includes moral, mental, and industrial work under a religious atmosphere that is enlightening and elevating, inspiring the young to become honorable and useful citizens.[67]

Then the booklet mentions the buildings which grew slowly under the most pressing financial difficulties: the main boys' buildings, where classrooms, chapel, museum, office, post office, dining hall, and dormitories were under the same roof; a boys' kindergarten department and theater in another building; a new church standing in a pretty park; a modern hospital with operating room; a girls' school with classrooms, music room, dining room, kitchen, dormitory, and laundry under one roof. The buildings had a water-works system supplied from Omak Creek. Kerosene lamps were supplanted now with an acetylene lighting system. The staff of instructors were three lay teachers in addition to Father and fifteen Lady Missionaries of St. Mary's.

> The courses of study include everything from the kindergarten to the College courses with the addition of manual training, agriculture, and music in all of its branches. . . .

---

[63] Bishop Schinner to De Rougé, April 30, 1915, Ms. copy, ADS.

[64] De Rougé to Bishop Schinner, May 8, 1915, Ms., ADS.

[65] *Book of Dedications,* Diocese of Spokane, 55, ADS.

[66] *Ibid.,* 5.

[67] Mr. F. A. De Vos, ed., *St. Mary's Mission High School* (information booklet printed by the *Omak Chronicle*), n.d., probably in 1914–1915.

Omak is not only proud of the Mission within its legal school district boundaries but deems it to be a leading factor of attraction and inducement for the newcomers who wish to settle in our town and community.[68]

A leaflet which seems to have had Father de Rougé for its author shows the variety of courses which were offered at St. Mary's Mission more than fifty years ago:

St. Mary's High School
Okanogan County, Washington
Railroad and Post Office, Omak, Wash.
Telephone Connections.

School for Boys

All classes including the Academic classes and first college classes. Program of studies same as in any college. Commercial courses, painting, music, photography, taxidermy, manual training, gardening, carpenter work, etc. Campus for foot ball and base ball, athletics. Room for sciences with apparatus for the Physic courses and models for Physiology, Natural History, etc. Library of over 2000 books.

School for Girls

Conducted by the Lady Missionaries of St. Mary. All school grades, Music, domestic science, fancy work, etc. Fifteen Lady Missionaries are in charge of the different departments. The Kindergarten is under the care of the Lady Missionaries. A special building is provided for white girls.

The Hospital

This is an up to date building separated from the others. First class nurses in charge. Modern equipment, operating room, etc. Good doctors in charge.

Requirements

A difference of creed is no bar for admittance. School starts the first of September and closes the last of June. No one is admitted except for the whole term. Tuition is very moderate, the school work is free, but board is to be paid in advance in two or more payments. Write for arrangements according to age, number of children in the same family or orphans. Music $5 a month. Hospital fees, doctor's bill etc. are extra. No one is to be excused from manual work. Short vacation or visits home will be allowed during the year. Each one to bring own blankets and have clothing marked and have white rubber collars.

For application write to Rev. Father Superior, Mission, Omak, P.O., Okanogan County, Washington.[69]

Missionary zeal drove Father de Rougé during the vacation months of 1915 again to the West Coast in order to instruct the other part of the Suiattle tribe. During his absence from the mission, Father J. M. Van de Walle again took his place. A letter to Bishop Schinner during that time

---

[68] De Vos, ed., *op. cit.*
[69] De Rougé, *St. Mary's High School* (advertisement, leaflet), OPA.

expresses great praise for the work of the Lady Missionaries and great concern about the state of health of Father de Rougé:

> Dear Bishop, if there are clouds in the Mission Sky its brightness is still more extensive, for we find some hidden saints in this place, women adorned by the spirit of sacrifice and abnegation. Poor Father de Rougé is a hard-working missionary, but despite the fact he is only 55 years of age he feels to be 80. At times he is so weak that it is hardly possible to say Mass. If he could have a robust helper a priest of some experience and of much abnegation, it would be of great benefit to this Mission. Father cannot depend on his men-teachers, and therefore it would be a blessing if his Provincial would send two teachers, scholastics, for example, from Gonzaga College.[70]

Considering Father Van de Walle's observations of Father de Rougé's health and the later description of the trip by the missionary himself we can imagine the heroism and complete trust in God needed for such a strenuous trip into the Pacific wilderness. Again the baptismal records tell us the results of Father's missionary trip. He baptized all his neophytes on July 11; another baptism followed the next day. Seven more baptisms are recorded on November 7, 1915.[71] The last mentioned people must have made the trip to St. Mary's Mission in order to be instructed. Two old picture cards, sent in 1915 from Sauk post office, show that boys from the Suiattle tribe were then enrolled in St. Mary's Boys' School. Beside the work for the Suiattle Indians Father had made quite an extensive exploratory trip on the Pacific Coast. He wrote to Bishop Schinner on July 23:

> I am just going home. . . . Would your Lordship object if I would take two of our sisters to come here among the Indians and help me to teach the catechism to the children? Bishop O'Dea is very anxious as I have converted a whole tribe, but they know very little and I cannot alone in these trips teach the children. We would also go to some other tribes well disposed *and no one to teach them*, it is very sad and we could do so much good and bring many to the church.[72]

As we mentioned, Father de Rougé had erected a special building for the white girls. It is the only building beside the church that still can be seen today. On October 2, 1915, Father wrote that he will have to take in more and more white children. He thinks he might lose some of his Indian children as so many government schools are being opened. He wants to make the separation between the white and Indian children more complete in order to forestall the excuse used by the white people for not

---

[70] Rev. J. M. Van de Walle to Bishop Schinner, July 12, 1915, Ms. ADS.
[71] *Baptismal Records of St. Mary's Mission* (Book II), 166–167.
[72] De Rougé to Bishop Schinner, July 23, 1915, Ms., ADS.

sending their children to the Mission.[73] All informants, Indians and white alumni of St. Mary's, have stated that always the most cordial relationships existed between the racial groups. At the boys' school, Indians sat on one side of the dining-room tables and the whites on the other; they had separate dormitories, however. The white boys helped the Indian boys improve their English vocabulary, while the Indian boys knew many things about nature that the white boys could profit by. Also the Indians' inborn feeling for color and design could be of benefit to their white brothers. It was a "give and take," a mutual stimulation, and a healthy competition that helped to plant Christian civilization and culture in the Okanogan Valley. Today where we feel the need for integration, more and more we realize that Father de Rougé was ahead of his time by trying to give to his Indian children not an isolated education, but to let them grow up side by side with their white brothers in order to be able later to take their place in the white man's society.

Father de Rougé enjoyed another visit from his Provincial during the end of November. Again Father Gleeson addressed a letter of appreciation to Mother Katherine:

> I have visited here the last of an Indian center. All along I have heard your name blessed by all Sisters and Fathers.
> Father de Rougé, whose work here is truly wonderful, is particularly eloquent in grateful praises. This morning by a particular Providence, the Thanksgiving Day and Feast of St. Katherine I sang a solemn Mass of Requiem to finish the Novena made monthly for the Benefactors of St. Mary's among the Okinagans. . . .
> Dear Father de Rougé is poorly — and no wonder after his 30 years of privations and labor up in this hard country. How he does love the Indians! And they with their child-like nature recognize and reciprocate it.[74]

During the last years of Father de Rougé's life he had found another benefactress in the person of Mrs. Wilhelmine F. Coulbaugh, who together with her sister, Mrs. A. C. Brown, contributed all the money for the building of the Sacred Heart Chapel which became an addition to the convent. Even the details of furnishings, plus the bell in the little belfry, were contributed by this generous lady. In gratitude Father de Rougé in his Christmas letter brings a detailed report about his second trip to the Pacific Coast that he had made last summer. It is the missionary's last big letter, yet it is filled with plans for the future. Referring to last year's excursion into the wilderness and the baptism of a part of a tribe, he continues:

---

[73] *Ibid.*, October 2, 1915.
[74] Vy. Rev. Gleeson to Mother Katherine, November 25, 1915, Ms., ABSS.

This year I went back, they had built a little rough board chapel for me but we had to make a camp fire outside to keep warm having no stove. In the spring we will improve things I hope and fix a place for the father to sleep and eat. Another trip I took [to] the Pacific, had to walk four miles to reach the camp. I had not much time to stay, only investigating things. Went to another place where long ago the old people were baptized, then abandoned. They make the sign of the cross, have made a religion of their own, received me well.

Another trip I went to the San Juan and the Pacific, there I found a large settlement of 1000 in two places. Never [had] they heard of the Catholic Church, [and] they came to me asked me many questions, asked me to come back, to instruct them and baptize them. I tell you it was sad to go and leave them so, but it was no use to even think of baptizing till I was sure I would get the means to come back, to build something for a start, and my plan is to bring two of our sisters here, Missionaries of St. Mary's and Catechists, to instruct the women and children and prepare them for baptism. I hope this winter by my letters to collect enough to start the work. Hope too to get yet more vocations at our convent so that I may take sisters along and not hurt the work here. . . . These places are 250 and 200 miles from here, trips cost too. . . . In all several thousand souls to save, thousands of children who never heard of God. What do you think of that? Our good Father Provincial approves the work, but said, How are you going to meet the expenses? To this all I would say: Providence must see to it. The Marquette League has promised me $125, a mere start, but glad to hear of it. . . .

Phil. has sent a chasuble and a chalice. I got another chasuble which I already left at the first chapel. . . . Last mail a letter from the Propa. of F. of N.Y. announced a chalice and $15 for beads. Such is my start: We will have 3 or 4 chapels to build in time, with little residences for the father and a separate one for the Sisters, at each place, till later a center can be established, and go from there to the other places. I have yet several settlements to visit, all abandoned too.[75]

In this letter we really see Father de Rougé in all his characteristic aspirations. We see him as the constant beggar, who knows how to appeal to the hearts of generous persons, because it is all for others; we see him as the perpetual builder whose plans for a new mission center and more chapels are made; we see him as the missionary who is constantly on the alert to win more souls for God; we see him as the priest who has already left a vestment in the new mission territory in order to be able to offer the sacrifice of the Mass through which he can make more men Christlike; we see him as the teacher and educator, ready to develop another part of the state of Washington and plant Christian culture there. About one fifth of the state of Washington was once his parish territory. Yet this humble

---

[75] De Rougé to Mrs. Wilhelmine Coulbaugh, St. Petersburg, Florida, December 22, [1915], Ms., OPA.

and saintly man knows no parish boundaries as long as he finds souls truly in need of the services of a priest. All that he has done since November of 1885 in the Okanogan Valley and many other places, the toil-filled thirty years are forgotten. He is ready to do them all over again. Father de Rougé standing on the threshold of death never thinks of rest. Will he ever reach the peak? Only when he has reached the highest one, Christ.

After revealing his plans for his new mission center at the Coast, Father de Rougé writes to Mrs. Coulbaugh about his work at St. Mary's Mission:

> In the same time here I have 100 children, started a school for the white girls this winter . . . our sanitarium of tuberculous, and my College!
> I try to get some young men to study for the priesthood and bring into them the vocation for these from the Indians if possible.
> I try to enroll others as Catechists to stay in the missions and help me and whoever I can get later to divide the work. These young men have no means and I have to support them. They are poorly lodged and I need bad[ly] to fix things a little better around. It is a miracle [that] we are even getting along. It would not take many like you to put me out of trouble. . . .[76]

In this letter the great plans for the continuation of Father's mission work are disclosed, but at the end of the letter comes the sad awareness of his state of health: "Unfortunately I am not well, and no more strong, the past has been very hard on me, and now I have to take great care of myself to be able to keep on. God is the Master."[77]

Several of Father's former students tell of stomach pains troubling the good priest. There is no record of his having gone to the West Coast in the spring as contemplated. During March and the beginning of April of 1916, Father's pains increased, and an operation was performed at Providence Hospital, Seattle. Father J. Tomkin, S.J., wrote reassuring news to Madame Luce at St. Mary's Mission from Seattle College:

> The operation as you are already aware, was very successful. Father went under the ether very quietly and never moved during the hour he was on the table. Heart and pulse action were splendid during the trial and remain so up to the present. He began to awake about four hours after the event and has been doing very well since. Up to this evening he has been sleeping or dozing all the time, and this is induced by the drugs given for that purpose as the doctor wants to make sure of the job. He will not be able to write for some days yet, but any communication he may wish to have conveyed to you will be attended to by,

Yours sincerely
[signed] J. Tomkin, S.J.[78]

---

[76] De Rougé to Mrs. Coulbaugh.   [77] *Ibid.*
[78] Rev. J. Tomkin, S.J., Seattle, to Mother Luce, St. Mary's Mission, April 9, 1916, Ms., OPA.

In addition to taking care of three building projects, in Keller, Nespelem, and Monse, Father Griva had been a great help to Father de Rougé during the last half year. He took charge of the spiritual affairs of the Mission during Father's illness, returning to Nespelem on April 29, 1916.[79]
. Father de Rougé was able to write a short note to Bishop Schinner on Good Friday from Providence Hospital. "Am here . . . doing well. Weak — Thanks for circular the other day and check today."[80] On Easter Sunday he conveyed Easter greetings to His Excellency, and expressed the hope that he would be home soon.[81] He went back to his rugged field of labor at St. Mary's Mission probably at the end of April, judging from the date of Father Griva's return to Nespelem. Work which only he could do had accumulated during his absence. He saw the children and their needs; how could he rest and recuperate? He was accustomed to patient endurance of pain during the years before his surgery. The daily routine started again. On the eighth of May, Father de Rougé acknowledged the last check sent to him by Mother Katherine. The following statement accompanied the check:

Board and tuition for 35 pupils	$ 825
Salary of cook	120
2 teachers	180
3 Lady Catechists	135
	$1260[82]

On the same day he wrote a letter to Father Griva stating that he is getting well.[83] The next day, the ninth of May, he was in extreme pain. One of the students visited him and, as always, Father was more concerned about the well-being of others than of himself. Twenty minutes after this visit, Father de Rougé was found lying on the floor. He had reached his peak: Christ his Master and eternity. Madam Luce at once notified Bishop Schinner by telegram.[84]

Many newspapers of the West paid tribute to the heroic missionary. *The Omak Chronicle* recalled that in early times Father had been the only man to uphold the Roman Catholic Faith in a radius of several hundred miles, his field extending far north into British Columbia and from Colville to Yakima. Then Mr. De Vos traced the development of Father's building projects:

---

[79] Griva, *History*, 133.
[80] De Rougé to Bishop Schinner, Good Friday, 1916, Ms., ADS.
[81] *Ibid.*, Easter Sunday, 1916.
[82] Mother Katherine repeated this statement to Father Caldi, June 16, Ms., OPA.
[83] Griva, *History*, 138.
[84] May 9, 1916, Ms., ADS.

From a crude log cabin, which the Father helped to build with his own hands and no one except Indians for helpers, has grown a wonderful institution of many buildings which include a main Boy's school, dormitory, chapel, museum, office, reception and dining halls under one roof, covering a space forty feet wide by three hundred long; boys' kindergarten and theater 30 x 150; manual training building 20 x 40; a beautiful church with a seating capacity of over 500 persons; a hospital building 36 x 100 which is modernly equipped throughout; a girls' school, laundry, dormitory and chapel 40 x 250; and a new building partly completed especially erected for the exclusive use of white girls in preparation for the opening of the South Half of the Colville Indian reservation this summer. But beside these main buildings, there are 11 of the necessary barns and outbuildings and surrounding fertile fields of Alfalfa.

The wonderful work is the accumulation of the life ambition of this noble man who spent his last drop of energy for the uplifting of both the Indians and the white settlers of this new country. Not one cent did he leave for anyone but his magnificent structures will stand as monuments in the land for years to come and the thousands of human beings who have come in contact with this man will continue to spread his good works as long as they live.[85]

The Spokesman Review, Spokane, Washington, stated that Father de Rougé's death "closes a career which for unselfish endeavor is almost without a parallel in the entire Northwest."[86] Another Spokane newspaper, probably *The Spokane Chronicle,* after announcing Father de Rougé's death, brought the information that Congressman Dill had on Thursday introduced a bill in the House giving to Father de Rougé's Mission the title to the sixty acres on which the mission is located, which he had held only in trust. The bill would also give to the Indian Bureau four sections of land instead of three, and fifty acres for cemeteries. It would also prohibit the introduction of intoxicating liquors on the reservation.[87] We doubt that Father de Rougé knew about the first step toward the realization of his ardent wishes. Father had died on Thursday; this bill was introduced the week before. Father de Rougé was deprived of the joy of seeing these wishes fulfilled.

Deep was the sorrow among Father's students, especially his former students who were not at the mission when he passed away. They still regret that news traveled so slowly; for many of them the funeral was over when they received the news of his death. Dr. Paschal Sherman, then a senior at St. Martin's College, Lacey, Washington, after having completed

---

[85] Mr. De Vos, ed., "Rev. E. de Rougé Dies Suddenly," *The Omak Chronicle,* May 12, 1916, n.p.

[86] *The Spokesman Review,* Spokane, Washington, May 11, 1916, n.p.

[87] "Pioneer Dies at Mission," *The Spokane Chronicle,* Spokane, Wash., May 9, 1916, n.p.

two years of college work under Father de Rougé, was the editor in chief of the school paper, *The Martian*. He published a "Tribute" to Father de Rougé from which we quote some excerpts:

> . . . He died in his room far away from the scenes to which education and station entitled. Renouncing first the right to a titled position in this world, he joined the Jesuits, and then gladly denied himself their constant companionship to enter upon a life of toil among the Indians of the Northwest. Surely the obscurity of his leave-taking must have been in keeping with the innermost wishes of such a man, but how it cast a pall of gloom over the community of which he was the beloved pastor!
> . . . they had learned to look upon him as a father and a friend in the truest sense of the word. I was one of them.
>
> .   .   .   .
>
> The field that Father de Rougé covered extended from Pentickton, B.C. down the Okanogan and Columbia Rivers, with stops of a day or two here and there, and across the Cascades to the Yakima country, — a stretch of territory at once vast and difficult of access . . . he often braved driving storms in winter and a thousand other discomforts which the hospitality of the Aborigines could not remove.
> . . . He welcomed the hundred and one little rebuffs that seemed to attend his every effort. To him it was the price of his salvation. . . to others it meant the firm establishment of Catholicism in that otherwise benighted corner of country. It meant the beating back of the forces of superstition and irreligion. . . .
> . . . "Give me two or three boys who will do what I tell them, and I will stay here in spite of difficulties," was the way he often voiced his determination to work in his chosen field as long as two or more individuals would really benefit by his presence. When . . . age had already dampened his more zestful enthusiasm long ago, still recently he had taken steps for the establishment of another mission, this time over there on the Sound at Neah Bay. . . . even a few moments before his sudden summons to his Lord, he was giving spiritual advice to a youngster, who had come to see about his condition, for all that day he had been complaining of severe internal pains.
> Many people including the writer, who is proud to have been his pupil, — now bless themselves for having known him. They sincerely feel that his coming about thirty-one years ago conferred an immeasurable good upon the community at large. . . . He founded a school that affords efficient instruction and academic training to Catholics as well as Non-Catholics, Indians as well as Whites . . . the school situated midst mountain splendor and in a thriving country, bids well to stand forever as a lasting monument to his memory . . . the life of Father de Rougé typifies the spirit and zest with which we should attend our ordinary duties of our state. It is one long sermon on Perseverance, Faith, Hope and Charity.[88]

---

[88] Dr. Paschal Sherman, "Father E. de Rouge, S.J., A Tribute," *The Martian* (Vol. II, No. 4, June, 1916), 198–200. Courtesy of Dr. Sherman.

It had been Father de Rougé's most ardent wish to be buried beneath the shrine of the Sorrowful Mother in St. Mary's cemetery. The Indian chiefs pleaded in vain to have their Father buried among them.[89] No other priest ever was able to fill the void in the hearts of the Indian people caused by the death of Father de Rougé who had worked and suffered for them until his heart stood still.

---

[89] Father de Rougé, S.J., is buried at Mount Michael's Cemetery, Spokane, Washington.

History Hidden in Baptismal Records

THE old *Baptismal Records* of St. Mary's Mission offer interesting historical data and are a reflection of the growth of Christian civilization. Many people had been baptized in the area quite some time before Father de Rougé took over. His predecessor, Father Urban Grassi, S.J., has 107 baptisms listed in the old *Baptismal Records* of St. Mary's dating from May 25, 1884, to December 25, 1885.[1]

Father de Rougé's entry of the first baptism from the Okanogan Valley took place on November 15, 1885. There are interesting similarities between the recordings of these two missionaries; for one thing they are incomplete. This may be due to several factors. The priests had first to learn the various dialects of the Okanogan language; in addition they needed to know the Yakima, the Moses, and the Nez Perce languages. The Indians were often known under different names and the sound of these names had to be translated into the white man's alphabet and then recorded. Often the hardworking missionaries had not the time to make the recordings complete when the Indians congregated around them for instruction. It is interesting to note the progress in civilization as the entries through the years slowly become more complete. First only the Christian baptismal names were recorded; even the sponsors' names are often only the first names of persons. Gradually a distinction needed to be made between persons with the same baptismal names; hence the Indian family names were added. These names appear under different spellings until gradually the white man's names were adopted. Names like the following hardly exist today: Nkrovalken, Klupakan, Sukantakan, Kalaskan, Niml-

---

[1] *Registrum Baptizatorum in Ecclesia Stae Mariae apud Okenakanos,* Nesqual-Dioecesis, Vancouver (Book I), 222–248. (Henceforth: BRSTM.)

kan, Seikukan, Raaskat, Orintaken, Pakeiamaken, Orumtaken, Koize, Kastize, Rilkarat, Selkize, Nranzi, Tromash, Kushrin, Nakapaths, Kaiama, and so on. Some of the Indian names were changed slightly and are still used today; for instance, Smitakan became Smitken, Tonaskat became Tonasket.

A great percentage of the women of the confederated tribes had very early intermarried with white men, many of whom had been employed by the fur companies. This accounts for the many French names used by the Okanogan Indians, such as Desautel, Francois, Marchand, Michel, Picard, Pichette, Pierre, Poitou, Toulou, etc. Other names were taken from the place where the Indian lived, for instance, Jim Wenatchee, Nespelem George, Columbia George, Jim Loop Loop. Sometimes a quality was added and became the family name as in Cultus Jim or Cultus Charley, cultus meaning bad; or Chief Long Jim, who was tall. As the contact with white people increased, a greater variety of all European languages was used in the new family names. As we will see, Father de Rougé once made the experiment of giving to his smart students the names of famous Americans.[2]

Father de Rougé seems to have been sometimes at a loss to name his neophytes. Among the twelve people he baptized on March 29, 1888, was one Sapie, whose son received the name Baptist Sapie. This entry tells us that Father had given this Indian the name which the Indians had given him: Sapie.[3] Another baptism on the same day of a son of Cultus Jim from Chelan, who was 21 years old, received Father's first name: Etienne.[4] We have been asked if ever an attempt has been made to convert the Chinese miners who worked the abandoned gold diggings in the Okanogan Valley. On July 21, 1890, Father de Rougé recorded that he baptized "Joseph Chinaman at Kettle River." The sponsor was Chief Antoine.[5] The real name of this Chinaman was very probably Joseph Chee Saw after whom the town of Chesaw was named.

Not only are the records incomplete as to names but also with reference to places. Where was the child born; where do his parents live? These questions were often a puzzle to the recording missionary. Many Indians lived scattered in the mountains as some still do today. Maybe the family was camping somewhere or they were hunting or fishing when the child was born. No definite map of Washington then existed, no post offices had been established at Indian settlements. As more white people

---

[2] Dr. Paschal Sherman, questionnaire, Mss.

[3] *BRSTM*, 41.

[4] *Ibid.*, 42.

[5] *Ibid.*, 59.

came into the area and the settlements and towns were established, Father de Rougé was able to make the entries in the baptismal records more complete. The pioneer priest is intimately connected with the growth of culture and civilization of this part of the State of Washington and British Columbia.

Father de Rougé's records give us an idea of the immensity of the distances he had to travel. Places were hundreds of miles from each other; we read: Alma, Kettle River, Loomis, Wenatchee, Shelan, Katar, Sanpoil, Ellensburg, Conconully, Waterville, Pine Creek, Mouth of Columbia River, Similkameen, B. C., Hedley, B. C., Pateros, Old Mission, St. Mary's, Brewster, Methow, Colville, Columbia, Chesaw, Molson, Golden, Kipling, Curlew, Keller, Tunk Creek, Bonaparte, Winthrop, Ophir, Ruby, Condon's Ferry, Tulalip, Silver, Metrom, Night Hawk, Malott, Yakima, Ignace Valley, White Stone, Omak, Oroville, Tonasket, Bridgeport, Inkameep, B. C., Neah Bay, Kettle Falls, Disautel, Pateros, Colville Valley, Okanogan, South Half Reservation, Antoine Valley, Monse, Sauk, Fruitland, Addie, French Valley, Sound, etc. The great heroism lies not in the number of baptisms recorded but in the distances traveled in a wilderness before the missionary could gather his harvest. Father de Rougé's entries show that some white settlers came from Spokane, Boston, Sidley, others came from as far away as Austria or Alaska.

Absences of Father de Rougé from his mission for any long period of time can be checked from the *Baptismal Records.* For instance: on August 30, 1887, he baptized Madeleine Antoine at the Okanogan Valley.[6] On September 12, November 20, and December 25, of the same year, he recorded a baptism on each of these days at St. Francis Regis Mission.[7] This shows us that Father did not stay all the time at the Okanogan Mission during the beginning years of his missionary activities. On February 19, 1888, he was at the Omak camp, where he baptized a daughter of Chief Smitkin.[8] From there he made a missionary journey to the Chelans and the Wenatchees.[9] Father Parodi took Father's place during his absence in 1888–1889 and had eleven baptisms.[10]

Although the history of a great part of eastern Washington can be gleaned from the *Baptismal Records of St. Mary's Mission,* the entries of baptisms and marriages recorded are only a fractional part of the immense work of Christianization and civilization undertaken by the Jesuit Fathers. From November 15, 1885, to February 18, 1916, when Father de Rougé

---

[6] *BRSTM,* 34.
[7] *Baptismal Records of St. Francis Regis Mission,* (1867–1887), 139.
[8] *BRSTM,* 36.
[9] *Ibid.,* 40–43.
[10] *Ibid.,* 249–251.

recorded his last baptism, we count 1461 baptisms by Father de Rougé and 124 by visiting Jesuit priests. Father de Rougé blessed 412 marital unions. He seems not to have recorded the burials; not all the dead could be brought to St. Mary's.

Baptisms and marriages can be counted in human figures but not the prayers and sacrifices needed until the missionary was able to gain another soul for Christ. These are figures recorded by God alone.

CHAPTER XX

History Told in a Questionnaire

THE most scholarly of Father de Rougé's former students or, we might say, the one who had the best opportunities for academic advancement, is Dr. Paschal Sherman. He is a full-blooded Indian who worked for the Federal Veteran Administration in Washington, D. C., and is now in retirement. This gentleman's answers to the author's questionnaire are invaluable and because of their historical interest we have decided to set them down in full, even though some repetition of the text does occur.

Name:
Paschal Sherman, A.B., A.M., PHD., LL.B., M.P.L. (Master of Patent Law).

Did you attend St. Mary's Mission School?
Yes. 1907–1914 (returned to public schools in 1908 for one year).

Who has been your teacher?
Father Etienne de Rougé, Christian Brothers, Brothers of Mary, laymen teachers and a "Madam" who taught me piano.

What do you remember about Father de Rougé?
Father de Rougé was a member of the French nobility. The French representative at an international meeting of the Red Cross in Washington, D. C., in the late 1920's or the early 1930's was a Count de Rougé. I was unable to see him.
Father de Rougé had the gift in a rare degree of dealing with people in a way that moved, that evoked loyalties, that left lasting impressions. He understood people. . . .
He learned the Indian language well, Okanogan dialect of the Salishan stock, so that sometimes he preached first in English and then in Indian.
He knew the prayers in Indian and could lead the congregation in their recitation. How much of these prayers he composed, I do not know.

372

They were inspiring, beautiful, and poetic. He heard confessions in Indian, English, and French. (Some of his Indian parishioners were partly of French extraction.)

Early he turned to advantage the Indian instinct to follow chiefs by developing the leadership of prominent tribesmen in church matters. This was directed in the main to external affairs or to matters of public interest. The leaders would be called together, for example, to discuss federal government aid to Indian education, to remove or to prevent scandals, etc. It was recognized that the woman, the mother, was the main force at home and in the church in religious matters. For this purpose women "Leaders in Prayer" (translation of the Indian word used) were invested with the office in a sodality-like ceremony before the altar rail. This system waned somewhat toward the end of the era represented.

By reason of this system and community spirit that it developed, Indians in faraway places would gather on Sundays to say prayers and sing hymns in Indian by themselves since the priest could visit the different communities only occasionally, usually once a year, in the early days of his pastorate. Later school duties and the administration of the growing St. Mary's Mission, his permanent station, greatly restricted these calls. The Indians on the shores of Lake Chelan would go in families many miles to say prayers and sing hymns at a church twice during the day on Sundays and feast days. On these occasions the local chief, Wapato John, would preach sometimes to his people on doing good and carrying out their religious duties. In case of death they conducted funerals, in the absence of the priest, with appropriate prayers in the church and at the graveside.

On most feast days, however, the Indians went to the Mission by horseback or in rigs, some traveling three or four days, with full camp accoutrements. The Mission then became an encampment of 150 to 300 souls. To the services the faithful were called by the ringing of the church bell, as on every Sunday, and often in the old church there was not enough room in the pews. The tribal chiefs on Corpus Christi, with the throng foregathered on the campus beneath Japanese lanterns, delivered addresses on signal from Father de Rougé. I was thrilled by these addresses, delivered in different Indian dialects, eloquent, some fierce and forceful in manner, always inspiring and moving in the sentiments and counsel so warmly proceeding from the heart. We might say Father de Rougé's far-flung flock was in the heyday of their religious enthusiasm.

Father Caldi was the immediate successor of Father de Rougé. He was of a different mold and personality. He spoke Indian well, the Okanogan dialect, which, of course, helped to bring the Indians closer to him.

But it was unfortunate that apparently on his advent he made no effort to ascertain who was who among his parishioners. He lost the active support of Coxit George, a leader widely known and revered among the Indians, by a chill reception and dismissal of the latter who had called to pay respects. Later he designated leaders of his own chosen from families who were neither prominent nor exceptionally active in church affairs. He never did obtain quite the hold in the hearts of the people that Father de Rougé did. The old order and ways of thinking, the rapport between the Indians and their "Black Robe," started breaking up.

Father Caldi pastured calves and other livestock on the beautiful lawn of Father de Rougé, telling me that the Bishop could snub him for maintaining a park in the country. Pigs were penned against the big school building tò facilitate their feeding. The appearance of the old mission was changing.

The non-English speaking Indians were passing, and the English speaking generation was rising. Many of the latter's children now, even though full-blood, cannot speak Indian. They and their parents think in English and speak in English. In dealings with the Whites the old Indians used a jargon language called Chinook. Historians say that Chinook was a trading language among the Indians in the Northwest long before the coming of the white man. It must be remembered that there are dialectical differences among Indian languages of the same stock and that languages of different stocks may have little or nothing in common. The fur companies adopted the Chinook for use in trading with the northwestern Indians (although some Wisconsin Indians are known to speak Chinook) and added words of English or French derivation. The successors of Father Caldi did not stop to learn Indian, at least to the extent of its use in the confessional, on the grounds that all Indians used English well enough to be understood.

What do you remember about the Madams?

The "Madams" evolved at the mission about 1909. Whether the first group was composed of local women, I am not sure, but to my knowledge the first head of the Madams was Mrs. La Londe, a local widow, whose son worked at the Mission and whose daughters married in Omak and in the surrounding community. It is believed that Madams were recruited from faraway places by advertising in religious publications. One was a sure-enough Sister, a Benedictine, who took charge of the infirmary, as she was a trained nurse. After two or three years she left to establish a religious house in Oroville, Washington, taking along one of the Madams who was an accomplished pianist. A few years later, while I was at the Catholic University of America, the freewheeling Sister appeared at one of the Benedictine convents near the campus and called me up. I had a fine visit with her. She was still seeking recruits for her establishment.

Why Father de Rougé called them "Madams," I do not know. I rather think it was because certain religious women were so called in Europe. We have in this area The Sacred Heart of Mary Religious, a teaching order with a mother-house in Belgium, who are addressed as "Mesdames" and not as "Sisters."

The Madams were women of various skills, knowledges and accomplishments. They formed a well-balanced teaching staff. I took piano lessons from one, a benign old soul, who seemingly used to doze as she sat beside me while I was playing a lesson and would wake with a start when I purposely struck a false note.

What other helpers were then at the Mission?
Did you know the Christian Brothers? What was their job?
Their names? When and why did they leave?

Two sets of religious Brothers served at the Mission at different times to my certain knowledge. There may have been a third set with a house of studies in Southampton, England. I received a letter from a Brother upon his return to Southampton. Without a Catholic Directory available for reference, I am unable to identify the orders of the Brothers with any degree of certainty.

The first group of three, whom we called Christian Brothers, were already at the Mission when I first came there in 1907. One of them had served at a mission in Alaska. A Brother Celestine (the names of the others I do not recall) taught and led the school band. He was a fine musician (although, strangely enough, he never told me that in playing the base tuba, I had to keep time with the base drum, which I discovered by myself after some painful sessions in which I was accused of being hopeless). These Brothers returned to Plattsburg, New York, and in the 1920's I called there, while on vacation, for a visit with Brother Celestine and was told that he had gone to Belgium as world head of the organization. They were still at the Mission when Halley's Comet passed by in 1910, which I recall as causing quite a commotion among the Brothers one night, and they must have left in 1911 or 1912. We called them "Christian Brothers" but if they were so, they did not belong to the same congregation or institute as the Christian Brothers wearing a different type of habit and running St. John's High School (Military), Washington, D. C., and their normal or preparatory institute at Ammendale, Maryland.

The succeeding group of Brothers, three in number and whom we shall call "Brothers of Mary," stayed about two years. One of them was a nonteaching member who took charge of the farm and manual work. They left to establish, or left to an established, school for boys in southeast Seattle.

Why these Brothers came and left, I do not know. I can think of three reasons: (1) they came to look and decide; (2) they saw; and (3) they decided that the conditions were not right for carrying on a religious community life and for running a school for boys on a long-term basis.

About 1913 Father de Rougé brought in young men whom he called "Catechists." They served as teachers in the lower grades or as "prefects" who took charge of the boys on work details or during the hours of recreation. Father de Rougé had some idea, apparently not well formulated, of placing them in studies leading toward the priesthood. I overheard the fragment of an earnest discussion between the good Father and the bishop who pointed out that he would have to have the certification of a seminary before he could give orders or ordain. The Catechists were serious young men who served their stint and went their ways. One, Ernest Burtle of Glenarm, Illinois, later got an A.B. degree in 1918 from Georgetown University of Washington, D. C., and went on to Webster Groves, Missouri, where he completed his studies for the priesthood in the early 1920's. Upon ordination he served in various pastorates in Illinois. Another of a German family in Philadelphia, whose name I do not recall, joined the Christian Brothers who run St. John's High School in Washington, D. C., and an institute at Ammendale, Maryland.

From time to time laymen were hired from various walks of life to serve as instructors. A carpenter from Omak and son-in-law of Madam La Londe, Ernest Middleton, presided over a shop to teach the boys general and bench (Furniture-making) carpentry. A Mr. John St. Onge came from Quebec to teach band, violin, and piano music. He was a good musician and left to take a similar post at St. Martin's College, Lacey, Washington. One of the most colorful was a half-breed, Samuel McLean, who taught oil painting and penmanship and was one of the stars on the famous Carlisle football teams of Jim Thorpe's time. We had a representative of Oxford University in William Gannon who was an excellent teacher of English and who left to accept an instructorship in Gonzaga University.

What subjects were taught?

English, French, History (Bible, American, Modern, and Ancient), Geography, Arithmetic, Algebra, Trigonometry, Latin, Greek, Music (Piano, Strings, and Brass), Art (Drawing and Oil Painting), Bookkeeping, Penmanship, Science, Physics, Carpentry, Elocution (including Drama).

What sports program did the Mission then have?

Baseball, football, and track. Basketball sporadically — nobody coached basketball in my time.

How many months of school did you have at that time?

About eight months.

How many hours a day were the children in school then?

About six hours.

How many children were at the Mission?

About fifty (boys) and girls. More sometimes.

What jobs did you have to do?

Outside of classroom and recreation hours, all boys had something to do on the farm and indoors. An establishment as large as the Mission, with farming and stock raising operators, required a lot of hands to keep it going.

On the whole, as I recall it, the boys accepted the work as a matter of course and rather cheerfully. Few of them paid tuition fees. Their labors had a twofold purpose: To teach them agriculture, stock raising and such crafts as running the establishment afforded, including carpentry, plumbing, etc., and in the process, to produce beef, vegetables, and fruit for the school. At that time the school produced considerable of its own food since the surrounding country was sparsely settled with the transportation of supplies by steamer or wagon freight rather difficult and expensive.

The regular stints of work was good discipline and to that extent was character molding. The boys worked singly, by twos, or in groups, depending on what was to be done. Where the work was in groups, usually one of the teachers or Brothers served as supervisor or "Prefect." Some had indefinite assignments or assignments over given periods, such as feeding the stock or helping the farmer in charge and the hired hands during particular seasons, planting and harvesting the crops. The younger boys took turns at housekeeping chores, sweeping the halls, classrooms and dormitories, helping the cook, washing and drying dishes, etc.

The boys' school had lay cooks, generally Japanese in my time. They were good cooks. We had a warren of rabbits and I recall the delicious rabbit stews we had on feast days. The main meal on these days was invariably a banquet, to which we looked forward, with a delightful variety of food well prepared.

I have done all sorts of work, including the repair of frozen pipes outdoors in winter in zero weather. One of the Brothers was a taxidermist and among my occasional chores was going out with a shotgun to hunt for coyotes or other small game and hawks or ducks for the museum. Strangely enough, I never was assigned to assist the Brother in stuffing animals or birds. But other boys were taught the process.

To afford a glimpse of one facet of Mission life, I may say I served as "trusty" in various capacities and assignments. I was not always true to my role. For example, it was my duty at about eight thirty o'clock at night to go to the convent and fetch a pitcher of the finest broth that the Madams could make for Father de Rougé and, miserable dictu, I never scrupled from partaking of the wonderful treat en route. I took turns in doing paper work in the good Father's office, but in my time his confidential secretary was John B. Cleveland, now prominent in politics as a Democrat and a well-to-do farmer in the Monse area of Okanogan County. Not too long ago Mr. Cleveland was a delegate to the Democratic State Convention in Spokane.

As a general rule, Father de Rougé made the work assignments or told a lay teacher or Brother what was to be done. The latter then carried out the details, selecting the boys and seeing that the work was done smoothly without undue burden on anyone.

What were the girls' jobs?

The work of the girls was indoors, attending to the school laundry, sewing on buttons, dressmaking, etc. I am not aware of the schedule of training that they followed. It was rare that they did any weeding and other light work on the farm.

What crops were raised at the Mission?

Wheat, alfalfa, vegetables.

What kind of orchards did the Mission have?

Apples, cherries, pears.

What stock did they have then?

Cattle, horses.

Where was the first chapel?

Believe across the creek from present site.

Where was the first church?

See diagram attached.

Did you help build the new church? When?

Yes. Believe in 1912.

Who were the most influential Indians at the Mission at your time?

In my time the most influential Indians at the Mission were Coxit George, Alexander Smitkin and Alex Nicholson. George and Smitkin were comparatively wealthy at one time in horse and cattle herds. They were looked upon by the Indians as leaders because of their uncommon good sense and sterling reputations. Alex Nicholson was a half-breed with unusually good judgment for one with little formal education. He, too, was exemplary in character and was always at the service of the mission.

How did they help the Mission? What did they think about the Mission?

They helped the Mission in various ways. They served as consultors to Father de Rougé in matters of church discipline, on support of the mission and in dealings with the government. The government gave a subsidy of some kind to the mission for Indian children enrolled,[1] and it was in connection with matters like this that the aid of the leaders named was enlisted.

In the earlier days when the machinery of county, state, and federal governments was not well organized, the mission was the focal point for settlement of Indian disputes by the "Black Robe." On the other hand, the latter felt free to call for reciprocal help as occasion required. No formal procedures were followed. Indian police (federally appointed and paid) were subject to the call of the good Father to pursue, overtake, and return runaway boys and girls. These consulters and other leaders were sometimes called upon, in matters of church discipline, to see that children were sent to the Mission for schooling, that the laws of the church on marriage were observed as far as possible, that the medicine man and his ceremonials did not hold sway in their communities, etc. By the way, the medicine man who in emergencies or in situations of great moment called upon the power of his spirit, represented by some animate or inanimate object, to effect cures or to bring about some eventuality at a critical time was anathema. He was not allowed in the church during services. The Catholic Indian while avoiding the medicine man, nevertheless feared him and believed in his remarkable powers. The medicine man had practiced his art and ministrations for centuries among the Indians and generally among primitive peoples the world over.

---

[1] As correspondence of Father Caldi with the Indian Agent shows, the government sometimes issued clothing to the Mission for needy children. Reference to other aids could not be found.

During feast days certain men were invested with "police" authority on the mission grounds and in the church to guide processions or to maintain proper order and reverence among the worshipers. Following a European custom and for as long as I can remember, women were seated on the left side of the church and men on the right. The advice of leaders like George or Smitkin were sometimes sought for designation of these monitors.

We saw that leaders like George, Smitkin, and Nicholson helped weld the people into closely-knit communities and to make the Mission the center of community regulations. They formed the core of the lay apostolate among the Indians. Others followed their example as leaders in wholesome respect for the "Black Robe." Before these Indians, the older generation, were aware of legal "rights" and legal subterfuges, when the guilty one can hide behind procedural machinery and a confusion of evidence, a question often asked by those who were on the verge of doing something out of the way or who were advising against its commission: "What will the Black Robe say?" The word of the Black Robe carried far and was deeply felt by the Catholic people.

The leaders were responsible for many material contributions to the Mission in money, logs, and cordwood, beef, etc. With the types of transportation available donations of this kind were comparatively infrequent. As stated elsewhere, the mission produced considerable of its own needs.

How do you think did the education the Mission offered helped to raise the living standards of the different tribes involved?

It may not be said that the education offered by the Mission raised the standard of living of entire tribes, which depended on the economic development of the community and state, but undoubtedly it did raise the standards of living of the individual Indian educated.

Do you think the religious training the children received at the Mission contributed to a good Catholic family life?

Yes.

Do you think that those who were educated here at the Mission continue after leaving the Mission to practice their Catholic Faith?

Generally yes. There were exceptions and will continue to be exceptions. It is my impression that the children of past generations practiced their faith more, mostly because their parents were better Christians.

Can you describe some of the old buildings which were at the Mission when you were a Mission pupil?

See diagram attached.

What kind of shrines were down by the Omak Creek?

Of the Blessed Virgin and, if I recall correctly, of St. Joseph.

Do you know something about the college?

The question of the early college is not understood. It may be more proper to ask what college courses were given? We did not have a college as such with official authority to confer college credits and degrees. Yet the pursuit of the college courses produced great results and carried great weight so that practical recognition was given to it in assigning a Mission student to the proper class in college elsewhere.

The courses of college rank given at the Mission were: Algebra; Trigonometry; Geometry, plane and analytical; Latin; Greek; French; English; History, modern and ancient. There was some reading in the sciences but we lacked equipment for experimentation. Some paraphernalia for experimentation in physics were bought and were demonstrated to classes by one of the Brothers. In due course for lack of space and for lack of teachers, they were placed in the school museum. The music taught particularly by Professor St. Onge was of a high order.

For the serious student, as a rule, opportunities abound in virtually any school for improvement of mind and for increase in knowledge over and beyond those afforded by the courses taken. So it was at the mission where the studies may not have followed standard curricula but were supplemented by independent reading so that the education obtained was substantial and practical. With what I learned in this way I felt perfectly at home later in the academic circles of St. Martin's College and the Catholic University of America.

William F. Hill, now in the insurance business in Spokane [now in Tonasket], required only about two years at St. Martin's College, Lacey, Washington, to earn an A.B. degree in 1914. I entered Junior Class at the same college in the fall of 1914, merrily taking up the philosophy course with Latin textbooks in three volumes. In my Senior year I won a Knights of Columbus graduate scholarship at the Catholic University, Washington, D. C., in an international competitive examination. I could not have won except for the education obtained at the Mission, with the concomitant sharpening of my perception and wits, because the tests included Latin, French, English, and Ancient History, on which I obtained very little additional learning at St. Martin's. Indeed, with no additional French courses taken at the University, I passed the German and French tests for the Ph.D. degree some years later at the Catholic University. In the scholarship examination I do not think I received favorable consideration on nonacademic grounds: for example, the Catholic University, which graded the results of the tests, did not know I was an Indian until I reported to the registrar's office.

The college courses at the mission were not given in terms of years. How much time was devoted to any course depended on individual capacity and opportunity. In my time we had boys older, up to 19 years, than those now attending the Mission. We were old enough and good enough to play championship baseball against town teams in the Okanogan valley. Most of these boys were good students and made the most of their opportunities to acquire an education. If given the material support needed, students like Ross Hilleary and John B. Cleveland would have made good "with a bang" in any college or university. While I made my way through St. Martin's first by doing such chores as sweeping halls, washing dishes, etc, and later by teaching Latin, I did have some home support for transportation, clothes and books. Of course, the latter day classes at the Mission have produced some notable representatives like Peter Campbell now in the second year of a five year architecture course at the Catholic University [1960].

We are proud of the achievements of Moses George, who came to the Mission as a little boy about the time I left. [He is] a road building engineer with headquarters at Wenatchee, Washington. He learned the use of the transit in surveying and the principles of road engineering virtually on his own and is now a high official in this field in the state of Washington. Sammy Smith, one of the three Smith brothers at the school, became immensely wealthy in cattle operations.

Were you present at one of the fires?

Yes.

Can you remember some incidents in connection with the fire?

A fire started at the convent in 1913 or 14. I gave the alarm and the fire was put out by the combined effort of the boys at the school.

How were the great feast days of the Church celebrated at the Mission?

The feast days celebrated at the Mission to which the Indians came from far and near in a great throng were Christmas, Easter, and Corpus Christi. The Indians knew Corpus Christi as the "Flower" feast because of the profusion of flower decorations and the flowers strewn along the paths of the solemn procession on that occasion. Holy Week, except as incident to Easter, and Christ the King were not attended by worshipers in such force.

I am not familiar with the rubrics and canons of the Church. But on these feast days Father de Rougé said High Mass. The servers (with two of the boys deaconized, as it were), were well trained in the responses. A well-drilled choir was always in attendance. One of the Madams, a choir member, had a remarkable soprano voice. Two young boys, Willie Carden and Willie Edwards (both long since deceased), also stand out in my memory as first rate sopranos who would have made good, I think, in any boys choir — and I have heard some notable organizations of boys choirs in my life. For the most of my career at the Mission I was the organ player, and I recall the intensive drills we used to have under the conducting of Father de Rougé, one of the Brothers, or Professor St. Onge.

(Apropos of nothing, I may mention that once while playing the organ alone in the choir loft a church mouse ran into my view on the right, apparently unaware of me and facing the altar, got on its haunches or hind legs still facing the altar as though in prayerful worship, and then after a minute or two descended to all fours to return to wherever it came from.)

The congregation of older Indians with whom I was familiar understood the various parts of the Holy Sacrifice of the Mass quite well and some of its members could give the responses of High Mass and nearly all at Benediction.

Mention was made of rubrics and canons because a priest once implied that Father de Rougé had no right to say the High Mass. I gathered from his passing remark that Father de Rougé should have had priest servers. While I attended the celebration of High Mass in suburban Washington without priests as servers, some doubts have been raised in my mind by what followed after Father de Rougé's passing. On feast days his successors said three Low Masses in succession without High Mass. One of the older Indians, who could not speak English, once told me that when he asked Father Caldi in Indian why High Mass was not said, the latter replied (his Indian translated): "It would be as though a lie was being told."

Easter and Corpus Christi were celebrated with processions. After European fashion Father de Rougé employed the ceremonials to impress the worshipers with the solemnity of the holy days. Of course, the processions had their place in Church ritual. A canopy was carried over the Sacred Host in procession supported at the four corners by such leaders as Smitkin wearing ceremonial sashes. At the elevation of the Host, a sacred and solemn moment, at midnight High Mass on Christmas a salute was fired at the door of the Church outside by the discharge of two shots in quick succession from a revolver or gun. Once when Bishop O'Dea of Seattle was proceeding up the Omak Creek road toward the mission a troop of mounted Indians was sent down to meet him and escort him in state to the church in time for him to preside at Benediction. In his remarks at the services he expressed deep appreciation for the gesture of honor.

Perhaps in this day of sophistication, ceremonials of this kind may be, in the words of Father Caldi, "as though a lie was being told."

When was the hospital built? Who took care of the patients?

1911 or 1912. A doctor and the Mesdames.

Can you remember some names of doctors or Sisters who took care of sick pupils?

Dr. Lane and Madam La Londe.

How many white children attended St. Mary's when you were there?

Most about six at any time.

What kind of food was served to the children?

Meats, (fish on days of abstinence), vegetables, fruits, cereals, breads, etc., standard foods usually well cooked.

Do you remember something about Father de Rougé's cave?

Don't recall any such thing as a cave.
There may have been one.

Who took care of the girls?

The Mesdames.

Who took care of the boys?

The Brothers or laymen teachers.

What rewards or punishments were given?

    Rewards: Medals and prizes, (books, etc.).

    Punishments: Usually no play during recreation hours. (One of the Brothers could slap resoundingly and convincingly.)

*   *   *

Addition to the Questionnaire: *Some Highlights of Memory.*

Father de Rougé was the dramatic department of the mission. Fired by histrionic instincts, he was enthusiasm and patience personified in his tireless efforts to develop the talents of a troupe of young players carefully chosen for stage productions. Shows were given in the school auditorium during feast days and at the closing exercises of the school year. Special performances were also given for important personages or for overnight visitors of distinction.

It was evident that Father de Rougé himself had excellent instruction and coaching in dramatics. His gestures and stage techniques were along classical lines: He expounded what I took to be his interpretation of Delsarte's principles on dramatic expression. From a book I read in the school library, I saw remarkable parallelism between the art of the mid-nineteenth century Delsarte in Paris and that of his flawless disciple in the western wilds.

We played abridged Moliere's, Handy Andy, and other standbys. We learned by heart "The Bear Story" of James Whitcomb Riley and other recitable masterpieces. We were always ready to entertain on any occasion. Besides we were given the advantage of speaking before people at almost every opportunity. Once I gave an address "Mon Reverend Pere" in French (composed by one of the Brothers) to the good Father on some anniversary before the assembled students and friends. We played in the brass and in the orchestra. On occasions I, among others, presented the aboriginal version of a piano vituoso in the public recital of a Chopin or a Liszt.

All this gave us a sense of presence, and power and humor. Conspicuous in the troupe were William F. Hill, Ross Hilleary, John B. Cleveland, Arnold Morris, Lawrence Morris, and Louie Smitkin who played, as I recall, some kid roles. On the world as a stage, Hill became a public figure in county and state cattle associations, as a county-commissioner, as Democratic committeeman in state politics, and in civic activities; Cleveland also became a public figure in county political and civic activities and is noted as a forceful and effective speaker; Ross Hilleary is a successful Farmer in the Coeur D'Alene region of Idaho; and the late Louie Smitkin several years ago was in the trucking business and a baseball great in Okanogan county. As for me, one of the first times in my career I looked back to this training with a bit of solid gratification was when a newspaper in 1924, dubbed my address to a jury in the Superior Court, Everett, Washington, as — "Eloquent."

*   *   *

Indian names are no more jawbreaking than the Scandinavian or the Slavic. But except for the Cherokees, alphabets were not devised and used for the different Indian tribes. It was extremely difficult to render the linquals, the labials and other sounds of the northwest Indian languages into the phonetics of our English-Roman alphabet. Since the names of the northwesterners did not run to combinations of meaning translatable into such euphemisms as the Sioux "Sitting Bull" or "Rain-In The Face," the results obtained in the construction of equivalents in vowels and consonants for the sounds of Indian names were not too satisfactory. The syllabification was conducive neither to easy nor to uniform pronunciation, among other things, and not infrequently the Indian seemed to be the goat of his own name.

No doubt by reason of these difficulties Father de Rougé decided in 1907 or 1908 to change the last names of certain students to English names distinctive in American history. We gleefully entered into the spirit of the thing and looked forward toward the moment when we would be presented with our new monikers. I recall one of the older boys already with a civilized name, Favel, insisted on having a new name, too, but he was not included in the select list. For some reason the Smitkin boys, Paul and Louie, also were not included. Perhaps their parents had objected. So far as I know, the parents of the others were not consulted, for one reason or another the new names were later dropped. The few still carried are reminders of a well-intentioned experiment which was not repeated.

My family name is Wapato which means potato in Chinook jargon and which my grandfather acquired when he became a potato king. He raised large crops of potatoes on the shores of Lake Chelan and transported them by mule-train overland for sale in Portland, Oregon, and other Columbia River settlements. My brother, Paul, was given a new name, too, but upon return to the public schools the following year he reverted to the family name. The new names were written on slips of paper and drawn from a hat. My brother and I were made to draw separate names but happily no internecine strife followed, for we were on the same side of the war — he became *Grant* and I *Sherman.*

*   *   *

The school infirmary was the only hospital for miles around in the county. But it was not open for the public generally, although some county patients were admitted. By the way, some boys, in trouble with the law were paroled to the Mission for a year or two. The physicians who called from Okanogan or Omak at such times as was necessary were under contract to the federal government. One Madam and a Benedictine Sister were trained nurses and could attend at operations.

I recall the death of two students, Gussie and Agapith (last names I cannot think of at this time), who were given impressive funerals. Gussie was a boarding student and died in the infirmary. Agapith, a day student, died by the creek in a house across from the Mission. During the funerals the church bell tolled at minute intervals, and the school band played stately music like the *Miserere of Il Trovatore* by Verdi, characterized by the masterful performance of the cornetists, John B. Cleveland and Paul Baima.

Before the building of the infirmary Father de Rougé had his assortment of drugs and first aid equipment on his shelves. In the days when Okanogan and Omak were way stations and the only physician in the neighborhood was a rancher for whom Pogue's Flat was named, seldom available in emergencies because he was frequently out on calls, the good Father rose to the heights of skill in some critical situations. Once a boy, Sam Wellington by name, while in a hearty guffaw accidentally caught in his mouth the blade of a hoe swung by another student. His tongue was slashed almost in half. Through the skillful treatment of Father de Rougé, the physician of body and soul, he recovered and was none the worse for the harrowing experience.

We had the usual childhood epidemics at the school, mumps at the boys' and chicken pox at the girls'. The visiting doctor on different occasions examined the children for bad eyesight and bad tonsils. As a result glasses and tonsillectomies were prescribed wholesale. Some of the boys were able to go through the operations without anesthetic of any kind. I decided I wasn't going to be made to wear glasses, and so while awaiting my turn for examination I memorized the eye chart which I could see within a few feet from the antechamber. I missed the last line purposely but the doctor declared I had perfect eyesight. I was in the infirmary twice, and the second occasion stands out in my memory because I and the older boys stole apples from the kitchen. When the nurse came storming in to accuse us, we blamed it on the patients who were completely innocent but who were too young to defend themselves convincingly.

*   *   *

I came on the scene when the mission was in the heyday of its glory as an educational and religious oasis under Father de Rougé's regime. The era 1907–1914 was memorable for many things. There was considerable building activity. The old boys' school and church were torn down and a larger building and a new church constructed. The infirmary was put up and the girls' school started and enlarged. A gymnasium, where school exercises were held, was built near the boys' school. The grounds were well laid out and took on a parklike appearance with beautiful lawns, flower beds, and full-grown shade trees. In this era there came together a group of boys gifted in various ways more than in the average run of registrations. Fortunately, too, there came teachers who seemed really interested in trying to develop those gifts to the best advantage possible.

I have visited many Indian schools since, including Bacone College, Muskogee, Oklahoma, and the impression is invariably given that the students are taught and handled with a patronizing attitude on the part of the non-Indian teaching staff. Whatever a student may do well is "good for an Indian, you know." And there seemed lacking the rapport of mutual respect and confidence between instructor and pupil so necessary to bring out the best in the latter.

Father de Rougé singled out the boys who showed unusual promise of achievement in the courses of study available. He took charge of the

Latin and Greek classes. He was a sort of indoor peripatetic supplementing the instruction and exercises in these languages with discussions of various academic subjects of interest, which I can say, as I look back from the vantage point of a liberal education, were really enlightening and broadening. He inspired reading in fine literature, history, and philosophy — at least, in me to an extent that I was strong in these subjects and in college and at the university. Besides tests in Latin, English, French, and History, my major ordeal for the Knights of Columbus graduate scholarship was a three hour examination in philosophy.

Students with a special bent for music were encouraged to play in the band or orchestra. Our band practice, individual as well as ensemble, was usually intensive, and succeeded in bringing our playing to a high pitch of excellence. We were so told by outsiders who were themselves experienced band players and we were acclaimed by crowds in Omak and at the Mission.

On Sundays and during holidays the morning study hours were given to painting, drawing, penmanship, and piano practice. Boys with a flair for painting were placed before easels for incursions into the world of art under the personal supervision of Father de Rougé. One of the Brothers was a particularly apt teacher of drawing with crayon and pencil. Agapith whose last name I do not recall and whose career was so short lived became a master penman through correspondence courses that the boys took in penmanship.

I received more than my time alloted for piano practice because of my way with the ivory keys. Likewise one of the teachers whose name I cannot recall gave me special attention in geometry and I remember some novel discussions we had on theorems, which helped sharpen my wits. He used to spend from one-half to three-quarters of an hour lecturing us in philosophy, and I knew something about such things as the simple apprehension in Logic long before I went to St. Martin's College. Another teacher, Luergenmiller by name, a former seminarian, was particularly good as an instructor in the courses of college rank and he seemed to take genuine delight in giving impetus to the progress of students with more than ordinary aptitudes.

In this era the boys who stood out in all-around excellence in the classroom, on the playing field, and in the school activities generally were Francis Favel, Max Favel, John B. Cleveland, William F. Hill, Ross Hilleary, the Morris brothers, and a few others whose names I cannot call to mind at this time.

Having read Dr. Sherman's contributions to the history of St. Mary's Mission we can only express our deepest regret that Father de Rougé, the born educator, had to leave his promising field of labor so soon.

CHAPTER XXI

Father de Rougé's Legacy

FATHER de Rougé's early death at the age of 57 proved to be a calamity for his Indian parishioners. Father had left a mark on the country, but was it lasting? He had continued the work of the early missionaries coming from St. Paul's, St. Francis Regis, and from old St. Joseph's at Yakima. He had tried to give all that Christianity was able to give, knowledge of God and His Commandments, the love of this God, culture, and schooling seen from the Christian point of view, works of charity as the outgrowth of Christianity. But what could one man alone do? His schools could only accept a small fraction of the tribal youth. Could anyone ever attempt to civilize a great part of a country in not quite two generations since the coming of the first missionaries? The European tribes had needed centuries. Yet, Father de Rougé's influence had been so great and so far-reaching that he accomplished more than any other missionary before him.

It was of utmost importance that the Jesuit superiors would find a successor for him who would speak the languages of the tribes and who would have some of Father de Rougé's qualities. The Indians were sore at heart; it needed great prudence to attempt to fill Father de Rougé's place. Father S. M. Filippi, S.J., coming from St. Francis Regis Mission helped out until Father Celestine Caldi, S.J., was chosen as the successor.[1] This new missionary arrived at the Mission on the first Friday of June, 1916.[2]

The new superior of the Mission had previously been the traveling missionary for Barnabee, Inchelium, Hall, Monaghan, San Poel, Lafleur, Daisy, Hunters, Fruitland, Republic, Curlew and many smaller stations.[3]

---

[1] Ledovina, Rev. C. B., to Bishop Schinner, June 14, 1916, Ms. Also: Ledovina to Rev. S. M. Filippi, S.J., St. Mary's Mission, Omak, Ms., ADS.

[2] Madam Luce to Bishop Schinner, June, 1916, Ms., ADS.

[3] *Litterae annuae a die Julii 1914 as diem 1. Julii, 1915.* Ms., OPA. Also: Caldi to Father Provincial, July 29, 1915, Ms., OPA.

He was a hardworking man but he felt that he had his limitations. Mr. De Vos writes:

> Father Caldi was as keen a chap as Father de Rouge but he began his time under sad handicaps. He had no personal funds, or estate to help him and he came to Omak to ask me how a man who did not know a growing turnip from a potatoe vine could feed 140 youngsters from what looked like a good farm. He admitted he knew a pig was not a cow but what care [to give them] and how to use them was beyond him and he had to make the place carry all expenses. The solution was easy, however. Tell no one of your farming ignorance, turn the farm over to Mr. Smith, the girls to your top Sister and handle the boys' school and administration yourself. It worked. . . .[4]

In the meantime Father de Rougé's last building project, the Sacred Heart Chapel for his Madams, was completed and Father Caldi asked Bishop Schinner if it would be possible for his Lordship to come on the Feast of the Sacred Heart to bless the new chapel.[5] His Excellency was unable to come.

The outlook for keeping the Mission going was not quite as gloomy as Father Caldi saw it. Good Mother Katherine was ready again with her help. On June 29, 1916, she writes to tell Father Caldi that she received the news of his appointment; at the same time she acquaints him with the arrangements made with Father de Rougé:

> We sent quarterly teacher's salaries, etc. as follows:
>
> | for 1 Quarter 2 teachers | 180 |
> |---|---|
> | 1 man | 90 |
> | 3 Lady Catechists | 135 |
> | Cook | 120 |
> | | 525 |
>
> In addition to this we sent payment for a number of girl pupils not exceeding an average of 40.[6]

The salaries for the teachers and other hired help as well as the girls' school were provided for. A certain number of boys received some help from the Catholic Bureau; besides, Bishop Schinner contributed whatever he was able. Most of the building projects were outwardly completed.

A very significant point easily overlooked is that on the same day when the *Omak Chronicle* announced Father de Rougé's death, it also brought the news that Omak had been chosen as the only registration point for the opening of the reservation.[7] Father de Rougé had prepared for the

---

[4] De Vos to the author.

[5] Rev. C. Caldi, S.J., to Rt. Rev. Schinner, June 14, 1916, Ms., ADS.

[6] Mother Katherine to Caldi, June 29, 1916, Ms. copy, ABSS.

[7] "Omak Made Registration Point Last Week — Now Gets U.S. Commissioner," *The Omak Chronicle,* May 12, 1916.

white man's children; his schools were ready to receive them. Here was an opportunity to establish a permanent school on the higher level for the incoming white population that would have helped to maintain a certain number of Indian children. But now the long-time educator of the Okanogan Valley had closed his eyes and his successor was unable to fill this gap. For two or three years the attendance at St. Mary's Mission School was enormous; often there were more nonboarding white children than Indians. With the decline in scholarship came the decline of the school.

As letters show, in the same year that Father de Rougé died Bishop Schinner had asked the Benedictines to take over the Mission.[8] Abbot Placidus from St. Benedict's Abbey, St. Benedict, Oregon, however, was short of priests and needed the consent of his Council. We were not able to ascertain the reasons for Bishop Schinner's request.[9] But the following quote taken from Abbot Placidus' letter of October 16, 1917, wherein he answers Bishop Schinner's letter of October 7, seems to give us the answer:

> I have placed the matter of taking over the Mission before the Council, but did not meet with any favor, their main objection being that the place must be on the verge of ruin, or the Jesuits would not want to give it up; why should we take over something the Jesuits do not want any longer?[10]

Bishop Schinner must have been aware of the changing conditions at St. Mary's Mission. He asked the Fathers of the Divine Word, Techny, Illinois, if they would be willing to take over St. Mary's Mission. Again he was unsuccessful.[11] Abbot Placidus himself would have liked to take over the Mission. As correspondence shows, the Abbot and Bishop Schinner together visited the Mission during January of 1918. Referring to this visit Abbot Placidus suggested that the Sisters' proposition to send two of them to the Beaverton Sisters to make their novitiate be accepted, as the Jesuit Fathers had formulated the rules of these Sisters. They "should be instrumental in correcting & straightening this matter, before they drop it & step out."[12] But Bishop Schinner did not like to take

---

[8] Rt. Rev. Abbot Placidus, O.S.B., to Bishop Schinner, December 7, 1916, Ms., ADS.

[9] Rev. Martin Pollard, O.S.B., Prior of Mount Angel Abbey (formerly St. Benedict's Abbey), St. Benedict, Oregon, to the author, October 8, 1962, stated that either Abbot Placidus tore up his letters or they must have been lost in the fire of 1926. During those early decades the tendency of the superiors was to overextend the activities; the calls for help of all kinds were frequent.

[10] Abbot Placidus to Bishop Schinner, October 16, 1917, Ms., ADS.

[11] Rev. J. A. Burgumer, S.V.D., to Bishop Schinner, December 24, 1917, Ms., ADS.

[12] Abbot Placidus to Bishop Schinner, January 24, 1918, Ms., ADS.

this step before anything definite had been arranged. "If some other society were to take charge after you have refused, which I hope you will not, that society might prefer some other community with which to affiliate."[13] The last correspondence on the subject is dated May 23, 1918, when Abbot Placidus told Bishop Schinner that he had intended to visit St. Mary's Mission. The chapter is "not in favor, until a miracle takes place." But there was a Benedictine priest on the way coming from Monte Casino. Maybe, he could be inducted to go to St. Mary's Mission.[14]

While Bishop Schinner still was looking for other priests to take over the mission, Father Caldi was trying to secure help in finally acquiring a patent in fee for the mission lands by writing to Senator Miles Poindexter, Washington, D. C. This letter shows that the very next school year after Father de Rougé's death the high school subjects had been dropped. The beautiful gardens and parks now had become cattle pastures; about eight to ten big iron gates ruined the scenery. We quote from Father Caldi's letter:

> Much of the land is fenced in, about 200 acres have been planted in grain and some acreage in alfalfa. There is an orchard of 200 fruit trees and some gardens are cultivated to furnish the vegetables. The boys are taught farming and gardening and in this way contribute much to their support while the girls are taught the domestic arts of Cooking, Sewing, Laundry and Nursing.
>
> A corps of thirteen teachers is employed in the schools to teach the children the simpler courses in English and Arithmetic with a good working knowledge of Typewriting, Painting, Mechanical Drawing, Hygiene and Physics, together with some carpenter, blacksmith and dairy work for the boys. The boys take care of the machinery of the place such as the gasoline engines and automobile, and the machinery of the laundry.[15]

During Father de Rougé's time, Christian education was the number one factor and all other aspects of the Mission life were geared to this objective. Now work became the important business of the Mission. We cannot entirely blame Father Caldi for this attitude. People who lived through the end of the First World War and the years that followed know how hard it was to earn a livelihood. The inhabitants of the Mission had first to live; however, Father Caldi should have considered that he had to deal with children of grade-school age only. The thirteen teachers he mentioned included every adult person at the Mission.

---

[13] Bishop Schinner to Abbot Placidus, January 25, 1918, Ms. copy, ADS.

[14] Abbot Placidus to Bishop Schinner, May 23, 1918, Ms., ADS.

[15] Caldi to Honorable Miles Poindexter, United States Senator, Washington, D. C., December 15, 1917. Ms., *Records of the Bureau of Indian Affairs*, Classified Files, Portion of 9834–1910, File #313, NA, Record Group 75.

Whatever may have been the shortcomings of Father Caldi, he saw early that the arrangement with the Ladies Catechists Missionaries was not just. Quite a few of them had to leave the Mission on account of sickness they had contracted while working under unhealthful conditions. Yet the Mission was too poor to provide for them. Father Caldi asked Mother Katherine about this matter:

> I consider it advisable at this junction of our history of St. Mary's to put the little community on a sound financial basis for the time to come; to establish a certain dependable income so the dear Sisters who sacrifice themselves heroically for the salvation of these Indians, may be made sure of the future.
>
> Three years ago, when I was put here at St. Mary's I gathered from your letters that your assistance may fail us, should God be pleased to crown you some day and bring you closer to Him.[16]

Mother Katherine's answer is not preserved. There was no provision made for the Madams. After the clothing they had brought to the Mission was in the course of years worn out, there was difficulty in replacing it. Madam Foster needed a new warm coat; Father Caldi gave her a man's coat, which she wore during the days, and during the nights she used it as a blanket. It must have been at times very embarrassing for women who were not married to completely depend on Father. What does a man know about a woman's needs?[17]

Father Caldi was a nervous and easily excitable person; he was quick to scold and to punish. Public relations were not his major strength, not with his pupils and their parents and not with Mother Katherine. Formerly we were able to trace all the building projects through the letters Father de Rougé wrote to Mother Katherine; Father Caldi's letters never betray what he is doing. His style becomes cold and businesslike. Slowly the attitude of his pupils changed.

On Sunday morning, October 5, 1919, as the inhabitants of the Mission prepared to go to Mass, a sudden fire alarm was given. The pride of the Mission, Father de Rougé's college, was aflame. The bell kept on tolling and all the surrounding neighbors, including Mrs. Helen Toulou and Alec Nicholson, hurried to the scene. The boys wanted to form a bucket brigade but Father Caldi slapped two boys and closed the door.[18] Was he afraid for the lives of the boys or did he then have already one of his mental spells? All of Father de Rougé's famous school went up in flames; not many items were saved. Gone was the famous museum, the library with over 2000 books which constituted in those pioneer days a

---

[16] Caldi to Mother Katherine, August 4, 1919, Ms., ABSS.
[17] Sister M. Michael, O.P., interview.
[18] John B. Cleveland, interview.

great treasure, all the school equipment, except the musical instruments which the boys saved.[19] The building itself had a value of $75,000 and what had been in the building about $25,000.[20] Destroyed also was a great historical treasure, the correspondence Father de Rougé had received.

Father Caldi wrote the sad news to Mother Katherine:

> It grieves me immensely to have to notify your maternity, that our St. Mary's Mission, suffered heavy loss by fire, last Sunday morning October 5th. The Indian boys' school known as the College, is in ashes today. It was about 300 feet long, some 40 feet wide and stories [sic] high; embellished by three large towers, one in the center, and one on either end.
>
> No one was injured and the fire was so controlled that it did not spread to other buildings. The wisdom of dear Father de Rougé was far-sighted in greatly isolating the various buildings of the Mission. We have moved to the hospital building. We go on as usual with our devotions, with our classes and with our regular mission-routine.
>
> We do not need to tell your Maternity that we have suffered great loss. Our stores, our Commissary department, were in the building; clothes, underwear, shoes, hardware, machines, and the tools for vocational training. We had bought our supplies, provisions and groceries for the winter; we had established an Electric Light Plant and had finished and fitted almost to perfection the vast building. Two dear Sisters and some twenty-five boys, have nothing left except what they wear, that being mighty little, because of the early hour of the fire viz., 8 a.m.[21]

How did the fire start? Nobody seemed to know. Years after a guilty boy came to Father Griva and told him that he was the one who started it. He had been strongly reprimanded by Father Caldi the previous day and had tried to get even.[22]

It was fortunate that the Mission had the hospital building, which now for the time being became the boys' house. Other remodeling had to be done at the Sisters' convent. The Madams, who during Father de Rougé's time taught the kindergarten boys during the days and had never to take care of the boys' dormitory, had been made responsible for any kind of work, be it teaching or outside work.[23] Two of the Madams were living in the boys' house when it burned. These ladies proved to be heroic souls who most certainly earned their heaven. There was no special room for

---

[19] The musical instruments were still there when our Sisters took over in 1936.

[20] Caldi to Bishop Schinner, May 27, 1920, Ms., ADS.

[21] Caldi to Mother Katherine, October 11, 1919, Ms., ABSS.

[22] Sister M. Michael, the former Madam Foster, was told this personally by Father Griva.

[23] Louie Morris, interview. As one of the bigger boys, Louis had to bring the smaller boys to bed.

the Madam to sleep when she had the supervision of the boys' dorm in the hospital. She retreated to a corner and improvised some means of privacy until years later when the new dormitories were built.[24]

After the big fire Father Caldi had not much time to meditate on the smoking embers; the mission had to go on. He did not take the rest his state of health would have needed; neither did he give rest to anybody else on his Mission. He set to work and made plans for more fireproof buildings which in due time became the third set of buildings, the ones still in use at the Mission. He was fond of machinery, especially of his automobile; it is therefore not surprising that the first building erected by him was a big "garage," thirty by sixty with five divisions. In one part was the Delco light plant with its thirty-two large glass batteries; another part was for his 1917–1918 Franklin car; a third was for the Model T Ford truck; a fourth section served as storage space for a Cletrac tractor. In the last division was the machine shop of Madame Fraser.[25] Everything that had to do with the car or with repairs was supplied at the Mission even when other necessary things were wanting. The carlift had to be operated not by Father himself but by Madam Foster; our Sister Richildis had to do it later. This was a job for Sundays only — for on Saturdays still heavier work had to be done.[26]

The enrollment of the grade school fluctuated according to attendance records. Only thirteen Indian girls were enrolled in the boarding school during the quarter ending December 31, 1918, but more white day students attended the school then. Ages ranged from twenty-three years to two years; one was from the Nespelem Tribe, three from the Wenatchees, four from the Colvilles and four from the Okanogans.[27] During the summer vacation month of 1919, just before the fire, the girls' school had twenty-two boarders. The following is one of the quarterly reports sent to Mother Katherine.

Names	Tribe	Blood	Age	Attendance
Anderson, Agnes	Nespelem	1/4	10 yrs.	31 days
Atkins, Josie	Wenatchee	4/4	13 "	26 "
Armstrong, Nancy	Nespelem	4/4	9 "	14 "
Antoine, Pauline	Wenatchee	4/4	7 "	8 "
Corbonaro, Mary	Okanogan	1/2	6 "	92 "
Corbonaro, Edith	Okanogan	1/2	6 "	92 "
Corbonaro, Elizabeth	Okanogan	1/2	5 "	92 "
Corbonaro, Annie	Okanogan	1/2	3 "	92 "
Corbonaro, Lucy	Okanogan	1/2	1, 9 mo.	92 "
Carden, Lucy	Okanogan	4/4	10 y.	10 "

---

[24] Sister M. Michael, O.P., interview.
[25] Joseph Jung and Anthony Walters, interviews.
[26] Sister M. Richildis, O.P., interview at Spokane, January 3, 1960.
[27] Caldi, *Quarterly Report* to Mother Katherine, December 31, 1918, Ms., ABSS.

Daniels, Ferne	Colville	1/8	13 "	30 "
George, Isabelle	Okanogan	4/4	13 "	25 "
George, Margaret	Okanogan	4/4	11 "	25 "
George, Margaret	Okanogan	4/4	8 "	3 "
Geojon, Irene	Okanogan	1/2	7 "	65 "
Martin, Caroline	Colville	4/4	3 "	31 "
Nicholson, Ellen	Colville	4/4	8 "	3 "
Nahumpshun, Catherine	Okanogan	4/4	8 "	18 "
Smitheran, Mildred	Okanogan	4/4	6 "	92 "
Smitheran, Grace	Okanogan	1/2	5 "	92 "
Steel, Mary	Okanogan	1/2	11 "	16 "
Stelkia, Lizzie	Okanogan	4/4	13 "	2 "[28]

We notice the many small children whose proper place would be at home.
The five Corbonaro children might have been orphans.

Another quarterly report for 1920, the year after the fire, gives the
number of pupils attending as forty-seven girls and twelve boys.[29] These
few grade-school boys were the workmen of the Mission. Perry Green,
fourteen, and Lawrence Walters, twelve years old, had to wire the church
for electric light. During the winter of 1920 Father Caldi wanted another
road built. Anthony Walters stated that he had been the oldest person
working at that road; he was then eight years old. More and more classes
were suspended, for "Father Caldi was a builder but not an educator."[30]
Madame Foster was the truck driver. She was working for months with
the boys in the sandpit loading and hauling the sand for the cement. The
second all-cement building was a two room school building with another
two room addition for the priest's office and sleeping quarters. This was
erected in about 1922–1923, thirty by seventy. The big quantities of
cement had to be mixed without machinery. Once during a recess from
mixing cement the exhausted boys ate some wild parsnips; one died in
fifteen minutes; the others became very sick.[31]

The next project of Father Caldi was the erection of dormitories, concerning which Father wrote to Bishop Shinner:

> In my last letter to the Indian Commissioner I stated our need of a
> boys' dormitory which we shall be able to put up with about $3000 and
> I then asked $1000 for fuel and supplies and $1000 for the purpose of
> domestic water.[32]

Meant was the Commissioner of the Catholic Indian Bureau, in Washington, D. C. He sent a check of $3500 as "a donation by the Indian Bureau

---

[28] Caldi, Report to Mother Katherine, September 30, 1919, Ms., ABSS.

[29] *Quarterly School Report,* Ms., SM.

[30] Sister M. Michael, interviews.

[31] Anthony Walters, interview.

[32] Caldi to Bishop Schinner, January 4, 1923, Ms., ADS.

for St. Mary's Mission."[33] Another check of $500 followed April 22, 1924.[34] The dormitory very probably was built during 1923–1924. It was quite a big building, one hundred ten by thirty four feet, which after its completion was not used for the boys but for the girls. During the summer of 1925 an auditorium and assembly hall, ninety by thirty, was erected which later also housed the library and the administration office. The barn which formerly was at a distance from the Mission was rebuilt near the other buildings, forty by seventy.[35] This shows again the utilitarian attitude of Father Caldi; beauty had no value for him.

The Indian agent, Upchurch, requested certain information from Father Caldi during August of 1922. We quote from the answer of the priest:

1. Incorporated name: The Pioneer Educational society, Headquarters, Mt. St. Michael's, Spokane.

2. . . . .

3. Religious work is supplemented by industrial training, domestic science, farming demonstrations etc. at the schools. Employees in charge, A. Berg, M. Fitzgibbon, A. Foster.[36]

4. Communicants approximately 500. The work is progressing and meeting with apparent . . . success.

5. Improvements: a magnificent church, a beautiful chapel, four large buildings, shops, machine and wagon sheds, a power laundry and three substantial barns, an orchard of about 200 fruit trees and some small fruit of every kind. 60 acres in alfalfa or grain (200 acres [of] the Mission farm, in grain). All the Mission land within fence, and subdivided into fields and pastures according to the lay of the country, every part of the land being used to its full extent and advantage. The value of all improvements amounting to over $100,000.

6. The writer does not know of any local conditions working against the welfare of the Indians. . . . However 1. The evil of divorce may be pointed out as the undoing of many a home. 2. At apple picking the Indians and Half breeds camp out in large numbers in the vicinity of Omak. Some of the White men bring them whiskey, and join the Indians in their gambles. Results are bad as the entire camp is a witness to the ensuing disorders.[37]

From the report we glean that the buildup of the Mission is foremost in Father's mind. In number four he speaks of apparent success which

---

[33] *Correspondence* of Rt. Rev. Ledovina to Bishop Schinner, January 7, 19, 24; April 22, 1924, Ms., ADS.

[34] Ledovina to Bishop Schinner, *op. cit.*

[35] "New Buildings Mark Growth of Historic Mission Near Omak," *IECM* (Vol. 11:4, January, 1929). Also: "Statue Erected to Founder of Mission," *The Northwest Progress,* January 8, n.p.

[36] The two last named were Madams who did not receive salaries and could not be counted as employees.

[37] Caldi to Indian Agent Upchurch, August 19, 1922, Ms., copy SM.

really was only apparent. Father de Rougé had to build up his Mission center twice; yet what a difference in attitude. His boys experienced the joy that a well-done job can give because their educator knew how to appeal to them and how to show them that the Mission was their own home. Love had been the guiding force behind Father de Rougé's actions; it had found its response in the minds of his students. Father Caldi's grade school boys experienced only the laboriousness and the toil of the daily work. Father Caldi was not the man to talk things over. He only commanded. Indians are individualists who have their own ideas; one has to know how to approach them in order to secure cooperation. It is a very sad fact that from the many Indians interviewed not one had to say a good word for the hardworking Father Caldi. He had no hold on their hearts; they rather followed the bad example of the whites. Only six years after Father de Rougé's death Father Caldi had to report on the evil of divorce. Many Indians became completely estranged toward the Mission generally; yet, Father Caldi most certainly did not build all the houses for himself.

What child is there who loves a constantly scolding and excited man? The fire was not the only time when a boy wanted to get even with Father Caldi, who used the strap quite frequently on his boys. One of the boys finally was tempted to collect all the straps and anything Father could use for punishment. While Father was saying Mass, he made an investigation of Father's office and then and there found a secret trap door under which the mass wine was hidden. Of course, the temptation was great and the boy was found drunk right there. On another occasion the boys pushed some farm machinery down a hill and gleefully watched Father looking for it.[38]

Any superior visiting the Mission for any length of time, observing Father's management and character, would have realized that here was a sick priest literally working himself to death. High blood pressure and the signs of a mental illness were showing themselves periodically. How did it happen that these factors were only taken note of after twenty years and after Father Caldi had destroyed much that Father de Rougé had built up? The shortage of priests, especially of those who knew the Indian dialects, and the great distance from other Jesuit establishments might be some answers. Father Caldi knew how to conceal his state of health and how to get rid of high ranking visitors. When Bishop White would visit the Mission, Father would give his orders: "Let him feel that the Mission is poor; give him a bed like anybody else has." The Bishop had to sleep in one of the old hard beds of the hospital. But no matter what they gave Bishop White, he never would show the least signs of dissatisfaction.[39]

[38] Anthony Walters, interview.
[39] Sister M. Richildis, O.P., interview.

Under Father de Rougé's management hospitality was a great virtue. The boys had made and handcarved all the furniture of the guest room, called the "Bishop's Room." How different things were now! After a night's visit when the guest would come into Father's office, he would find him very occupied, hardly looking up. Then Father Caldi's farewell wishes sounded about like this, "Well, Bishop, we were glad to have you. You have seen the Mission now; we are very busy and — Good Bye."[40]

The Bishop was not allowed to see the Sisters' building; its condition would have been too much of a shock. Father Caldi was his own school law and school superintendent. When he found any work to be done he would ring a bell and all would run out of classes, teachers included. Usually the hard work, like hauling the logs for firewood six or more miles from the mountains, was for the morning hours. The afternoons when all were tired were good enough for sitting in the classrooms. Old, exhausted and sick Madam Fitzgibbon would fall asleep at her desk many times. The children then would keep respectfully silent; they knew the Mission was no place to be sick. The educational standards of the Mission deteriorated so that children who were transferred had to be put back in the grades in other schools.[41] As the number of Madams decreased, no qualified teachers took their place. We have found no indication that Father Caldi ever hired teachers, although Mother Katherine sent the salary for them. He seems to have used all these contributions to build up the Mission plant. It is easy, of course, to criticize. How many of those who had their children at St. Mary's Mission and expected all kinds of services for their children contributed to the upkeep of the mission?

Miss Wilhelmine Coolbaugh, whom we have mentioned as giving Father de Rougé the means to build the Sacred Heart Chapel for the Madams at the convent, had considerable correspondence with Father Caldi. She kept on sending Mass stipends and had "a Father de Rougé Fund" for orphan children established. This fund was in the form of two thousand dollars in bonds from which she wanted Father to use the interest for his children.[42] Later she kept on adding to the Fund until it was ten thousand dollars.[43]

It was Wilhelmine Coolbaugh who wanted a memorial statue of Father de Rougé erected on the mission grounds.

I am very anxious to have the memorial inscription because every Indian, white person or child looking at the little monument erected

---

[40] Rev. Joseph Balfe, S.J., interview.
[41] Sister M. Richildis, interview. Also: Walters, interview.
[42] Coolbaugh to Caldi, October 26, 1920, Ms., OPA.
[43] *Ibid.*, August 17, 1921, Ms., OPA.

to the sainted memory of good Fr. de Rougé should know why it was put there and who this great missionary was.[44]

A letter written by Miss Coolbaugh seems to indicate that she visited the Mission during August, 1924.[45] The completed statue, which was made by a German artist from a photograph, arrived at the Mission on October 22, 1925; Miss Coolbaugh paid $200 for the statue, with a "balance for [the] children's Christmas."[46] Unfortunately this helper of the Mission met her death by drowning in 1933.[47] Faithful to St. Mary's Mission, she left $10,000 in her last will to the Mission, $990 of which was taken by the State of Illinois in inheritance tax.[48]

Few letters of Mother Katherine to St. Mary's are preserved. The Archives of the Oregon Province, however, treasure the following one:

> Enclosed herewith please find check in the sum of $987.50 for the quarter ended December 31, 1923, covering board and tuition for 22 pupils and salary of teacher and cook.
>
> I was pleased to hear about the Christmas festivities at St. Mary's and particularly glad that so many from afar do attend to their religious duties. This must have been a great consolation to you.
>
> May I ask that you will be good enough to extend to the children the expression of my grateful appreciation of their beautiful Christmas letter and the kind wishes expressed therein. Let them be assured that every day they all receive a remembrance in the prayers of all the Sisters here at the Mother House where we have the inestimable privilege of daily Exposition of the Most Blessed Sacrament. Two Sisters are on adoration all day praying for the Colored and the Indian Missions, begging God to send down upon the people of these missions the graces that will save them.[49]

We have seen how the enrollment of the girls had shrunk. The Indians still traveled long distances to St. Mary's for the celebrations of the great feasts.

Right Reverend Monsignor William Hughes thanked the boys a year later for the Christmas letter of 1924. The contents acquaint us with further improvement made by Father Caldi:

> I would like to have been with you when you were making that fine swimming pool. Better than that, I would like to be there to enjoy it when the warm weather comes.
>
> That was the best kind of an accident when you struck water near the convent. The new well must be a blessing to your school and to the Fathers and the Sisters who take care of all you boys and girls. See how

---

44 *Ibid.*, March 3, 1924, Ms., OPA.
45 Coolbaugh to Caldi, summer of 1924, Ms., SM.
46 *Ibid.*, end of October, 1925, Ms., SM.
47 Most Rev. Thomas A. Welch, *Telegram* to Caldi, November 18, 1933, Ms., SM.
48 L. C. Gilbertson, Personal Trust Officer, The First National Bank of Chicago, to St. Mary's Mission, Omak, Washington, May 2, 1935, Trust No. 17841, Ms., SM.
49 Mother M. Katherine to Caldi, January 10, 1924, Ms., OPA.

God watches over your Mission school when He lets you find this precious gift deep down in the ground.[50]

Father Caldi had added a sacristy to the church and had the hospital repaired.[51] Renovations during 1927 consisted of painting the outside of the church, repairing the church tower, erecting cement foundations under various buildings, laying new floors, and adding to the cold-storage space for apples.[52]

A new boys' dormitory was built about 1930–1931. Father Caldi had made an appeal for help to the President of the American Board of Catholic Missions, Cardinal Mundelein. Father wanted $10,000.[53] We were not able to ascertain the results of the appeal, but we know that as a result of it he was able to erect a large brick dormitory. A few yards from this large dormitory Father Caldi constructed his last building, a brick gymnasium, forty by one hundred twelve feet. This building was built by Ernest Hubbert for $2,095.00 for labor. The bricks came from Wenatchee and their cost was $5,838.55.[54]

After the buildings were completed Father contemplated taking more children. He asked the caretaker of the closed Chemawa Indian School, Oregon, for additional bedsprings.[55] He says he has sixty children at St. Mary's and wants to have eighty. Since the new assembly hall had been erected the children were treated with free shows paid for by the Mission.[56] As letters of the girls to Mother Katherine tell, all was not joyless at the Mission.[57] There were outings and other diversions. The swimming pool also was used quite frequently during the summer months. Now that Father Caldi had his Mission built up, we assume that at least during the winter there was more time spent in the classrooms. Even if the educational standards of the Mission under Father Caldi were lowered, many of the children attending the Mission still received a far better training than they could have had at home.

For the past seventeen years Father Caldi had known no rest until the third set of buildings at the Mission were completed. About 1933, he became aware of serious consequences if not enough helpers could be secured to care for these buildings and for the children. Only three Ladies

[50] Rt. Rev. Monsignor Hughes, Director of the Indian Bureau, to the Boys of St. Mary's Mission, January 26, 1925, Ms., OPA.
[51] Caldi to Bishop Schinner, May 27, 1920, Ms., ADS.
[52] Caldi, *Report of 1927*, Ms., OPA.
[53] Caldi to Most Rev. Charles D. White of Spokane, October 11, 1930, Ms., ADS.
[54] Caldi, *Estimate Cost of Material on Gymnasium*, Ms., OPA.
[55] Caldi to Chemawa Indian School, Oregon, October 13, 1933, Ms. copy, POA.
[56] Caldi to D. C. Millward, Cosmopolitan Film Exchange, Seattle, Wash., October 27, 1933. Ms. copy, OPA.
[57] St. Mary's Girls to Mother Katherine, December 16, 1923, Ms., ABSS.

Catechists Missionaries had entered while he was in charge of the Mission: Madam Euphrasia Jacobs came in 1917, Madam Kemper in 1924, and Madam Mary Carroll in 1927. Buried at St. Mary's were Madams Clark, La Londe, Blake, Luce, and Dumont. Only six Madams were left in 1933; all others had gone. Of the six, two were seriously ill.

We saw that the Ursulines and other Sisters had been asked to come to the Mission before the Madams were put in charge of the girls. On June 19, 1933, Bishop White was considering the Providence Sisters when he wrote to Father Caldi:

> Today I spoke to the Mother General about having their Sisters take over the Mission school, but without success. She told me that you had spoken to her about this a few days ago.[58]

A copy of Father Caldi's letter from November 2 of the same year shows how desperately he is looking for Sisters:

> It is with feeling of diffidence, yet most earnest expectation that I send your Maternity these few lines. You have been so kind and generous to St. Mary's Mission since I have been in charge [beginning in] June, 1916 and for a long time before, during the lifetime of Rev. Father de Rougé, S.J., the founder.
>
> The dear Sisters, Lady Missionaries of St. Mary's have now reduced to six in number. . . . I have good reason to know and to be convinced that His Excellency would be much pleased if your Sisters were to come to our assistance in looking after our children and adopting our Sisters into your Community. My Rev. Father Provincial, Rt. Rev. Father Fitzgerald, S.J., is much pleased with my proposal.
>
> Of course my plan is at your mercy. At present date we have fifty-three girls and 25 boys. A truly beautiful Mission, or plant, no debts, no encumbrance. We have the love of the people who offer us the fruits of their orchards in season's abundance.
>
> Our dear Sisters rejoice at the possibility of becoming your daughters, remaining at their post and being incorporated according to Canon Law.[59]

But with the many missions Mother Katherine had founded and supplied with her Sisters, she could not spare any professed Sisters. Six months later Father Caldi tells Mother Katherine: "We are reduced to five Sisters. . . . The dear Lady Missionaries are in charge of boys as well as of girls. We are praying for vocations of genuine Missionaries and of course, assistance."[60] Later in the year another Madam died. Both Madam Fitzgibbon and Madam Kemper died in 1934, and only four heroic souls were left for all the work of housing, feeding, and teaching the Indian children.

[58] Bishop White to Caldi, June 19, 1933, Ms., SM.
[59] Caldi to Mother Katherine, November 2, 1933, Ms. copy, OPA.
[60] Caldi to Mother Katherine, July 18, 1934, Ms., ABSS.

St. Mary's Mission, Omak, Washington, founded in 1886 by Fr. Etienne de Rougé, S.J., as it looks today.

Fire of 1938.

One of the "church houses" that stood on both sides of Omak Creek.

Dining room of the smaller children.

Mr. Arthur Lund, the "Father" of Tonasket, a great benefactor.

Dr. Paschal Sherman, Washington, D. C., one of the honor students of Father de Rougé, S.J., at early St. Mary's Mission.

The present Bishop of Spokane,
His Excellency Bishop
Bernard J. Topel, Ph.D., D.D.

Bishop Charles D. White, Bishop
of Spokane, and Father Joseph
Balfe, S.J. (1938).

The last elected chief,
Jim James, and his wife,
Lucy. (Courtesy of
Chelan County
Historical Society.)

Camping ground for the July tribal celebrations at Nespelem,
Washington.

(Top left) From left: Thomas Wilson, Nez Perce, and Moses Ned Cleveland and Charlie Williams, grandsons of Chief Kamakin of the Yakimas.

(Top right) "Liege" Williams, Nez Perce tribal leader, wearing historical regalia of his forefathers, in the 1957 Circle Ground Parade on July 4 in Nespelem, Washington.

(Left) Harry Owhi, Yakima and Palouse.

(Bottom left) Bertha Covington — Russel, a college graduate.

(Bottom right) Jessie Jim, daughter of Long Jim. (Courtesy of Chelan County Historical Society.)

(*Top left*) *Eloise Orr-King, Yakima-Menatchee.*

(*Top right*) *Antoine Francis. (Courtesy of Chelan County Historical Society.)*

(*Left*) *Katherine Lot, Nez Perce.*

(*Bottom*) *Salmon Jumping at Kettle Falls, Washington (Photo by Saunders Shoppe.)*

From left: Peter Dan Moses; Senator Toby Morris of Oklahoma, Chairman of the Subcommittee of the Committee on Indian Affairs; Chief Jim James; Congressman Walt Horan from Washington.

Logging operation on the Colville Reservation on the San Poil Region near Keller.

The Grand Coulee Dam. At the right center is the world's largest pumping plant which raises water 280 feet through ten giant flumes into the world's largest irrigation canal, feeding water to the storage reservoir. The water then is conducted to over a million acres of semi-arid land in the Columbia Basin Irrigation Project.

Father Caldi then found out that a little community of Dominican Sisters had just established themselves in their new Provincial House of Our Lady of the Valley Convent which had been from 1873–1921 the Sacred Heart School for Indians and whites in the Colville Valley. These Sisters had answered the repeated call of Bishop Carroll of Helena, Montana, to come and aid his hard-pressed diocesan high school and college and take care of the domestic department. This was not the purpose for which the Community had been founded, but after nearly two years of debates and difficulties the first group of the Poor School Sisters of St. Dominic had crossed the Atlantic, coming from Speyer, Germany. They were in charge of the domestic department at Carroll College and had two hospitals erected, one at Conrad, Montana, and the other at Chewelah, Washington. Mother Mary Bonaventura, O.P., had been very much concerned that the first purpose of the Institute, to teach the girls, be followed as soon as possible. Some of the teachers had come from Germany and had attended college and others were attending colleges to readjust themselves to American conditions. The Sisters experienced very poor beginnings. It was then that the following letter from Father Caldi was received:

Ven. Mother Bonaventura
Meyers Falls, Washington
Rev. Mother:
  You probably have heard of St. Mary's Mission and school. Our average enrollment is about eighty Indian children. The Lady Missionaries of St. Mary's with the aid of the pupils and a faithful workman are doing all the work connected with the Mission except the financing of same. The Lady Missionaries are six in number [four] one of them being rather sick at the present writing.
  I wonder if you could consider helping us out in our need, . . . We need at least two accredited teachers and more other Sisters. I have confidence that you will make a success of the work and make it prosper.
  At present under the patronage of St. Joseph we have all we need except Sisters, neither debts nor obligations of any kind.
  St. Mary's Mission is a little over one hundred and fifty miles from your present home. Kindly consider the matter in your prayers and try and give me a cheering answer.[61]

No answer to this letter of Father Caldi by Mother Bonaventura can be found. These must have been some of her thoughts, however, whatever she might have said in any reply to Father Caldi: How could she take over an institution and write about it to Mother General without having seen the place and knowing all that was expected of

[61] Caldi to Rev. Mother Mary Bonaventura, O.P., September 19, 1934, Ms., ADSK.

her Sisters? Could she afford, when she was deeply in debt with her hospitals and with the Provincial House, to pay the high cost of board and room and of education for her Sisters and then send them to a mission that had not one cent left for the Sisters — she who had not the money for a stamp when her Sisters wanted to write home? For the time being Mother Bonaventura was busy renovating the old acquired house at Kettle Falls.

Father Caldi at St. Mary's Mission became more desperate. During the spring of 1935, he had quite a correspondence with Mother Katherine as his notes show. A letter addressed to Mother Mercedes brings an invitation of Father Caldi to Mother Katherine to visit the Mission. He reveals that he is not without a sense of humor:

> If Very Reverend Mother could persuade herself to come thus far she will find the way very easy and herself recompensed by the grandness of the country and the harvest of souls. . . .
> I will be present at the Mission any day, hour, she may select, I suggest route via San Francisco practically as short and more comfortable than any other. Pullman all the way to Wenatchee, comfortable coach from there to Omak, warm hearts, four and half miles to St. Mary's Mission.[62]

Father Caldi had enclosed the train schedule from San Francisco to Omak. Mother Katherine was then on a visitation of her missions in the South of the United States. On April 12, 1935, Mother Katherine thought she had found better train connections and wrote to Father Caldi.[63] This plan was changed again as a letter from Xavier University, New Orleans, shows:

> I told you that if I changed my plans as outlined to you in my letter of April 12th, I would let you know. I find there is no train leaving Stockton for Portland at the time mentioned. In place of this, we will stay in San Francisco, leaving there 7:40 A.M. and going straight through to Seattle. The train arrives 2:30 P.M. We will hope to meet you there.[64]

Father Caldi met Mother Katherine in Seattle and traveled with her and her companion, Sister M. Agatha, to Wenatchee. There, according to Father's orders, Madame Euphrasia was waiting with the car that brought the guests to St. Mary's Mission. Mother Katherine was impressed by the Latin responses in unison by the whole congregation as she attended Mass the next day. This being Sunday, the Indians had filled the church and wanted to see their great benefactress. The rest

---

[62] Caldi to Rev. Mother Mercedes, Cornwells Heights, Pennsylvania, March 19, 1935, Ms. copy, OPA.
[63] Mother Katherine to Caldi, April 12, 1935, Ms., OPA.
[64] *Ibid.*, April 20, 1935.

of the day was spent in serious discussions with Father Caldi about the future of the Mission. On Monday Mother Katherine surprised the missionary, Father Griva, at Nespelem with a visit. He writes:

On the 13th (May 1935) I had the visit of Mother Katherine Drexel, foundress of the congregation of the Sisters of perpetual adoration. She came with Sister Agatha of this congregation and Father Caldi and Sister Euphrasia of St. Mary's Mission. This Mother had been so good as to give one thousand dollars for the church at Nespelem. . . . After they had seen the church at Nespelem Father Caldi brought Mother and the Sisters to Coulee Dam to make them see the wonderful work that had been done there. And all went back to St. Mary's on the same day.[65]

On the fourteenth of May, Father Caldi brought his visitors to Spokane to see the Jesuit Provincial, Very Reverend W. J. Fitzgerald, and Bishop White. Mother Katherine and her companion stayed overnight at Holy Names Academy as the *Diary* of this institution shows. The outcome of her visit is told in a speech Mother Katherine gave after her return to Cornwells Heights:

We had traveled by rail from Port Arthur, Texas, and by auto along the edge of a precipice from Wenatchee to Omak, Washington, and were now discussing with Rev. Celestine Caldi, Jesuit Indian missionary, the fate of the only remaining Catholic mission school among the Okinagon Indians. "Can we save these Indians by means of instruction given in the country day school, Father?" I asked. "Come and see the nearest day school, Mother," Father Caldi insisted. So we went — over mountain trails and through forests where winter travel would be extremely difficult, if not impossible. That answered my question.

On our Colored missions in the South, from which we had just come, rural and urban elementary and high schools, and our Xavier University, were keeping and giving the faith. Among the Indians, the educational problem is vastly different where villages are widely scattered over large reservations, and home conditions primitive. Moreover, the new Government educational program for Indians has given rise to an emergency which called us from Texas to New Mexico, for a consultation with the Fathers and Sisters engaged in work among the Navajo. A summer schedule of catechetical and social welfare work was mapped out ere we took our departure for the Pacific Coast, thence straight north to Seattle, bound for Omak. Here we hoped to dispense with St. Mary's Mission boarding school, could we devise means of carrying on the work by follow-up and instruction given to the children attending county schools. This would effect an economy in favor of the constantly increasing expenses of our own thirty-four foundations with sixty-five schools, and this new emergency on our Indian missions.

It was with real sorrow that we contemplated the change after we had seen the permanent fruit of the work of Father Caldi and the

[65] Griva, *History*, 326.

Sisters are doing to preserve in the Okinagon the Faith brought to them
by the early missionaries, many of whom I knew personally or by correspondence, especially Father de Rougé, founder of the mission, who
taught the Indian boys to build their own mission home, and Father
Cataldo, one time Superior of the Indian missions of the Rocky Mountains. I remember well a visit from the latter to our home at St. Michael's,
Torresdale. His birthplace was near Sorrento, Italy. My two sisters and
I had just been to Sorrento, likewise to the Indian missions in Washington, in behalf of which Father Cataldo had now come to the East
to seek our help. As I listened to his earnest pleading, and recalled the
beauty of Sorrento, recalled the barren desert of the Indian country,
I thought, "My God, is it possible that he left this beautiful homeland
to come and live in a desert?"

We left Omak without having come to a decision, but went on to
see His Excellency, the Most Reverend Bishop of Seattle [Spokane]. En
route, Father Caldi brought us to St. Michael's Scholasticate, Hillyard,
where we wished to see the Jesuit Provincial on the errand. . . . Pres-
ently, I found myself beside the graves of those heroic Indian missionaries
whom I had known. Father Cataldo was there — "Thrice-Broken," the
Indians named him after he had sustained serious injuries three times on
his missionary journeys. . . . His plea in behalf of his beloved Indians
re-echoed in my memory as I stood beside his grave. . . . We departed
for the Episcopal residence, where before long I had the privilege of
asking, "What is going to become of these Indians, Your Excellency?"
"I do not know," was his grave and troubled reply; "I can not get help
for them." Then and now, the thought forces itself upon me: "If only
our good Catholic people knew, they would not allow the work of these
heroic missionaries to be lost to the Church." St. Mary's is our "Last
Stand" among the Okinagon. Must it be sacrificed?[66]

After reaching her Mother House, Mother Katherine assembled the
Council General to consider the problems of St. Mary's. The Council
Mothers regretted very much that they were unable to take over the
mission on account of the shortage of Sisters. However, the members
of the Council were in sympathy with the four remaining Madams at
St. Mary's:

The only thing we can do and this we are willing to do if it is in
accord with the wishes of your Excellency and agreeable to the Jesuit
Fathers, would be to take these four Sisters into our Congregation as we
would take any other applicants, have them make their postulantship
and novitiate with us according to our Constitutions and at the end of
the period of probation if they have been satisfactory, to admit them to
Profession of Temporary vows. At the end of five years of Temporary
vows if still satisfactory they would like the other Sisters make their
final vows.

---

[66] Mother M. Katherine Drexel, "If Only Our Good Catholic People Knew,"
The News Bulletin of Mission Fields At Home (1:5, July–August, 1915). Courtesy
of the Blessed Sacrament Sisters, Cornwells Height, Pa.

The receiving of the Sisters into our Congregation would be caring for them, but it would not be taking care of the Mission which I feel is a matter of deep concern to Your Excellency.

While at St. Mary's visitation of the mission Your Excellency did mention some other Order in the Diocese that would be willing to take over the work and these Sisters and thus preserve and continue the excellent work that has been done there all these years. . . .[67]

How Bishop White could speak of this "other Order" taking over the Mission is not clear. He had not spoken yet with Mother M. Bonaventura, the Provincial of the Poor School Sisters of St. Dominic; he knew, however, that the Dominican Sisters were preparing to take over their first school in the country. A letter of Reverend W. J. Fitzgerald, S.J., to Mother Katherine showed that Bishop White wanted the Provincial of the Jesuit Fathers to come to Spokane, for important discussions.[68] Meanwhile Mother Bonaventura had written to her Mother House in Speyer, Germany, to inform Mother General Aquinata, O.P., about Father Caldi's request.

When nobody else wanted to take over the hard work at the Mission and this place was in danger of being closed, Bishop White called on good-hearted Mother Bonaventura, O.P., and asked her to help him out of trouble. She herself had not even seen the mission but she promised to do what she could. No answer yet had come back from Germany. Permission was later granted, but the Community never obliged itself formally to have its Sisters always there. No formal or legal obligation with the Jesuit Fathers or with the Bishop of Spokane was ever signed by the Community. Also the Community cannot be expected to increase its Sisters simultaneously when the Mission authorities decide to increase the enrollment of the Mission School. The statement in the *1940 Financial Report* that, "Bishop White himself engaged the Sisters now laboring at St. Mary's Mission, determining what they were to receive, etc,"[69] is very ambiguous. What the Sisters did and still do is charity freely given. Bishop White saw a solution of his problem in Mother Bonaventura's mission enthusiasm and informed Father Caldi about the meeting:

Today I was talking over the matter with Mother M. Bonaventura O.P. of Our Lady of the Valley Convent, Meyers Falls. She had written to Mother House for authorization of the Mother General, but owing to the distracted state of things in Germany a reply to her petition had not yet been received. However she was confident that the authorization will be easily obtained and that at least a year from now her Dominican

[67] Mother Katherine to Bishop White, June 13, 1935, Ms., ADS.
[68] Rev. W. J. Fitzgerald, S.J., to Mother Katherine, July 6, 1935, Ms., ABSS.
[69] 1940 *Financial Report of St. Mary's Mission,* Ms., OPA.

Sisters can take over the work. I feel that this will be the real solution of the problem which is causing me some anxiety as well as your devoted self. I advised Mother Bonaventura to visit the Mission in the near future and to obtain a better idea of the place and of the work. She is indeed interested, and I pray our Lord that if it be His will, we shall see these Sisters at the Mission, and that at the same time an arrangement be made that the present remaining Madams will be properly cared for, most likely as co-laborers with the Sisters.[70]

On the same day of the meeting Bishop addressed a letter to Mother Bonaventura in which he speaks about the future of the Madams, and he hopes arrangements can be made to satisfy the free will of the Madams.[71]

In answering Mother Katherine's letter of June 13, Bishop White informed her about the conference with Mother Bonaventura and about his hope "since it is impossible for your Sisters to come among us in this time of emergency" of working "out a plan with the community in question."[72] Mother Katherine answered that her "heart rejoiced," when she heard from his Excellency the news that the "Good Mother Superior in Spokane" gave him hope that she would be able to take over the Mission.[73]

Father Caldi under date of August 7, 1935, told Bishop White: "We shall be pleased to welcome Rev. Mother M. Bonaventura, O.P., and trust that everything here will meet her kind approval and interest."[74] While Mother Bonaventura inspected the place Father kept the Madams away, being afraid they would talk too much about the real situation of the Mission which he wanted to conceal. Mother even perceived a glimpse of his regimentation and the angry voice when handling the hardworking Madams. Was nobody aware of the precarious state of Father's health? Madam Carroll, now Sister Mary Ann, O.P., has stated that Father Caldi was the kindest man as long as his health permitted him to react normally to situations, but that he was "two people," easily irritated and aroused. Perhaps Mother Bonaventura thought that when her Sisters would come, they would have their own superior and would not depend on Father Caldi. In the meantime a group of enthusiastic mission-minded Sisters were preparing to cross the ocean coming from Germany. They arrived at the end of 1935 to increase the numbers of the small community.

70 Bishop White to Caldi, July 25, 1935, Ms., copy, ADS.

71 Bishop White to Mother Bonaventura, O.P., July 25, 1935, Ms., ADSK.

72 Bishop White to Mother Katherine, July 26, 1935, Ms., ABSS.

73 Mother Katherine to Caldi, August 9, 1935, Ms. copy, ABSS.

74 Caldi to Bishop White, August 7, 1935, Ms., ADS.

Father Caldi kept good Mother Katherine in suspense concerning the future of the Mission and of the Madams. He wrote:

> The reef on which our four Sisters are clinging is a problem and a study. The four have been at St. Mary's the last twenty years[75] and love the place; they love to go to you however. They are very grateful for your Maternity's offer.
>
> If they went now, in a few days or weeks the little Indians would swarm in, in desolation indeed. . . . No one has come to replace the four Sisters. They would rather wait one year. Of their own choosing they suggest that I write to your Maternity.[76]

Father Caldi did not know what he should do about receiving the pupils for the new term, nor if Mother Katherine would support the school.[77] The benefactress answered that she did not know what she could do in the matter of supporting the school until Father finds out from his provincial what he wants to do. She had learned from Bishop White that he thinks there is some religious order that might take over the mission. Then she added:

> I think when I saw your former Provincial with you at Spokane that I understood him to say that the Provincial would have to be consulted as to any Sisterhood that the Bishop would suggest. . . .[78]

Father's letter on September 16 clearly indicates the progress of his mental sickness. He asked Mother Katherine to send Sister Agatha and enough Sisters to aid the workers at the Mission. Then he speaks about the change; that the Dominican Sisters are willing to come. "Take the school, work at the Mission, give us Noviciate and Vows. [Take us] into their Order and made one Community with us." He writes as if the Madams themselves were writing and signs his name to it. The Madams were free to choose any kind of life they wanted. They were given the opportunity to see the Provincial House and there personally applied for admittance into the Institute of the Poor School Sisters. Father makes it sound as if they were forced to enter:

> Wonderful as this proposition is, a much better offering than we would have ever aspired at in the past, the fact remains that we Sisters do our distant cry. Very Reverend Mother Katherine bear in mind that this had been our Mission since the days of dear Fr. de Rougé (these last twenty-five years), and that His Excellency, Rt. Rev. Chas. D. White, D.D. asked you most earnestly to come and aid we Indians [sic] in his diocese. . . .[79]

---

[75] Only Sister Michael had been there twenty years.
[76] Caldi to Mother Katherine, August 19, 1935, Ms., ABSS.
[77] Ibid.
[78] Mother Katherine to Caldi, August 28, 1935, Ms. copy, ABSS.
[79] Caldi to Mother Katherine, September 16, 1935, Ms., ABSS.

Mother Katherine again was visiting her missions in the South when Father Caldi's letter was forwarded to her. Since Father Caldi had not written about the four Sisters, Mother Katherine thought they did not want to come. However, she interpreted the letter presumably written by the Sisters and signed by Father as expressing the wish to come. Mother Katherine urged Father Caldi to let her know definitely if the Sisters wanted to come.

She then stated again that taking over the Mission by her Sisters would be wholly out of the question. The third point tells about the reducing of the allowance:

> For the continued financial assistance towards the Mission I explained to you, dear Father, when I visited St. Mary's last year, the uncertainty and in fact the impossibility of our giving what we had been able to do in previous years. We are compeled to curtail and reduce the allowance in almost every place where we have been helping.[80]

However, Mother Katherine promised to pay for this scholastic year according to the enrollment of the girls not exceeding forty girls. She felt sorry that she had to make these statements which had become obligatory. Then she added:

> I feel that I must make this clearly understood now, dear Father, so that the hopes of the good Sisters who may assume the work of St. Mary's, may not be raised so as to count on what we have been able to do in the past, as a guarantee that they can look forward to it for the future.[81]

Suffice it to say that the Dominican Sisters were left in the dark about any arrangement whatever concerning Mother Katherine's contributions.

Was Father Caldi afraid to tell Mother Katherine clearly that the Madams did not want to enter a convent in the East? Finally in November he wrote more definitely. "As you realize our request for your coming to take charge was most sincere & most pressing. The four Sisters have decided to remain at St. Mary's Mission. . . ."[82] Then the long letter enumerates all the work to be done at the Mission. Thanks are expressed to the Mothers of the Council and especially to Mother Katherine for all her generous help. She is reminded that "This was your own Mission from the start as well as his," meaning Father de Rougé.[83]

It would have been impossible for Father de Rougé and for Father Caldi to build the various houses of the Mission in the course of the

---

[80] Mother Katherine to Caldi, October 16, 1935, Ms., OPA.
[81] Ibid.
[82] Caldi to Mother Katherine, November 19, 1935, Ms., ABSS.
[83] Ibid.

years without Mother Katherine's generous help. The financial contributions of Father de Rougé and his relations are considerably exaggerated. He had built the first small house and house chapel after his return from France in 1889 with money he had collected there and alms from his relatives. From then on he needed the help of others; he was very honest about his poverty and his needs. The Indians paid for the first school house. Mother Katherine had supported the mission with small donations in the early 1900's and then from 1905 on regularly every quarter. It is touching to read about the amounts of money that arrived at the Mission. We give some examples of checks received at different times during the years:

July 15,	1916	$1125.00
January 16,	1916	$1375.00
July 17,	1918	$1100.00
January 9,	1920	$1225.00
April 7,	1929	$1112.50
October 14,	1929	$1437.50
April 4,	1936	$1362.50[84]

Mother Katherine had to stop her contributions at the end of the school year of 1936. She was then 77 years of age and felt rightly that she had to provide first for all the missions she herself had founded as the interest from her inheritance was only hers as long as she lived. Altogether she had spent on St. Mary's Mission for the Colville Confederated Tribes a total of $137,631.00.[85] This sum would have today more than ten times the value it had then. We can say that St. Mary's Mission received for the Indians from Mother Katherine more than one and a half million dollars in today's money value.

It must have been like a ray from heaven when the struggling Madams received this letter from Mother Bonaventura:

Very dear Sisters,

I guess you are very glad that the school year is soon over. We understand it; for indeed, we often remembered you, dear Sisters, and your hard work. But, as we have promised, we shall soon come to relieve you.

You paid us a visit last year for the purpose to communicate to us your intention to join our Community, to become our dear Sisters in St. Dominic, and dear children of the Blessed Mother whose devoted Son St. Dominic was.[86]

[84] *File on St. Mary's Mission*, Ms., OPA.

[85] *Records of St. Elizabeth's Convent*, Cornwells Heights, Mss., ABSS. Kindness of Mother General M. Anselm.

[86] Mother Bonaventura, O.P., to the Madams of St. Mary's Mission, June 30, 1936, Ms., ADSK.

The Madams then were asked for their written requests to become members of this Community.

Bishop White was waiting anxiously for more workers at St. Mary's Mission. On June 30, 1936, he wrote to Mother Bonaventura telling her that he is asking permission from Rome to accept the Madams as they were over forty years of age. Then he continued:

> I understand that on tomorrow, the feast of the Most Precious Blood, you will begin your missionary work at St. Mary's Mission, Omak. Accordingly I shall offer the Holy Sacrifice tomorrow for God's Blessing on this very meritorious work, and His special blessing on your community that all its members may grow daily in the love of Our Lord and be enlightened and strengthened to do His holy will in all things. I shall indeed include in my intentions the devoted women who now petition to be received into your congregation and who for so many years have labored with so much zeal for our little Indian children; nor shall I forget those of their little band who have already been called by Our Lord to receive their eternal reward.[87]

Europeans generally have a high regard for mission work, for teaching and nourishing the Faith, for planting Christian culture in pagan lands. On July 1, 1936, four enthusiastic German Sisters arrived at St. Mary's Mission. They were Sisters M. Eugenia, M. Richildis, M. Donatilla, and M. Reginalda, O.P. These Sisters were to prepare the place for the opening of the next school year. Everything they found in the old convent was in a most primitive condition. Poor Mother Bonaventura, who had no cent to spare, had first to buy dishes for her Sisters, otherwise they would have lost their appetite with what they found. There was no place to hang clothes; the Sisters pounded nails into the wall of the old rooms, something that Father Caldi quickly forbade. The Sisters scrubbed and cleaned for months to remove the dirt that had accumulated in years. In their first missionary enthusiasm they rose at three o'clock in the morning to work in the fields until Father Caldi laughed at them. It did not take long until serious encounters with the mentally sick priest were registered. For the time being he was glad that relief had come. "We were fortunate enough to receive four Sisters from the old Colville Mission. They seem very fervent in their work for the Indians," he wrote to Mother Katherine.[88]

The four Madams were still at the Mission to help the Sisters to get acquainted with the work to be done. Sister Richildis recalls how she followed Madam Foster wherever she went:

---

[87] Bishop White to Mother Bonaventura, June 30, 1936, Ms., ADSK.

[88] Caldi to Mother Katherine, July 20, 1936, Ms., ABSS.

Madam Foster, now Sister M. Michael, was fearless of snakes. She gave me a ride through a potato field. Accidentally I must have stepped on the tail of a blue racer and the snake jumped up and bit in my gimp. Coldly Madam Foster hit the snake and told me, "Come on, forget about it." I was stiff for fear because it was my first encounter with a snake.[89]

Madam Foster had to report to Father in his office after coming back from the potato field. Sister Richildis followed. Madam stood as straight and rigid as a soldier before his inspecting commander. "Where have you been?" "In the potato field." "Is the work done?" "Yes." Then Madam made a stiff right turn and out she marched.[90] There was no room for womanliness under Father Caldi.

About 1915, the Mission storekeeper had moved to East Omak, where he owned a house and two or three lots. As he grew older and sickly he gave the house and the land to the Mission and moved up into the Mission hospital, where he died. Gradually a settlement grew around the Biles and Coleman Lumber Mill; also the apple pickers would camp there during the picking season. Sister Mary Ann, O.P., remembers that she was instrumental in having this house converted into St. Joseph's Church of East Omak. She had in 1931 suggested to Father Caldi that the house be used for Mass during the apple harvesting season.[91] Sister Richildis remembers her first religious vacation school that was taught in this house at East Omak. The altar stone and what was needed for Mass had to be brought along. The altar was the store counter. The truck driver, Madam Foster, would travel every day through the Indian settlements and bring the children to the former store.[92] Later Father Joseph Balfe, S.J., had the house converted into a church, and Father Edward Griva, S.J., contributed to the interior improvements and asked Bishop Schinner to bless the new St. Joseph's Church at East Omak on April 18, 1941.[93] This church has been enlarged in recent years.

The second group of Dominican Sisters arrived at St. Mary's at the end of August, 1936. Now the four Madams were finally excused to follow their desires. Madam Euphrasia went home to her native Alaska; the other three entered a short postulancy at Our Lady of the Valley Convent, Kettle Falls, Washington, before they were received as Sisters into the Community. The school at St. Mary's started the first week of September. Mother Seraphica, O.P., the Provincial Assistant herself, was the superior and taught second, third, and fourth grades. Sister Francis

[89] Sister M. Richildis, O.P., interview.
[90] *Ibid.*
[91] Sister Mary Ann., OP., interviews.
[92] Sister M. Richildis, interview.
[93] Griva, *History*, 353, 361.

de Sales taught the fifth to the eighth grades inclusive. Sisters Aristella instructed the first graders, while Sister Richildis had charge of the music. Sister Donatilla worked in the sewing room; Sister Reginalda was the first cook, and Sister Marina was in charge of the laundry.

These Sisters had their own superior and were not the subjects of Father Caldi. When Mother Seraphica went to Father's office to introduce herself, as the superior of the Sisters, lightning seemed to gleam in the eyes of the priest. He emphatically remarked, "I am the Superior." She was considered an enemy from the beginning, as taking away his authority. Once Father saw Sister Superior carrying an open umbrella. Perhaps he had never seen one in this rough pioneer country. He screamed at her, "What kind of a precious nun are you?"[94] The Sisters were afraid of him and avoided him whenever possible. His mental health gave way more and more until on September 15, 1936, he was replaced by Father Dumbeck, S.J. Briefly he dropped in again at the beginning of October to take care of the Indians, as he spoke their language. After that he had to be taken to Townsend, Washington, by Father Dumbeck, and later admitted at Eastern State Mental Hospital, where he died on February 3, 1938.[95]

It is a tragic story that this hardworking priest had to stay at his post until his health gave way completely. He had been sick during November, 1928. It was first believed to have been a stroke; perhaps it was, considering his high blood pressure. Father himself attributed it to poisoning by carbon monoxide gas in the car.[96] Let us not minimize Father Caldi's merits. Had he not built all the present buildings of St. Mary's except the church, there might not be a St. Mary's Mission today. Father de Rougé did not own land when he died; it was Father Caldi who finally increased the holdings to 1280 acres.[97] Not only Father de Rougé but Father Caldi also made the supreme sacrifice for the Indians.

Since Father Caldi's time, seven more Jesuit priests have ruled the destinies of St. Mary's. During the last decades a few assistant priests also have worked hard at the Mission. Father Dumbeck, Father Caldi's successor, had remarked:

> One of the things that must be done this Fall is a new roof on the Sisters' building. The present shingles are so cracked and curled out of shape that they cannot shed water. I hate to think of putting that much in

---

[94] Sister Richildis, interview.

[95] *Vitae Functi*, Provincae Oregoniensis, June 1, 1954.

[96] *The Caldi Papers*, Mss., OPA.

[97] See *Map on Mission Lands*. Also: correspondence from NA Mss.

the old building. They need decent new Quarters. Well, Deus Providebit.[98]

God provided but not in the way the Sisters would have liked it. They had just put the last jars of canned apricots in the cellars and felt a certain relief after weeks of hard work. Fresh cinnamon rolls and bread were baking. It was the Feast of St. Ignatius, the thirty-first of July, 1938. The Superior, Father Joseph Balfe, was on his way to Omak when he heard the sirens scream and was told that his Mission was on fire. The heat from the canning together with the heat of the season had started a fire in the old chimney which had known more than one blaze. Father John Balfe, S.J., the brother of the superior being on vacation at the Mission, saved the Blessed Sacrament. We let Father Joseph Balfe tell the story:

About half past nine Saturday morning, dense smoke poured out through the roof of the kitchen. As fast as we could, we got a ladder, a hoe and an axe, and the hired man climbed to the roof. He could do very little because by that time, the flames had broken through the shingles in two or three places, and it was far too hot to get close enough to cut through so that we might douse water into the space between the roof and the ceiling. The water pressure was low, very low (it had been an unusual year, no rain since April) so there was not much help from there.

The kitchen was located near the center of the service building which includes, besides the kitchen, all the dining rooms, the Sisters' quarters, laundry, cellar, two classrooms and the chapel. The wind was not very strong, but in spite of that the fire rapidly spread both north and south along the line of the building and within thirty minutes the entire Service Building was either ablaze or melting down in a terrific heat. In fact, within a hour's time the building had taken the outline of a ruin, and that is what it is today. . . .

The fire department from Omak, seven miles away sent up a truck and some men, and later on, a truckload of C.C.C. boys came. With this help we did something to prevent the fire spreading to nearby outhouses. Twice the little shed which houses our light plant caught fire from the intense heat and the showers of sparks and flying embers, but we fought the blaze down, so the plant is safe and is working all right. A long line of woodsheds with a good deal of wood burnt up, as did some farm machinery which we parked in a shed not far from the laundry.

Now the chapel was the last building to go on the south end of the doomed line. We saved the vestments, except our Benediction cope, the organ (Two Old Indians climbed to the choir loft for that), a few other things and of course, the Blessed Sacrament, but aside from those articles, the chapel sank into ashes.

Here is what caused comment from people who later viewed the ruins. The girls' dormitory was built jam up against the chapel — that

[98] Rev. I. J. Dumbeck, S.J., to Bishop White, October 5, 1936, Ms., ADS.

is, about five feet of one side wall of the dormitory touched the chapel. Blazing brands and embers fell constantly on the tin roof and stuccoed sides of the dormitory, but in spite of the fact that we had to watch a somewhat dangerous porch at the rear of the dormitory, that building never caught fire, and it is there today, sound and cool and unmarked, practically as if there had been no fire. So we have that building, thank the Lord, and also the Administration Building, where my office is located, another fireproof building nearby which houses two classrooms, the boys' dormitory and the Gymnasium.

The loss is considerable, especially the loss of the contents of the burnt building. All kitchen equipment was destroyed, as was that of the laundry, dining rooms, Sisters' quarters, (the Sisters saved only what they wore), the girls' class room equipment, and what was in the chapel, excepting what I have mentioned as salvaged. The Sisters had canned a good deal of apricots from our own orchards, but the fruit and jars melted down.

Today the water reservoir is still burning. Fire got into the sawdust insulation between the tank and the outer protecting wall, and the smouldering heat burst the bricks out in so many places that the whole thing will have to be rebuilt.

The Sisters are getting reorganized down in the gymnasium, as well as they can, and although we cannot be sure just what is best to do yet, most likely if quarters are re-established for them it will be there in the gymnasium.[99]

The Sisters mention there had been no immediate answer from the Omak fire department. The Mission that time was considered to be outside the city limits. Water had to be carried in buckets from the swimming pool. Many things happened in the excitement when even a man "lost his head." The farm hand took the big mirror from the sewing room and threw it out of the window. The shoes saved were either all the right ones or the left ones. One Sister threw the statue of St. Joseph into the swimming pool saying, "Here, St. Joseph, swim." He swam all right and lost his color. The Sister worried about Sister Rose Francis, the former Madam Riedmiller. Nobody had seen her. She returned hours later. She had a heart condition, and when the fire started she took her little suitcase, went to an Indian farmer who lived near the mission to stay till the fire was over, thus avoiding too much excitement. Father Balfe estimated the value of the loss about $50,000. The house was only partially insured. This was now the second of Father de Rougé's buildings, his girls' school and convent, that was leveled by the flames.

Good friends from Omak brought blankets and food, but the Sisters had no pots and no dishes. Sisters Reginalda and Michael took the

[99] Rev. Joseph Balfe, S.J., "Fire Discovered in Kitchen of St. Mary's Mission," *The Calumet* (Autumn Number, October, 1938), n.p.

pickup and went on a begging tour; they returned with pots, dishes, furnishings, etc. The Sisters were fortunate that a stove had been placed on one side of the gymnasium. This building was hurriedly converted into an all purpose building: convent, chapel, kitchen, dining rooms, sewing room, classroom, laundry, and storage space. School started again in October, 1938, and the mission work went on. Nobody ever seemed to have thought of the loss the poor Sisters endured, who had lost all their personal possessions. They had brought the required items from home when they entered the convent, even their bed linens. Mother Bonaventura was too poor to replace all this. Very valuable musical instruments such as violins and flutes were lost and never replaced.

Our Sisters tell how they went to catechize at Camp Six and at Disautel, places about eleven miles from St. Mary's. Prior to 1917, some Indians living near Disautel had a small sawmill for cutting lumber to build their homes. About 1917 they sold the mill to Roy Meader and other fruit growers who manufactured apple boxes. These in turn sold out in 1920 to Harry L. Bennett of Seattle. In 1928, Biles and Coleman acquired the mill after theirs in Omak had been destroyed by fire. The firm operated Camp Six about two miles west of Disautel and later moved their logging headquarters to Disautel. The name was misspelled when the government established a post office; the place had been named after the Desautel family. In 1929–1930 this place had a population of about two hundred and seventy-five people. A little Catholic church was built under the direction of Father J. Balfe in 1938. The means for building had been donated by a lady through the Marquette League.[100] Disautel and East Omak were connected by a logging railroad, the tracks of which crossed part of the Mission property. Once Sister Francis de Sales wanted to get Christmas trees and took some boys along. The boys saw the logging train coming, jumped on the train, and waved good-bye to Sister and arrived at the depot of Disautel. The railroad was discontinued in 1948 when the floodwaters of Omak Creek had destroyed nearly all the bridges. In 1957, the logging camp at Disautel was closed.[101] During the years of operation of the camps the Fathers and the Sisters would go twice every month to Disautel until gradually the place became deserted. The unused little church still stands there.

The Indians were very happy when in 1939, Father Griva was named assistant to Father J. Balfe. Father Griva knew the Indian languages, and visited the old Indian people again as Father de Rougé had done.

---

[100] Griva, *History*, 354.

[101] Emmit R. Aston, Logging Manager, Biles-Coleman Lumber Company, to the author, June 10, 1960, Ms.

A new religious fervor was experienced at St. Mary's Mission. The good Indian people today still regret very much that Father Griva had not been made the successor of Father de Rougé.

Now the mission had the two accredited teachers Father Caldi had asked for but the Sisters did not find an accredited school. They were still considered to a great extent farm workers instead of teachers. It was only under Father Paul Corkery that the Mission School was accredited.[102] The work of the Dominican Sisters at St. Mary's was hard and discouraging at times. Only God knows how much the Sisters' strength and endurance were taxed during the hard beginning, especially as they did not know Indian psychology. To send Sisters to St. Mary's Mission was indeed a very heroic act of Mother Bonaventura. It is no overstatement to say that the charity done at St. Mary's Mission by this small Community, to the children and to the many Fathers who during the course of the decades came to make their retreats at St. Mary's, also to the Mission Fathers who used the Sisters' hospital facilities in Tonasket, exceeds the golden mean. In a time when their hospitals and the Provincial House were deep in debt and when they had an insufficient number to staff their own houses, more than fifteen percent of the Sisters were working for mere subsistence, while the Order had to hire helpers and pay the high salaries. Even this subsistence was very poor during the beginnings. The Sisters remember how Mother Bonaventura sent food to aid her Sisters in maintaining their strength for the hard work.

After the fire, fellow Sisters had opened their trunks to help the Mission Sisters, but in a few years these articles were worn out, too. Dated January 31, 1942, we find a letter written by Father Fletcher to Mother Bonaventura:

> Sister Superior informed me you were kind enough to advance money for clothing etc., etc.
>
> Kindly let me know the various expenses, as Sister Superior is somewhat bashful about money matters.[103]

The Archives of Our Lady of the Valley Convent treasure a single "thank you letter" written during Father Leo J. Robinson's term of office as Provincial. The Sisters then had been eight years at St. Mary's:

> Recently we had the pleasure of paying an official visit to the Indian Mission at Omak, Washington. While there, it was abundantly clear how truly important your Sisters are to that Mission. There generosity, self-

---

[102] Chronicle of St. Mary's Mission, September 3, 1948, Ms., SM.
[103] Rev. A. Fletcher, S.J., to Mother Bonaventura, January 31, 1942, Ms., ADSK.

sacrifice and resourcefulness contribute enormously to the success of the good work being done at Omak.[104]

Father Caldi had expected the Dominican Sisters to take care of the boys as the Madams had done. It is a sheer impossibility to do a good job in the classroom and in addition supervise the boys all day long outside of class hours and even during the nights in the dormitory. Some of the Indian boys are advanced in years and cannot be properly called grade-school boys. Mother Arsenia finally had this arrangement changed as the following letter shows:

> For eleven years our dear Sisters have devoted all their energy to the worthy cause of the education and salvation of the Indian children. Most of our Sisters who entered so enthusiastically upon their mission are still at St. Mary's. Very few changes have been made. The Sisters are getting older and their strength is decreasing. It is especially difficult for the Sisters in charge of the boys, to do justice to their religious duties, and to enrich their teaching with the necessary preparation because the adequate supervision of the boys outside of school hours as well as in the dormitory demands every moment of time.
> Last year I told His Excellency, the Most Reverend Charles D. White, Bishop of Spokane, that the work on the Mission is too hard, and he suggested that the supervision of the boys outside school hours be given to men. I have informed Reverend Father Gleeson of this. Nothing was done.
> May I renew my petition this year, dear Reverend Father Provincial, and ask that the burden of supervision of the boys be taken from the Sisters. The Sisters would be greatly relieved and could perform the remaining duties more satisfactorily and adequately.[105]

Father Robinson saw to it that the Sisters were relieved of the boys' dorm.

Another great strain was lifted from the teaching Sisters when Sister Consuelo complained to Father Corkery that the Sisters had absolutely no community life. Then it was decided that the Fathers should supervise the evening study halls. Father Corkery himself did not stay in his office, but helped wherever need of supervision showed itself, be it in one of the dining rooms or during study hall.

As Washington State requires five years of college work for the Standard Certificate and our small Community does not own higher educational institutions, the education of the Sisters teaching at St. Mary's represents a financial burden. The present high cost of education and

[104] Rev. Leo J. Robinson, S.J., to Mother M. Arsenia, O.P., October 6, 1944, Ms., ADSK.
[105] Mother M. Arsenia, O.P., to Vy. Rev. L. Robinson, S.J., July 14, 1947, Ms. copy, ADSK.

of living during the five years of study amount to $10,000 to $12,000. Nobody ever has offered a scholarship or a reduction in education costs to the Sisters working at the Mission to enable them to continue their heroic work. However, Father Balfe, S.J., during recent years showed himself very generous in providing a monthly allowance to the Sisters. The number of Sisters has decreased considerably during the last two years. The Mission could not continue its work without the lay helpers who give a year of their life for mission work. This becomes a yearly problem for the Mission.

Fire has been one of the greatest scourges in St. Mary's history. Father Caldi's brick gymnasium had been, after the fire in 1938, converted into a service building. A new gym was needed. Father Paul Corkery with the financial assistance of Mr. Morier from Yakima erected a quonset structure. It had served only a few years when on August 29, 1955, it was leveled by fire. It was about eleven o'clock in the evening when Father John O'Brien's faithful dog kept scratching on Father's door. Father O'Brien looking for the cause saw the old hospital building ablaze. It had been closed as a hospital since 1926, but was now converted into a dormitory for the older girls. It took quite some shaking to awake the sleeping children of the mission farm foreman, whose family lived in the adjoining house. From there the fire jumped over to the new gymnasium where all the children's gym suits, sports equipment, a new piano, and other furnishings were destroyed with the new building. The fire was attributed to a short circuit in electric lines between the gymnasium and the old hospital. The Sisters were afraid that the church might catch fire when they saw the burning embers and the direction of the wind. All valuables from the sacristy were carried into the parlors. It was fortunate that the school had not started yet and the nearby classroom building was unharmed.

A winter which was more severe than any since followed. High snows came down at the end of September and stayed until May. For six months all was white. Who can describe the restlessness of Indian children in a classroom if they have no place "to let off steam"? The teachers had to have them either in the classrooms or in the dorms after school hours. Again Father Corkery went to work and planned a much bigger building that would serve other purposes as well. Completed in 1956, its size was one hundred sixty by sixty feet with a big stage, lounge, and sleeping quarters for twenty older girls on one end of the building, and boys' playrooms, shower rooms, office and guest rooms on the other end. The center was the gymnasium with ample room to practice basketball with six baskets. The building had not been in use for two years when on January 4, 1958, it, too, became a sacrifice to the flames. The loss was estimated to be nearly $100,000 including all the equipment. Mr. and Mrs. John Gallagher of Dash-point, Washington, had shortly before presented to the Mission all new mattresses for the older girls' dormitory. Mr. Morier had spent between $150,000 and $200,000 on the mission and again there was no gymnasium left.[106] A third one was built by Father Corkery on the foundation of the first and the one that had burned in 1955. It is the one now in use. It is understandable that such big losses so close together nearly undermined the Mission's economy.

Just then the Lord sent some more good benefactors in the persons of Mr. Ed. Figlensky and his wife and their friends. A new cooling and freezing unit was added to the kitchen and Mr. Figlensky helps to fill it. Without him many a piece of meat would not be on the children's menu.

Considering all the sacrifices brought by Father de Rougé and other Jesuit priests, by the Madams, the Christian Brothers, the Dominican Sisters, who have offered their health and their lives filled with hard work, plus the generosity of all the many benefactors throughout the Mission's long history, their great sacrifices so urgently needed in order to keep the doors open for the children — do the accomplishments of the Mission and appreciation and cooperation of the Indians themselves warrant such a big price? This is a question many people have asked. Let us try to answer some aspects of it.

Mr. Chris C. Smith of Bridgeport, Washington, who attended St. Mary's from 1913–1916 as a white day student, answered the following questions:

How do you think did the education the Mission offered help to raise the living standards of the different tribes involved?

It helped to prepare the young people to find their place in the white man's society. Unscrupulous whites, some merchants, would not let an Indian alone until they got almost all of their Treaty Money.

Do you think the religious training the children received at the Mission contributed to a good Catholic family life?

It had quite an influence on some of them, especially grace before meals and blessing after.

Do you think that those who were educated here at the Mission continue after leaving the Mission to practice their faith?

Most of them did altho some of them became quite lax, but I don't think many ever gave up their Faith entirely and in talking to them I

[106] Rev. J. Balfe, interview.

have never heard one who did not have love and respect for St. Mary's Mission.[107]

Mr. De Vos has the following to say:

> While attending the 1959 Indian celebration at Nespelem, I made it my business to talk with all the Indians I could find who had attended St. Mary's under de Rougé. With only one exception, male or female, all were strong in their praise of the benefits they had received. Many of this generation had found it possible to leave the reservation and integrate into better homes and living conditions. It gave me real joy.[108]

The following letter is from Mrs. Ruby Babcock who attended St. Mary's as an eighth grader in 1939 when Fathers J. Balfe and Griva and the Dominican Sisters were at the mission:

> Our first acquaintance with St. Mary's began when two Sisters came to Monse to teach Summer school. Most of their students were in the upper grammar grades. I was just entering the eighth grade the summer that Sister Francis de Sales invited us to tour the Mission. The people of Monse vicinity were depression poor. None of the homes had any more than cold running water and felt fortunate if they had that. St. Mary's was quite a contrast to our homes — we felt it would be a luxurious place to live.
>
> Sister said that perhaps we could come and sure enough about one week after, we received a card saying we could come. We had made hints to our public school teacher and she seemed displeased so rather than face her we slipped our books out and didn't go back. The two Smith girls, Pearl and Marie, and I were the three who went to the Mission. This was in the fall of 1939.
>
> Life did seem luxurious to us there, although we were very lonely at times. My memories are not so much of the every day living there as the contrast between the spiritual poverty we had been raised in and the wonderful truths that we learned at the Mission. We were among those unfortunate children who are allowed to grow up too soon. We were very wise in the ways of the world by the time we attended St. Mary's. I remember many times as a child wondering just what this life was all about and feeling an uneasiness and restlessness in my ignorance. . . . We did learn that there must be discipline of the soul. I have always looked back on my year at St. Mary's as the holiest year of my life. Not that I was holy, but that for the first time I lived with people who were close to God — people who were goodness itself.
>
> In later years, my own spiritual life was to undergo many ups and downs. The memory of St. Mary's and the knowledge of God learned there was the only life preserver I had. If God in His goodness and Mercy should spare my soul and the souls of my family I am certain beyond doubt that St. Mary's will deserve the credit.[109]

---

[107] Mr. Chris C. Smith, questionnaire, Ms.
[108] De Vos to the author.
[109] Mrs. Ruby Babcock, letter to the author, September 20, 1960, Ms.

The following is a report of a visit to St. Mary's Mission fifteen years later, in 1954, by a tribal committee:

On April 30th, a committee from the Business Council consisting of Nellie Rima, Louis Orr, Harry Owhi, Henry Covington and Superintendent Phillis, made a special visit to St. Mary's Mission in Omak for information and other purposes. (The writer of this discourse was able to pull a few strings to accompany the committee on their tour). What started out to be a routine business survey, turned out to be a delightful excursion, full of surprises and pleasantries.

After a briefing from Father Corkery, our genial host, we visited the 7th and 8th grade classroom where they were in the midst of demonstrating "How to figure interest on loans." The committee along with the writer, were completely baffled by the speed and accuracy which the boys and girls demonstrated in working the problems out on the blackboard. . . . The classes also gave a few highlights of the English language. Adverbs, nouns, objects of prepositions, etc. were flying all over the place. We were pleased to see the children so eager and bright in their class participation. . . .

In all the other classes that we visited during the day we received the same surprises. The courtesy and respect that the children showed to their teachers and to us was something that I thought had died some time ago. But here in St. Mary's Mission, it is very much alive and practiced every minute of the day. There is a spirit of willingness and helpfulness in the attitude of the students.

It was near lunch time when our footsteps led us toward the dining hall. Little did we know that we were in for a delicious surprise by the Home Economics class. We were served a full course banquet by Sally Swan, Agnes George, and Lorraine Robinette. . . .

Our next stop was the exhibit of the sewing classes. I have never seen such beautiful work as those students had on display in this particular classroom. . . .

The dorms of the children were visited by the committee and all were in neat order. The older girls have their own dorm, apart from the younger girls. The boys are to be commended in the neat appearance of their dorm. It is pretty hard for a boy to get interested in the fine art of making a bed with square corners and without a wrinkle.[110]

The report then enumerates the various recreational activities going on at the Mission; mention is made of the glee club, the school paper, the high standards of the teachers' qualifications.

At St. Mary's Mission the physical well-being of the pupils is not neglected. Sports are considered an essential part of their education. The record of the school's 1957–1958 basketball season given to the

---

[110] Charles DePoe, Executive Secretary of the Business Council of the Colville Confederated Tribes, *Report,* April 30, 1954.

author by Reverend William Bishoff, S.J.,[111] reveals the success of one part of the sports program.

All aspects of physical health were checked by the regular visit of the County Health Nurse, who vaccinated the children against the various communicable diseases. In addition, the government dental officer from Nespelem spent many days at St. Mary's giving the children proper dental care. A report by Dr. Ralkowski reveals how much dental work was needed.[112]

Conditions at the Mission today are vastly different from what they were during Father de Rougé's time. Many parishes have been established in the area and each one of them seeks to teach and deepen the faith of its members through the Confraternity of Christian Doctrine. A boarding school for children if a good home is at hand represents an abnormal condition. The purpose of the Mission School, to plant and deepen the faith through a good Christian education, has somewhat changed during the last decades in the eyes of some parents. In 1959, 2751 persons of the Colville Reservation were living on the reserve and 1669 persons had their homes outside the reservation. We said that during Father de Rougé's time there were no divorces among his Indian parishioners. Today about one third of the families living on the reservation have broken homes.[113] From this one third come two-thirds of the Mission children. It is to be deeply regretted that three-fourths of the children attending St. Mary's have not the good example of their parents and other relatives to take them to church on Sundays. For these people the Mission is merely a cheap place to have their children fed and raised. They have lost sight of the purpose for which the Mission has been founded and for which the Fathers and the Sisters are sacrificing themselves. With the Confraternity of Christian Doctrine established in every parish of the diocese, those who want to study their religion can easily take advantage of the study hours offered.

Father de Rougé had said that whiskey would be the ruin of the Indians. The United States gave the Indians the freedom to drink whiskey even before it gave them freedom from federal supervision and control. The Mission educators could tell many sad tales of mental agony endured by children of parents who are habitually intoxicated. Observation of the two greatest problems of the Colville Reservation shows that the whiskey

---

[111] Then in charge of the sports at the Mission.

[112] Dr. H. N. Ralkowski, *Report Of The Activities Of The Dental Branch,* Colville Indian Hospital, November 4 through December 11, 1957, Ms.

[113] Jessie A. Bloodworth, *Human Resources Survey Of The Colville Confederated Tribes* (A Field Report Of The Bureau Of Indian Affairs Portland Area Office, Colville Agency), June, 1959, 58.

problem and the broken home problem are interrelated and that each broken home seems in turn to create as many broken homes as there are children in the family. The Mission educators are working here against forces that they are not able to control.

St. Mary's at the present time is unable to offer more than grade school education. When the children graduate from grade school they are in the most dangerous years of their lives. More schooling, guidance and a good Christian home would be needed. Children from broken homes feel stranded. There are hardly any job opportunities on the Reservation. Especially for the boys this proves very dangerous; they become the loafers of the Reservation and before long they will be in trouble with the law. If a girl under similar circumstances smiles at them, they marry, they themselves still being children. They feel that this togetherness will substitute for their feeling of loneliness and insecurity. The children arrive; the parents are not mature enough to shoulder responsibility, or they find out as they develop more maturity that they are incompatible. Another broken home is created. It would take another Father de Rougé to fill the need for an all-boys' high school, completely separated from the mission; of course the Mission could be converted into one. It would save many a home if the responsible provider, the man of the family, could be kept in school until he is more mature. Only if he has adequate education can the Indian compete with his white brother and secure a livelihood outside the Reservation. The present high cost of living makes it very difficult for talented Indian students to obtain board and room near educational institutions in cities, even if schools provide scholarships.

All charitable institutions depend on the generosity of private individuals. The Mission has not had the financial assistance of Mother Katherine since 1936. It would be impossible today to start extensive building programs as Father de Rougé and Father Caldi did. As records show, Father Balfe applied in 1938 to the Tribal Council of the Confederated Colville Tribes for some assistance to St. Mary's Mission.[114] Some agency officials objected to giving money to private schools as had been done by several other tribes as soon as the contract system of the government was discontinued. The Colvilles placed some of their children with the Providence Sisters at Coeur d'Alene. These Sisters, too, needed tribal assistance. The Father of Sister Providentia, Mr. John Tolon, Representative from California, was asked to handle the matter. Mr. Tolon wrote back that he had tried to approach this directly through Congress and

---

[114] Rev. J. Balfe, S.J., to Mr. Albert Orr, Chairman Tribal Council, Colville Tribe, November 5, 1938, Ms. copy.

that the United States Supreme Court had settled this question. He quoted from the Court of Appeal, speaking about the Indians' trust money:

> . . . and while these monies are not delivered to them in hand, yet the money must not only be provided but be expended for their benefit and in part for education; it seems inconceivable that Congress should have intended to prohibit them from receiving religious education *at their own cost* if they so desired it; such an intent would be one 'to prohibit the free exercise of religion' amongst Indians. . . .[115]

After this difficulty had been cleared away there arose others from members of the Tribal Council who opposed the giving of any aid to St. Mary's Mission. The missionaries had laid down their lives in order to plant the Faith among this people, yet many remained through the years opposed to any aid. Finally around 1942, the first assistance of $5,000 was divided among the two schools, St. Mary's and Sacred Heart at Coeur d'Alene. During 1946 attempts were made by members of the Tribal Council to cut this allowance by nearly $2,000. The *Chronicle of St. Mary's Mission* tells us that Father Green had come from Nespelem on the twenty-fourth of May, 1948, and "brought the news that the Colville Reservation Indians had voted against tribal money given for the church."[116] From 1949 to 1952, $8,000 was given yearly to both schools, while from 1952 on to the present St. Mary's received tribal assistance of $15,000 per year.[117] In the meantime the operating costs of St. Mary's have risen to between $60,000 and $70,000 yearly.[118]

During a special session of the Colville Business Council on August 12–13, 1958, when Father Corkery attempted to have the tribal assistance raised, a certain woman member of the Council made the remark "that the payment per pupil should be lowered so that more students would be able to enroll at St. Mary's." The old rates remained.[119] Again St. Mary's Mission tried to have the tribal contributions increased when the Tribal Committee on Health, Education, and Welfare met on July 6, 1960. Father Schiller from the Catholic Charities had been invited by St. Mary's Mission. The main subject of the discussion was the disposition of $15,000 contributed to St. Mary's Mission. In the course of the discussion the question was raised: "Is the majority of the people in favor of this grant?" One of the members of the Committee then slowly stood up and said that some of the older people do not favor it,

---

115 John H. Tolon, M.G. quoting Court of Appeal to Colville Tribal Council, February 9, 1940, Ms. copy. Courtesy of Mrs. Ruby Babcock.

116 *Chronicle of St. Mary's Mission,* May 25, 1948, Ms.

117 Courtesy of Charles DePoe, Executive Secretary, Colville Tribal Council.

118 Rev. J. Balde, S.J., interview.

119 Minutes of the Colville Business Council, Special Session, August 12–13, 1958.

because their memories under Father Caldi are not entirely pleasant, because the Mission then was not what it is now.[120] The Mission subject was tabled.

Father Caldi most certainly had meant well; he could not help being sick. Father P. Corkery had died just two years before. He had built three gyms and saw two go up in flames. It was no easy job to provide for one hundred sixty youngsters who filed into the dining rooms three times a day. After the second gymnasium had burned, Mr. John Cleveland suggested in Tribal Council that a grant of $10,000 be made to the Mission to help meet the emergency, but this too had been voted down.[121] Because "The Mission under Father Caldi was not what it is now," the Mission as it is now did not receive the money for their own children. It took some more time-consuming meetings and some more worries at St. Mary's until the grant of $15,000 was given to the Mission without a raise. In justice and appreciation we mention that the members of the Tribal Council during recent years have been most cooperative, helpful, and generous toward St. Mary's Mission and also to the author of this history. The Mission will receive a $5,000 raise, that means $20,000 of tribal contributions from 1965 on.

St. Mary's Mission today is the only Catholic Indian Boarding School still operating in the State of Washington. In its long and colorful history it has brought culture, education, charity, and Christianity to Indians and whites when no other instruction existed. The Mission School has had its ups and downs, but it has kept on struggling courageously under the most trying circumstances to give to the children and especially those poorest of God's children, the ones from broken homes, a good Christian education and a sense of security and of being wanted. Often what the Mission educators build up in nine months of schooling is completely ruined during three months of vacation by the want of love and guidance and the insecurity of broken homes. Quite a few under-nourished and neglected children return to the Mission and are glad when school starts again. After an evening meal and a shower, one little girl who had just come back, and was resting comfortably in her clean bed, called to a Sister who was passing by, "Oh, I am so glad and happy that I may sleep in a bed again." "Where have you slept during the last three months?" Sister inquired. "Under a tree," was the reply. Once an eighth grader fainted after returning from his weekend on Sunday evening. Realizing how strange it was that a strong boy should faint, one of the Sisters asked, "Did you eat when you were home?" "I had

---

[120] Sister M. Consuelo, O.P., who was present, interview.
[121] John Cleveland, interview.

a bottle of coke since I left the Mission," said the boy.

Father de Rougé's educational institutions where he trained the minds of his beloved Indians so carefully have ceased to exist. His hospital where he tried to heal the sick bodies burned in 1955. But the center of the Mission, the Home of the Lord, the Mission church, still stands. Father J. Balfe, S.J., had it renovated for the seventy-fifth jubilee of the founding of the Mission. It is as if Father de Rougé would say: "Here is my legacy to you. Fill this church again as your forefathers did and bring the Faith back to the parents of the children, only then will the purpose of the Mission be fulfilled and the education of your children be fruitful."

CHAPTER XXII

Current Problems and Developments

THE rightful claims the Indians possessed against the United States government had always been a sore spot in the hearts and minds of the Indian people. The right to possess property is inherent in human nature. Chief James Bernard of the Colvilles was one of the first chiefs who realized the moral obligations of the United States government toward its Indian wards. This chief had attended school for some time at the former Pinkney City, near Mill Creek in the Colville Valley. He could read and write, and he founded a movement to fight for the rights of the tribes on a legal basis. His letters in the National Archives show that he signed his letters as "President of the Colville Indian Association." All his most precious possessions, even his home ranch, were sacrificed in his battle for the rights of his people.

The right to have the services of an attorney was controlled by the Bureau of Indian Affairs. The American Indians had "no right to institute or press claims against the Government," until a special act by Congress granted that right. This "jurisdictional bill" was passed by Congress on February 18, 1925, but failed to become law on account of President Calvin Coolidge's pocket veto. His objections were that it would not be fair to undertake to litigate claims of such ancient origin, and that these claims seem to rest under the general objection which justified all statutes of limitation.

On November 2, 1925, President Coolidge received an answer to his objections, which had been formulated by the assembled chiefs and headmen of the various tribes at a council at Spokane, Washington, on October 31, 1925. It is addressed:

TO OUR GREAT WHITE FATHER
THE PRESIDENT OF THE UNITED STATES

We, the older Indians and Chiefs of the Colville and Okanogan tribes of Indians of the State of Washington, open our hearts to you, our great White Father at Washington. We tell you about our body, about our lands; we speak for all our people, the men, the women, the children, and the children that are not yet born. This is what our fathers considered; this is what we consider, this is what we want you to consider.

We will tell you how we regard the white man according to our view of things. We will speak the truth; we will speak plain so that you can understand us. Those that speak the truth are not afraid to speak plain; those who speak the truth do not need to speak with a forked tongue. We speak the truth. You do not understand the Indians, and poke fun at them every day. They always seem to have something to say about the Indians and don't understand them — even at the odor of the Indians you turn up your nose. We smell of the clean wood fire, of the woods. Now, we do not like the smell of the white people. We don't like the ways of the white people, but we have said nothing about that.

We will tell you about this Indian Country. This was our country. God created this Indian Country, and it was like he spread out a big blanket, and he put the Indians on it. The Indians were created here in this country, truly and honestly, and that was the time our rivers started to run. Then God put fish in the rivers, and he put deer and elk in the mountains and buffalo upon the plains, and roots and berries in the field, and God made laws through which there came the increase of fish and game. When the Creator gave us Indians life, we awakened and as soon as we saw the fish and the game we knew that they were made for us. For the men God gave the deer, the elk and the buffalo to hunt for food and hides; for the women God made the roots and the berries for them to gather, and the Indians grew and multiplied as a people, and gave their thanks to the Creator. When we were created we were given our ground to live on, and from that time these were our rights.

This is all true. Our mothers gathered berries; our fathers fished and killed game. These words are ours and they are true. It matters not how long we live, we cannot change these thoughts. This land was ours, and our strength and our blood is from the fish and the game, the roots and the berries. These are the essence of our life. We were not brought here from a foreign country; we did not come here. We were put here by the Creator. The Creator did not plan the Indian to plow up the fields or to live as White Man. We had no cattle, no hogs, no grain — just berries and roots, and fish and game. We never thought we would be troubled by these things. Whenever the season opened we raised our hearts in thanks to the Creator for his bounty that his food was given us.

When we came into the world, we came from a woman, our Mother. She, before we were born, saved rabbit skins for us, and when we came into the world she placed us in skin. That was our dress. She fed and cared for us. This country was like our Mother. Here our fathers were

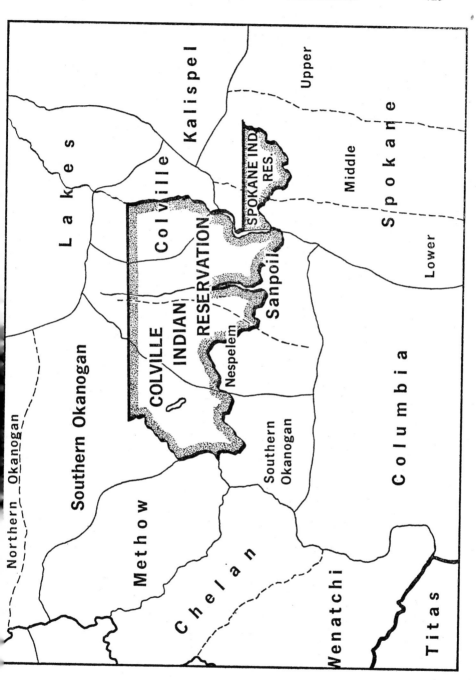

born. Here we were born. It provided us with food and cared for us. This country was like our Mother; we did not want to leave it. We never saw a better country. We are satisfied. It was Indian country long before the White Man came. We were poor Indians, but we were content to stay here in our country. Here were good roots; the camas, the couse, the bitter-root. Here many salmon came; came in the spring and again came when the grass was dry. Here the game, the deer and the birds multiplied. Here the good sun shone brightly, and the trails led to our friends the Flatheads and the Nez Perces, and across the Mountains to the buffalo grounds. This country God gave to our fathers. Our game food God placed upon this land for our fathers to eat. God provided here for our fathers, the Indians, their food in season; the game, the berries, the roots and the fish. God Gave to the Indians here all they needed; God gave us here all we desired, all we needed. Therefore, we believe that we the Indians were favored of God; and according to this understanding, and our views of things we regard the White Man as thus beneath us, in creation and in standing before God.

We thought of our Maker and prayed hard. In the morning our fathers had their prayers and asked God to give them pure water from heaven that the grass might grow. They asked for pure water so that nothing unclean would be in them; also that they would be provided with plenty to eat.

Our Fathers taught us to pray that way. Our fathers taught us to be kind to little children, to be kind to one another, to be friends upon our lands and to have strong hearts. Their words were true and like to the light. We are telling you the truth. Now you will understand: that is something you didn't understand before. We will tell you of our fathers. Our fathers were great in the days gone by, and their past will last forever and ever. Our fathers did not have books. Our fathers did not need books. The Indian did not write down his words on paper, or in a book, and then place his words on a shelf to be covered with dust, forgotten and unknown to his children. The Indian wrote his words, his promises in his memory; in his children's memory, and in the memory of his children's children, Our fathers lived here in happiness. They had hearts that were strong; they regarded them the same as a mountain. Our fathers taught us never to kill things foolishly, but to take for use only, to kill only for food. Our fathers allowed the white man to come as our fathers were good and kind to everyone. Our Maker, the Great God, told us when everything was full grown and had full growth; when the birds' eggs had hatched, and the birds grown; when the deer and the buffalo had calves on strong legs; calves that ate the grass, then we should kill the game.

Our fathers' roads were straight no matter where they went; their roads were always open never closed; and their words were true.

The White Man has brought a change in this, our country. Since our fathers' time even the rocks and trees that our fathers were accustomed to have disappeared. You have killed off or destroyed all that we used for food. Our game food God placed here upon this land for us to eat — you have killed off, have killed it off foolishly; the Indian game food that they lived on; the buffalo you have killed for hides; the deer and the game birds you have killed off by poison or wantonly hunted and killed for pleasure. You have done this without asking us, and you have taken away our country by force, against our will; you see how you have done with us and we have just watched you do away with our things. You have done away with our beautiful land that long ago we roamed over, free as a bird. All these things you have done; all these things you have taken away; all the things that were beautiful to the Indians. We calmly looked on. We had not been here a little while; we had always been here. When the world was made, God gave everyone a country. God did not forget the Indian. God gave the Indians this country. He placed the great waters of the ocean between us, to separate the lands he gave to the Indians from the lands he gave the White Men. You came and you took our lands. One part came from the cold side of heaven (the Canadians) and said, this is all my land down to this line; another party came from the warm side of heaven (Americans) and said this is all my land up to this line. They did us, the Indians, a great wrong. When the President and the Queen of England made their line dividing the Indian Country they did not consult us. You came after us; you should have consulted us.

Before white people came we lived here in peace and were content. We heard that wonderful persons were to come among us. We were pleased; we thought you would help us. When you came we found you were only men like ourselves. Your skin is white but your blood was red like our own. We found that the white men did not come to help the Indians, but to take from the Indian his country. As soon as you white people came and put your feet in our country we began to be miserable. Your children got their eyes on the ground and they coveted it. When they saw this country of ours they liked it. They did not care for the poor Indian. They wanted our country and they put their feet in our very tracks. When you came we welcomed you. You did not ask for what is ours. You took what was ours. You fenced our trails; you took our gardens; you took away our homes by force; you plowed up our fathers' graves; you killed our game. Had it not been for our fathers; had it not been for the teachings of our fathers, of our priests, had it not been that our hearts were big, the white people would not have been so plentiful here for the Indians have strong hearts like the mountain. Now you white people have grown up on our country, and are rich in everything. Our fathers told us to be good, to do right; did you do right to the Indians? You have taken all that we had; what have you given us?

Our fathers taught us water was the only thing we should drink; water was the only thing we had to drink. Your fire water the Indians did not make. The Indians did not have fire water. Your fire water makes men into beasts. You knew that your fire water even kills you, yet you gave it to the Indian, you white people. You made Indians into beasts with fire water; you killed Indians with fire water. No Indian ever made fire water. You had bad diseases and sicknesses that God had not given to or meant for the Indians, his children. You inflicted us with them; you killed us with them. You white people stole and debauched our women, our wives, our sisters, our daughters, and when you were done with them you sent them back to our teepees with their half white children for us to support; we from whom you had taken everything. You wanted our land; you took it from us. You have killed our game; you have destroyed our fisheries; our great fishery at the Kettle Falls where when we were young, all the tribes gathered and we gave fish to all who came; even to the tribes east of the mountains. You have plowed up our camas and couse grounds and our berry fields. You have trampled over the graves of our fathers.

We have sat broken hearted because of what you did; we have sat with empty bellies, and watched you while our children cried. Watched you and your children enjoy that which you took from us. That which you took from us and have not paid us for. We are men. Men with different skins than yours, different thoughts than yours; but we are men. We did not fight you. We are men with strong hearts, hearts like mountains. We were told it was wrong to fight. We watched you.

You put your laws upon us. Your laws say that we men are children, and that we cannot manage the little you left to us. By your laws you say that we are but children; that we have no minds, that we cannot do as we wish with what is ours — that little that you have not taken yet from us. That we cannot ask you to pay us for what you owe us, unless we, your children, first ask and get consent from your great council of Congress. After many years, many long years, your council of Congress this Spring voted us Indian consent. Your Council of Congress said that we Indians could ask you in your Court of Claims to pay us what is right for you to pay for that you took from us.

We are now told that you, the President, have said that we should have asked you to pay us in that Court before; that our claims are too old — that we have waited too long. We have waited long; we have waited very long. We cannot ask you to pay, only when your Council of Congress says we may. When did Congress say we could ask? Our fathers told us to pay our debts; to pay all our debts. Our fathers did not tell us we need not pay the old debts, our fathers told us if they could not pay their debts then, we their children must pay them, or our childrens' children, else we and our children, and our fathers are disgraced.

We are broken hearted because we are treated like children. We wait to know about our claims; we have waited very long. We ask you to now treat us as men; to deal with us as men. Do so now. Make glad our hearts; make whole the broken promises of Stevens.

About this land it all belonged to the Indians. You were more numerous than we; as numerous as are all the ants in all the ant hills. You were stronger than we. You put your feet in all our tracks. You crowded us out. You took our land away. We were sorry. Our hearts were heavy. They are yet heavy. We never started to offend the whites, but they have continually done wrong towards us. We never gave to you, we never sold our lands to you; we have never agreed on a treaty. We have never given you any writing for these lands. We were willing to be big hearted towards you; we would have selected the best of our lands and reserved our homes and the graves of our fathers, and we would have been liberal with you, so that the poor white men who had no lands and were hungry for Indian lands might settle on what was left of our lands. We so often told your commissioners.

You took our lands from us. Without our consent, wholly without consulting us, General Grant, the President, selected some of our lands; not our homes, not our best lands, not where our fathers were buried, but some of the poor lands, mostly rocks and mountains. We did not select those lands. We were not consulted. We did not consent to go on those lands. We had other lands, good lands. We then lived on those lands. We cultivated them. Our fathers were buried on those lands. There we wanted to live. But the white man wanted those same lands, wanted them because they were good lands, the best lands. The white men did not want the rocks and the mountains where the President said we should have a reservation. The white men crowded us out. They threatened us. They seized our lands and improvements; they threatened us. The Indian Agents you sent to us told us we had to move from our homes to that Reservation that the President had selected. You sent your soldiers among us. We did not fight you. Our priests taught us it was wrong to steal; that it was wrong to fight. We did not fight. We obeyed you. We left our homes. We left the graves of our fathers. We left with heavy hearts and we went on those poor rocky lands that you left to us as a Reservation; the poor lands that the White Men did not want. We went unwillingly.

You had told us that our lands and rights would not be taken from us without our consent. We believed you. We trusted you. You said you were our friend and protector. Our lands were taken from us without our consent. The great chief, Governor Isaac I. Stevens, who first came among us and who held councils with us said that he was our friend; that whatever was done about our lands would be done by talking and agreeing, both sides being satisfied. He said that our rights were our rights; that we would not be deprived of them, and that our lands should not be taken away from us without our consent. We spoke with one tongue. He spoke for you. We, the poor ignorant Indians believed him. He went away to the great war you had, long, long ago. We are told he was killed in battle. Had he lived we believe he would have kept his words unbroken. His words are broken words. The Indian Agents, the Commissioners, and other big men that you sent to us for many years after that handed you the broken words of Stevens. They told you that you had no right to our lands; told you that our lands had not been given to you, told you that no agreement had been made between us, told you that you had not bought our lands, that you had not paid for them, told you that our Indian title to our lands was not wiped out.

When these Agents, these Commissioners, these Big Men spoke thus to us and to you, you had other agents surveying our lands, you were inviting white men to settle upon them; you were giving them away to the railroads, to the State, to the Schools and Colleges, to whoever wanted them until now all the Indian lands, that you made free lands are gone. All our lands you have given away, and you did not own them;

you did not buy them from us; you have not paid us for them.

We never gave you what you took. These lands were taken away from us by you — our friend, our protector, our guardian. These lands were not taken from us in war, we never fought you, we were always your friend. What you took was ours, so claimed by us, so recognized by our neighbors, so recognized by you; you have never paid us for what you took.

On this land of ours your children have built great towns; over it they have run railroads; from the belly of the earth they have dug our silver, gold, lead and copper. They have cut down and used the great forests that grew on our hills, they have built great dams across our salmon streams and harnessed the lightning to do their work. They have made farms and orchards out of our root fields and our hunting grounds. Your people have multiplied and grown rich on our lands; these lands that you our friend, took from us without our consent; these lands that you have never paid us for.

You are our guardian. You govern us by your laws. We cannot employ attorneys without your consent. We cannot act without your consent. By your laws we cannot urge a claim against you without your consent; we cannot ask you for justice in your own courts, unless you first make a law granting us that right.

The first time you spoke to us Indians about our lands was in the day of our fathers, when we were children or infants in our Mothers arms, you were yet talking to us about our lands and our rights when we were young men. We have talked ever since. Our hair is now gray and we are becoming old, some of us are now very old, and we will see but few winters. We are old and we have not long to wait here. We would like to have this matter settled before we meet our fathers; before we meet Governor Isaac I. Stevens. We do not want to tell them that Stevens' promises, that our promises are yet broken; that the Indian lands were taken for the whites without the consent of the Indians; that the whites have multiplied and grown rich on the Indians lands; and that the poor Indians from whom they were taken without consent, without agreement, without treaty, have never been settled with or paid for the lands taken from them.

After many years we secured your consent to employ a lawyer, familiar with your customs, to present our claim.

The sub chief in the two great councils of Congress made a law that our claims should, with your consent, be submitted to and heard by your Court of Claims. This proposed law was designated as H.R. 9160. It was submitted to you, you did NOT approve it, and unless you approve the law, the poor Indian cannot go into your courts; cannot secure justice.

We are told that you, the President have said that our claims are too old. Who made them old? Who delayed the settlement? We are your children; we are your wards; we can do nothing without your consent. We have been — we are now helpless unless you act. We cannot bring suit against you in your courts. If settlement with us has been delayed, it has been due to your own fault. It is not the fault of the poor, ignorant, helpless Indian. Will you take advantage of your own fault? Will you say, I delayed a long time settling with my children; now because I delayed so long I will not settle with them at all? An Indian does not so pay his debt. If he cannot pay it his children pay it. We cannot believe, that you, the President, meant to take advantage of the poor Indian, and refuse to pay him because of your own delay.

We have also been told that you have said that our claim is too large. We have never put any price on our lands, or on the rights you took away from us without our consent. All we have asked, all we now ask is that the matter be settled; that you permit your Court of Claims to decide whatever it is just for you to pay us. Are you not willing to pay that; are you not willing to pay whatever you justly owe; whether it is big or little? We are told that you are the head of the wealthiest nation in the whole world; that the United States is a benevolent nation, that has given hundreds of thousands of dollars — great sums that the poor Indian cannot comprehend, to the poor people across the ocean in the countries where the great world war was fought, and where our own sons fought, bled and died fighting shoulder to shoulder with your own sons. Whatever your courts may decide and fix upon as the amount justly due us, for the lands and rights taken from us will be as but a leaf from the great tree of your wealth; it will be but as a small twig from the branch that you broke off and gave away. Is not the Heart that gives away big enough to move you to pay the just debt, be it little or big, that you owe to us poor Indians?

An Indian pays his debts before he gives a potlatch.

We have studied our situation. We have watched you. We are wise with the wisdom of our fathers. We know that the Indian as an Indian must cease. We see that the day of the Indian has passed; the Sun set on the old Indian life when you killed our game, destroyed our fisheries, and took away our lands. We now know that the Indians if they continue to exist must become White Men in their manner of living.

We have some of us read your history. We learn that it has taken two thousand years to change the Helvatians of France; the Germanians and the Goths, and the Britons and the Picts of England, into you white people of today. We know that the Indian cannot be wholly changed into White Men in a generation or in a short time. We know that the mind and way of thinking has to be changed and we know that the bodies of the Indians have to be changed. We who lived by fishing and the chase must learn to work as White Men and our muscles and the bones of our bodies must change. Our bellies must accept and be content with strange foods; our skins must grow accustomed to our wearing the White Mens' clothes and our lungs that only knew the clean free air must become accustomed to the air of closed houses. While we change into White Men we must suffer in body and in spirit. We must fight in our bodies all your diseases which we as Indian never knew, and for which our Indian medicines are not good. Our women must learn to have children and to keep them well under new and changed conditions so that they grow into strong men and women.

We see you White Men work and gather money and property together

for your children. We have children. We love these children. We think
of our childrens' children who will be White Men and Women like your-
selves — but with red skins — less red than ours. What was ours, what
our fathers left to us you have taken. Taken without our consent, for
that we want pay. This is our right. This is our need. We want this that
we may care for ourselves and our children while the Indian changes into
a White Man. That we may care for and make provision for our children,
just as you White Men do. This is our right.

Now about our Claims. We want them settled now while we yet live.
When they are settled we can continue changing into White Men and
they will be forgotten. Now these claims are in our minds. We keep
thinking about them.

Why do you not settle this matter, why do you not let your Court of
Claims decide what is justly due us?

It is not because of lack of time for the life time of man has passed
since we first began to talk about our lands. It is not because you do not
know of our claims and of their right and justness, for commencing with
Governor Stevens, your own Commissioners and Agents have often told
us of our rights, and have often written them out in the records of your
doings that you keep in your great office at Washington. Why do you not
settle this matter? We are very old. The lands, the rights you took were
OURS. We have never agreed that you should have them. They were
valuable, valuable to us and more valuable to you. You took them. You
have never settled with us for them. We want nothing but what is just,
nothing but what your own Court of Claims may freely say is ours. What
are you going to do?

We have spoken. That is All.[1]

This simple, straightforward address of the old Indian chiefs to President Coolidge is indeed a touching, and in places eloquent, memorial of
the injustices done to an aboriginal people. Through the many repetitions
of the same grievances the chiefs wanted to make sure that they would
finally be understood, although it would have been absurd not to understand, in the light of George Washington's statement to the Six Nations
of the early, honest democratic ideals of the United States government:
"The general government will never consent to your being defrauded but
will protect you in all your rights."[2]

Again Senator W. L. Jones and Congressman Sam B. Hill sponsored
another jurisdiction act, S. 3185, which passed both Houses of Congress
on June 23, 1926. Again President Coolidge did not return it within
ten days after it was presented to him. This forced the tribal attorney,
William S. Lewis, to follow the advice of the sponsoring Congressmen

[1] Chiefs of the Colville and Okanogan Tribes quoted in H.R. 3855. "Claims of
the Colville and Okanogan Indian Tribes of Washington against the United States,"
House of Representatives, Sixty-Ninth Congress, First Session, 3–12.

[2] *American State Papers, Indian Affairs*, L, 142.

and follow suit in the Court of Claims under the conviction that the bill became a law through failure of the Executive to return it on time.[3] As papers from the National Archives show, the matter finally went to the Supreme Court in 1929.[4]

As formulated by their attorney, W. S. Lewis, the claims of the Colville Confederated Tribes are:

1. Okanogan and Methow Tribes, for lands lying west of the Okanogan River from the International boundary line south to the Columbia River and west to the summit of the Cascades, estimated ....   1,800,000 Acres

2. Okanogan and Sanpoil Tribes, including the Nespelem band — for lands south of the Columbia River and north of the lands of the Yakima Tribe as fixed by treaty there within of June 9, 1855 (12 Stat. 951), estimated ....   500,000 Acres

3. Sanpoil Tribe, including the Nespelem Band — lands lying north of the Columbia River and east of the Okanogan River and partly within the Colville Indian Reservation, estimated as containing ....   1,000,000 Acres

4. Colville and Lake Tribes — lands lying east of the Columbia River and north of the Spokane River and bounded on the east by the summit of the Kalispell Mountains, estimated ....   1,238,144 Acres

5. All of said tribes and bands — hunting and grazing rights within their claimed territory, supra, and also hunting rights in the "common hunting grounds" under the treaty with the Blackfeet Nation of Oct. 17, 1855 (11 Stat. 657) $1,000,000

6. All of said tribes and bands — fishing rights in "their old fishing grounds" .... $1,000,000[5]

Compensation was not to exceed $1.25 per acre.[6] These were only rough estimates and were more definitely computed by the tribal attorney. Accordingly the Okanogan acreage is 1,997,500; the Sanpoil and Okanogan had lost 570,000 acres; the compensation asked for fishing rights was

---

[3] William S. Lewis, letter to Hon. Chas. Burke, Commissioner of Indian Affairs, April 1, 1927, Ms. NA, Record No. 75, 2295-23-052 Colville.

[4] William S. Lewis, to Office of Indian Affairs, Washington, D. C., April 4, 1929. Mr. Lewis argued the case of the Okanogan and Colville Indians before the Supreme Court on March 11, 1929.

[5] Hubert Work, Secretary of the Interior, to Hon. Scott Leavitt, Chairman Committee on Indian Affairs, quoting W. S. Lewis. Hearing before Subcommittee of the Committee on Indian Affairs, April 6, 1926. *House of Representatives, Sixty-Ninth Congress, First Session,* H.R. 9270.

[6] *Ibid.*

considerably higher, while the common hunting ground claim was computed to be $9,399,999.00.[7]

Duncan McDonald, the son of the former Hudson's Bay Company trader of Forts Colville and Conah, who lived with his family for long years at Fort Colville on the Columbia River, was a witness to the fishing and hunting claims of the Colville Confederated Tribes. Under oath he stated:

> The principal source of food and products for barter of these tribes came from their fisheries, which originally supplied them with more than half their annual food supply as well as a surplus for trade. As first known to me the fisheries of these tribes on the Columbia River at Kettle Falls and on the tributaries of that river within the territories of these Indians literally swarmed with salmon and other fish, which were caught and cured by the thousands in number and by tons and tons in weight. . . .
>
> I am also familiar with the common use made by these tribes of Indians with the Flathead, Nez Perce and other Indians in the "common hunting grounds" lying east of the summit of the Rocky Mountains in the basin of the Three Forks of the Missouri River to Yellow Stone Park and the Big Hole Country on the South. In the fifties and sixties this hunting ground was literally filled with game, there were millions and millions of buffalo, thousands upon thousands of antelope, elk, big horn sheep, and other game. . . .
>
> . . . These Spokane and Colville tribes sent out hunting parties to this region, usually once a year, in the fall. These would stay living off of the country four or five months and come back in the Spring. Sometimes Summer parties went to this common hunting ground. . . .
>
> These hunting parties from the Colville and Spokane tribes usually consisted of about fifty families. They took with them dried salmon and other articles of barter to trade with the Eastern tribes. . . . Returning often with their pack animals loaded down with meat and hides they had cured and roots and other articles of food and use they had dug or bartered for.[8]

Duncan McDonald went on to say that wealthy families might bring back eighteen or twenty horses, each loaded with two hundred pounds, while others had less, or some might have their horses stolen by the Blackfeet Indians. From this common hunting ground the Colville Confederated Tribes got their bulk robes for tents, bedding, saddle blankets, as well as other items for barter with the coast Indians. They also had their living while away. McDonald had visited this hunting ground in 1858 with his father, Angus McDonald.

The possessory rights of the Colville tribes had been very early definitely

---

[7] W. S. Lewis, letter to Hon. Chas. H. Burke, April 1, 1927, *op. cit.*

[8] Duncan McDonald, certified statement, September 22, 1927, to Office of Indian Affairs, Washington, D. C., Ms., NA, Record Group 75, 2295-23-052.

established. Governor Isaac I. Stevens had the outer boundaries in a general way on his first map in 1853; he also considered these lands in the Walla Walla Council in 1855, which was attended by designated members of the nontreaty Colville tribes.

In vain did the attorneys quote the meaning of the Fifth Amendment of the Constitution, which forbids the taking of private property without just compensation; the policy of the Indian Department and of President Coolidge were fixed:

> It is recommended that these bills do not receive your favorable consideration. The Director of the Bureau of the Budget has advised that the proposed legislation in H.R. 9270 is in conflict with the financial program of the President.[9]

President Hoover also supported Coolidge's action and refused to help. All efforts of the tribal attorneys for the next two decades were without result. The claims of the Colville Confederated Tribes had been dismissed. Chief James Bernard was several times in Washington, D. C., but could do nothing.

The *Minutes* of the Meetings of the Tribal Business Council in the 1940's show renewed attempts of the tribes to create understanding of their problems. Meetings were held in all the districts of the Reservation. Finally, after years of preparatory work a ten man delegation was chosen to represent the tribes before the Subcommittee on Indian Affairs. Old tribal chiefs and leaders, who had lived through their history and were delegated, were: Jim James, Peter Dan Moses, Billy Curlew, and Victor Nicholas. Younger leaders chosen were: John B. Cleveland, Joe Monaghan, Albert Orr, Peter J. Gunn, and Frank George.

In the meantime the acreage of tribal possessions had changed. The building of Coulee Dam also changed original boundaries. Land holdings in the Colville Reservation as of December 31, 1941, consisted of:

	Acres
Fee patented ceded lands no longer under Indian jurisdiction	223,368
Trust patented allotments (still restricted)	258,851
Lands ceded under the Act of March 22, 1906, which were undisposed of and vacant, temporarily withdrawn by Secretarial order of September 19, 1934	818,277
Remaining tribal lands and reserves	84,590
Gross area of the diminished Colville Reservation	1,385,086[10]

[9] Hubert Work, Secretary of the Interior, Report to Chairman, Committee on Indian Affairs, April 2, 1926, quoted in Hearing Before a Subcommittee of the Committee on Indian Affairs, *House of Representatives, Sixty-Ninth Congress, First Session,* on H.R. 9270, 3.

[10] Colville Business Council, *Resolution of July 9–10, 1943.* Ms., Tribal Office, Nespelem, Wash.

A more democratic spirit toward the American Indian developed after World War II. The Indian Claims Commission Act was passed on August 13, 1946.[11] During World War I more than 12,000 American Indians had died for their country; this number was much bigger during World War II. Now the work to do a bit of justice to the original Americans, who had fought side by side with their white brothers, began.

By interlocutory order, dated February 29, 1956, the Commission had adjudged that the United States is liable to the following tribes: Lakes, Colville, Sanpoils, Nespelems, Okanogans, and Methows. The value of the respective tracts of land less the part that lay within the Reservation established for these and other tribes by Executive Order of July 2, 1872, was to be measured by the value of July 2, 1872, less any offsets allowed by law. Two different appraisal experts were at work; the different acreage between the two was enormous. Also civil engineers and soil scientists were employed. Boundaries that lay midstream on the Columbia and Okanogan Rivers were changed to the shorelines; this amounted to 17,225 acres less. The aboriginal lands taken from the mentioned tribes together were finally computed to be approximately 1,700,000 acres. The award made by the Indian Claims Commission was $1,000,000, after offsets of $61,000. It represents about sixty-one cents per acre. These claims had been filed under Docket 181.[12]

More legal battles were necessary before the money was to be paid. Since the Wheeler-Howard Act was passed on June 18, 1934, as we will see, the individual tribes had ceased to exist as far as the government was concerned. Instead they were called now "The Confederated Colville Tribes" against the wishes of the Indian people. The Indian Claims Commission Act mentioned that the money should be awarded to the individual tribes. Another act of Congress now settled this matter: any award given to one tribe will be shared by all. If the Moses Tribe or the Nez Perce members, who were placed on the Colville reservation, will be given their judgment funds, it will be given to all the tribes.

What to do with the awarded $1,000,000 became a controversy that took more than three years to solve. Should the money be used by the Secretary of the Interior to develop the Reservation, or should it be paid to the people in a per capita payment? The people had voted that they needed the money in a per capita payment; the Reservation is an economically depressed area; and finally through the efforts of the Colville

---

[11] *Indian Claims Commission Act*, (60 Stat. 1949).

[12] *Before the Indian Claims Commission, Docket 181, The Confederated Tribes of the Colville Reservation* et al Plaintiffs v. *The United States of America,* copy in Tribal Office, Nespelem, Wash. Also: *Minutes of Mass Meeting, November 14, 1964.*

Indian Association a $350 per capita payment was granted under S. 1169.[13]

More judgments funds are to be awarded in the near future. The tribes are paying ten percent of the judgments awarded and other expenses to their attorneys. Now that the legal machinery is established let us hope that the rest of the grievances of the Colville Confederated Tribes versus the United States will be settled soon. To pay at the present time for land on the basis of its value in 1872 is again a great injustice to the tribes, but it represents a beginning in more democratic procedures. Could we buy an acre of land to build a home, or could we acquire an acre of finest timberland for fifty cents? These were prices the good Indian people were supposed to vote on at a meeting concerning the land claims of the Chelan, Entiat, Wenatchee, Columbia, and Palus Indians, who were considered subject to the Walla Walla Treaty of 1855, but rather moved to the Colville Reservation instead of to the Yakima. This judgment fund will be based on the 1859 price per acre, the date when the Yakima Treaty was ratified.

The Indian people are generally distrustful of the century-old system of the United States Indian Bureau. Among its employees have been wonderful field workers and teachers who had the good of the Indians at heart, but they have been a minority. It is more or less their job to follow and execute the policy of those who hold the key positions in the Indian Service. The Indian people are justified in being resentful of the Indian Bureau's actions. Throughout the many years of its existence the Bureau has dominated nearly every aspect of tribal life. The aboriginal Americans had to feel that they were the outlaws and illegal occupants of lands which the white man wanted. By chicanery and fraud reservations were assigned to them, and then even these were gradually diminished and agreements shamefully violated. Moral and legal obligations were pushed aside. Except during the past twenty years or so, the government has proved to be a faithless guardian of its Indian wards.

One of the blackest pages in United States history is the use of the Indian's trust money. Researches and investigations of former Senator William H. King of Utah brought to light some shocking figures. We can only bring some small excerpts from the gentleman's speech before the

---

[13] "Hearings Before the Subcommittee on Indian Affairs on the Committee on Interior and Insular Affairs, United States Senate," *Eighty-Seventh Congress, First Session*, on S. 2123 and H.R. 8236, August 15, and September 13, 1961 (U. S. Government Printing Office, Washington, D. C.: 1961).

Also: *ibid., Eighty-Eighth Congress, First Session*, on S. 1442 and S. 1169, Oct. 24, 25, 26, and November 20, 1963 (U. S. Government Printing Office, Washington, D. C.: 1964).

United States Senate, February 8, 1933. Congress in 1929, had appropriated for Indian Service a total of $18,247,122:

> But the Bureau had actually spent, in the fiscal year 1929, $21,635,478, or $3,388,356 in excess of the total of specific appropriations. . . . This part of the overexpenditure, $1,734,247, had been simply lifted by the Indian Bureau out of tribal trust funds. . . .[14]

> Congress and the Indian Bureau have used the Indian capital assets for Indian Bureau maintenance, and the expenditures have been lavish. They have totaled more than $110,000,000 since 1900, and this misappropriation of the Indian estate — its diversion to unproductive administrative uses — continues today and is eating up a larger proportion of the available liquid capital than in 1920 or 1910. The Bureau used for its own maintenance (exclusive of per capita payments) $30,930,540 of Indian tribal funds in the 7 fiscal years 1926–32, inclusive. It has used in the fiscal year 1932, 76 percent of the total tribal income of 1932.[15]

Indian trust monies have totaled more than "$500,000,000 since 1887." They were derived from sales of land, timber, oil, and minerals. Proper trusteeship would have reinvested that money to conserve the principal, but the Indian Bureau did not do so. Senator King continues to say:

> Never, either to the Indian tribes or to Congress, has the Bureau made an accounting for its use of these hundreds of millions of dollars. The records are imperfect and are not compiled. Suits for accounting by the Indian tribes would probably be defeated through the absence of records.[16]

We saw how under Bureau administration the wealth of the Indians diminished and how from the tribal income for 1932 only 24 percent were left for the Indian owners.

The Indian Bureau is also accused of having too many employees. During 1932 the ratio of Bureau employees to Indians was 1–25. In 1933 we have "1 Federal employee for every 23 Indians, and 1 employee for every 6 children in the schools."[17] Senator King recommended a radical change in the attitude of the government toward its Indian wards and a complete reorganization of the Indian Bureau. He remarks:

> A trustee who squanders the inheritance of his ward or who is indifferent to the latter's welfare merits the condemnation of all who desire

---

[14] Hon. William H. King, speech before the Senate of the U. S. February 8, 1933, quoted in "Hearings Before a Subcommittee of the Committee on Indian Affairs United States Senate, *Seventy-Sixth Congress*, "Survey of Conditions of the Indians in the United States," Part 37, 21406.

[15] *Ibid.*, 21419.

[16] *Ibid.*

[17] *Ibid.*, 21408.

justice, and subjects himself to the corrective power of the courts.[18]

The squandering of tribal trust money also took place on the Colville Reservation. The Colville Indian Association is on record as having protested against this on March 25, 1933:

> We the Colville Indian Association, strongly object to the Indian Bureau spending about twice as much as our tribal income.
> We ask our President, Franklin D. Roosevelt, to dismiss two thirds of these government employees on our reservation as we do not wish to go in debt for Bureau employees salaries. . . .[19]

The Association had asked Congress to come and investigate. This subcommittee came toward the end of October of the same year and found that the Agency for the Colville Tribes alone had 41 employees. Senator Frazier told the Indians:

> . . . According to this report $27,305.90 of your tribal funds were spent for the Colville agency general support. You want to see to it that you get enough of that money to build homes for every Indian that wants a home out of the timber, instead of letting that money be used to pay salaries of these employees.[20]

Let us now consider some of the more important Indian legislation of the last decades. In 1924 all Indians became citizens of the United States. As the Committee on Indian Affairs had stated, it had been very difficult for an Indian to obtain citizenship without either being allotted and getting a patent of fee simple, or leaving the Reservation and taking up his residence apart from any tribe of Indians.[21] Under this bill as amended by Congress, citizenship was given directly to all Indians, thus ruling out all Bureau interference.[22] The Indians were now citizens, but still they had no rights and no freedom.

One of the most controversial laws ever passed by Congress was the Wheeler-Howard Act, later called the Indian Reorganization Act. Volumes have been filled with the testimony given before Congressional committees of serious grievances of various Indian tribes who were subjected to intimidations, false promises, punishments, and other unlawful means in order to vote for the acceptance of this Act.

---

[18] Hon. William H. King, speech, *op. cit.*, 21404.

[19] James Bernard and others, letter of March 25, 1933, to the president, quoted in "Hearings Before a Subcommittee of the Committee on Indian Affairs, United States Senate," *Seventy-Second Congress, First Session, Part 32*, 17141–17142.

[20] Senator Lynn J. Frazer, *ibid.*, 17109.

[21] *House of Representatives 222, Sixty-Eighth Congress, First Session*, February 22, 1924, on H.R. 6355.

[22] S. Rept. 441, *Sixty-Eighth Congress, First Session*, April 21, 1924, Also: *Sixty-Fifth Congressional Record*, 8621–8622, 9303–9304. *Forty-Third Stat.* 253, 8 U.S.C. 3.

The Wheeler-Howard Act represented a reversal of United States policy of land ownership. It had been the Indian policy of the United States government to break up the ties of aboriginal communal ownership, to allot certain acres of land for the individual families and put the Indians on reservations. Now they were supposed to band together again in corporations and to relinquish their allotments. Any business was to be done in groups. Also there was overemphasis on having the Indians make a living on their old arts and crafts. It would have meant turning the clock back 150 years to restore and perpetuate the tribal communal life in a modern society. This Indian Reorganization Act was, according to Commissioner John Collier, intended to give the tribes more self-government. In reality every important decision was subject to approval by the Commissioner of Indian Affairs.

The honorable gentlemen Wheeler and Howard had nothing to do with the Act except that they introduced it by request. We learn more about this law that was made without consent of the Indians from a *Speech* by Honorable Virginia E. Jenckes, of Indiana, before the House of Representatives, on May 14, 1935:

> The Indians alleged that the Wheeler-Howard Act which the present Commissioner propagandized through the last Congress under the guise of bestowing self-government upon the Indians' citizenship of the United States, not only does not grant them self-government, but that it goes further toward entrenching Bureau control of their affairs than any previous legislation of Congress; that in the face of the Citizenship Act of 1924 this bill is unconstitutional; they further allege that it had its origin and was sponsored as early as 1932 by the American Civil Liberties Union, whose headquarters are located in New York City. Their contention is that this organization is one of the most active communistic organizations in the United States and that all legislation flowing from that source is decidedly communistic. The Indians further contend that the Wheeler-Howard Act is being administered largely through the Indian Bureau and Interior Department officials, now or formerly identified with the American Civil Liberties Union.[23]

The original Wheeler-Howard Act had been drafted by the Solicitor of the Interior Department, Nathan R. Margold, the former chairman of the Indian Committee of the American Civil Liberties Union.[24] This organization put on a vigorous campaign to have the bill passed by Congress. The original Wheeler-Howard Bill contained forty-eight printed pages. Congress amended it the very next year of its passage. It had some good

---

[23] Hon. Virginia E. Jenkes, speech, House of Representatives, May 14, 1935, quoted in "Hearings," Part 37, 20729.

[24] Commissoner Collier quoted by O. K. Chandler, *ibid.,* 20471.

points, but as a whole it still violated the personal dignity of the individual Indian.

The Nez Perce tribe in a telegram to the Chairman of the Indian Committee accused the Commissioner of having muzzled the press; only the good points of the Act were stressed. They protested the unjust elections where votes which had not been cast were counted as in favor of the bill, disfranchising those who had voted against it. They deplored the proposal to go back to the old pagan religious ceremonial with its immorality, which would close the mouth of every minister or missionary. They also protested that this bill would take away their independence as citizens of the United States.[25]

Being members of an investigating committee and hearing the reactions of the various Indian tribes, Senators Wheeler and Frazier in 1937, introduced S. 1736, Seventy-Fifth Congress, First Session, a bill to have the whole Indian Reorganization Act repealed.[26] He was not successful. Attorney Albert A. Grorud, who served for many years as legal counsel in Congress, enumerated three bills that were introduced during the Seventy-Fourth Congress and eight bills that were introduced during the Seventy-Fifth Congress. These wanted either the Wheeler-Howard Act repealed for certain reservation, or states, or for all the Indians of the United States. Many more bills were introduced during the following Congresses up to 1954–1955. They were opposed by Commissioner Collier and the New Deal Administration, and Congress was powerless.[27]

How did the tribes on the Colville Reservation react when this Indian Reorganization Act was put to the test by the domineering Bureau? These tribes had more or less kept their tribal identity. There had been very early intermarriages between members of the tribes living near Fort Okanogan and Fort Colville and white men. The Skoelpi and the Lake tribes have generally been earlier exposed to the Christian white man's civilization. Also, the different bands of the Okanogans had made wonderful progress, but still all these tribes in their tribal life listened for guidance to their rightfully elected chiefs. Intertribal friction developed when by Executive Orders of April 19, 1879, and March 6, 1880, lands claimed by the Okanogan and Methow tribes were set apart for Chief Moses and his people and named the Columbia reservation, as we have seen. This land in turn, as we mentioned before, was a few years later declared public domain and Moses and his people with a few exceptions were induced to move to the Colville reservation. The Okanogans had

---

[25] Nez Perce Indians, Nez Perce Reservation, telegram, quoted in "Hearings," Part 37, 20727–20728.

[26] Ibid., 20908. Bill S. 1736, *Seventy-Fifth Congress, First Session.*

[27] Albert A. Grorud, attorney, to Mrs. Alyce Hallenius, June 28, 1965, Ms.

been the rightful owners, but it was Moses who received a yearly sum of $1,000, another $1,000 to build a house for himself, one hundred head of cows for himself, plus all the help each head of a family of his tribe received in return for relinquishing the Columbia reservation. Chief Sarsapkin, who wanted to stay on the Columbia reservation, was allowed to have 2500 acres or four square miles of land, and each male adult or head of a family one square mile, while the rightful owners received later only about eighty or one hundred sixty acres depending on the kind of land they wanted. The second cause of friction came from placing Chief Joseph with about one hundred twenty of his people as prisoners of war on the Colville Reservation. The Moses people and especially these Nez Perces have stood pretty well aloof from the rest of the Colville population. It was not their fault that they were placed there. They have the highest number of full-bloods. We can imagine the reaction when they were told to form cooperatives, farm chapters, and a common tribal government under Bureau control. Nevertheless, they listened to the superintendent's explanations of the Wheeler-Howard Act and used their own reasoning powers.

The National Archives show extensive correspondence on the subject between Commissioner Collier and agency superintendent and influential tribal leaders. Chief James Bernard showed his concern about proper election procedures; he wanted polling places that were accessible to the members of each district; he also wanted to know if the vote of the two hundred Canadians who were then enrolled on the Colville Reservation and who were absent, would be counted.[28] Commissioner Collier instructed Superintendent Harvey K. Meyer to explain to the chief that the Act "is already in effect and the Indians must vote themselves out, so to speak; that means that a majority of the eligible adult Indians must vote to exclude themselves."[29] Also instructions had been given to group leaders as to the eligibility of absentee members. Chief James Bernard later announced that the Colvilles were ready to vote for or against the Wheeler-Howard Bill. If adopted, then they would go ahead "making new plans under the new legislation and receive the benefits such as expenses for organizing, forming the constitution and bylaws."[30]

The Wheeler-Howard Act had authorized Congress to appropriate $10,000,000, from which only $2,000,000 were to be used per annum.

[28] Chief James Bernard, letter, October 23, 1934, to Hon. John Collier, Commissioner of Indian Affairs, Washington, D. C., Ms., NA, Record Group 75, 9557-36-066 Colville. All the correspondence on this subject is filed under the above number.

[29] John Collier to Harvey K. Meyer, carbon from Ms., NA.

[30] James Bernard to Collier, Ms.

Too much emphasis was put on this promise; in reality the Indian tribes generally did not receive much of these benefits, or none.

Strong opposition came from the Monse and Nespelem areas. These people wanted the "North-half Indians" excluded from voting. Also A. G. Wilson, Supervisor of the Elections, had told the Indians, "If less than a majority vote against the act — even if negative votes should outnumber the affirmative ones, the act still applies." Cleveland Kamiakin, Willie Redstar, Johnny Frank, L. C. Wapato, and Mathew Srimpt were the signers of the protest sent to Collier.[31] Some of the above leaders did not trust the secret ballot system; they had heard about cheating; they warned the Commissioner, that if they failed to exclude themselves from the new law, they would employ attorneys to preserve their rights.[32]

The tribal members went to the polls on April 6, 1936. In answering an inquiry of Louie Timentwa and Cleveland Kamiakin, Collier gives the results of the voting:

> We have just received a report from your superintendent showing that out of a population of 1659, 421 Indians voted yes and 562 voted no. However, the negative vote is not sufficient to exclude the Indians from the application of the act as at present construed by the Solicitor.[33]

On June 15, 1935, Congress passed the law that the voting to exclude a reservation from the act, or voting for new constitutions and bylaws required the vote of a majority. According to the new law the Indian Reorganization Act did not apply to the Colville Reservation. Section 18 of the Indian Reorganization Act also had stated that a majority of adult voters would be sufficient to exclude the tribes from the application of the act.[34] It shows us the pressure put on by the Commissioner of Indian Affairs and his subordinates to overrule Congress and to have the act adopted by the tribes.

In spite of all this the Indians were induced to establish some form of self-government and to vote on a constitution and bylaws. Only twenty-four percent voted on June 20, 1936, whereas at least a vote of thirty percent of the adult population was necessary to adopt a constitution as required by Congress. A field agent was employed by the Bureau, yet strong opposition continued to have a tribal council transact the business of all the tribes. The Moses and Nez Perce tribes were on the side of the opposition. Voting for the revised constitution was on February 26, 1938,

[31] L. C. Wapato and others, to Collier, April 1, 1935, Mss.

[32] Cleveland Kamiakin, Willie Andrews Red Starr, Charlie Simpson, to Collier, April 5 and 6, 1935, Mss.

[33] Collier to Louie Timentwa and Cleveland Kamiakin, April 30, 1935, Ms. carbon.

[34] See: Wheeler-Howard Act, *Public Law 383, Seventy-Third Congress*, S. 3645, 19 sections.

authorized and dominated by the Bureau. Now more than thirty percent of the eligible voters participated; five-hundred three voted for and seventy-six voted against. So far, five amendments to the constitution have been made by the tribes and have been approved by the Commissioner.

Under the new constitution the tribes lost their identity and were now named by the government: the Colville Confederated Tribes; yet, they never have been confederated. From now on the Colvilles were governed by a business council of fourteen members elected from the four districts. These council members must have lived in their district for one year. This excludes all who are not living within the reservation boundaries; however, these may participate in the elections by absentee ballots. The council is so arranged that some of its members are completing their two-year terms every year. To be an enrolled member of the tribes the degree of Indian blood may not be below one-fourth degree, as voted on by the Indian people. This was approved by Commissioner John R. Nichols, but not the other measure the Indian people wanted, that of reservation-wide voting.

The Colville Indians through the years have been subject, like other tribes, to the changing and experimental policies of the Department of the Interior and its Indian Bureau. After the war years the problems on our home fronts received better attention; one of the greatest was the Indian problem. The Indian Reorganization Act had delayed for a time the earlier work of Congress toward more freedom for its Indian wards. Since about 1950, the policy has been to equip the Indians to earn their livelihood side by side with other Americans. The Eighty-Third Congress initiated the historic policy of terminating several Indian tribes that had been neglected and were not prepared. Strong protest arose from Indians all over the country. They wanted to initiate their own legislation if they felt they were ready for the last step — that of complete freedom. But this action of Congress gave the impetus to work during this transition period toward termination generally.

A positive, far-reaching program was initiated by Congress for the Indians, especially in the fields of health and education. Since July 1, 1955, all medical work and Indian health problems were placed under the Public Health Service of the United States.[35] To relinquish this aspect of Indian care the Bureau had been under pressure of public opinion for quite some time. Greater sums were appropriated by Congress, and marked improvements in Indian health care resulted.

Great advances have been made during the past twenty years by the Bureau of Indian Affairs in the education of the Indian people. Mis-

---

[35] Acts of April 3, 1952 (66 *Stat.* 935).

sionaries had been the first educators of the Indians as we have seen. The Johnson-O'Malley Act of April 16, 1934, authorized state-federal co-operation, whereby the state receives certain sums for the education of Indian children in public schools, due to the tax-exempt status of Indian lands.[36] Since 1935, the State of Washington has such a contract. Great emphasis is placed on having the Indian students complete their high school education. Promising scholars are encouraged and helped to seek admission in one of the federal Indian boarding schools on the basis of ability and need. However, the number of students that can be admitted from the various tribes is limited. There exists a need on the Colville Reservation for help to students from broken homes. Many of these young people have only average mentality; their cultural background is poor. Many of the low I.Q.'s could be raised by placing these young people in better environments. How can these boys and girls from underprivileged homes compete for job opportunities in our complex, diploma-conscious society?

The Colville Confederated Tribes have been concerned about the educational opportunities of their younger members; the *Minutes* of the 1942 Tribal Council meetings show discussions about loans given for education. These loans became outright grants during the following six years. Recently, college scholarships were given annually. Four of them were four-year, $2,600 grants and two were $1,500 scholarships. Scholarships for the school year 1965–1966 amounted to $28,200; now six four-year, three three-year, and four two-year scholarships are granted. Of the fifteen grants, thirteen were major grants of more than $1,000. The tribe also awards ten $200 scholarships to high school graduates for vocational training and a number of grants to worthy college students. The basis for this program is need, scholastic achievement, and character. A more recent adult vocational training is made possible by ten special $200 scholarships from tribal funds.

The tribal funds are supplemented by federal grants and loans. The education specialist of the Colville Indian Agency at Coulee Dam, Washington, takes great pains in order to interview students, help and advise them toward their future goals. Booklets are available to students telling about grants from various organizations and individuals and where to apply for help and how to budget their financial resources. Colville tribal members are attending colleges and universities all over the country. The following statistics show the increase during the past years only. Besides these there are college graduates among the older members of the tribes. To say that the Colville Confederated Tribes lack enough education to run their own

---

[36] Johnson-O'Malley Act (*48 Stat.* 596).

business and to be terminated is an effrontery. The tribes took care of their own affairs before the white man came. St. Mary's Mission today serves mostly children from underprivileged homes. The observations of Mission authorities cannot be taken to apply to the tribes as a whole. Only one-fourth of the about 4800 members are living on the Reservation, one-fourth have their homes nearby, and the rest are scattered in thirty-five states.

EDUCATIONAL STATISTICAL INFORMATION

	1960–1	1961–2	1962–3	1963–4	1964–5
College Students	5	11	30	39	69
Federal Boarding School Vocational Students	7	11	25	30	17
Federal Boarding School High School Students	1	4	20	41	33

	Year	Number		Year	Number
High School Graduates	1964	53	Elementary 1964–65		1055
Anticipated High School Graduates	1965	70	students		
			Secondary 1964–65		395

College Seniors (academic) 1964–5   9

Colville Tribal Scholarships 1964–5 $29,600   30% of College students are from
and Grants   off The Reservation 1964–65
                                                                school year.
Spokane Tribal Scholarships 1964–5   5,000
and Grants

Federal Educational Grants 1964–5   16,000

High School Diplomas earned through Adult Educational   40
Program

Certificates earned by adults from General Educational
Development Tests through adult Educational Program   51

[37]

The efforts of Congress toward granting the Indians complete citizenship rights have resulted in the repeal of some discriminatory laws against the Indians. During two wars the Indian veterans laid down their lives for the country, yet if they wanted to shoot a deer for meat, they could not have a rifle. In 1953, an old law prohibiting the selling of firearms to Indians was repealed.[38] In the same year the Indian Liquor Law was

---

[37] Courtesy of Elmer Anderson, Education Specialist, Colville Indian Agency, Coulee Dam, Washington.
[38] 67 Stat. 590.

declared repealed if it was in conformity with the state laws.[39] The Colville Tribal Council adopted an ordinance permitting the sale of liquor on the Reservation by a vote of twelve for and zero against on October 9, 1953.[40] However, the freedom to drink intoxicants is partly abused. Intoxication has become a certain escape mechanism from the miserable realities of life the underprivileged and jobless have in living on the Reservation. We believe the same observation applies to our city slums.

Under Public Law 772, enacted by Congress on July 24, 1956, about 818,000 acres of ceded tribal lands not disposed of were restored to tribal ownership. Most of the tribal members favored restoration, but many were against the payment of $40,000 to the Okanogan and Ferry Counties in lieu of taxes for this land. They contend that they had to pay for their own lands. The same act of Congress in accordance with the Resolution of April 8, 1955, under Section 5 provided that "the Colville Business Council, submit to the Secretary of the Interior within five years of enactment of this Act proposed legislation providing for the termination of Federal supervision . . ."[41] Accordingly the Department of the Interior caused a number of surveys to be made in order to provide the tribes and its tribal council with the needed information on the varied Reservation potentials. These surveys were published under the following titles: "Soil and Grazing Resources Inventory of the Colville Indian Reservation"; "Forest Resources Inventory of the Colville Reservation"; "Human Resources Survey of the Colville Confederated Tribes," all in 1959. Adjudication of some 11,066 mining claims was started; by June 27, 1961, 10,920 claims had been disposed of; others were still pending. By June 30, 1961, approximately $600,000 had been expended for these surveys, we suppose from tribal money.[42]

The business council then wanted to have an economic analysis that would relate to the following termination plans:

(a) Continue the reservation resources as a group endeavor without development;
(b) Undertake a program to develop the reservation resources; and
(c) Liquidate all assets and distribute the pro rata shares to all members.

The Stanford Research Institute of Menlo Park, California, was given a

---

[39] Public Law 277, *Eighty-Third Congress.*

[40] Courtesy of Stanley T. Poch, Colville Indian Agency, Coulee Dam.

[41] Act of July 24, 1956 (*70 Stat.* 626).

[42] John A. Carver, Assistant Secretary of the Interior, to Hon. Henry M. Jackson, Chairman, Committee on Interior and Insular Affairs, U. S. Senate, May 29, 1963, quoted in "Hearings Before the Subcommittee on Indian Affairs of the Committee on Interior and Insular Affairs," *United States Senate, Eighty-Eighth Congress, First Session,* on S. 1442 and S. 1169, 4–6.

$30,000 contract for this analysis. Some of the most important conclusions, which seem to point to termination and to individualizing the assets of the reservation, were: that the tribes have an insufficient number of trained and experienced managers and supervisors for the development and for managing the assets of the reservation as a whole; that heavy taxes might become a burden unless special provision for tax relief were developed; and that financing a development program would depend on how many members wished to liquidate. Borrowing capacity is $20 million; if more than twenty-five percent of the members wanted to liquidate, the tribes might be obliged to sell some of their assets to pay off these people. The Institute's statistics showing the estimated income from various conditions revealed that the per capita gain is the highest if, after liquidation, the capital is invested.[43]

To form a tribal corporation a board of directors would be needed. The Bureau of Indian Affairs has in its one hundred years of tutelage hampered the initiative of the Indian leaders; every important decision needed the authorization of the Bureau.

After studying the Stanford analysis, interested Indian people went to work and drafted proposed legislation toward termination. The first termination bill was introduced by the Colville Indian Association in 1962. This H.R. 6801 died in committee. The Tribal Business Council introduced S. 1442 and its companion bill H.R. 8469 during the Eighty-Seventh Congress, but no action was taken. It was reintroduced during the Eighty-Eighth Congress, read twice and died also in committee. The Colville Indian Association opposed this two-stage bill; one of the members made the statement before the Senate subcommittee, that the government had tried to educate the Indians for one hundred fifty years. The association did not think that the Indians needed two stages. The Petitioners Party of the Colville Confederated Tribes wanted the reservation preserved as a reservation and formally included in the President's conservation of national resources program.

After this meeting and hearing on the bill, some members of the Colville Indian Association split away and founded the Liquidators in order to work more speedily for termination. Some of their members were elected into the Tribal Council; now there was a majority working for the same aims. A new legislative bill was drafted, introduced into Congress as S. 1413, and hearings were held April 5 and 6, 1965, in Washington, D. C. Mention was made in this bill that tribal members who do not want to leave the Reservation, could continue under federal trustee-

---

[43] *An Analysis of Economic Development Possibilities of the Colville Indian Reservation,* 7–23.

ship. Also, it was suggested that Congress take over the greatest assets of the tribes, the forests, and add them to the Colville National Forest. The Colville Indian Association agreed with certain parts, but wanted definite amendments. The entire tribal land should be terminated. Fear was expressed that those who would stay under federal supervision might be considered not competent. All of the Indians should have the right to buy the lands they wanted and stay where they wished to be. Minors and incompetents should have bonded guardians, and their shares should be placed in savings instead of a trust. The forests which comprise ninety percent of the tribal assets should be divided into units and sold to the highest bidder. The Colville Indian Association's bill was introduced on January 16, 1965, and the first hearing on the bill took place on June 18, 1965. The Petitioners Party renewed their former statements.[44] Their fear of losing the valuable forests is understandable: history shows how the Indians were cheated.

This difference of opinion of the members of the Colville Confederated Tribes is an indication of their real democratic spirit with free speech and personal thinking. Step by step they had to fight for their rights.

How did the Indian Bureau and its Commissioner respond to the proposed termination legislation of the Colville Confederated Tribes? The Joint Legislative Committee of the Business Council sent the following opinion poll to every member eligible to vote:

> The Bureau of Indian Affairs has reported to Congress a proposed plan for economic development of the entire Colville Reservation under continued federal trusteeship. The plan calls for borrowing about $14,000,000 (fourteen million Dollars) by mortgaging reservation assets. That money would be used to build and operate tribal mills for processing of all reservation timber in the hope of increasing employment and per capita payments to tribal members. Future enrollment with Confederated Tribes of the Colville Reservation would be closed.
> What is your opinion of the above proposal of the Bureau of Indian Affairs?[45]

The answer by secret ballot was 93.15 percent against it.

There are about sixteen mills operating in areas surrounding the Reservation; this would make the building of additional mills on the Reservation unnecessary. It would destroy the economy of several counties. Why was such a program not initiated about fifty years ago? And why has the

---

[44] See: "Hearings Before the Subcommittee on Indian Affairs of the Committee on Interior and Insular Affairs," *United States Senate, Eighty-Ninth Congress, First Session,* on S. 11413.

[45] Opinion poll, Joint Legislative Committee Colville Business Council, Colville Confederated Tribes, Ms.

entire Reservation to be mortgaged for more than half of the borrowing capacity? Where is the money of the Colville Confederated Tribes that is supposed to be held in trust by the United States government? What about the sales of the ceded lands to interested people and what about the big lumber sales of years gone by?

Let us hope that the integrity of our lawmakers will prevail and that legislation soon may be enacted that would be beneficial to all concerned. The Colville tribes have made substantial advances during recent years. The Tribal Council assists in all worthwhile projects. A youth camp is available near Twin Lakes, Inchelium, to give our Indian youth educational and recreational opportunities free of charge. Important sanitation projects are undertaken, loans are given. Law and order enforcement has been transferred already by the Tribal Council to the State of Washington authorities, fishing and hunting excluded. Also the Bureau of Indian Affairs has a social worker employed for various services. Advances have been made by the County Extension Agents in training courses for leaders in all branches of Reservation economy.

What is needed is complete freedom to exercise citizenship; it will result in increased initiative of tribal members to work for betterment of their economic and educational status. This freedom should not be denied in view of some who might end up one day to be the charges of public welfare.

And now, one more important question: what is that territory that once was the aboriginal home of the Colville Confederated Tribes like now? To say the least, it has become a sportman's paradise and a great tourist attraction. There is the beautiful Colville Valley; historic Chewelah with its great Magnesite Company; Colville, that keeps the name of historic Fort Colville alive; St. Francis Regis Mission in the Colville Valley; Our Lady of the Valley Convent, once the earliest educational center of the region; Old St. Paul's Mission, now one of Washington's historic monuments, and the city of Kettle Falls with its recreational facilities near Roosevelt Lake. Traveling up and down the Columbia River we see the fertile aboriginal lands of the Colville and Lake tribes.

A state highway leads over the mountains from Kettle Falls over Sherman Creek to Republic, famous for its Knob Hill gold mine; from here we could take roads in all directions through scenic mountains and valleys. The Okanogan Valley, the home of several bands of Indians, is famous for its dry and sunny climate. Lumber, mining, and cattle industries keep the economy going. All along the valley from Wenatchee to far up into Canada are apple and soft-fruit orchards, that provide seasonal work for many people.

Tourists come to see the Wenatchee Apple Blossom Festival, the scenic Lake Chelan region, the building of Wells Dam, Chief Joseph Dam near Bridgeport, and the historic Fort Okanogan Museum near Brewster. It is very worthwhile to visit the Okanogan Fair, the annual Omak Stampede, the Biles and Coleman Lumber Mill and their extensive tree farms. Here we find also Omak's earliest historic place, St. Mary's Mission; nearby we could take a swim or have a boat ride in the medicinal waters of Omak Lake. All up the valley are mountain lakes and streams stocked with fish. Tonasket invites the travelers to its city park for a picnic and nearby Whitefish Lake and Conconully State Park have much to offer in recreational facilities. To visit Oroville and then have a ride along Lake Osoyous and all along Lake Okanogan, to see the striving communities in Canada, once the territory of the mighty Okanogan tribe, will be rewarding.

Others might want to attend the week-long July celebrations in Nespelem and see the old Indian costumes and teepes. Nearby famous Coulee Dam is lighted up in brilliant colors during evening darkness. On a guided tour inside the dam anyone would be amazed at the immensity of this wonder of modern technical engineering.

All these lands the Indians have given away; we have seen how this was done and what they received for it. The Black Robes still try to help these tribes on the last frontier. Civilization is moving on. What could the white man do to help the Indians attain their rights and their complete integration into modern society?

Conclusion

WE HAVE attempted to trace the history of the planting of Christian civilization and culture in an important part of our Pacific Northwest. From all the influences exerted by the various groups of white men who came into contact with the aboriginal population, the Indians, the most conspicuous and most unselfish ones were the missionaries representing the Catholic Church. The fur traders, the miners, the cattlemen, the sheepmasters, the settlers, and farmers, all these came for the sake of material gain.

The unsung heroes who made the problems of the Indians their very own and tried to Christianize and elevate the natives were the Jesuit Missionaries. They had left the countries of their birth with the expressed purpose of serving the Indians in the far Northwest. The preceding pages have shown the heroism practiced in daily courageous self-sacrifice and saintliness; the superhuman fortitude and fearlessness in the face of seemingly insurmountable obstacles, day by day, year after year; the utter self-forgetfulness of their former education and station in life.

While all the missionaries mentioned in this history have contributed their share in the development of Christian culture in our Northwest, the one whose contribution is especially striking is Father de Rougé. His brother, in resketching the early life of Father Etienne de Rougé, reminds us of the high station in life that the future missionary was born into. He names the persons of rank and nobility present at Etienne's baptism. "He was held over the baptismal font by Herve de Rougé, Marquis of Plessis-Belliere, first cousin of his father, and by Victoria de Bagneux, Countess of Chanieres, his mother's mother."[1] Two of Father de Rougé's brothers and a sister were married to persons of the old French nobility, while one of his sisters became a Benedictine nun of Solesmes. Vicomte Olivier de Rougé also mentioned examples of saintliness and virtue among the nearest relatives of Father de Rougé. His father's sister was a pious religious; his grandfather's brother was a Jesuit who closed his life with a holy death in Rome; his grandfather's sister was the pious Erminia, a companion of St. Sophie Madeleine Barat; his great-grandmother, the Countess de Rougé, nee de Lignerare-Caylus, led a very ascetical life. We are further told how the boy Etienne built himself a hermitage in

[1] Olivier de Rougé, to Father Van de Walle, May 4, 1923, *Mes Souvenirs de l'enfance et de la jeunesse du Père Etienne de Rougé, missionnaire,* Mss. OPA.

the forest behind the chateau of his parents. He wanted to become a missionary and a priest, and this secret place became a refuge for the missionary where he could be alone to meditate. The young Etienne was a prey to continual headaches, but his "sweetness never altered, sweetness painfully acquired by effort, for there was in his character that same violence that carried him towards God."[2]

The young Count de Rougé was a novice of the Jesuit Novitiate at Angers in France when the persecution of religious broke out. The mansion of his parents served as a refuge for the Jesuits for three weeks until new quarters at Aberdovey, Wales, were ready for them. Soon came the departure from Wales to America, where he remained for nine years, returning to make his tertianship in Slough, Buckinghamshire, England. This was followed by a visit home. As his brother wrote, this was the last time he saw France. He then "definitely returned to the missions, and consummated the last sacrifice by a last adieu to the home of his ancestors, to his family, to France; he followed his vocation to go and rest in God."[3] This disproves the statement that "Father de Rougé returned several times to France in order to collect money." We have seen that he was not the "millionaire" some people would like to make him. All had to be acquired bit by bit for his many building projects, and it required great heroism to stick to his plans until they were completed.

Heroism in its truest sense also was practiced by the cheated Indians during long years of patient suffering. Inhumanity has played its part in our "Great Northwest." Complete justice is still wanting. The aboriginal owners of the Colville and Okanogan Valleys heroically kept the peace with their white brothers in spite of encroachments upon their God-given rights. What would have happened without the influence of the men who fought and won the "battles" on the home front, the missionaries?

Father de Rougé's early death was a blow for higher education of the Indians. What he had built up with so much sacrifice was discontinued the very next year. Surveys show quite a gap in higher education years after his death; there was nothing to replace it. Okanogan's first educator also had established schools for the incoming white population, the children of the pioneer settlers. He accepted in his schools students of every race and religious denomination; he was ahead of his time in this respect. How different the history of St. Mary's Mission and also that of the surrounding country and the Colville Reservation might have been if Father de Rougé had remained alive and active until the time of the opening of the Reservation for settlement.

---

[2] Oliver de Rougé to Van de Walle.
[3] Ibid.

The priestly pioneer educator and missionary is still gratefully remembered by Indians and whites in a large part of the State of Washington and British Columbia. Mention of his name suffices to enkindle a certain gleam in the eyes of people of various denominations. They recall the heroism of this priest in caring for the human needs of body and soul; they remember and appreciate the cultural values they received at Father's Mission; they also treasure the supernatural outlook on life which he implanted in all who came in contact with him by his words and by his deeds.

May this history be a token of gratitude to all who planted faith and goodness in our great State of Washington; may it also be a memorial to the members of the Colville Confederated Tribes, its present Chairman Narcisse Nicholson, Jr., and the members of the Business Council, who unanimously voted a loan that the big history could be printed. May these good Indian people, their children and children's children never forget their ancient heritage as well as the values they received from the mission centers.

Bibliography

I. PRIMARY SOURCES

A. Archival Material

Anonymous, *Notes* on Father Grassi, S.J., Mss., OPA.

Balfe, Rev, Joseph, S.J., to Mr. Albert Orr, Chairman Tribal Council, November 5, 1938, Ms. carbon copy.

Blanchet, Most Rev. A. M. A., *Report on Confirmations at the Colville Mission, 1879,* Ms., AAS.

Burke, Chas. H., Commissioner of Indian Affairs, to the Secretary of the Interior, April 7, 1924. (Request for patent in fee to the Pioneer Educational Society.) 1946-816.2, Record Group 75, NA.

———— to the Secretary of the Interior, June 28, 1924. (Permit to erect a boat-house on "lake Omache.") NA.

———— and others, correspondence with Father Celestine Caldi, S.J., May 10, 19, 20, 1924; June 18, 28, 1924; July 19, 1924, Mss., SM.

Burgumer, Rev. J. A., S.V.D., Techny, Illinois, to Most Rev. P. F. Schinner, Bishop of Spokane, December 24, 1917, Ms., ADS.

Caldi, Rev. Celestine, S.J., *Caldi Papers,* Mss., OPA.

———— to Most Rev. P. F. Schinner, *Correspondence, 1916–1925,* Mss., ADS.

———— to Most Rev. Charles D. White, Bishop of Spokane, *Correspondence, 1928–1936,* Mss., ADS.

———— to Honorable Miles Poindexter, United States Senator, Washington, D. C., December 15, 1917, 19461-10-816.2, NA.

———— to Rev. Mother Mary Bonaventura, O.P., Provincial of the Poor School-sisters of St. Dominic, Kettle Falls, Wash., September 19, 1934, Ms., ADSK.

———— *Attendance Records of St. Mary's Mission School,* Omak, Wash.

———— *Letters and Attendance Records* to Mother M. Katherine, 1916–1936, Mss., ABSS.

———— *Annual Reports* to Most Rev. Schinner, September 1, 1919; May 27, 1920, Mss., ADS.

———— *Historia Domus Missionis Sanctae Mariae apud Okanogan,* [1919], 1922–1923, Mss., OPA.

———— *Correspondence* with Superintendent O. D. Upchurch, Colville Indian Agency, 1921–1922, Mss., OPA.

———— *Annual Report of 1927,* Ms., OPA.

———— to His Eminence Cardinal Mundelein, President of the American Board of Catholic Missions, October 13, 1930, Ms., ADS.

———— *Estimate Cost of Material on Gymnasium,* Ms., OPA.

———— to Chemawa Indian School, Oregon, October 13, 1933, Ms. copy, OPA.

———— to Mother Mary Mercedes, Cornwells Heights, Pa., March 19, 1935, Ms. copy, OPA.

Cataldo, Rev. Joseph M., "Nes Perce History," *The Cataldo Papers,* Mss., OPA.

Colville Confederated Tribes Business Council, *Minutes of Special Session, August 12–13, 1958,* Ms. copy.

Condon, Rt. Rev. W. J., to Rev. C. Caldi, S.J., February 26, 1928, Ms., OPA.

Coulbaugh, Mrs. Wilhelmine F., *Correspondence* with Rev. Etienne de Rougé, S.J., 1915–1916; with Rev. Celestine Caldi, S.J., 1916–1933, Mss., OPA, SM.

Cunningham, Madame, to Most Rev. Schinner, August 25, 1915, Ms., ADS.

D'Aste, Rev. Jerome, S.J., *Diary*, Mss., OPA.

De Poe, Executive Secretary, Colville Tribal Committee, *Report of Visit to St. Mary's Mission, Omak, Wash., April 30*, [*1954*], Ms., SM.

——— *Contributions of Colville Confederated Tribes to St. Mary's Mission, Omak, Wash.*

De Smet, Rev. Pierre, S.J., to J. N. Nicolet, Washington, D. C., April 21, 1840. Autographed Ms., Archives Northwest Room, Main Public Library, Spokane, Wash.

Dillon, Very Rev. F. C., S.J., *Annual Report for 1898, St. Francis Regis Mission,* Ms., ADS.

Diocese of Spokane, *Book of Dedications*, Mss., ADS.

Drexel, Rev. Mother Mary Katherine, *Correspondence* with Rev. Etienne de Rougé, S.J., 1905–1916; with Rev. Celestine Caldi, S.J., 1916–1936, Mss., OPA. (Very incomplete.)

——— to Most Rev. Edward John O'Dea, D.D., Bishop of Nisqually, Wash., February 1, 1901, Ms., ADS.

——— *Correspondence* with Most Rev. Charles D. White, Bishop of Spokane, 1935–1936, Mss., ADS.

Dumbeck, Rev. Ignatius, S.J., to Most Rev. White, October 5, 1936, Ms., ADS.

Favel, Francis, Secretary of Father de Rougé, to Mother M. Katherine Drexel, October 11, 1909, Ms., ABSS.

Fletcher, Rev. A., S.J., to Rev. Mother Provincial M. Bonaventura, O.P., Kettle Falls, Wash., January 31, 1942, Ms., ADSK.

Fitzgerald, Rev. M. J., S.J., to Most Rev. White, January 4, 1937, Ms., ADS.

——— to Rev. Mother M. Katherine, July 6, 1935, Ms., ABSS.

Gilbertson, L. C., Personal Trust Officer, The First National Bank, Chicago, Ill., to St. Mary's Mission, Omak, Wash., May 2, 1935, Trust No. 17841, Ms., SM.

Girls of St. Mary's Mission, Omak, Wash., to Mother M. Katherine, December 16, 1923, Mss., ABSS.

Gleeson, Very Rev., A. S., S.J., to Mother M. Katherine, December 3, 1914; November 25, 1915, Mss, ABSS.

Gottrell, William V., to Rev. Paul Corkery, St. Mary's Mission, Omak, Wash., May 20, 1958, Ms., SM.

Grassi, Rev. Urban, S.J., to Rev. Joseph Giorda, S.J., November 10, 1874, Ms., OPA.

——— to Father Superior, June 29, 1876, Ms., OPA.

——— to Rev. Joseph M. Cataldo, S.J., April 23, 1878; April 19, 1881, Mss., OPA.

Griva, Rev. Edward M., S.J., *Building Account*, Ms., SM.

——— *Fifty Years of My Missionary Life Among Indians and Whites From July 1894 Till the End of September 1944*, Mss., OPA.

Groh, Rev. Mother Mary Bonaventura, O.P., to the Ladies Catechists Missionaries of St. Mary's Mission, Omak, Wash., May 12, 1936, Ms., ADSK.

——— *Correspondence* with Most Rev. Charles D. White, September 8, 1936; November 28, 1936, Mss., ADS. Also: Ms. copies, ADSK.

Gwydir, Rickard D., U. S. Indian Agent, Colville Agency, to Hon. J. D. C. Atkins, Commissioner of Indian Affairs, Washington, D. C., November 24, 1887. Record Group 75, 19461/10-816.2, NA, 473.

Hielborn, Bent E., Secretary of Senator Poindexter, to Father de Rougé, S.J., April 23, 1912, Ms., OPA.

Hughes, Rt. Rev. Msgr. William, Director of Bureau of Catholic Indian Missions, Washington, D. C., December 31, 1927, to Most Rev. Charles D. White, Ms., ADS.

——— *Correspondence* with Rev. C. Caldi, S.J., 1925–1928, Mss, ADS.

———— to the Boys of St. Mary's Mission, Omak, Wash., January 26, 1925, Ms., OPA.

Hunt, Clair, Special Allotting Agent, to the Commissioner of Indian Affairs, April 30, 1912. Church lands, St. Mary's Mission, NA.

———— April 30, 1912. Allotments of Indians along Omak Creek-Powersite withdrawals. Portions of 9834-1910 Colville, Record Group 75, NA.

———— to Hon, E. J. Cannon, Spokane, March 9, 1915, Ms., OPA.

Johnson, J. M., Superintendent, Colville Agency, to the Commissioner of Indian Affairs, Washington, D.C., September 25, 1912, 19461/10-816.2. Record Group 75, NA.

———— to Rev. E. de Rougé, S.J., St. Mary's Mission, February 26, April 23, 1912, Mss., OPA.

Joset, Rev. Joseph, S.J., The Joset Papers, Mss., OPA.

Ketcham, Rt. Rev. William H., Director of the Bureau of Catholic Indian Missions, Washington, D. C., to the Commissioner of Indian Affairs, September 28, 1906, Records of Bureau of Indian Affairs, Classified Files, Portions of 19451/10-816.2, Record Group 75, NA.

———— to Father de Rougé, S.J., February, 1914, Ms., ADS.

La Motte, Rev. George De, S.J., Diary, Mss., OPA.

———— Letters to Mother M. Katherine Drexel, January 31, 1905; May 17, 1905; June 9, 1905, Mss., ABSS.

Lane, Franklin K., Secretary of the Interior, to Henry K. Ashburn, Chairman, Committee on Indian Affairs, February 6, 1918, 19461/10-816.2, NA.

Larrabee, C. F., Acting Commissioner, Office of Indian Affairs, to Rt. Rev. William H. Ketcham, Director of the Bureau of Catholic Indian Missions, Washington, D. C., November 2, 1918, 19461/10-816.2, NA.

Ledovina, Rev. C. B., Vice-President and General Secretary of the Catholic Church Extension Society, to Rev. S. M. Filippi, S.J., St. Mary's Mission, Omak, Wash., June 8, 1916, Ms. copy, ADS.

———— to Most Rev. P. F. Schinner, Bishop of Spokane, June 17, July 20, 1916, Mss., ADS.

Luce, Madam, Telegram to Bishop Schinner, May 9, 1916, ADS.

Luyton, Rev. Joseph, Financial Statement for 1906, Ms., ADS.

McHugh, Paul, and Chief Smitakan, Agreement, November 26, 1909, Ms., OPA.

Merit, E. B., Assistant Commissioner of Indian Affairs, to the Secretary of the Interior, April 11, 1924, 19461/10-816.2.

Meyer, Harvey K., Superintendent of Colville Agency, to Rev. Celestine Caldi, S.J., March 19, 1927; July 12, 1929, Mss., OPA.

Moses Se-qua-tal-coo-sum, Head Chief of the Isle de Pierre Indians, Speech at the Council at the mouth of the Okanogan River, June 30, 1870. Washington Superintendency Letters Received, 1861–1874, RBIA, NA.

Novits, S. G., to Rev Etienne de Rougé, S.J., February 26, 1914, Ms., ADS.

O'Dea, Most Rev. E. J., Bishop of Seattle, to John J. McCauley, November 29, 1910, Ms., ADS.

———— Correspondence with Rev. E. de Rougé, S.J., 1897–1914, Ms. copies, ADS.

———— to Brother Bruno, Brothers of Our Lady of Lourdes, Seattle, December 23, 1910, Ms., ADS.

O'Sullivan, James M., S.J., The O'Sullivan Papers, "Extracts from the Roman Archives on the Missionary Labors of Father Nobili, S.J.," Mss., OPA.

Parodi, Aloysius, S.J., Reminiscences, Ms., OPA.

———— Memoirs, Mss., OPA.

Placidus, Abbot, O.S.B., St. Benedict's Abbey, St. Benedict, Oregon, Correspondence with Most Rev. Schinner, 1916–1918, Mss., ADS.

Pok-pok-o-Kine, Chief of the Sanpoil, *Speech:* Sanpoile River, W.T., June 26, 1870, *Letters Received, 1861–1874,* RBIA.

Quatal-i-Kim, Head Chief of the Sanpoils and Nespelems, *Speech:* Sanpoile River, W.T., June 26, 1870, *Letters Received, 1861–1874,* RBIA.

Riedmiller, Sister Rose Francis, O.P., *Letter* to Mrs. Monda, Wenatchee, Wash., September, 1944, Ms.

Robinson, Rev. Leo J., S.J., to Rev. Mother Provincial, Dominican Sisters, Kettle Falls, October 6, 1944, Ms., ADSK.

Rougé, Rev. Etienne de, S.J., *Correspondence* with Mother M. Katherine Drexel, Cornwells Heights, Pa., 1905–1916, Mss., ABSS.

—— *Original Map of Mission Territory,* OPA.

—— *Water Claims,* 1905, Ms., SM. Also: Department of Conservation and Development, Olympia, Wash.

—— *Annual Reports* to Most Rev. O'Dea, 1896–1910, Mss., ADS.

—— *Correspondence* with Most Rev. O'Dea, 1907–1914, Mss., ADS.

—— *Correspondence* with Most Rev. A. F. Schinner, Bishop of Spokane, 1914–1916, Ms. copies, ADS.

—— to Rev. Joseph M. Cataldo, S.J., March 21, 1886; March 20 [1883], Mss., OPA.

—— *St. Mary's Mission.* (A description of the mission in 1890.) Ms., OPA.

—— *Historia Domus* [1909]; [1913], Mss., OPA.

—— to Sister M. Mercedes, Cornwells Heights, Pa., Sept. 27, 1906, Ms., ABSS.

—— *Formula of Vows for Ladies Catechists Missionaries of St. Mary's,* Ms., OPA.

—— *Brief Statement of the Organization of the Ladies Catechists Missionaries of St. Mary's Mission,* Mss., ADS.

—— to Mother M. James, Cornwells Heights, Pa., 1908, 1909, 1912, Mss., ABSS.

—— to Mrs. Wilhelmine F. Coulbaugh, St. Petersburg, Florida, December 22 [1915], Ms., OPA.

—— to James Monaghan, Spokane, Wash., October 13, 1913, Ms., OPA.

—— to Very Rev. E. R. Dyer, S.S., D.D., March 12, 1915, Ms. copy, ADS; March 12, 1914, Ms., ADS.

—— to Bureau of Catholic Indian Missions, Washington, D. C., December 15, 1900, Ms., ADS.

—— *St. Mary's Mission 25 Years Ago and Today,* mimeographed copy, ABSS.

—— to Honorable Commissioner of Indian Affairs, Washington, D. C., January 27, 1910, 19461/10-816.2, Record Group 75, NA.

—— to J. M. Johnson, Colville Indian Agency, Miles, Wash., April 4, 1910, 19461/10-816.2, Record Group 75, NA.

—— to Miss Luce, April 21, May 28, July 4, 1911, Mss., OPA.

Rougé, Vicomte Oliver de, *Mes Souvenirs de l'enfance et de la jeunesse du Père Etienne de Rougé, missionnaire,* May 4, 1923, to Father Vandewalle [Van de Walle], Mss., OPA.

Schinner, Most Rev. A. F., Bishop of Spokane, *Correspondence* concerning St. Mary's Mission, Omak, Wash., with the Rev. E. B. Ledovina, Vice-President of the Catholic Church Extension Society, 1910–1915, Ms. copies, ADS.

—— *Correspondence* with Rev. E. de Rougé, S.J., 1914–1916, Ms. copies, ADS.

—— to Abbot Placidus, St. Benedict's Abbey, St. Benedict, Oregon, January 25, 1918, Ms. copy, ADS.

Sells, Cato, Commissioner of Indian Affairs, Washington, D. C., to Hon. Miles Poindexter, United States Senator, January 24, 1918, 19461/10–816.2, Record Group 75, NA.

Stalter, Mother M. Arsenia, O.P., to Very Rev. Leo Robinson, S.J., Provincial, July 14, 1947, Ms. copy, ADSK.

Stevens, Isaac I., to Father J. Joset, S.J., November 28, 1855, Ms., OPA.

Streamer, Frank Marion, *The Streamer Papers*, Mss., AWHS.

St. Francis Regis Mission, Ward, Wash., *Rapports des Missionnaires, depui 1870 jusqua 1876 inclusivement*, Ms., AAS.

———— *Liber Baptizatorum in Missione S. Francis Regis, Colville (St. Paul's)*, Book III, 1867–1887, OPA.

———— *Historia Domus, Residentia et scholae S. Francisci Regis a Julio 1907 ad Julium 1910*, Mss., OPA.

———— *Litterae annuae a die Julii 1914 ad diem 1, Julii, 1915*, Ms., OPA.

———— *Ad litteras annuas pro annois scholasticis 1895–1896; 1896–1897; 1897–1898*, Mss., OPA.

———— *School Reports*, Mss., OPA.

———— *Diary of St. Francis Regis Mission, 1870–1892*, Mss., OPA.

———— *Historia Domus*, Book I: May 20, 1900–June 27, 1904; Book II: –April 10, 1908; Book III: –February 16, 1912; Book IV: –1916; Book V: –1919; Book VI: –1926; Book VII: –1932, OPA.

———— *Mission de Colville*, 1870 (Statistics), Ms., AAS.

———— *Sauvages Catholiques*, W. T., 1873, Ms., AAS.

———— *Chroniques De La Providence Du Sacre Coeur, Colville, W.T., Depuis 1re Juillet 1873 Jusqu a Juillet* [1918], Mss. Archives, St. Ignatius Province of the Providence Sisters, Spokane, Wash.

St. Mary's Mission, Omak, Wash., *House Diary*, January 1, 1944–January 25, 1950, Mss., SM.

———— *Registrum Batizatorum in Ecclesia Stae Mariae Okenakanos*, Book I, 1884–October 20, 1901; Book II, –April, 1931; Book III: –1931–.

———— *Maps of Mission Lands*, 1924, 19461/10-816.2, NA.

———— *Map of Present Mission Lands*, Okanogan County Courthouse Files, 1961.

———— *Map of Mission Lands*, n.d., SM.

St. Paul's Mission, Kettle Falls, Wash., *Church Records*, Book I: 1842–1852; Book II: –1866, OPA.

St. Onge, John, *Record of Study and Teaching*, Ms., Archives of St. Martin's Abbey, Lacey, Wash.

———— to Father Superior, St. Martin's Abbey, Lacey, Wash., January 16, 1914, Ms., Archives of St. Martin's Abbey.

Tennelly, Rt. Rev. J. B., *Correspondence* with Father Caldi, S.J., 1926–1936, Mss., OPA.

———— *Correspondence* concerning St. Mary's Mission with Most Rev. Bishop Charles D. White, Bishop of Spokane, Mss., ADS.

Tolon, John H., Representative from California to the Tribal Council, Colville Confederated Tribes, February 9, 1940, Ms. copy, tribal files.

Tomaskut, Head Chief of the Okanogans, *Speech* at Council held at Soo-yoo-oos [Osoyoos, B.C.], July 3, 1870, *Washington Superintendency Letters Received, 1861–1874*, RBIA.

Tomkin, Rev. J., S.J., Seattle, Wash., to Mother Luce, St. Mary's Mission, Omak, Wash., April 9, 1916, Ms., OPA

Tosi, Rev. P., S.J., *Recensement dans les Missions des R.R. PP. Jesuites 1877, Missions des Indians*, Ms., AAS.

Upchurch, O. P., Superintendent of Colville Agency, to Hon. Malcolm McDonald, member, Board of Indian Commissioners, Washington, D. C., September 25, 1920, Ms. copy, OPA.

———— *Correspondence* with Father C. Caldi, S.J., 1920–1924, Ms., OPA.

———— to Joanna F. Blake, St. Mary's Mission, *Note* accompanying patent in Fee No. 901698, January 13, 1923, Ms., SM.

Valentine, R. G., Commissioner of Indian Affairs, to the Hon. Secretary of the Interior, n.d. (Land Contract 24900-1899, 19461-1910, 36097–1910, Mission Land, Colville Reservation), approved June 11, 1910, Frank Pierce, First Asst. Sec., NA.

———— to Captain John McA. Webster, Superintendent Colville Indian School, Fort Spokane, Wash., June 24, 1910, 19461/10-816.2, Record Group 75, NA.

Van de Walle, Rev. J. M., to Bishop Schinner, July 12, September 15, September 20, 1915, Mss., ADS.

Webster, J. McA., Captain, United States Indian Agent, Fort Spokane, Wash., *Correspondence* with Father de Rougé, S.J., 1909–1910, Mss., OPA.

Wee-ah-pe-Kun or Kis-a-wee-likh, Subchief of the Okanogans, *Speech,* July 3, 1870. *Washington Superintendency Letters Received, 1861–1874,* RBIA.

Weibel, Rev. George, S.J., *The Weibel Papers,* Mss., OPA.

Welch, Most Rev. Thomas A., *Telegram* to Rev. C. Caldi, S.J., November 18, 1933, ADS.

White, Most Rev. Charles D., *Correspondence* concerning St. Mary's Mission and Lady Catechists with Mother M. Bonaventura, O.P., Our Lady of the Valley Convent, Kettle Falls, Wash., 1935–1936, Mss., ADSK.

———— *Correspondence* with Father C. Caldi, S.J., 1928–1935, Ms. copies, ADS; Mss., OPA.

———— to Messrs. Winston, Strawn, and Shaw, Chicago, November 25, 1933, Ms. copy, ADS.

Winston, Strawn, and Shaw, to Rt. Rev. Theodore M. Ryan, November 18, 1933, Ms., ADS.

B. Oral Interviews of Eyewitnesses

Arcasa, Mrs. Isabel, Nespelem, April 16, 1961.

Balfe, Rev. Joseph, S.J., St. Mary's Mission, Omak, Wash., August 14, 1961.

Beal, John, Loomis, Wash., July 15, 1961.

Bottomley Miss Maggie, with Mrs. K. Lacey, Oroville, Wash., March 15, 1961; with the author, July 13, 1961.

Brown, William Compton, Judge, Okanogan, Wash., October 17, and 24, 1959; January 29, 1961.

Buber, Mr. Jerry, St. Mary's Mission, August 20, 1960.

Carroll, Sister Mary Ann, O.P., Tonasket, September 14, 1960; Kettle Falls, March, 1963.

Caulfield, Mrs. Audrey, Spokane, September 20, 1961.

Cleveland, Mr. John, St. Mary's Mission, April 24, March 15, August 12, 1960.

Fancher, Mrs. Wanda, Tonasket, with Mrs. Nellie Picken, July 11, 1961.

Fatcher, Sister M. Reginalda, O.P., Spokane, June 18, 1961.

Favel, Mr. Francis, St. Mary's Mission, November 8, 1959; Spokane, June 30, 1961; July 27, 1961.

Figlenski, Mr. Edward, Tunk Valley, July 13, 1961.

Figlenski, Mr. John, St. Mary's Mission, October 16, 1960.

Foster, Sister Mary Michael, O.P., Spokane, throughout 1959–1961.

Fissler, Sister M. Consuelo, O.P., Spokane, September 4, 1960.

George, Mrs. Christine, Katar Valley, May 3, 1960.

Green, Mr. Harry, St. Mary's Mission, November 9, 1959.

Herbott, Sister M. Aristella, O.P., Tonasket, October 30, 1960.

Herbott, Sister M. Richildis, O.P., Spokane, January 3, 1961.

Heider, Rt. Rev. Abbot Raphael, O.S.B., St. Martin's Abbey, Lacey, Wash., July 31, 1962.

Hill, Mr. William F., Spokane, June 16, September 18, 1960; July 19, 20, 22, 25, 1961.

Hirst, Mr. Richard, St. Mary's Mission, January 27, 1961.

James, Chief Jim of the Sanpoel Tribe, Keller, Wash., January 28, 1961.

Jung, Mr. Joseph, St. Mary's Mission, October 16, 1960.

Lacey, Mrs. Katie, Osoyoos, B.C., January 27, 1960; July 11, 1961.

Loudon, Mr. Paul, *interview* with Mrs. Lacey, Loomis, Wash., March 15, 1961.

Louie, Mr. John, Disautel, January 31, 1961.

Lund, Mr. Arthur, Tonasket, October 10, 1960; July 9, 1961.

Marchant, Mrs. Josephine, St. Mary's Mission, May 28, 1960.

Morris, Mr. Louie, Brewster, August 23, 1960.

Morris, Mrs. Louie (Celestine Moomaw), Brewster, August 23, 1960.

Nicholson, Narcisse, Ellisforde, with Mrs. Katie Lacey, March 24, 1961, with the author, St. Mary's Mission, May 10, Sept. 12, 1960; Ellisforde, January 30, July 15, 1961.

Opel, Mrs. Florence Bernier, Seattle, June 4, 1960.

Pierre, Mr. Louie, St. Mary's Mission, April 20, 1961.

Pierre, Mrs. Mary Therese, St. Mary's Mission, April 5, 1961.

Quill, Mrs. Florence, St. Mary's Mission, May 4, 1960; East Omak, August 22, 1960.

Picken, Mr. Robert L., Tonasket, July 12, 1961.

Runnels, Mr. Lewis, Tonasket, July 14, 1961.

Smitkin, Mrs. Agnes, Monse, August 23, 1960.

St. Peter, Mrs. Maggie, Omak, May 1, 1960.

Swimpkin, Mrs. Therese, St. Mary's Mission, May 28, 1960.

Teobasket, Mrs. Suzette, Similkameen Reserve, with Mrs. Katie Lacey, March 15, 1961.

Toulou, Mrs. Helen, St. Mary's Mission, November 3, 1959; April 14, 1960.

Van Coelen, Mr. Harry A., St. Mary's Mission, May 8–11, 1960.

Walters, Mr. Joseph, St. Mary's Mission, October 16, 1960.

Waters, Mrs. Louise, St. Mary's Mission, December 15, 1959.

White, Mr. Cull, Spokane, January 7, 1960; St. Mary's Mission, January 27–29, 1961.

Zacherle, Mrs. Pauline, St. Mary's Mission, November 8, 15, 1959; also several times during 1960–1961.

C. Letters of Eyewitnesses to the Author

Arcasa, Mrs. Isabel, Nespelem, April 16, 1961.

Babcock, Mrs. Ruby, Okanogan, September 20, 1960.

Buber, Mr. Jerry, Puyallup, November 11, 1960.

Cleveland, John B., Monse, December 5, 1960; July 28, 1961.

De Vos, Mr. A., Soap Lake, Wash., November 4, 1960; December 18, 1960.

Dignan, Mrs. Edna, Brentwood Bay, B.C., November 23, 1959; April 15, October 3, 1960.

Hill, Mrs. William F., Spokane, Wash., *Questionnaire Answers* and *Letters,* February 3, 1960.

Lacey, Mrs. Katie, Osoyoos, B.C., *Correspondence,* 1961–1963.

Lund, Mr. Arthur, Tonasket, January 11, 1961.

Nelson, Mrs. H. F., Curlew, July 12, 1961.

Nicholson, Mr. Narcisse, Ellisforde, fall of 1960.

Opel-Bernier, Mrs. Florence, Seattle, April 11, 1960.

Runnels, Lewis A., Tonasket, September 27, December 10, 22, 1960; January 19, 1961.

Russel, Robert H., Assistant Supervisor of Water Resources, Olympia, June 1, 1960.

Sherman, Paschal, Ph.D., Washington, D. C., March 21, 1960, May 8, 1960,

October 15, 1960; March 4, 1963. *Letters, Questionnaire Answers, Some High-lights of Memory, Documents From the National Archives in Photostats, Hand-drawn Maps.*

Smith, Chris C., Bridgeport, *Questionnaire Answers,* September, 1961.

Tennelly, Rt. Rev. J. B., Director, Bureau of Catholic Indian Missions, Washington, D. C., December 15, 1959.

Trodden, Mr. J. P., Bellingham, August 24, 1960.

Toulou, Mrs. Helen, Kewa, *Manuscript Book on Tribal History,* 1959–1960.

Van Coelen, Harry, Portland, Ore., *Plan of the First Set of Buildings at St. Mary's Mission, Omak, Notes on Historical Facts,* May 8–11, 1960.

White, Mr. Cull, Ephrata, Wash., May 24, 1960; March 19, 1961.

D. Primary Sources: Published Material

Anonymous, "The Missions of the Rocky Mountains in 1881," *WL* (12:1, 1883), 43–56.

——— "Obituary: Father Grassi," *WL* (19:2, June, 1890), 266–270.

Balfe, Rev. Joseph, S.J., "Fire Discovered in Kitchen of St. Mary's Mission," *The Calumet* (October, 1938), n.p.

Blanchet, Most Rev. Francis Norbert, *Historical Sketches of the Catholic Church in Oregon.* Portland, Ore.: The Sentinel Press, 1878.

——— *Historical Notes and Reminiscences of Early Times in Oregon.* Portland, Ore.: The Sentinel Press, 1883.

Caldi, Rev. Celestine, S.J., "Keeping the Faith Among the Okanogans," "The First Christmas Among the Wenatchees," *The Indian Sentinel,* I (Winter, 1929–1930), 1–2.

——— "Lettera del P.C. Caldi al R.P. Provinciale, 10 Settembre 1901," *LPT,* Torino: Tipografia Ditto G. Derossi, 1902, 92–101.

——— "Indian Missionaries: Father de Rougé, S.J.," *The Indian Sentinel* (1:3, January, 1917), 37–38.

Caruana, Rev. J. M., S.J., to Father Cataldo, S.J., Superior General of the Rocky Mountain Missions, n.d., *WL* (11:3, September, 1882), 269–275.

——— to Father Cataldo, S.J., April 17, 1882, *WL* (12:1, January, 1883), 49–51.

——— *Diary,* quoted by Historicus [Rev. George Weibel, S.J.], in "Fifty Years of Peaceful Conquest," *Gonzaga Magazine* (Vol. 5, May 8, 1914), 414–418.

Colville Business Council, *Minutes of Special Session, August 12–13, 1958* (carbon copy of Ms.).

Covington, Henry, *Tape Recording on Chief Skolaskan,* by Cull White.

Cox, Ross, *Adventures on the Columbia River, Including a Residence of Six Years on the Western Side of the Rocky Mountains.* New York: J. & J. Harper, 1832.

De Smet, Rev. Pierre Jean, S.J., *Lettres Choisies,* Bruxelles: M. Clossen Et Cie. Editeurs, 26, Rue De Jonker, 1877.

——— *Letters and Sketches With a Narrative of a Year Residence Among the Indian Tribes of the Rocky Mountains.* Philadelphia: M. Fithian, 1843.

——— *Oregon Missions and Travels Over the Rocky Mountains, in 1845–46.* New York: Edward Dunigan, 1847.

——— *New Indian Sketches.* New York: D. & J. Sadlier, 1885. (Also P. J. Kenedy, 1895.)

——— *Western Missions and Missionaries: A Series of Letters.* New York: J. B. Kirker, 1863. (Also Kenedy, 1859.)

Drexel, Mother M. Katherine, "If Only Our Good Catholic People Knew," *Mission Fields at Home* (New Bulletin, 1:5, July–August, 1935), 1.

Diomedi, Rev. Alexander, S.J., "Extract From a Letter of a Rocky Mountain Jesuit Missionary," *The Indian Sentinel* (No. 7, 1906), 28–48.

———— "Sketches of Modern Indian Life," *WL* (32:2, July, 1893), 231–256; (32:3, December, 1893) 353–378; (33:1, April, 1894), 23–49.

Grassi, Urban, S.J., to Father Cataldo, S.J., October 4, 1873, "On Indian Missions, the Simpesquensi, etc.," *WL* (3:1, January, 1874), 68–73; (3:3, September, 1874), 213–214.

———— to Father Cataldo, S.J., April 23, 1878 (on Indian Missions, W.T.), *WL* (7:3, September, 1878), 174–178.

———— to Father Valente, S.J., May 26, 1874, *WL* (3:3, 1874), 214–216.

Griva, Rev. Edward M., S.J., "Lettera del P. Edoardo Griva al R.P. Provinciale, St. Francis Regis Mission, Meyers Falls, Wash., 22 July, 1903," *LPT*, Torino: Tipografia Ditto G. Derossi, 1904.

———— "Missions of the Sacred Heart at Nespelem," *WL* (48:2, June, 1919), 210–216.

Ladies Catechists Missionaries of St. Mary's Mission, *School of the Ladies Catechists of St. Mary, Mission, P.O., O'Kanagan Co., Wash.* (mimeographed copy in possession of Mrs. Frank Mechtel, Wenatchee).

Landerholm, Carl, trans. and ed., *Notices & Voyages of the Famed Quebec Mission to the Pacific Northwest. Being the Correspondence, Notices, etc. of Fathers Blanchet and Demers, together with those of Father Bolduc and Langlois.* Portland, Ore.: Champoeg Press, Inc., 1956.

Nobili, Rev. John, S.J., to Father Goetz, "Two Old Letters," *WL* (18:1, February, 1889), 77–79.

Parker, Samuel, *Journal of an Exploring Tour Beyond the Rocky Mountains, Under the Direction of the A.B.C.F.M., Performed in the Years 1835, '36, and '37.* Ithaca: N. Y.: Mak, Andrus and Woodruff, Printers, 1838.

Pypers, Rt. Rev. Theophilus, M. J., *History of St. Ann's Parish, Spokane, Washington. 1902–1941. And Stories from the Big Bend Mission, 1901–1906.* Spokane, Wash., n.d.

Ross, Alexander, *Adventures of the First Settlers on the Oregon or Columbia River.* London: Smith, Elder and Co., 1849. (Also edited by Milton Quaife, Chicago: R. R. Donnelly & Sons, 1923, and R. G. Thwaites, ed., in *Early Western Travels,* VII, Cleveland, Ohio, 1904.)

———— *Fur Hunters of the Far West: A Narrative of Adventure in the Oregon and Rocky Mountains,* 2 vols. London: Smith Elder and Co., 1885. (Also edited by Kenneth A. Spalding, Norman: University of Oklahoma Press, 1956.)

Rougé, Rev. Etienne de, S.J., "Lettera del P. Stefano de Rouge al R.P. Cataldo, 9 maggio 1886," *MDPT*, 87–89. Original manuscript in OPA.

———— "Estratta d'una lettera del P. de Rouge al P. Canestrelli, 8 maggio 1886," *MDPT*, 86–87. Original manuscript in OPA.

———— "Estratta d'una lettera del P. de Rougé al F. G. De La Motte, Luglio-agosto 1886," *MDPT*, 91–97. Original manuscript in OPA.

———— "Lettera Del P.E. de Rouge al R.P. Provinciale, Missione di S. Maria — Washington, 26 Settembre 1903," *LPT*, 1904, 129–130. Original manuscript in OPA.

———— *I Smemeies, I Nkaumen, I Sukuenzin L Okenakan Nkolkoeltens. Preces in Linguam Indorum Okenagan Versae.* Paris: 1442 Imp. G. Picquoin, 54, Rue De Lille.

———— *Circular to Ladies Applicants,* May 6, 1911, OPA.

———— *Information Concerning the Ladies Missionaries,* mimeographed copy, OPA.

———— *Ladies Catechists Are Needed at St. Mary's Mission,* mimeographed copy, OPA.

———— *Applicants as Catechists Missionaries to St. Mary's Mission. To Ladies Applicants as Catechists Missionaries. To Applicants Catechists Missionaries Coming to St. Mary's Mission,* mimeographed copies, OPA.

—— *St. Mary's Mission High School,* leaflet, mimeographed, OPA.

—— *St. Mary's Mission High School,* Omak Chronicle Press, 1914–1915.

—— "St. Mary's Mission, Omak, Washington," Richard F. Steele, ed. in *History of North Washington,* Spokane, Wash.: Western Historical Publishing Company, 1904.

—— "The Conversion of the Wenatchee," *The Indian Sentinel,* 1912, 42–44.

—— *St. Mary's Mission,* brochure, mimeographed copy, in possession of Mrs. Frank Mechtel, Wenatchee, Wash.

—— "The Conversion of an Indian Tribe," "The Sodality of an Indian Tribe," *WL* (44:1, February, 1915), 35–38.

Rouget, Etienne de, S.J., "L' Indien du Nord Quest Recit deun missionnaire de montagnes Rocheuses," *Les Etudes Religieuses Philosophiques Historiques at Litteraires* (49, Mar 1890), 470–500.

Sherman, Paschal, Ph.D., "Father E. de Rougé, S.J., A Tribute," *The Martian,* St. Martin's College, Lacy, Wash. (2:4, June, 1916), 198–200.

Waring, Guy, *My Pioneer Past.* Boston: Bruce Humphries, Inc., 1936.

Wilkes, Charles, *Narrative of the United States Exploring Expedition During the Years 1838, 1839, 1840, 1841, 1842,* Vol. IV. Philadelphia: Lea & Blanchard, 1845.

E. Government Publications

Annual Report of the Commissioner of Indian Affairs to the Secretary of the Interior. Washington, D. C.: Government Printing Office, 1869–1960.

Bloodworth, Jessie A., *Human Resources Survey of the Colville Confederated Tribes. A Field Report of the Bureau of Indian Affairs Portland Area Office, Colville Agency, June 1959.*

Butler, Hon. Hugh, "Speech in Senate of the United States, January 22, 1951," *Transfer of Title to Certain Lands to the Colville Indians, Washington* (9365-38519), 4.

Cain, Sen. Harry P., "Pertaining Facts Concerning the Colville Reservation in the State of Washington and the Indians Belonging Thereto," *Congressional Record: Proceedings and Debates of the Eighty-Second Congress, Second Session* (220775-44328), U. S. Government Printing Office, 1952.

Cohen, Felix S., *Handbook of Federal Indian Law.* Washington, D. C.: U. S. Government Printing Office, 1945.

A Compilation of the Messages and Papers of the Presidents, 20 vols. New York: Bureau of National Literature, Inc. [Copyrights: 1911–1917].

Curry, A. P., General, *Report on the Indian Troubles in Okanogan County to General R. G. O'Brien, Adjutant General, N.G.W., Olympia,* Spokane Falls, January 24, 1891.

Eberly, John H., Commissioner of Indian Affairs, "School Contracts With Bureau of Catholic Indian Missions," in "Report of the Secretary of the Interior," *House Executive Document 1, Fiftieth Congress, Second Session* (Vol. II, Part 5), XV.

Executive Orders Relating to Indian Reservations From May 14, 1885 to July 1, 1912. Washington, D. C.: Government Printing Office, 1912.

Harney, General, to General Scott, June 1, 1859 (Letter 40), 140–141; (Letter 41), June 3, 1859; De Smet to Captain A. Pleasenton, May 28, 1859 (41 a), 147–149; May 25, 1859, (40 a) 141–143. Pleasenton to De Smet, June 1, 1859. (40 e) 145." *Executive Document No. 65, Thirty-Sixth Congress, House of Representatives, First Session, Affairs in Oregon,* Serial No. 1051.

Hattan, Elton M., Office of the Regional Solicitor, Portland, to Supt. Colville Agency, October 15, 1956. *Mineral Rights under Stock-Raising Homesteads* — B.L.M. Files, Colville Reservation.

Hayes, R. B., "Executive Order" in "Report of the Secretary of the Interior," *House Executive Document 1, Forty-Sixth Congress, Second Session* (Vol. I, Part 5), 323.

Horan, Walt, Congressman, "History of the Colville Reservation," in *Hearings Before the Subcommittee on Indian Lands of the Committee on Public Lands, House of Representatives and the Committee on Interior and Insular Affairs, United States Senate, Eighty-First Congress, First Session,* on H.R. 2432. (Serial No. 19).

James, Chief Jim, "Testimony Before the Subcommittee on Indian Affairs," *Eighty-First Congress, First Session,* H.R. 2432 (Serial No. 19).

Kappler, Charles, comp. and ed., *Indian Affairs: Laws and Treaties.* Washington, D. C.: Government Printing Office, 1904–1941, 5 vols.

Milroy, R. H., to Hon. E. P. Smith, Commissioner of Indian Affairs, October 20, 1873, "Report 62," *Executive Document 4, Forty-Third Congress, First Session, 1873–1874.* (Vol. IV, Part 5), 664–665. Washington, D. C.: Government Printing Office, 1874.

Office of Indian Affairs, *Bulletin 8* (1923).

Public Laws of the United States of America Passed by the Fifty-Ninth Congress, 1905–1907.

Ralkowski, Dr. H. N., *Report of the Dental Office, Colville Agency Hospital Nespelem to the Bureau of Indian Affairs* (November 4–December 11, 1957).

"Report of the Secretary of the Interior," *House Executive Documents, Fiftieth Congress, Second Session, 1888–1889.* (Vol. II, 1888–1889), 222. Washington, D. C.: Government Printing Office, 1889.

"Report of the Secretary of the Interior," *House Executive Documents, Forty-Eighth Congress, Second Session, 1884–1885* (Vol. II). Washington, D. C.: Government Printing Office, 1885.

"Reports of Explorations and Surveys to Ascertain the Most Practicable and Economical Route for a Railroad From the Mississippi River to the Pacific Ocean. Made Under the Direction of the Secretary of War, in 1853–55." *Executive Document No. 56, House of Representatives, Thirty-Sixth Congress, First Session.* (Vol. XII, Book One.) Washington, D. C.: Thomas H. Ford, Printer, 1860.

Shanks, J. P. C., to Hon. T. W. Bennet and H. W. Reed, Gentlemen of the Special Commission, August 14, 1873. *Executive Documents, Forty-Third Congress, First Session, 1873–1874* (Vol. 4, Part 5), 529–530. Washington, D. C.: Government Printing Office, 1874.

The Statutes at Large of the United States of America From December, 1905, to March, 1907 (Vol. XXXIV in Three Parts). Washington, D. C.: Government Printing Office, 1907.

Stevens, Isaac I., "Report," in "Report of the Secretary of the Interior," *Executive Documents, The Senate of the United States, Second Session, Thirty-Third Congress* (Vol. I), 448 ff. Washington, D. C.: Beverly Tucker, Senate Printer, 1855.

Survey of Conditions of the Indians in the United States. Hearings Before a Subcommittee of the Committee on Indian Affairs, United States Senate, Seventy-Second Congress, First Session, Part 32. Washington, D. C.: Government Printing Office, 1934.

—————— *Seventy-Sixth Congress,* Part 37. Washington, D. C.: Government Printing Office: 1940.

Symons, Lieut. Thomas W., "Report of an Examination of the Upper Columbia River and the Territory in Its Vicinity in September and October, 1881," *Senate Executive Document No. 186, Forty-Seventh Congress, First Session.* Washington, D. C.: Government Printing Office, 1882.

Teller, Hon. Senator, *Congressional Records: Containing the Proceedings and Debates of the Fifty-First Congress, First Session. Also Special Session of the Senate* (XXI), 7651.

Tidball, John C., Colonel, aide-de-camp, brevet brigadier general, Washington, D. C., October 27, 1883, Comp., "Report of Journey Made by General Sherman in the North, West and Middle Parts of the United States in 1883," in "Report of the Secretary of War," *Forty-Eighth Congress, First Session, 1883. Index to the Executive Documents of the House of Representatives for the First Session of the Forty-Eighth Congress* (91883-1884). Washington, D. C.: Government Printing Office, 1884.

U. S. Congress, *Hearings Before the Subcommittee on Indian Affairs of the Committee on Public Lands, House of Representatives and the Committee on Interior and Insular Affairs United States Senate, Eighty-First Congress, First Session,* on H.R. 2432. (A Bill Restoring to Tribal Ownership Certain Lands Upon the Colville Indian Reservation, Wash., February 9, March 23, April 27, May 3, July 20 and 29, 1949.) Washington, D. C.: United States Government Printing Office, 1949.

———— *Hearings Before the Subcommittee on Indian Affairs of the Committee on Interior and Insular Affairs United States Senate, Eighty-Seventh Congress, First Session,* on S. 2123 and H.R. 8236. "Legislation to Authorize the Use of Funds Arising From Judgments in Favor of Any of the Confederated Tribes of the Colville Reservation," August 15 and September 13, 1961. Washington, D. C.: U. S. Printing Office, 1961.

———— *Hearings Before the Subcommittee on Indian Affairs of the Committee on Interior and Insular Affairs, Eighty-Eighth Congress, First Session,* Hearings held at Spokane, Nespelem, and Seattle, and in Washington, D. C., October 24, 25, 26; November 20, 1963. Washington, D. C.: U. S. Government Printing Office, 1964.

———— *Hearing Before the Subcommittee on Indian Affairs of the Committee on Interior and Insular Affairs, United States Senate, First Session,* on S. 1169, S. 1442, H.R. 4918. Hearings held at Spokane, Nespelem, Seattle, and Washington, D. C., October 24, 25, 26; November 20, 1963. Washington, D. C.: U. S. Government Printing Office, 1964.

———— *Hearing Before the Subcommittee on Indian Affairs of the Committee on Interior and Insular Affairs, Eighty-Ninth Congress, First Session,* on S. 1413. Washington, D. C.: U. S. Government Printing Office, 1965.

Vest, Hon. Senator, in *Congressional Records Containing the Proceedings and Debates of the Fifty-Sixth Congress, First Session* (Serial No. 356, XXXIII), 3884–3886.

Watkins, E. C. and others, "Report Regarding Consolidation of Indian Agencies in Colville County, etc.," *Senate Executive Document No. 20, Firty-Fifth Congress, Second Session* (Serial No. 1780), 1–8.

II. SECONDARY SOURCES

A. Books and Pamphlets

Allaire, L'Abbé J. B. A., *Dictionaire Biographique Du Clerge Canadian-Francais.* Montreal: Des Sowods-Muets, 1910.

Allen, Paul, *History of the Expeditions Under the Command of Lewis and Clark,* 2 vols. New York: Harper and Brothers, 1901.

———— *Meriwether Lewis and William Clark, Pioneers of the Great American Northwest,* 2 vols. Akron, Ohio: The Werner Company, 1901.

Bagley, Clarence Booth, *Indian Myths of the Northwest.* Seattle, Wash.: Lowman & Hanford, 1930.

———— ed. *Early Catholic Missions in Old Oregon,* 2 vols. Seattle, Wash.: Lowman & Hanford Company, 1932.

Blankenship, Russel, *And There Were Men*. New York: Alfred A. Knopf, 1942.

Bancroft, Hubert Howe, *History of Washington, Idaho and Montana, 1845–1889*, Vol. XXXI of *History of the Northwest States*. San Francisco: The History Company, 1890.

——— *The Native Races, Myths and Languages*. San Francisco: A. L. Bancroft & Company, 1883.

——— *The New Pacific*. New York: A. L. Bancroft Company, 1900.

Barnet, H. G., *Indian Shakers: A Messianic Cult of the Pacific Northwest*. Carbondale: Southern Illinois Press, 1957.

Barto, Harold E., *History of the State of Washington*. Chicago: D. C. Heath & Company, 1947.

Begg, Alexander, *History of British Columbia*. Toronto: William Briggs, 1894.

Bischoff, Rev. William Norbert, S.J., *The Jesuits in Old Oregon*. Caldwell, Idaho: The Caxton Printers, 1945.

Bowden, Angio Burt, *Early Schools in Washington Territory*. Seattle, Wash.: Lowman & Hanford, 1935.

Bourne, Edward Gaylord, "The Legend of Marcus Whitman," in *Essays in Historical Criticism*. New York: Charles Scribner's Sons, 1901.

Brown, William Compton, *Early Okanogan History*. Okanogan, Wash.: Press of the Okanogan Independent, 1911.

Brown, William Compton, *The Indian Side of the Story*. Spokane, Wash.: C. W. Hill Printing Co., 1961.

——— *Chief Tonasket*, mimeographed Ms.

Burpee, Lawrence, *The Search for the Western Sea*. New York: The Macmillan Company, 1902.

Burton, Katherine, *The Golden Door: The Life of Mother Katherine Drexel*. New York: Kenedy, 1957.

Bryan, Enoch A., *Orient Meets Occident*. Pulman, Wash.: The Student Book Corporation, 1936.

Bryce, George, *The Remarkable History of the Hudson's Bay Company, Including That of the French Traders of North-Western Canada and of the North West, XY, and Astor Fur Companies*. London: Sampson Low Marston and Company, 1902.

Catlin, George, *The North American Indians*, Vol. II. London: Tilt and Bugue, 1842.

Caywood, Louis R., *Excavation at Two Fort Okanogan Sites, 1952. With Appendix on Artifacts* by Leonard R. Butler. San Francisco: United States Department of the Interior, National Park Service, Region Four, 1954.

Centenary and Silver Jubilee Souvenir Book for Spokane and the Inland Empire, 1838–1913–1938. Spokane: The Inland Catholic Press, 1938.

Chittendon, Hiram Martin, and Alfred Talbot Richardson, *Life, Letters and Travels of Father Pierre-Jean De Smet, S.J., 1801–1873*. New York: Francis P. Harper, 1905.

Cline, Walter, and others; Leslie Spier, ed., *The Sinkaietk or Southern Okanogan of Washington*. Menasha, Wis.: George Banta Publishing Company Agent, 1938.

Collier, Donald, Alfred E. Hudson, and Arlo Ford, *Archaeology of the Upper Columbia Region*. Seattle, Wash.: University of Washington Press, 1942.

Cooke, Robert, *Sketches of the Life of Msgr. de Mazenod, 1782–1861, Founder of the Oblates of Mary Immaculate*. Dublin: Dollard, 1914.

Coues, Elliott, ed., *New Light on the Early History of the Greater Northwest. The Manuscript Journals of Alexander Henry, Fur Trader of the Northwest Company and of David Thompson, Official Geographer and Explorer of the Same Company, 1799–1814*, 3 vols. New York: Francis P. Harper, 1897.

Curtis, Edward S., *The North American Indian*, Vol. VII, Frederick Webb Hodge, ed. Norwood, Mass.: The Plimpton Press [Copyright 1911].

Dryden, Cecil, *Up the Columbia for Furs*. Caldwell, Idaho: The Caxton Printers, 1949.

Dunn, J. B., Jr., *Massacre of the Mountains. A History of the Indian Wars of the Far West*. New York: Archer House, Inc., 1866.

Durkin, Rev. Joseph, S.J., *General Sherman's Son*. New York: Farrar, Strauss and Cudahy, 1959.

Fee, Chester Anders, *Chief Joseph: The Biography of a Great Indian*. New York: Wilson-Erickson, Inc., 1936.

Fleming, R. Harvey, ed., *Minutes of Council Northern Department of Rupert Land, 1821–1831*, Vol. 3. Toronto: The Champlain Society for the HBRS, 1940.

Franchere, Gabriel, *Narrative of a Voyage to the Northwest Coast of America in the Years 1811, 1812, 1813 and 1814 or the First American Settlement on the Pacific*, J. V. Huntington, tr. and ed. Cleveland: Redfield, 1904.

Fries, U. E., and Emil B. Fries, *From Copenhagen to Okanogen*. Caldwell, Idaho: The Caxton Printers, 1951.

Fraser, Geo. J., *The Story of Osoyoos*, September, 1811, to December, 1952. Penticton: The Penticton Herald Press, 1952.

Fuller, George W., *The Inland Empire of the Pacific Northwest*, 3 vols. Spokane: H. G. Linderman, 1928.

——— *A History of the Pacific Northwest. With special emphasis on the Inland Empire*. New York: Alfred A. Knopf, 1946 (rev. ed.).

Galbraigth, John S., *The Hudson's Bay Company as an Imperial Factor, 1821–1869*. Berkeley and Los Angeles: University of California Press, 1957.

Garraghan, Gilbert J., S.J., *The Jesuits in the Middle United States*, 3 vols. New York: The America Press, 1938.

——— *Chapters in Frontier History*. Milwaukee: The Bruce Publishing Company, 1934.

Gates, Charles Marvin, *Readings in Pacific Northwest History, 1790–1895*. Seattle, Wash.: University Bookstore, 1941.

Guilday, Peter, *A History of the Councils of Baltimore (1791–1884)*. New York: Macmillan Company, 1932.

Glassley, Ray Hoard, *Pacific Northwest Indian Wars*. Portland, Ore.: Binford and Mort, Publishers, 1953.

Glazebrook, G. P., ed. *The Hargrave Correspondence, 1821–1843*, Vol. XXIV. Toronto: The Champlain Society, 1938.

Glimpses of Pioneer Life, *A Series of Biographies, Experiences, and Events Intimately Concerned with the Settlement of Okanogan County, Washington*. The Okanogan Independent Press, 1924.

Goddard, John W., *Washington, the Evergreen State*. Chicago: Charles Scribner's Sons, 1942.

Haines, Francis, *Red Eagles of the Northwest. The Story of Chief Joseph and His People*. Portland, Ore.: The Scholastic Press, 1939.

Heffelfinger, C. H., and George A. Custer, *The Evergreen Citizen*. Caldwell, Idaho: The Caxton Printers, 1943.

Hesse, Marie Louise, and Cecelia Somday, *A Short History of the Catholic Church in Ferry County*, printed in December, 1958.

Hodge, Frederick Webb, *Handbook of American Indians*. Part I, Washington, D. C.: Government Printing Office, 1907 (Smithsonian Institution Bulletin 30 of the American Bureau of Ethnology). Part II, New York: Pageant Book Inc., 1950.

Holbrook, Steward H., *The Columbia*. New York: Rinehart and Co., Inc., 1956.

Holliday, C. W., *The Valley of Youth*. Caldwell, Idaho: The Caxton Printers, 1948.

Hooker, Sir W. J., *Companion to the Botanical Magazine*, Vol. II. "Brief Memoir of the Life of Mr. David Douglas With Extracts From His Letters," 79–161. London: Edward Couchman, 1836.

Howard, Major-General O. O., *My Life and Experience Among Our Hostile Indians.* Hartford, Conn.: A. D. Northington & Company, 1907.

Hull, Lindley, comp. and ed., *A History of the Famous Wenatchee, Entiat, Chelan and Columbia Valleys.* Spokane, Wash.: Shaw & Borden, 1929.

Hulbert, A. B., and D. P. Hulbert, *The Oregon Crusade*, 5 vols. The Steward Commission of Colorado and the Denver Public Library [Copyright 193?].

——— *Marcus Whitman, Crusader*, 3 vols. The Steward Commission of Colorado and the Denver Public Library [Copyright, 1936–1941].

Hubert, Archer Butler, *The Call of the Columbia*, Vol. IV. The Steward Commission of Colorado and the Denver Public Library, 1934.

HUM-ISHU-MA, "Mourning Dove," *CO-GE-WE-A, The Half-Blood.* Boston: The Four Seas Company, 1927.

Johansen, Dorothy O., and Charles M. Gates, *Empire of the Columbia.* New York: P. F. Collier & Sons, 1868.

Irving Washington, *Astoria* in *The Works of Washington Irving*, Vol. VII. New York: P. F. Collier & Sons, 1868.

Jung, A. M., *Jesuit Missions Among the American Tribes of the Rocky Mountains.* Spokane, Wash.: Gonzaga University Press, 1925.

Judson, Katherine Berry, *Myths and Legends of the Pacific Northwest.* Chicago, Ill.: A. C. McClurg and Co., 1910.

Journal Kept by David Douglas During His Travel in North America, 1823–1827. New York: Antiquarian Press, 1959.

Kane, Paul, *Wanderings of an Artist Among the Indians of North America.* Toronto: The Radisson Society of Canada, Limited, 1925.

Kerr, Harry J., *A History of Okanogan.* The Okanogan Independent Press, 1931.

Laveille, Rev. E., *Life of Father De Smet.* New York: Kenedy, 1915.

Lavender, David, *Land of Giants.* Garden City, N. Y.: Doubleday & Company, Inc., 1958.

Lyman, William D., *The Columbia River.* New York: G. P. Putnam's Son, 1909.

Lyons, Sister Laetitia Mary, M.A., *Francis Norbert Blanchet and the Founding of the Oregon Missions (1838-1848).* Washington, D. C.: The Catholic University of America Press, 1940.

Magaret, Helene, *Father De Smet, Pioneer Priest of the Rockies.* New York: Farrar & Rinehart, Inc., 1940.

Marshall, William Isaac, *Acquisition of Oregon and Long-Suppressed Evidence About Marcus Whitman*, 2 vols. Seattle: Lowman and Hanford Co., 1911.

Martin, Chester, *Lord Selkirk's Work in Canada.* Oxford Historical and Literary Studies, VII. Oxford: University Press, 1916.

Mauring, B. F., *The Conquest of the Coeur d'Alenes, Spokanes and Palouses.* Spokane, Wash.: John W. Graham & Co., 1912.

Meany, Edmond S., *History of the State of Washington.* New York: The Macmillan Company, 1924.

Meeker, Ezra, *Seventy Years of Progress in Washington.* Tacoma, Wash.: Allstrum Printing Company, 1921.

Merk, Frederick, ed., *Fur Trade and Empire. George Simpson's Journal; Remarks Connected With the Fur Trade in the Course of a Voyage From York Factory to Fort George and Back to York Factory 1824–1825, Together With Accompanying Documents,* Harvard Historical Studies, XXXI. Cambridge, Mass.: University Press, 1931.

Metz, Rev. W. J., *History of the Catholic Church and Schools in Washington,* comp. by Herman Winter, 1936 (mimeographed copy at Crosby Library, Gonzaga University, Spokane).

Mooney, James, "The Smohalla Religion of the Columbia Region; Chief Joseph as a 'Dreamer'; Tribes of the Columbia, etc." (1893), in *14th Annual Report of the*

Bureau of Ethnology, Pt. 2 (708–885). Washington, D. C.: Government Printing Office, 1896.

Morice, Rev. A. G., *History of the Catholic Church in Western Canada*, 2 vols. Toronto: The Musson Book Company, Limited, 1910.

McGucken, William, S.J., *The Catholic Way in Education*. Milwaukee: The Bruce Publishing Company, 1934.

McLaughlin, James, *My Friend the Indian*. Boston: Houghton Mifflin Co., 1910.

McWhorter, L. V., ed., *Yellow Wolf: His Own Story*. Caldwell, Idaho: The Caxton Printers, 1940.

———— *Hear Me My Chiefs*, Ruth Bordin, ed. Caldwell, Idaho: The Caxton Printers, 1952.

Nichols, M. Leona, *The Mantle of Elias. The Story of Fathers Blanchet and Demers in Early Oregon*. Portland, Ore.: Binford & Mort, Publishers [Copyright, 1914].

Oakshott, Thomas I., *Colville: City of Proud Heritage*. Colville: Statesman-Examiner Press, 1950.

Oakshott, Thomas I., and others, *The Book of the Counties, 1953*. Washington State Association of County Commissioners and County Engineers in Cooperation With the State College of Washington.

O'Hara, Rt. Rev. E. V., *Pioneer Catholic History of Oregon*. Portland, Ore.: Glass & Pruhomme, 1911. Also: Paterson, N. J.: St. Anthony Guild Press, 1939.

Palladino, Rev. L. B., S.J., *Indian and White in the Northwest, or a History of Catholicity in Montana*. Baltimore: John Murphy & Company, 1894.

———— *Education for the Indian*. New York: Benziger Brothers, 1892.

Peace River: A Canoe Voyage From Hudson's Bay to the Pacific by the Late Sir George Simpson in 1828. Journal of the Late Chief Factor Archibald McDonald (Hon. Hudson's Bay Company) Who Accompanied Him. Toronto: Adam Stevenson, 1872.

Pollard, Lancaster, *A History of the State of Washington*. Portland, Ore.: Binford & Mort, Publishers, 1943.

Pollard, Lancaster, and Lloyd Spencer, *A History of the State of Washington*, 4 vols. New York: American Historical Society, 1937.

Pope Pius XI, "Encyclical on Christian Education," in *Five Great Encyclicals*, Rev. Gerald Treacy, ed. New York: The Paulist Press, 1952.

Priest, Loring B., *Uncle Sam's Stepchildren. The Reformation of the United States Indian Policy, 1865–1887*. New Brunswick: Rutgers University Press, 1942.

Pritchell, John Perry, *The Red River Valley, 1811–1849. A Regional Study*. New Haven: Yale University Press, 1942.

Pronty, Andrew, ed., *Centennial of the Diocese of Seattle, 1850–1950*. Seattle: Northwest Progress Press, 1950.

Rahill, Peter J., *The Catholic Indian Missions and Grant's Peace Policy, 1870–1884*. Washington, D. C.: The Catholic University of America Press, 1935.

Ray, Verne F., *The Sanpoil And Nespelems. Salishan Peoples of Northeastern Washington*. Seattle, Wash.: The University of Washington Press, 1932.

Relander, Click, *Drummers and Dreamers*, with a Foreword by Dr. Frederick Webb Hodge. Caldwell, Idaho: The Caxton Printers, 1956.

Rich, E. E. ed., *Part of Dispatch From George Simpson Esqr. Governor of Ruperts Land to the Governor & Committee of the Hudson's Bay Company, London. March 1, 1829, Continued and Completed March 24 and June 5, 1829*, Vol. 10. Toronto: The Champlain Society for the HBRS, 1947.

———— *The Letters of John McLaughlin From Fort Vancouver to the Governor and Committee (First Series, 1828–38)*, HBRS, Vol. 4. Toronto: The Champlain Society, 1941.

———— *(Second Series, 1838–44)*, HBRS, Vol. 6. Toronto: The Champlain Society, 1943.

—— (*Third Series, 1844–46*), HBRS, Vol. 7. Toronto: The Champlain Society, 1944.

—— *The History of the Hudson's Bay Company,* Vol. II (1763–1870). London: HBRS, 1959.

Rushmore, Elsie Mitchel, *The Indian Policy During Grant's Administration.* Jamaica, Queenborough, New York: The Marion Press, 1914.

Schoolcraft, Henry R., L.L.D., *Historical and Statistical Information Respective the History, Condition and Prospects of the Indian Tribes of the United States,* collected and prepared under the direction of the Bureau of Indian Affairs per act of Congress of March 3, 1847. Philadelphia: Lippincott Grambo & Co. With *Index to Schoolcraft's Indian Tribes of the United States.* Nichols, Frames S., comp., *Smithsonian Institution Bureau of Ethnology, Bulletin 152.* Washington, D. C.: Government Printing Office, 1954.

Shea, John Gilmary, *History of the Catholic Church in the United States,* 4 vols. New York: McVey, 1919.

Snowden, Clinton A., *A History of Washington,* 4 vols. New York: The Century History Company, 1909.

Spier, Leslie, *Tribal Distribution in Washington.* Menasha, Wis,: George Banta Publishing Co., 1936.

Splawn, Andrew Jackson, *KA-MI-AKIN: The Last Hero of the Yakimas.* Portland, Ore.: Kilham Stationary & Printing Co., 1917.

Steele, Richard F., and A. P. Rose, *An Illustrated History of Stevens, Ferry, Okanogan and Chelan Counties, State of Washington.* Spokane, Wash.: Western Historical Publishing Company, 1904.

Stevens, Hazard, *Life of Isaac Ingall Stevens,* 2 vols. New York: Houghton Mifflin and Company, 1901.

Teit, James A., "The Salishan Tribes of the Western Plateaus," Franz Boas, ed., in *Forty-Fifth Annual Report of the Bureau of American Ethnology, 1927–1928,* 23–396. Washington, D. C.: Government Printing Office, 1930.

Thwaites, Reuben Gold, ed., *Early Western Travels, 1836–1841,* Vol. 22. Cleveland, Ohio: The Arthur H. Clarck Company, 1904–07.

Tyrell, Joseph B., ed., *David Thompson's Narrative of His Explorations in Western America, 1784–1812,* Vol. 12. Toronto: The Publications of the Champlain Society, 1916.

Willson, Beckles, *The Great Company. Being a History of the Honourable Company of Merchants — Adventurers Trading Into Hudson's Bay.* Toronto: The Copp, Clarck Company, 1899.

Winans, W. P., *Stevens County, Washington, Its Creation, Addition, Subtraction and Division* (mimeographed copy, n.d.). Spokane, Wash.: Northwest Room, Public Library.

Winther, Oscar Odburn, *The Great Northwest.* New York: Alfred A. Knopf, 1956.

Writers of the Works Project Administration, comp., *Washington, a Guide to the Evergreen State.* Portland, Ore.: Binford & Mort [1941].

Wood, D. E., and others, *Okanogan Highlands Echoes. Molson-Knob-Hill-Chesaw Community Study* (mimeographed copy), 1962.

The Yakima Valley Catholic Centennial, 1847–1947.

B. Periodicals

American Indians and American Life, Vol. 311 (May, 1957), of *The Annals of the American Academy of Political and Social Science.*

Annals of the Catholic Indian Missions of America, Vol. I (January, 1877).

Barry, Neilson J., "The Indians in Washington, Their Geographic Distribution of Linguistic Families," *OHQ* (28:1, March, 1927), 49–61.

———— "Astorians Who Became Permanent Settlers," *WHQ* (24:3, July, 1933), 222–231; (24:4, October, 1933), 280–301.

———— "The Indians in Washington, Their Distribution by Languages," *OHQ* (28:2, June, 1927), 147–162.

Brown, William Compton, "Old Fort Okanogan and the Okanogan Trail," *OHQ* (15:1, March, 1914), 1–38.

Burgunder, Ben, "Recollections of the Inland Empire," *WHQ* (17:3, July, 1926), 190–210.

Burns, Robert Ignatius, S.J., "Pere Joset's Account of the Indian War of 1858," *PNQ* (38:4, October, 1947), 285–307.

———— "The Jesuits, the Northern Indians and the Nez Perce War of 1877," *PNQ* (42:1, January, 1951), 40–73.

———— "A Jesuit in the War Against the Northern Tribes," reprint from *The Records of the American Catholic Historical Society,* Philadelphia (LXI:1, March, 1950).

Carpenter, John A., "General Howard and the Nez Perce War of 1877," *PNQ* (49:4, October, 1958), 129–145.

Clement, Percy, "Early Days of Kelowna And District," *The Twenty-Third Report of the Okanogan Historical Society* (1936), 19–20.

Davis, William L., S.J., "Peter John De Smet: The Journey of 1840," *PNQ* (35:1, January, 1944), 29–73.

Deutsch, Herman J., "Indian and White in the Inland Empire; The Contest for the Land, 1880–1912," *PNQ* (47:6, April, 1956), 44–51.

Ermatinger, C. O., "The Columbia River Under Hudson's Bay Company Rule," *WHQ* (5:3, July, 1914), 192–206.

Elliott, T. C., "Journal of John Work, June–October, 1825," *WHQ* (5:2, April, 1914), 85–116; "Journal of September 7th–December 14th, 1825" (5:3, July, 1914), 163–191; "Journal of December 15th–June 12th, 1826" (5:4, October, 1914), 258–287.

———— "The Fur Trade in the Columbia River Basin, Prior to 1811," *WHQ* (6:1, January, 1915), 310.

———— "Journal of David Thompson," *OHQ* (15:1, March, 1914), 39–63.

———— "The Strange Case of Jonathan Carver and the Name of Oregon," *OHQ* (22:3, September, 1920), 341–368.

Esvelt, John P., "Upper Columbia Chinese Placering," *Pacific Northwesterner* (2:3, Summer, 1958), 6–11.

Gwydir, R. D., "A Report of the San Poel Indians," *WHQ* (8:4, October, 1917), 243–250.

Harvey, A. G., "David Stuart: Okanogan Pathfinder — Founder of Kamloops," BCHQ (9, October, 1945), 277–288.

Historicus [Rev. George Weibel, S.J.], "Fifty Years of Peaceful Conquest," *Gonzaga Magazine* (1913–1914), 18–25, 70–78, 125–133, 179–187, 232–241, 293–303, 344–356, 407–418, 455–464, 520–532, Volume V.

Howay, F. W., "The Introduction of Intoxicating Liquors Amongst the Indians of the Northwest Coast," BCHQ (6, July, 1942), 157–169.

Howay, F. W., and T. C. Elliott, "Reprint of Boit's Log of the Columbia, 1790–1793," *OHQ* (22:4, December, 1921), 265–365.

Judge, Louis, "Wenatchee Indians Ask Justice," *WHQ* (16:1, January, 1925), 20–28.

Lacey, Mrs. Katie, "Tonasket, Chief of the Okanogans," *The Twenty-Third Report of The Okanogan Historical Society 1959,* 19–20.

Lewis, W. L., "Information Concerning the Establishment of Fort Colville," *WHQ* (16:2, April, 1925), 102–107.

Lewis, W. L., and Jacob A. Meyers, eds., "Life at Old Fort Colville."

WHQ (16:3, July, 1925), 198–205. (From the papers of Angus McDonald, Late Chief Trader.)

McGloin, Rev. John B., S.J., "The New Caledonia Years, 1845–1848," *The Owl* (40:8, May, 1953), 6 ff.

Nelson, Denys, "Father Pandosi and the Establishment of Okanogan Mission," *The Seventeenth Report of the Okanogan Historical Society*, 1953, 53–66, 67–86.

O'Brien, John M., "The Story of Old Ruby," *The Pacific Northwesterner* (4:2, Spring, 1960), 27–32.

Oliphant, J. Orin, "Old Fort Colville," *WHQ* (15:2, April, 1925), 83–101.

Sherwood, S. F., "The Cunning of Chief Moses," *The Washington Historian* (1:4, July, 1900), 172–173.

Tennelly, Rt. Rev. J. B., "Annual Report of the Secretary of the Commission for the Catholic Missions Among the Colored People and the Indians," *Our Negro and Indian Missions* (January, 1928), 42.

Wagget, Rev. George M., "The Oblates of Mary Immaculate in the Pacific Northwest of U. S. A.," *Etudes Oblates* (6:1, Janvier-Mars, 1947), 7–83.

White, Hester E., "General Sherman at Osoyoos," *Fifteenth Report of the Okanogan Historical Society* (1951), 44–66.

Young, F. G., "John Boit's Log of the Columbia, 1790–1793," *OHQ* (22:4, December, 1921), 258–356.

C. Newspapers

The Inland Empire Catholic Messenger, Spokane.
The Catholic Northwest Progress, Seattle.
The Omak Chronicle, Omak, Wash.
The Okanogan Independent, Okanogan, Wash.
The Ruby Miner, Ruby, Wash.
The Seattle Daily Times, Seattle.
The Spokane Daily Chronicle, Spokane.
The Spokesman-Review, Spokane
The Statesman-Examiner, Colville.
The Walla Walla Statesman, Walla Walla, Wash.

D. Encyclopedias and Directories

Catholic Directory, 1877. New York: D. & J. Sadlier & Co.
The Catholic Encyclopedia, Vol. 7. New York: Robert Appleton Company [Copyright, 1910].
Chelan, Douglas, Grant and Okanogan Counties Directories, 1910–1911. Seattle: R. L. Polk & Co., Inc.
The Metropolitan Catholic Almanac, 1861. Baltimore: John Murphy & Co.
The Official Catholic Directory (Series 1881–1919). Different Publishers, Chancery, Seattle.
Official Catholic Directory of the Diocese of Spokane, 1916.

Index